The American Intellectual Tradition

The American Intellectual Tradition

A Sourcebook
Volume I: 1620–1865

Edited by

DAVID A. HOLLINGER
University of Michigan

and

CHARLES CAPPER
University of North Carolina at Chapel Hill

New York Oxford
OXFORD UNIVERSITY PRESS
1989

Oxford University Press

Oxford   New York   Toronto
Delhi   Bombay   Calcutta   Madras   Karachi
Petaling Jaya   Singapore   Hong Kong   Tokyo
Nairobi   Dar es Salaam   Cape Town
Melbourne   Auckland

and associated companies in
Berlin   Ibadan

Library of Congress Cataloging-in-Publication Data
The American intellectual tradition.
Contents: v. 1. 1620–1865—v.
2. 1865 to the present.
1. United States—Intellectual life—Sources.
I. Hollinger, David A.   II. Capper, Charles
E169.1.A47218 1989   973   88-12632
ISBN 0-19-505774-0 (set)
ISBN 0-19-504461-4 (v. 1)
ISBN 0-19-504462-2 (v. 2)

2 4 6 8 9 7 5 3 1

Printed in the United States of America
on acid-free paper

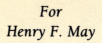

For
Henry F. May

Preface

If a tradition is a family of disagreements, the American intellectual tradition is a very extended family. Its members include arguments inspired by the interests and ideals of a variety of communities within the United States as well as arguments concerned with the national community itself. The family also embraces arguments responsive to Western, if not universal, issues in philosophy, science, religion, politics, literature, and the arts. Some of the most influential members of this family are highly conscious of their European ancestry, whereas others have married into European families and still others remain always preoccupied with the family's Americanness. The family is currently quite content with its extended state; it is happy to count among its many arguments those voiced against the Unitarians by Ralph Waldo Emerson, against Booker T. Washington by W.E.B. Du Bois, and against John Stuart Mill by B. F. Skinner. But the family is vague on just what makes it a family to begin with. And the family is divided, if not confused, over exactly which of its members ought to supervise the education of its young. What disagreements are primary? How should the tradition be structured for the purposes of its continuation and critical revision? What specific artifacts of discourse have played the greatest role historically in developing the American intellectual tradition?

Answers to these questions are necessarily implied by any sourcebook for the study of the American intellectual history. In deciding what to include in this collection, we have been aware of the dynamism and diversity of our subject as well as highly conscious of the differing constructions of it offered by various scholars. We have sought the advice of numerous colleagues and have designed *The American Intellectual Tradition* to make easily available to students many of the documents now routinely assigned—often through photocopies of uncertain legality—by teachers of this subject in American colleges and universities. Hence these volumes are chiefly practical devices, not outlines of a systematic, comprehensive interpretation of American intellectual history. Yet certain priorities have shaped these volumes, and it is appropriate to make them explicit.

The American Intellectual Tradition is frankly intellectual in orientation. Most of the documents collected herein are the result of someone's effort to perform an analysis and to persuade others of the correctness of that analysis. Although these documents express "attitudes" and embody "ideas," we have been more sensitive to their status as *arguments*. Hence most of our selections are of the genres classically associated with purposive discourse: sermon, address, letter, treatise, and essay. We have sought to identify pieces of argumentation that became prominent points of reference for contemporaries or for Americans of later generations. In so doing, we have necessarily been drawn again and again to the work of men and women normally regarded as intellectual leaders: people who were relatively effective at making arguments.

Arguments can be addressed to an infinite number of issues, but the writings collected herein respond to issues that have persistently generated extensive intellectual discussion. The bulk of our selections concern the theoretical basis for religious, scientific, artistic, political, social, and economic practice. Because the United States is above all a polity, the American family of disagreements includes a high proportion of arguments about the basis of politics. Because the public culture of America has often been caught up in the distinctive ethos of Protestant Christianity, many of our selections—especially in volume I—are directed at religious issues. Because modern America has been a peculiarly science-preoccupied civilization, many of the selections in volume II address the character of the scientific enterprise and debate the implications of scientific knowledge.

In order to give these issues historical shape, we have organized the documents around general themes or movements, which we address briefly in introductions preceding each main section. Were this a textbook rather than a sourcebook, we would have sought more consistently to indicate the entire structure of discourse surrounding the texts we discuss; here we can do no more than hint at this, leaving it to the instructor to fill in the missing arguments and counterarguments. In framing our selections, we have also sought to avoid what seems to us a failing in many previous anthologies: the packaging of each source as an example of a particular doctrine or movement. Throughout we have tried to promote the recognition that most intellectual works are dynamic and multifaceted and therefore have meaning in more than one frame of reference. With this in mind, we have written headnotes that emphasize the dense interiority of each document as well as the setting in which it was produced.

Wherever possible we have sought to include countervailing voices in this anthology, along with newer voices just beginning to be heard—or heard again—by historians. Yet one could easily list a fair number of creative American intellectuals whose names do not appear in our contents. The obvious solution would have been to expand our list. We have resisted this temptation for two reasons. First, not all formulations and figures were equally original or influential in the American intellectual tradition. Second, to have included a large number of individuals would have required reproducing only snippets. But reducing these texts to snippets would have all but eliminated their complexity and integrity, or the very qualities that define their character as intellectual sources. Also, because their complexity opens them to varying interpretations, reducing them to brief excerpts would have diminished their value as practical teaching devices. Hence, whenever we have been obliged to choose between reflecting the social and cultural diversity of American intellectual life and giving students an opportunity to confront a substantial piece of argumentation by a major thinker, we have most often chosen the second of these alternatives. Occasionally we have selected sections from a book or a letter, but most of the documents in these volumes are complete or nearly complete essays, addresses, or chapters.

The American Intellectual Tradition appears at a time when the study of intellectual history in American colleges and universities has recently been enlivened by vigorous methodological debate and conceptual innovation. We want to call attention to three especially cogent discussions of the state of the art: John E. Toews, "Intellectual History After the Linguistic Turn: The Autonomy of Meaning and the Irreducibility of Experience," *American Historical Review,* 92 (October 1987), 879–907; Donald R. Kelley, "Horizons of Intellectual History: Retrospect, Circumspect, Prospect," *Journal of the History of Ideas,* 48 (January–March 1987), 143–69; and Michael

Ermarth, "Mindful Matters: The Empire's New Codes and the Plight of Modern European Intellectual History," *Journal of Modern History,* 57 (1985), 506–27. Students interested in the ongoing discussions of intellectual historians can consult the *Intellectual History Newsletter,* published at Boston University under the editorship of David D. Hall.

For advice in relation to this sourcebook, we wish to thank the following individuals: Robert C. Bannister of Swarthmore College; Thomas Bender of New York University; Ruth H. Bloch of the University of California, Los Angeles; Paul Boyer of the University of Wisconsin–Madison; Charles Lloyd Cohen of the University of Wisconsin–Madison; George Cotkin of California State Polytechnic University at San Luis Obispo; David Brion Davis of Yale University; John P. Diggins of the University of California, Irvine; Richard Wightman Fox of Reed College; George M. Fredrickson of Stanford University; James B. Gilbert of the University of Maryland; Samuel Haber of the University of California, Berkeley; Thomas L. Haskell of Rice University; Hugh Hawkins of Amherst College; E. Brooks Holifield of Emory University; James Hoopes of Babson College; Daniel Walker Howe of the University of California, Los Angeles; David Johnson of Portland State University; John F. Kasson of the University of North Carolina at Chapel Hill; Linda K. Kerber of the University of Iowa; James T. Kloppenberg of Brandeis University; Bruce Kuklick of the University of Pennsylvania; Henry F. May of the University of California, Berkeley; Donald B. Meyer of Wesleyan University; Robert Moates Miller of the University of North Carolina at Chapel Hill; Lewis Perry of Vanderbilt University; Daniel T. Rodgers of Princeton University; Dorothy Ross of the University of Virginia; Joan Shelly Rubin of the State University College of New York at Brockport; Barbara Sicherman of Trinity University; Daniel Singal of Hobart and William Smith Colleges; Wilson Smith of the University of California, Davis; James Turner of the University of Michigan; and Daniel Wilson of Muhlenberg College. Some of these colleagues would have preferred a somewhat different contents ("An anthology for American intellectual history without Henry Adams? . . . a contradiction in terms!"), but without their counsel *The American Intellectual Tradition* would be less representative than it is of current teaching practice.

For assistance in the preparation of this sourcebook we wish to thank Thomas Baker, Martin Burke, James Jennings, and Brian Lloyd. The project was supported by grants from the University Research Council and the College of Arts and Sciences of the University of North Carolina at Chapel Hill. We also wish to express our appreciation for the advice and assistance of Nancy Lane of Oxford University Press.

The editors have worked closely at every stage of the preparation of *The American Intellectual Tradition,* but responsibility for volume I belongs to Charles Capper and for volume II to David Hollinger.

Ann Arbor, Mich.   D.A.H.
Chapel Hill, N.C.   C.C.
  June 1988

Note on the Texts in Volume I

The date assigned to a text other than a letter is the date of first regular publication or, in the case of an address or sermon, initial delivery. If the date of first publication varies significantly from the date of composition, the latter is given in parentheses preceding the text. Letters are identified by date of composition. Except for the modern "s" in place of the archaic "f," the original spelling, capitalization, and punctuation of all texts have been retained.

Contents

Part One: The Puritan Vision

Part Two: Republican Enlightenment

Part Three: Evangelical Democracy

Part Four: Romanticism and Reform

Part Five: The Quest for Union

Part One

The Puritan Vision

Introduction

To consider Puritan thinkers as part of an ongoing tradition of American intellectuals might seem perversely anachronistic. The very noun "intellectual" was never used by them, and key concepts commonly found in the writings represented in these volumes, such as "self-sufficient reason" or "the independent thinker," would have seemed to them absolutely abhorrent. Yet if the Puritans were not moderns, they were not archaic obscurantists either. The outpouring of scholarship on American Puritanism in the last fifty years has taught us to marvel at the highly articulated intellectuality of Puritan culture in both Old and New England. Nor should this be surprising. The Puritans were enthusiastic inheritors not only of Christian and biblical scholarship, but also of the new learning and culture of Renaissance humanism. From both sources they took materials that they strenuously manipulated in order to achieve the highest cultural goal of the religious intellectual—a justification of the ways of God to man and woman. Out of this striving necessarily came a complex synthesis of supernatural, rationalistic, and emotional elements that has remained—in large part *because* of its great strength and complexity—a powerful influence in American intellectual life down to the twentieth century.

At the bottom of this Puritan synthesis was the idea of the covenant. This was a concept, developed first by late sixteenth- and early seventeenth-century continental and English reformed theologians, that defined the relationship between God and humankind as being based on a covenant—a series of divinely ordained yet understandable rules and mutual responsibilities. So defined, the covenant or "federal" idea obviously had wide-ranging applicability, as is well shown in the first two selections. John Winthrop, in his lay sermon on Christian charity, used the concept both to expound a complete theory of political authority and social relations and to explain the world-historical significance of the entire New England venture. Samuel Willard's theological statement of the covenant idea was no less comprehensive. In his lectures Willard defined in sweeping terms the biblical, moral, and psychological character of God's promises to humankind, along with men and women's covert but nonetheless critical role in helping to fulfill them.

New England Puritan convenantal thought, although vast in scope, was frought with ambiguity and tensions. When conflict among its formulators therefore broke out in the first years of the Massachusetts Bay settlement, although the dissenters were few, the dissension brought into sharp focus some of the most basic elements of the Puritan intellectual vision. None of these was more basic than the ultimate evangelical questions, What must I do to be saved? and (almost as momentous) How do I *know* that I am saved? The selection from the General Court's examination of Anne Hutchinson dramatically reveals the astonishingly broad range of answers that Puritan intellectuals sometimes gave to those questions. Religious dissension naturally raises the issue of toleration, a problem addressed by the Bay Colony's other great religious dissenter, Roger Williams. But for Williams the issue was not the familiar modern secular one of mutual tolerance achieved through rational discourse, but rather one that went, like Hutchinson's dissent, although from a different angle, to the heart of the New England covenantal way. In his essay on Indian conversions, Williams argued that the authenticity of Puritan piety and hopes for fulfillment of God's promises were undermined by the very exercise of political authority over religion that the Massachusetts colony's intellectual leaders believed was essential to the implementation of God's word in this world.

By the end of the seventeenth century, much of the social and political basis of the New England way had eroded. The Puritan monopoly of political power in the Massachusetts Bay Colony had been broken with the new charter's substitution of property for church membership as the basis for suffrage, non-Puritan sects were growing in numbers, and competing Enlightenment currents were increasingly attracting the allegiance of Puritan and non-Puritan intellectuals. Meanwhile, ministers continued to preach jeremiads over what they saw as clear evidence of rising worldliness in their society. In this context a host of third- and fourth-generation New England Puritan leaders, like their Protestant counterparts in other parts of America and in Europe, lent support to organized efforts to revitalize their region's piety. The last selections by the two leading Puritan intellectual figures of their respective generations demonstrate the range of responses to these turbulent times. Cotton Mather, in his essay on the doing of good, sought feverishly to find in voluntaristic moral efforts avenues to Godly piety and community solidarity. By contrast Jonathan Edwards, in his sermon in defense of divine determinism and especially in his treatise defending the spiritual character of religious emotions, both creatively adapted and radically subverted emerging modern rationalistic and moralistic intellectual currents in order to restore the ethical and psychological integrity of a God-intoxicated Christian faith.

Recommendations for Further Reading

Perry Miller, *The New England Mind,* vol. 1: *The Seventeenth Century* (New York, 1939), and vol. 2: *From Colony to Province* (Cambridge, Mass., 1953); Edmund S. Morgan, *Visible Saints: The History of a Puritan Idea* (New York, 1963); Norman Pettit, *The Heart Prepared: Grace and Conversion in Puritan Spiritual Life* (New Haven, 1966); T. H. Breen, *The Character of the Good Ruler: A Study of Puritan Political Ideas in New England, 1630–1730* (New Haven, 1970); Stephen Foster, *Their Solitary Way: The Puritan Social Ethic in the First Century of Settlement in New England* (New Haven, 1971); Robert Middlekauff, *The Mathers: Three Generations of Puritan Intellectuals, 1596–1728* (New York, 1971); David D. Hall, *The Faithful Shepherd: A History of the New England Ministry in the Seventeenth Century* (Chapel Hill, 1972); Larzer Ziff, *Puritanism in America: New Culture in a New World* (New York, 1973); E. Brooks Holifield, *The Covenant Sealed: The Development of Puritan Sacramental Theology in Old and New England, 1570–1720* (New Haven, 1974); Sacvan Bercovitch, *The Puritan Origins of the American Self* (New Haven, 1975); Sacvan Bercovitch, *The American Jeremiad* (Madison, Wis., 1978); William K. B. Stoever, *'A Faire and Easie Way to Heaven': Covenant Theology and Antinomianism in Early Massachusetts* (Middletown, Conn., 1978); Norman Fiering, *Moral Philosophy at Seventeenth-Century Harvard: A Discipline in Transition* (Chapel Hill, 1981); Charles E. Hambrick-Stowe, *The Practice of Piety: Puritan Devotional Disciplines in Seven-*

teenth-Century New England (Chapel Hill, 1982); Philip F. Gura, *A Glimpse of Sion's Glory: Puritan Radicalism in New England, 1620–1660* (Middletown, Conn., 1984); David S. Lovejoy, *Religious Enthusiasm in the New World: Heresy to Revolution* (Cambridge, Mass., 1985); Charles Lloyd Cohen, *God's Caress: The Psychology of Puritan Religious Experience* (New York, 1986); Harry S. Stout, *The New England Soul: Preaching and Religious Culture in Colonial New England* (New York, 1986).

JOHN WINTHROP

"A Modell of Christian Charity"
1630

As the first and very often annually reelected governor of the Massachusetts Bay Colony until his death, John Winthrop (1588–1649) was New England's preeminent political leader. He was also the region's leading political theorist. His speeches on the limits of popular liberty and the importance of special prerogatives for elected magistrates constitute the most important body of governmental theory in the first years of settlement. But his most philosophical discourse was by far the extraordinary one he wrote and probably delivered while on board the Puritan flagship *Arbella* as it sailed across the Atlantic bound for New England. In it he envisioned a polity that, however consensual in form and sometimes contractual in language, was strongly organic and theocratic. The ideal state, in Winthrop's schema, rested on a covenant with God, who both determined the fundamental moral laws regulating society and, through Christ's infusion of the power of love, created in the elect their desire to carry out His commandments. What gave Winthrop's abstract model its peculiar power, though, were two additional themes that he grafted onto it: his organically imaged and Bible-derived injunctions concerning the proper social and economic behavior befitting a community "knitt together" by Christ and his strangely cosmic image of this tiny Puritan outpost bearing alone in the world the terrible responsibility for fulfilling—or not fulfilling—God's plan for human redemption. Edmund S. Morgan's *The Puritan Dilemma: The Story of John Winthrop* (Boston, 1958) presents a classic portrait of Winthrop's career and worldview. Loren Baritz has a thoughtful chapter on Winthrop's political ideas in his *City on a Hill: A History of Ideas and Myths in America* (New York, 1964), 3–45. For a challenging interpretation of the "Modell" as a foreshadowing of a dominant American rhetoric and ideology, see Sacvan Bercovitch, *The American Jeremiad* (Madison, Wis., 1978), 3–30.

God Almightie in his most holy and wise providence hath soe disposed of the Condicion of mankinde, as in all times some must be rich some poore, some highe and eminent in power and dignitie; others meane and in subieccion.

The Reason Hereof.

1. REAS: *First,* to hold conformity with the rest of his workes, being delighted to shewe forthe the glory of his wisdome in the variety and differance of the Creatures and the glory of his power, in ordering all these differences for the preservacion and good of the whole, and the glory of his greatnes that as it is the glory of princes to haue many officers, soe this great King will haue many Stewards counting himselfe more honoured in dispenceing his guifts to man by man, then if hee did it by his owne immediate hand.

2. REAS: *Secondly,* That he might haue the more occasion to manifest the worke of his Spirit: first, vpon the wicked in moderateing and restraineing them: soe that the riche and mighty should not eate vpp the poore, nor the poore, and dispised rise vpp against theire superiours, and shake off theire yoake; 2ly in the regenerate in exerciseing his graces in them, as in the greate ones, theire loue mercy, gentlenes, temperance etc., in the poore and inferiour sorte, theire faithe patience, obedience etc:

3. REAS: Thirdly, That every man might haue need of other, and from hence they might be all knitt more nearly together in the Bond of brotherly affeccion: from hence it appeares plainely that noe man is made more honourable then another or more wealthy etc., out of any perticuler and singuler respect to himselfe but for the glory of his Creator and the Common good of the Creature, Man; Therefore God still reserues the propperty of these guifts to himselfe as Ezek: 16. 17. he there calls wealthe his gold and his silver etc. Prov: 3. 9. he claimes theire seruice as his due honour the Lord with thy riches etc. All men being thus (by divine providence) rancked into two sortes, riche and poore; vnder the first, are comprehended all such as are able to liue comfortably by theire owne meanes duely improued; and all others are poore according to the former distribution. There are two rules whereby wee are to walke one towards another: JUSTICE and MERCY. These are allwayes distinguished in theire Act and in theire obiect, yet may they both concurre in the same Subiect in eache respect; as sometimes there may be an occasion of shewing mercy to a rich man, in some sudden danger of distresse, and allsoe doeing of meere Justice to a poor man in regard of some perticuler contract etc. There is likewise a double Lawe by which wee are regulated in our conversacion one towardes another: in both the former respects, the lawe of nature and the lawe of grace, or the morrall lawe or the lawe of the gospell, to omitt the rule of Justice as not propperly belonging to this purpose otherwise then it may fall into consideracion in some perticuler Cases: By the first of these lawes man as he was enabled soe withall [is] commaunded to loue his neighbour as himselfe vpon this ground stands all the precepts of the morrall law, which concernes our dealings with men. To apply this to the works of mercy this lawe requires two things first that every man afford his help to another in every want or distresse Secondly, That hee performe this out of the same affeccion, which makes him carefull of his owne good according to that of

Source: Winthrop Papers, vol. 2 (Boston: Massachusetts Historical Society, 1931), 282–95. Notes altered. Reprinted by permission of the Massachusetts Historical Society, Copyright © 1931.

our Saviour Math: [7.12] Whatsoever ye would that men should doe to you. This was practised by Abraham and Lott in entertaineing the Angells and the old man of Gibea.

The Lawe of Grace or the Gospell hath some differance from the former as in these respectes first the lawe of nature was giuen to man in the estate of innocency; this of the gospell in the estate of regeneracy: 2ly, the former propounds one man to another, as the same fleshe and Image of god, this as a brother in Christ allsoe, and in the Communion of the same spirit and soe teacheth vs to put a difference betweene Christians and others. Doe good to all especially to the household of faith; vpon this gound the Israelites were to putt a difference betweene the brethren of such as were strangers though not of the Canaanites. 3ly. The Lawe of nature could giue noe rules for dealeing with enemies for all are to be considered as freinds in the estate of inno-cency, but the Gospell commaunds loue to an enemy. proofe. If thine Enemie hunger feede him; Loue your Enemies doe good to them that hate you Math: 5. 44.

This Lawe of the Gospell propoundes likewise a difference of seasons and occa-sions there is a time when a christian must sell all and giue to the poore as they did in the Apostles times. There is a tyme allsoe when a christian (though they giue not all yet) must giue beyond theire abillity, as they of Macedonia. Cor: 2. 6. likewise community of perills calls for extraordinary liberallity and soe doth Community in some speciall seruice for the Churche. Lastly, when there is noe other meanes whereby our Christian brother may be releiued in this distresse, wee must help him beyond our ability, rather than tempt God, in putting him vpon help by miraculous or extraordi-nary meanes.

This duty of mercy is exercised in the kindes, Giueing, lending, and forgiueing.

QUEST. What rule shall a man observe in giueing in respect of the measure?

ANS. If the time and occasion be ordinary he is to giue out of his aboundance— let him lay aside, as god hath blessed him. If the time and occasion be extraordinary he must be ruled by them; takeing this withall, that then a man cannot likely doe too much especially, if he may leaue himselfe and his family vnder probable meanes of comfortable subsistance.

OBIECTION. A man must lay vpp for posterity, the fathers lay vpp for posterity and children and he is worse then an Infidell that prouideth not for his owne.

ANS: For the first, it is plaine, that it being spoken by way of Comparison it must be meant of the ordinary and vsuall course of fathers and cannot extend to times and occasions extraordinary; for the other place the Apostle speakes against such as walked inordinately, and it is without question, that he is worse then an Infidell whoe throughe his owne Sloathe and voluptuousnes shall neglect to prouide for his family.

OBIECTION. The wise mans Eies are in his head (saith Salomon) and foreseeth the plague, therefore wee must forecast and lay vpp against euill times when hee or his may stand in need of all he can gather.

ANS: This very Argument Salomon vseth to perswade to liberallity. Eccle: [11.1.] cast thy bread vpon the waters etc.: for thou knowest not what euill may come vpon the land Luke 16. make you freinds of the riches of Iniquity; you will aske how this shall be? very well. for first he that giues to the poore lends to the lord, and he will repay euen in this life an hundred fold to him or his. The righteous is ever mercifull and lendeth and his seed enioyeth the blessing; and besides wee know what advantage it will be to vs in the day of account, when many such Witnesses shall stand forthe for vs to witnesse the improuement of our Tallent. And I would knowe of those whoe pleade soe much for layeing vp for time to come, whether they hold that to be Gospell Math: 16. 19. Lay not vpp for yourselues Treasures vpon Earth etc. if they acknowl-edge it what extent will they allowe it; if onely to those primitiue times lett them consider the reason wherevpon our Saviour groundes it, the first is that they are subiect to the moathe, the rust the Theife. Secondly, They will steale away the hearte, where the treasure is there will the heart be allsoe. The reasons are of like force at all times therefore the exhortacion must be generall and perpetuall which [applies] all-wayes in respect of the loue and affeccion to riches and in regard of the things them-selues when any speciall seruice for the churche or perticuler distresse of our brother doe call for the vse of them; otherwise it is not onely lawfull but necessary to lay vpp as Joseph did to haue ready vppon such occasions, as the Lord (whose stewards wee are of them) shall call for them from vs: Christ giues vs an Instance of the first, when hee sent his disciples for the Asse, and bidds them answer the owner thus, the Lord hath need of him; soe when the Tabernacle was to be builte his [servant] sends to his people to call for their silver and gold etc.; and yeildes them noe other reason but that it was for his worke, when Elisha comes to the widowe of Sareptah and findes her prepareing to make ready her pittance for herselfe and family, he bids her first provide for him, he challengeth first gods parte which shee must first giue before shee must serue her owne family, all these teache vs that the lord lookes that when hee is pleased to call for his right in any thing wee haue, our owne Interest wee haue must stand aside, till his turne be serued, for the other wee need looke noe further then to that of John 1. he whoe hath this worlds goodes and seeth his brother to neede, and shutts vpp his Compassion from him, how dwelleth the loue of god in him, which comes punctually to this Conclusion: if thy brother be in want and thou canst help him, thou needst not make doubt, what thou shouldst doe, if thou louest god thou must help him.

QUEST: What rule must wee obserue in lending?

ANS: Thou must obserue whether thy brother hath present or probable, or possible meanes of repayeing thee, if ther be none of these, thou must giue him according to his necessity, rather then lend him as hee requires; if he hath present meanes of repayeing thee, thou art to looke at him, not as an Act of mercy, but by way of Com-merce, wherein thou arte to walke by the rule of Justice, but, if his meanes of repaye-ing thee be onely probable or possible then is hee an obiect of thy mercy thou must lend him, though there be danger of looseing it Deut: 15. 7. If any of thy brethren be poore etc. thou shalt lend him sufficient that men might not shift off this duty by the apparent hazzard, he tells them that though the Yeare of Jubile were at hand (when he must remitt it, if hee were not able to repay it before) yet he must lend him and that chearefully: it may not greiue thee to giue him (saith hee) and because some might obiect, why soe I should soone impoverishe my selfe and my family, he adds with all thy Worke etc. for our Saviour Math: 5. 42. From him that would borrow of thee turne not away.

QUEST: What rule must wee obserue in forgiueing?

ANS: Whether thou didst lend by way of Commerce or in mercy, if he haue noe-thing to pay thee [thou] must forgiue him (except in cause where thou hast a surety or a lawfull pleadge) Deut. 15. 2. Every seaventh yeare the Creditor was to quitt that which hee lent to his brother if hee were poore as appeares ver: 8[4]: saue when there shall be noe poore with thee. In all these and like Cases Christ was a generall rule

Math: 7. 22. Whatsoever ye would that men should doe to you doe yee the same to them allsoe.

Quest: What rule must wee obserue and walke by in cause of Community of perill?

Ans: The same as before, but with more enlargement towardes others and lesse respect towards our selues, and our owne right hence it was that in the primitiue Churche they sold all had all things in Common, neither did any man say that that which he possessed was his owne likewise in theire returne out of the Captiuity, because the worke was greate for the restoreing of the church and the danger of ene-mies was Common to all Nehemiah exhortes the Jewes to liberallity and readines in remitting theire debtes to theire brethren, and disposeth liberally of his owne to such as wanted and stands not vpon his owne due, which hee might haue demaunded of them, thus did some of our forefathers in times of persecucion here in England, and soe did many of the faithfull in other Churches whereof wee keepe an honourable remembrance of them, and it is to be obserued that both in Scriptures and latter stories of the Churches that such as haue beene most bountifull to the poore Saintes especially in these extraordinary times and occasions god hath left them highly Commended to posterity, as Zacheus, Cornelius, Dorcas, Bishop Hooper, the Cuttler of Brussells and divers others obserue againe that the scripture giues noe causion to restraine any from being over liberall this way; but all men to the liberall and cherefull practise hereof by the sweetest promises as to instance one for many, Isaiah 58. 6: Is not this the fast that I haue chosen to loose the bonds of wickednes, to take off the heavy burdens to lett the oppressed goe free and to breake every Yoake, to deale thy bread to the hungry and to bring the poore that wander into thy house, when thou seest the naked to cover them etc. then shall thy light breake forthe as the morneing, and thy healthe shall growe speedily, thy righteousnes shall goe before thee, and the glory of the lord shall embrace thee, then thou shalt call and the lord shall Answer thee etc. 2. 10: If thou power out thy soule to the hungry, then shall thy light spring out in darknes, and the lord shall guide thee continually, and satisfie thy Soule in draught, and make fatt thy bones, thou shalt be like a watered Garden, and they shall be of thee that shall build the old wast places etc. on the contrary most heavy cursses are layd vpon such as are straightened towards the Lord and his people Judg: 5. [23] Cursse ye Meroshe because the[y] came not to help the Lord etc. Pro: [21. 13] Hee whoe shutteth his eares from hearing the cry of the poore, he shall cry and shall not be heard: Math: 25. [41] Goe ye curssed into everlasting fire etc. [42.] I was hungry and ye fedd mee not. Cor: 2. 9. 16. [6.] He that soweth spareingly shall reape spareingly.

Haueing allready sett forth the practise of mercy according to the rule of gods lawe, it will be vsefull to lay open the groundes of it allsoe being the other parte of the Commaundement and that is the affeccion from which this exercise of mercy must arise, the Apostle tells vs that this loue is the fulfilling of the lawe, not that it is enough to loue our brother and soe noe further but in regard of the excellency of his partes giueing any motion to the other as the Soule to the body and the power it hath to sett all the faculties on worke in the outward exercise of this duty as when wee bid one make the clocke strike he doth not lay hand on the hammer which is the immediate instrument of the sound but setts on worke the first mouer or maine wheele, knoweing that will certainely produce the sound which hee intends; soe the way to drawe men to the workes of mercy is not by force of Argument from the goodnes or necessity of the worke, for though this course may enforce a rationall minde to some present Act of mercy as is frequent in experience, yet it cannot worke such a habit in a Soule as shall make it prompt vpon all occasions to produce the same effect but by frameing these affeccions of loue in the hearte which will as natiuely bring forthe the other, as any cause doth produce the effect.

The diffinition which the Scripture giues vs of loue is this Loue is the bond of perfection. First, it is a bond, or ligament. 2ly, it makes the worke perfect. There is noe body but consistes of partes and that which knitts these partes together giues the body its perfeccion, because it makes eache parte soe contiguous to other as thereby they doe mutually participate with eache other, both in strengthe and infirmity in pleasure and paine, to instance in the most perfect of all bodies, Christ and his church make one body: the severall partes of this body considered aparte before they were vnited were as disproportionate and as much disordering as soe many contrary quall-ities or elements but when christ comes and by his spirit and loue knitts all these partes to himselfe and each to other, it is become the most perfect and best propor-tioned body in the world Eph: 4. 16. "Christ by whome all the body being knitt together by every ioynt for the furniture thereof according to the effectuall power which is in the measure of every perfeccion of partes a glorious body without spott or wrinckle the ligaments hereof being Christ or his loue for Christ is loue 1 John: 4. 8. Soe this definition is right Loue is the bond of perfeccion.

From hence wee may frame these Conclusions.

1 first all true Christians are of one body in Christ 1. Cor. 12. 12. 13. 17. [27.] Ye are the body of Christ and members of [your?] parte.

2ly. The ligaments of this body which knitt together are loue.

3ly. Noe body can be perfect which wants its propper ligamentes.

4ly. All the partes of this body being thus vnited are made soe contiguous in a speciall relacion as they must needes partake of each others strength and infirmity, ioy, and sorrowe, weale and woe. 1 Cor: 12. 26. If one member suffers all suffer with it, if one be in honour, all reioyce with it.

5ly. This sensiblenes and Sympathy of each others Condicions will necessarily infuse into each parte a natiue desire and endeavour, to strengthen defend preserue and comfort the other.

To insist a little on this Conclusion being the product of all the former the truthe herof will appeare both by precept and patterne 1. John. 3. 10. yee ought to lay downe your liues for the brethren Gal: 6. 2. beare ye one anothers burthens and soe fulfill the lawe of Christ.

For patterns wee haue that first of our Saviour whoe out of his good will in obe-dience to his father, becomeing a parte of this body, and being knitt with it in the bond of loue, found such a natiue sensiblenes of our infirmities and sorrowes as hee willingly yeilded himselfe to deathe to ease the infirmities of the rest of his body and soe heale theire sorrowes: from the like Sympathy of partes did the Apostles and many thou-sands of the Saintes lay downe theire liues for Christ againe, the like wee may see in the members of this body among themselues. 1. Rom. 9. Paule could haue beene con-tented to haue beene seperated from Christ that the Jewes might not be cutt off from the body: It is very obseruable which hee professeth of his affectionate part[ak]eing with every member: whoe is weake (saith hee) and I am not weake? whoe is offended and I burne not; and againe. 2 Cor: 7. 13. therefore wee are comforted because yee were comforted. of Epaphroditus he speaketh Phil: 2. 30. that he regarded not his owne life to [do] him seruice soe Phebe. and others are called the seruantes of the Churche, now it is apparant that they serued not for wages or by Constrainte but out of loue, the like wee shall finde in the histories of the churche in all ages the sweete Sympathie of affeccions which was in the members of this body one towardes another, theire chearfullnes in serueing and suffering together how liberall they were without repineing harbourers without grudgeing and helpfull without reproacheing and all from hence they had feruent loue amongst them which onely make[s] the practise of mercy constant and easie.

The next consideration is how this loue comes to be wrought; Adam in his first estate was a perfect modell of mankinde in all theire generacions, and in him this loue was perfected in regard of the habit, but Adam Rent in himselfe from his Creator, rent all his posterity allsoe one from another, whence it comes that every man is borne with this principle in him, to loue and seeke himselfe onely and thus a man continueth till Christ comes and takes possession of the soule, and infuseth another principle loue to God and our brother. And this latter haueing continuall supply from Christ, as the head and roote by which hee is vnited get the predominency in the soule, soe by little and little expells the former 1 John 4. 7. loue cometh of god and every one that loueth is borne of god, soe that this loue is the fruite of the new birthe, and none can haue it but the new Creature, now when this quallity is thus formed in the soules of men it workes like the Spirit vpon the drie bones Ezek. 37. [7] bone came to bone, it gathers together the scattered bones or perfect old man Adam and knitts them into one body againe in Christ whereby a man is become againe a liueing soule.

The third Consideracion is concerning the exercise of this loue, which is twofold, inward or outward, the outward hath beene handled in the former preface of this discourse, for vnfolding the other wee must take in our way that maxime of philosophy, Simile simili gaudet or like will to like; for as it is things which are carued [1] with disafeccion to eache other, the ground of it is from a dissimilitude or [*blank*] ariseing from the contrary or different nature of the things themselues, soe the ground of loue is an apprehension of some resemblance in the things loued to that which affectes it, this is the cause why the Lord loues the Creature, soe farre as it hath any of his Image in it, he loues his elect because they are like himselfe, he beholds them in his beloued sonne: soe a mother loues her childe, because shee throughly conceiues a resemblance of herselfe in it. Thus it is betweene the members of Christ, each discernes by the worke of the spirit his owne Image and resemblance in another, and therefore cannot but loue him as he loues himselfe: Now when the soule which is of a sociable nature findes any thing like to it selfe, it is like Adam when Eue was brought to him, shee must haue it one with herselfe this is fleshe of my fleshe (saith shee) and bone of my bone shee conceiues a greate delighte in it, therefore shee desires nearenes and familiarity with it: shee hath a great propensity to doe it good and receiues such content in it, as feareing the miscarriage of her beloued shee bestowes it in the inmost closett of her heart, shee will not endure that it shall want any good which shee can giue it, if by occasion shee be withdrawne from the Company of it, shee is still lookeing towardes the place where shee left her beloued, if shee heare it groane shee is with it presently, if shee finde it sadd and disconsolate shee sighes and mournes with it, shee

1. The text is here evidently corrupt.

hath noe such ioy, as to see her beloued merry and thriueing, if shee see it wronged, shee cannot beare it without passion, shee setts noe boundes of her affeccions, nor hath any thought of reward, shee findes recompence enoughe in the exercise of her loue towardes it, wee may see this Acted to life in Jonathan and David. Jonathan a valiant man endued with the spirit of Christ, soe soone as hee Discovers the same spirit in David had presently his hearte knitt to him by this linement of loue, soe that it is said he loued him as his owne soule, he takes soe great pleasure in him that hee stripps himselfe to adorne his beloued, his fathers kingdome was not soe precious to him as his beloued David, Dauid shall haue it with all his hearte, himselfe desires noe more but that hee may be neare to him to reioyce in his good hee chooseth to converse with him in the wildernesse even to the hazzard of his owne life, rather then with the greate Courtiers in his fathers Pallace; when hee sees danger towards him, hee spares neither care paines, nor perill to divert it, when Iniury was offered his beloued David, hee could not beare it, though from his owne father, and when they must parte for a Season onely, they thought theire heartes would haue broake for sorrowe, had not theire affeccions found vent by aboundance of Teares: other instances might be brought to shewe the nature of this affeccion as of Ruthe and Naomi and many others, but this truthe is cleared enough. If any shall obiect that it is not possible that loue should be bred or vpheld without hope of requitall, it is graunted but that is not our cause, for this loue is allwayes vnder reward it never giues, but it allwayes receiues with advantage: first, in regard that among the members of the same body, loue and affection are reciprocall in a most equall and sweete kinde of Commerce. 2ly [3ly], in regard of the pleasure and content that the exercise of loue carries with it as wee may see in the naturall body the mouth is at all the paines to receiue, and mince the foode which serues for the nourishment of all the other partes of the body, yet it hath noe cause to complaine; for first, the other partes send backe by secret passages a due proporcion of the same nourishment in a better forme for the strengthening and comforteing the mouthe. 2ly the labour of the mouthe is accompanied with such pleasure and content as farre exceedes the paines it takes: soe is it in all the labour of loue, among christians, the partie loueing, reapes loue againe as was shewed before, which the soule covetts more then all the wealthe in the world. 2ly [4ly]. noething yeildes more pleasure and content to the soule then when it findes that which it may loue fervently, for to loue and liue beloued is the soules paradice, both heare and in heaven: In the State of Wedlock there be many comfortes to beare out the troubles of that Condicion; but let such as haue tryed the most, say if there be any sweetnes in that Condicion comparable to the exercise of mutuall loue.

From the former Consideracions ariseth these Conclusions.

1 First, This loue among Christians is a reall thing not Imaginarie.

2ly. This loue is as absolutely necessary to the being of the body of Christ, as the sinewes and other ligaments of a naturall body are to the being of that body.

3ly. This loue is a divine spirituall nature free, actiue strong Couragious permanent vnder valueing all things beneathe its propper obiect, and of all the graces this makes vs nearer to resemble the virtues of our heavenly father.

4ly, It restes in the loue and wellfare of its beloued, for the full and certaine knowledge of these truthes concerning the nature vse, [and] excellency of this grace, that which the holy ghost hath left recorded 1. Cor. 13. may giue full satisfaccion which is needfull for every true member of this louely body of the Lord Jesus, to worke vpon theire heartes, by prayer meditacion continuall exercise at least of the speciall [power] of this grace till Christ be formed in them and they in him all in eache other knitt together by this bond of loue.

It rests now to make some applicacion of this discourse by the present designe which gaue the occasion of writeing of it. Herein are 4 things to be propounded: first the persons, 2ly, the worke, 3ly, the end, 4ly the meanes.

1. For the persons, wee are a Company professing our selues fellow members of Christ, In which respect onely though wee were absent from eache other many miles, and had our imploymentes as farre distant, yet wee ought to account our selues knitt together by this bond of loue, and liue in the excercise of it, if wee would haue comforte of our being in Christ, this was notorious in the practise of the Christians in former times, as is testified of the Waldenses from the mouth of one of the adversaries Aeneas Syluius, mutuo [solent amare] pene antequam norint, they vse to loue any of theire owne religion even before they were acquainted with them.

2ly. for the worke wee haue in hand, it is by a mutuall consent through a speciall overruleing providence, and a more then an ordinary approbation of the Churches of Christ to seeke out a place of Cohabitation and Consorteshipp vnder a due forme of Government both ciuill and ecclesiasticall. In such cases as this the care of the publique must oversway all private respects, by which not onely conscience, but meare Ciuill pollicy doth binde vs; for it is a true rule that perticuler estates cannott subsist in the ruine of the publique.

3ly. The end is to improue our liues to doe more seruice to the Lord the comforte and encrease of the body of christe whereof wee are members that our selues and posterity may be the better preserued from the Common corrupcions of this euill world to serue the Lord and worke out our Salvacion vnder the power and purity of his holy Ordinances.

4ly for the meanes whereby this must bee effected, they are 2fold, a Conformity with the worke and end wee aime at, these wee see are extraordinary, therefore wee must not content our selues with vsuall ordinary meanes whatsoever wee did or ought to haue done when wee liued in England, the same must wee doe and more allsoe where wee goe: That which the most in theire Churches maineteine as a truthe in profession onely, wee must bring into familiar and constant practise, as in this duty of loue wee must loue brotherly without dissimulation, wee must loue one another with a pure hearte feruently wee must beare one anothers burthens, wee must not looke onely on our owne things, but allsoe on the things of our brethren, neither must wee think that the lord will beare with such faileings at our hands as hee dothe from those among whome wee haue liued, and that for 3 Reasons.

1. In regard of the more neare bond of mariage, betweene him and vs, wherein he hath taken vs to be his after a most strickt and peculiar manner which will make him the more Jealous of our loue and obedience soe he tells the people of Israell, you onely haue I knowne of all the families of the Earthe therefore will I punishe you for your Transgressions.

2ly, because the lord will be sanctified in them that come neare him. Wee know that there were many that corrupted the seruice of the Lord some setting vpp Alters before his owne, others offering both strange fire and strange Sacrifices allsoe; yet there came noe fire from heaven, or other sudden Judgement vpon them as did vpon Nadab and Abihu whoe yet wee may thinke did not sinne presumptuously.

3ly When God giues a speciall Commission he lookes to haue it strictly obserued in every Article, when hee gaue Saule a Commission to destroy Amaleck hee indented with him vpon certaine Articles and because hee failed in one of the least, and that vpon a faire pretence, it lost him the kingdome, which should haue beene his reward, if hee had obserued his Commission: Thus stands the cause betweene God and vs, wee are entered into Covenant with him for this worke, wee haue taken out a Commission, the Lord hath giuen vs leaue to drawe our owne Articles wee haue professed to enterprise these Accions vpon these and these ends, wee haue herevpon besought him of favour and blessing: Now if the Lord shall please to heare vs, and bring vs in peace to the place wee desire, then hath hee ratified this Covenant and sealed our Commission, [and] will expect a strickt performance of the Articles contained in it, but if wee shall neglect the observacion of these Articles which are the ends wee haue propounded, and dissembling with our God, shall fall to embrace this present world and prosecute our carnall intencions, seekeing greate things for our selues and our posterity, the Lord will surely breake out in wrathe against vs be revenged of such a periured people and make vs knowe the price of the breache of such a Covenant.

Now the onely way to avoyde this shipwracke and to provide for our posterity is to followe the Counsell of Micah, to doe Justly, to loue mercy, to walk humbly with our God, for this end, wee must be knitt together in this worke as one man, wee must entertaine each other in brotherly Affeccion, wee must be willing to abridge our selues of our superfluities, for the supply of others necessities, wee must vphold a familiar Commerce together in all meekenes, gentlenes, patience and liberallity, wee must delight in eache other, make others Condicions our owne reioyce together, mourne together, labour, and suffer together, allwayes haueing before our eyes our Commission and Community in the worke, our Community as members of the same body, soe shall wee keepe the vnitie of the spirit in the bond of peace, the Lord will be our God and delight to dwell among vs, as his owne people and will commaund a blessing vpon vs in all our wayes, soe that wee shall see much more of his wisdome power goodnes and truthe then formerly wee haue beene acquainted with, wee shall finde that the God of Israell is among vs, when tenn of vs shall be able to resist a thousand of our enemies, when hee shall make vs a prayse and glory, that men shall say of succeeding plantacions: the lord make it like that of New England: for wee must Consider that wee shall be as a Citty vpon a Hill, the eies of all people are vppon vs; soe that if wee shall deale falsely with our god in this worke wee haue vndertaken and soe cause him to withdrawe his present help from vs, wee shall be made a story and a by-word through the world, wee shall open the mouthes of enemies to speake euill of the wayes of god and all professours for Gods sake; wee shall shame the faces of many of gods worthy seruants, and cause theire prayers to be turned into Cursses vpon vs till wee be consumed out of the good land whether wee are goeing: And to shutt vpp this discourse with that exhortacion of Moses that faithfull seruant of the Lord in his last farewell to Israell Deut. 30. Beloued there is now sett before vs life, and good, deathe and euill in that wee are Commaunded this day to loue the Lord our God, and to loue one another to walke in his wayes and to keepe his Commaundements and his Ordinance, and his lawes, and the Articles of our Covenant with him that wee may liue and be multiplyed, and that the Lord our God may blesse vs in the land whether wee goe to possesse it: But if our heartes shall turne away soe that wee will not obey, but shall be seduced and worshipp [serue *cancelled*] other Gods our pleasures, and proffitts, and serue them; it is propounded vnto vs this day, wee shall surely perishe out of the good Land whether wee passe over this vast Sea to possesse it;

> Therefore lett vs choose life,
> that wee, and our Seede,
> may liue; by obeyeing his
> voyce, and cleaueing to him,
> for hee is our life, and
> our prosperity.

SAMUEL WILLARD

Selection from *A Compleat Body of Divinity*
1688

Of the leading divines of New England's second generation, Samuel Willard (1640–1707) was probably the most learned. Although a prolific lecturer and for his last six years the acting president of Harvard College, he achieved his most enduring fame as the author of the most systematic exposition of Puritan theology ever published in the American colonies. In this one-thousand-page tome, originally delivered as a marathon series of 250 lectures over nearly twenty years, he brought to bear on all the major questions of the Westminster Catechism a large fund of the logical, metaphysical, and rhetorical learning of the Western world of his day. In the two lectures included here, Willard delineated the history and character of God's two convenants with humankind. The second convenant, the convenant of grace, appeared in Willard's rendering as executed by God without regard to human "works," but also as "a Rule of Happiness" both eminently just and carefully adjusted to man and woman's reasonable and responsible nature. For a thorough explication of Willard's theological thought, see Ernest Benson Lowrie, *The Shape of the Puritan Mind: The Thought of Samuel Willard* (New Haven, 1974). Perry Miller, "The Marrow of Puritan Divinity," in Miller's *Errand into the Wilderness* (Cambridge, Mass., 1956), 48–98, is the classic formulation of the convenant idea in Puritan theology. But for a recent, well-supported contrasting interpretation, see Michael McGiffert, "Grace and Works: The Rise and Division of Covenant Divinity in Elizabethan Puritanism," *Harvard Theological Review,* 75 (1982), 463–502.

Sermon *IV*.

QUESTION II.

*W H A T   R U L E hath God given to direct us,
how we may glorify and enjoy Him ?*

ANSWER.

The *W O R D* of God (which is contained in
the Scriptures of the *Old & New Testament*) is
the *O N L Y* Rule to direct us, how we may
glorify and enjoy Him.

E V E R Y wise Agent always observes this method : he first propounds an *End* to
himself, and fixeth upon it, and then he sets himself to study and find out proper &
sutable *Means,* which he may improve in his regular pursuance of it. This Scheme,
Idea, or Exemplar of the means, and the way rightly to apply them to his purpose, is
that which is called his *Rule of Operation.* And such a Rule is requisite in order to the
practice of every *Art ;* and he that is throughly acquainted with it, and dexterous at it,
may only be called an *Artist.* Such a method as this is followed in our *Catechism,* in
laying down the Doctrine of *Religion* or *Divinity.* Having therefore rightly stated and
limitted man's great *End,* in the *former* question, there remains nothing but to set him
in the *Way* to his unfailing obtainment of it ; which is the design of all that follows.
And there are two things here requisite, *viz.* that we be *satisfied about our Rule,* and
that we be well *acquainted with the Contents of it.* The former is endeavoured in the
Question we are now upon ; the latter is pursued in those that follow after.

T H E main scope then of the present Inquiry, is about *the Rule itself.* Man's happiness is a great and momentous thing ; if he miss of that, he hath laboured in vain.
He had need therefore have a *sure & unerring* Rule, to direct him thereunto, that he
be not deceived & disappointed ; because his loss will be irreparable. We are therefore
here pointed to this Rule, and have it characterized unto us.

F O R a right Understanding, and full Explication of this Question and Answer ;
there are these things will call for our distinct Consideration. (1.) That Man *must* have
a *Rule* to direct him, or else he can never attain to his chief end. (2). That this Rule
can be but *one.* (3.) That the *Word of God* is the *only* Rule. (4.) That this word, which
is the Rule, is contained in the *Scriptures* of the *Old* and New *Testament.*

Prop. I. *T H A T* Man *must have a* R U L E *to direct him, with which he is well
acquainted* ; or else he can never attain to his chief End. There are two things contained
in the Proposition. (1.) That there must be a *Rule.* (2.) That we must have *Acquaintance*
with it. Both these may be evidenced.

Article 1. *T H E R E must be a Rule.* Man cannot be led to his End *without* one.
The necessity of Man's having a Rule, may be argued from two Considerations.

[1.] F R O M the Consideration of *the Respect which Man bears to his End* : and
that whether lookt upon in a state of *Integrity* or of *Apostasy.*

Source: Samuel Willard, *A Compleat Body of Divinity in Two Hundred and Fifty Expository Lectures on the
Assembly's Shorter Catechism* (Boston: B. Green & S. Kneeland, 1726), 10–16.

(1.) L O O K upon him in his *Primitive Perfection,* standing in his Integrity ; and here he could never reach his End without a Rule. The following Conclusions will evidence the Truth of this Assertion.

1. *M A N was not made happy.* That Man was (strictly speaking) neither happy nor miserable in his *first* state, is a Truth undeniable, if we do but acknowledge his happiness to consist in his *attaining his chief End,* and his misery in his *missing* or falling short of it. He was *fitted for* happiness, inasmuch as he had all that stock of Grace put into his hands, which was sufficient by improvement to make him happy. There was nothing wanting in that Image of God, which he had stamped upon him : And yet he was *capable of losing* his felicity, and becoming *unhappy;* being made muta-ble, and capable of losing that Image, as the Event unhappily proved. *Man* was there-fore at first made a *Probationer* for happiness : and that by the law of special Government.

2. *H A P P I N E S S was proposed to Man at first in a Covenant-Way.* That there was a Covenant between *God & Adam,* the Scripture assures us, and gives us an account of the Nature and Terms of it. Now in a Covenant there are always those two things, *Something promised* upon condition on one part, and the *conditions required* on the other part, in order to the obtaining it. The *Thing* proposed to Man in the first Covenant was *Happiness.* The *manner* of proposing it, was by telling him *how he was to come by it,* if ever he expected to become the owner of it. The Terms therefore so run, *Do & Live,* Rom. 10.5.

3. *H E N C E there was a fixed or stated way, to which Man's being made happy was restrained.* For, if Happiness were not promised to man *absolutely,* but *hypotheti-cally,* it must needs *depend* upon that hypothesis ; and the performance of the Condi-tion is the *way* to his felicity : and that this was fixed, is therein evident, because together with a firm *Promise* made to him, That if he obeyed, he should be happy, there was as strong a *Threatning,* That if he came short of it, he should undoubtedly be miserable, *Gen.* 2.17.

4. *H E could neither find nor keep this way, without a Rule of direction* ; and con-sequently could never have reached blessedness. He could never have known, when he *served* to his end, or when he *mist* of it. He had been lost in a wilderness, out of which he could not have gotten, but must have been at an utter Loss. In summ, there was a *Medium* between a state of *Innocence,* and a state of *Felicity* : there was a way to pass safe to it, and a way to miss of it. And to enable him to chuse the one, and avoid the other, he must have a Rule.

(2.) M U C H more does Man need a Rule, if we look upon him in his state of *Apostasy.* And this is that which we are mostly concerned in ; for that is the Condition of all *Adam's* Posterity. That *fallen* Man needs a Rule to guide him to Salvation, will appear if we consider, ———

1. *T H A T Sin hath made him truly & wofully* Miserable *and* Wretched. He is not only not happy, but he is fallen from that *Nearness* to it, in which he once stood, into a great *Distance* from Felicity. He is separated from his end, is *fallen short of the Glory of God,* (Rom. 3.23.) and is removed from the *Enjoyment* of him, (Isai. 59.2.) and because in these Two, his Blessedness did consist, the *loss* of them declares him wretched.

2. *T H A T if ever fallen Man recover happiness, he must be* brought back *again to this great End of his.* As long as he is out of his road, nothing but *destruction* and *misery are in his ways,* (Rom 3.16.) He can never be truly blessed, but only in

the glorifying God, and enjoying him ; because happiness is only in reaching his chief end.

3. *T H E R E is something* required *of man, in order to his recovering his Felicity.* He is not only to be passive, but *active* too in this affair. There is *Faith* in Christ, and new *Obedience* requisite, as will afterwards appear. As man was at first made capable of being happy in a Covenant-way : So fallen man is recovered to Blessedness in a Covenant-way. Hence the terms are declared in the Gospel. See *Mark* 16. 16. *Rom.* 8. 13. *Heb.* 12. 14.

4. *H E N C E he must have a* Rule *for this.* The *Gospel* must have its Precepts, as well as the Law. Fallen Man cannot steer his course without a Compass. The *gate is strait,* and *the way is narrow,* and *few find it.* (Mat. 7. 14.) It is vain for him to endeavour it, unless he have a Clue to direct him.

T H A T Man must have a Rule further appears, ———

[2.] F R O M the Consideration *of the nature of a Rule.* A Rule is nothing else but *that whereby a man is guided so to do his Work, as to sute it to the End and Use for which he doth it* : and the reason of it is, because he may else miss, and so lose his Labour. There is necessarily requisite a *Sutableness* between the *Means,* and the *End,* for which they are used : Else means are vain. The right suting of them, 'tis the nature of a Rule to discover : and no man can be an *Artist* in any employment without it. And how then shall Man work out his Salvation, if he have no such Direction ?

Articl. 2. *T H A T Man must have Acquaintance with this Rule.* It is not enough that there *be* one, but *he* must be *skilled* in it. To clear this, Consider ———

1. *M A N is made* a Cause by Counsel *of his own Actions.* God hath given him an *understanding,* capable of discerning ; and a *will,* able to choose his way. This is a priviledge bestowed upon Man above all other Creatures in this lower World. Job 35. II. *God teacheth us more than the beasts of the earth, and maketh us wiser then the fowls of heaven.*

2. *G O D deals with man in a way that is* suited *to his Nature.* He treats him as a *Reasonable* Creature. He sutes his state to his *Constitution,* accommodates it to such a sort of Being. Inferior Beings have a Rule, as well as Man: But God guides them only by Instinct. *They* cannot *know* their Rule. It is sufficient for them, that *He* knows it, and hath imprinted it upon their Natures. But God deals with Man in a way of *Precepts, Promises, & Threatnings,* which is a *Moral* Way. The whole Scripture gives us account of this manner of God's treating Man.

3. *H E N C E Man can never attain his End, without he* knows *his Rule.* The Service God expects of Man is a *reasonable Service,* (Rom. 12, 1.) He must be *voluntary* in his Obedience : God requires the *Heart.* He must *choose* the ways of God : And how can he do so, except he *knows* them ? For this reason it is said, that *without knowledge* the mind of Man cannot be *good,* and that a people are *destroyed* for lack of Knowledge. There is no such thing as blind Obedience in Religion.

Prop. II. *T H A T this Rule can be but* ONE. This Proposition is not so to be understood, as if there were not *many particular Rules* prescribed, to be followed by men, in order to Salvation. Out of doubt, so many several *Precepts* as are laid down in Scripture, are so many particular Rules to direct us in our way. But the meaning is, that there is but one *System* or *Body of Rules* ; but one Directory, according to which he can so order his way as to be happy. This is called a *Rule,* Gal. 6. 16. And that this is but *One,* will appear, if we consider these Arguments.

1. *T H A T Man's Happiness depends upon his performing the* Conditions *of the*

Covenant, in which it is offered to him. God is the Author of Blessedness, and it is his free gift. He therefore hath sovereign arbitrary Authority to propose the Terms on which he will bestow it : and having so done, if Man expects to be happy, he must see to the fulfilment of *these* Terms; else he can never lay Claim or pretend a Title to it. Nay, if he miss of the *Condition* of the promise, he presently brings himself under the *Threatning* ; and for this reason Precepts are not only given affirmatively, but *negatively* too.

2. *T H A T there is but* one Way, *in one* Covenant, *according to which God hath engaged to make Man happy.* It is true, there are two Covenants, in which God hath been concerned with Man ; the Covenant of *Works,* and the Covenant of *Grace* : and these have their *several* ways and rules. In the *first,* Man was to be made happy by *Works* : in the *second,* by *Grace.* The former depended upon man's *personal Obedience* : the latter upon *Christ's.* The former called for *doing,* the other for *believing.* But each of them have their *limited* way. And man being *fallen* from the first Covenant-Condition, and set it against him, and having lost his strength, it can *no more* be a Rule of Happiness to him. It is now only by the *New* Covenant, that he can ever hope to obtain Life & Salvation : and the Way to it, according to this Covenant, is determined ; and therefore the Rule can be but one. For,

1. *T H E R E is no Salvation without* Reconciliation *to God.* As long as God and He are Enemies, He is unhappy. God only can save him ; and he will save him only in the way of Reconciliation. Nay, he cannot be happy but in the *Enjoyment* of God ; which how can he come at, till reconciled ? Till then, he is *without God,* Eph. 2. 12.

2. *T H E R E is but* one Mediator *of reconci[li]ation,* and that is *Jesus Christ,* as the Apostle tells us expressly, 1 *Tim.* 2. 4. There is no coming to God but *by him* : out of him God is a *Consuming Fire.* He only hath satisfy'd provoked Justice, and pulled down the wall of partition. Thro' him then, and in no other way must we obtain Reconciliation.

3. *T H E R E is but* one way *to become* interested *in the Satisfaction of Christ,* and partake in reconciliation by him ; and that is by *believing* in him. Joh. 3. 36. *He that believeth on the Son, hath everlasting life : and he that believeth not the Son, shall not see life ; but the wrath of God abideth on him.* Christ is not *actually* a Saviour to *all* men indiscriminatively, but *only* to Believers. He therefore bad his Disciples to preach *That,* as the *Sum* of the Gospel. Mark 16. 15, 16. *Preach the gospel to every creature. He that believeth and is baptized, shall be saved ; but he that believeth not shall be damned.*

4. *T H E R E is but* one way of serving God *in new & evangelical* Obedience, and that is by *living to the will of God.* (1 *Pet.* 4.2.) God hath told man *what* is his Will, wherein he expects to be served by him, (*Mic.* 6. 8) and this only hath a *Promise* given to it : without which, it is bold *presumption* for a man to challenge to himself a reward of Blessedness.

A N D here we have an easy Resolution to that case which some so perplex themselves about, viz,

Quest. W H E T H E R Man may be saved in any *Religion, provided he be* true to *the observance of it ?*

Answ. T O bring this Case to the *Premisses,* I'll lay down these few following Conclusions ;

1. T H A T, if there be but *one Rule* guiding to blessedness, and Man must *know* that Rule, or he cannot be blessed, then no Religion can save a Man, but that only in which this Rule is made known. Hence therefore the Word of God discovers the *misery*

of men who are *Strangers* to this Rule. The Apostle argues, Rom. 10. 14. *How shall they believe in him of whom they have not heard ?* How shall man guide his steps to Life, if he have not a discovery of the *Way* ? Or guide them right, if he have not the *true Way* ? The Wise Man tells us, *Where there is no Vision, the people perish*, Prov. 29. 18.

2. T H A T there may be *different Sects* in Religion, and yet men may be *saved* in them. We are to distinguish between *diverse* Religions, and *Diversity in* Religion. Through our knowing *but in part*, it is come to pass, that Professors of Christianity have been of diverse Opinions in many things ; and their difference hath occasioned several *Denominations* ; but while they agree in the *Foundation*, they may be saved. So *Paul* assures us, 1 *Cor.* 3. 11, 12, &c.

3. T H A T there are *Religions* in the World, that not only have *no discoveries* of this *one* Rule, but prescribe to men Rules *contradictory* thereunto. The Truth of this Assertion cannot be suspected, by him that hath but a little Acquaintance with the several Religions, which the Children of Men have taken up, and followed. If we look upon all the Sects of the *Gentile* Religion, we shall not find in them any the least footsteps of man's Salvation by *Christ*, and faith in him. They have set up *Idolatrous* Worship, and served gods of their own making, bowed down to stocks and stones : among Twenty Thousand gods, have mist of the *true One* ; have betook themselves to moral *Vertues*, as the way to felicity ; and though they had *Sacrifices*, yet they neither used them as *typical* shadows of *Christ*, nor did they offer them to G O D, but to *Devils*. If we look upon the *Mahometan* ; though they do in word acknowledge *God* and *Christ*, yet they neither acknowledge Christ as a *Redeemer*, nor do they prescribe *faith* in him as necessary, nor yet do they acknowledge his *Laws* : but set up *their own* in Opposition to his. If we consider the *Anti-Christian* ; whatever pretence they make, yet they have *subverted* this Rule, in the foundations of it ; inasmuch as they have joyned *other* Mediators unto Christ ; have *enervated* faith in his Righteousness for Justification & Salvation; and brought back a Covenant of *Works* ; have set up their own *Canons*, not only in equality with, but in *Opposition* to his Commands ; and because they loved not the Truth, have been left to *believe Lies*.

4. H E N C E the *closer* such men follow *these Religions*, the further they are from *Happiness* ; because they thereby keep at the greater *distance* from the *only Rule* of Salvation. They mistake, that think *conscientious* following an erroneous Rule, is a *Salve* for the Errors of it. Ignorance is a damning evil ; and Ignorance in the Understanding will beget *Error* in the *Conscience*, and there is no reason why God should not punish Sin in the *Conscience*, as well as Sin in the *Will*.

I T therefore tells us, that it is a matter of great, yea infinite Concernment to us, that we labour to be *rightly acquainted* with the Rule we are to follow in our pursuit of happiness : and therefore that we do not take it upon Credit ; but make *diligent inquiry* to know, what is the good & perfect and acceptable Will of God, left otherwise to take a great deal of pains to *no purpose*, and following a *false* guide, do in the end miss of, and finally fall altogether short of our desired Salvation.

[APRIL 24. 1688.]

Sermon V.

Prop. I I I. *T H A T the* W O R D of G O D *is this only Rule.* If Man cannot be happy, without a Rule that can direct him to it, it must needs be his great concernment to know it, and not be mistaken. Now when the Word of God is said to be the Rule, it is a *metonymical* Expression, and intends that it is therein *contained* & no where else. Here therefore, two things are to be considered. (1.) What we understand by the Word of God? (2.) How it appears to be the only Rule?

Q. 1. *W H A T are we to understand by the Word of God?*

A. T H I S Expression is *variously* used in Scripture : Especially,

1. For *the Son of God,* who is the *Eternal Word,* (*Joh.* 1. 1, 14.) So called, because by him God hath been pleased to make himself *known* to his People. Ver. 18. *No man hath seen God at any time ; the only begotten Son, which is in the bosom of the Father, he hath declared him.*

2. F O R *the Eternal Decree* or Ordinance, in which God laid out and determined the works of Efficiency. So *Psal.* 148. 8.

3. F O R God's powerful *Administration* of the Works of Creation & Providence. There is a *Creating* Word (*Psal.* 33. 6.) and there is a *Preserving* Word, (*Mat.* 4. 4. *Heb.* 1. 3.) But neither of these is here applicable[.]

4. F O R *the Revelation or Discovery of his approving Will.* The proper use of *Speech* or *Words* among men, is to communicate their minds & thoughts one to another : and hence 'tis metaphorically applied to God, in respect of those *manifestations,* which he makes to the Children of men, of himself ; and is more especially restrained to those discoveries, wherein he lets them know what is their *Duty,* and wherein they may be capable of pleasing him. And this is the most frequent use of the Word in Scripture. In what way soever God sees meet to make known his mind to us, in that way he may be said to *speak* to us ; which the Apostle tells us hath been in *divers manners.* Heb. 1. 1.

Q. 2. *H O W does it appear to be the only Rule?*

A. W E may here (to expedite this matter) call to mind, that there have been *two Covenants,* in which God hath traded with men about their happiness, *viz.* that of *Works,* and that of *Grace.* As to the *former,* or that of works, there needs no applying of this Consideration to it, because man is no longer to expect felicity by it. If fallen man could have attained his end according to the tenour of that, the second had been *superfluous.* Gal. 3. 21. *Is the law then against the promises of God? God forbid : for if there had been a law given which could have given life, verily Righteousness should have been by the law.* That Covenant stands armed with *Curses,* and all that are under it can expect nothing else : Ver. 10. *For as many as are of the works of the law, are under the curse : for it is written, Cursed is every one that continueth not in all things which are written in the book of the law to do them.* And yet if there were need, it might be evidenced that God's Word was Man's only Rule there : but because *Adam's* apostate Children can expect Life & Salvation only according to the tenour of the Covenant of *Grace,* it will suffice to make it appear, that the Word of God is the only Rule, to direct us to glorify and enjoy him, in the way of *this* Covenant[.] And this will be manifest by these Propositions.

1. T H A T Man by his fall *mist* of the happiness offered in the first Covenant, & brought himself under a condition of *misery.* Man's happiness consists in the *glorifying* of God, & *enjoying* him : and the fall cut him off from both. From the former, Rom. 3. 23. *For all have sinned, and come short of the glory of God* : From the latter. Isa. 59[.] 2. *Your iniquities have separated between you and your God.* And hence he fell from Life into a state of Death : for therein did the Curse consist. Gen. 2. 17. *In the day that thou eatest thereof, thou shalt surely die.* So that all the Children of men are not only born

capable of Misery : But they are born *actually* miserable. Hence this *Death* is said to be *past upon all men,* Rom. 5. 12.

2. T H A T fallen man is *no longer capable* of being made *happy* by *that* Covenant. For, though his happiness be still in attaining his end, and his end be still the fame that ever it was, yet it is not to be advanced by him *in that way* wherein it was at *first* prescribed : and this, not by reason of any default in the Law or Covenant, (that is holy, & just and good) but by reason of *his own Impotency.* Rom. 7. 13, 14. *Was then that which is good, made death unto me ? God forbid. For we know that the law is spiritual : but I am carnal, sold under sin.* And here is a double Impotency exprest in the two Phrases : — *Carnal,* i. e. Sinful *naturally* and *habitually* ; and so not able to *keep the Law,* by which God may be glorified, and I perform the Condition of Life : ———— *Sold under Sin,* i. e. under the *Sentence* of Condemnation ; not able to *make Satisfaction,* and remove the Curse. So that this Covenant speaks nothing but *terrour* and *despair* to all those that are held under the Conditions of it.

3. T H A T hence, if ever the undone Creature be *restored* to happiness, by attaining his end, there must be *another way* found out for it. If blessedness can be no longer *by the law,* then either man must *never* be blessed ; Or, there must be a *new law* of blessedness provided for him ; Or he must be made blessed *without any,* which cannot be ; for, if he could not be happy when he was *innocent,* but by closing with his Rule, and reaching his End, much less can he be so now he is *miserable,* unless there be a way to rid him of his misery, and bring him back to felicity. If therefore the law of *works* cannot, something *else* must, or otherwise he must needs perish. And if there be another *way,* there must of necessity be another *Rule* ; This being a directory suited to the way, and therefore cannot but vary accordingly. Hence that, Heb. 7. 12. *For the priesthood being changed, there is made of necessity a change also of the law.*

4. T H A T the *Recovery* of fallen man from this Misery, is an act of *God's sovereign Pleasure.* It derives from hence, and hath its dependance here. If, when man had come short of his end, and lost his happiness, he had left him there without hopes forever, he could not have done him any *injury* ; it had been but an Hell of *his own* procuring. Hence the Original of man's Recovery is referred to *God's Will.* Eph. 1. 5. *Having predestinated us to the adoption of children by Jesus Christ to himself, according to the good pleasure of his will.* God had once brought himself under an Obligation to give him life in case of Obedience ; but he had not obliged himself to deliver him, if he should cast himself away.

5. T H A T hence the *Way,* in which this recovery is to be obtained, *depends upon* that Pleasure of His. He that might have chosen, whether *ever* he would have saved us, hath the liberty of prescribing (as he sees meet) *how* he will bring it about, and upon what *Terms* we may expect it. If *he* do not restore us, none can : and if he do, it is *free Grace.* Who then shall prescribe to him? Or who shall make his terms for him ? And for this reason it is, that *Salvation* is said to *belong to God.*

6. T H A T as God *purposed* from Eternity to bring back a number of fallen Men, so he provided a *new Covenant-way* to accomplish it in. God hath a company of *Elect* or chosen ones among the ruins of the fall, whom he appointed to felicity in the days of Eternity, before the World was, (*Eph.* 1.6.) And when he appointed them to the *End,* he also allotted the *Means,* by which they should reach it. Eph. 1. 4. *According as he hath chosen us in him before the foundation of the world, that we should be holy, and without blame before him in love.* The new and living way was then fixed, & preemptorily resolved upon ; and it was but *one* way that was then determined, unto the

which the terms of the new Covenant are in the publication of it restrained. Mark 16. 16. *He that believeth and is baptized shall be saved ; but he that believeth not, shall be damned.*

7. T H A T *except God had revealed* this Way and Rule, it could *never* have been *known* in the World. Men nor Angels could not have so much as *published* that good news, *that there is such a thing,* unless he had first declared it: much less could they have given a *draught* of it. Hence it is, that where there is none of this Revelation, a People are in a state of Perdition, Prov. 29. 18. *Where there is no vision, the people perish : but he that keepeth the law, happy is he.* Rom. 10. 14. *How then shall they call on him in whom they have not believed ? and how shall they believe in him of whom they have not heard ? and how shall they hear without a preacher ?* For who should be able to know the mind of God, or enter into the secrets of the decree, till God was pleased to break them open ? Hence when *Peter* confessed Christ, he tells him, as Matth. 16. 17. *Blessed art thou Simon Barjona : for flesh and blood hath not revealed it unto thee, but my father which is in heaven.*

8. T H A T *in what way soever* God reveals this will of his, *that* is to be accounted his *Word.* For Gods word is nothing else but his *making his mind known* to his Creature. Now there have been *divers ways,* that God hath taken thus to inform his people of their duty ; sometimes by *Oracles,* giving vocal Commands to them ; sometimes by *Urim & Thummim* ; partly by *Angels* appearing in humane Shape, & by the *Son of God* before his Incarnation, who often came to his Servants of Old : partly by *Visions* and *Dreams,* appearing to them in sleep, in raptures, and trances : and partly by *Prophets* and extraordinary men sent and spirited by him : and partly by appointing such men to *write down* his Will for the use of his People : of all which ways we have an account given unto us in the holy Scriptures.

9. T H A T *nothing but what* G O D hath thus *revealed* to his People, doth or can belong to the *Rule.* That there *needs* no more, will be afterwards considered, when we come to observe the Perfection of Scripture : But here we observe, that there *can* be no more. We are therefore severely *forbidden* to *add.* Prov. 30. 5, 6. *Every word of God is pure.* — *Add thou not unto his words, lest he reprove thee, and thou be found a liar.* For, if the *Salvation* of fallen man depends meerly on the *good pleasure* of God, the *knowledge* of it necessarily depends upon his *revelation.* How else should it possibly come to be known ? Hence we have that challenge, Rom. 11. 34. *For who hath known the mind of the Lord, or who hath been his counseller ?* None was admitted to fit at Council-Table with him, or hear what he purposed in the Days of Eternity, or read those Records of his Decrees. Till *he* told it, it was a *secret.* For any therefore of their own head to make any addition to this Rule, is a bold Intrusion upon the Divine Prerogative ; an imposing upon God, which he will never admit of : nor shall they find any other thanks from God, but a severe Demand, *Who required these things at your hands ?*

H E R E I shall take into Consideration a C A S E controverted among many viz.

Quest. W H E T H E R *the* Light of Nature, *which Men bring with them into the world, may not be* improved, *so as to be a* sufficient *Rule to guide them to their chief End ?*

Answ. W E are here to consider Man in his *lapsed* Estate, and the Light of Nature *as* it is to be found in him in this estate of his : And *thus* taken, the Answer is in the *Negative.* For the full Illustration whereof, let these things be thought upon.

1. T H A T the light of Nature *at the first* only discovered to Man *the Rule,* by

which he was to attain his end, according to a *Covenant of Works*. It was properly adapted to the first covenant, in which man was by his *personal* Obedience to serve to God's glory, and secure his favour. Hence it contained in it only the *moral* law, or the substance of what was contained in the ten Commandments. Rom. 2.14, 15. *The Gentiles which have not the law, do by nature the things contained in the law, these having not the law, are a law unto themselves. Which shew the work of the law written in their hearts.* It said, These things ought to be done, and those to be avoided; & if thou so do, thou shalt be happy. It was accommodated to the Image of God, that was imprinted on man, and served to guide him in the right improvement of it. It was the candle of the Lord, set up in him to light him in his way wherein he ought to go.

2. T H A T though the light of Nature clearly discovered to man his *Obligation to God,* yet it did not show him *every point of the Rule,* by which God would be served by him. There were some things *positive* required, which were not to be particularly found in it, but were made known to man by Revelation. Man knew, that God was to be obeyed in whatsoever he should enjoyn him, by the light of Nature : but this did not tell him that the Tree of life & knowledge were *sacramental,* and that it was *Death* to eat of the latter. The difference between the trees was arbitrary, and not natural. Possibly that might tell him, a *Sabbath* was due to be kept ; but that *one* day of seven, or *this* day of seven was it, he had by revelation: God is therefore said to *sanctify* it.

3. T H A T this light in *fallen* man is wofully *impaired.* Man knock't his head in his fall, and craz'd his understanding, as to divine Truths. It is but a little that he knows of that Rule. Some broken fragments, & moth-eaten registers, old rusty outworn monuments there are; but so imperfect & illegible, that there are but very few of them, that he can spell out what they mean, and in others he is mistaken. For this, we have that good Man's confession, Prov. 30. 2. *Surely I am more brutish than any man, and have not the understanding of a man.* For this reason, a state of Nature is called a state of *Darkness,* and natural men said to be *brutish.* Hence Divine Revelation is necessary to the right & thorough discerning of what was required in the old Covenant ; in which a mistake is a capital crime, *Gal.* 3. 10.

4. T H A T if the light of Nature, were as *clear* in man *now* as it was at *first,* yet his *Inability* to follow it, renders it *unprofitable* to him. The impotency, which is in natural men, to obey the demands of the Law, cuts them off from a capacity of improving the greatest discoveries they can make of it, to their advantage & happiness. For if men know & do not, their *Guilt* is *aggravated* ; but fallen man can not do, not so much as the thing which he knows ought to be done. Whereas happiness is not in bare knowing, but doing. Joh. 13. 17. *If ye know these things, happy are ye if ye do them.* So that the utmost that this light doth for the man, is to let him see that he is *undone* : and the more discoveries he makes by it, the more conviction he hath of his great Infelicity.

5. T H A T the light of Nature makes *no* discovery to man of *any other way* to attain his end and be happy, besides what was exhibited in the Covenant of *works.* And here let it be observed, ———

1. T H A T man by the light of Nature could *never have known,* that there was *any other possible way* for God to be glorified in man's salvation. Fallen *Adam* knew himself to be miserable, cursed, under a sentence of Condemnation ; that Justice was engaged against him: but how Justice could be satisfyed, Holiness be maintained, and yet Mercy be magnified, was beyond his reach. How God should punish sin, and yet

love the sinner ; take vengeance on men's Inventions, and yet extend grace to their Persons, was above the discoveries of Nature, a Riddle beyond all it's Rules & Principles to expound. It had it's notions about *happiness,* but none about *salvation.* Hence that is asserted concerning all natural men, Rom. 3.17. *The Way of peace have they not known.*

2. T H A T *much less* are there any footsteps of the *Way it self,* to be found in the hearts of men : there are no umbrages of any such Discovery to be found there. If we should follow the whole method of it, step by step, and ask nature what it can say to it, it must be altogether silent. I shall instance only in three things that are most comprehensive.

1. I T hath no notices of the *Person* of Christ, and the *Redemption* wrought out by him. It might speak something of a *Trinity* of Persons in the God-head once ; though, of that there is scarce any thing to be found in the relicts of it since the Fall: but that the second Person should be made *Man,* and subject himself to the Law, and make satisfaction for sin, and make way that man might be justified by his imputed Righteousness, and saved by his merits,—here was a deep silence. Some would have *Adam* to be a Type of *Christ* ; but if he were, he was an arbitrary, and not a natural one. Others would have us to believe, that *Adam* before his fall knew of the Incarnation of the Son of God : but we have no evidence for this in Scripture ; and if he did, it must be by revelation. Others have thought that the *Gentiles Sacrifices* intimate some dark apprehensions of Satisfaction by another : but it is certain, sacrificing was handed down to the World by Tradition from *Noah,* and not by the light of nature; and that the Heathen lookt upon them as satisfactions *ex Opere operato,* and not as shadows of a better Sacrifice. Hence the preaching of a Christ is so far from the gust of humane reason, that it hath the reputation of *foolishness* by it. 1 Cor. 1. 23. *But we preach Christ crucified, unto the Jews a stumbling-block, and unto the Greeks, foolishness.*

2. I T gives no direction about *Gospel-Faith.* Faith in *God* is a great Duty of the first Commandment, and was clearly written in the law of nature ; and fallen man hath natural Convictions of it as a Duty : But to believe in *Christ,* to rest in God for life and salvation upon the score of *Christ's* Righteousness, under a deep sense that we have none of our own, and to depend upon a *Promise* in so doing, it is so far from bearing any witness to it, that it looks upon it with greatest contempt : and for this very reason it is, that men who make highest pretences to Reason, speak most contemptuously of it, as is obvious in *Socinians, Pelagians, Arminians,* and such like men. And hence such endeavours to confound the Doctrines of Justification & Sanctification in one : because nature's light hath notions of a *Personal* Righteousness, but knows nothing of a *Relative* one.

3. I T is altogether a stranger to *Evangelical Obedience.* If it could afford any thing to man's information, it is here ; but it is as much at a loss in this, as any thing. For, tho' it knows something of moral Duty (and that is but a little) yet it gives fallen man no information how to *please God* by his Obedience, and when he hath followed it to the highest, it leaves him unprofitable, (*Luk.* 17.10.) and his Duties are but painted Abominations. It may convince man of wofull flaws in his Obedience, but how to mend them it tells them not. Moral Obedience and Deeds of Sanctification, are vastly different things. Now, it tells not man where he may get a new Principle of Spiritual Life, to enable him to live to and please God. It sets not open before him the Fountain, in which his Uncleanness may be washed away : where he may be furnished with grace

to serve God, and live to his glory : nor how his imperfect Duties may find acceptance with an holy God, and receive his approbation ; or where he may fetch those continual supplies of renewed strength to conquer his Corruptions, to deny Ungodliness, &c.

N O W all these things are *essential* to that Rule, by which fallen man may be guided to glorify God, and enjoy him : and to be mistaken about them, or not to be acquainted with them, will undoubtedly leave him short of happiness. And this shews us their great folly, who will measure Divinity by natural Light, and will admit nothing in Religion, which will not stoop to the test and trial of human Reason. And it tells us, how deeply we are engaged to God for his word of Revelation !

[MAY 22. 1688.]

"The Examination of Mrs. Anne Hutchinson at the Court at Newtown"

1637

In discussing the covenant of grace, Willard made it clear that although the working of salvation was *caused* by God, it was necessarily *conditioned* by the individual's faith. This idea, although orthodox doctrine for most seventeenth-century Puritan theologians, was vigorously challenged in the first years of the Massachusetts settlement. John Cotton (1584–1652), the foremost minister of the first generation of Puritan colonists, preached instead a gospel of salvation by a free grace that was neither conditioned by human effort, including even that by which a striving soul merely prepared herself to receive grace, nor evidenced by sanctification (a saint's outward good behavior). These views were not "Antinomian" or (as the term literally meant) "against the law" in any strictly heretical sense; Cotton always insisted that justified saints were just as much bound by the Mosaic and other moral laws as reprobates even though their moral or "legal" actions had nothing to do with their salvation. Anne Hutchinson (1591–1643), an ardent follower of Cotton and a sophisticated religious teacher in her own right, went further. First, she claimed that because almost all the ministers other than Cotton made the covenant of grace conditional, they preached a covenant of works, or the heresy that a person could *earn* salvation through human efforts. In addition she seems to have sometimes taught that a saint's inward sense of holiness, rather than being (as most Puritan divines taught) at least somewhat testable by objective means, was totally unmediated by reason, nature, or (as she suggests in the selection that follows) biblical texts. For persisting in speaking these ideas, she was banished from the colony and, Cotton himself having abandoned her, soon thereafter excommunicated from his church. She went to Rhode Island and a few years later to New York, where she and most of her family were killed in an Indian raid. For a recent persuasive interpretation of Antinomian theology, see William K. B. Stoever, 'A Faire and Easie Way to Heaven': Covenant Theology and Antinomianism in Early Massachusetts (Middletown, Conn., 1978). For a good introduction to John Cotton's intellectual development, see Larzer Ziff, The Career of John Cotton: Puritanism and the American Experience (Princeton, 1962). The ideas of Anne Hutchinson and her followers are surveyed in two recent studies: Philip F. Gura, A Glimpse of Sion's Glory: Puritan Radicalism in New England, 1620–1660 (Middletown, Conn., 1984), 237–75; and David S. Lovejoy, Religious Enthusiasm in the New World: Heresy to Revolution (Cambridge, Mass., 1985), 62–86. David D. Hall has edited an indispensable collection of documents on the Hutchinson controversy, from which this selection is taken. The selection picks up the discussion at the point where it shifts from arguments about the legality of Hutchinson's meetings with women—which she parried with great effectiveness—to questions about her theological positions. Apart from Cotton and Hutchinson, the speakers are either members of the Court, including, most prominently, Governor Winthrop and Deputy Governor Thomas Dudley, or the accusing ministers.

[November 1637]

Dep. gov. I would go a little higher with Mrs. Hutchinson. About three years ago we were all in peace. Mrs. Hutchinson from that time she came hath made a disturbance, and some that came over with her in the ship did inform me what she was as soon as she was landed. I being then in place dealt with the pastor and teacher of Boston and desired them to enquire of her, and then I was satisfied that she held nothing different from us, but within half a year after, she had vented divers of her strange opinions and had made parties in the country, and at length it comes that Mr. Cotton and Mr. Vane were of her judgment, but Mr. Cotton hath cleared himself that he was not of that mind, but now it appears by this woman's meeting that Mrs. Hutchinson hath so forestalled the minds of many by their resort to her meeting that now she hath a potent party in the country. Now if all these things have endangered us as from that foundation and if she in particular hath disparaged all our ministers in the land that they have preached a covenant of works, and only Mr. Cotton a covenant of grace, why this is not to be suffered, and therefore being driven to the foundation and it being found that Mrs. Hutchinson is she that hath depraved all the ministers and hath been the cause of what is fallen out, why we must take away the foundation and the building will fall.

Mrs. H. I pray Sir prove it that I said they preached nothing but a covenant of works.

Dep. Gov. Nothing but a covenant of works, why a Jesuit may preach truth sometimes.

Mrs. H. Did I ever say they preached a covenant of works then?

Dep. Gov. If they do not preach a covenant of grace clearly, then they preach a covenant of works.

Mrs. H. Not Sir, one may preach a covenant of grace more clearly than another, so I said.

D. Gov. We are not upon that now but upon position.

Mrs. H. Prove this then Sir that you say I said.

D. Gov. When they do preach a covenant of works do they preach truth?

Mrs. H. Yes Sir, but when they preach a covenant of works for salvation, that is not truth.

D. Gov. I do but ask you this, when the ministers do preach a covenant of works do they preach a way of salvation?

Mrs. H. I did not come hither to answer to questions of that sort.

D. Gov. Because you will deny the thing.

Mrs. H. Ey, but that is to be proved first.

D. Gov. I will make it plain that you did say that the ministers did preach a covenant of works.

Mrs. H. I deny that.

D. Gov. And that you said they were not able ministers of the new testament, but Mr. Cotton only.

Mrs. H. If ever I spake that I proved it by God's word.

Source: The Antinomian Controversy, 1636–1638: A Documentary History, ed. David D. Hall (Middletown, Conn.: Wesleyan University Press, 1968), 317–19, 321, 323–26, 332, 333–38, 340–45, 347–48. Editor's notes altered. Reprinted by permission of the Wesleyan University Press, Copyright © 1968.

Court. Very well, very well.

Mrs. H. If one shall come onto me in private, and desire me seriously to tell them what I thought of such an one. I must either speak false or true in my answer.

D. Gov. Likewise I will prove this that you said the gospel in the letter and words holds forth nothing but a covenant of works and that all that do not hold as you do are in a covenant of works.

Mrs. H. I deny this for if I should so say I should speak against my own judgment.

. . . . . .

Mr. Weld. Being desired by the honoured court, that which our brother Peters had spoken was the truth and things were spoken as he hath related and the occasion of calling this sister and the passages that were there among us. And myself asking why she did cast such aspersions upon the ministers of the country though we were poor sinful men and for ourselves we cared not but for the precious doctrine we held forth we could not but grieve to hear that so blasphemed. She at that time was sparing in her speech. I need not repeat the things they have been truly related. She said the fear of man is a snare and therefore I will speak freely and she spake her judgment and mind freely as was before related, that Mr. Cotton did preach a covenant of grace and we a covenant of works. And this I remember she said we could not preach a covenant of grace because we were not sealed, and we were not able ministers of the new testament no more than were the disciples before the resurrection of Christ.

. . . . . .

Mr. Shephard. I am loth to speak in this assembly concerning this gentlewoman in question, but I can do no less than speak what my conscience speaks unto me. For personal reproaches I take it a man's wisdom to conceal. Concerning the reproaches of the ministry of our's there hath been many in the country, and this hath been my thoughts of that. Let men speak what they will not only against persons but against ministry, let that pass, but let us strive to speak to the consciences of men, knowing that if we had the truth with us we shall not need to approve our words by our practice and our ministry to the hearts of the people, and they should speak for us and therefore I have satisfied myself and the brethren with that. Now for that which concerns this gentlewoman at this time I do not well remember every particular, only this I do remember that the end of our meeting was to satisfy ourselves in some points. Among the rest Mrs. Hutchinson was desired to speak her thoughts concerning the ministers of the Bay. Now I remember that she said that we were not able ministers of the new testament. I followed her with particulars, she instanced myself as being at the lecture and hearing me preach when as I gave some means whereby a christian might come to the assurance of God's love. She instanced that I was not sealed. I said why did she say so. She said because you put love for an evidence. Now I am sure she was in an error in this speech for if assurance be an holy estate then I am sure there are not graces wanting to evidence it.

Mr. Eliot. I am loth to spend time therefore I shall consent to what hath been said. Our brethren did intreat us to write and a few things I did write the substance of which hath been here spoken and I have it in writing therefore I do avouch it.

Mr. Shephard. I desire to speak this word, it may be but a slip of her tongue, and I hope she will be sorry for it, and then we shall be glad of it.

Dep. Gov. I called these witnesses and you deny them. You see they have proved this and you deny this, but it is clear. You said they preached a covenant of works and that they were not able ministers of the new testament; now there are two other things that you did affirm which were that the scriptures in the letter of them held forth nothing but a covenant of works and likewise that those that were under a covenant of works cannot be saved.

Mrs. H. Prove that I said so. (*Gov.*) Did you say so?

Mrs. H. No Sir it is your conclusion.

D. Gov. What do I do charging of you if you deny what is so fully proved.

Gov. Here are six undeniable ministers who say it is true and yet you deny that you did say that they did preach a covenant of works and that they were not able ministers of the gospel, and it appears plainly that you have spoken it, and whereas you say that it was drawn from you in a way of friendship, you did profess then that it was out of conscience that you spake and said The fear of man is a snare wherefore should I be afraid, I will speak plainly and freely.

Mrs. H. That I absolutely deny, for the first question was thus answered by me to them. They thought that I did conceive there was difference between them and Mr. Cotton. At the first I was somewhat reserved, then said Mr. Peters I pray answer the question directly as fully and as plainly as you desire we should tell you our minds. Mrs. Hutchinson we come for plain dealing and telling you our hearts. Then I said I would deal as plainly as I could, and whereas they say I said they were under a covenant of works and in the state of the apostles why these two speeches cross one another. I might say they might preach a covenant of works as did the apostles, but to preach a covenant of works and to be under a covenant of works is another business.

Dep. Gov. There have been six witnesses to prove this and yet you deny it.

Mrs. H. I deny that these were the first words that were spoken.

Gov. You make the case worse, for you clearly shew that the ground of your opening your mind was not to satisfy them but to satisfy your own conscience.

Mr. Peters. We do not desire to be so narrow to the court and the gentlewoman about times and seasons, whether first or after, but said it was.

Dep. Gov. For that other thing I mentioned for the letter of the scripture that it held forth nothing but a covenant of works, and for the latter that we are in a state of damnation, being under a covenant of works, or to that effect, these two things you also deny. Now the case stands thus. About three quarters of a year ago I heard of it, and speaking of it there came one to me who is not here, but will affirm it if need be, as he did to me that he did hear you say in so many words. He set it down under his hand and I can bring it forth when the court pleases. His name is subscribed to both these things, and upon my peril be it if I bring you not in the paper and bring the minister (meaning Mr. Ward) to be deposed.

Gov. What say you to this, though nothing be directly proved, yet you hear it may be.

Mrs. H. I acknowledge using the words of the apostle to the Corinthians unto him, that they that were ministers of the letter and not the spirit did preach a covenant of works. Upon his saying there was no such scripture, then I fetched the Bible and shewed him this place 2 Cor. iii. 6. He said that was the letter of the law. No said I it is the letter of the gospel.

Gov. You have spoken this more than once then.

Mrs. H. Then upon further discourse about proving a good estate and holding it out by the manifestation of the spirit he did acknowledge that to be the nearest way, but yet said he, will you not acknowledge that which we hold forth to be a way too wherein we may have hope; no truly if that be a way it is a way to hell.

    Gov. Mrs. Hutchinson, the court you see hath laboured to bring you to acknowledge the error of your way that so you might be reduced, the time now grows late, we shall therefore give you a little more time to consider of it and therefore desire that you attend the court again in the morning.

The Next Morning.

. . . . . .

    Dep. Gov. Let her witnesses be called.
    Gov. Who be they?
    Mrs. H. Mr. Leveret and our teacher and Mr. Coggeshall.

. . . . . .

    Gov. Mr. Cotton, the court desires that you declare what you do remember of the conference which was at that time and is now in question.

    Mr. Cotton. I did not think I should be called to bear witness in this cause and therefore did not labour to call to remembrance what was done; but the greatest passage that took impression upon me was to this purpose. The elders spake that they had heard that she had spoken some condemning words of their ministry, and among other things they did first pray her to answer wherein she thought their ministry did differ from mine, how the comparison sprang I am ignorant, but sorry I was that any comparison should be between me and my brethren and uncomfortable it was, she told them to this purpose that they did not hold forth a covenant of grace as I did, but wherein did we differ? why she said that they did not hold forth the seal of the spirit as he doth. Where is the difference there? say they, why saith she speaking to one or other of them, I know not to whom. You preach of the seal of the spirit upon a work and he upon free grace without a work or without respect to a work, he preaches the seal of the spirit upon free grace and you upon a work. I told her I was very sorry that she put comparisons between my ministry and their's, for she had said more than I could myself, and rather I had that she had put us in fellowship with them and not have made that discrepancy. She said, she found the difference. Upon that there grew some speeches upon the thing and I do remember I instanced to them the story of Thomas Bilney in the book of martyrs how freely the spirit witnessed unto him without any respect unto a work as himself professes. Now upon this other speeches did grow. If you put me in mind of any thing I shall speak it, but this was the sum of the difference, nor did it seem to be so ill taken as it is and our brethren did say also that they would not so easily believe reports as they had done and withal mentioned that they would speak no more of it, some of them did; and afterwards some of them did say they were less satisifed than before. And I must say that I did not find her saying they were under a covenant of works, nor that she said they did preach a covenant of works.

    Gov. You say you do not remember, but can you say she did not speak so———
Here two lines again defaced.

    Mr. Cotton. I do remember that she looked at them as the apostles before the ascension.

    Mr. Peters. I humbly desire to remember our reverend teacher. May it please you to remember how this came in. Whether do you not remember that she said we were not sealed with the spirit of grace, therefore could not preach a covenant of grace, and she said further you may do it in your judgment but not in experience, but she spake plump that we were not sealed.

Mr. Cotton. You do put me in remembrance that it was asked her why cannot we preach a covenant of grace? Why, saith she, because you can preach no more than you know, or to that purpose, she spake. Now that she said you could not preach a covenant of grace I do not remember such a thing. I remember well that she said you were not sealed with the seal of the spirit.

Mr. Peters. There was a double seal found out that day which never was.

Mr. Cotton. I know very well that she took the seal of the spirit in that sense for the full assurance of God's favour by the holy ghost, and now that place in the Ephesians doth hold out that seal.

Mr. Peters. So that was the ground of our discourse concerning the great seal and the little seal.

Mr. Cotton. To that purpose I remember somebody speaking of the difference of the witness of the spirit and the seal of the spirit, some to put a distinction called it the broad seal and the little seal. Our brother Wheelwright answered if you will have it so be it so.

Mrs. H. Mr. Ward said that.

Some three or four of the ministers. Mr. Wheelwright said it.

Mr. Cotton. No, it was not brother Wheelwright's speech but one of your own expressions, and as I remember it was Mr. Ward.

Mr. Peters. . . . . . .

Mr. Cotton. Under favour I do not remember that.

Mr. Peters. Therefore her answer clears it in your judgment but not in your experience.

Mrs. H. My name is precious and you do affirm a thing which I utterly deny.

D. Gov. You should have brought the book with you.

Mr. Nowell. The witnesses do not answer that which you require.

Gov. I do not see that we need their testimony any further. Mr. Cotton hath expressed what he remembred, and what took impression upon him, and so I think the other elders also did remember that which took impression upon them.

Mr. Weld. I then said to Mrs. Hutchinson when it was come to this issue, why did you let us go thus long and never tell us of it?

Gov. I should wonder why the elders should move the elders of our congregation to have dealt with her if they saw not some cause.

Mr. Cotton. Brother Weld and brother Shepard, I did[1] then clear myself unto you that I understood her speech in expressing herself to you that you did hold forth some matter in your preaching that was not pertinent to the seal of the spirit———*Two lines defaced.*

Dep. Gov. They affirm that Mrs. Hutchinson did say they were not able ministers of the new testament.

Mr. Cotton. I do not remember it.

Mrs. H. If you please to give me leave I shall give you the ground of what I know to be true. Being much troubled to see the falseness of the constitution of the church

---

1. Later editions of Hutchinson's *History* include a "not": "I did not."

of England, I had like to have turned separatist; whereupon I kept a day of solemn humiliation and pondering of the thing; this scripture was brought unto me—he that denies Jesus Christ to be come in the flesh is antichrist—This I considered of and in considering found that the papists did not deny him to be come in the flesh, nor we did not deny him—who then was antichrist? Was the Turk antichrist only? The Lord knows that I could not open scripture; he must by his prophetical office open it unto me. So after that being unsatisfied in the thing, the Lord was pleased to bring this scripture out of the Hebrews. He that denies the testament denies the testator, and in this did open unto me and give me to see that those which did not teach the new covenant had the spirit of antichrist, and upon this he did discover the ministry unto me and ever since. I bless the Lord, he hath let me see which was the clear ministry and which the wrong. Since that time I confess I have been more choice and he hath let me to distinguish between the voice of my beloved and the voice of Moses, the voice of John Baptist and the voice of antichrist, for all those voices are spoken of in scripture. Now if you do condemn me for speaking what in my conscience I know to be truth I must commit myself unto the Lord.

Mr. Nowell. How do you know that that was the spirit?

Mrs. H. How did Abraham know that it was God that bid him offer his son, being a breach of the sixth commandment?

Dep. Gov. By an immediate voice.

Mrs. H. So to me by an immediate revelation.

Dep. Gov. How! an immediate revelation.

Mrs. H. By the voice of his own spirit to my soul. I will give you another scripture, Jer. 46. 27, 28—out of which the Lord shewed me what he would do for me and the rest of his servants.—But after he was pleased to reveal himself to me I did presently like Abraham run to Hagar. And after that he did let me see the atheism of my own heart, for which I begged of the Lord that it might not remain in my heart, and being thus, he did shew me this (a twelvemonth after) which I told you of before. Ever since that time I have been confident of what he hath revealed unto me.

Obliterated | another place out of Daniel chap. 7. and he and for us all, wherein he | shewed me the sitting of the judgment and the standing of all high and low before the Lord and how thrones and kingdoms were cast down before him. When our teacher came to New-England it was a great trouble unto me, my brother Wheelwright being put by also. I was then much troubled concerning the ministry under which I lived, and then that place in the 30th of Isaiah was brought to my mind. Though the Lord give thee bread of adversity and water of affliction yet shall not thy teachers be removed into corners any more, but thine eyes shall see thy teachers. The Lord giving me this promise and they being gone there was none then left that I was able to hear, and I could not be at rest but I must come hither. Yet that place of Isaiah did much follow me, though the Lord give thee the bread of adversity and water of affliction. This place lying I say upon me then this place in Daniel was brought unto me and did shew me that though I should meet with affliction yet I am the same God that delivered Daniel out of the lion's den, I will also deliver thee.———Therefore I desire you to look to it, for you see this scripture fulfilled this day and therefore I desire you that as you tender the Lord and the church and commonwealth to consider and look what you do. You have power over my body but the Lord Jesus hath power over my body and soul, and assure yourselves thus much, you do as much as in you lies to put the Lord Jesus Christ from you, and if you go on in this course you begin you will bring a curse upon you and your posterity, and the mouth of the Lord hath spoken it.

Dep. Gov. What is the scripture she brings?

Mr. Stoughton. Behold I turn away from you.

Mrs. H. But now having seen him which is invisible I fear not what man can do unto me.

Gov. Daniel was delivered by miracle do you think to be deliver'd so too?

Mrs. H. I do here speak it before the court. I look that the Lord should deliver me by his providence.

Mr. Harlakenden. I may read scripture and the most glorious hypocrite may read them and yet go down to hell.

Mrs. H. It may be so.

. . . . . .

Mr. Endicot. I would have a word or two with leave of that which hath thus far been revealed to the court. I have heard of many revelations of Mr.[2] Hutchinson's, but they were reports, but Mrs. Hutchinson I see doth maintain some by this discourse, and I think it is a special providence of God to hear what she hath said. Now there is a revelation you see which she doth expect as a miracle. She saith she now suffers and let us do what we will she shall be delivered by a miracle. I hope the court takes notice of the vanity of it and heat of her spirit. Now because her reverend teacher is here I should desire that he would please to speak freely whether he doth condescend to such speeches or revelations as have been here spoken of, and he will give a great deal of content.

Mr. Cotton. May it please you Sir. There are two sorts of revelations, there are [defaced] or against the word besides scripture both which [defaced] tastical and tending to danger more ways than one———there is another sort which the apostle prays the believing Ephesians may be made partakers of, and those are such as are breathed by the spirit of God and are never dispensed but in a word of God and according to a word of God, and though the word revelation be rare in common speech and we make it uncouth in our ordinary expressions, yet notwithstanding, being understood in the scripture sense I think they are not only lawful but such as christians may receive and God bear witness to it in his word, and usually he doth express it in the ministry of the word and doth accompany it by his spirit, or else it is in the reading of the word in some chapter or verse and whenever it comes it comes flying upon the wings of the spirit.

Mr. Endicot. You give me satisfaction in the thing and therefore I desire you to give your judgment of Mrs. Hutchinson; what she hath said you hear and all the circumstances thereof.

Mr. Cotton. I would demand whether by a miracle she doth mean a work above nature or by some wonderful providence for that is called a miracle often in the psalms.

Mrs. H. I desire to speak to our teacher. You know Sir what he doth declare though he doth not know himself [*something wanting.*] now either of these ways or at

2. Apparently a misprint for "Mrs."

this present time it shall be done, yet I would not have the court so to understand me that he will deliver me now even at this present time.

Dep. Gov. I desire Mr. Cotton to tell us whether you do approve of Mrs. Hutchinson's revelations as she hath laid them down.

Mr. Cotton. I know not whether I do understand her, but this I say, if she doth expect a deliverance in a way of providence—then I cannot deny it.

Dep. Gov. No Sir we did not speak of that.

Mr. Cotton. If it be by way of miracle then I would suspect it.

Dep. Gov. Do you believe that her revelations are true?

Mr. Cotton. That she may have some special providence of God to help her is a thing that I cannot bear witness against.

Dep. Gov. Good Sir I do ask whether this revelation be of God or no?

Mr. Cotton. I should desire to know whether the sentence of the court will bring her to any calamity, and then I would know of her whether she expects to be delivered from that calamity by a miracle or a providence of God.

Mrs. H. By a providence of God I say I expect to be delivered from some calamity that shall come to me.

Gover. The case is altered and will not stand with us now, but I see a marvellous providence of God to bring things to this pass that they are. We have been hearkening about the trial of this thing and now the mercy of God by a providence hath answered our desires and made her to lay open her self and the ground of all these disturbances to be by revelations, for we receive no such   made out of the ministry of the word   and so one scripture after another, but all this while there is no use of the ministry of the word nor of any clear call of God by his word, but the ground work of her revelations is the immediate revelation of the spirit and not by the ministry of the word, and that is the means by which she hath very much abused the country that they shall look for revelations and are not bound to the ministry of the word, but God will teach them by immediate revelations and this hath been the ground of all these tumults and troubles, and I would that those were all cut off from us that trouble us, for this is the thing that hath been the root of all the mischief.

Court. We all consent with you.

Gov. Ey it is the most desperate enthusiasm in the world, for nothing but a word comes to her mind and then an application is made which is nothing to the purpose, and this is her revelations when it is impossible but that the word and spirit should speak the same thing.

Mr. Endicot. I speak in reference to Mr. Cotton. I am tender of you Sir and there lies much upon you in this particular, for the answer of Mr. Cotton doth not free him from that way which his last answer did bring upon him, therefore I beseech you that you'd be pleased to speak a word to that which Mrs. Hutchinson hath spoken of her revelations as you have heard the manner of it. Whether do you witness for her or against her.

Mr. Cotton. This is that I said Sir, and my answer is plain that if she doth look for deliverance from the hand of God by his providence, and the revelation be in a word or according to a word, that I cannot deny.

Mr. Endicot. You give me satisfaction.

Dep. Gov. No, no, he gives me none at all.

Mr. Cotton. But if it be in a way of miracle or a revelation without the word that

I do not assent to, but look at it as a delusion, and I think so doth she too as I understand her.

Dep. Gov. Sir, you weary me and do not satisfy me.

Mr. Cotton. I pray Sir give me leave to express my self. In that sense that she speaks I dare not bear witness against it.

Mr. Nowell. I think it is a devilish delusion.

Gover. Of all the revelations that ever I read of I never read the like ground laid as is for this. The Enthusiasts and Anabaptists had never the like.

Mr. Cotton. You know Sir, that their revelations broach new matters of faith and doctrine.

Gover. So do these and what may they breed more if they be let alone. I do acknowledge that there are such revelations as do concur with the word but there hath not been any of this nature.

Dep. Gov. I never saw such revelations as these among the Anabaptists, therefore am sorry that Mr. Cotton should stand to justify her.

Mr. Peters. I can say the same and this runs to enthusiasm, and I think that is very disputable which our brother Cotton hath spoken [*wanting*] an immediate promise that he will deliver them [*wanting*] in a day of trouble.

Gover. It overthrows all.

Dep. Gov. These disturbances that have come among the Germans have been all grounded upon revelations, and so they that have vented them have stirred up their hearers to take up arms against their prince and to cut the throats one of another, and these have been the fruits of them, and whether the devil may inspire the same into their hearts here I know not, for I am fully persuaded that Mrs. Hutchinson is deluded by the devil, because the spirit of God speaks truth in all his servants.

Gov. I am persuaded that the revelation she brings forth is delusion.

All the court but some two or three ministers cry out, we all believe it—we all believe it.

Mr. Endicot. I suppose all the world may see where the foundation of all these troubles among us lies.

Mr. Eliot. I say there is an expectation of things promised, but to have a particular revelation of things that shall fall out, there is no such thing in the scripture.

Gov. We will not limit the word of God.

Mr. Collicut. It is great burden to us that we differ from Mr. Cotton and that he should justify these revelations. I would intreat him to answer concerning that about the destruction of England.

Gov. Mr. Cotton is not called to answer to any thing but we are to deal with the party here standing before us.

Mr. Bartholomew. My wife hath said that Mr. Wheelwright was not acquainted with this way until that she imparted it unto him.

Mr. Brown. Inasmuch as I am called to speak, I would therefore speak the mind of our brethren. Though we had sufficient ground for the censure before, yet now she having vented herself and I find such flat contradiction to the scripture in what she saith, as to that in the first to the Hebrews—God at sundry times spake to our fathers—For my part I understand that scripture and other scriptures of the Lord Jesus Christ, and the apostle writing to Timothy saith that the scripture is able to make one perfect—therefore I say the mind of the brethren—I think she deserves no less a censure than hath been already past but rather something more, for this is the foundation of all mischief and of all those bastardly things which have been overthrowing by that great meeting. They have all come out from this cursed fountain.

Gov. Seeing the court hath thus declared itself and hearing what hath been laid to the charge of Mrs. Hutchinson and especially what she by the providence of God hath declared freely without being asked, if therefore it be the mind of the court, looking at her as the principal cause of all our trouble, that they would now consider what is to be done to her.———

Mr. Coddington. I do think that you are going to censure therefore I desire to speak a word.

Gov. I pray you speak.

Mr. Coddington. There is one thing objected against the meetings. What if she designed to edify her own family in her own meetings may none else be present?

Gov. If you have nothing else to say but that, it is pity Mr. Coddington that you should interrupt us in proceeding to censure.

Mr. Coddington. I would say more Sir, another thing you lay to her Charge is her speech to the elders. Now I do not see any clear witness against her, and you know it is a rule of the court that no man may be a judge and an accuser too. I do not speak to disparage our elders and their callings, but I do not see any thing that they accuse her of witnessed against her, and therefore I do not see how she should be censured for that. And for the other thing which hath fallen from her occasionally by the spirit of God, you know the spirit of God witnesses with our spirits, and there is no truth in scripture but God bears witness to it by his spirit, therefore I would entreat you to consider whether those things you have alledged against her deserve such censure as you are about to pass, be it to banishment or imprisonment. And again here is nothing proved about the elders, only that she said they did not teach a covenant of grace so clearly as Mr. Cotton did, and that they were in the state of the apostles before the ascension. Why I hope this may not be offensive nor any wrong to them.

Gov. Pass by all that hath been said formerly and her own speeches have been ground enough for us to proceed upon.

Mr. Coddington. I beseech you do not speak so to force things along, for I do not for my own part see any equity in the court in all your proceedings. Here is no law of God that she hath broken nor any law of the country that she hath broke, and therefore deserves no censure, and if she say that the elders preach as the apostles did, why they preached a covenant of grace and what wrong is that to them, for it is without question that the apostles did preach a covenant of grace, though not with that power, till they received the manifestation of the spirit, therefore I pray consider what you do, for here is no law of God or man broken.

. . . . . .

Gov. The court hath already declared themselves satisfied concerning the things you hear, and concerning the troublesomeness of her spirit and the danger of her course amongst us, which is not to be suffered. Therefore if it be the mind of the court that Mrs. Hutchinson for these things that appear before us is unfit for our society, and if it be the mind of the court that she shall be banished out of our liberties and imprisoned till she be sent away, let them hold up their hands.

All but three.

Those that are contrary minded hold up yours,

    Mr. Coddington and Mr. Colborn, only.

Mr. Jennison. I cannot hold up my hand one way or the other, and I shall give my reason if the court require it.

Gov. Mrs. Hutchinson, the sentence of the court you hear is that you are banished from out of our jurisdiction as being a woman not fit for our society, and are to be imprisoned till the court shall send you away.

Mrs. H. I desire to know wherefore I am banished?

Gov. Say no more, the court knows wherefore and is satisfied.

ROGER WILLIAMS

Christenings Make Not Christians
1645

Roger Williams (c. 1603–83), the banished Massachusetts minister who founded the colony of Rhode Island, is rightly remembered for his bold stand in favor of religious toleration. But even more interesting than the stance itself were the ingenious ways he derived it from Bible-based Puritan concepts. His heterodox reasoning was particularly well shown in his remarkable essay on Indian conversions. Here not only did he scornfully denounce, as he did in his famous *Bloudy Tenent of Persecution,* the use of any coercion to force religious conformity as a flagrant contradiction of the purely spiritual weapons of Jesus Christ, but he also called into question even preaching for conversion. This practice, he insisted, was both biblically unwarranted and grossly manipulative of delicate and humanly untouchable states of consciousness. The outcome of Williams's radical disjunction of the sacred and profane was paradoxical: he suggested a broad definition of acceptable cultural norms, as in the case of the Indians, whereas he narrowed what was acceptable in religion—what he cared most about—to the point of witnessing, prophesying, and awaiting Christ's second coming and the restoration of the apostolic church. Although corrected by recent scholarship, the best general work on Williams as a religious thinker is Perry Miller, *Roger Williams: His Contribution to the American Tradition* (Indianapolis, 1953). Edmund S. Morgan, *Roger Williams: The Church and the State* (New York, 1967) is an excellent study of Williams's political ideas. For a knowledgeable discussion of Williams's eschatology, see W. Clark Gilpin, *The Millenarian Piety of Roger Williams* (Chicago, 1979).

A Briefe Discourse concerning that name *Heathen,* commonly given to the INDIANS

As also concerning that great point of their *CONVERSION.*

I shall first be humbly bold to inquire into the name *Heathen,* which the English give them, & the Dutch approve and and practise in their hame HEYDENEN, signifying Heathen or Nations.

How oft have I heard both the English and Dutch (not onely the civill, but the most debauched and profane) say, These *Heathen* Dogges, better kill a thousand of them then that we *Christians* should be indangered or troubled with them; Better they were all cut off, & then we shall be no more troubled with them: They have spilt our *Christian* bloud, the best way to make riddance of them, cut them all off, and so make way for Christians.

I shall therefore humbly intreat my country-men of all sorts to consider, that although men have used to apply this word *Heathen* to the Indians that go naked, and have not heard of that One-God, yet this word *Heathen* is most improperly sinfully, and unchristianly so used in this sence. The word *Heathen* signifieth no more then *Nations* or *Gentiles;* so do our Translations from the Hebrew כרים and the Greeke ἔϑνη, in the old and New Testament promiscuously render these words *Gentiles, Nations, Heathens.*

Why Nations? Because the Jewes being the onely People and Nation of God, esteemed (and that rightly) all other People, not only those that went naked, but the famous BABYLONIANS, CALDEANS, MEDES, and PERSIANS, GREEKES and ROMANES, their stately Cities and Citizens, inferiour themselves, and not partakers of their glorious privileges, but Ethnicke, Gentiles, Heathen, or the Nations of the world.

Now then we must enquire who are the People of God, his *holy nation,* since the coming of the Lord Jesus, and the rejection of his first typicall holy Nation the Jewes.

It is confest by all, that the CHRISTIANS the followers of Jesus, are now the onely People of God, his *holy nation,* &c. ἔϑνος ἅγιον I, Πευ, 2,9,

Who are then the *nations, heathen,* or *gentiles,* in opposition to this *People of God?* I answer, All People, *civilized* as well as *uncivilized,* even the most famous States, Cities, and the Kingdomes of the World: For all must come within that distinction. I. Cor. 5. *within* or *without.*

Within the *People of God,* his Church at CORINTH: *Without* the City of CORINTH worshipping *Idols,* and so consequently all other People, HEATHENS, or NATIONS, opposed to the people of God, the true *Jewes:* And therefore now the naturall *Jewes*

Source: *The Complete Writings of Roger Williams,* vol. 7, ed. Perry Miller (New York: Russell & Russell, 1963), 31–41. Reprinted by permission of Russell & Russell/Atheneum, Copyright © 1963.

themselves, not being of this People, are *Heathens, Nations* or *Gentiles.* Yea, this will by many hands be yeelded, but what say you to the *Christian world?* What say you to *Christ endome?* I answer, what do you thinke *Peter* or *John,* or *Paul,* or any of the first Messengers of the Lord Jesus; yea if the Lord Jesus himselfe were here, (as he will be shortly) and were to make answer, what would they, what would he say to a CHRISTIAN WORLD? To CHRISTENDOME? And otherwise then what He would speak, that is indeed what he hath spoken, and will shortly speake, must no man speak that names himselfe a Christian.

Herdious in his Map of his CHRISTIAN WORLD takes in all *Asia, Europe,* a vaste part of *Africa,* and a great part also of *America,* so far as the *Popes Christnings* have reached to.

This is the CHRISSION WORLD, or Christendome, in which respect men stand upon their tearmes of *high opposition* between the CHRISTIAN and the TURKE, (the Christian shore, and the Turkish shore) between the CHRISTIANS of this Christian WORLD and the JEW, and the CHRISTIAN and the HEATHEN, that is the naked *American.*

But since *Without* is turned to be *Within,* the WORLD turned CHRISTIAN, and atheittle *flocke* of JESUS CHRIST hath [marvelously] increased in such wonderfull conversions, let me be bold to aske what is Christ? What are the Christians? The Hebrew משיא and the Greeke χοισυος will tell us that Christ was and in (is) the *Anointed* of God, whom the prophets and Kings and preists of Israel in their *anointings* did prefigure and type out; whence his followers are called χριστιανοι christians, that is *Anointed* also: So that indeed to be a *christian* implyes two things, first, to be a follower of that anointed one in all his Offices; secondly, to pertake of his anointings, for the Anointing of the Lord Jesus (like the anointings of AARON, to which none might make the like on pain of death) descend to the skirt of his garments.

To come nearer to this Christion world, (where the world becomes christian holy, anointed, Gods People, &c.) what saith John? What saith the Angel? Yea, what saith Jesus Christ and his Father (from whom the Revelation came *Revel* I.I.? What say they unto the Beast and his Worshippers Revel. 13.

If that beast be not the *Turke,* nor the *Roman Emperour* (as the grossest interpret) but either the generall councels, or the catholike church of *Rome,* or the Popes or Papacy (as the most refined interpret) why then all the *world, Revel.* 13. ὄλη ἡ γῆ wonders after the *Beast,* worships the *Beast,* followeth the *Beast,* and boasts of the *Beast,* that there is none like him, and all People, Tongues, and Nations, come under the power of this Beast, & no man shall buy nor sell, nor live, who hath not the marke of the *Beast* in his *Fore-head,* or in his hand, or the number of his name.

If this *world* or *earth* then be not intended of the whole terrestriall Globe, *Europe, Asia, Africa* and *America,* (which sence and experience denyes) but of the *Roman earth,* or world, and the People, Languages, and Nations, of the *Roman Monarchy,* transferred from the *Roman* Emperour to the *Roman* Popes, and the Popish *Kingdomes,* branches of that ROMAN-ROOT, (as all *history* and content of time make evident.)

Then we know by this time what the Lord Jesus would say of the Christian world and of the *Christian:* Indeed what he saith *Revel.* 14. If any man worship the *Beast* or his *picture,* he shall drinke &c. even the dread fullest cup that the whole Booke of God ever held forth to sinners.

Grant this, say some of *Popish* Countries, that notwithstanding they make up Christendome, or Christian world, yet submitting to that *Beast,* they are the *earth* or *world* and must drinke of that most dreadfull cup: But now for those nations that have withdrawn their necks from that *beastly yoke,* & protesting against him, are not Papists, but Protestants, shall we, may we thinke of them, that they, or any of them may also be called (in true Scripture sence) *Heathens,* that is Nations or Gentiles, in opposition to the People of God, which is the onely holy Nation.

I answer, that all Nations now called *Protestants* were at first part of that whole Earth, or main (ANTICHRISTIAN) Continent, that wondered after, worshipped the Beast, &c. This must then with holy feare and trembling (because it concernes the KINGDOME of God, and salvation) be attended to, Whether such a departure from the *Beast,* and coming out from ANTICHRISTIAN abominations, from his markes in a false conversion, and a false constitution, or framing of NATIONALL CHURCHES in false MINISTERIES, and ministrations of BAPTISME, *Supper of the Lord, Admonitions, Excommunications* as amounts to a true perfect Hand, cut off from that Earth which wondered after and worshipped the *Beast:* or whether, not being so cut off, they remaine not *Peninsula* or necks of land, contiguous and joyned still unto his *Christendome?* If now the bodies of Protestant Nations remaine in an unrepentant, unregenerate, naturall estate, and so consequently farre from hearing the admonitions of the Lord Jesus, Math 18. I say they must sadly consider and know (least their profession of the name of Jesus prove at last but an aggravation of condemnation) that Christ Jesus hath said, they are but as *Heathens* and *Publicanes,* vers. 17. How might I therefore humbly beseech my country men to consider what deepe cause they have to search their conversions from that *Beast* and his *Pisture?* And whether having no more of Christ then the name (beside the invented wayes of worship, derived from, or drawn after *Romes pattern*) their hearts and conversations will not evince them unconverted and *unchristian Christians,* and not yet knowing what it is to come by true Regeneration within, to the true spirituall Jew from without amongst the Nations, that is *Heathens* or *Gentiles.*

How deeply and eternally this concerns each soule to search into! yea, and much more deeply such is professe to be Guides, Leaders, and Builders of the HOUSE of God.

First, as they look to *Formes* and *Frame* of Buildings, or Churches.

Secondly, as they attend to *Meanes* and *Instruments,* &c.

Thirdly, as they would lay sure Foundations; and lasting Groundsells.

Fourthly, as they account the cost and charge such buildings will amount unto.

Fifthly, so they may not forget the true spirituall matter and materials of which a true House, Citty, Kingdome, or Nation of God, now in the new Testament are to be composed or gathered.

Now Secondly, for the hopes of CONVERSION, and turning the People of *America* unto God: There is no respect of Persons with him, for we are all the worke of his hands; from the rising of the Sunne to the going downe thereof, his name shall be great among the nations from the East & from the West, &c. If we respect their sins, they are far short of *European* sinners: They neither abuse such corporall mercies for they have them not; nor sin they against the Gospell light, (which shines not amongst them) as the men of *Europe* do: And yet if they were greater sinners then they are, or greater sinners then the *Europeans,* they are not the further from the great *Ocean* of mercy in that respect.

Lastly, they are intelligent, many very ingenuous, plaine-hearted, inquisitive and (as I said before) prepared with many convictions, &c.

Now secondly, for the Catholicks conversion, although I believe I may safely hope that God hath his in Rome, in Spaine, yet if Antichrist be their false head (as most true it is) the body, faith, baptisme, hope (opposite to the true, Ephes. 4.) are all false also; yea consequently their preachings, conversions, salvations (leaving secret things to God) must all be of the same false nature likewise.

If the reports (yea some of their owne *Historians*) be true, what monstrous and most inhumane conversions have they made; baptizing thousands, yea ten thousands of the poore Natives, sometimes by wiles and subtle devices, sometimes by force compelling them to submit to that which they understood not, neither before nor after such their monstrous Christning of them. Thirdly, for our *New-england* parts, I can speake uprightly and confidently, I know it to have been easie for my selfe, long ere this, to have brought many thousands of these Natives, yea the whole country, to a far greater Antichristian conversion then ever was yet heard of in *America*. I have reported something in the Chapter of their Religion, how readily I could have brought the whole Country to have observed one day in seven; I adde to have received a *Baptisme* (or washing) though it were in *Rivers* (as the first *Christians* and the Lord *Jesus* himselfe did) to have come to a *stated Church meeting*, maintained priests and formes of prayer, and a whole forme of *Antichristian* worship in life and death. Let none wonder at this, for *plausible perswasions* in the mouths of those whom naturall men esteem and love: for the power of prevailing forces and armies hath done this in all the *Nations* (as men speake) of *Christendome*. Yea what lamentable experience have we of the *Turnings* and *Turnings* of the *body* of this Land in point of Religion in few yeares?

When *England* was all *Popish* under Henry the seventh, how easie is conversion wrought to halfe Papist halfe-Protestant under *Henry* the eighth?

From halfe-Protestanisme halfe-Popery under *Henry* the eight, to absolute Protestanisme under Edward the sixth: from absoluer Protestation under *Edward* the sixt to absalute popery under Quegne *Mary,* and from absolute Popery under Queene *Mary,* (just like the Weathercocke, with the breath of every Prince) to absolute Protestanisme under Queene *Elizabeth* &c.

For all this, yet some may aske, why hath there been such a price in my hand not improved? why have I not brought them to such a conversion as I speake of? I answer, woe be to me, if I call light darknesse, or darknesse light; sweet bitter, or bitter sweet; woe be to me if I call that conversion unto God, which is indeed subversion of the soules of Millions in *Christendome,* from one false worship to another, and the prophanation of the holy name of God, his holy Son and blessed Ordinances. *America* (as *Europe* and all nations) lyes dead in sin and trespasses: It is not a suite of crimson Satten will make a dead man live, take off and change his crimson into white he is dead still, off with that, and shift him into cloth of gold, and from that to cloth of diamonds, he is but a dead man still: For it is not a forme, nor the change of one forme into another, a finer, and a finer, and yet more fine, that makes a man a convert I meane such a convert as is acceptable to God in Jesus Christ, according to the visible Rule of his last will and Testament. I speake not of Hypocrites, (which may but glister, and be no solid gold as *Simon Magus, Judas* &c.) But of a true externall conversion; I say then, woe be to me if intending to catch men (as the Lord Jesus said to *Peter*) I should pretend conversion) and the bringing of men as misticall fish, into a *Church-estate,* that is a converted estate, and so build them up with *Ordinances* as a converted Christian People, and yet afterward still pretend to catch them by an after conversion. I question not but that it hath pleased God in his infinit pitty and patience, to suffer this among us, yea and to codvert thousands, whom all men, yea and the persons (in their personall estates converted) have esteemed themselves good converts before.

But I question whether this hath been so frequent in these late yeares, when the times of ignorance (which God pleaseth to passe by) are over, and now a greater light concerning the Church, Ministery, and conversion, is arisen. I question whether if such rare talents, which God hath betrusted many of his precious Worthies with, were laid out (as they shall be in the Lord's most holy season) according to the first pattern; I say, I question whether or no, where there hath been one (in his personall estate converted) there have not been, and I hope in the Lords time shall be, thousands truly converted from *Antichristian Idols* (both in *person* and *worship*) to serve the living and true God.

And lastly, it is out of question to me, that I may not pretend a *false conversion,* and *false state* of *worship,* to the true Lord Jesus.

If any noble *Berean* shall make inquiry what is that true conversion I intend; I answer first negatively.

First, it is not a conversion of a People from one false worship to another, as *Nebuchadnezzer* compeld all Nations under his Monarchy.

Secondly, it is not to a mixture of the manner or worship of the true God, the God of Israel, with false gods & their worships, as the People were converted by the King of *Assyria,* 2, Kin. 17. in which worship for many Generations did these *Samaritans* continue, having a forme of many wholsome truths amongst them, concerning God and the *Messiah,* Joh. 4.

Thirdly, it is not from the true to a false, as Jereboam turned the ten Tribes to their ruine and dispersion unto this day, I. Kin. 12.

Fourthly, it must not be a conversion to some externall submission to Gods Ordinances upon earthly respects, as JACOBS sons converted the *Sichemites, Gen.* 34.

Fiftly, it must not be, (it is not possible it should be in truth) a conversion of People to the worship of the Lord Jesus, by force of Armes and swords of steele: So indeed did *Nebuchadnezzer* deale with all the world, *Dan.* 3. so doth his *Antitype* and *successor* the *Beast* deal with all the earth, *Rev.* 13. &c.

But so did never the Lord Jesus bring any unto his most pure worship, for he abhorres (as all men, yea the very *Indians* doe) an unwilling Spouse, and to enter into a forced bed: The will in worship, if true, is like a free Vote, nec cogic, nec cogitur: JESUS CHRIST compells by the mighty perswasions of his Messengers to come in, but otherwise with earthly weapons he never did compell nor can be compelled.

The not discerning of this truth hath let out the bloud of thousands in civill combustions in all ages; and made the whore drunk, & the Earth drunk with the bloud of the Saints, and witnesses of Jesus.

And it is yet like to be the destruction & and dissolution of (that which is called) the Christian world, unless the God of peace and pity looke downe upon it, and satisfy the soules of men, that he hath not so required. I should be far yet from unsecuring the peace of a City, of a Land, (which I confesse ought to be maintained by civill weapons, & which I have so much cause to be earnest with God for) Nor would I leave a gap open to any mutinous hand or tongue, nor wish a weapon left in the hand of any known to be mutinous and peace-breakers.

I know (lastly) the consciences of many are otherwise perswaded, both from Israels state of old, and other Allegations; yet I shall be humbly bold to say, I am able to present such considerations to the eyes of all who love the Prince of truth and Peace, that shall discover the weaknesse of all such allegations, and answer all objections, that have been, or can be made in this point. So much negatively.

Secondly, affirmatively: I answer in generall, A true Conversion (whether of *Americans* or *Europeans*) must be such as those Conversions were of the first pattern, either of the Jewes or the Heathens; That Rule is the golden *Mece wand* in the hand of the Angell or Messenger, *rev.* II. I. beside which all other are leaden and crooked.

In particular: First, it must be by the free proclaiming or preaching of Repentance & forgivenesse of sins. Luk. 24. by such Messengers as can prove their lawfull sending and Commission from the Lord Jesus, to make Disciples out of all nations: and so to baptize or wash them εἰς τὸ ὄνομα into the *name* or *profession* of the holy Trinity, *Mat,* 28. 19 Rom. 10. 14. 15.

Secondly, such a conversion (so farre as mans Judgement can reach which is fallible, (as was the judgement of the first Messengers, as in *Simon Magus,* &c.) as is a turning of the whole man from the power of *Sathan* unto God, *act.* 26. Such a change, as if an old man became a new Babe B 2 *Joh.* 3. yea, as amounts to Gods new creation in the soule, *Ephes,* 2. 10.

Thirdly, Visibly it is a turning from Idols not only of *conversation* but of *worship* (whether *Pagan,* Turkish, Jewish, or ANTICHRISTIAN) to the Living and true God in the waies of his holy worship, appointed by his Son, I Thes. I. 9.

I know Objections use to be made against this, but the *golden Rule,* if well attended to, will discover all crooked *swervings* and *aberrations.*

If any now say unto me, Why then if this be *Conversion,* and you have such a *Key* of *Language,* and such a dore of *opportunity,* in the knowledge of the Country and the inhabitants, why proceed you not to produce in *America* some patternes of such conversions as you speake of?

I answer, first, it must be a great deale of practise, and mighty paines and hardship undergone by my selfe, or any that would proceed to such a further degree of the Language, as to be able in propriety of speech to open matters of salvation to them.

In matters of Earth men will helpe to spell out each other, but in matters of Heaven (to which the soule is naturally so averse) how far are the Eares of man hedged up from listening to all improper Language?

Secondly, my desires and endeavours are constant (by the helpe of God) to attaine a propriety of Language.

Thirdly, I confesse to the honour of my worthy Countrymen in the *Bay of Massachuset,* and elsewhere, that I received not long since expressions of their holy desires and proffers of assistance in the worke, by the hand of my worthy friend Colonell *Humphreys,* during his abode there.

Yet fourthly, I answer, if a man were as affectionate and zealous as *David* to build an house for God, and as wise and holy to advise and incourage, as *Nathan,* attempt this worke without a *Word, Warrant* and *Commission,* for *matter,* and *manner,* from GOD himselfe, they must afterwards heare a voice (though accepting good desires, yet reproving want of Commission) *Did I ever speak a word saith the Lord?* &c. 2. *Sam.* 7.7.

The truth is, having not been without (through the mercy of God) abundant and constant thoughts about a true Commission for such an Embassie and Ministery. I must ingenuously confesse the restlesse unsatisfiednesse of my soule in divers *main particulars:* As first whether (since the Law must go forth from *Zion,* and the word of the Lord from *Jerusalem*) I say whether Gods great businesse between Christ Jesus the holy Son of God and Antichrist the man of sin and Sonne of perdition, must not be first over, and *Zion* and *Jerusalem* be rebuilt and re-established, before the Law and word of life be sent forth to the rest of the Nations of the World, who have not heard of Christ: The Prophets are deep concerning this.

Secondly since there can be no preaching (according to the last Will and Testament of Christ Jesus) without a true sending *Rom.* 14. 15. Where the power and authority of *sending* and *giving* that *Commission Math.* 28 &c. I say where that power now lyes?

It is here unseasonable to number up all that lay claime to this *Power,* with their grounds for their pretences, either those of the *Romish* sort, or those of the *Reforming* or *Re-building* sort, and the mighty controversies which are this day in all parts about it: in due place (haply) I may present such sad *Queries* to consideration, that may occasion some to cry with DANIEL (concer-JERUSALEMS desolation *Dan.* 9) *Under the whole Heaven hath not been done, as hath been* done to JERUSALEM: and with JEREMY in the same respect, Lam. 2. 12. *Have you no respect all you that passe by, behold and see if there were ever sorrow like to my sorrow, wherewith the Lord hath afflicted me in the day of his fierce wrath.*

That may make us ashamed for all that wee have done, *Ezek.* 43 and loath our selves, for that (in whorish worships) wee have broken him with our whorish hearts *Ezek.* 9. To fall dead at the feet of JESUS, *Rev.* I. as JOHN did, and to weepe much as hee *Rev.* 5. that so the Lamb may please to open unto us that WONDERFUL BOOK and the seven SEALED MYSTERIES thereof.

Your unworthy Country-man
ROGER WILLIAMS.

FINIS.

COTTON MATHER

Selection from *Bonifacius*
1710

If Roger Williams sought to narrow the scope of religion in order to preserve its authenticity, Cotton Mather (1663–1728) strove heroically to expand it, it would seem, almost infinitely. Theories have abounded concerning the sources of this trait or (more controversially) compulsion, beginning, naturally, with his extraordinary lineage as the son and grandson of three of Puritan New England's greatest ministers. But whatever the causes, the result seems clear enough: Mather's voracious passion to experience the power of his Christian faith through a multiplicity of forms animated, for better or worse, virtually all his far-flung works, from his ill-fated search for evidences of witchcraft to his enthusiastic embrace of the new natural science. One can also see this drive operating in his influential *Bonifacius*. Most of this tract was taken up with various benevolent and (to a modern eye) meddling practical proposals for "doing good." But in these opening and closing chapters, Mather was both bolder and more revealing. He carefully asserted the orthodox basis of his good works in the saving grace of God while showing how the doing of good might bring about social cohesion, worldwide political change, and a joyful fulfillment of a faith so anguished as to seem otherwise almost unbearable. For an excellent discussion of Mather's religious thought, see Robert Middlekauff, *The Mathers: Three Generations of Puritan Intellectuals, 1596–1728* (New York, 1971), 191–367. The historical and theological significance of Mather's pietism is cogently discussed in Richard F. Lovelace, *The American Pietism of Cotton Mather: Origins of American Evangelicalism* (Grand Rapids, Mich., 1979). Mather is the subject of two splendid biographies that shed much light on his intellectual life and character: David Levin, *Cotton Mather: The Young Life of the Lord's Remembrancer, 1663–1703* (Cambridge, Mass., 1978); and Kenneth Silverman, *The Life and Times of Cotton Mather* (New York, 1984).

[Chapter One:] Essays to Do Good

Such *glorious things are spoken* in the oracles of our good God, concerning them who *devise good,* that A BOOK OF GOOD DEVICES may very reasonably demand attention and acceptance from them that have any impressions of the most *reasonable religion* upon them. I am *devising* such a BOOK; but at the same time offering a sorrowful demonstration, that if men would set themselves to *devise good,* a world of *good* might be done, more than there is, in this *present evil world.* It is very sure, the world has *need enough.* There needs abundance to be done, that the great GOD and His CHRIST may be more known and served in the world; and that the *errors* which are *impediments* to the *acknowledgments* wherewith men ought to glorify their Creator and Redeemer, may be rectified. There needs abundance to be done, that the *evil manners* of the world, by which men are *drowned in perdition,* may be reformed; and mankind rescued from the epidemical corruption and slavery which has overwhelmed it. There needs abundance to be done, that the *miseries* of the world may have *remedies* and *abatements* provided for them; and that miserable people may be relieved and comforted. The world has according to the computation of some, above seven hundred millions of people now living in it. What an ample field among all these, to *do good* upon! In a word, *the kingdom of God* in the world calls for innumerable *services* from us. To do SUCH THINGS is to Do GOOD. Those men DEVISE GOOD, who shape any DEVICES to do things of such a tendency; whether the things be of a *spiritual* importance, or of a *temporal.* You see, Sirs, the general matter, appearing as yet but as a *chaos,* which is to be wrought upon. *Oh! that the good Spirit of God may now fall upon us, and carry on the glorious work which lies before us!*

§2. 'Tis to be supposed, my readers will readily grant, that it is an excellent, a virtuous, a laudable thing to be full of *devices,* to bring about such *noble purposes.* For any man to deride, or to despise my proposal, *that we resolve and study to do as much good in the world as we can,* would be so black a character, that I am not willing to make a supposal of it in any of those with [whom] I am concerned. Let no man pretend unto the name of *a Christian,* who does not approve the proposal of *a perpetual endeavor to do good in the world.* What pretension can such a man have to be *a follower of the Good One?* The primitive *Christians* gladly accepted and improved the name, when the pagans by a mistake styled them, *Chrestians;* because it signified, *useful ones.* The *Christians* who have no ambition to be so, shall be condemned by the pagans, among whom it was a term of the highest honor, to be termed, *a benefactor;* to have *done good,* was accounted *honorable.* The philosopher being asked why everyone desired so much to look upon a fair object, he answered, that *it was a question of a blind man.* If any man ask, as wanting the sense of it, "What is it worth the while to *do good* in the world?," I must say, "It sounds not like the question of a good man." The Αιθησις πνευματικη, as *Origen* calls it, the *spiritual taste* of every good man will make him have an unspeakable *relish* for it. Yea, unworthy to be discoursed as a *man,* is he, who is not for *doing of good among men.* An enemy to the proposal, *that mankind may be the better for us,* deserves to be reckoned, little better than, *a common enemy of mankind.* How cogently do I bespeak, a good reception of what is now designed! I

Source: Cotton Mather, *Bonifacius: An Essay upon the Good,* ed. David Levin (Cambridge, Mass.: Harvard University Press, Belknap Press, 1966), 17–34, 138–44, 149–51, 152. Editor's notes altered. Reprinted by permission of The Belknap Press of Harvard University Press, Copyright © 1966 by The President and Fellows of Harvard College.

produce not only *religion,* but even *humanity* itself, as full of a *fiery indignation against the adversaries of the design.* Excuse me, Sirs; I declare, that if I could have my choice, I would never *eat* or *drink,* or *walk,* with such an one as long as I live; or, look on him as any other than one by whom *humanity* itself is debased and blemished. A very *wicked writer,* has yet found himself compelled by the force of *reason,* to publish this confession. "To love the public, to study an universal good, and to promote the interest of the whole world, as far as is in our power, is surely the highest of goodness, and makes that temper, which we call Divine." And, he goes on: "Is the doing of good for glory's sake so divine a thing? [Alas, too much *humane,* Sir!] Or, is it not a diviner to do good, even where it may be thought inglorious? Even unto the ungrateful, and unto those who are wholly insensible of the good they receive!" A man must be far gone in *wickedness,* who will open his mouth, against such *maxims* and *actions!* A better pen has remarked it; yea, the man must be much a stranger in history, who has not made the remark. *To speak truth, and to do good, were in the esteem even of the heathen world, most God-like qualities.* God forbid, that in the esteem of the *Christian world* for those qualities, there should be any abatement!

§3. I won't yet propose the *reward* of *well-doing,* and the glorious things which the *mercy* and *truth* of God will do, for them who *devise good,* because I would have to do with such, as will esteem it, a sufficient *Reward* unto itself. I will imagine that generous ingenuity, in my readers, which will dispose them to count themselves *well-rewarded* in the thing itself, if God will accept them to *do good* in the world. It is an invaluable *honor,* to *do good;* it is an incomparable *pleasure.* A man must look upon himself as *dignified* and *gratified* by GOD, when an *opportunity* to *do good* is put into his hands. He must embrace it with *rapture,* as enabling him directly to answer the great END of his being. He must manage it with *rapturous delight,* as a most suitable business, as a most precious privilege. He must *sing in those ways of the Lord,* wherein he cannot but find himself, while he is *doing of good.* As the saint of old sweetly sang, "I was glad, when they said unto me, Let us go into the House of the Lord." Thus ought we to be *glad,* when any *opportunity* to *do good,* is offered unto us. We should need no *arguments,* to make us entertain the offer; but we should *naturally* fly into the matter, as most agreeable to the *divine nature* whereof we are *made partakers.* It should *oblige* us wonderfully! An ingot of gold presented unto us, not more obliging! Think, Sirs, *Now I enjoy what I am for! Now I attain what I wish for!* Some servants of God have been so strongly disposed this way, that they have cheerfully made a tender of any *recompense* that could be desired (yea, rather than fail, a *pecuniary* one) unto any friend that would *think* for them, and *supply* the *barrenness* of their thoughts, and *suggest* unto them any special and proper *methods,* wherein they may be *serviceable.* Certainly, to *do good,* is a thing that brings its own *recompense,* in the opinion of those, who reckon a kind *information* of a point wherein they may *do good,* worthy to be by them requited with a *recompense* to the *informer.* I will only say: "If any of you are strangers unto such a disposition as this, to look upon an *opportunity* to *do good,* as a thing that *enriches* you, and to look upon yourselves as *enriched,* and *favored* of God, when He does employ you to *do good:* I have done with you." I would pray them, to lay the *book* aside; it will disdain to carry on any further conversation with 'em! It handles a subject on which the wretches of the house of *Caleb,* will not be conversed withal. It is content with one of Dr. *Stoughton's* Introductions: "It is enough to me, that I speak to wise men, whose reason shall be my rhetoric, to Christians, whose conscience shall be my eloquence."

§4. Though the assertion fly never so much like a *chainshot* among us, and rake down all before it, I will again, and again assert it; *that we might every one of us do more good than we do.* And therefore, this is the FIRST PROPOSAL, to be made unto us: *to be exceedingly humbled, that we have done so little good in the world.* I am not *uncharitable,* in saying: I know not that *assembly* of Christians upon earth, which ought not to be a *Bochim,* in this consideration. Oh! tell me, what *Utopia* I shall find it in! Sirs, let us begin to bring forth some *good fruit,* by lamenting our own *great unfruitfulness.* Verily, *sins of omission* must be confessed and bewailed; else we add unto the number of them. The most *useful* men in the world, have gone out of it, crying to God, "Lord, let my sins of omission be forgiven to me!" Men that have made more than ordinary conscience about well-spending of their *time,* have had their deathbed made uneasy by this reflection: *The loss of time now sits heavy upon me.* Be sure, all *unregenerate* persons are, as our Bible has told us, *unprofitable* persons. 'Tis not for nothing, that the comparison of *thorns,* and *briars,* has been used, to *teach* us, what they are. An unrenewed sinner, alas, he never did *one good work* in all his *life!* In all his *life,* did I say? You must give me that word again! He is *dead* while he *lives;* he is *dead in sins;* he has never yet begun to *live unto God:* and, as is he, so are *all the works of his hands;* they are *dead works.* Ah! wretched *good-for-nothing.* Wonder, wonder at the patience of Heaven, which yet forbears *cutting down* such a *cumberer of the ground.* The best, and the first advice, to be given unto such persons, is, *immediately to do their best, that they may get out of their woeful unregeneracy.* Let them *immediately* acknowledge the *necessity* of their turning to God, but how *unable* they are to do it, and how *unworthy* that God should make them *able. Immediately* let them lift up their *cry* unto sovereign *grace,* to *quicken* them; and let them then *try,* whether they cannot with *quickened* Souls, *plead* the *sacrifice* and *righteousness* of a glorious CHRIST for their happy reconciliation to God; seriously resolve upon a life of *obedience* to God, and *serious religion;* and resign themselves up unto the *Holy Spirit,* that He may possess them, instruct them, strengthen them, and *for His name's sake lead them in the paths of holiness.* There will no *good* be done, till this be done. The very *first-born* of all *devices to do good,* is in being *born again,* and in *devising means, that a banished* soul may no longer be *expelled* from the presence of God. But you that have been brought home to God, have sad cause, not only to deplore the *dark days* of your unregeneracy, wherein you did none but the *unfruitful works of darkness;* but also, that you have done so *little,* since God has quickened you and enabled you, to *do,* the things that should be done. How little, how little have you lived up, to the strains of *gratitude,* which might have been justly expected, since God has brought you *into His marvellous light!* The best of us may mourn in our complaint: "Lord, how little good have I done, to what I might have done!" Let the sense of this cause us to *loathe* and *judge* ourselves before the Lord: let it fill us with shame, and abase us wonderfully! How can we do any other, than with *David,* even make a cauldron of our couch, and a bath of our tears, when we consider how little *good* we have done! *Oh! that our heads were waters,* because they have been so *dry* of all thoughts to *do good! Oh! that our eyes were a fountain of tears,* because they have been so little upon the *lookout* for objects and methods to *do good* upon! For the *pardon* of this *evil-doing,* let us fly to the Great *Sacrifice,* which is our only *expiation.* Plead the *blood* of that *Lamb of God,* whose universal *usefulness* is one of those admirable properties, for which He has been called, *a lamb.* The *pardon* of our *barrenness* at *good works* being thus obtained, by faith in that *blood which cleanses from all sin,* that is the way for us to be rescued from a condemnation to *perpetual barrenness.* The dreadful sentence of, *Let no fruit grow on thee forever!* will be reversed and prevented, by such a *pardon.* Sirs, a true, right, evangelical procedure to *do good,* must have this *repentance* laid in the foundation of it! We do not *handle the matter wisely,* if a *foundation* be not laid thus *low,* and in the deepest *self-abasement.*

§5. How full, how full of *devices* are we, for our own *secular advantage!* And how *expert* in *devising* many *little things,* to be done for ourselves! We apply our thoughts, with a mighty assiduity, unto the old question, *What shall I eat and drink, and wherewithal shall I be clothed?* It is with a very strong application of our thoughts, that we study, what we shall do for ourselves, in our *marriages,* in our *voyages,* in our *bargains,* and in many, many other concerns, wherein we are solicitous to have our condition easy. We solicitously *contrive,* that we may accomplish *good bargains,* and that we may steer clear of ten thousand *inconveniences,* to which, without some *contrivance,* we may lie obnoxious. The *business* of our *personal callings* we carry on with numberless thoughts, how we may *do well,* in what is to be done. To accomplish our temporal *business,* in affairs that cannot be numbered, we *find out witty inventions.* But, O rational, immortal, Heaven-born SOUL, are thy wonderous faculties capable of no greater improvements, no better employments? Why should a *soul* of such high capacities, a *soul* that may arrive to be clothed in the bright *scarlet* of *angels,* yet *embrace a dunghill!* O let a *blush* coloring beyond *scarlet,* be thy clothing for thy being found so meanly occupied! Alas, *in the multitude of thy thoughts within thee,* hast thou no dispositions to raise thy soul, unto some thoughts, *what may be done for* GOD, *and* CHRIST, *and for my own* SOUL, *and for the most considerable interests?* How many hundreds of *thoughts* have we, how to obtain or secure some trifle for ourselves; to *one,* how we may serve the interests of the glorious LORD, and of His people in the world? How can we now pretend, that we *love Him,* or, that a carnal, and criminal *self-love,* has not the dominion over us? I again come in, upon a *soul* of an Heavenly extract, and *smite* it, as the angel did the sleeping prisoner: *Awake, shake off thy shackles, lie no longer fettered in a base confinement unto nothing but a meaner sort of business.* Assume and assert the liberty of now and then thinking on the *noblest question* in the world: *What good may I do in the world?* There was a time, when it was complained by no less a man, than *Gregory* the Great (the Bishop of *Rome): I am sunk into the world!* It may be the complaint of a *soul,* that minds all other things, and rarely calls to mind that *noblest question. Ah! star, fallen from Heaven,* and choked in dust, rise and soar up to something answerable to thy original. Begin a *course of thoughts,* which when begun, will be like a *resurrection from the dead.* They *which dwell in the dust, wake and sing,* and little anticipate the life which we are to live at the *resurrection of the dead,* when they livelily set themselves to think: *How may I be a blessing in the world?* And, *What may I do, that righteousness may more dwell in the world?*

§6. How much *hurt* may be done by *one wicked man?* Yea, sometimes *one wicked man,* of but small abilities, becoming an *indefatigable tool of the Devil,* may do an incredible deal of mischief in the world. We have seen some wretched instruments of *cursed memory,* ply the intention of *doing mischief,* at a strange rate; until they have undone a whole country; yea, unto the undoing of more than three kingdoms. 'Tis a melancholy consideration, which I am now upon: and I may say, an astonishing one! You will hardly find *one of a thousand,* who does near so much, to serve God and Christ, and his own soul, as you may see done by thousands to serve the Devil. *An horrible thing!*

"O my soul; thy *Maker,* and thy *Saviour,* so worthy of thy love, and thy all! A Lord, whose infinite goodness, will follow all that thou doest for Him, with remunerations, beyond all apprehension glorious! How little, how little, is it that thou doest for Him! At the same time, look into thy neighborhood; see there a monster of wickedness, who to his uttermost will serve a Devil, that will prove a *destroyer* unto him, and all whose *wages* will be *torments.* He *studies* how to serve the *Devil;* he is never weary of his *drudgery;* he racks his *invention* to go through with it. He *shames* me, he *shames* me wonderfully! *O my God, I am ashamed, and blush to lift up my face unto thee, my God.*"

There is a man, of whom we read: "He deviseth mischief upon his bed, he sets himself in a way that is not good." Now I beseech you, why should not we be as *active,* as *frequent,* as *forward,* in *devising of good;* and as full of *exquisite contrivance?* Why should not we be as *wise to do good,* as any people are *wise to do evil?* I am sure, we have a *better cause;* and there is more of *reason* for it. My friend, thou are one that makes but a *little figure* in the world, and a *brother of low degree,* behold, a vast encouragement! A *little* man may do a great deal of *hurt.* And then, why may not a *little* man, do a great deal of *good!* It is possible the *wisdom of a poor man,* may start a proposal, that may *save a city,* serve a nation! A *single hair* applied unto a *flyer,* that has other wheels depending on it, may pull up an *oak,* or pull down an *house.*

It is very observable, that when our Lord JESUS CHRIST would recommend the *zeal,* with which the *Kingdom of Heaven* is to be served, He did not mention an example of *honest wisdom;* no, but of an unrighteous and scandalous *dishonesty* (as of an *unjust steward*) for our emulation. The *wisdom* of our Lord in this matter, is much to be observed. His design is, not only to represent the *prudence,* but also the vast industry, ingenuity, resolution, and *heroic effort of soul,* necessary in them, that would seek and serve the Kingdom of Heaven. There is nowhere to be found among men, that *vivacity of spirit* in *lawful* actions, which there is to be found in *unlawful* ones. The ways of *honesty* are plain to men, and they require not so much *uneasiness* in the minds of men to manage them. Whereas your *thieves* and *cheats,* and men that follow courses of *dishonesty,* take ways that are full of difficulties: the *turns* and the *tricks* with which they must be carried through them, are innumerable. Hence among such fellows, you find the exercise of the most extraordinary *subtlety.* There is no such cunning, and nimble *application* to be anywhere else met withal. 'Tis very emphatical, to fetch from hence the colors of *heavenly wisdom!* That which I would now be at, is this: that we *do good* with as much *application,* as any men alive can use in *evil-doing.* When *wickedness proceeds from the wicked,* it is often done *with both hands,* and *greedily.* Why may not we proceed in our *usefulness,* even *with both hands,* and *greedily* watching for opportunities? We have no occasion for any *ill arts,* that we may carry on our designs to *do good.* God forbid, that we should ever imagine the uniting of such *inconsistencies.* But why cannot we carry on our *designs,* with as much, and as deep, and as copious *thought,* as the men of *ill arts?* And why may not we lay out our spirits, with as transporting a vigor, to do the things that will be *acceptable* to God, and *profitable* to men, as any wretches have, when they *weary themselves to commit iniquity?* To reprehend certain ecclesiastical drones, who had little inclination to *do good,* Father *Latimer* employed a coarse expression of this importance: "If you won't learn of good men, for shame learn of the Devil! He is never idle. He goes about, seeking what hurt he may do!" Truly, the indefatigable prosecution of their designs, which we may see in some, whom the Holy Word of God has called, *the children of the Devil,* may exceedingly put us to the blush. Our *obligations* to *do good* are infinite: they *do evil* against all *obligations*. The *compensations* made unto them who *do good,* are encouraging beyond all expression; they who *do evil,* get nothing to boast of; but *evil pursues the sinners.* If the *Devil* do *go about,* and people inspired by him also *go about, seeking what hurt they may do,* why do not we *go about,* and *seek,* and think, where and how to *do good?* Verily, 'twere a character for a *good angel,* to do so. O thou *child of God,* and *lover of all righteousness:* how canst thou find in thy heart at any time to *cease* from doing all the *good,* that can be done, in the *right ways of the Lord?* Methinks, that *Word of the Lord,* may be a *burden* unto us; if we have any true *honor* in us, it will be so! *The children of this world, are in* (and *for*) *their generation, wiser than the children of light.* Yea, they pursue the *works of darkness* more livelily, than any of us *walk in the light,* wherewith our Great Saviour has favored us.

§7. To the title of GOOD WORKS there do belong, those *essays to do good,* which are now urged for. To produce them, the *first* thing, and indeed the ONE thing, that is *needful,* is, a glorious work of GRACE on the soul, renewing and quickening of it, and *purifying* of the sinner, and rendering him *zealous of good works:* a *workmanship of God* upon us, *creating* us over again, by JESUS CHRIST, *for good works.* And then, there is needful, what will necessarily follow upon such a *work:* that is, a *disposition* to *do good works* upon true, genuine, generous, and evangelical *principles.* Those *principles* are to be *stated,* before we can go any further; when they are *active,* we shall go a great deal further.

It is in the first place, to be taken for granted: that the *end* for which we do *good works* must not be, to afford the matter of our *justification,* before the Law of the holy GOD. Indeed, no *good works* can be done by any man until he be *justified.* Until a man be united unto the glorious CHRIST, who is *our life,* he is a *dead man.* And, I pray, what *good works* to be expected from such a man? They will all be *dead works.* For, "Severed from me ye can do nothing," saith our Savior. The *justification of a* sinner, *by faith, before good works, and in order to them,* is one of those truths, which may say to the Popish innovations, "With us are the gray-headed, and very aged men, much elder than they Father." It was an old maxim of the faithful, *Bona opera sequuntur justificatum, non præcedunt justificandum.*[1] It is the *righteousness* of the *good works* done by our Saviour and *Surety,* not our own, that *justifies* us before God, and answers the demands of His Law upon us. We do by *faith* lay hold on those *good works* for our *justifying righteousness* before we arrive to do our own. 'Tis not our *faith* itself, either as doing of *good works,* or as being itself one of them, which entitles us to the *justifying righteousness* of our Saviour. But it is *faith,* only *as* renouncing of our own righteousness, and relying on that of our Saviour, provided for the *chief of sinners,* by which we are *justified.* Sir, all your attempts at *good works* will come to nothing, till a *justifying faith* in your Saviour, shall carry you forth unto them. This was the divinity of the ancients; *Jerome* has well expressed it: *Sine Christo omnis virtus est in vitie.*[2] Nevertheless; first, you are to look upon it, as a glorious truth of the Gospel, that the *moral law* (which prescribes and requires *good works*) must by every Christian alive be made the *rule* of his life. *Do we make void the Law through faith? God forbid. Yea, we establish the Law.* The *rule,* by which we are to *glorify* God, is given us in the law of *good works,* which we *enjoy* (I will express it *so!*) in the *Ten Commandments.* It is impossible for

---

1. Good works follow justification; they do not precede justification.
2. Without Christ, all virtue is vice.

us, to be released from all obligations to glorify God by a conformity to this *rule;* sooner shall we cease to be creatures. The *conformity* to that rule in the *righteousness,* which our Saviour by His obedience to it, has *brought in,* to *justify* us, has forever *magnified the Law, and made it honorable.* Though our Saviour has furnished us, with a perfect and spotless *righteousness,* when His obedience to the *Law,* is placed unto our account; yet it is a *sin* for us at all to fall short in our own obedience to the *Law:* we must always loathe and judge ourselves for the *sin.* We are not under the *Law* as a *covenant of works.* Our own exactness in doing of *good works,* is not now the *condition* of our *entering into life. Woe unto us if it were!* But still, the *Covenant of Grace* holds us to it, as our *duty;* and if we are in the *Covenant of Grace,* we shall make it our *study,* to *do* those *good works* which once were the terms of our *entering into life. Manet lex tota pietatis;*[3] that was the divinity in *Tertullian's* days! There must be such an esteem for the *law* of *good works* retained forever in all the *justified:* a law never to be abrogated; never to be abolished! And then, secondly, though we are *justified* by a *precious faith* in the *righteousness of God our Saviour,* yet good works are demanded of us, to *justify* our *faith;* to *demonstrate,* that it is indeed that *precious faith.* A *justifying faith* is a *jewel,* which may be *counterfeited.* But now the *marks* of a *faith,* which is no counterfeit, are to be found in the *good works* whereto a servant of God is inclined and assisted by his *faith.* It is by a *regenerating work* of the Holy Spirit, that *faith* is wrought in the souls of the chosen people. Now the same *work* of God, and of *grace,* which does in a *regeneration* dispose a man to make his flight by *faith,* unto the *righteousness* of his only Saviour, will also dispose him to the *good works* of a *Christian life.* And the same *faith* which goes to the Saviour for a part in His *righteousness,* will also go to Him, for an heart and strength to do the *good works,* which are *ordained, that we should walk in them.* If our *faith* be not such a *faith,* 'tis a *lifeless* one, and it will not bring to *life.* A *workless faith* is a *worthless faith.* My friend, suppose thyself standing before the *Judgment-seat* of the glorious LORD. A needful, a prudent, supposal; it ought to be a very *frequent* one. The *Judge* demands, "What hast thou to plead, for a portion in the blessedness of the righteous?" The plea must be:

"O my glorious Judge, Thou hast been my sacrifice. Oh! Judge of all the earth, give poor dust and ashes leave to say, 'My righteousness is on the bench. Surely in the Lord I have my righteousness. O my Saviour, I have received it, I have secured it, upon Thy gracious offer of it.'"

The *Judge* proceeds:

"But what hast thou to plead, that thy faith should not be rejected, as the faith and hope of the hyprocrite?"

Here the plea must be:

"Lord, my faith was Thy work. It was a faith which disposed me to all the good works of Thy holy religion. My faith sanctified me. It carried me to Thee, O my Saviour, for grace to do the works of righteousness. It embraced that for my Lord as well as for my Saviour. It caused me with sincerity to love and keep Thy commandments; with assiduity to serve the interests of Thy Kingdom in the world." Thus you have *Paul* and *James* reconciled. Thus you have *good works* provided for. The aphorism of the physician, is, *Per brachium fit judicium de corde.* The *doings* of men are truer and surer indications, than all their *sayings,* of what they are *within.* But there is yet a further consideration, upon which you must be *zealously affected* for them. You must

---

3. The entire law of duty [or obedience to God] remains.

consider *good works,* as the *way* to, yea, as a *part* of, the *great salvation,* which is purchased and intended for you, by your blessed Saviour. Without an *holy heart* you can't be fit for an *holy heaven; meet for the inheritance of the holy ones* in that *light,* which admits no *works of darkness,* where none but *good works* are done for eternal ages. But an *holy heart* will cause a man to do *good works* with all his heart. The motto on the gates of the Holy City is: NONE BUT THE LOVERS OF GOOD WORKS TO ENTER HERE. 'Tis implied, in what we read, *without holiness no man shall see the Lord.* Yea, to be *saved* without *good works,* were to be *saved* without *salvation.* Much of our *salvation* lies in doing of *good works.* When our *souls* are *enlarged* and *unfettered,* it is that we may *do* such things. *Heaven* is begun upon *earth* in the doing of them. Doubtless, no man shall come up to *Heaven,* who is not so persuaded. I will mention but one more of those *principles,* which *good works* grow upon. 'Tis that noble one, of GRATITUDE. The believer cannot but inquire, "What shall I render to my Saviour?" The result of the inquiry will be, *with good works to glorify Him.* We read, "Faith works by love." Our *faith* will first show us the matchless and marvelous *love* of God, in saving us. And the *faith* of this *love* will work upon our hearts, until it has raised in us, an unquenchable flame of *love* unto Him that hath so *loved* us, and *saved* us.

These, these are to be our dispositions:

"O my Saviour, hast Thou done so much for me? Now will I do all I can for Thy Kingdom, and people in the world? Oh! What service is there that I may now do for my Saviour, and for His people in the world!"

These are the principles to be proceeded on! And on them, I will observe to you a notable thing. 'Tis worthy of observation, that there are no men in the world, who so abound in *good works,* as the men who have most of all abandoned all pretense to *merit* by their *works.* There are *Protestants* who have outdone *Papists,* in our days, as well as in Dr. *Willet's.* No *merit-mongers* have gone beyond some holy Christians, who have done *good works,* upon the *assurance* of their being already justified and entitled unto life eternal.

I take notice, that our Apostle, casting a just contempt on the *endless genealogies,* and long, intricate, perplexed pedigrees, which the *Jews* of his time, stood so much upon; proposes instead thereof to be studied, *charity, out of a pure heart, and a good conscience, and faith unfeigned.* As if he had said, I will give you a *genealogy* worth ten thousand of theirs, first, from *faith unfeigned* proceeds a *good conscience*: from a *good conscience* proceeds a *pure heart*: from a *pure heart* proceeds a *charity* to all about us. 'Tis admirably stated!

§8. It is to be feared, that we too seldom *inquire* after our OPPORTUNITIES TO DO GOOD. Our *opportunities to do good* are our TALENTS. An awful account must be rendered unto the great GOD, concerning our use of the TALENTS, wherewith He has entrusted us, in these precious *opportunities.* We do not *use* our *opportunities,* many times because we do not *know* what they are; and many times, the reason why we do not *know,* is because we do not *think.* Our *opportunities to do good,* lie by unregarded, and unimproved, and so 'tis but a mean account that can be given of them. We *read* of a thing, which we *deride* as often as we behold: *there is, that maketh himself poor, and yet has great riches.* It is a thing too frequently exemplified, in our *opportunities to do good,* which are some of our most valuable *riches.* Many a man seems to reckon himself destitute of those *talents;* as if there were *nothing* for him to do: he pretends he is not in a condition to *do* any *good.* Alas! poor man; *what can he do?* My friend, *think* again; *think* often. *Inquire* what your *opportunities* are. You will doubtless find them, to be more than you were *aware* of. *Plain men dwelling in tents,* persons of a very *ordinary character,* may in a way of bright piety, prove persons of *extraordinary usefulness.* A poor *John Urich* may make a *Grotius* the better for him. I have read of a pious *Weaver,* of whom some eminent persons would say, "Christ walked as it were alive upon the Earth in that man." And a world of *good* was done by that man. A mean *mechanic,* who can tell what an *engine* of *good* he may be, if humbly and wisely applied unto it!

This then is the next PROPOSAL. Without abridging yourselves of your *occasional thoughts* on the question, often every day, *What good may I do?,* state a *time* now and then for more *deliberate thoughts* upon it. Can't you find a *time* (suppose once a week, yea, and how agreeably, on the *Lord's* day) to take that question into your consideration: WHAT IS THERE THAT I MAY DO, FOR THE SERVICE OF THE GLORIOUS LORD, AND FOR THE WELFARE OF THOSE, FOR WHOM I OUGHT TO BE CONCERNED? Having implored the *direction* of God, who is the *Father of Lights,* and the Author and Giver of *good thoughts, consider* on the matter, in the various aspects of it. *Consider* till you have *resolved* on something. The *resolutions* which you *take up,* immediately *write down.* Examine what *precept* and what *promise,* you can find in the Word of God, that may countenance the intentions, in these your *memorials.* Look over the *memorials* at proper seasons afterwards, to see how far you have proceeded in the execution of them. The advantages of these *reserved* and *revised* MEMORIALS, no *rhetoric* will serve to commend them, no *arithmetic* to number them. There are some *animals,* of whom we say, "They do not know their own strength." *Christians,* why should you be *they?*

§9. Let us descend unto PARTICULARS. But in doing so, let it not be imagined, that I pretend unto an enumeration of all the GOOD DEVICES, that are to be thought upon. Indeed, not a *thousandth* part of them, need or can be now enumerated. The *essay,* which I am now upon, is, only to dig open the several *springs* of *usefulness;* which having once begun to run, will spread into *streams,* which no *human foresight* can comprehend. *Spring up, O well!* So will every true *Israelite* sing, upon every PROPOSAL here exhibited. And the *nobles of Israel* can do nothing more agreeable to their own character, than to fall to work upon it. Perhaps almost every *proposal* to be now mentioned, may be like a *stone* falling on a *pool; reader,* keep thy mind *calm,* and see, whether the effect prove not so! That one *circle* (and *service*) will produce another, until they extend, who can tell, how far? and they cannot be reckoned up. The men who give themselves up to GOOD DEVICES, and who take a due notice of their *opportunities to do good,* usually find a strange growth of their *opportunities.* The gracious and faithful Providence of the glorious Lord, grants this recompense unto His diligent servants, that He will *multiply* their *opportunities* to be *serviceable.* And when ingenious men have a little used themselves unto *contrivances,* in this or that way of pursuing the best intentions, their ingenuity will sensibly improve, and there will be more of *exquisiteness,* more of *expansion,* in their diffusive applications. Among all the dispensations of *special Providence,* in the government of the world, there is none more *uninterrupted,* than the accomplishment of that word, UNTO HIM THAT HATH, SHALL BE GIVEN. I will say this: O *useful Man,* take that for thy *motto:* HABENTI DABITUR. And, in a lively use of thy *opportunities to do good,* see how notably, it will be accomplished! Sir, see what accomplishment of that word will at last surprise you: "Though thy beginning were small, yet thy latter end shall greatly increase."

. . . . . .

[Chapter Twelve: Desiderata]

§22. We will not propose, that our *essays to do good,* should ever come to an end. But we will now put an end unto this, of tendering PROPOSALS for it. It shall conclude with a *catalogus desideratorum,* or a mention of some obvious, and general *services* for the Kingdom of God among mankind, whereto 'twere to be desired, that religious and ingenious men might be awakened.

A CATALOGUE OF DESIRABLES, waiting for the *zeal of good men* to prosecute them.

(Difficilem rem optas; generis humani innocentiam!)[4]

I. The propagation of the holy and glorious *religion of* CHRIST; a religion which *emancipates* mankind from the worst of slaveries and miseries, and wonderfully *ennobles* it; and which alone prepares men for the blessedness of another world: why is this no more endeavored by the professors of it? PROTESTANTS, why will you be out-done by *popish idolaters!* Oh! the vast pains which those *bigots,* have taken, to carry on the *Romish* merchandises and idolatries! No less than six hundred clergymen, in that one order of the *Jesuits,* did within a few years, at several times, embark themselves for *China,* to win over that mighty nation unto their bastard-Christianity. No less than five hundred of them lost their *lives,* in the difficulties of their enterprise; and yet the survivors go on with it; expressing a sort of trouble, that it fell not unto their share to make a sacrifice of their *lives,* in enterprising the propagation of religion. *O my God, I am ashamed, and blush to lift up my face unto thee my God!* It were but a *Christian,* but a *grateful,* but an *equal* thing; but who can foretell what *prosperity* might be the recompense! If our *companies* and *factories,* would set apart a more considerable part of their *gains* for this work, and set upon a more vigorous prosecution of it. *Gordon's* proposal, unto all men of estates, to set apart a small part of their estates for this purpose (at the end of his *Geography*), should be taken into further consideration. What has been done by the *Dutch* missionaries at *Ceylon,* and what is doing by the *Danish* missionaries at *Malabar,* one would think, might animate us, to imitate them!

If men of a spirit for *evangelizing,* and *illuminating* a woeful world, would learn the *languages* of some nations that are yet *ungospellized,* and wait on the Providence of Heaven, to lead them to, and own them in, some *apostolical undertakings,* who can tell what might be done? We know, what *Ruffinus* relates concerning the conversion of the *Iberians;* and what *Socrates,* concerning the things done by *Frumentius* and *Ædesius,* in the *inner India.*

But on this *desirable* there are two things *remarkable.*

First, it is the conjecture of some *seers,* that until the *Temple* be *cleansed,* there will be no general appearance of the *nations* to worship in it. And the truth is, there will be danger, until then, that many persons active in *Societies for the Propagation of Religion,* may be more intent upon propagating their own little *forms* and *fancies* and *interests,* than the more *weighty matters of the Gospel.* Yea, 'twill be well, if they be not unawares imposed upon, to hurt *Christianity* where 'tis well-established, while places wholly *ungospellized* in the neighborhood may lie neglected. Let us therefore do what we can towards the Church's *reformation,* in order to its *dilatation.*

Secondly, it is probable, that the *Holy Spirit* in operations, like those of the first ages, whereby Christianity was first *planted,* will be again conferred from our *ascended*

---

4. You choose a difficult thing, the righteousness of mankind.

Lord, for the *spreading* of it. The *Holy Spirit,* who has withdrawn from the *apostate church,* will come, and *abide* with us, and render this world like a *watered garden.* His irresistible influences will cause whole *nations* to be *born at once;* He will not only *convert* but *unite,* His people. By Him, God shall *dwell with men.* Would not the *Heavenly Father give His Holy Spirit,* if it were more *asked* of Him!

II. 'Tis lamentable to see the *ignorance* and *wickedness,* yet remaining, even in many parts of the *British* dominions: in *Wales;* in the *Highlands;* and in *Ireland.* Are the *Gouges* all dead? There are pretended *shepherds,* in the world, that will never be able to answer before the Son of God, for their laying so little to heart, the *deplorable* circumstances, of so many people, whom they might, if they were not scandalously negligent, bring to be more acquainted with the only Saviour. And there might be more done, that some of the *American* colonies, may no longer be such *Cimmerian* ones.

III. Why is no more done, for the poor *Greeks,* and *Armenians,* and *Muscovites,* and other Christians, who have little *preaching,* and no *printing* among them? If we sent *Bibles,* and *Psalters,* and other *books of piety* among them, in their own languages, they would be *noble* presents, and, God knows, how *useful* ones!

IV. Poor *sailors,* and poor *soldiers,* call for our pity. They meet with *great and sore troubles.* Their *manners* are too commonly such, as discover no very good effects of their *troubles.* What shall be done to make them a *better sort of men?* There must, besides more *books of piety* distributed among them, other methods be thought upon; *Cadit asinus et est qui sublevat. Perit anima, et non est qui manum apponat!*[5] Let *Austin* awaken us.

V. The *Tradesman's Library* needs to be more enriched. We have seen, *Husbandry Spiritualized;* and, *Shepherdy Spiritualized;* and, *Navigation Spiritualized;* we have seen, the *weaver* also accommodated, with agreeable meditations. To spread the *nets of salvation* for men, in the ways of their *personal callings,* and convey good thoughts unto them, in the *terms* and *steps,* of their daily business, is a real service to the interests of piety. A BOOK also, that shall be an *onomatologia monitoria,* and shall advise people how to make their *names* become unto them, the *monitors* of their duty; might be of much use to the *Christened* world. And, a BOOK, that shall be, *The Angel of Bethesda,* and shall instruct people how to improve in agreeable points of piety, from the several maladies, which their *bodies* may be diseased withal; and at the same time, inform them of the most experimented, natural, specific *remedies* for their diseases, might be very useful to mankind. These two subjects, if not undertaken by any other hand, may be so shortly by that which now writes; except the glorious Lord of my life, immediately put an end unto it; and *my days are past, my purposes are broken off, even the thoughts of my heart!*

VI. *Universities* that shall have more *collegia pietatis* in them, like those of the excellent *Franckius* in the lower *Saxony;* oh! that there were more of them!—seminaries in which the scholars may have a most polite education; but not be sent forth with recommendations for the evangelical ministry, till it be upon a strict examination found, that their souls are fired with the *fear* of God, and the *love* of Christ, and a *zeal* to do good, and a *resolution* to bear poverty, and obloquy, and all sorts of temptations, in the service of our holy religion; they would be the *wonders* of the world, and what *wonders* might they do in the world!

---

5. An ass falls, and there is someone to help lift him up. A soul dies, and there is no one to help it.

Let the *charity-schools*, also, *increase and multiply; charity-schools* which may provide subjects for the great Saviour, blessings for the next generation; *charity-schools*, not perverted unto the ill purposes of introducing a *defective Christianity*.

VII. Those things, that so far as we *understand by the books* of the sacred Prophecies, are to be, *the works of our day;* 'Tis *wisdom* to observe and pursue. When the time was arrived, that the *Antichrist* must enter his last *half-time*, one poor monk proves a main instrument of ravishing *half* his empire from him. Thus to fall in with the designs of the *Divine Providence*, is the way to be wonderfully prospered and honored. One small man, thus *nicking the time* for it, may do wonders!

I take the *works of our day* to be:

1. The *reviving of primitive Christianity;* to study and restore everything, of the *primitive* character. The *apostasy* is going off. The time for *cleansing the Temple* comes on. More *Edwardses* would be vast blessings, where the *primitive doctrines of Christianity* are depraved.

2. The persuading of the *European* powers, to shake off the chains of *popery*. This argument—there is no *popish nation*, but what by embracing the *Protestant religion*, would *ipso facto*, not only assert themselves into a glorious *liberty*, but also *double their wealth* immediately—'tis marvellous, that it is no more yet hearkened unto! Sirs, prosecute it, with more of *demonstration*. One shows, that the abolishing of popery in *England*, is worth at least eight millions of pounds yearly to the nation. Let the argument be tried with other nations, the argument, *ab utili*.

3. The *forming* and *quickening* of that People, that are to be, The Stone Cut Out of the Mountain. Here, as well as in some other things, *none of the wicked shall understand, but the wise shall understand*. God will do His own work, in His own time, and in His own way. And *Austin* tells me, *Utile est ut taceatur aliquod verbum, propter incapaces.*[6]

[Chapter Thirteen:] The Conclusion

The *zeal of the Lord of Hosts will perform these things:* a *zeal* inspired and produced by the *Lord of Hosts* in His faithful servants, will put them upon the performance of such things. Nothing has been yet proposed, that is impracticable; *Non fortia loquor, sed possibilia.*[7] But, *Eusebius* has taught me, *Vere magnum est magna facere, et teipsum putare nihil.*[8] Sirs, under and after a course of such *actions*, which have a true glory in them, and really are more glorious than all the *actions* and *achievements*, whereof those bloody plunderers, whom we call *conquerors*, have made a wretched ostentation: and perhaps made inscriptions like those of *Pompey* on his Temple of *Minerva*—still *humility*, must be the *crown* of all. All, nothing without *humility*; nothing without a sense that you are *nothing*, a consent to be made *nothing*. You must first, most humbly acknowledge unto the great God, *that after you have done all, you are unprofitable servants;* and make your humble confession, that not only you have *done but that which was your duty to do*, but also that you have exceedingly fallen short of doing your *duty*.

6. It is prudent to refrain from speaking some words to men who are incapable of understanding.
7. I speak not of difficult things but of possibilities.
8. It is certainly noble to do great things and to think nothing of yourself.

If God abase you with very *dark dispensations* of His Providence, after all your inde-fatigable and your disinterested essays to *glorify* Him, humble yourselves before Him; yet abate nothing of your *essays;* hold on, saying, "My God will humble me, yet will I glorify Him. Lord, Thou art righteous; but still I will do all I can to serve thy glorious Kindgom." This indeed, is a more easy *humiliation;* but then there is one to be demanded, of much greater difficulty: that is, that you humbly submit unto all the *diminutions,* among *men,* that God shall order for you. Your admirable Saviour was one who *went about* ever *doing of good;* mankind was never visited by such a *benefac-tor.* And yet we read, "He was One spoken against." Never anyone so vilified! Had He been the worst *malefactor* in the world, He could not have been worse dealt withal. He expostulated, "For which of my good works is it that you treat me so?" Yet they went on; they hated Him, they reproached Him, they murdered Him. *Austin* said very truly, *Remedium elationis est contuitus Dominicae crucis.*[9] It will also be the remedy of discouragement; it will keep you from *sinking,* as well as being *lifted up.* You are con-formed unto your Saviour, in your watchful endeavors to *do good,* and be *fruitful in every good work.* But your conformity unto Him, yet *lacks one thing;* that is, after all, to be *despised and rejected of men;* and patiently to bear the contempt, and malice, and abuses of an *untoward generation.* One of the fathers, who sometimes wanted a little of this grace, could say, *Nihil est quod nos ita et hominibus et Deo gratos facit, quam si vitae merito magni, et humilitate infimi simus.*[10] 'Tis an excellent thing to come to *noth-ing.* If you hear the hopes of disaffected men, to see you *come to nothing, hear* it with as much of satisfaction as they can *hope* it. Embrace *exinanitions;* embrace *annihila-tions.* I find a zealous and famous *doer of good,* much affected with the picture of a devout man, to whom a voice comes down from Heaven, *Quid vis fieri pro te?* Whereto he replies, *Nihil, Domine, nisi pati et contemni pro te.*[11] Sirs, let it be seen somewhere else than in *picture;* be you the *substance* of it. Thus, *let patience have its perfect work!*

. . . . . .

Ye *useful men,* your *acceptance* with your Saviour, and with God through your Saviour, and *recompense* in the world to come, is to carry you cheerfully through all your *essays* at *usefulness.* To be *reprobate for every good work,* is a character, from which 'twill be the *wisdom* of all men, to fly with all the dread imaginable. But then, to be *always abounding in the work for the Lord,* this is always the truest and the highest *wisdom.* 'Tis the *wisdom which is from above,* that is full of *mercy and good fruits.* The *sluggards* who do no good in the world, are *wise in their own conceit;* but the men who are diligent in *doing* of good, can give such a *reason* for what they do, as proves them to be *really wise.* Men *leave off to be wise,* when they *leave off to do good.* The *wisdom* of it appears in this: 'tis the best way of spending our *time;* 'tis *well-spent,* when spent in *doing of good.* It is also a sure way, a sweet way, effectually to bespeak the *blessings*

9. The remedy for pride is the contemplation of the Cross.

10. Nothing makes us more pleasing to God and men that being low in humility even if we achieve greatness in our lives.

11. What do you want me to do for you? . . . Nothing, Lord, but that I may suffer and be despised for your sake.

of God on ourselves. Who so likely to *find blessings,* as the men that *are blessings?* It has been said, *Qui bene vivit, semper orat;*[12] so I will say, *Qui bene agit, bene orat.*[13] Every *action* we do for the *Kingdom* of God, is in the efficacy of it, a *prayer* for the *kindness* of God. While we are *at work* for God, certainly, He will be *at work* for us, and ours: He will do for us, more than ever we have *done* for Him; far *more than we can ask or think!* There is a *voice* in every *good thing* that is done; 'tis that, *Oh! do good unto them that are good!* Thus my BONIFACIUS anon comes to wear the name of BENE-DICTUS also. Yea, and there may be this more particular effect of what we do. While we *employ* our *wits* for the interests of God, it is very probable, that we shall *sharpen* them for our own. We shall become the more *wise for ourselves,* because we have been *wise to do good.* And of the man who is a *tree that brings forth fruit,* we read, *whatsoever he doth shall prosper.* Nor can a man take a readier way to *live joyfully, all the days of the life of our vanity, which God has given us under the sun.* For, now our *life* will not be thrown away in *vanity;* we don't *live in vain.* My friend, *go thy way* and be joyful; *for God accepteth thy works.* Our *few* and *evil* days are made much less so, by our *doing* of *good* in every one of them, as it rolleth over us. Yea, the Holy *Spirit* of God who is the *quickener* of them who *do good without ceasing,* will be their *comforter.* Every day of our *activity* for the Kingdom of God, will be in some sort a day of *Pentecost* unto us, a day of the Holy Spirit's coming upon us. The *consolations of God,* will *not be small,* with the man, who is full of *contrivances for God,* and for His Kingdom. In short, we read, "The valleys are covered over with corn; they shout for joy, they also sing." We may be in *low* circumstances: but if we abound in the fruits of *well-doing,* and if we feed many with our services, we are *covered over with corn.* We shall *shout for joy, and also sing,* if we be so. The *conscience* of what we do, and of what we aim to do, will be a *continual feast* unto us. *Our rejoicing is this, the testimony of our conscience!* And, *Recte fecisse merces est.*[14] Yea, the *pleasure* in doing of *good offices,* 'tis inexpressible; 'tis unparalleled; 'tis *angelical;* more to be envied than any *sensual pleasure;* a most *refined* one. Pleasure was long since defined, *the result of some excellent action.* 'Tis, a sort of *holy Epicurism.* O most *pitiable* they that will continue strangers to it! But, *memineris,* was the constant word of encouragement unto a soldier. I say, *remember;* there's more to be *remembered.*

When the *serviceable* man comes to his *Nunc Dimittis,*[15] then, he who did *live desired,* shall *die lamented.* It shall be witnessed and remembered of him, *that he was one who did good in Israel.* An *epitaph* the glory whereof is beyond that of the most superb and stately *pyramid!* When [i.e., then] the calumniators, who once *licked the file* of his reputation, shall have only the impotence of their defeated malice to reflect upon.

. . . . . .

. . . I will conclude with a TESTIMONY that I shall abide by. 'Tis this: were a man able to write in *seven languages:* could he converse daily with the sweets of all the

---

12. He who lives well is always praying.
13. He who does good, prays well.
14. Virtue is its own reward.
15. Permission to depart—that is, his death—in contentment that he has done all he can do.

liberal sciences, that more polite men ordinarily pretend unto; did he entertain himself with all ancient and modern *histories;* and could he feast continually on the *curiosities* which all sorts of learning may bring unto him; none of all this would afford the ravishing satisfaction, much less would any grosser delights of the *senses* do it; which he might find, in relieving the distresses of a poor, mean, *miserable neighbor;* and which he might much more find, in doing any *extensive service* for the Kingdom of our great SAVIOUR in the world; or anything to redress the miseries under which mankind is generally languishing.

JONATHAN EDWARDS

"The Justice of God in the Damnation of Sinners"
1734

Selection from *A Treatise Concerning Religious Affections*
1746

In his early years Jonathan Edwards (1703–58) achieved considerable fame as a successful preacher and a moderate champion of the religious revivals that swept through the American colonies in the 1730s and 1740s. After that spiritual outpouring receded, Edwards composed a series of major treatises that would eventually establish him as American Puritanism's greatest theologian and America's foremost systematic philosopher before the Civil War. At the center of these works was the traditional Augustinian–Calvinist triad of divine excellency, human depravity, and grace-producing salvation for the divinely chosen few. Undergirding this triad, however, was a complex web of philosophical arguments that were deeply responsive to the same modern thinkers, beginning with Descartes and ending with the post-Lockean sentimentalist humanitarians, that were to prove the system's undoing. In the first of the two selections presented here—a sermon delivered on the eve of the revivals that foreshadowed much of the argumentation of his later famous work, *The Freedom of the Will*—Edwards demonstrated one approach he sometimes took: he counterattacked. In particular, he argued, the humanitarian assertion of the self-determination of the will was self-contradictory and opposed to the very moral responsibility that the anti-Calvinists charged the orthodox position with promoting. In his treatise on the religious affections, Edwards displayed a more imaginative response to modern challenges. To a large extent, of course, this treatise was a continuation of his earlier defenses of emotions from aspersions cast by intellectualist ministers who had tried to discredit the revivals by equating their emotionalism with irrationalism. Edwards argued, on the contrary, that affections were the "spring of men's actions" and therefore at the center of all true religion. Furthermore, he contended, not all religious affections were truly religious, and most of the treatise was taken up by a discussion of various "signs" by which one might discern the difference. But Edwards's most important strategy—and the element that raised his treatise, philosophically speaking, above almost anything he ever wrote—was his construction of a new model of the human mind, which allowed him, as is shown in these extracts from *Religious Affections*, to root truly spiritual affections in a new sense of the heart. This new sense was, in true modern experimental idiom, a datum of consciousness but, unlike the materialist senses of Locke, was also an indwelling principle that allowed the soul to see and desire holiness. This holiness was therefore both a new kind of moral and aesthetic knowledge of being and a new inclination of the heart toward that knowledge. It was, in sum, grace in a new garb. Conrad Cherry's *Theology of Jonathan Edwards: A Reappraisal* (Garden City, N.Y., 1966) is excellent on the theological aspects of Edwards's thought. For an erudite and powerful study of Edwards's moral philosophy in relation to that of his European philosophical antecedents and contemporaries, see Norman Fiering, *Jonathan Edwards's Moral Thought and*

Its British Context (Chapel Hill, 1981). A good, brief overall account of Edwards's philosophy may be found in the chapter on Edwards in Elizabeth Flower and Murray G. Murphey, *A History of Philosophy in America,* vol. 1 (New York, 1977), 137–99. James Hoopes, "Jonathan Edwards's Religious Psychology," *Journal of American History,* 69 (March 1983), 849–65 is a discerning discussion of various interpretations of Edwards's psychology and metaphysics. For a valuable discussion of the role of Edwardsian thought in the development of an influential post-Calvinist tradition of philosophical theology, see Bruce Kuklick, *Churchmen and Philosophers: From Jonathan Edwards to John Dewey* (New Haven, 1985).

"The Justice of God in the Damnation of Sinners"
1734

"It is just with God eternally to cast off and destroy sinners."——For this is the punishment which the law condemns to.—The truth of this doctrine may appear by the joint consideration of two things, *viz.* Man's *sinfulness,* and God's *sovereignty.*

I. It appears from the consideration of man's sinfulness. And that whether we consider the infinitely evil nature of all sin, or how much sin men are guilty of.

1. If we consider the infinite evil and heinousness of sin in general, it is not unjust in God to inflict what punishment is deserved; because the very notion of deserving any punishment is, that it may be justly inflicted. A deserved punishment and a just punishment are the same thing. To say that one *deserves* such a punishment, and yet to say that he does not *justly* deserve it, is a contradiction; and if he justly deserves it, then it may be justly *inflicted.*

Every crime or fault deserves a greater or less punishment, in proportion as the crime itself is greater or less. If any fault deserves punishment, then so much the greater the fault, so much the greater is the punishment deserved. The faulty nature of any thing is the formal ground and reason of its desert of punishment; and therefore the more any thing hath of this nature, the more punishment it deserves. And therefore the terribleness of the degree of punishment, let it be never so terrible, is no argument against the justice of it, if the proportion does but hold between the heinousness of the crime and the dreadfulness of the punishment; so that if there be any such thing as a fault infinitely heinous, it will follow that it is just to inflict a punishment for it that is infinitely dreadful.

A crime is more or less heinous, according as we are under greater or less *obligations* to the contrary. This is self-evident; because it is herein that the criminalness or faultiness of any thing consists, that it is contrary to what we are obliged or bound to, or what *ought* to be in us. So the faultiness of one being hating another, is in proportion to his obligation to love him. The crime of one being despising and casting contempt on another, is proportionably more or less heinous, as he was under greater or less obligations to honour him. The fault of disobeying another, is greater or less, as any one is under greater or less obligations to obey him. And therefore, if there be any being that we are under infinite obligations to love, and honour, and obey, the contrary towards him must be infinitely faulty.

Our obligation to love, honour, and obey any being, is in proportion to his loveliness, honourableness, and authority; for that is the very meaning of the words. When we say any one is very lovely, it is the same as to say, that he is one very much to be

Source: The Works of President Edwards, ed. Edward Williams and Edward Parsons, vol. 6 (London: James Black & Son, 1817), 363–69.

loved. Or if we say such a one is more honourable than another, the meaning of the words is, that he is one that we are more obliged to honour. If we say any one has great authority over us, it is the same as to say, that he has great right to our subjection and obedience.

But God is a being *infinitely* lovely, because he hath infinite excellency and beauty. To have infinite excellency and beauty, is the same thing as to have infinite loveliness. He is a Being of infinite greatness, majesty, and glory; and therefore he is infinitely honourable. He is infinitely exalted above the greatest potentates of the earth, and highest angels in heaven; and therefore he is infinitely more honourable than they. His authority over us is infinite; and the ground of his right to our obedience is infinitely strong; for he is infinitely worthy to be obeyed himself, and we have an absolute, universal, and infinite dependence upon him.

So that sin against God, being a violation of infinite obligations, must be a crime infinitely heinous, and so deserving of infinite punishment.—Nothing is more agreeable to the common sense of mankind, than that sins committed against any one, must be proportionably heinous to the dignity of the being offended and abused; as it is also agreeable to the word of God, 1 Sam. ii. 25. "If one man sin against another, the Judge shall judge him;" (*i.e.* shall judge him, and inflict a finite punishment, such as finite judges can inflict;) "but if a man sin against the Lord, who shall intreat for him?" This was the aggravation of sin that made Joseph afraid of it, Gen. xxxix.9. "How shall I commit this great wickedness, and sin against God?" This was the aggravation of David's sin, in comparison of which he esteemed all others as nothing, because they were infinitely exceeded by it. Psalm li. 4. "Against thee, thee only, have I sinned."—The *eternity* of the punishment of ungodly men renders it infinite; and it renders it no more than infinite; and therefore renders no more than proportionable to the heinousness of what they are guilty of.

If there by *any* evil or faultiness in sin against God, there is certainly *infinite* evil; for if it be any fault at all, it has an infinite aggravation, *viz.* that it is against an infinite object. If it be ever so small upon other accounts, yet if it be any thing, it has one infinite dimension; and so is an infinite evil. Which may be illustrated by this: If we suppose a thing to have infinite length, but no breadth and thickness, (a mere mathematical line,) it is nothing: but if it have *any* breadth and thickness, though never so small, and infinite length, the quantity of it is infinite; it exceeds the quantity of any thing, however broad, thick, and long, wherein these dimensions are all finite.

So that the objections made against the *infinite* punishment of sin, from the necessity, or rather previous certainty of the futurition of sin, arising from the unavoidable original corruption of nature, if they argue any thing, argue against *any* faultiness at all; for if this necessity or certainty leaves *any* evil at all in sin, that fault must be *infinite* by reason of the infinite object.

But every such objector as would argue from hence, that there is no fault at all in sin, confutes himself and shews his own insincerity in his objection. For at the same time that he objects, that men's acts are necessary, and that this kind of necessity is inconsistent with faultiness in the act, his own practice shews that he does not believe what he objects to be true: otherwise why does he at all *blame* men? Or why are such persons at all displeased with men, for abusive, injurious and ungrateful acts towards them? Whatever they pretend, by this they shew that indeed they do believe that there is no necessity in men's acts that is inconsistent with blame. And if their objection be this, that this previous certainty is by God's own ordering, and that where God orders an antecedent certainty of acts, he transfers all the fault from the actor on himself; their practice shews, that at the same time they do not believe this, but fully believe the contrary: For when they are abused by men, they are displeased with *men,* and not with *God* only.

The light of nature teaches all mankind, that when an injury is *voluntary,* it is faulty, without any consideration of what there might be previously to determine the futurition of that evil act of the will. And it really teaches this as much to those that object and cavil most as to others; as their universal practice shews. By which it appears, that such objections are insincere and perverse. Men will mention others' corrupt nature when they are injured, as a thing that aggravates their crime, and that wherein their faultiness partly consists. How common is it for persons, when they look on themselves greatly injured by another, to inveigh against him, and aggravate his baseness, by saying, "He is a man of a most perverse spirit: he is natually of a selfish, niggardly, or proud and haughty temper: he is one of a base and vile disposition." And yet men's natural corrupt dispositions are mentioned as an excuse for them, with respect to their sins against God, as if they rendered them blameless.

2. That it is just with God eternally to cast off wicked men, may more abundantly appear, if we consider how much sin they are guilty of. From what has been already said, it appears, that if men were guilty of sin but in one particular, that is sufficient ground of their eternal rejection and condemnation. If they are *sinners,* that is enough. Merely this, might be sufficient to keep them from ever lifting up their heads, and cause them to smite on their breasts, with the publican that cried, "God be merciful to me a sinner." But sinful men are full of sin; principles and acts of sin; their guilt is like great mountains, heaped one upon another, till the pile is grown up to heaven. They are totally corrupt, in every part, in all their faculties; in all the principles of their nature, their understandings and wills; and in all their dispositions and affections. Their heads, their hearts, are totally depraved; all the members of their bodies are only instruments of sin; and all their senses, seeing, hearing, tasting, &c. are only inlets and outlets of sin, channels of corruption. There is nothing but sin, no good at all. Rom. vii. 18. "In me (that is, in my flesh,) dwelleth no good thing." There is all manner of wickedness. There are the seeds of the greatest and blackest crimes. There are principles of all sorts of wickedness against men; and there is all wickedness against God. There is pride; there is enmity; there is contempt; there is quarrelling; there is Atheism; there is blasphemy. There are these things in exceeding strength; the heart is under the power of them, is sold under sin, and is a perfect slave to it. There is hard-heartedness, hardness greater than that of a rock, or an adamant-stone. There is obstinacy and perverseness, incorrigibleness and inflexibleness in sin, that will not be overcome by threatenings or promises, by awakenings or encouragements, by judgments or mercies, neither by that which is terrifying, nor that which is winning. The very blood of God our Saviour will not win the heart of a wicked man.

And there are actual wickednesses without number or measure. There are breaches of every command, in thought, word, and deed: a life full of sin; days and nights filled up with sin; mercies abused, and frowns despised; mercy and justice, and all the divine perfections, trampled on; and the honour of each person in the Trinity trod in the dirt. Now if one sinful word or thought has so much evil in it, as to deserve eternal destruction, how do they deserve to be eternally cast off and destroyed, that are guilty of so much sin!

II. If with man's sinfulness, we consider God's *sovereignty,* it may serve further to clear God's justice in the eternal rejection and condemnation of sinners, from men's cavils and objections. I shall not now pretend to determine precisely what things are, and what things are not, proper acts and exercises of God's holy sovereignty; but only, that God's sovereignty extends to the following things.

1. That such is God's sovereign power and right, that he is originally under no *obligation* to keep men from sinning; but may in his providence permit and *leave* them to sin. He was not obliged to keep either angels or men from falling. It is *unreasonable* to suppose, that God should be obliged, if he makes a reasonable creature capable of knowing his will, and receiving a law from him, and being subject to his moral government, at the same time to make it *impossible* for him to sin, or break his law. For if God be obliged to this, it destroys all use of any commands, laws, promises, or threatenings, and the very notion of any moral government of God over those reasonable creatures. For to what purpose would it be, for God to give such and such laws, and declare his holy will to a creature, and annex promises and threatenings to move him to his duty, and make him careful to perform it, if the creature at the same time has this to think of, that God is *obliged* to make it *impossible* for him to break his laws? How can God's threatenings move to care or watchfulness, when, at the same time, God is obliged to render it impossible that he should be exposed to the threatenings? Or, to what purpose is it for God to give a law at all? For according to this supposition, it is God, and not the creature, that is under law. It is the lawgiver's care, and not the subject's, to see that his law is obeyed; and this care is what the lawgiver is absolutely obliged to! If God be *obliged* never to *permit* a creature to fall, there is an end of all divine laws, or government, or authority of God over the creature; there can be no manner of use of these things.

God *may permit* sin, though the being of sin will *certainly* ensue on that permission; and so, by permission, he may dispose and order the event. If there were any such thing as chance, or mere contingence, and the very notion of it did not carry a gross absurdity, (as might easily be shewn that it does,) it would have been very unfit that God should have left it to mere chance, whether man should fall or no. For chance, if there should be any such thing, is undesigning and blind. And certainly it is more fit that an event of so great importance, and which is attended with such an infinite train of great consequences, should be disposed and ordered by infinite *wisdom,* than that it should be left to blind *chance.*

If it be said, that God need not have interposed to render it impossible for man to sin, and yet not leave it to mere contingence or blind chance neither; but might have left it with man's *free-will,* to determine whether to sin or no: I answer, if God did leave it to man's free-will, without any *sort of disposal, or ordering* [or rather, *adequate cause*] in the case, whence it should be previously *certain* how that free-will should determine, then still that first determination of the will must be merely contingent or by chance. It could not have any antecedent act of the will to determine it; for I speak now of the very first act or motion of the will, respecting the affair that may be looked upon as the prime ground and highest source of the event. To suppose this to be determined by a foregoing act is a contradiction. God's disposing this determination of the will by his *permission,* does not at all infringe the liberty of the creature. It is in no respect any more inconsistent with liberty, than mere chance or contingence. For if the determination of the will be from blind, undesigning chance, it is no more from the agent himself, or from the will itself, than if we suppose, in the case, a wise divine disposal by permission.

2. It was fit that it should be at the ordering of the divine wisdom and good pleasure, whether every particular man should stand for himself, or whether the first father of mankind should be appointed as the moral and federal head and representative of the rest. If God has not liberty in this matter to determine either of these two as he pleases, it must be because determining that the first father of men should represent the rest, and not that every one should stand for himself, is *injurious* to mankind. For if it be not injurious, how is it unjust? But it is not injurious to mankind; for there is nothing in the nature of the case itself, that makes it better that each man should stand for himself, than that all should be represented by their common father; as the least reflection or consideration will convince any one. And if there be nothing in the nature of the thing that makes the former better for mankind than the latter, then it will follow, that they are not hurt in God's choosing and appointing the latter, rather than the former; or, which is the same thing, that it is not injurious to mankind.

3. When men are fallen, and become sinful, God by his sovereignty has a right to determine about their redemption as he pleases. He has a right to determine whether he will redeem any, or not. He might, if he had pleased, have left all to perish, or might have redeemed all. Or, he may redeem some, and leave others; and if he doth so, he may take whom he pleases, and leave whom he pleases. To suppose that all have forfeited his favour, and deserved to perish, and to suppose that he may not leave any one individual of them to perish, implies a contradiction; because it supposes that such an one has a claim to God's favour, and is not justly liable to perish; which is contrary to the supposition.

It is meet that God should order all these things according to his own pleasure. By reason of his greatness and glory, by which he is infinitely above all, he is worthy to be sovereign, and that his pleasure should in all things take place. He is worthy that he should make himself his end, and that he should make nothing but his own wisdom his rule in pursuing that end, without asking leave or counsel of any, and without giving account of any of his matters. It is fit that he who is absolutely perfect, and infinitely wise, and the Fountain of all wisdom, should determine every thing [that he effects] by his own will, even things of the greatest importance. It is meet that he should be thus sovereign, because he is the first being, the eternal being, whence all other beings are. He is the creator of all things; and all are absolutely and universally dependent on him; and therefore it is meet that he should act as the sovereign possessor of heaven and earth.

Selection from *A Treatise Concerning Religious Affections*
1746

1 PET. 1:8: *Whom having not seen, ye love: in whom, though now ye see him not, yet believing, ye rejoice with joy unspeakable, and full of glory.*

In these words, the Apostle represents the state of the minds of the Christians he wrote to, under the persecutions they were then the subjects of. These persecutions are what he has respect to, in the two preceding verses, when he speaks of the trial of their faith, and of their being in heaviness through manifold temptations.

. . . . . .

. . . [T]he proposition or doctrine, that I would raise from these words is this,
DOCT. True religion, in great part, consists in holy affections.
We see that the Apostle, in observing and remarking the operations and exercises of religion, in the Christians he wrote to, wherein their religion appeared to be true and of the right kind, when it had its greatest trial of what sort it was, being tried by persecution as gold is tried in the fire, and when their religion not only proved true, but was most pure, and cleansed from its dross and mixtures of that which was not true, and when religion appeared in them most in its genuine excellency and native beauty, and was found to praise, and honor, and glory; he singles out the religious affections of love and joy, that were then in exercise in them: these are the exercises of religion he takes notice of, wherein their religion did thus appear true and pure, and in its proper glory.

. . . . . .

. . . It may be inquired, what the affections of the mind are?
I answer, the affections are no other, than the more vigorous and sensible exercises of the inclination and will of the soul.
God has indued the soul with two faculties: one is that by which it is capable of perception and speculation, or by which it discerns and views and judges of things; which is called the understanding. The other faculty is that by which the soul does not merely perceive and view things, but is some way inclined with respect to the

Source: The Works of Jonathan Edwards, ed. Perry Miller. Vol. 2, *Religious Affections*, ed. John E. Smith (New Haven: Yale University Press, 1959), 93, 95, 96–97, 191, 197–213, 240–43, 249–53. Reprinted by permission of Yale University Press, Copyright © 1959.

things it views or considers; either is inclined to 'em, or is discinclined, and averse from 'em; or is the faculty by which the soul does not behold things, as an indifferent unaffected spectator, but either as liking or disliking, pleased or displeased, approving or rejecting. This faculty is called by various names: it is sometimes called the *inclination:* and, as it has respect to the actions that are determined and governed by it, is called the *will:* and the *mind,* with regard to the exercises of this faculty, is often called the *heart.*

The exercises of this faculty are of two sorts; either those by which the soul is carried out towards the things that are in view, in approving of them, being pleased with them, and inclined to them; or those in which the soul opposes the things that are in view, in disapproving them, and in being displeased with them, averse from them, and rejecting them.

And as the exercises of the inclination and will of the soul are various in their kinds, so they are much more various in their degrees. There are some exercises of pleasedness or displeasedness, inclination or disinclination, wherein the soul is carried but a little beyond a state of perfect indifference. And there are other degrees above this, wherein the approbation or dislike, pleasedness or aversion, are stronger; wherein we may rise higher and higher, till the soul comes to act vigorously and sensibly, and the actings of the soul are with that strength that (through the laws of the union which the Creator has fixed between soul and body) the motion of the blood and animal spirits begins to be sensibly altered; whence oftentimes arises some bodily sensation, especially about the heart and vitals, that are the fountain of the fluids of the body: from whence it comes to pass, that the mind, with regard to the exercises of this faculty, perhaps in all nations and ages, is called the *heart.* And it is to be noted, that they are these more vigorous and sensible exercises of this faculty, that are called the *affections.*

. . . . . .

Shewing What Are Distingushing Signs of Truly Gracious and Holy Affections

[*First Sign*]

. . . . . .

I. Affections that are truly spiritual and gracious, do arise from those influences and operations on the heart, which are *spiritual, supernatural* and *divine.*

I will explain what I mean by these terms, whence will appear their use to distinguish between those affections which are spiritual, and those which are not so.

We find that true saints, or those persons who are sanctified by the Spirit of God, are in the New Testament called spiritual persons. And their being spiritual is spoken of as their peculiar character, and that wherein they are distinguished from those who are not sanctified. This is evident because those who are spiritual are set in opposition to natural men, and carnal men. Thus the spiritual man, and the natural man, are set in opposition one to another; "The natural man receiveth not the things of the Spirit of God, for they are foolishness unto him; neither can he know them; because they are spiritually discerned. But he that is spiritual judgeth all things" (I Cor. 2:14–15).

The Scripture explains itself to mean an ungodly man, or one that has no grace, by a natural man: thus the apostle Jude, speaking of certain ungodly men, that had crept in unawares among the saints, ver. 4 of his Epistle, says, ver. 19: "These are sensual, having not the Spirit." This the Apostle gives as a reason why they behaved themselves in such a wicked manner as he had described. Here the word translated "sensual," in the original is ψυκικοι; which is the very same, which in those verses in I Cor. ch. 2 is translated "natural." In the like manner, in the continuation of the same discourse, in the next verse but one, spiritual men are opposed to carnal men: which the connection plainly shows mean the same, as spiritual men and natural men, in the foregoing verses: "and I, brethren, could not speak unto you, as unto spiritual, but as unto carnal"; i.e. as in a great measure unsanctified. That by carnal the Apostle means corrupt and unsanctified, is abundantly evident, by Rom. 7:25 and 8:1, 4–9, 12, 13; Gal. 5:16 to the end; cf. Col. 2:18. Now therefore, if by natural and carnal, in these texts, he intended "unsanctified"; then doubtless by spiritual, which is opposed thereto, is meant "sanctified" and gracious.

And as the saints are called spiritual in Scripture, so we also find that there are certain properties, qualities, and principles, that have the same epithet given them. So we read of a spiritual mind, Rom. 8:6–7 and of spiritual wisdom, Col. 1:9 and of spiritual blessings, Eph. 1:3.

Now it may be observed that the epithet "spiritual," in these and other parallel texts of the New Testament, is not used to signify any relation of persons or things to the spirit or soul of man, as the spiritual part of man, in opposition to the body, which is the material part: qualities are not said to be spiritual, because they have their seat in the soul, and not in the body: for there are some properties that the Scripture calls carnal or fleshly, which have their seat as much in the soul, as those properties that are called spiritual. Thus it is with pride and self-righteousness, and a man's trusting to his own wisdom, which the Apostle calls fleshy (Col. 2:18). Nor are things called spiritual, because they are conversant about those things that are immaterial, and not corporeal. For so was the wisdom of the wise men, and princes of this world, conversant about spirits, and immaterial beings; which yet the Apostle speaks of as natural men, totally ignorant of those things that are spiritual (I Cor. ch. 2). But it is with relation to the Holy Ghost, or Spirit of God, that persons or things are termed spiritual, in the New Testament. "Spirit," as the word is used to signify the third person in the Trinity, is the substantive, of which is formed the adjective "spiritual," in the Holy Scriptures. Thus Christians are called spiritual persons, because they are born of the Spirit, and because of the indwelling and holy influences of the Spirit of God in them. And things are called spiritual as related to the Spirit of God; "Which things also we speak, not in the words which man's wisdom teacheth, but which the Holy Ghost teacheth, comparing spiritual things with spiritual. But the natural man receiveth not the things of the Spirit of God" (I Cor. 2:13–14). Here the Apostle himself expressly signifies, that by spiritual things, he means the things of the Spirit of God, and things which the Holy Ghost teacheth. The same is yet more abundantly apparent by viewing the whole context. Again, "To be carnally minded is death: but to be spiritually minded is life and peace" (Rom. 8:6). The Apostle explains what he means by being carnally and spiritually minded, in what follows in the 9th verse, and shows that by being spiritually minded, he means a having the indwelling and holy influences of the Spirit of God in the heart. "But ye are not in the flesh, but in the Spirit, if so be the Spirit of God dwell in you. Now if any man have not the Spirit of Christ, he is none of his."

The same is evident by all the context. But time would fail to produce all the evidence there is of this, in the New Testament.

And it must be here observed, that although it is with relation to the Spirit of God and his influences, that persons and things are called spiritual; yet not all those persons who are subject to any kind of influence of the Spirit of God, are ordinarily called spiritual in the New Testament. They who have only the common influences of God's Spirit, are not so called, in the places cited above, but only those, who have the special, gracious and saving influences of God's Spirit: as is evident, because it has been already proved, that by spiritual men is meant godly men, in opposition to natural, carnal and unsanctified men. And it is most plain, that the Apostle by spiritually minded, Rom. 8:6, means graciously minded. And though the extraordinary gifts of the Spirit, which natural men might have, are somethimes called spiritual, because they are from the Spirit; yet natural men, whatever gifts of the Spirit they had, were not, in the usual language of the New Testament, called spiritual persons. For it was not by men's having the gifts of the Spirit, but by their having the virtues of the Spirit, that they were called spiritual; as is apparent, by Gal. 6:1: "Brethren, if any man be overtaken in a fault, ye which are spiritual restore such an one in the spirit of meekness." Meekness is one of those virtues which the Apostle had just spoken of, in the verses next preceding, showing what are the fruits of the Spirit. Those qualifications are said to be spiritual in the language of the New Testament, which are truly gracious and holy, and peculiar to the saints.

Thus when we read of spiritual wisdom and understanding (as in Col. 1:9: "We desire that ye may be filled with the knowledge of his will, in all wisdom and spiritual understanding"). Hereby is intended that wisdom which is gracious, and from the sanctifying influences of the Spirit of God. For doubtless, by spiritual wisdom, is meant that which is opposite to what the Scripture calls natural wisdom; as the spiritual man is opposed to the natural man. And therefore spiritual wisdom is doubtless the same with that wisdom which is from above, that the apostle James speaks of, "The wisdom that is from above, is first pure, then peaceable, gentle," etc. (Jas. 3:17), for this the Apostle opposes to natural wisdom, ver. 15: "This wisdom descendeth not from above, but is earthly, sensual," the last word in the original is the same that is translated "natural," in I Cor. 2:14.

So that although natural men may be the subjects of many influences of the Spirit of God, as is evident by many Scriptures, as Num. 24:2; I Sam. 10:10 and 11:6 and 16:14; I Cor. 13:1–3; Heb. 6:4–6 and many others; yet they are not in the sense of the Scripture, spiritual persons; either are any of those effects, common gifts, qualities or affections, that are from the influence of the Spirit of God upon them, called spiritual things. The great difference lies in these two things.

1. The Spirit of God is given to the true saints to dwell in them, as his proper lasting abode; and to influence their hearts, as a principle of new nature, or as a divine supernatural spring of life and action. The Scriptures represent the Holy Spirit, not only as moving, and occasionally influencing the saints, but as dwelling in them as his temple, his proper abode, and everlasting dwelling place (I Cor. 3:16; II Cor. 6:16; John 14:16–17). And he is represented as being there so united to the faculties of the soul, that he becomes there a principle or spring of new nature and life.

So the saints are said to live by Christ living in them (Gal. 2:20). Christ by his Spirit not only is in them, but lives in them; and so that they live by his life; so is his

Spirit united to them, as a principle of life in them; they don't only drink living water, but this living water becomes a well or fountain of water, in the soul, springing up into spiritual and everlasting life (John 4:14), and thus becomes a principle of life in them; this living water, this Evangelist himself explains to intend the Spirit of God (ch. 7:38–39). The light of the Sun of Righteousness don't only shine upon them, but is so communicated to them that they shine also, and become little images of that Sun which shines upon them; the sap of the true vine is not only conveyed into them, as the sap of a tree may be conveyed into a vessel, but is conveyed as sap is from a tree into one of its living branches, where it becomes a principle of life. The Spirit of God being thus communicated and united to the saints, they are from thence properly denominated from it, and are called spiritual.

On the other hand, though the Spirit of God may many ways influence natural men; yet because it is not thus communicated to them, as an indwelling principle, they don't derive any denomination or character from it; for there being no union it is not their own. The light may shine upon a body that is very dark or black; and though that body be the subject of the light, yet, because the light becomes no principle of light in it, so as to cause the body to shine, hence that body don't properly receive its denomination from it, so as to be called a lightsome body. So the Spirit of God acting upon the soul only, without communicating itself to be an active principle in it, can't denominate it spiritual. A body that continues black, may be said not to have light, though the light shines upon it; so natural men are said not to have the Spirit, Jude 19: "sensual," or natural (as the word is elsewhere rendered) "having not the Spirit."

2. Another reason why the saints and their virtues are called spiritual (which is the principal thing), is that the Spirit of God, dwelling as a vital principle in their souls, there produces those effects wherein he exerts and communicates himself in his own proper nature. Holiness is the nature of the Spirit of God, therefore he is called in Scripture the Holy Ghost. Holiness, which is as it were the beauty and sweetness of the divine nature, is as much the proper nature of the Holy Spirit, as heat is the nature of fire, or sweetness was the nature of that holy anointing oil, which was the principal type of the Holy Ghost in the Mosaic dispensation; yea, I may rather say that holiness is as much the proper nature of the Holy Ghost, as sweetness was the nature of the sweet odor of that ointment. The Spirit of God so dwells in the hearts of the saints, that he there, as a seed or spring of life, exerts and communicates himself, in this his sweet and divine nature, making the soul a partaker of God's beauty and Christ's joy, so that the saint has truly fellowship with the Father, and with his Son Jesus Christ, in thus having the communion or participation of the Holy Ghost. The grace which is in the hearts of the saints, is of the same nature with the divine holiness, as much as 'tis possible for that holiness to be, which is infinitely less in degree; as the brightness that is in a diamond which the sun shines upon, is of the same nature with the brightness of the sun, but only that it is as nothing to it in degree. Therefore Christ says, John 3:6: "That which is born of the Spirit is spirit"; i.e. the grace that is begotten in the hearts of the saints, is something of the same nature with that Spirit, and so is properly called a spiritual nature; after the same manner as that which is born of the flesh is flesh, or that which is born of corrupt nature is corrupt nature.

But the Spirit of God never influences the minds of natural men after this manner. Though he may influence them many ways, yet he never, in any of his influences, communicates himself to them in his own proper nature. Indeed he never acts disagreeably to his nature, either on the minds of saints or sinners: but the Spirit of God may act upon men agreeably to his own nature, and not exert his proper nature in the acts and exercises of their minds: the Spirit of God may act so, that his actions may be agreeable to his nature, and yet may not at all communicate himself in his proper nature, in the effect of that action. Thus, for instance, the Spirit of God moved upon the face of the waters, and there was nothing disagreeable to his nature in that action; but yet he did not at all communicate himself in that action, there was nothing of the proper nature of the Holy Spirit in that motion of the waters. And so he may act upon the minds of men many ways, and not communicate himself any more than when he acts on inanimate things.

Thus not only the manner of the *relation* of the Spirit, who is the operator, to the subject of his operations, is different; as the Spirit operates in the saints, as dwelling in them, as an abiding principle of action, whereas he doth not so operate upon sinners; but the influence and *operation itself* is different, and the effect wrought exceeding different. So that not only the persons are called spiritual, as having the Spirit of God dwelling in them; but those qualifications, affections and experiences that are wrought in them by the Spirit, are also spiritual, and therein differ vastly in their nature and kind from all that a natural man is or can be the subject of, while he remains in a natural state; and also from all that men or devils can be the authors of: 'tis a spiritual work in this high sense; and therefore above all other works is peculiar to the Spirit of God. There is no work so high and excellent; for there is no work wherein God does so much communicate himself, and wherein the mere creature hath, in so high a sense, a participation of God; so that it is expressed in Scripture by the saints being made "partakers of the divine nature" (2 Pet. 1:4), and having God dwelling in them, and they in God (I John 4:12, 15–16, and ch. 3:21), and having Christ in them (John 17:21; Rom. 8:10), being the temples of the living God (2 Cor. 6:16), living by Christ's life (Gal. 2:20), being made partakers of God's holiness (Heb. 12:10), having Christ's love dwelling in them (John 17:26), having his joy fulfilled in them (John 17:13), seeing light in God's light and being made to drink of the river of God's pleasures (Ps. 36:8–9), having fellowship with God, or communicating and partaking with him (as the word signifies) (I John 1:3). Not that the saints are made partakers of the essence of God, and so are "Godded" with God, and "Christed" with Christ, according to the abominable and blasphemous language and notions of some heretics; but, to use the Scripture phrase, they are made partakers of God's fullness (Eph. 3:17–19; John 1:16), that is, of God's spiritual beauty and happiness, according to the measure and capacity of a creature; for so it is evident the word "fullness" signifies in Scripture language. Grace in the hearts of the saints, being therefore the most glorious work of God, wherein he communicates of the goodness of his nature, it is doubtless his peculiar work, and in an eminent manner, above the power of all creatures. And the influences of the Spirit of God in this, being thus peculiar to God, and being those wherein God does, in so high a manner, communicate himself, and make the creature partaker of the divine nature (the Spirit of God communicating itself in its own proper nature). This is what I mean by those influences that are divine, when I say that truly gracious affections do arise from those influences that are spiritual and divine.

The true saints only have that which is spiritual; others have nothing which is divine, in the sense that has been spoken of. They not only have not these communications of the Spirit of God in so high a degree as the saints, but have nothing of that nature or kind. For the apostle James tell us, that natural men have not the Spirit;

and Christ teaches the necessity of a new birth, or a being born of the Spirit, from this, that he that is born of the flesh, has only flesh, and no spirit (John 3:6). They have not the Spirit of God dwelling in them in any degree; for the Apostle teaches, that all who have the Spirit of God dwelling in them are some of his (Rom. 8:9–11). And an having the Spirit of God is spoken of as a certain sign that persons shall have the eternal inheritance; for 'tis spoken of as the earnest of it (2 Cor. 1:22 and 5:5; Eph. 1:14), and an having anything of the Spirit is mentioned as a sure sign of being in Christ, "Hereby know we that we dwell in him, because he hath given us of his Spirit" (I John 4:30). Ungodly men, not only han't so much of the divine nature as the saints, but they are not partakers of it; which implies that they have nothing of it; for a being partaker of the divine nature is spoken of as the peculiar privilege of the true saints (II Pet. 1:4). Ungodly men are not partakers of God's holiness (Heb. 12:10). A natural man has no experience of any of those things that are spiritual: the Apostle teaches us that he is so far from it, that he knows nothing about them, he is a perfect stranger to them, the talk about such things is all foolishness and nonsense to him, he knows not what it means, "The natural man receiveth not the things of the Spirit of God; for they are foolishness to him; neither can he know them; because they are spiritually discerned" (I Cor. 2:14). And to the like purpose Christ teaches us that the world is wholly unacquainted with the Spirit of God, "Even the Spirit of truth, whom the world cannot receive; because it seeth him not, neither knoweth him" (John 14:17). And 'tis further evident, that natural men have nothing in them of the same nature with the true grace of the saints because the Apostle teaches us that those of them who go furthest in religion, have no charity, or true Christian love (I Cor. ch. 13). So Christ elsewhere reproves the Pharisees, those high pretenders to religion, that they had not the love of God in them (John 5:42). Hence natural men have no communion or fellowship with Christ, or participation with him (as these words signify), for this is spoken of as the peculiar privilege of the saints (I John 1:3, together with verses 6, 7, and I Cor. 1:8–9). And the Scripture speaks of the actual being of a gracious principle in the soul, though in its first beginning, as a seed there planted, as inconsistent with a man's being a sinner (I John 3:9). And natural men are represented in Scripture as having no spiritual light, no spiritual life, and no spiritual being; and therefore conversion is often compared to opening the eyes of the blind, raising the dead, and a work of creation (wherein creatures are made entirely new), and becoming newborn children.

From these things it is evident, that those gracious influences which the saints are subjects of, and the effects of God's Spirit which they experience, are entirely above nature, altogether of a different kind from anything that men find within themselves by nature, or only in the exercise of natural principles; and are things which no improvement of those qualifications, or principles that are natural, no advancing or exalting them to higher degrees, and no kind of composition of them, will ever bring men to; because they not only differ from what is natural, and from everything that natural men experience, in degree and circumstances; but also in kind; and are of a nature vastly more excellent. And this is what I mean by supernatural, when I say, that gracious affections are from those influences that are supernatural.

From hence if follows, that in those gracious exercises and affections which are wrought in the minds of the saints, through the saving influences of the Spirit of God, there is a new inward perception or sensation of their minds, entirely different in its nature and kind, from anything that ever their minds were the subjects of before they were sanctified. For doubtless if God by his mighty power produces something that is new, not only in degree and circumstances, but in its whole nature, and that which could be produced by no exalting, varying or compounding of what was there before, or by adding anything of the like kind; I say, if God produces something thus new in a mind, that is a perceiving, thinking, conscious thing; then doubtless something entirely new is felt, or perceived, or thought; or, which is the same thing, there is some new sensation or perception of the mind, which is entirely of a new sort, and which could be produced by no exalting, varying or compounding of that kind of perceptions or sensations which the mind had before; or there is what some metaphysicians call a new simple idea. If grace be, in the sense above described, an entirely new kind of principle; then the exercises of it are also entirely a new kind of exercises. And if there be in the soul a new sort of exercises which it is conscious of, which the soul knew nothing of before, and which no improvement, composition or management of what it was before conscious or sensible of, could produce, or anything like it; then it follows that the mind has an entirely new kind of perception or sensation; and here is, as it were, a new spiritual sense that the mind has, or a principle of new kind of perception or spiritual sensation, which is in its whole nature different from any former kinds of sensation of the mind, as tasting is diverse from any of the other senses; and something is perceived by a true saint, in the exercise of this new sense of mind, in spiritual and divine things, as entirely diverse from anything that is perceived in them, by natural men, as the sweet taste of honey is diverse from the ideas men get of honey by only looking on it, and feeling of it. So that the spiritual perceptions which a sanctified and spiritual person has, are not only diverse from all that natural men have, after the manner that the ideas or perceptions of the same sense may differ one from another, but rather as the ideas and sensations of different senses do differ. Hence the work of the Spirit of God in regeneration is often in Scripture compared to the giving a new sense, giving eyes to see, and ears to hear, unstopping the ears of the deaf, and opening the eyes of them that were born blind, and turning from darkness unto light. And because this spiritual sense is immensely the most noble and excellent, and that without which all other principles of perception, and all our faculties are useless and vain; therefore the giving this new sense, with the blessed fruits and effects of it in the soul, is compared to a raising the dead, and to a new creation.

This new spriritual sense, and the new dispositions that attend it, are no new faculties, but are new principles of nature. I use the word "principles," for want of a word of a more determinate signification. By a principle of nature in this place, I mean that foundation which is laid in nature, either old or new, for any particular manner or kind of exercise of the faculties of the soul; or a natural habit or foundation for action, giving a person ability and disposition to exert the faculties in exercises of such a certain kind; so that to exert the faculties in that kind of exercises, may be said to be his nature. So this new spiritual sense is not a new faculty of understanding, but it is a new foundation laid in the nature of the soul, for a new kind of exercises of the same faculty of understanding. So that new holy disposition of heart that attends this new sense, is not a new faculty of will, but a foundation laid in the nature of the soul, for a new kind of exercises of the same faculty of will.

The Spirit of God, in all his operations upon the minds of natural men, only moves, impresses, assists, improves, or some way acts upon natural principles; but gives no new spiritual principle. Thus when the Spirit of God gives a natural man visions, as he did Balaam, he only impresses a natural principle, viz. the sense of seeing, immediately exciting ideas of that sense; but he gives no new sense; neither is there anything supernatural, spiritual or divine in it. So if the Spirit of God impresses on a man's imagination, either in a dream, or when he is awake, any outward ideas of any of the senses, either voices, or shapes and colors, 'tis only exciting ideas of the same kind that he has by natural principles and senses. So if God reveals to any natural man, any secret fact; as for instance, something that he shall hereafter see or hear; this is not infusing or exercising any new spiritual principle, or giving the ideas of any new spiritual sense; 'tis only impressing, in an extraordinary manner, the ideas that will hereafter be received by sight and hearing. So in the more ordinary influences of the Spirit of God on the hearts of sinners, he only assists natural principles to do the same work to a greater degree, which they do of themselves by nature. Thus the Spirit of God by his common influences may assist men's natural ingeniosity, as he assisted Bezaleel and Aholiab in the curious works of the tabernacle: so he may assist men's natural abilities in political affairs, and improve their courage, and other natural qual- ifications; as he is said to have put his Spirit on the seventy elders, and on Saul, so as to give him another heart: so God may greatly assist natural men's reason, in their reasoning about secular things, or about the doctrines of religion, and may greatly advance the clearness of their apprehensions and notions of things of religion in many respects, without giving any spiritual sense. So in those awakenings and convictions that natural men may have, God only assists conscience, which is a natural principle, to do that work in a further degree, which it naturally does. Conscience naturally gives men an apprehension of right and wrong, and suggests the relation there is between right and wrong, and a retribution: the Spirit of God assists men's consciences to do this in a greater degree, helps conscience against the stupefying influence of worldly objects and their lusts. And so there are many other ways might be mentioned wherein the Spirit acts upon, assists and moves natural principles; but after all, 'tis no more than nature moved, acted and improved; here is nothing supernatural and divine. But the Spirit of God in his spiritual influences on the hearts of his saints, operates by infusing or exercising new, divine and supernatural principles; principles which are indeed a new and spiritual nature, and principles vastly more noble and excellent than all that is in natural men.

From what has been said it follows, that all spiritual and gracious affections are attended with, and do arise from some apprehension, idea or sensation of mind, which is in its whole nature different, yea exceeding different from all that is or can be in the mind of a natural man; and which the natural man discerns nothing of, and has no manner of idea of (agreeable to I Cor. 2:14), and conceives of no more than a man without the sense of tasting can conceive of the sweet taste of honey, or a man without the sense of hearing can conceive of the melody of a tune, or a man born blind can have a notion of the beauty of the rainbow.

But here two things must be observed in order to the right understanding of this.

1. On the one hand it must be observed, that not everything which in any respect appertains to spiritual affections, is new and entirely different from what natural men can conceive of, and do experience; some things are common to gracious affections with other affections; many circumstances, appendages and effects are common. Thus a saint's love to God has a great many things appertaining to it, which are common with a man's natural love to a near relation: love to God makes a man have desires of the honor of God, and a desire to please him; so does a natural man's love to his friend

make him desire his honor, and desire to please him: love to God causes a man to delight in the thoughts of God, and to delight in the presence of God, and to desire conformity to God, and the enjoyment of God; and so it is with a man's love to his friend; and many other things might be mentioned which are common to both. But yet that idea which the saint has of the loveliness of God, and that sensation, and that kind of delight he has in that view, which is as it were the marrow and quintessence of his love, is peculiar, and entirely diverse from anything that a natural man has, or can have any notion of. And even in those things that seem to be common, there is something peculiar: both spiritual love and natural, cause desires after the object beloved; but they be not the same sort of desires; there is a sensation of soul in the spiritual desires of one that loves God, which is entirely different from all natural desires: both spiritual love and natural love are attended with delight in the object beloved; but the sensations of delight are not the same, but entirely and exceedingly diverse. Natural men may have conceptions of many things about spiritual affections; but there is something in them which is as it were the nucleus, or kernel of them, that they have no more conceptions of, than one born blind has of colors.

It may be clearly illustrated by this: we will suppose two men; one is born without the sense of tasting, the other has it; the latter loves honey and is greatly delighted in it because he knows the sweet taste of it; the other loves certain sounds and colors: the love of each has many things that appertain to it, which is common; it causes both to desire and delight in the object beloved, and causes grief when it is absent, etc.: but yet, that idea or sensation which he who knows the taste of honey, has of its excellency and sweetness, that is the foundation of his love, is entirely different from anything the other has or can have; and that delight which he has in honey, is wholly diverse from anything that the other can conceive of; though they both delight in their beloved objects. So both these persons may in some respects love the same object: the one may love a delicious kind of fruit, which is beautiful to the eye, and of a delicious taste; not only because he has seen its pleasant colors, but knows its sweet taste; the other, perfectly ignorant of this, loves it only for its beautiful colors: there are many things seem, in some respect, to be common to both; both love, both desire, and both delight; but the love, and desire, and delight of the one, is altogether diverse from that of the other. The difference between the love of a natural man and spiritual man is like to this; but only it must be observed, that in one respect it is vastly greater, viz. that the kinds of excellency which are perceived in spiritual objects, by these different kinds of persons, are in themselves vastly more diverse, than the different kinds of excellency perceived in delicious fruit, by a tasting and a tasteless man; and in another respect it may not be so great, viz. as the spiritual man may have a spiritual sense or taste, to perceive that divine and most peculiar excellency, but in small beginnings, and in a very imperfect degree.

2. On the other hand, it must be observed, that a natural man may have those religious apprehensions and affections, which may be in many respects very new and surprising to him, and what before he did not conceive of; and yet what he experiences be nothing like the exercises of a principle of new nature, or the sensations of a new spiritual sense: his affections may be very new, by extraordinarily moving natural principles, in a very new degree, and with a great many new circumstances, and a new cooperation of natural affections, and a new composition of ideas; this may be from some extraordinary powerful influence of Satan and some great delusion; but there is

nothing but nature extraordinarily acted. As if a poor man, that had always dwelt in a cottage, and had never looked beyond the obscure village where he was born, should in a jest, be taken to a magnificent city and prince's court, and there arrayed in princely robes, and set in the throne, with the crown royal on his head, peers and nobles bowing before him, and should be made to believe that he was now a glorious monarch; the ideas he would have, and the affections he would experience, would in many respects be very new, and such as he had no imagination of before; but all is no more, than only extraordinarily raising and exciting natural principles, and newly exalting, varying and compounding such sort of ideas, as he has by nature; here is nothing like giving him a new sense.

Upon the whole, I think it is clearly manifest, that all truly gracious affections do arise from special and peculiar influences of the Spirit, working that sensible effect or sensation in the souls of the saints, which are entirely different from all that it is possible a natural man should experience, not only different in degree and circumstances, but different in its whole nature: so that a natural man not only cannot experience that which is individually the same, but can't experience anything but what is exceeding diverse, and immensely below it, in its kind; and that which the power of men or devils is not sufficient to produce the like of, or anything of the same nature.

I have insisted largely on this matter, because it is of great importance and use, evidently to discover and demonstrate the delusions of Satan, in many kinds of false religious affections, which multitudes are deluded by, and probably have been in all ages of the Christian church; and to settle and determine many articles of doctrine, concerning the operations of the Spirit of God, and the nature of true grace.

Now therefore, to apply these things to the purpose of this discourse.

From hence it appears that impressions which some have made on their imagination, or the imaginary ideas which they have of God, or Christ, or heaven, or anything appertaining to religion, have nothing in them that is spiritual, or of the nature of true grace. Though such things may attend what is spiritual, and be mixed with it, yet in themselves they have nothing that is spiritual, nor are they any part of gracious experience.

Here, for the sake of the common people, I will explain what is intended by impressions on the imagination, and imaginary ideas. The imagination is that power of the mind, whereby it can have a conception, or idea of things of an external or outward nature (that is, of such sort of things as are the objects of the outward senses), when those things are not present, and be not perceived by the senses. It is called imagination from the word "image"; because thereby a person can have an image of some external thing in his mind, when that thing is not present in reality, nor anything like it. All such kind of things as we perceive by our five external senses, seeing, hearing, smelling, tasting and feeling, are external things: and when a person has an idea, or image of any of these sorts of things in his mind, when they are not there, and when he don't really see, hear, smell, taste, nor feel them; that is to have an imagination of them, and these ideas are imaginary ideas: and when such kind of ideas are strongly impressed upon the mind, and the image of them in the mind is very lively, almost as if one saw them, or heard them, etc. that is called an impression on the imagination. Thus colors, and shapes, and a form of countenance, they are outward things; because they are that sort of things which are the objects of the outward sense of seeing: and therefore when any person has in his mind a lively idea of any shape, or color, or form of countenance; that is to have an imagination of those things. So if he has an idea of such sort of light or darkness, as he perceives by the sense of seeing; that is to have an idea of outward light, and so is an imagination. So if he has an idea of any marks made on paper, suppose letters and words written in a book; that is to have an external and imaginary idea of such kind of things as we sometimes perceive by our bodily eyes. And when we have the ideas of that kind of things which we perceive by any of the other senses, as of any sounds or voices, or words spoken; this is only to have ideas of outward things, viz. of such kind of things as are perceived by the external sense of hearing, and so that also is imagination: and when these ideas are livelily impressed, almost as if they were really heard with the ears, this is to have an impression on the imagination. And so I might go on, and instance in the ideas of things appertaining to the other three senses of smelling, tasting and feeling.

Many who have had such things have very ignorantly supposed them to be of the nature of spiritual discoveries. They have had lively ideas of some external shape, and beautiful form of countenance; and this they call spiritually seeing Christ. Some have had impressed upon them ideas of a great outward light; and this they call a spiritual discovery of God's or Christ's glory. Some have had ideas of Christ's hanging on the cross, and his blood running from his wounds; and this they call a spiritual sight of Christ crucified, and the way of salvation by his blood. Some have seen him with his arms open ready to embrace them; and this they call a discovery of the sufficiency of Christ's grace and love. Some have had lively ideas of heaven, and of Christ on his throne there, and shining ranks of saints and angels; and this they call seeing heaven opened to them. Some from time to time have had a lively idea of a person of a beautiful countenance smiling upon them; and this they call a spiritual discovery of the love of Christ to their souls, and tasting the love of Christ. And they look upon it as sufficient evidence that these things are spiritual discoveries, and that they see them spiritually, because they say they don't see these things with their bodily eyes, but in their hearts; for they can see them when their eyes are shut. And in like manner, the imaginations of some have been impressed with ideas of the sense of hearing; they have had ideas of words, as if they were spoke to them; sometimes they are the words of Scripture, and sometimes other words: they have had ideas of Christ's speaking comfortable words to them. These things they have called having the inward call of Christ, hearing the voice of Christ spiritually in their hearts, having the witness of the Spirit, and the inward testimony of the love of Christ, etc.

The common, and less considerate and understanding sort of people, are the more easily led into apprehensions that these things are spiritual things, because spiritual things being invisible, and not things that can be pointed forth with the finger, we are forced to use figurative expressions in speaking of them, and to borrow names from external and sensible objects to signify them by. Thus we call a clear apprehension of things spiritual by the name of light; and an having such an apprehension of such or such things, by the name of seeing such things; and the conviction of the judgment, and the persuasion of the will, by the word of Christ in the gospel, we signify by spiritually hearing the call of Christ: and the Scripture itself abounds with such like figurative expressions. Persons hearing these often used, and having pressed upon them the necessity of having their eyes opened, and having a discovery of spiritual things; and seeing Christ in his glory, and having the inward call, and the like, they ignorantly look and wait for some such external discoveries, and imaginary views as have been spoken of; and when they have them, are confident that now their eyes are opened, now Christ has discovered himself to them, and they are his children; and hence are exceedingly affected and elevated with their deliverance and happiness, and many kinds of affections are at once set in a violent motion in them.

But it is exceeding apparent that such ideas have nothing in them which is spiritual and divine, in the sense wherein it has been demonstrated that all gracious experiences are spiritual and divine. These external ideas are in no wise of such a sort, that they are entirely, and in their whole nature diverse from all that men have by nature, perfectly different from, and vastly above any sensation which 'tis possible a man should have by any natural sense or principle, so that in order to have them, a man must have a new spiritual and divine sense given him, in order to have any sensations of that sort: so far from this, that they are ideas of the same sort which we have by the external senses, that are some of the inferior powers of the humane nature; they are merely ideas of external objects, or ideas of that nature, of the same outward sensitive kind; the same sort of sensations of mind (differing not in degree, but only in circumstances) that we have by those natural principles which are common to us, with the beasts, viz. the five external senses. This is a low, miserable notion of spiritual sense, to suppose that 'tis only a conceiving or imagining that sort of ideas which we have by our animal senses, which senses the beasts have in as great perfection as we; it is, as it were, a turning Christ, or the divine nature in the soul, into a mere animal. There is nothing wanting in the soul, as it is by nature, to render it incapable of being the subject of all these external ideas, without any new principles. A natural man is capable of having an idea, and a lively idea of shapes and colors and sounds when they are absent, and as capable as a regenerate man is: so there is nothing supernatural in them. And 'tis known by abundant experience, that 'tis not the advancing or perfecting humane nature, which makes persons more capable of having such lively and strong imaginery ideas, but that on the contrary, the weakness of body and mind, and distempers of body, makes persons abundantly more susceptive of such impressions.

. . . . . .

[Second Sign]

. . . . . .

II. The first objective ground of gracious affections, is the transcendently excellent and amiable nature of divine things, as they are in themselves; and not any conceived relation they bear to self, or self-interest.

I say that the supremely excellent nature of divine things, is the first, or primary and original objective foundation of the spiritual affections of true saints; for I do not suppose that all relation which divine things bear to themselves, and their own particular interest, are wholly excluded from all influence in their gracious affections. For this may have, and indeed has, a secondary and consequential influence in those affections that are truly holy and spiritual; as I shall show how by and by.

It was before observed, that the affection of love is as it were the fountain of all affection; and particularly, that Christian love is the fountain of all gracious affections: now the divine excellency and glory of God, and Jesus Christ, the Word of God, the works of God, and the ways of God, etc. is the primary reason, why a true saint loves these things; and not any supposed interest that he has in them, or any conceived benefit that he has received from them, or shall receive from them, or any such imagined relation which they bear to his interest, that self-love can properly be said to be the first foundation of his love to these things.

Some say that all love arises from self-love; and that it is impossible in the nature of things, for any man to have any love to God, or any other being, but that love to himself must be the foundation of it. But I humbly suppose it is for want of consideration, that they say so. They argue, that whoever loves God, and so desires his glory, or the enjoyment of him, he desires these things as his own happiness; the glory of God, and the beholding and enjoying his perfections, are considered as things agreeable to him, tending to make him happy; he places his happiness in them, and desires them as things, which (if they were obtained) would be delightful to him, or would fill him with delight and joy, and so make him happy. And so, they say, it is from self-love, or a desire of his own happiness, that he desires God should be glorified, and desires to behold and enjoy his glorious perfections. But then they ought to consider a little further, and inquire how the man came to place his happiness in God's being glorified, and in contemplating and enjoying God's perfections. There is no doubt, but that after God's glory, and the beholding his perfections, are become so agreeable to him, that he places his highest happiness in these things, then he will desire them, as he desires his own happiness. But how came these things to be so agreeable to him, that he esteems it his highest happiness to glorify God, etc.? Is not this the fruit of love? A man must first love God, or have his heart united to him, before he will esteem God's good his own, and before he will desire the glorifying and enjoying of God, as his happiness. 'Tis not strong arguing, that because after a man has his heart united to God in love, as a fruit of this, he desires his glory and enjoyment as his own happiness, that therefore a desire of this happiness of his own, must needs be the cause and foundation of his love: unless it be strong arguing, that because a father begat a son, that therefore his son certainly begat him. If after a man loves God, and has his heart so united to him, as to look upon God as his chief good, and on God's good as his own, it will be a consequence and fruit of this, that even self-love, or love to his own happiness, will cause him to desire the glorifying and enjoying of God; it will not thence follow, that this very exercise of self-love, went before his love to God, and that his love to God was a consequence and fruit of that. Something else, entirely distinct from self-love might be the cause of this, viz. a change made in the views of his mind, and relish of his heart; whereby he apprehends a beauty, glory, and supreme good, in God's nature, as it is in itself. This may be the thing that first draws his heart to him, and causes his heart to be united to him, prior to all considerations of his own interest or happiness, although after this, and as a fruit of this, he necessarily seeks his interest and happiness in God.

There is such a thing, as a kind of love or affection, that a man may have towards persons or things, which does properly arise from self-love; a preconceived relation to himself, or some respect already manifested by another to him, or some benefit already received or depended on, is truly the first foundation of his love, and what his affection does wholly arise from; and is what precedes any relish of, or delight in the nature and qualities inherent in the being beloved, as beautiful and amiable. When the first thing that draws a man's benevolence to another, is the beholding those qualifications and properties in him, which appear to him lovely in themselves, and the subject of them, on this account, worthy of esteem and goodwill, love arises in a very different manner, than when it first arises from some gift bestowed by another, or depended on from him, as a judge loves and favors a man that has bribed him; or from the relation he supposes another has to him, as a man who loves another because he looks upon him as his child. When love to another arises thus, it does truly and properly arise from self-love.

That kind of affection to God or Jesus Christ, which does thus properly arise from self-love, cannot be a truly gracious and spiritual love; as appears from what has been said already: for self-love is a principle entirely natural, and as much in the hearts of devils as angels; and therefore surely nothing that is the mere result of it, can be super-natural and divine, in the manner before described. Christ plainly speaks of this kind of love, as what is nothing beyond the love of wicked men, Luke 6:32: "If ye love them that love you, what thank have ye? For sinners also love those that love them." And the devil himself knew that that kind of respect to God which was so mercenary, as to be only for benefits received or depended on (which is all one), is worthless in the sight of God; otherwise he never would have made use of such a slander before God, against Job, as in Job 1:9–10: "Doth Job serve God for nought? Hast thou not made an hedge about him, and about his house?" etc. Nor would God ever have implicitly allowed the objection to have been good, in case the accusation had been true, by allowing that that matter should be tried, and that Job should be so dealt with, that it might appear in the event, whether Job's respect to God was thus mercenary or no, and by putting the proof of the sincerity and goodness of his respect, upon that issue.

'Tis unreasonable to think otherwise, than that the first foundation of a true love to God, is that whereby he is in himself lovely, or worthy to be loved, or the supreme loveliness of his nature. This is certainly what makes him chiefly amiable. What chiefly makes a man, or any creature lovely, is his excellency; and so what chiefly renders God lovely, and must undoubtedly be the chief ground of true love, is his excellency. God's nature, or the divinity, is infinitely excellent; yea 'tis infinite beauty, brightness, and glory itself. But how can that be true love of this excellent and lovely nature, which is not built on the foundation of its true loveliness? How can that be true love of beauty and brightness, which is not for beauty and brightness' sake? How can that be a true prizing of that which is in itself infinitely worthy and precious, which is not for the sake of its worthiness and preciousness? This infinite excellency of the divine nature, as it is in itself, is the true ground of all that is good in God in any respect; but how can a man truly and rightly love God, without loving him for that excellency in him, which is the foundation of all that is in any manner of respect good or desirable in him? They whose affection to God is founded first on his profitableness to them, their affection begins at the wrong end; they regard God only for the utmost limit of the stream of divine good, where it touches them, and reaches their interest; and have no respect to that infinite glory of God's nature, which is the original good, and the true fountain of all good, the first fountain of all loveliness of every kind, and so the first foundation of all true love.

. . . . . .

And as it is with the love of the saints, so it is with their joy, and spiritual delight and pleasure: the first foundation of it, is not any consideration or conception of their interest in divine things; but it primarily consists in the sweet entertainment their minds have in the view or contemplation of the divine and holy beauty of these things, as they are in themselves. And this is indeed the very main difference between the joy of the hypocrite, and the joy of the true saint. The former rejoices in himself; self is the first foundation of his joy: the latter rejoices in God. The hypocrite has his mind pleased and delighted, in the first place, with his own privilege, and the happiness which he supposes he has attained, or shall attain. True saints have their minds, in the first place, inexpressibly pleased and delighted with the sweet ideas of the glorious and amiable nature of the things of God. And this is the spring of all their delights, and the cream of all their pleasures; 'tis the joy of their joy. This sweet and ravishing entertainment, they have in the view of the beautiful and delightful nature of divine things, is the foundation of the joy that they have afterwards, in the consideration of their being theirs. But the dependence of the affections of hypocrites is in a contrary order: they first rejoice, and are elevated with it, that they are made so much of by God; and then on that ground, he seems in a sort, lovely to them.

The first foundation of the delight a true saint has in God, is his own perfection; and the first foundation of the delight he has in Christ, is his own beauty; he appears in himself the chief among ten thousand, and altogether lovely: the way of salvation by Christ, is a delightful way to him, for the sweet and admirable manifestations of the divine perfections in it; the holy doctrines of the gospel, by which God is exalted and man abased, holiness honored and promoted, and sin greatly disgraced and discouraged, and free and sovereign love manifested; are glorious doctrines in his eyes, and sweet to his taste, prior to any conception of his interest in these things. Indeed the saints rejoice in their interest in God, and that Christ is theirs; and so they have great reason; but this is not the first spring of their joy: they first rejoice in God as glorious and excellent in himself, and then secondarily rejoice in it, that so glorious a God is theirs: they first have their hearts filled with sweetness, from the view of Christ's excellency, and the excellency of his grace, and the beauty of the way of salvation by him; and then they have a secondary joy, in that so excellent a Saviour, and such excellent grace is theirs.

But that which is the true saint's superstructure, is the hypocrite's foundation. When they hear of the wonderful things of the gospel, of God's great love in sending his Son, of Christ's dying love to sinners, and the great things Christ has purchased, and promised to the saints, and hear these things livelily and eloquently set forth; they may hear with a great deal of pleasure, and be lifted up with what they hear: but if their joy be examined, it will be found to have no other foundation than this, that they look upon these things as theirs, all this exalts them, they love to hear of the great love of Christ so vastly distinguishing some from others; for self-love, and even pride itself, makes 'em affect great distinction from others: no wonder, in this confident opinion of their own good estate, that they feel well under such doctrine, and are pleased in the highest degree, in hearing how much God and Christ makes of 'em. So that their joy is really a joy in themselves, and not in God.

And because the joy of hypocrites is in themselves, hence it comes to pass, that in their rejoicings and elevations, they are wont to keep their eye upon themselves; having received what they call spiritual discoveries or experiences, their minds are taken up about them, admiring their own experiences: and what they are principally taken and elevated with, is not the glory of God, or beauty of Christ, but the beauty of their experiences. They keep thinking with themselves, what a good experience is this! What a great discovery is this! What wonderful things have I met with! And so they put their experiences in the place of Christ, and his beauty and fullness; and instead of rejoicing in Christ Jesus, they rejoice in their admirable experiences: instead of feeding and feasting their souls in the view of what is without them, viz. the innate, sweet, refreshing amiableness of the things exhibited in the gospel, their eyes are off from these things, or at least they view them only as it were sideways; but the object that fixes their contemplation, is their experience; and they are feeding their souls, and feasting a selfish principle with a view of their discoveries: they take more comfort in their discoveries than in Christ discovered, which is the true notion of living upon experiences and frames; and not a using experiences as the signs, on which they rely for evidence of their good estate, which some call living on experiences: though it be very observable, that some of them who do so, are most notorious for living upon experiences, according to the true notion of it.

The affections of hypocrites are very often after this manner; they are first, much affected with some impression on their imagination, or some impulse, which they take to be an immediate suggestion, or testimony from God, of his love and their happiness, and high privilege in some respect, either with or without a text of Scripture; they are mightily taken with this, as a great discovery; and hence arise high affections. And when their affections are raised, then they view those high affections, and call them great and wonderful experiences; and they have a notion that God is greatly pleased with those affections; and this affects them more; and so they are affected with their affections. And thus their affections rise higher and higher, till they sometimes are perfectly swallowed up: and self-conceit, and a fierce zeal rises withal; and all is built like a castle in the air, on no other foundation but imagination, self-love and pride.

And as the thoughts of this sort of persons are, so is their talk; for out of the abundance of their heart, their mouth speaketh. As in their high affections, they keep their eye upon the beauty of their experiences and greatness of their attainments; so they are great talkers about themselves. The true saint, when under great spiritual affections, from the fullness of his heart, is ready to be speaking much of God, and his glorious perfections and works, and of the beauty and amiableness of Christ, and the glorious things of the gospel; but hypocrites, in their high affections, talk more of the discovery, than they do of the thing discovered; they are full of talk about the great things they have met with, the wonderful discoveries they have had, how sure they are of the love of God to them, how safe their condition is, and how they know they shall go to heaven, etc.

A true saint, when in the enjoyment of true discoveries of the sweet glory of God and Christ, has his mind too much captivated and engaged by what he views without himself, to stand at that time to view himself, and his own attainments: it would be a diversion and loss which he could not bear, to take his eye off from the ravishing object of his contemplation, to survey his own experience, and to spend time in thinking with himself, what an high attainment this is, and what a good story I now have to tell others. Nor does the pleasure and sweetness of his mind at that time, chiefly arise from the consideration of the safety of his state, or anything he has in view of his own qualifications, experiences, or circumstances; but from the divine and supreme beauty of what is the object of his direct view, without himself; which sweetly entertains, and strongly holds his mind.

As the love and joy of hypocrites, are all from the source of self-love; so it is with their other affections, their sorrow for sin, their humiliation and submission, their religious desires and zeal: everything is as it were paid for beforehand, in God's highly gratifying their self-love, and their lusts, by making so much of them, and exalting them so highly, as things are in their imagination. 'Tis easy for nature, as corrupt as it is, under a notion of being already some of the highest favorites of heaven, and having a God who does so protect 'em and favor 'em in their sins, to love this imaginary God that suits 'em so well, and to extol him, and submit to him, and to be fierce and zealous for him. The high affections of many are all built on the supposition of their being eminent saints. If that opinion which they have of themselves were taken away, if they thought they were some of the lower form of saints (though they should yet suppose themselves to be real saints), their high affections would fall to the ground. If they only saw a little of the sinfulness and vileness of their own hearts, and their deformity, in the midst of their best duties and their best affections, it would knock their affections on the head; because their affections are built upon self, therefore self-knowledge would destroy them. But as to truly gracious affections, they are built elsewhere: they have their foundation out of self, in God and Jesus Christ; and therefore a discovery of themselves, of their own deformity, and the meanness of their experiences, though it will purify their affections, yet it will not destroy them, but in some respects sweeten and heighten them.

Part Two

Republican Enlightenment

Introduction

That massive Western intellectual reorientation known as the Enlightenment that began to emerge in the second half of the seventeenth century rested principally on two revolutionary ideas: that it was possible to understand the universe through the use of human faculties and that such understanding could be put to use to make society more rational and humane. In America a moderate version of the first of these ideas gradually entered the intellectual mainstream with little overt opposition. By the second half of the eighteenth century, even many Calvinistic intellectuals found it fairly easy to square revelation with some form of experiential reason. Simultaneously, under the influence of rising hopes fueled by the American Revolution, an increasing number of secular-minded intellectuals readily embraced the second idea of enlightened social amelioration. Yet the fact remains that however politically liberal, by European standards, the American Enlightenment was intellectually comparatively tame. Even its most worldly spokesmen, like Franklin and Jefferson, rarely felt the necessity of making a public issue of their dismissal of Christian revelation. Nor did any American Hume or Voltaire come forward to suggest the corrosive power of empirical reason on commonly held beliefs in objective truth or morality.

Such intellectual ubiquity and moderation have sometimes led European writers to assert that the American Enlightenment meant simple blandness. This is obviously false. On the contrary, a good argument can be made to suggest that what made Enlightenment intellectuals in America so intriguing, not to mention influential, was precisely their ingenuity in absorbing and refashioning powerful religious and political currents that later generations would consider quite alien to the Enlightenment faith in reason and experiment. In the area of morality, no enlightened American intellectual exhibited these dialectical traits in more multiform ways than Benjamin Franklin. It is therefore fitting that Part Two open with a selection from Franklin's legendary narrative of post-Puritan ethics. In this section of his *Autobiography,* he showed through the guise of one of the most luminous personas in American literature how it was possible to make out of one's life an experiment in the ways to psychic autonomy and upward mobility.

Implicit in Franklin's moral code was a liberal, entrepreneurial yet public service–minded social and political vision that would have a long life in American culture. More immediately, American political thought was shaped by a more stringent complex of ideas that eighteenth-century thinkers called republicanism. In its full-blown ideological form, it asserted that the health of a polity was, on the one hand, dependent on "virtue"—or the self-sufficiency and public spiritedness of its citizens—and, on the other hand, threatened by "corruption" promoted by overweening executive "power" in league with its self-seeking, luxury-loving minions. This ideology was a luxuriant tree with many roots and branches. It was linked with the civic humanism of ancient Greek and Roman authors as revived by Renaissance, Puritan commonwealth, and English parliamentary reform writers. In the American colonies it intertwined itself with Puritan and evangelical notions of the covenanted and benevolent faithful marching against the Antichrist in step with God's millennial scheme. Moreover, in the circumstances of the British-American colonial conflict, it gave lurid meaning to British encroachments. But in the hands of Revolutionary Enlightenment intellectuals, republicanism received a secular and to some extent liberal reshaping, as is well shown in the three great Revolutionary texts presented here. In his "Dissertation on the Canon and the Feudal Law," John Adams argued that it was knowledge and understanding that animated the brightly New England form of liberty and power, whereas ignorance and superstition fueled their feudal and, by implication, partly British form. Likewise, although more positively, Thomas Paine and Thomas Jefferson based their republican prescriptions for (in Paine's case) a monarchless state and (in Jefferson's) revolution on rationally agreed on "common sense" and "self-evident truths."

The contradictory post-Revolutionary legacy of American republicanism has been much debated recently by historians. No better entry into this problem can be found than a sampling of the writings of America's two great republican intellectuals, John Adams and Thomas Jefferson. In his letters to Samuel Adams and Jefferson, John Adams earnestly pleaded his reasons for thinking that liberty was both nurtured and threatened by the people *and* aristocracies, and he advanced as a solution a republicanized version of a mixed government resting on different orders. Jefferson, on the other hand, in the selection from his *Notes on the State of Virginia* and in his letter to John Adams, presented a contrasting case for a more egalitarian polity, although one that also admitted, on both Enlightenment and republican grounds, its own kind of noblesse oblige. Finally, because a good deal of what was nobly liberal about Jefferson and, to a lesser extent, John Adams derived from their ethical and religious outlook, three letters on these subjects conclude this set of Adams–Jeffersoniana.

Historically, of course, the most important political fruit of enlightened republicanism was the Constitution, the intellectual significance of which was well illuminated by the contentious debate over its ratification. After four years of post-Revolutionary political conflicts and rising fears for the security of the republic, political intellectuals were forced to contend with the greatest difficulty of a modern republican polity—how to reconcile conflicts of interest so that public virtue would remain intact. In addressing this problem, different thinkers arrived at sometimes very different conclusions. George Mason, in his sketch of objections to the Constitution, argued that the adoption of many of the document's federal ideas would inevitably lead to a betrayal of important republican ideals. Alexander Hamilton, on the other hand, in his speech to the Constitutional Convention gave his reasons for believing that only a more national and authoritative republican system would sufficiently protect the national government from self-seeking interests and promote the republic's public warfare. And in *The Federalist* numbers 10 and 51, James Madison, the Constitution's leading architect, constructed a dynamically symmetrical representation of the new federal state that would be so extended and divided as to nurture a social pluralism and a popularly elected governing class that would work together to control liberty's vices. No greater monument to the American enlightened mind was produced than this passionately dispassionate discourse over the best rational model for the preservation of a virtuous republic.

Recommendations for Further Reading

Henry F. May, *The Enlightenment in America* (New York, 1976); Donald H. Meyer, *The Democratic Enlightenment* (New York, 1976); Henry Steele Commager, *The Empire of Reason: How Europe Imagined and America Realized the Enlightenment* (Garden City, N.Y., 1977); Roy Porter and Mikuláš Teich, eds., *The Enlightenment in National Context* (Cambridge, 1981); Emory Elliott, *Revolutionary Writers: Literature and Authority in the New Republic, 1725–1810* (New York, 1982); Jay Fliegelman, *Prodigals and Pilgrims: The American Revolution Against Patriarchal Authority, 1750–1800* (Cambridge, 1982); Alan Heimert, *Religion and the American Mind: From the Great Awakening to the Revolution* (Cambridge, Mass., 1966); Nathan O. Hatch, *The Sacred Cause of Liberty: Republican Thought and the Millennium in Revolutionary New England* (New Haven, 1977); Sidney E. Mead, *The Old Religion in the Brave New World: Reflections on the Relation Between Christendom and the Republic* (Berkeley, 1977); Ruth H. Bloch, *Visionary Republic: Millennial Themes in American Thought, 1756–1800* (Cambridge, 1985); Patricia U. Bonomi, *Under the Cope of Heaven: Religion, Society, and Politics in Colonial America* (New York, 1986); Bernard Bailyn, *The Ideological Origins of the American Revolution* (Cambridge, Mass., 1967); Gordon S. Wood, *The Creation of the American Republic, 1776–1787* (Chapel Hill, 1969); J.G.A. Pocock, *The Machiavellian Moment: Florentine Political Thought and the Atlantic Republican Tradition* (Princeton, 1975); Lester H. Cohen, *The Revolutionary Histories: Contemporary Narratives of the American Revolution* (Ithaca, N.Y., 1980); Linda K. Kerber, *Women of the Republic: Intellect and Ideology in Revolutionary America* (Chapel Hill, 1980); Drew R. McCoy, *Political Economy in Jeffersonian America* (Chapel Hill, 1980); John P. Diggins, *The Lost Soul of American Politics: Virtue, Self-Interest, and the Foundations of Liberalism* (New York, 1984); Joyce Appleby, ed., "Republicanism in the History and Historiography of the United States," Special Issue of *American Quarterly,* 37 (Fall 1985), 461–598; Forrest McDonald, *Novus Ordo Seclorum: The Intellectual Origins of the Constitution* (Lawrence, Kans., 1985); J.G.A. Pocock, *Virtue, Commerce, and History: Essays on Political Thought and History, Chiefly in the Eighteenth Century* (Cambridge, 1985); Steven Watts, *The Republic Reborn: War and the Making of Liberal America, 1790–1820* (Baltimore, 1987).

BENJAMIN FRANKLIN

Selection from *The Autobiography*
(1784–88)

Scientist, businessman, statesman, journalist, diplomat, man of letters, and international celebrity, Benjamin Franklin (1706–90) was the American Enlightenment's Proteus. In none of these roles, however, did Franklin achieve as much popular influence as in his moral writings, and of these none was more important than his *Autobiography*. Here one can see in its fully nuanced complexity—as one cannot in his set pieces or cleverly sententious maxims—his essential message: virtue is or should be both a code and an expression of life. In the selections that follow, written, like most of his memoir, in the last years of his life, Franklin advanced a large assortment of virtues drawn from a host of ancient and modern Western traditions, although he placed particular emphasis on the Puritan values of frugality, temperance, and industry. The means and ends of these virtues, of course, were quite unPuritan. Not scrupulous introspection, but the alteration of habit was the way to virtue. Likewise, not holiness but human happiness—defined primarily as a condition of independence, self-control, and the power to promote the public welfare, and to be *seen* as such—appeared as, if not the highest, at least a perfectly sufficient goal. And throughout Franklin maintained a tone of warm but ironic appreciation of the self of his narrative, suggesting to the reader that this Franklin was perhaps every man or woman as *"Free and Easy"* as himself. Alfred Owen Aldridge, *Benjamin Franklin and Nature's God* (Durham, N.C., 1967) is a solid study of Franklin's religion. Franklin's ethics are explored in three excellent essays: David Levin, *"The Autobiography of Benjamin Franklin*: The Puritan Experimenter in Life and Art," *Yale Review,* 53 (Winter 1964), 258–75; Norman Fiering, "Benjamin Franklin and the Way to Virtue," *American Quarterly,* 30 (Summer 1978), 199–223; and J.A. Leo Lemay, "Benjamin Franklin, Universal Genius," in Lemay's *The Renaissance Man in the Eighteenth Century* (Los Angeles, 1978), 1–44. Drew R. McCoy, "Benjamin Franklin's Vision of a Republican Political Economy for America," *William and Mary Quarterly,* 35 (October 1978), 605–28, cogently places Franklin's economic thought in the context of republican ideology. For a recent interesting discussion of Franklin's project to create an exemplary self, see Mitchell Robert Breitwieser, *Cotton Mather and Benjamin Franklin: The Price of Representative Personality* (Cambridge, 1984), 171–305.

Continuation of the Account of my Life. Begun at Passy, 1784.

It is some time since I receiv'd the . . . Letters, but I have been too busy till now to think of complying with the Request they contain. It might too be much better done if I were at home among my Papers, which would aid my Memory, and help to ascertain Dates. But my Return being uncertain, and having just now a little Leisure, I will endeavour to recollect and write what I can; if I live to get home, it may there be corrected and improv'd.

Not having any Copy here of what is already written, I know not whether an Account is given of the means I used to establish the Philadelphia public Library, which from a small Beginning is now become so considerable, though I remember to have come down to near the Time of that Transaction, 1730. I will therefore begin here, with an Account of it, which may be struck out if found to have been already given.

At the time I establish'd myself in Pennsylvania, there was not a good Bookseller's Shop in any of the Colonies to the Southward of Boston. In New York and Philadelphia the Printers were indeed Stationers, they sold only Paper, etc., Almanacs, Ballads, and a few common School Books. Those who lov'd Reading were oblig'd to send for their Books from England. The Members of the Junto had each a few. We had left the Alehouse where we first met, and hired a Room to hold our Club in. I propos'd that we should all of us bring our Books to that Room, where they would not only be ready to consult in our Conferences, but become a common Benefit, each of us being at Liberty to borrow such as he wish'd to read at home. This was accordingly done, and for some time contented us. Finding the Advantage of this little Collection, I propos'd to render the Benefit from Books more common by commencing a Public Subscription Library. I drew a Sketch of the Plan and Rules that would be necessary, and got a skillful Conveyancer Mr. Charles Brockden to put the whole in Form of Articles of Agreement to be subscribed, by which each Subscriber engag'd to pay a certain Sum down for the first Purchase of Books and an annual Contribution for increasing them. So few were the Readers at that time in Philadelphia, and the Majority of us so poor, that I was not able with great Industry to find more than Fifty Persons, mostly young Tradesmen, willing to pay down for this purpose Forty shillings each, and Ten Shillings per Annum. On this little Fund we began. The Books were imported. The Library was open one Day in the Week for lending them to the Subscribers, on their Promissory Notes to pay Double the Value if not duly returned. The Institution soon manifested its Utility, was imitated by other Towns and in other Provinces, the Libraries were augmented by Donations, Reading became fashionable, and our People having no public Amusements to divert their Attention from Study became better acquainted with Books, and in a few Years were observ'd by Strangers to be better instructed and more intelligent than People of the same Rank generally are in other Countries.

When we were about to sign the above-mentioned Articles, which were to be binding on us, our Heirs, etc. for fifty Years, Mr. Brockden, the Scrivener, said to us, "You are young Men, but it is scarce probable that any of you will live to see the Expiration of the Term fix'd in this Instrument." A Number of us, however, are yet

Source: Benjamin Franklin's Autobiography: An Authoritative Text, Backgrounds, Criticism, ed. J. A. Leo Lemay and P. M. Zall (New York: W. W. Norton & Co., 1986), 62–79. Editors' notes altered. Reprinted by permission of W. W. Norton & Company, Inc., Copyright © 1986.

living. But the Instrument was after a few Years rendered null by a Charter that incorporated and gave Perpetuity to the Company.

The Objections, and Reluctances I met with in Soliciting the Subscriptions, made me soon feel the Impropriety of presenting oneself as the Proposer of any useful Project that might be suppos'd to raise one's Reputation in the smallest degree above that of one's Neighbors, when one has need of their Assistance to accomplish that Project. I therefore put myself as much as I could out of sight, and stated it as a Scheme of *a Number of Friends,* who had requested me to go about and propose it to such as they thought Lovers of Reading. In this way my Affair went on more smoothly, and I ever after practic'd it on such Occasions; and from my frequent Successes, can heartily recommend it. The present little Sacrifice of your Vanity will afterwards be amply repaid. If it remains a while uncertain to whom the Merit belongs, someone more vain than yourself will be encourag'd to claim it, and then even Envy will be dispos'd to do you Justice, by plucking those assum'd Feathers, and restoring them to their right Owner.

This Library afforded me the Means of Improvement by constant Study, for which I set apart an Hour or two each Day; and thus repair'd in some Degree the Loss of the Learned Education my Father once intended for me. Reading was the only Amusement I allow'd myself. I spent no time in Taverns, Games, or Frolics of any kind. And my Industry in my Business continu'd as indefatigable as it was necessary. I was in debt for my Printing-House, I had a young Family coming on to be educated, and I had to contend with for Business two Printers who were establish'd in the Place before me. My Circumstances however grew daily easier: my original Habits of Frugality continuing. And My Father having among his Instructions to me when a Boy, frequently repeated a Proverb of Solomon, *"Seest thou a Man diligent in his Calling, he shall stand before Kings, he shall not stand before mean Men."* I from thence consider'd Industry as a Means of obtaining Wealth and Distinction, which encourag'd me: tho' I did not think that I should every literally stand before Kings, which however has since happened; for I have stood before five, and even had the honor of sitting down with one, the King of Denmark, to Dinner.

We have an English Proverb that says,

> He that would thrive
> Must ask his Wife,

it was lucky for me that I had one as much dispos'd to Industry and Frugality as myself. She assisted me cheerfully in my Business, folding and stitching Pamphlets, tending Shop, purchasing old Linen Rags for the Paper-makers, etc., etc. We kept no idle Servants, our Table was plain and simple, our Furniture of the cheapest. For instance my Breakfast was a long time Bread and Milk, (no Tea,) and I ate it out of a twopenny earthen Porringer with a Pewter Spoon. But mark how Luxury will enter Families, and make a Progress, in Spite of Principle. Being Call'd one Morning to Breakfast, I found it in a China Bowl with a Spoon of Silver. They had been bought for me without my Knowledge by my Wife, and had cost her the enormous Sum of three and twenty Shillings, for which she had no other Excuse or Apology to make, but that she thought *her* Husband deserv'd a Silver Spoon and China Bowl as well as any of his Neighbors. This was the first Appearance of Plate and China in our House, which afterwards in a Course of Years as our Wealth increas'd, augmented gradually to several Hundred Pounds in Value.

I had been religiously educated as a Presbyterian; and tho' some of the Dogmas of that Persuasion, such as the Eternal Decrees of God, Election, Reprobation, etc. appear'd to me unintelligible, others doubtful, and I early absented myself from the Public Assemblies of the Sect, Sunday being my Studying-Day, I never was without some religious Principles; I never doubted, for instance, the Existence of the Deity, that he made the World, and govern'd it by his Providence; that the most acceptable Service of God was the doing Good to Man; that our Souls are immortal; and that all Crime will be punished and Virtue rewarded either here or hereafter; these I esteem'd the Essentials of every Religion, and being to be found in all the Religions we had in our Country I respected them all, tho' with different degrees of Respect as I found them more or less mix'd with other Articles which without any Tendency to inspire, promote or confirm Morality, serv'd principally to divide us and make us unfriendly to one another. This Respect to all, with an Opinion that the worst had some good Effects, induc'd me to avoid all Discourse that might tend to lessen the good Opinion another might have of his own Religion; and as our Province increas'd in People and new Places of worship were continually wanted, and generally erected by voluntary Contribution, my Mite for such purpose, whatever might be the Sect, was never refused.

Tho' I seldom attended any Public Worship, I had still an Opinion of its Propriety, and of its Utility when rightly conducted, and I regularly paid my annual Subscription for the Support of the only Presbyterian Minister or Meeting we had in Philadelphia. He us'd to visit me sometimes as a Friend, and admonish me to attend his Administrations, and I was now and then prevail'd on to do so, once for five Sundays successively. Had he been, *in my Opinion,* a good Preacher perhaps I might have continued, notwithstanding the occasion I had for the Sunday's Leisure in my Course of Study: But his Discourses were chiefly either polemic Arguments, or Explications of the peculiar Doctrines of our Sect, and were all to me very dry, uninteresting and unedifying, since not a single moral Principle was inculcated or enforc'd, their Aim seeming to be rather to make us Presbyterians than good Citizens. At length he took for his Text that Verse of the 4th Chapter of Philippians, *Finally, Brethren, Whatsoever Things are true, honest, just, pure, lovely, or of good report, if there be any virtue, or any praise, think on these Things;* and I imagin'd in a Sermon on such a Text, we could not miss of having some Morality: But he confin'd himself to five Points only as meant by the Apostle, viz. 1. Keeping holy the Sabbath Day. 2. Being diligent in Reading the Holy Scriptures. 3. Attending duly the Public Worship. 4. Partaking of the Sacrament. 5. Paying a due Respect to God's Ministers.—These might be all good Things, but as they were not the kind of good Things that I expected from that Text, I despaired of ever meeting with them from any other, was disgusted, and attended his Preaching no more. I had some Years before compos'd a little Liturgy or Form of Prayer for my own private Use, viz, in 1728, entitled, *Articles of Belief and Acts of Religion.* I return'd to the Use of this, and went no more to the public Assemblies. My Conduct might be blameable, but I leave it without attempting farther to excuse it, my present purpose being to relate Facts, and not to make Apologies for them.

It was about this time that I conceiv'd the bold and arduous Project of arriving at moral Perfection. I wish'd to live without committing any Fault at anytime; I would conquer all that either Natural Inclination, Custom, or Company might lead me into. As I knew, or thought I knew, what was right and wrong, I did not see why I might not *always* do the one and avoid the other. But I soon found I had undertaken a Task of more Difficulty than I had imagined: While my Care was employ'd in guarding against one Fault, I was often supris'd by another. Habit took the Advantage of Inattention. Inclination was sometimes too strong for Reason. I concluded at length, that the mere speculative Conviction that it was our Interest to be completely virtuous, was not sufficient to prevent our Slipping, and that the contrary Habits must be broken and good Ones acquired and established, before we can have any Dependence on a steady uniform Rectitude of Conduct. For this purpose I therefore contriv'd the following Method.

In the various Enumerations of the moral Virtues I had met with in my Reading, I found the Catalogue more or less numerous, as different Writers included more or fewer Ideas under the same Name. Temperance, for Example, was by some confin'd to Eating and Drinking, while by others it was extended to mean the moderating every other Pleasure, Appetite, Inclination or Passion, bodily or mental, even to our Avarice and Ambition. I propos'd to myself, for the sake of Clearness, to use rather more Names with fewer Ideas annex'd to each, than a few Names with more Ideas; and I included after Thirteen Names of Virtues all that at that time occurr'd to me as necessary or desirable, and annex'd to each a short Precept, which fully express'd the Extent I gave to its Meaning.

These Names of Virtues with their Precepts were

1. TEMPERANCE.
Eat not to Dulness. Drink not to Elevation.

2. SILENCE.
Speak not but what may benefit others or your self. Avoiding trifling Conversation.

3. ORDER.
Let all your Things have their Places. Let each Part of your Business have its Time.

4. RESOLUTION.
Resolve to perform what you ought. Perform without fail what you resolve.

5. FRUGALITY.
Make no Expense but to do good to others or yourself: i.e. Waste nothing.

6. INDUSTRY.
Lose no Time. Be always employ'd in something useful. Cut off all unnecessary Actions.

7. SINCERITY.
Use no hurtful Deceit. Think innocently and justly; and, if you speak, speak accordingly.

8. JUSTICE.
Wrong none, by doing Injuries or omitting the Benefits that are your Duty.

9. MODERATION.
Avoid Extremes. Forbear resenting Injuries so much as you think they deserve.

10. CLEANLINESS.
Tolerate no Uncleanness in Body, Clothes or Habitation.

11. TRANQUILITY.
Be not disturbed at Trifles, or at Accidents common or unavoidable.

12.   CHASTITY.

Rarely use Venery but for Health or Offspring; Never to Dulness, Weakness, or the Injury of your own or another's Peace or Reputation.

13.   HUMILITY.

Imitate Jesus and Socrates.

My intention being to acquire the *Habitude* of all these Virtues, I judg'd it would be well not to distract my Attention by attempting the whole at once, but to fix it on one of them at a time, and when I should be Master of that, then to proceed to another, and so on till I should have gone thro' the thirteen. And as the previous Acquisition of some might facilitate the Acquisition of certain others, I arrang'd them with that View as they stand above. *Temperance* first, as it tends to procure that Coolness and Clearness of Head, which is so necessary where constant Vigilance was to be kept up, and Guard maintained, against the unremitting Attraction of ancient Habits, and the Force of perpetual Temptations. This being acquir'd and establish'd, *Silence* would be more easy, and my Desire being to gain Knowledge at the same time that I improv'd in Virtue, and considering that in Conversation it was obtain'd rather by the Use of the Ears than of the Tongue, and therefore wishing to break a Habit I was getting into of Prattling, Punning and Joking, which only made me acceptable to trifling Company, I gave *Silence* the second Place. This, and the next, *Order,* I expected would allow me more Time for attending to my Project and my Studies; RESOLUTION once become habitual, would keep me firm in my Endeavours to obtain all the subsequent Virtues; *Frugality* and *Industry,* by freeing me from my remaining Debt, and producing Affluence and Independence would make more easy the Practice of *Sincerity* and *Justice,* etc. etc. Conceiving then that agreeable to the Advice of Pythagoras in his Golden Verses, daily Examination would be necessary, I contriv'd the following Method for conducting that Examination.

I made a little Book in which I alloted a Page for each of the Virtues, I rul'd each Page with red Ink so as to have seven Columns, one for each Day of the Week, marking each Column with a Letter for the Day. I cross'd these Columns with thirteen red Lines, marking the Beginning of each Line with the first Letter of one of the Virtues, on which Line and in its proper Column I might mark by a little black Spot every Fault I found upon Examination, to have been committed respecting that Virtue upon that Day.

I determined to give a Week's strict Attention to each of the Virtues successively. Thus in the first Week my great Guard was to avoid every the least Offence against Temperance, leaving the other Virtues to their ordinary Chance, only marking every Evening the Faults of the Day. Thus if in the first Week I could keep my first Line marked T clear of Spots, I suppos'd the Habit of that Virtue so much strengthen'd and its opposite weaken'd, that I might venture extending my Attention to include the next, and for the following Week keep both Lines clear of Spots. Proceeding thus to the last, I could go thro' a Course complete in Thirteen Weeks, and four Courses in a Year. And like him who having a Garden to weed, does not attempt to eradicate all the bad Herbs at once, which would exceed his Reach and his Strength, but works on one of the Beds at a time, and having accomplish'd the first proceeds to a second; so I should have, (I hoped) the encouraging Pleasure of seeing on my Pages the Progress

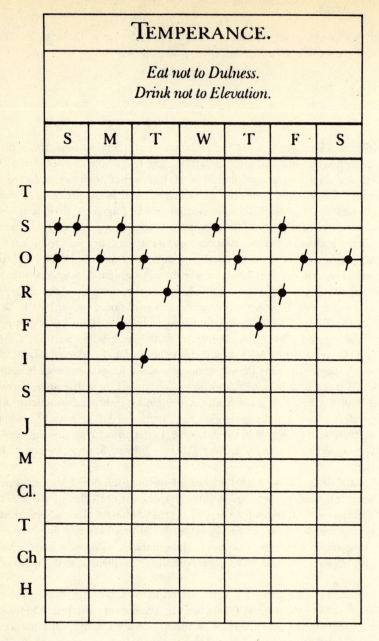

	S	M	T	W	T	F	S
T							
S	✦✦	✦			✦	✦	
O	✦	✦	✦		✦	✦	✦
R			✦			✦	
F		✦			✦		
I			✦				
S							
J							
M							
Cl.							
T							
Ch							
H							

I made in Virtue, by clearing successively my Lines of their Spots, till in the End by a Number of Courses, I should be happy in viewing a clean Book after a thirteen Weeks' daily Examination.

   This my little Book had for its Motto these Lines from *Addison's Cato,*

> Here will I hold: If there is a Pow'r above us,
>   (And that there is, all Nature cries aloud

Thro' all her Works) he must delight in Virtue,
And that which he delights in must be happy.

Another from *Cicero*.

O Vitæ Philosophia Dux! O Virtutum indagatrix, expultrixque vitiorum! Unus dies bene, et ex preceptis tuis actus, peccanti immortalitati est anteponendus.[1]

Another from the Proverbs of Solomon speaking of Wisdom or Virtue;

Length of Days is in her right hand, and in her Left Hand Riches and Honors; Her Ways are Ways of Pleasantness, and all her Paths are Peace.

III, 16, 17

And conceiving God to be the Fountain of Wisdom, I thought it right and necessary to solicit his Assistance for obtaining it; to this End I form'd the following little Prayer, which was prefix'd to my Tables of Examination, for daily Use.

O Powerful Goodness! bountiful Father! merciful Guide! Increase in me that Wisdom which discovers my truest Interests; Strengthen my Resolutions to perform what that Wisdom dictates. Accept my kind Offices to thy other Children, as the only Return in my Power for thy continual Favors to me.

I us'd also sometimes a little Prayer which I took from *Thomson's* Poems, viz.

Father of Light and Life, thou Good supreme,
O teach me what is good, teach me thy self!
Save me from Folly, Vanity and Vice,
From every low Pursuit, and fill my Soul
With Knowledge, conscious Peace, and Virtue pure,
Sacred, substantial, neverfading Bliss!

The Precept of *Order* requiring that *every Part of my Business should have its allotted Time,* one Page in my little Book contain'd the following Scheme of Employment for the Twenty-four Hours of a natural Day.

I enter'd upon the Execution of this Plan for Self-examination, and continu'd it with occasional Intermissions for some time. I was surpris'd to find myself so much fuller of Faults than I had imagined, but I had the Satisfaction of seeing them diminish. To avoid the Trouble of renewing now and then my little Book, which by scraping out the Marks on the Paper of old Faults to make room for new Ones in a new Course, became full of Holes: I transferr'd my Tables and Precepts to the Ivory Leaves of a Memorandum Book, on which the Lines were drawn with red Ink that made a durable Stain, and on those Lines I mark'd my Faults with a black Lead Pencil, which Marks I could easily wipe out with a wet Sponge. After a while I went thro' one Course only in a Year, and afterwards only one in several Years; till at length I omitted them entirely, being employ'd in Voyages and Business abroad with a Multiplicity of Affairs, that interfered. But I always carried my little Book with me.

My Scheme of ORDER, gave me the most Trouble, and I found, that tho' it might be practicable where a Man's Business was such as to leave him the Disposition of his

---

1. "O, Philosophy, guide of life! O teacher of virtue and corrector of vice. One day of virtue is better than an eternity of vice."

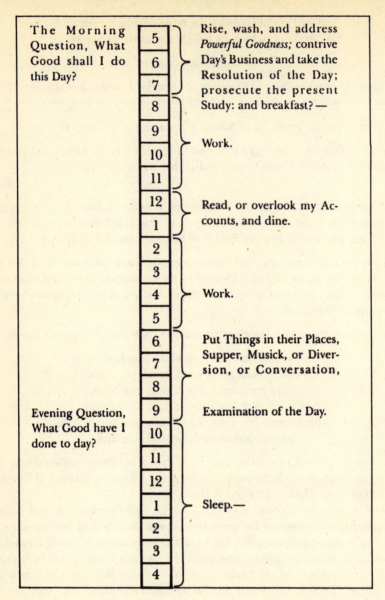

The Morning Question, What Good shall I do this Day?

5	Rise, wash, and address *Powerful Goodness;* contrive Day's Business and take the Resolution of the Day; prosecute the present Study: and breakfast? —
6	
7	
8	
9	Work.
10	
11	
12	Read, or overlook my Accounts, and dine.
1	
2	Work.
3	
4	
5	
6	Put Things in their Places, Supper, Musick, or Diversion, or Conversation,
7	
8	
9	Examination of the Day.
10	
11	
12	
1	Sleep.—
2	
3	
4	

Evening Question, What Good have I done to day?

Time, that of a Journeyman Printer for instance, it was not possible to be exactly observ'd by a Master, who must mix with the World, and often receive People of Business at their own Hours. *Order* too, with regard to Places for Things, Papers, etc. I found extremely difficult to acquire. I had not been early accustomed to it, and having an exceeding good Memory, I was not so sensible of the Inconvenience attending Want of Method. This Article therefore cost me so much painful Attention and my Faults in it vex'd me so much, and I made so little Progress in Amendment, and had such frequent Relapses, that I was almost ready to give up the Attempt, and content myself with a faulty Character in that respect. Like the Man who in buying an Axe of a Smith my Neighbor, desired to have the whole of its Surface as bright as the Edge; the Smith consented to grind it bright for him if he would turn the Wheel. He turn'd while the Smith press'd the broad Face of the Axe hard and heavily on the Stone, which made the Turning of it very fatiguing. The Man came every now and then from the Wheel to see how the Work went on; and at length would take his Axe as it was without farther Grinding. No, says the Smith, Turn on, turn on; we shall have it bright by and by; as yet 'tis only speckled. Yes, says the Man; but—*I think I like a speckled Axe best.*—And I believe this may have been the Case with many who having for want of some such Means as I employ'd found the Difficulty of obtaining good, and breaking bad Habits, in other Points of Vice and Virtue, have given up the Struggle, and concluded that *a speckled Axe was best.* For something that pretended to be Reason was every now and then suggesting to me, that such extreme Nicety as I exacted of myself might be a kind of Foppery in Morals, which if it were known would make me ridiculous; that a perfect Character might be attended with the Inconvenience of being envied and hated; and that a benevolent Man should allow a few Faults in himself, to keep his Friends in Countenance.

In Truth I found myself incorrigible with respect to *Order;* and now I am grown old, and my Memory bad, I feel very sensibly the want of it. But on the whole, tho' I never arrived at the Perfection I had been so ambitious of obtaining, but fell far short of it, yet I was by the Endeavour made a better and a happier Man than I otherwise should have been, if I had not attempted it; As those who aim at perfect Writing by imitating the engraved Copies, tho' they never reach the wish'd for Excellence of those Copies, their Hand is mended by the Endeavour, and is tolerable while it continues fair and legible.

And it may be well my Posterity should be informed, that to this little Artifice, with the Blessing of God, their Ancestor ow'd the constant Felicity of his Life down to his 79th Year in which this is written. What Reverses may attend the Remainder is in the Hand of Providence: But if they arrive, the Reflection on past Happiness enjoy'd ought to help his Bearing them with more Resignation. To *Temperance* he ascribes his long-continu'd Health, and what is still left to him of a good Constitution. To *Industry* and *Frugality* the early Easiness of his Circumstances, and Acquisition of his Fortune, with all that Knowledge which enabled him to be an useful Citizen, and obtain'd for him some Degree of Reputation among the Learned. To *Sincerity* and *Justice* the Confidence of his Country, and the honorable Employs it conferr'd upon him. And to the joint Influence of the whole Mass of the Virtues, even in their imperfect State he was able to acquire them, all that Evenness of Temper, and that Cheerfulness in Conversation which makes his Company still sought for, and aggreeable even to his younger Acquaintance. I hope therefore that some of my Descendants may follow the Example and reap the Benefit.

It will be remark'd that, tho' my Scheme was not wholly without Religion there was in it no Mark of any of the distinguishing Tenets of any particular Sect. I had purposely avoided them; for being fully persuaded of the Utility and Excellency of my Method, and that it might be serviceable to People in all Religions, and intending some time or other to publish it, I would not have anything in it that should prejudice anyone of any Sect against it. I purposed writing a little Comment on each Virtue, in which I would have shown the Advantages of possessing it,[2] and the Mischiefs attending its

2. "Nothing so likely to make a Man's Fortune as Virtue." [BF memo]

opposite Vice; and I should have called my Book the ART *of Virtue,* because it would have shown the *Means and Manner* of obtaining Virtue; which would have distinguish'd it from the mere Exhortation to be good, that does not instruct and indicate the Means; but is like the Apostle's Man of verbal Charity, who only, without showing to the Naked and the Hungry *how* or where they might get Clothes or Victuals, exhorted them to be fed and clothed. *James* II, 15, 16.

But it so happened that my Intention of writing and publishing this Comment was never fulfilled. I did indeed, from time to time put down short Hints of the Sentiments, Reasonings, etc. to be made use of in it; some of which I have still by me: But the necessary close Attention to private Business in the earlier part of Life, and public Business since, have occasioned my postponing it. For it being connected in my Mind with a *great and extensive Project* that required the whole Man to execute, and which an unforeseen Succession of Employs prevented my attending to, it has hitherto remain'd unfinish'd.

In this Piece it was my Design to explain and enforce this Doctrine, that vicious Actions are not hurtful because they are forbidden, but forbidden because they are hurtful, the Nature of Man alone consider'd: That it was therefore every one's Interest to be virtuous, who wish'd to be happy even in this World. And I should from this Circumstance (there being always in the World a Number of rich Merchants, Nobility, States and Princes, who have need of honest Instruments for the Management of their Affairs, and such being so rare) have endeavoured to convince young Persons, that no Qualities were so likely to make a poor Man's Fortune as those of Probity and Integrity.

My List of Virtues contain'd at first but twelve: But a Quaker Friend having kindly inform'd me that I was generally thought proud; that my Pride show'd itself frequently in Conversation; that I was not content with being in the right when discussing any Point, but was overbearing and rather insolent; of which he convinc'd me by mentioning several Instances; I determined endeavouring to cure myself if I could of this Vice or Folly among the rest, and I added *Humility* to my List, giving an extensive Meaning to the Word. I cannot boast of much Success in acquiring the *Reality* of this Virtue; but I had a good deal with regard to the *Appearance* of it. I made it a Rule to forbear all direct Contradiction to the Sentiments of others, and all positive Assertion of my own. I even forbid myself, agreeable to the old Laws of our Junto, the Use of every Word or Expression in the Language that imported a fix'd Opinion; such as *certainly, undoubtedly,* etc. and I adopted instead of them, I *conceive,* I *apprehend,* or I *imagine* a thing to be so or so, or it so appears to me at present. When another asserted something that I thought an Error, I denied myself the Pleasure of contradicting him abruptly, and of showing immediately some Absurdity in his Proposition; and in answering I began by observing that in certain Cases or Circumstances his Opinion would be right, but that in the present case there *appear'd* or *seem'd* to me some Difference, etc. I soon found the Advantage of this Change in my Manners. The Conversations I engag'd in went on more pleasantly. The modest way in which I propos'd my Opinions, procur'd them a readier Reception and less Contradiction; I had less Mortification when I was found to be in the wrong, and I more easily prevail'd with others to give up their Mistakes and join with me when I hapen'd to be in the right. And this Mode, which I at first put on, with some violence to natural Inclination, became at length so easy and so habitual to me, that perhaps for these Fifty Years past no one has ever heard a dogmatical Expression escape me. And to this Habit (after my Character of Integrity) I think it principally owing, that I had early so much Weight with my Fellow Citizens, when I proposed new Institutions, or Alterations in the old; and so much Influence in public Councils when I became a Member. For I was but a bad Speaker, never eloquent, subject to much Hesitation in my choice of Words, hardly correct in Language, and yet I generally carried my Points.

In reality there is perhaps no one of our natural Passions so hard to subdue as *Pride*. Disguise it, struggle with it, beat it down, stifle it, mortify it as much as one pleases, it is still alive, and will every now and then peep out and show itself. You will see it perhaps often in this History. For even if I could conceive that I had completely overcome it, I should probably be proud of my Humility.

Thus far written at Passy, 1784.

I am now about to write at home, August 1788, but cannot have the help expected from my Papers, many of them being lost in the War. I have however found the following.

Having mentioned *a great and extensive Project* which I had conceiv'd, it seems proper that some Account should be here given of that Project and its Object. Its first Rise in my Mind appears in the following little Paper, accidentally preserv'd, viz.

Observations on my Reading History in Library, May 9, 1731.

"That the great Affairs of the World, the Wars, Revolutions, etc. are carried on and effected by Parties.

"That the View of these Parties is their present general Interest, or what they take to be such.

"That the different Views of these different Parties, occasion all Confusion.

"That while a Party is carrying on a general Design, each Man has his particular private Interest in View.

"That as soon as a Party has gain'd its general Point, each Member becomes intent upon his particular Interest, which thwarting others, breaks that Party into Divisions, and occasions more Confusion.

"That few in Public Affairs act from a mere View of the Good of their Country, whatever they may pretend; and tho' their Actings bring real Good to their Country, yet Men primarily consider'd that their own and their Country's Interest was united, and did not act from a Principle of Benevolence.

"That fewer still in public Affairs act with a View to the Good of Mankind.

"There seems to me at present to be great Occasion for raising an united Party for Virtue, by forming the Virtuous and good Men of all Nations into a regular Body, to be govern'd by suitable good and wise Rules, which good and wise Men may probably be more unanimous in their Obedience to, than common People are to common Laws.

"I at present think, that whoever attempts this aright, and is well qualified, cannot fail of pleasing God, and of meeting with Success.

B.F."

Revolving this Project in my Mind, as to be undertaken hereafter when my Circumstances should afford me the necessary Leisure, I put down from time to time on Pieces of Paper such Thoughts as occur'd to me respecting it. Most of these are lost; but I find one purporting to be the Substance of an intended Creed, containing as I thought the Essentials of every known Religion, and being free of everything that might shock the Professors of any Religion. It is express'd in these Words, viz.

"That there is one God who made all things.

"That he governs the World by his Providence.

"That he ought to be worshipped by Adoration, Prayer and Thanksgiving.

"But that the most acceptable Service of God is doing Good to Man.

"That the Soul is immortal.

"And that God will certainly reward Virtue and punish Vice either here or hereafter."

My Ideas at that time were, that the Sect should be begun and spread at first among young and single Men only; that each Person to be initiated should not only declare his Assent to such Creed, but should have exercis'd himself with the Thirteen Weeks' Examination and Practice of the Virtues as in the before-mention'd Model; that the Existence of such a Society should be kept a Secret till it was become considerable, to prevent Solicitations for the Admission of improper Persons; but that the Members should each of them search among his Acquaintance for ingenuous well-disposed Youths, to whom with prudent Caution the Scheme should be gradually communicated: That the Members should engage to afford their Advice, Assistance and Support to each other in promoting one another's Interest, Business and Advancement in Life: That for Distinction we should be call'd the Society of the *Free and Easy;* Free, as being by the general Practice and Habit of the Virtues, free from the Dominion of Vice, and particularly by the Practice of Industry and Frugality, free from Debt, which exposes a Man to Confinement and a Species of Slavery to his Creditors. This is as much as I can now recollect of the Project, except that I communicated it in part to two young Men, who adopted it with some Enthusiasm. But my then narrow Circumstances, and the Necessity I was under of sticking close to my Business, occasion'd my Postponing the farther Prosecution of it at that time, and my multifarious Occupations public and private induc'd me to continue postponing, so that it has been omitted till I have no longer Strength or Activity left sufficient for such an Enterprise: Tho I am still of Opinion that it was a practicable Scheme, and might have been very useful, by forming a great Number of good Citizens: and I was not discourag'd by the seeming Magnitude of the Undertaking, as I have always thought that one Man of tolerable Abilities may work great Changes, and accomplish great Affairs among Mankind, if he first forms a good Plan, and, cutting off all Amusements or other Employments that would divert his Attention, makes the Execution of that same Plan his sole Study and Business.

In 1732 I first published my Almanac, under the Name of *Richard Saunders,* it was continu'd by me about 25 Years, commonly call'd *Poor Richard's Almanac.* I endeavour'd to make it both entertaining and useful, and it accordingly came to be in such Demand that I reap'd considerable Profit from it, vending annually near ten Thousand. And observing that it was generally read, scarce any Neighborhood in the Province being without it, I consider'd it as a proper Vehicle for conveying Instruction among the common People, who bought scarce any other Books. I therefore filled all the little Spaces that occur'd between the Remarkable Days in the Calendar, with Proverbial Sentences, chiefly such as inculcated Industry and Frugality, as the Means of procuring Wealth and thereby securing Virtue, it being more difficult for a Man in Want to act always honestly, as (to use here one of those Proverbs) *it is hard for an empty Sack to stand upright*. These Proverbs, which contained the Wisdom of many Ages and Nations, I assembled and form'd into a connected Discourse prefix'd to the Almanac of 1757, as the Harangue of a wise old Man to the People attending an Auction. The bringing all these scatter'd Counsels thus into a Focus, enabled them to make greater Impression. The Piece being universally approved was copied in all the Newspapers of the Continent, reprinted in Britain on a Broadside to be stuck up in Houses, two Translations were made of it in French, and great Numbers bought by the Clergy and Gentry to distribute gratis among their poor Parishioners and Tenants. In Pennsylvania, as it discouraged useless Expense in foreign Superfluities, some thought it had its share of Influence in producing that growing Plenty of Money which was observable for several Years after its Publication.

JOHN ADAMS

"A Dissertation on the Canon and the Feudal Law"
1765

Vain, irritable, inordinately suspicious, yet disinterested, profound, scrupulously honest, and so passionate in his devotion to the right as to be lovable—so wrote Thomas Jefferson of the personality traits of his friend and comrade and soon to be political enemy John Adams (1735–1826). These characteristics, which his biographers have come to denominate as quintessentially "Puritan" ones, also suffused a good deal of Adams's political writings, and nowhere more so than in his pre-Revolutionary "Dissertation" justifying American opposition to the Stamp Act. The act, in Adams's view, was nothing less than an assault on the New England way. But to make his case, he had to republicanize his region's myth; liberty more than godliness, in Adams's reading, inspired Winthrop's "City upon a Hill." Even this version the enlightened Adams recast by making the passion for knowledge, which he ambiguously linked with "power," both the fundamental spring and the end of liberty. Finally, Adams portrayed such a starkly oppressive countersystem of priestcraft and feudal oppression that even small elements of such a system—like the Stamp Act—seemed plausibly tantamount to "a direct and formal design . . . to enslave all America." For a good introduction to the development of Adams's political ideas, see John R. Howe, Jr., *The Changing Political Thought of John Adams* (Princeton, 1966). Paul Conkin delineates the Puritan cast of Adams's outlook in his *Puritans and Pragmatists: Eight Eminent American Thinkers* (New York, 1968), 109–48. Trevor Colbourn includes a useful chapter on the relation of Adams's views of history to his politics in *The Lamp of Experience: Whig History and the Intellectual Origins of the American Revolution* (Chapel Hill, 1965), 83–106.

"Ignorance and inconsideration are the two great causes of the ruin of mankind."
This is an observation of Dr. *Tillotson,* with relation to the interest of his fellow-men,
in a future and immortal state: But it is of equal truth and importance, if applied to
the happiness of men in society, on this side the grave. In the earliest ages of the world,
absolute monarchy seems to have been the universal form of government. Kings, and
a few of their great counsellors and captains, exercised a cruel tyranny over the people
who held a rank in the scale of intelligence, in those days, but little higher than the
camels and elephants, that carried them and their engines to war.

By what causes it was bro't to pass, that the people in the middle ages, became
more *intelligent* in general, would not perhaps be possible in these days to discover:
But the fact is certain; and wherever a general knowledge and sensibility have prevail'd among the *people,* arbitrary government, and every kind of oppression, have
lessened and disappeared in proportion. Man has certainly an exalted soul! and the
same principle in humane nature, that aspiring noble principle, founded in benevolence, and cherished by knowledge, I mean the love of power, which has been so often
the cause of *slavery,* has, whenever freedom has existed, been the cause of *freedom.* If
it is this principle, that has always prompted the princes and nobles of the earth, by
every species of fraud and violence, to shake off, all the *limitations* of their power; it
is the same that has always stimulated the common people to aspire at independency,
and to endeavor at confining the power of the great within the lmits of *equity* and
reason.

The poor people, it is true, have been much less successful than the great. They
have seldom found either leisure or opportunity to form an union and exert their
strength—ignorant as they were of arts and letters, they have seldom been able to
frame and support a regular opposition. This, however, has been known, by the great,
to be the temper of mankind, and they have accordingly laboured, in all ages, to wrest
from the populace, as they are contemptuously called, the knowledge of their rights
and wrongs, and the power to assert the former or redress the latter. I say RIGHTS,
for such they have, undoubtedly, antecedent to all earthly government—*Rights* that
cannot be repealed or restrained by human laws—*Rights* derived from the great legislator of the universe.

Since the promulgation of christianity, the two greatest systems of tyranny, that
have sprung from this original, are the *cannon* and the *feudal* law. The desire of dominion, that great principle by which we have attempted to account for so much good,
and so much evil, is, when *properly restrained,* a very useful and noble movement in
the human mind: But when such restraints are taken off, it becomes an incroaching,
grasping, restless and ungovernable power. Numberless have been the systems of iniquity, contrived by the great, for the gratification of this passion in themselves: but in
none of them were they ever more successful, than in the invention and establishment
of the *cannon* and the *feudal* law.

By the *former* of these, the most refined, sublime, extensive, and astonishing constitution of policy, that ever was conceived by the mind of man, was framed by the
Romish clergy for the aggrandisement of their own order. All the epithets I have here
given to the Romish policy are just: and will be allowed to be so, when it is considered,

Source: Papers of John Adams, ed. Robert J. Taylor. Vol. 1, ed. Robert J. Taylor, Mary-Jo Kline, and Gregg
L. Lint (Cambridge, Mass.: Harvard University Press, 1977), 111–28. Editors' notes and section titles omitted. Reprinted by permission of Harvard University Press, Copyright © 1977.

that they even persuaded mankind to believe, faithfully and undoubtingly, that GOD almighty had intrusted *them* with the keys of heaven; whose gates *they* might open and close at pleasure—with a power of dispensation over all the rules and obligations of morality—with authority to licence all sorts of sins and crimes—with a power of deposing princes, and absolving subjects from allegiance—with a power of procuring or withholding the rain of heaven and the beams of the sun—with the management of earthquakes, pestilence and famine. Nay with the mysterious, awful, incomprehensible power of creating out of bread and wine, the flesh and blood of God himself. All these opinions, they were enabled to spread and rivet among the people, by reducing their minds to a state of sordid ignorance and staring timidity; and by infusing into them a *religious* horror of letters and knowledge. Thus was human nature chained fast for ages, in a cruel, shameful and deplorable servitude, to him and his subordinate tyrants, who, it was foretold, would exalt himself above all that was called God, and that was worshipped.

In the latter, we find another system similar in many respects, to the former: which altho' it was originally formed perhaps, for the necessary defence of a *barbarous* people, against the inroads and invasions of her neighbouring nations; yet, for the same purposes of tyranny, cruelty and lust, which had dictated the *cannon* law, it was soon adopted by almost all the princes of Europe, and wrought into the constitutions of their *government*. It was originally, a code of laws, for a vast army, in a perpetual encampment. The general was invested with the sovereign propriety of all the lands within the territory. Of *him,* as his servants and vassals, the first rank of his great officers held the lands: and in the same manner, the other subordinate officers held of *them:* and all ranks and degrees held their lands, by a variety of *duties* and *services,* all tending to bind the chains the faster, on *every* order of mankind. In this manner, the common people were held together, in herds and clans, in a state of *servile* dependance on their lords; bound, even by the tenure of their lands to follow them, whenever they commanded, to their wars; and in a state of total ignorance of every thing divine and human, excepting the use of arms, and the culture of their lands.

But, another event still more calamitous to human liberty, was a wicked confederacy, between the *two systems* of tyranny above described. It seems to have been even *stipulated* between them, that the *temporal* grandees should contribute every thing in their power to maintain the ascendency of the *priesthood;* and that the spiritual grandees, in their turn, should employ that ascendency over the *consciences* of the *people,* in impressing on their minds, a *blind, implicit* obedience to civil magistracy.

Thus, as long as this confederacy lasted, and the people were held in ignorance; Liberty, and with her, Knowledge, and Virtue too, seem to have deserted the earth; and one age of darkness, succeeded another, till GOD, in his benign providence, raised up the champions, who began and conducted the *reformation.* From the time of the reformation, to the first settlement of *America,* knowledge gradually spread in Europe, but especially in *England;* and in proportion as *that* increased and spread among the people, *ecclesiastical* and *civil* tyranny, which I use as synonimous expressions, for the *cannon* and *feudal* laws, seem to have lost their strength and weight. The people grew more and more sensible of the wrong that was done them, by these systems; more and more impatient under it; and determined at all hazards to rid themselves of it; till, at last, under the *execrable* race of the *Steuarts,* the struggle between the people and the confederacy aforesaid of temporal and spiritual tyranny, became formidable, violent and bloody.

It was this great struggle, that peopled America. It was not religion *alone,* as is commonly supposed; but it was a love of *universal Liberty,* and an hatred, a dread, an horror of the infernal confederacy, before described, that projected, conducted, and accomplished the settlement of America.

It was a resolution formed, by a sensible people, I mean the *Puritans,* almost in despair. They had become intelligent in general, and many of them learned. For this fact I have the testimony of archbishop *King* himself, who observed of that people, that they were more intelligent, and better read than even the members of the church whom he censures warmly for that reason. This people had been so vexed, and tortured by the powers of those days, for no other crime than their knowledge, and their freedom of enquiry and examination, and they had so much reason to despair of deliverance from those miseries, on that side the ocean; that they at last resolved to fly to the *wilderness* for refuge, from the temporal and spiritual principalities and powers, and plagues, and scourges, of their *native* country.

After their arrival here, they began their settlements, and formed their plan both of ecclesiastical and civil government, in *direct opposition* to the *cannon* and the *feudal* systems. The leading men among them, both of the clergy and the laity, were men of sense and learning: To many of them, the historians, orators, poets and philosophers of *Greece* and *Rome* were quite familiar: and some of them have left libraries that are still in being, consisting chiefly of volumes, in which the wisdom of the most enlightened ages and nations is deposited, written however in languages, which their great grandsons, *tho' educated in European Universities,* can scarcely read.

Thus accomplished were many of the first Planters of these Colonies. It may be thought polite and fasionable, by many modern fine Gentlemen perhaps, to deride the Characters of these Persons, as enthusiastical, superstitious and republican: But such ridicule is founded in nothing but foppery and affectation, and is grosly injurious and false. Religious to some degree of enthusiasm it may be admitted they were; but this can be no peculiar derogation from their character, because it was at that time almost the universal character, not only of England, but of Christendom. Had this however, been otherwise, their enthusiasm, considering the principles in which it was founded, and the ends to which it was directed, far from being a reproach to them, was greatly to their honour: for I believe it will be found universally true, that no great enterprize, for the honour or happiness of mankind, was ever achieved, without a large mixture of that noble infirmity. Whatever imperfections may be justly ascribed to them, which however are as few, as any mortals have discovered their judgment in framing their policy, was founded in wise, humane and benevolent principles; It was founded in revelation, and in reason too; It was consistent with the principles, of the best, and greatest, and wisest legislators of antiquity. Tyranny in every form, shape, and appearance was their disdain, and abhorrence; no fear of punishment, not even of *Death* itself, in exquisite tortures, had been sufficient to conquer, that steady, manly, pertenacious spirit, with which they had opposed the tyrants of those days, in church and state. They were very far from being enemies to monarchy; and they knew as well as any men, the just regard and honour that is due to the character of a dispenser of the misteries of the gospel of Grace: But they saw clearly, that popular powers must be placed, as a guard, a countroul, a ballance, to the powers of the monarch, and the priest, in every government, or else it would soon become the man of sin, the whore of Babylon, the mystery of iniquity, a great and detestable system of fraud, violence, and usurpation. Their greatest concern seems to have been to establish a government of the church more consistent with the scriptures, and a government of the state more agreable to the dignity of humane nature, than any they had seen in Europe: and to transmit such a government down to their posterity, with the means of securing and preserving it, for ever. To render the popular power in their new government, as great and wise, as their principles and theory, i.e. as human nature and the christian religion require it should be, they endeavored to remove from it, as many of the feudal inequalities and dependencies, as could be spared, consistently with the preservation of a mild limited monarchy. And in this they discovered the depth of their wisdom, and the warmth of their friendship to human nature. But the first place is due to religion. They saw clearly, that of all the nonsense and delusion which had ever passed thro' the mind of man, none had ever been more extravagant than the notions of absolutions, indelible characters, uninterrupted successions, and the rest of those phantastical ideas, derived from the common law, which had thrown such a glare of mystery, sanctity, reverence and right reverence, eminence and holiness, around the idea of a priest, as no mortal could deserve, and as always must from the constitution of human nature, be dangerous in society. For this reason, they demolished the whole system of Diocesan episcopacy and deriding, as all reasonable and impartial men must do, the ridiculous fancies of sanctified effluvia from episcopal fingers, they established sacerdotal ordination, on the foundation of the bible and common sense. This conduct at once imposed an obligation on the whole body of the clergy, to industry, virtue, piety and learning, and rendered that whole body infinitely more independent on the civil powers, in all respects than they could be where they were formed into a scale of subordination, from a pope down to priests and fryars and confessors, necessarily and essentially a sordid, stupid, wretched herd; or than they could be in any other country, where an archbishop held the place of an universal bishop, and the vicars and curates that of the ignorant, dependent, miserable rabble aforesaid; and infinitely more sensible and learned than they could be in either. This subject has been seen in the same light, by many illustrious patriots, who have lived in America, since the days of our fore fathers, and who have adored their memory for the same reason. And methinks there has not appeared in New England a stronger veneration for their memory, a more penetrating insight into the grounds and principles and spirit of their policy, nor a more earnest desire of perpetuating the blessings of it to posterity, than that fine institution of the late chief justice Dudley, of a lecture against popery, and on the validity of presbyterian ordination. This was certainly intended by that wise and excellent man, as an eternal memento of the wisdom and goodness of the very principles that settled America. But I must again return to the feudal law.

The adventurers so often mentioned, had an utter contempt of all that dark ribaldry of hereditary indefeasible right—the Lord's anointed—and the divine miraculous original of government, with which the priesthood had inveloped the feudal monarch in clouds and mysteries, and from whence they had deduced the most mischievous of all doctrines, that of passive obedience and non resistance. They knew that government was a plain, simple, intelligible thing founded in nature and reason and quite comprehensible by common sense. They detested all the base services, and servile dependencies of the feudal system. They knew that no such unworthy dependences took place in the ancient seats of liberty, the republic of Greece and Rome: and they tho't all such slavish subordinations were equally inconsistent with the constitution of human nature and that religious liberty, with which Jesus had made them free. This was certainly the opinion they had formed, and they were far from being singular or extravagant in thinking so. Many celebrated modern writers, in Europe, have espoused the same sentiments. Lord Kaim's, a Scottish writer of great reputation, whose authority in this case ought to have the more weight, as his countrymen have not the most worthy ideas of liberty, speaking of the feudal law, says, "A constitution so contradictory to all the principles which govern mankind, can never be brought about, one should imagine, but by foreign conquest or native usurpations." Brit. Ant. P. 2. Rousseau speaking of the same system, calls it "That most iniquitous and absurd form of government by which human nature was so shamefully degraded." Social Compact, Page 164. It would be easy to multiply authorities, but it must be needless, because as the original of this form of government was among savages, as the spirit of it is military and despotic, every writer, who would allow the people to have any right to life or property, or freedom, more than the beasts of the field, and who was not hired or inlisted under arbitrary lawless power, has been always willing to admit the feudal system to be inconsistent with liberty and the rights of mankind.

To have holden their lands, allodially, or for every man to have been the sovereign lord and proprietor of the ground he occupied, would have constituted a government, too nearly like a commonwealth. They were contented therefore to hold their lands of their King, as their sovereign Lord, and to him they were willing to render homage: but to no mesne and subordinate Lords, nor were they willing to submit to any of the baser services. In all this, they were so strenuous, that they have even transmitted to their posterity, a very general contempt and detestation of holdings by quit rents: As they have also an hereditary ardor for liberty and thirst for knowledge.

They were convinced by their knowledge of human nature derived from history and their own experience, that nothing could preserve their posterity from the encroachments of the two systems of tyranny, in opposition to which, as has been observed already, they erected their government in church and state, but knowledge diffused generally thro' the whole body of the people. Their civil and religious principles, therefore, conspired to prompt them to use every measure, and take every precaution in their power, to propagate and perpetuate knowledge. For this purpose they laid, very early the foundations of colleges, and invested them with ample priviledges and emoluments; and it is remarkable, that they have left among their posterity, so universal an affection and veneration for those seminaries, and for liberal education, that the meanest of the people contribute chearfully to the support and maintenance of them every year, and that nothing is more generally popular than projections for the honour, reputation and advantage of those seats of learning. But the wisdom and benevolence of our fathers rested not here. They made an early provision by law, that every town consisting of so many families, should be always furnished with a grammar school. They made it a crime for such a town to be destitute of a grammar school master, for a few months, and subjected it to an heavy penalty. So that the education of all ranks of people was made the care and expence of the public in a manner, that I believe has been unknown to any other people ancient or modern.

The consequences of these establishments we see and feel every day. A native of America who cannot read and write is as rare an appearance, as a Jacobite or a Roman Catholic, i.e. as rare as a Comet or an Earthquake. It has been observed, that we are all of us, lawyers, divines, politicians and philosophers. And I have good authorities to say that all candid foreigners who have passed thro' this country, and conversed freely with all sorts of people here, will allow, that they have never seen so much knowledge and civility among the common people in any part of the world. It is true, there has been among us a party for some years, consisting chiefly not of the descendants of the first settlers of this country but of high churchmen and high statesmen, imported since, who affect to censure this provision for the education of our youth as a needless expence, and an imposition upon the rich in favour of the poor—and as an institution productive of idleness and vain speculation among the people, whose time and attention it is said ought to be devoted to labour, and not to public affairs or to examination into the conduct of their superiors. And certain officers of the crown, and certain other missionaries of ignorance, foppery, servility and slavery, have been most inclined to countenance and increase the same party. Be it remembred, however, that liberty must at all hazards be supported. We have a right to it, derived from our Maker. But if we had not, our fathers have earned, and bought it for us, at the expence of their ease, their estates, their pleasure, and their blood. And liberty cannot be preserved without a general knowledge among the people, who have a right from the frame of their nature, to knowledge, as their great Creator who does nothing in vain, has given them understandings, and a desire to know—but besides this they have a right, an indisputable, unalienable, indefeasible divine right to that most dreaded, and envied kind of knowledge, I mean of the characters and conduct of their rulers. Rulers are no more than attorneys, agents and trustees for the people; and if the cause, the interest and trust is insidiously betray'd, or wantonly trifled away, the people have a right to revoke the authority, that they themselves have deputed, and to constitute abler and better agents, attorneys and trustees. And the preservation of the means of knowledge, among the lowest ranks, is of more importance to the public, than all the property of all the rich men in the country. It is even of more consequence to the rich themselves, and to their posterity. The only question is whether it is a public emolument? and if it is, the rich ought undoubtedly to contribute in the same proportion, as to all other public burdens, i.e. in porportion to their wealth which is secured by public expences. But none of the means of information are more sacred, or have been cherished with more tenderness and care by the settlers of America, than the Press. Care has been taken, that the art of printing should be encouraged, and that it should be easy and cheap and safe for any person to communicate his thoughts to the public. And you, Messieurs Printers, whatever the tyrants of the earth may say of your paper, have done important service to your country, by your readiness and freedom in publishing the speculations of the curious. The stale, impudent insinuations of slander and sedition, with which the gormandizers of power have endeavor'd to discredit your paper, are so much the more to your honour; for the jaws of power are always opened to devour, and her arm is always stretched out if possible to destroy, the freedom of thinking, speaking and writing. And if the public interest, liberty and happiness have been in danger, from the ambition or avarice of any great man or number of great men, whatever may be their politeness, address, learning, ingenuity and in other respects integrity and humanity, you have done yourselves honour and your country service, by publishing and pointing out that avarice and ambition. These views are so much the more dangerous and pernicious, for the virtues with which they may be accompanied in the same character, and with so much the more watchful jealousy to be guarded against.

"Curse on such virtues, they've undone their country."

Be not intimidated therefore, by any terrors, from publishing with the utmost freedom, whatever can be warranted by the laws of your country; nor suffer yourselves to be wheedled out of your liberty, by any pretences of politeness, delicacy or decency. These as they are often used, are but three different names, for hypocrisy, chicanery and cowardice. Much less I presume will you be discouraged by any pretences, that malignant's on this side the water will *represent* your paper as factious and seditious, or that the Great on the other side the water will take offence at them. This Dread of *representation,* has had for a long time in this province effects very similar to what the physicians call an hydropho, or dread of water. It has made us delirious. And we have rushed headlong into the water, till we are almost drowned, out of simple or phrensical fear of it. Believe me, the character of this country has suffered more in Britain, by the pusillanimity with which we have borne many insults and indignities from the creatures of power at home, and the creatures of those creatures here, than it ever did or ever will by the freedom and spirit that has been or will be discovered in writing, or action. Believe me my countrymen, they have imbibed an opinion on the other side the water, that we are an ignorant, a timid and a stupid people, nay their tools on this side have often the impudence to dispute your bravery. But I hope in God the time is near at hand, when they will be fully convinced of your understanding, integrity and courage. But can any thing be more ridiculous, were it not too provoking to be laughed at, than to pretend that offence should be taken at home for writings here? Pray let them look at home. Is not the human understanding exhausted there? Are not reason, imagination, wit, passion, senses and all, tortured to find out satyr and invective against the characters of the vile and futile fellows who sometimes get into place and power? The most exceptionable paper that ever I saw here, is perfect prudence and modesty, in comparison of multitudes of their applauded writings. Yet the high regard they have for the freedom of the Press, indulges all. I must and will repeat it, your Paper deserves the patronage of every friend to his country. And whether the defamers of it are arrayed in robes of scarlet or sable, whether they lurk and skulk in an insurance office, whether they assume the venerable character of a Priest, the sly one of a scrivener, or the dirty, infamous, abandoned one of an informer, they are all the creatures and tools of the lust of domination.

The true source of our sufferings, has been our timidity.

We have been afraid to think. We have felt a reluctance to examining into the grounds of our privileges, and the extent in which we have an indisputable right to demand them against all the power and authority, on earth. And many who have not scrupled to examine for themselves, have yet for certain prudent reasons been cautious, and diffident of declaring the result of their enquiries.

The cause of this timidity is perhaps hereditary and to be traced back in history, as far as the cruel treatment the first settlers of this country received, before their embarkation for America, from the government at Home. Every body knows how dangerous it was to speak or write in favour of any thing in those days, but the triumphant system of religion and politicks. And our fathers were particularly, the objects of the persecutions and proscriptions of the times. It is not unlikely therefore, that, although they were inflexibly steady in refusing their positive assent to any thing against their principles, they might have contracted habits of reserve, and a cautious diffidence of asserting their opinions publickly. These habits they probably brought with them to America, and have transmitted down to us. Or, we may possibly account for this appearance, by the great affection and veneration, Americans have always entertained for the country from whence they sprang—or by the quiet temper for which they have been remarkable, no country having been less disposed to discontent than this—or by a sense they have, that it is their duty to acquiesce, under the administration of government, even when in many smaller matters gravaminous to them, and until the essentials of the great compact are destroy'd or invaded. These peculiar causes might operate upon them; but without these we all know, that human nature itself, from indolence, modesty, humanity or fear, has always too much reluctance to a manly assertion of its rights. Hence perhaps it has happened that nine tenths of the species, are groaning and gasping in misery and servitude.

But whatever the cause has been, the fact is certain, we have been excessively cautious of giving offence by complaining of grievances. And it is as certain that American governors, and their friends and all the crown officers have avail'd themselves of this disposition in the people. They have prevailed on us to consent to many things, which were grosly injurious to us, and to surrender many others with voluntary tameness, to which we had the clearest right. Have we not been treated formerly, with abominable insolence, by officers of the navy? I mean no insinuation against any gentleman now on this station, having heard no complaint of any one of them to his dishonor. Have not some generals, from England, treated us like servants, nay more like slaves than like Britons? Have we not been under the most ignominious contribution, the most abject submission, the most supercilious insults of some custom house officers? Have we not been trifled with, browbeaten, and trampled on, by former governors, in a manner which no king of England since James the second has dared to indulge towards his subjects? Have we not raised up one family, in them placed an unlimitted confidence, and been soothed and battered and intimidated by their influence, into a great part of this infamous tameness and submission? "These are serious and alarming questions, and deserve a dispassionate consideration."

This disposition has been the great wheel and the mainspring in the American machine of court politicks. We have been told that "the word 'Rights' is an offensive expression." That "the King his ministry and parliament will not endure to hear Americans talk of their Rights." That "Britain is the mother and we the children, that a filial duty and submission is due from us to her," and that "we ought to doubt our own judgment, and presume that she is right, even when she seems to us to shake the foundations of government." That "Britain is immensely rich and great and powerful, has fleets and armies at her command, which have been the dread and terror of the universe, and that she will force her own judgment into execution, right or wrong." But let me intreat you Sir to pause and consider. Do you consider your self as a missionary of loyalty or of rebellion? Are you not representing your King his ministry and parliament as tyrants, imperious, unrelenting tyrants by such reasoning as this? Is not this representing your most gracious sovereign, as endeavouring to destroy the foundations of his own throne? Are you not putting language into the royal mouth, which if fairly pursued will shew him to have no right to the crown on his own sacred head? Are you not representing every member of parliament as renouncing the transactions at Runningmede, and as repealing in effect the bill of rights, when the Lords and Commons asserted and vindicated the rights of the people and their own rights, and insisted on the King's assent to that assertion and vindication? Do you not represent them as forgetting that the prince of Orange, was created King William by the People, on purpose that their rights might be eternal and inviolable? Is there not something extremely fallacious, in the common-place images of mother country and children colonies? Are we the children of Great-Britain, any more than the cities of London, Exeter and Bath? Are we not brethren and fellow subjects, with those in Britain, only under a somewhat different method of legislation, and a totally different method of taxation? But admitting we are children; have not children a right to complain when their parents are attempting to break their limbs, to administer poison, or to sell them to enemies for slaves? Let me intreat you to consider, will the mother, be pleased, when you represent her as deaf to the cries of her children? When you compare her to the infamous miscreant, who lately stood on the gallows for starving her child? When you resemble her to Lady Macbeth in Shakespear, (I cannot think of it without horror)

> Who "had given suck, and knew
> How tender 'twas to love the Babe that milk'd her."
> But yet, who could
> "Even while 'twas smiling in her Face,
> Have pluck'd her Nipple from the boneless Gums,
> And dash'd the Brains out."

Let us banish forever from our minds, my countrymen, all such unworthy ideas of the King, his ministry and parliament. Let us not suppose, that all are become luxurious effeminate and unreasonable, on the other side the water, as many designing persons would insinuate. Let us presume, what is in fact true, that the spirit of liberty, is as ardent as ever among the body of the nation, though a few individuals may be corrupted. Let us take it for granted, that the same great spirit, which once gave Cæsar so warm a reception; which denounced hostilities against John 'till Magna Charta was signed; which severed the head of Charles the first from his body, and drove James the second from his kingdom; the same great spirit (may heaven preserve it till the earth shall be no more) which first seated the great grand father of his present most gracious Majesty, on the throne of Britain, is still alive and active and warm in England; and that the same spirit in America, instead of provoking the inhabitants of that country, will endear us to them for ever and secure their good will.

This spirit however without knowledge, would be little better than a brutal rage. Let us tenderly and kindly cherish, therefore the means of knowledge. Let us dare to read, think, speak and write. Let every order and degree among the people rouse their attention and animate their resolution. Let them all become attentive to the grounds and principles of government, ecclesiastical and civil. Let us study the law of nature; search into the spirit of the British constitution; read the histories of ancient ages; contemplate the great examples of Greece and Rome; set before us, the conduct of our own British ancestors, who have defended for us, the inherent rights of mankind, against foreign and domestic tyrants and usurpers, against arbitrary kings and cruel priests, in short against the gates of earth and hell. Let us read and recollect and impress upon our souls, the views and ends, of our own more immediate forefathers, in exchanging their native country for a dreary, inhospitable wilderness. Let us examine into the nature of that power and the cruelty of that oppression which drove them from their homes. Recollect their amazing fortitude, their bitter sufferings! The hunger, the nakedness, the cold, which they patiently endured! The severe labours of clearing their grounds, building their houses, raising their provisions amidst dangers from wild beasts and savage men, before they had time or money or materials for commerce! Recollect the civil and religious principles and hopes and expectations, which constantly supported and carried them through all hardships, and patience and resignation!. Let us recollect it was liberty! The hope of liberty for themselves and us and ours, which conquered all discouragements, dangers and trials! In such researches as these let us all in our several departments chearfully engage! But especially the proper patrons and supporters of law, learning and religion.

Let the pupil resound with the doctrines and sentiments of religious liberty. Let us hear the danger of thraldom to our consciences, from ignorance, extream poverty and dependance, in short from civil and political slavery. Let us see delineated before us, the true map of man. Let us hear the dignity of his nature, and the noble rank he holds among the works of God! that consenting to slavery is a sacriligious breach of trust, as offensive in the sight of God, as it is derogatory from our own honor or interest or happiness; and that God almightly has promulgated from heaven, liberty, peace, and good-will to man!

Let the Bar proclaim, "the laws, the rights, the generous plan of power," delivered down from remote antiquity; inform the world of the mighty struggles, and numberless sacrifices, made by our ancestors, in defence of freedom. Let it be known, that British liberties are not the grants of princes or parliaments, but original rights, conditions of original contracts, coequal with prerogative and coeval with government.—That many of our rights are inherent and essential, agreed on as maxims and establish'd as preliminaries, even before a parliament existed. Let them search for the foundations of British laws and government in the frame of human nature, in the constitution of the intellectual and moral world. There let us see, that truth, liberty, justice and benevolence, are its everlasting basis; and if these could be removed, the superstructure is overthrown of course.

Let the colleges join their harmony, in the same delightful concern. Let every declamation turn upon the beauty of liberty and virtue, and the deformity, turpitude and malignity of slavery and vice. Let the public disputations become researches into the grounds and nature and ends of government, and the means of preserving the good and demolishing the evil. Let the dialogues and all the exercises, become the instruments of impressing on the tender mind, and of spreading and distributing, far and wide, the ideas of right and the sensations of freedom.

In a word, let every sluice of knowledge be open'd and set a flowing. The encroachments upon liberty, in the reigns of the first James and the first Charles, by turning the general attention of learned men to government, are said to have produced the greatest number of consummate statesmen, which has ever been seen in any age, or nation. Your Clarendons, Southamptons, Seldens, Hampdens, Faulklands, Sidneys, Locks, Harringtons, are all said to have owed their eminence in political knowledge, to the tyrannies of those reigns. The prospect, now before us, in America, ought in the same manner to engage the attention of every man of learning to matters of power and of right, that we may be neither led nor driven blindfolded to irretrievable destruction. Nothing less than this seems to have been meditated for us, by somebody or other in Great-Britain. There seems to be a direct, and formal design on foot, to enslave all America. This however must be done by degrees. The first step that is intended seems to be an entire subversion of the whole system of our Fathers, by an introduction of the cannon and feudal law, into America. The cannon and feudal systems tho' greatly mutilated in England, are not yet destroy'd. Like the temples and palaces, in which the great contrivers of them, once worship'd and inhabited, they exist in ruins; and much of the domineering spirit of them still remains. The designs and labours of a certain society, to introduce the former of them into America, have been well exposed to the public by a writer of great abilities, and the further attempts to the same purpose that may be made by that society, or by the ministry or parliament, I leave to the conjectures of the thoughtful. But it seems very manifest from the S---p A-t itself, that a design is form'd to strip us in a great measure of the means of knowledge, by loading the Press, the Colleges, and even an Almanack and a News-Paper, with restraints and duties; and to introduce the inequalities and dependances of the feudal system, by taking from the poorer sort of people all their little subsistance, and conferring it on a set of stamp officers, distributors and their deputies. But I must proceed no further at present. The sequel, whenever I shall find health and leisure to pursue it, will be a "disquisition of the policy of the stamp act." In the mean time however let me add, These are not the vapours of a melancholly mind, nor the effusions of envy, disappointed ambition, nor of a spirit of opposition to government: but the emanations of an heart that burns, for its country's welfare. No one of any feeling, born and educated in this once happy country, can consider the numerous distresses, the gross indignities, the barbarous ignorance, the haughty usurpations, that we have reason to fear are meditating for ourselves, our children, our neighbours, in short for all our countrymen and all their posterity, without the utmost agonies of heart, and many tears.

THOMAS PAINE

Selection from *Common Sense*
1776

An English Quaker staymaker's son, American revolutionary pamphleteer, and elected deputy of the French revolutionary National Convention, Thomas Paine (1737–1809) was the American Enlightenment's cosmopolitan radical. His radicalism, however, consisted less in the character of his life or his specific political positions—which in France were comparatively moderate—than in the fervent, self-assured way in his writings he assaulted inherited traditions that seemed to him to stand in the way of the free and rational ordering of human belief and conduct in accordance with Nature's laws. In his *Age of Reason* (1794–95) he furiously attacked Christianity on just these grounds, and it nearly destroyed his reputation in America. By contrast his earlier *Common Sense,* published on the eve of the American Revolution, made him overnight the most widely read and popularly acclaimed author in the colonies, although this work, too, fundamentally assaulted an important American tradition: the English constitution and its mixed government of king, lords, and commons. Practically, of course, this position was revolutionary because it called for a break not just with Parliament, as did most resistance leaders, but with the king himself. More importantly, Paine's uniquely thoroughgoing assault on all forms of hereditary rule proclaimed the necessity for a wholly new form of republican government. Rather than promulgating the traditional radical Whig idea of preserving liberty and virtue in the state by dividing it into three separate and mutually checking branches resting on three distinct orders in society, Paine advocated the creation of a directly representative government produced by a social compact of equal individuals desirous of preserving their freedom and security and rationally pursuing their reciprocal commercial interests. It was this liberal ideal—together with Paine's secularized millennial appeals to God as monarch and America as "an asylum for mankind"—that made *Common Sense* such an uncommon revolutionary treatise. For an excellent brief intellectual portrait of Paine, see the sketch by Crane Brinton in the *Dictionary of American Biography* (New York, 1934), vol. 7, 159–66. Eric Foner, *Tom Paine and Revolutionary America* (New York, 1976) is suggestive on the ideological significance of Paine's political thought. A. Owen Aldridge usefully discusses the intellectual background and character of Paine's American writings in *Thomas Paine's American Ideology* (Newark, Del., 1984).

Of the Origin and Design of Government in General, with Concise Remarks on the English Constitution

Some writers have so confounded society with government, as to leave little or no distinction between them; whereas they are not only different, but have different origins. Society is produced by our wants, and government by our wickedness; the former promotes our happiness *positively*, by uniting our affections; the latter *negatively*, by restraining our vices. The one encourages intercourse, the other creates distinctions. The first is a patron, the last a punisher.

Society in every state is a blessing, but government, even in its best state, is but a necessary evil; in its worst state, an intolerable one; for when we suffer, or are exposed to the same miseries *by a government,* which we might expect in a country *without government,* our calamity is heightened by reflecting that we furnish the means by which we suffer.

Government, like dress, is the badge of lost innocence; the palaces of kings are built on the ruins of the bowers of paradise. For, were the impulses of conscience clear, uniform, and irresistibly obeyed, man would need no other lawgiver; but that not being the case, he finds it necessary to surrender up a part of his property to furnish means for the protection of the rest; and this he is induced to do by the same prudence which in every other case, advises him out of two evils to choose the least.

Wherefore, security being the true design and end of government, it unanswerably follows, that whatever *form* thereof apears most likely to ensure it to us with the least expense and greatest benefit, is preferable to all others.

In order to give a clear and just idea of the design and end of government, let us suppose a small number of persons settled in some sequestered part of the earth, unconnected with the rest; they will then represent the first peopling of any country, or of the world. In this state of natural liberty, society will be their first thought. A thousand motives will excite them thereto; the strength of one man is so unequal to his wants, and his mind so unfitted for perpetual solitude, that he is soon obliged to seek assistance and relief of another, who in his turn requires the same.

Four or five united would be able to raise a tolerable dwelling in the midst of a wilderness; but *one* man might labor out the common period of life without accomplishing anything; when he had felled his timber he could not remove it, nor erect it after it was removed; hunger in the meantime would urge him from his work, and every different want call him a different way. Disease, nay even misfortune, would be death; for though neither might be mortal, yet either would disable him from living, and reduce him to a state in which he might rather be said to perish than to die.

Thus necessity, like a gravitating power, would soon form our newly-arrived emigrants into society, the reciprocal blessings of which would supersede and render the obligations of law and government unnecessary while they remained perfectly just to each other: but as nothing but heaven is impregnable to vice, it will unavoidably happen, that in proportion as they surmount the first difficulties of emigration, which bound them together in a common cause, they will begin to relax in their duty and

Source: *Life and Writings of Thomas Paine,* ed. Daniel E. Wheeler, vol. 2 (New York: Vincent Parke & Co., 1908), 1–13, 19–21, 29, 51–54, 54–58. Editor's notes omitted.

attachment to each other; and this remissness will point out the necessity of establishing some form of government to supply the defect of moral virtue.

Some convenient tree will afford them a state-house, under the branches of which the whole colony may assemble to deliberate on public matters. It is more than probable that their first laws will have the title only of *Regulations,* and be enforced by no other penalty than public disesteem. In this first parliament every man, by natural right, will have a seat.

But as the colony increases, the public concerns will increase likewise, and the distance at which the members may be separated, will render it too inconvenient for all of them to meet on every occasion as at first, when their number was small, their habitations near, and the public concerns few and trifling. This will point out the convenience of their consenting to leave the legislative part to be managed by a select number chosen from the whole body, who are supposed to have the same concerns at stake which those have who appointed them, and who will act in the same manner as the whole body would were they present.

If the colony continue increasing, it will become necessary to augment the number of representatives, and that the interest of every part of the colony may be attended to, it will be found best to divide the whole into convenient parts, each part sending its proper number; and that the *elected* might never form to themselves an interest separate from the *electors,* prudence will point out the propriety of having elections often; because as the *elected* might by that means return and mix again with the general body of the *electors* in a few months, their fidelity to the public will be secured by the prudent reflection of not making a rod for themselves. And as this frequent interchange will establish a common interest with every part of the community, they will mutually and naturally support each other, and on this (not on the unmeaning name of king) depends the *strength of government and the happiness of the governed.*

Here, then, is the origin and rise of government; namely, a mode rendered necessary by the inability of moral virtue to govern the world; here, too, is the design and end of government, viz., freedom and security. And however our eyes may be dazzled with show, or our ears deceived by sound; however prejudice may warp our wills, or interest darken our understanding; the simple voice of nature and reason will say, it is right.

I draw my idea of the form of government from a principle in nature, which no art can overturn, viz., that the more simple anything is, the less liable it is to be disordered, and the easier repaired when disordered; and with this maxim in view, I offer a few remarks on the so much boasted Constitution of England. That it was noble for the dark and slavish times in which it was erected, is granted. When the world was overrun with tyranny, the least remove therefrom was a glorious rescue. But that it is imperfect, subject to convulsions, and incapable of producing what it seems to promise, is easily demonstrated.

Absolute governments (though the disgrace of human nature) have this advantage with them, that they are simple; if the people suffer, they know the head from which their suffering springs; they know likewise the remedy, and are not bewildered by a variety of causes and cures. But the Constitution of England is so exceedingly complex, that the nation may suffer for years together without being able to discover in which part the fault lies; some will say in one and some in another, and every political physician will advise a different medicine.

I know it is difficult to get over local or long-standing prejudices, yet if we will suffer ourselves to examine the component parts of the English Constitution, we shall find them to be the base remains of two ancient tyrannies, compounded with some new republican materials.

First—The remains of monarchical tyranny in the person of the King.

Secondly—The remains of aristocratical tyranny in the persons of the Peers.

Thirdly—The new republican materials in the persons of the Commons, on whose virtue depends the freedom of England.

The two first, by being hereditary, are independent of the people; wherefore in a *constitutional sense* they contribute nothing toward the freedom of the state.

To say that the Constitution of England is a *union* of three powers, reciprocally *checking* each other, is farcical; either the words have no meaning, or they are flat contradictions.

To say that the Commons is a check upon the King, presupposes two things:

First—That the King is not to be trusted without being looked after, or in other words, that a thirst for absolute power is the natural disease of monarchy.

Secondly—That the Commons, by being appointed for that purpose, are either wiser or more worthy of confidence than the Crown.

But as the same Constitution which gives the Commons a power to check the King by withholding the supplies, gives afterwards the King a power to check the Commons by empowering him to reject their other bills, it again supposes that the King is wiser than those whom it has already supposed to be wiser than him. A mere absurdity!

There is something exceedingly ridiculous in the composition of monarchy; it first excludes a man from the means of information, yet empowers him to act in cases where the highest judgment is required. The state of a king shuts him from the world, yet the business of a king requires him to know it thoroughly; wherefore the different parts, by unnaturally opposing and destroying each other, prove the whole character to be absurd and useless.

Some writers have explained the English Consitution thus: The King, say they, is one, the people another; the Peers are a house in behalf of the King, the Commons in behalf of the people.

But this hath all the distinctions of a house divided against itself; and though the expressions be pleasantly arranged, yet when examined, they appear idle and ambiguous; and it will always happen, that the nicest construction that words are capable of, when applied to the description of something which either cannot exist or is too incomprehensible to be within the compass of description, will be words of sound only, and though they may amuse the ear, they cannot inform the mind, for this explanation includes a previous question, viz.: *How came the King by a power which the people are afraid to trust, and always obliged to check?*

Such a power could not be the gift of a wise people, neither can any power, *which needs checking,* be from God; yet the provision, which the Constitution makes, supposes such a power to exist.

But the provision is unequal to the task; the means either cannot or will not accomplish the end, and the whole affair is a *felo de se;* for as the greater weight will always carry up the less, and as all the wheels of a machine are put in motion by one, it only remains to know which power in the Constitution has the most weight, for that will govern; and though the others, or a part of them, may clog, or, as the phrase is, check the rapidity of its motion, yet so long as they cannot stop it, their endeavors will be ineffectual; the first moving power will at last have its way, and what it wants in speed, is supplied by time.

That the Crown is this overbearing part in the English Constitution, needs not be mentioned, and that it derives its whole consequence merely from being the giver of places and pensions, is self-evident; wherefore, though we have been wise enough to shut and lock a door against absolute monarchy, we at the same time have been foolish enough to put the Crown in possession of the key.

The prejudice of Englishmen in favor of their own government by kings, lords and commons, arises as much or more from national pride than reason. Individuals are undoubtedly safer in England than in some other countries, but the *will* of a king is as much the *law* of the land in Britain as in France, with this difference, that instead of proceeding directly from his mouth, it is handed to the people under the more formidable shape of an act of Parliament. For the fate of Charles I hath only made kings more subtle—not more just.

Wherefore, laying aside all national pride and prejudice in favor of modes and forms, the plain truth is, that *it is wholly owing to the constitution of the people, and not to the constitution of the government,* that the Crown is not as oppressive in England as in Turkey.

An inquiry into the *constitutional errors* in English form of government is at this time highly necessary; for as we are never in a proper condition of doing justice to others, while we continue under the influence of some leading partiality, so neither are we capable of doing it to ourselves while we remain fettered by any obstinate prejudice. And as a man who is attached to a prostitute is unfitted to choose or judge of a wife, so any prepossession in favor of a rotten constitution of government will disable us from discerning a good one.

Of Monarchy and Hereditary Succession

Mankind being originally equals in the order of creation, the equality could only be destroyed by some subsequent circumstances; the distinctions of rich and poor may in a great measure be accounted for, and that without having recourse to the harsh, ill-sounding names of oppression and avarice. Oppression is often the *consequence,* but seldom or never the *means* of riches; and though avarice will preserve a man from being necessitously poor, it generally makes him too timorous to become wealthy.

But there is another and greater distinction, for which no truly natural or religious reason can be assigned, and that is, the distinction of men into KINGS and SUBJECTS. Male and female are the distinctions of nature, good and bad the distinctions of heaven; but how a race of men came into the world so exalted above the rest, and distinguished like some new species, is worth inquiring into, and whether they are the means of happiness or of misery to mankind.

In the early ages of the world, according to the Scripture chronology, there were no kings; the consequence of which was, there were no wars: it is the pride of kings which throws mankind into confusion. Holland without a king hath enjoyed more peace for this last century than any of the monarchical governments in Europe. Antiquity favors the same remark; for the quiet and rural lives of the first patriarchs hath a happy something in them, which vanishes away when we come to the history of Jewish royalty. ·

Government by kings was first introduced into the world by the heathens, from whom the children of Israel copied the custom. It was the most prosperous invention the devil ever set on foot for the promotion of idolatry. The heathens paid divine honors to their deceased kings, and the Christian world hath improved on the plan, by doing the same to their living ones. How impious is the title of *sacred majesty* applied to a worm who in the midst of his splendor is crumbling into dust!

As the exalting one man so greatly above the rest, cannot be justified on the equal rights of nature, so neither can it be defended on the authority of Scripture; for the will of the Almighty, as declared by Gideon and the prophet Samuel, expressly disapproves of the government by kings.

· · · · · ·

To the evil of monarchy we have added that of hereditary succession; and as the first is a degradation and lessening of ourselves, so the second, claimed as a matter of right, is an insult and imposition on posterity. For all men being originally equals, no *one* by *birth* could have a right to set up his family in perpetual preference to all others forever, and though himself might deserve *some* decent degree of honors of his contemporaries, yet his descendants might be far too unworthy to inherit them.

One of the strongest *natural* proofs of the folly of hereditary right of kings, is that nature disapproves it, otherwise she would not so frequently turn it into ridicule by giving mankind an *ass for a lion*.

Secondly, as no man at first could possess any other public honors than were bestowed upon him, so the givers of those honors could have no power to give away the right of posterity, and though they might say, "We choose you for *our* head," they could not, without manifest injustice to their children, say, "that your children and your children's children shall *reign* over ours for *ever*." Because such an unwise, unjust, unnatural compact might, perhaps, in the next succession put them under the government of a rogue or a fool.

Most wise men in their private sentiments have ever treated hereditary right with contempt; yet it is one of those evils, which when once established is not easily removed; many submit from fear, others from superstition, and the more powerful part shares with the king the plunder of the rest.

This is supposing the present race of kings in the world to have had an honorable origin; whereas it is more than probable, that, could we take off the dark covering of antiquity and trace them to their first rise, we should find the first of them nothing better than the principal ruffian of some restless gang, whose savage manners or preeminence in subtility obtained him the title of chief among plunderers; and who by increasing in power, and extending his depredations, overawed the quiet and defenseless to purchase their safety by frequent contributions. Yet his electors could have no idea of giving hereditary right to his descendants, because such a perpetual exclusion of themselves was incompatible with the free and unrestrained principles they professed to live by.

· · · · · ·

Thoughts on the Present State of American Affairs

. . . . . .

If there is any true cause of fear respecting independence, it is because no plan is yet laid down. Men do not see their way out; wherefore, as an opening into that business, I offer the following hints; at the same time modestly affirming, that I have no other opinion of them myself, than that they may be the means of giving rise to something better. Could the straggling thoughts of individuals be collected, they would frequently form materials for wise and able men to improve into useful matter.

Let the assemblies be annual, with a president only. The representation more equal. Their business wholly domestic, and subject to the authority of a continental congress.

Let each colony be divided into six, eight, or ten, convenient districts, each district to send a proper number of delegates to congress, so that each colony sends at least thirty. The whole number in congress will be at least three hundred and ninety. Each congress to sit. . . . . and to choose a president by the following method: When the delegates are met, let a colony be taken from the whole thirteen colonies by lot, after which, let the whole congress choose (by ballot) a president from out of the delegates of that province.

In the next congress, let a colony be taken by lot from twelve only, omitting that colony from which the president was taken in the former congress and so proceeding on till the whole thirteen shall have had their proper rotation. And in order that nothing may pass into a law but what is satisfactorily just, not less than three-fifths of the congress to be called a majority. He that will promote discord, under a government so equally formed as this, would have joined Lucifer in his revolt.

But as there is a peculiar delicacy, from whom or in what manner this business must first arise, and as it seems most agreeable and consistent that it should come from some intermediate body between the governed and the governors, that is, between the congress and the people, let a *Continental Conference* be held, in the following manner, and for the following purpose:

A committee of twenty-six members of congress, viz., two for each colony. Two members from each house of assembly, or provincial convention; and five representatives of the people at large, to be chosen in the capital city or town of each province, for and in behalf of the whole province, by as many qualified voters as shall think proper to attend from all parts of the province for that purpose; or, if more convenient, the representatives may be chosen in two or three of the most populous parts thereof.

In this conference, thus assembled, will be united, the two grand principles of business, *knowledge* and *power*. The members of congress, assemblies, or conventions, by having had experience in national concerns, will be able and useful counsellors, and the whole, being empowered by the people, will have a truly legal authority.

The conferring members being met, let their business be to frame a *Continental Charter,* or Charter of the United Colonies; (answering to what is called the Magna Charta of England) fixing the number and manner of choosing members of congress, and members of assembly, with their date of sitting, and drawing the line of business and jurisdiction between them: always remembering, that our strength is continental, not provincial: securing freedom and property to all men, and above all things, the free exercise of religion, according to the dictates of conscience; with such other matter as is necessary for a charter to contain.

Immediately after which, the said conference to dissolve, and the bodies which shall be chosen conformable to the said charter, to be the legislators and governors of this continent for the time being; whose peace and happiness, may God preserve, Amen.

. . . . . .

But where, say some, is the king of America? I'll tell you, friend, He reigns above, and doth not make havoc of mankind like the royal brute of Britain. Yet that we may not appear to be defective even in earthly honors, let a day be solemnly set apart for proclaiming the charter; let it be brought forth, placed on the divine law, the Word of God; let a crown be placed thereon, by which the world may know, that so far as we approve of monarchy, that in America *the law is king*.

For as in absolute governments the king is law, so in free countries the law ought to be king; and there ought to be no other. But lest any ill use should afterwards arise, let the crown at the conclusion of the ceremony be demolished and scattered among the people whose right it is.

A government of our own is our natural right: and when a man seriously reflects on the precariousness of human affairs, he will become convinced that it is infinitely wiser and safer to form a constitution of our own, in a cool deliberate manner, while we have it in our power, than to trust such an interesting event to time and chance. If we omit it now, some Masaniello may here after arise, who, laying hold of popular disquietudes, may collect together the desperate and the discontented, and by assuming to themselves the powers of government, may sweep away the liberties of the continent like a deluge.

Should the government of America return again into the hands of Britain, the tottering situation of things will be a temptation for some desperate adventurer to try his fortune; and in such a case, what relief can Britain give? Ere she could hear the news, the fatal business might be done; and ourselves suffering like the wretched Britains under the oppression of the Conqueror. Ye that oppose independence now, ye know not what ye do; ye are opening a door to eternal tyranny, by keeping vacant the seat of government.

There are thousands and tens of thousands who would think it glorious to expel from the continent that barbarous and hellish power which hath stirred up the Indians and negroes to destroy us; the cruelty hath a double guilt; it is dealing brutally by us and treacherously by them. To talk of friendship with those in whom our reason forbids us to have faith, and our affections, (wounded through a thousand pores,) instruct us to detest, is madness and folly. Every day wears out the little remains of kindred between us and them; and can there be any reason to hope that as the relationship expires the affection will increase, or that we shall agree better when we have ten times more and greater concerns to quarrel over than ever?

Ye that tell us of harmony and reconciliation, can ye restore to us the time that is passed? Can ye give to prostitution its former innocence? Neither can ye reconcile Britain and America. The last cord now is broken; the people of England are presenting addresses against us. There are injuries which nature cannot forgive; she would cease to be nature if she did. As well can the lover forgive the ravisher of his mistress, as the continent forgive the murders of Britain. The Almighty hath implanted in us these unextinguishable feelings for good and wise purposes. They are the guardians of His image in our hearts. They distinguish us from the herd of common animals. The social compact would dissolve and justice be extirpated from the earth, or have only a casual existence, were we callous to the touches of affection. The robber and the murderer would often escape unpunished, did not the injuries which our tempers sustain, provoke us into justice.

O ye that love mankind! Ye that dare oppose, not only the tyranny, but the tyrant, stand forth! Every spot of the old world is overrun with oppression. Freedom hath been hunted round the globe. Asia and Africa have long expelled her, Europe regards her like a stranger, and England hath given her warning to depart. O! receive the fugitive, and prepare in time an asylum for mankind.

THOMAS JEFFERSON

The Declaration of Independence
1776

The Declaration of Independence, as written by Thomas Jefferson (1743–1826) and amended and adopted by the Continental Congress, was *the* great political document of the American Enlightenment. This was not, of course, because of the originality of its particular ideas, which, as Jefferson later noted, were all stock notions of contemporary republican thought. What *was* original was the text as a whole: it was the first complete fusion in a public document of Enlightenment ideals and republican principles. After only the barest mention of "Nature's God," the Declaration boldly asserted as the foundation of its political principles "self-evident" truths that, because they were axiomatic, were to rational men "undeniable" (to use Jefferson's original adjective). Furthermore these rational truths were moral truths. They affirmed both the essential equality of men and certain individual human rights whose protection depended on forms of self-government that, as the "long train of abuses and usurpations" was meant to demonstrate, were sufficiently violated by the British king and his government as to evince "a design to reduce [the colonies] under absolute Despotism" and so justify a revolutionary separation. Finally, the Declaration announced the intention of the United States to establish for the first time in history a *nation* on the basis of these Enlightenment–republican principles. As such, the Declaration was both sweepingly universalistic and, as Jefferson later claimed, "an expression of the American mind." Carl Becker, *The Declaration of Independence: A Study in the History of Political Ideas* (New York, 1922) is a classic still worth consulting. Garry Wills, *Inventing America: Jefferson's Declaration of Independence* (Garden City, N.Y., 1978) is a richly stimulating but controversial reading of the Declaration in the context of Jefferson's intellectual world. For a contrasting and more technically philosophical interpretation, see Morton White, *The Philosophy of the American Revolution* (New York, 1978).

IN CONGRESS, JULY 4, 1776.

*THE UNANIMOUS DECLARATION OF THE THIRTEEN
UNITED STATES OF AMERICA,*

When in the Course of human events, it becomes necessary for one people to dissolve the political bands which have connected them with another, and to assume among the powers of the earth, the separate and equal station to which the Laws of Nature and of Nature's God entitle them, a decent respect to the opinions of mankind requires that they should declare the causes which impel them to the separation. We hold these truths to be self-evident, that all men are created equal, that they are endowed by their Creator with certain unalienable Rights, that among these are Life, Liberty and the pursuit of Happiness. That to secure these rights, Governments are instituted among Men, deriving their just powers from the consent of the governed, That whenever any Form of Government becomes destructive of these ends, it is the Right of the People to alter or to abolish it, and to institute new Government, laying its foundation on such principles and organizing its powers in such form, as to them shall seem most likely to effect their Safety and Happiness. Prudence, indeed, will dictate that Governments long established should not be changed for light and transient causes; and accordingly all experience hath shewn, that mankind are more disposed to suffer, while evils are sufferable, than to right themselves by abolishing the forms to which they are accustomed. But when a long train of abuses and usurpations, pursuing invariably the same Object evinces a design to reduce them under absolute Despotism, it is their right, it is their duty, to throw off such Government, and to provide new Guards for their future security. Such has been the patient sufferance of these Colonies; and such is now the necessity which constrains them to alter their former Systems of Government. The history of the present King of Great Britain is a history of repeated injuries and usurpations, all having in direct object the establishment of an absolute Tyranny over these States. To prove this, let Facts be submitted to a candid world. He has refused his Assent to Laws, the most wholesome and necessary for the public good. He has forbidden his Governors to pass Laws of immediate and pressing importance, unless suspended in their operation till his Assent should be obtained; and when so suspended, he has utterly neglected to attend to them. He has refused to pass other Laws for the accommodation of large districts of people, unless those people would relinquish the right of Representation in the Legislature, a right inestimable to them and formidable to tyrants only. He has called together legislative bodies at places unusual, uncomfortable, and distant from the depository of their public Records, for the sole purpose of fatiguing them into compliance with his measures. He has dissolved Representative Houses repeatedly, for opposing with manly firmness his invasions on the rights of the people. He has refused for a long time, after such dissolutions, to cause others to be elected; whereby the Legislative powers, incapable of Annihilation, have returned to the People at large for their exercise; the State remaining in the mean time exposed to all the dangers of invasion from without, and convulsions within. He has endeavoured to prevent the population of these States; for that purpose obstructing

Source: The Papers of Thomas Jefferson, vol. 1, ed. Julian P. Boyd, Lyman H. Butterfield, and Mina R. Bryan (Princeton: Princeton University Press, 1950), 429–32. Reprinted by permission of Princeton University Press, Copyright © 1950.

the Laws for Naturalization of Foreigners; refusing to pass others to encourage their migrations hither, and raising the conditions of new Appropriations of Lands. He has obstructed the Administration of Justice, by refusing his Assent to Laws for establishing Judiciary powers. He has made Judges dependent on his Will alone, for the tenure of their offices, and the amount and payment of their salaries. He has erected a multitude of New Offices, and sent hither swarms of Officers to harrass our people, and eat out their substance. He has kept among us, in times of peace, standing Armies without the Consent of our legislatures. He has affected to render the Military independent of and superior to the Civil power. He has combined with others to subject us to a jurisdiction foreign to our constitution, and unacknowledged by our laws; giving his Assent to their Acts of pretended Legislation: For Quartering large bodies of armed troops among us: For protecting them, by a mock Trial, from punishment for any Murders which they should commit on the Inhabitants of these States: For cutting off our Trade with all parts of the world: For imposing Taxes on us without our Consent: For depriving us in many cases of the benefits of Trial by Jury: For transporting us beyond Seas to be tried for pretended offences: For abolishing the free System of English Laws in a neighbouring Province, establishing therein an Arbitrary government, and enlarging its Boundries so as to render it at once an example and fit instrument for introducing the same absolute rule into these Colonies: For taking away our Charters, abolishing our most valuable Laws, and altering fundamentally the Forms of our Governments: For suspending our own Legislatures, and declaring themselves invested with power to legislate for us in all cases whatsoever. He has abdicated Government here, by declaring us out of his Protection and waging War against us. He has plundered our seas, ravaged our Coasts, burnt our towns, and destroyed the Lives of our people. He is at this time transporting large Armies of foreign Mercenaries to compleat the works of death, desolation and tyranny, already begun with circumstances of Cruelty & perfidy scarcely paralleled in the most barbarous ages, and totally unworthy the Head of a civilized nation. He has constrained our fellow Citizens taken Captive on the high Seas to bear Arms against their Country, to become the executioners of their friends and Brethren, or to fall themselves by their Hands. He has excited domestic insurrections amongst us, and has endeavoured to bring on the inhabitants of our frontiers, the merciless Indian Savages, whose known rule of warfare, is an undistinguished destruction of all ages, sexes and conditions. In every stage of these Oppressions We have Petitioned for Redress in the most humble terms: Our repeated Petitions have been answered only by repeated injury. A Prince, whose character is thus marked by every act which may define a Tyrant, is unfit to be the ruler of a free people. Nor have We been wanting in attentions to our Brittish brethren. We have warned them from time to time of attempts by their legislature to extend an unwarrantable jurisdiction over us. We have reminded them of the circumstances of our emigration and settlement here. We have appealed to their native justice and magnanimity, and we have conjured them by the ties of our common kindred to disavow these usurpations, which, would inevitably interrupt our connections and correspondence. They too have been deaf to the voice of justice and of consanguinity. We must, therefore, acquiesce in the necessity, which denounces our Separation, and hold them, as we hold the rest of mankind, Enemies in War, in Peace Friends.

We, therefore, the Representatives of the united States of America, in General Congress, Assembled, appealing to the Supreme Judge of the world for the rectitude of our intentions, do, in the Name, and by Authority of the good People of these Colonies, solemnly publish and declare, That these United Colonies are, and of Right ought to be Free and Independent States; that they are Absolved from all Allegiance to the British Crown, and that all political connection between them and the State of Great Britain, is and ought to be totally dissolved; and that as Free and Independent States, they have full Power to levy War, conclude Peace, contract Alliances, establish Commerce, and to do all other Acts and Things which Independent States may of right do. And for the support of this Declaration, with a firm reliance on the protection of divine Providence, we mutually pledge to each other our Lives, our Fortunes and our sacred Honor.

JOHN ADAMS

Letters to Samuel Adams, October 18, 1790; and to Thomas Jefferson, November 15, 1813; April 19, 1817

In the interval between his career as (in Jefferson's words) "the great Colossus" of the battle for independence in Congress and his presidency of the United States, John Adams published the two most systematic expositions of political theory produced in America before the nineteenth century. In his long, digressive but brilliantly pointed *Defence of the Constitutions of the United States* and *Discourses on Davila,* Adams spun out his arguments against the idea—first promulgated by Paine but recently promoted in a more statist form by French revolutionaries—that republics ought to be dominated by unitary legislative bodies consisting of representatives elected by an undifferentiated electorate of equal citizens. Adams earnestly argued that such a system, if adopted in America, would inevitably lead to a self-seeking, class-conflicted, liberty-devouring state and society. As an alternative he put forward a partly republicanized version of the mixed government of the English constitution—a state consisting of a mutually checking executive and upper and lower house. Besides being a vigorous theorist, Adams was also, along with his friend Jefferson, one of the finest letter writers of the greatest letter-writing age in history, and so two letters are included here in which he presented succinct versions of these political ideas. In his letter to his cousin, the former revolutionary militant Samuel Adams, John Adams gave his reasons for thinking that neither reason nor virtue but only a rational "political architecture" of a balanced government could keep liberty from subverting virtue. In the second letter, taken from his touching and fascinating late correspondence with his once comrade-turned-enemy but now intimate philosophical friend Jefferson, Adams analyzed with great subtlety and passion the many sources and varied guises of the one element he regarded as the most important in his system, the "aristocracy." In the 1817 letter to Jefferson, Adams poignantly sketched what probably lay behind much of his political outlook—his curiously skeptical yet warmly humanized post-Puritan faith in this "best of all possible Worlds." For a penetrating discussion of Adams's republicanism, see Gordon S. Wood, *The Creation of the American Republic, 1776–1787* (Chapel Hill, 1969), 567–92. Zoltan Haraszti, *John Adams and the Prophets of Progress* (Cambridge, Mass., 1952) is a captivating presentation of Adams's thought as revealed in his marginal comments on his reading. Henry F. May includes as the penultimate section of his *Enlightenment in America* (New York, 1976), 278–302, an excellent comparative rendering of the thought of Adams and Jefferson.

To Samuel Adams

NEW YORK, 18 October, 1790.

DEAR SIR,—I am thankful to our common friend, as well as to you, for your favor of the fourth, which I received last night. My fears are in unison with yours, that hay, wood, and stubble, will be the materials of the new political buildings in Europe, till men shall be more enlightened and friendly to each other.

You agree, that there are undoubtedly principles of political architecture. But, instead of particularizing any of them, you seem to place all your hopes in the universal, or at least more general, prevalence of knowledge and benevolence. I think with you, that knowledge and benevolence ought to be promoted as much as possible; but, despairing of ever seeing them sufficiently general for the security of society, I am for seeking institutions which may supply in some degree the defect. If there were no ignorance, error, or vice, there would be neither principles nor systems of civil or political government.

I am not often satisfied with the opinions of Hume; but in this he seems well founded, that all projects of government, founded in the supposition or expectation of extraordinary degrees of virtue, are evidently chimerical. Nor do I believe it possible, humanly speaking, that men should ever be greatly improved in knowledge or benevolence, without assistance from the principles and system of government.

I am very willing to agree with you in fancying, that in the greatest improvements of society, government will be in the republican form. It is a fixed principle with me, that all good government is and must be republican. But, at the same time, your candor will agree with me, that there is not in lexicography a more fraudulent word. Whenever I use the word *republic* with approbation, I mean a government in which the people have collectively, or by representation, an essential share in the sovereignty. The republican forms of Poland and Venice are much worse, and those of Holland and Bern very little better, than the monarchical form in France before the late revolution. By the republican form, I know you do not mean the plan of Milton, Nedham, or Turgot. For, after a fair trial of its miseries, the simple monarchical form will ever be, as it has ever been, preferred to it by mankind. Are we not, my friend, in danger of rendering the word *republican* unpopular in this country by an indiscreet, indeterminate, and equivocal use of it? The people of England have been obliged to wean themselves from the use of it, by making it unpopular and unfashionable, because they found it was artfully used by some, and simply understood by others, to mean the government of their interregnum parliament. They found they could not wean themselves from that destructive form of government so entirely, as that a mischievous party would not still remain in favor of it, by any other means than by making the words *republic* and *republican* unpopular. They have succeeded to such a degree, that, with a vast majority of that nation, a republican is as unamiable as a witch, a blasphemer, a rebel, or a tyrant. If, in this country, the word *republic* should be generally

Source: The Works of John Adams, ed. Charles Francis Adams, vol. 6 (Boston: Charles C. Little and James Brown, 1851), 414–20; *The Adams-Jefferson Letters: The Complete Correspondence Between Thomas Jefferson and Abigail and John Adams,* 2 vols., ed. Lester J. Cappon, vol. 2 (Chapel Hill: University of North Carolina Press, 1959), 397–402, 508–10. Editor's notes in Cappon altered. Reprinted by permission of The University of North Carolina Press, Copyright © 1959.

understood, as it is by some, to mean a form of government inconsistent with a mixture of three powers, forming a mutual balance, we may depend upon it that such
mischievous effects will be produced by the use of it as will compel the people of
America to renounce, detest, and execrate it as the English do. With these explana-
tions, restrictions, and limitations, I agree with you in your love of republican governments, but in no other sense.

With you, I have also the honor most perfectly to harmonize in your sentiments
of the humanity and wisdom of promoting education in knowledge, virtue, and benevolence. But I think that these will confirm mankind in the opinion of the necessity of
preserving and strengthening the dikes against the ocean, its tides and storms. Human
appetites, passions, prejudices, and self-love will never be conquered by benevolence
and knowedge alone, introduced by human means. The millennium itself neither supposes nor implies it. All civil government is then to cease, and the Messiah is to reign.
That happy and holy state is therefore wholly out of this question. You and I agree in
the utility of universal education; but will nations agree in it as fully and extensively
as we do, and be at the expense of it? We know, with as much certainty as attends
any human knowledge, that they will not. We cannot, therefore, advise the people to
depend for their safety, liberty, and security, upon hopes and blessings which we know
will not fall to their lot. If we do our duty then to the people, we shall not deceive
them, but advise them to depend upon what is in their power and will relieve them.

Philosophers, ancient and modern, do not appear to me to have studied nature,
the whole of nature, and nothing but nature. Lycurgus's principle was war and family
pride; Solon's was what the people would bear, &c. The best writings of antiquity
upon government, those, I mean, of Aristotle, Zeno, and Cicero, are lost. We have
human nature, society, and universal history to observe and study, and from these we
may draw all the real principles which ought to be regarded. Disciples will follow their
masters, and interested partisans their chieftains; let us like it or not, we cannot help
it. But if the true principles can be discovered, and fairly, fully, and impartially laid
before the people, the more light increases, the more the reason of them will be seen,
and the more disciples they will have. Prejudice, passion, and private interest, which
will always mingle in human inquiries, one would think might be enlisted on the side
of truth, at least in the greatest number; for certainly the majority are interested in the
truth, if they could see to the end of all its consequences. "Kings have been deposed
by aspiring nobles." True, and never by any other. "These" (the nobles, I suppose,)
"have waged everlasting war against the common rights of men." True, when they
have been possessed of the *summa imperii* in one body, without a check. So have the
plebeians; so have the people; so have kings; so has human nature, in every shape and
combination, and so it ever will. But, on the other hand, the nobles have been essential
parties in the preservation of liberty, whenever and wherever it has existed. In Europe,
they alone have preserved it against kings and people, wherever it has been preserved;
or, at least, with very little assistance from the people. One hideous despotism, as
horrid as that of Turkey, would have been the lot of every nation of Europe, if the
nobles had not made stands. By nobles, I mean not peculiarly an hereditary nobility,
or any particular modification, but the natural and actual aristocracy among mankind.
The existence of this you will not deny. You and I have seen four noble families rise
up in Boston,—the CRAFTS, GORES, DAWES, and AUSTINS. These are as really a nobility
in our town, as the Howards, Somersets, Berties, &c., in England. Blind, undistinguish-

ing reproaches against the aristocratical part of mankind, a division which nature has made, and we cannot abolish, are neither pious nor benevolent. They are as pernicious as they are false. They serve only to foment prejudice, jealousy, envy, animosity, and malevolence. They serve no ends but those of sophistry, fraud, and the spirit of party. It would not be true, but it would not be more egregiously false, to say that the people have waged everlasting war against the rights of men.

"The love of liberty," you say, "is interwoven in the soul of man." So it is, according to La Fontaine, in that of a wolf; and I doubt whether it be much more rational, generous, or social, in one than in the other, until in man it is enlightened by experience, reflection, education, and civil and political institutions, which are at first produced, and constantly supported and improved by a few; that is, by the nobility. The wolf, in the fable, who preferred running in the forest, lean and hungry, to the sleek, plump, and round sides of the dog, because he found the latter was sometimes restrained, had more love of liberty than most men. The numbers of men in all ages have preferred ease, slumber, and good cheer to liberty, when they have been in competition. We must not then depend alone upon the love of liberty in the soul of man for its preservation. Some political institutions must be prepared, to assist this love against its enemies. Without these, the struggle will ever end only in a change of impostors. When the people, who have no property, feel the power in their own hands to determine all questions by a majority, they ever attack those who have property, till the injured men of property lose all patience, and recur to finesse, trick, and stratagem, to outwit those who have too much strength, because they have too many hands to be resisted any other way. Let us be impartial, then, and speak the whole truth. Till we do, we shall never discover all the true principles that are necessary. The multitude, therefore, as well as the nobles, must have a check. This is one principle.

"Were the people of England free, after they had obliged King John to concede to them their ancient rights?" The people never did this. There was no people who pretended to any thing. It was the nobles alone. The people pretended to nothing but to be villains, vassals, and retainers to the king or the nobles. The nobles, I agree, were not free, because all was determined by a majority of their votes, or by arms, not by law. Their feuds deposed their "Henrys, Edwards, and Richards," to gratify lordly ambition, patrician rivalry, and "family pride." But, if they had not been deposed, those kings would have become despots, because the people would not and could not join the nobles in any regular and constitutional opposition to them. They would have become despots, I repeat it, and that by means of the villains, vassals, and retainers aforesaid. It is not family pride, my friend, but family popularity, that does the great mischief, as well as the great good. Pride, in the heart of man, is an evil fruit and concomitant of every advantage; of riches, of knowledge, of genius, of talents, of beauty, of strength, of virtue, and even of piety. It is sometimes ridiculous, and often pernicious. But it is even sometimes, and in some degree, useful. But the pride of families would be always and only ridiculous, if it had not family popularity to work with. The attachment and devotion of the people to some families inspires them with pride. As long as gratitude or interest, ambition or avarice, love, hope, or fear, shall be human motives of action, so long will numbers attach themselves to particular families. When the people will, in spite of all that can be said or done, cry a man or a family up to the skies, exaggerate all his talents and virtues, not hear a word of his weakness or faults, follow implicitly his advice, detest every man he hates, adore every man he loves, and knock down all who will not swim down the stream with them, where is your remedy? When a man or family are thus popular, how can you prevent them from being proud? You and I know of instances in which popularity has been a wind, a tide, a whirlwind. The history of all ages and nations is full of such examples.

Popularity, that has great fortune to dazzle; splendid largesses, to excite warm gratitude; sublime, beautiful, and uncommon genius or talents, to produce deep admiration; or any thing to support high hopes and strong fears, will be proud; and its power will be employed to mortify enemies, gratify friends, procure votes, emoluments, and power. Such family popularity ever did, and ever will govern in every nation, in every climate, hot and cold, wet and dry, among civilized and savage people, Christians and Mahometans, Jews and Heathens. Declamation against family pride is a pretty, juvenile exercise, but unworthy of statesmen. They know the evil and danger is too serious to be sported with. The only way, God knows, is to put these families into a hole by themselves, and set two watches upon them; a superior to them all on one side, and the people on the other.

There are a few popular men in the Massachusetts, my friend, who have, I fear, less honor, sincerity, and virtue, than they ought to have. These, if they are not guarded against, may do another mischief. They may excite a party spirit and a mobbish spirit, instead of the spirit of liberty, and produce another Wat Tyler's rebellion. They can do no more. But I really think their party language ought not to be countenanced, nor their shibboleths pronounced. The miserable stuff that they utter about the *well-born* is as despicable as themselves. The ἐυγενεῖς of the Greeks, the *bien nées* of the French, the *welgebohren* of the Germans and Dutch, the *beloved families* of the Creeks, are but a few samples of national expressions of the same thing, for which every nation on earth has a similar expression. One would think that our scribblers were all the sons of redemptioners or transported convicts. They think with Tarquin, *"In novo populo, ubi omnis repentina atque ex virtute nobilitas fit, futurum locum forti ac strenuo viro."*[1]

Let us be impartial. There is not more of family pride on one side, than of vulgar malignity and popular envy on the other. Popularity in one family raises envy in others. But the popularity of the least deserving will triumph over envy and malignity; while that which is acquired by real merit, will very often be overborne and oppressed by it.

Let us do justice to the people and to the nobles; for nobles there are, as I have before proved, in Boston as well as in Madrid. But to do justice to both, you must establish an arbitrator between them. This is another principle.

It is time that you and I should have some sweet communion together. I do not believe, that we, who have preserved for more than thirty years an uninterrupted friendship, and have so long thought and acted harmoniously together in the worst of times, are now so far asunder in sentiment as some people pretend; in full confidence of which, I have used this freedom, being ever your warm friend.

JOHN ADAMS.

---

1. Amongst a new people, where all rank was of sudden growth and founded on worth, there would be room for a brave and strenuous man." Livy, 1.34.6.

To Thomas Jefferson

Quincy November 15. [18]13

DEAR SIR

I cannot appease my melancholly commiseration for our Armies in this furious snow storm in any way so well as by studying your Letter of Oct. 28.

We are now explicitly agreed, in one important point, vizt. That "there is a natural Aristocracy among men; the grounds of which are Virtue and Talents."

You very justly indulge a little merriment upon this solemn subject of Aristocracy. I often laugh at it too, for there is nothing in this laughable world more ridiculous than the management of it by almost all the nations of the Earth. But while We smile, Mankind have reason to say to Us, as the froggs said to the Boys, What is Sport to you is Wounds and death to Us. When I consider the weakness, the folly, the Pride, the Vanity, the Selfishness, the Artifice, the low craft and meaning cunning, the want of Principle, the Avarice the unbounded Ambition, the unfeeling Cruelty of a majority of those (in all Nations) who are allowed an aristocratical influence; and on the other hand, the Stupidity with which the more numerous multitude, not only become their Dupes, but even love to be Taken in by their Tricks: I feel a stronger disposition to weep at their destiny, than to laugh at their Folly.

But tho' We have agreed in one point, in Words, it is not yet certain that We are perfectly agreed in Sense. Fashion has introduced an indeterminate Use of the Word "Talents." Education, Wealth, Strength, Beauty, Stature, Birth, Marriage, graceful Attitudes and Motions, Gait, Air, Complexion, Physiognomy, are Talents, as well as Genius and Science and learning. Any one of these Talents, that in fact commands or influences true Votes in Society, gives to the Man who possesses it, the Character of an Aristocrat, in my Sense of the Word.

Pick up, the first 100 men you meet, and make a Republick. Every Man will have an equal Vote. But when deliberations and discussions are opened it will be found that 25, by their Talents, Virtues being equal, will be able to carry 50 Votes. Every one of these 25, is an Aristocrat, in my Sense of the Word; whether he obtains his one Vote in Addition to his own, by his Birth Fortune, Figure, Eloquence, Science, learning, Craft Cunning, or even his Character for good fellowship and a bon vivant.

What gave Sir William Wallace his amazing Aristocratical Superiority? His Strength. What gave Mrs. Clark, her Aristocratical Influence to create Generals Admirals and Bishops? her Beauty. What gave Pompadour and Du Barry the Power of making Cardinals and Popes? their Beauty. You have seen the Palaces of Pompadour and Du Barry: and I have lived for years in the Hotel de Velentinois, with Franklin who had as many Virtues as any of them. In the investigation of the meaning of the Word "Talents" I could write 630 Pages, as pertinent as John Taylors of Hazelwood. But I will select a single Example: for female Aristocrats are nearly as formidable in Society as male.

A daughter of a green Grocer, walks the Streets in London dayly with a baskett of Cabbage, Sprouts, Dandlions and Spinage on her head. She is observed by the Painters to have a beautiful Face, an elegant figure, a graceful Step and a debonair. They hire her to Sitt. She complies, and is painted by forty Artists in a Circle around her. The scientific Sir William Hamilton outbids the Painters, sends her to Schools for a genteel Education and Marries her. This Lady not only causes the Tryumphs of the Nile of Copinhagen and Trafalgar, but seperates Naples from France and finally banishes the King and Queen from Sicilly. Such is the Aristocracy of the natural Talent of Beauty. Millions of Examples might be quoted from History sacred and profane, from Eve, Hannah, Deborah Susanna Abigail, Judith, Ruth, down to Hellen Madame de Maintenon and Mrs. Fitcherbert. For mercy's sake do not compell me to look to our chaste States and Territories, to find Women, one of whom lett go, would, in the Words of Holopherne's Guards "deceive to whole Earth."

The proverbs of Theognis, like those of Solomon, are Observations on human nature, ordinary life, and civil Society, with moral reflections on the facts. I quoted him as a Witness of the Fact, that there was as much difference in the races of Men as in the breeds of Sheep; and as a sharp reprover and censurer of the sordid mercenary practice of disgracing Birth by preferring gold to it. Surely no authority can be more expressly in point to prove the existence of Inequalities, not of rights, but of moral intellectual and physical inqualities in Families, descents and Generations. If a descent from, pious, virtuous, wealthy litterary or scientific Ancestors is a letter of recommendation, or introduction in a Mans his favour, and enables him to influence only one vote in Addition to his own, he is an Aristocrat, for a democrat can have but one Vote. Aaron Burr had 100,000 Votes from the single Circumstance of his descent from President Burr and President Edwards.

Your commentary on the Proverbs of Theognis reminded me of two solemn Charactors, the one resembling John Bunyan, the other Scarron. The one John Torrey: the other Ben. Franklin. Torrey a Poet, an Enthusiast, a superstitious Bigot, once very gravely asked my Brother Cranch, "whether it would not be better for Mankind, if Children were always begotten from religious motives only"? Would not religion, in this sad case, have as little efficacy in encouraging procreation, as it has now in discouraging it? I should apprehend a decrease of population even in our Country where it increases so rapidly. In 1775 Franklin made a morning Visit, at Mrs. Yards to Sam. Adams and John. He was unusally loquacious. "Man, a rational Creature"! said Franklin. "Come, Let Us suppose a rational Man. Strip him of all his Appetites, especially of his hunger and thirst. He is in his Chamber, engaged in making Experiments, or in pursuing some Problem. He is highly entertained. At this moment a Servant Knocks, "Sir dinner is on Table." "Dinner! Pox! Pough! But what have you for dinner?" Ham and Chickens. "Ham"! "And must I break the chain of my thoughts, to go down and knaw a morsel of a damn'd Hogs Arse"? "Put aside your Ham." "I will dine tomorrow."

Take away Appetite and the present generation would not live a month and no future generation would ever exist. Thus the exalted dignity of human Nature would be annihilated and lost. And in my opinion, the whole loss would be of no more importance, than putting out a Candle, quenching a Torch, or crushing a Firefly, *if in this world only We have hope.*

Your distinction between natural and artificial Aristocracy does not appear to me well founded. Birth and Wealth are conferred on some Men, as imperiously by Nature, as Genius, Strength or Beauty. The Heir is honours and Riches, and power has often no more merit in procuring these Advantages, than he has in obtaining an handsome face or an elegant figure. When Aristocracies, are established by human Laws and honour Wealth and Power are made hereditary by municipal Laws and political Institutions, then I acknowledge artificial Aristocracy to commence: but this never commences, till Corruption in Elections becomes dominant and uncontroulable. But this artificial Aristocracy can never last. The everlasting Envys, Jealousies, Rivalries, and

quarrells among them, their cruel rapacities upon the poor ignorant People their followers, compell these to sett up Caesar, a Demogogue to be a Monarch and Master,
pour mettre chacun a sa place ["to put each one in his place"]. Here you have the
origin of all artificial Aristocracy, which is the origin of all Monarchy. And both artificial Aristocracy, and Monarchy, and civil, military, political and hierarchical Despotism, have all grown out of the natural Aristocracy of "Virtues and Talents." We,
to be sure, are far remote from this. Many hundred years must roll away before We
shall be corrupted. Our pure, virtuous, public spirited federative Rupublick will last
for ever, govern the Globe and introduce the perfection of Man, his perfectability being
already proved by Price Priestly, Condorcet Rousseau Diderot and Godwin.

"Mischief has been done by the Senate of U.S." I have known and felt more of
this mischief, than Washington, Jefferson and Madison altoge[the]r. But this has been
all caused by the constitutional Power of the Senate in Executive Business, which
ought to be immediately, totally and eternally abolished.

Your distinction between the aristoi and pseudo aristoi, will not help the matter.
I would trust one as soon as the other with unlimited Power. The Law wisely refuses
an Oath as a witness in his own cause to the Saint as well as to the Sinner.

No Romance would be more amusing, than the History of your Virginian and our
new England Aristocratical Families. Yet even in Rhode Island, where there has been
no Clergy, no Church, and I had almost said, no State, and some People say no religion, there has been a constant respect for certain old Families. 57 or 58 years ago, in
company with Col. Counsellor, Judge, John Chandler, whom I have quoted before, a
Newspaper was brought in. The old Sage asked me to look for the News from Rhode
Island and see how the Elections had gone there. I read the List of Wantons, Watsons,
Greens, Whipples, Malbones etc. "I expected as much" said the aged Gentleman, "for
I have always been of Opinion, that in the most popular Governments, the Elections
will generally go in favour of the most ancient families." To this day when any of these
Tribes and We may Add Ellerys, Channings Champlins etc are pleased to fall in with
the popular current, they are sure to carry all before them.

You suppose a difference Opinion between You and me, on the Subject of Aristocracy. I can find none. I dislike and detest hereditary honours, Offices Emoluments
established by Law. So do you. I am for ex[c]luding legal hereditary distinctions from
the U.S. as long as possible. So are you. I only say that Mankind have not yet discovered any remedy against irresistable Corruption in Elections to Offices of great Power
and Profit, but making them hereditary.

But will you say our Elections are pure? Be it so; upon the whole. But do you
recollect in history, a more Corrupt Election than that of Aaron Burr to be President,
or that of De Witt Clinton last year. By corruption, here I mean a sacrifice of every
national Interest and honour, to private and party Objects.

I see the same Spirit in Virginia, that you and I see in Rhode Island and the rest
of New England. In New York it is a struggle of Family Feuds. A fewdal Aristocracy.
Pensylvania is a contest between German, Irish and old English Families. When Germans and Irish Unite, they give 30,000 majorities. There is virtually a White Rose and
a Red Rose a Caesar and a Pompey in every State in this Union and Contests and
dissentions will be as lasting. The Rivalry of Bourbons and Noailleses produced The
French Revolution, and a similar Competition for Consideration and Influence, exists
and prevails in every Village in the World.

Where will terminate the Rabies Agri ["madness for land"]? The Continent will be scattered over with Manors, much larger than Livingstons, Van Ranselaers or Phillips's. Even our Deacon Strong will have a Principality among you Southern Folk. What Inequality of Talents will be produced by these Land Jobbers?

Where tends the Mania for Banks? At my Table in Philadelphia, I once proposed to you to unite in endeavours to obtain an Amendment of the Constitution, prohibiting to the separate States the Power of creating Banks; but giving Congress Authority to establish one Bank, with a branch in each State; the whole limited to Ten Millions of dollars. Whether this Project was wise or unwise, I know not, for I had deliberated little on it then and have never thought it worth thinking much of since. But you spurned the Proposition from you with disdain.

This System of Banks begotten, hatched and brooded by Duer, Robert and Governeur Morris, Hamilton and Washington, I have always considered as a System of national Injustice. A Sacrifice of public and private Interest to a few Aristocratical Friends and Favourites. My scheme could have had no such Effect.

Verres plundered Temples and robbed a few rich Men; but he never made such ravages among private property in general, nor swindled so much out of the pocketts of the poor and the middle Class of People as these Banks have done. No people but this would have borne the Imposition so long. The People of Ireland would not bear Woods half pence. What Inequalities of Talent, have been introduced into this Country by these Aristtocratical Banks!

Our Winthrops, Winslows, Bradfords, Saltonstalls, Quincys, Chandlers, Leonards Hutchinsons Olivers, Sewalls etc are precisely in the Situation of your Randolphs, Carters, and Burwells, and Harrisons. Some of them unpopular for the part they took in the late revolution, but all respected for their names and connections and whenever they fall in with the popular Sentiments, are preferred, cetoris paribus to all others. When I was young, the Summum Bonum in Massachusetts, was to be worth ten thousand pounds Sterling, ride in a Chariot, be Colonel of a Regiment of Miltia and hold a seat in his Majesty's Council. No Mans Imagination aspired to any thing higher beneath the Skies. But these Plumbs, Chariots, Colonelships and counsellorships are recorded and will never be forgotten. No great Accumulations of Land were made by our early Settlers. Mr. Bausoin a French Refugee, made the first great Purchases and your General Dearborne, born under a fortunate Starr is now enjoying a large Portion of the Aristocratical sweets of them.

As I have no Amanuenses but females, and there is so much about generation in this letter that I dare not ask any one of them to copy it, and I cannot copy it myself I must beg of you to return it to me, your old Friend

JOHN ADAMS

To Thomas Jefferson

Quincy April 19 1817

DEAR SIR

My loving and beloved Friend, Pickering, has been pleased to inform the World that I have "few Friends." I wanted to whip the rogue, and I had it in my Power, if it had been in my Will to do it, till the blood come. But all my real Friends as I thought them, with Dexter and Grey at their Head insisted "that I should not say a Word." "That nothing that such a Person could write would do me the least Injury. That it would betray the Constitution and the Government, if a President out or in should enter into a Newspaper controversy, with one of his Ministers whom he had removed from his Office, in Justification of himself for that removal or any thing else." And they talked a great deal about *"The Dignity"* of the Office of President, which I do not find that any other Persons, public or private regard very much.

Nevertheless, I fear that Mr. Pickerings Information is too true. It is impossible that any Man should run such a Gauntlet as I have been driven through, and have many Friends at last. This "all who know me know" though I cannot say "who love me tell."

I have, however, either Friends who wish to amuse and solace my old age; or Ennemies who mean to heap coals of fire on my head and kill me with kindness: for they overwhelm me with Books from all quarters, enough to offuscate all Eyes, and smother and stifle all human Understanding. Chateaubriand, Grim, Tucker, Dupuis, La Harpe, Sismondi, Eustace[.] A new Translation of Herodotus by Belloe with more Notes than Text. What should I do, with all this lumber? I make my "Woman kind" as the Antiquary expresses it, read to me, all the English: but as they will not read the French, I am obliged to excruciate my Eyes to read it myself. And all to what purpose? I verily believe I was as wise and good, seventy Years ago, as I am now.

At that Period Lemuel Bryant was my Parish Priest; and Joseph Cleverly my Latin School Master. Lemuel was a jolly jocular and liberal Schollar and Divine. Joseph a Scollar and Gentleman; but a biggoted episcopalian of the School of Bishop Saunders and Dr. Hicks, a down right conscientious passive Obedience Man in Church and State. The Parson and the Pedagogue lived much together, but were eternally disputing about Government and Religion. One day, when the Schoolmaster had been more than commonly fanatical, and declared "if he were a Monark, *He would have but one Religion in his Dominions"* The Parson coolly replied "Cleverly! You would be the best Man in the World, if You had no Religion."

Twenty times, in the course of my late Reading, have I been upon the point of breaking out, "This would be the best of all possible Worlds, if there were no Religion in it."!!! But in this exclamati[on] I should have been as fanatical as Bryant or Cleverly. Without Religion this World would be something not fit to be mentioned in polite Company, I mean Hell. So far from believing in the total and universal depravity of human Nature; I believe there is no Individual totally depraved. The most abandoned Scoundrel that ever existed, never Yet Wholly extinguished his Conscience, and while Conscience remains there is some Religion. Popes, Jesuits and Sorbonists and Inquisitors have some Conscience and some Religion. So had Marius and Sylla, Caesar Cataline and Anthony, and Augustus had not much more, let Virgil and Horace say what they will.

What shall We think of Virgil and Horace, Sallust Quintillian, Pliny and even Tacitus? and even Cicero, Brutus and Seneca? Pompey I leave out of the question, as a mere politician and Soldier. Every One of these great Creatures has left indelible marks of Conscience and consequently of Religion, tho' every one of them has left abundant proofs of profligate violations of their Consciences by their little and great Passions and paltry Interests.

The vast prospect of Mankind, which these Books have passed in Review before me, from the most ancient records, histories, traditions and Fables that remain to Us, to the present day, has sickened my very Soul; and almost reconciled me to Swifts Travels among The Yahoo's. Yet I never can be a Misanthrope. Homo Sum ["I am a man"]. I must hate myself before I can hate my Fellow Men: and that I cannot and will not do. No! I will not hate any of them, base, brutal and devilish as some of them have been to me.

From the bottom of my Soul, I pitty my Fellow Men. Fears and Terrors appear to have produced an univer[s]al Credulity. Fears of Calamities in Life and punishments after death, seem to have possessed the Souls of all Men. But fear of Pain and death, here, do not seem to have been so unconquerable as fear of what is to come hereafter. Priests, Hierophants, Popes, Despots Emperors, Kings, Princes Nobles, have been as credulous as Shoeblacks, Boots, and Kitchen Scullions. The former seem to have believed in their divine Rights as sincerely as the latter. Auto de fee's in Spain and Portugal have been celebrated with as good Faith as Excommunications have been practiced in Connecticutt or as Baptisms have been refused in Phyladelphia.

How it is possible than [i.e., that] Mankind should submit to be governed as they have been is to me an inscrutable Mystery. How they could bear to be taxed to build the Temple of Diana at Ephesus, the Pyramyds of Egypt, Saint Peters at Rome, Notre Dame at Paris, St. Pauls in London, with a million Etceteras; when my Navy Yards, and my quasi Army made such a popular Clamour, I know not. Yet all my Peccadillos, never excited such a rage as the late Compensation Law!!![2]

I congratulate you, on the late Election in Connecticutt.[3] It is a kind of Epocha. Several causes have conspired. One which you would not suspect. Some one, no doubt instigated by the Devil, has taken it into his head to print a new Edition of "The independent Whig" even in Connecticut, and has scattered the Volumes through the State. These Volumes it is said, have produced a Burst of Indignation against Priestcraft Bigotry and Intollerance, and in conjunction with other causes have produced the late Election. When writing to you I never know when to Subscribe

JOHN ADAMS

2. In 1816 and 1817 Congress passed several invalid-pension bills for veterans of the War of 1812. Adams apparently refers to the bill enacted on March 3, 1817.

3. The campaign issue in the spring election of 1817 was "whether freemen shall be tolerated in the free exercise of their religious and political rights." Oliver Wolcott, father of the Constitution of 1818 (Connecticut's first), was elected governor.

THOMAS JEFFERSON

Selection from *Notes on the State of Virginia*
1787

Letters to John Adams, October 28, 1813;
to Benjamin Rush, with a Syllabus, April 21, 1803;
and to Thomas Law, June 13, 1814

No American figure—not even Franklin—was more devoted to or pursued more successfully the Enlightenment ideal of a many-sided intellectual life in the service of the public good than Thomas Jefferson. Nor does one work reflect more completely his varied activities as scientist, architect, philosopher, and statesman than *Notes on the State of Virginia,* the book he produced out of his answers to a questionnaire circulated by the secretary of the French legation at Philadelphia. The selection from the four queries presented herein illustrates what might be called Jefferson's political sociology, or his pioneering effort at integrating his enlightened views of society and culture with his democratic politics and ethics. In his discussion of blacks and slavery, his two sets of interests seem painfully and tragically, if not completely, at odds. By contrast, in his discussions of public education and religious freedom, he argued compellingly that a hierarchical but enlightened educational system and a free, experimental approach to religious belief undergirded republican self-government and social progress. But the tour de force of Jefferson's republican sociology was his famous answer to the query about manufactures. Here he maintained that the spring of social and political virtue was economic independence, which, in turn, was nurtured by a commercial yet nonetheless self-sufficient kind of farming made possible by America's "immensity of land." As Jefferson's most succinctly political statement on the role of talent and virtue in a democratic polity was *his* side of the exchange with Adams over the nature of an aristocracy, this letter is printed following the *Notes.* Finally, Jefferson's mature politics was most deeply rooted in his moral philosophy, which he developed in his usual serenely methodical, epistolary fashion. In his "Syllabus" on the doctrines of Jesus that he enclosed in his letter to Benjamin Rush, Jefferson argued for a severely ethicized and socialized Christianity that was as far from Paine's militantly rationalistic, anti-Christian deism as it was from Adams's skeptical pietism. But in his letter to Thomas Law, Jefferson presented his most developed case for the social efficacy of a moral philosophy. Jefferson's benevolent "moral sense" was as involuntary and democratic as any sense, yet tested, he conceded, by varying standards of "utility" and "general feeling." Adrienne Koch, *The Philosophy of Thomas Jefferson* (New York, 1943) is a still useful introduction to Jefferson's thought. And for a still challenging, although somewhat one-sided, study of Jefferson's naturalistic philosophy, see Daniel J. Boorstin, *The Lost World of Thomas Jefferson* (Boston, 1948). A recent provocative exchange on the character of Jeffersonian political ideology is found in Lance Banning, "Jeffersonian Ideology Revisited: Liberal and Classical Ideas in the New American Republic" and Joyce Appleby, "Republicanism in Old and New Contexts," *William and Mary Quarterly,* 43 (January 1986), 3–34. For two excellent contrasting interpretations of Jefferson's views on blacks and slavery, see Winthrop D. Jordan, *White over Black: American Attitudes Toward the*

Negro, 1550–1812 (Chapel Hill, 1968), 429–81; and David Brion Davis, *The Problem of Slavery in the Age of Revolution, 1770–1823* (Ithaca, N.Y., 1975), 164–212. Elizabeth Flower and Murray G. Murphey, in their *History of Philosophy in America*, vol. 1 (New York, 1977), 277–353, include a valuable discussion of Jefferson's ethics and metaphysics in the context of trends in eighteenth-century American philosophy. Charles B. Sanford, *The Religious Life of Thomas Jefferson* (Charlottesville, Va., 1984) is a balanced survey, but for a fine brief study of Jefferson's religion, see Eugene R. Sheridan, "Introduction," in *Jefferson's Extracts from the Gospels: "The Philosophy of Jesus" and "The Life and Morals of Jesus,"* ed. Dickinson W. Adams, *The Papers of Thomas Jefferson, Second Series*, ed. Charles T. Cullen (Princeton, 1983), 3–42.

Selection from *Notes on the State of Virginia*
1787

Q U E R Y   X I V .

Laws

The administration of justice and description of the laws?
. . . . . .

Many of the laws which were in force during the monarchy being relative merely to that form of government, or inculcating principles inconsistent with republicanism, the first assembly which met after the establishment of the commonwealth appointed a committee to revise the whole code, to reduce it into proper form and volume, and report it to the assembly. . . . The following are the most remarkable alterations proposed:

To change the rules of descent, so as that the lands of any person dying intestate shall be divisible equally among all his children, or other representatives, in equal degree.

To make slaves distributable among the next of kin, as other moveables.

To have all public expences, whether of the general treasury, or of a parish or county, (as for the maintenance of the poor, building bridges, court-house, &c.) supplied by assessments on the citizens, in proportion to their property.

To hire undertakers for keeping the public roads in repair, and indemnify individuals through whose lands new roads shall be opened.

To define with precision the rules whereby aliens should become citizens, and citizens make themselves aliens.

To establish religious freedom on the broadest bottom.

To emancipate all slaves born after passing the act. The bill reported by the revisors does not itself contain this proposition; but an amendment containing it was prepared, to be offered to the legislature whenever the bill should be taken up, and further directing, they they should continue with their parents to a certain age, then be

Source: Thomas Jefferson, *Notes on the State of Virginia,* ed. William Peden (Chapel Hill: University of North Carolina Press, 1955), 130, 136–37, 137–43, 146–49, 157, 159–65. Editor's notes omitted. Reprinted by permission of The University of North Carolina Press, Copyright © 1955.

brought up, at the public expence, to tillage, arts or sciences, according to their gen-iusses, till the females should be eighteen, and the males twenty-one years of age, when they should be colonized to such place as the circumstances of the time should render most proper, sending them out with arms, implements of houshold and of the handicraft arts, seeds, pairs of the useful domestic animals, &c. to declare them a free and independant people, and extend to them our alliance and protection, till they shall have acquired strength; and to send vessels at the same time to other parts of the world for an equal number of white inhabitants; to induce whom to migrate hither, proper encouragements were to be proposed. It will probably be asked, Why not retain and incorporate the blacks into the state, and thus save the expence of supplying, by importation of white settlers, the vacancies they will leave? Deep rooted prejudices enterained by the whites; ten thousand recollections, by the blacks, of the injuries they have sustained; new provocations; the real distinctions which nature has made; and many other circumstances, will divide us into parties, and produce convulsions which will probably never end but in the extermination of the one or the other race.—To these objections, which are political, may be added others, which are physical and moral. The first difference which strikes us is that of colour. Whether the black of the negro resides in the reticular membrane between the skin and scarf-skin, or in the scarf-skin itself; whether it proceeds from the colour of the blood, the colour of the bile, or from that of some other secretion, the difference is fixed in nature, and is as real as if its seat and cause were better known to us. And is this difference of no importance? Is it not the foundation of a greater or less share of beauty in the two races? Are not the fine mixtures of red and white, the expressions of every passion by greater or less suffusions of colour in the one, preferable to that eternal monotony, which reigns in the countenances, that immoveable veil of black which covers all the emotions of the other race? Add to these, flowing hair, a more elegant symmetry of form, their own judgment in favour of the whites, declared by their preference of them, as uniformly as is the preference of the Oran-ootan for the black women over those of his own species. The circumstance of superior beauty, is thought worthy attention in the propagation of our horses, dogs, and other domestic animals; why not in that of man? Besides those of colour, figure, and hair, there are other physical distinctions proving a difference of race. They have less hair on the face and body. They secrete less by the kidnies, and more by the glands of the skin, which gives them a very strong and disagreeable odour. This greater degree of transpiration renders them more tol-erant of heat, and less so of cold, than the whites. Perhaps too a difference of structure in the pulmonary apparatus, which a late ingenious experimentalist has discovered to be the principal regulator of animal heat, may have disabled them from extricating, in the act of inspiration, so much of that fluid from the outer air, or obliged them in expiration, to part with more of it. They seem to require less sleep. A black, after hard labour through the day, will be induced by the slightest amusements to sit up till mid-night, or later, though knowing he must be out with the first dawn of the morning. They are at least as brave, and more adventuresome. But this may perhaps proceed from a want of forethought, which prevents their seeing a danger till it be present. When present, they do not go through it with more coolness or steadiness than the whites. They are more ardent after their female: but love seems with them to be more an eager desire, than a tender delicate mixture of sentiment and sensation. Their griefs are transient. Those numberless afflictions, which render it doubtful whether heaven has given life to us in mercy or in wrath, are less felt, and sooner forgotten with them. In general, their existence appears to participate more of sensation than reflection. To this must be ascribed their disposition to sleep when abstracted from their diversions, and unemployed in labour. An animal whose body is at rest, and who does not reflect, must be disposed to sleep of course. Comparing them by their faculties of memory, reason, and imagination, it appears to me, that in memory they are equal to the whites; in reason much inferior, as I think one could scarcely be found capable of tracing and comprehending the investigations of Euclid; and that in imagination they are dull, tasteless, and anomalous. It would be unfair to follow them to Africa for this investigation. We will consider them here, on the same stage with the whites, and where the facts are not apocryphal on which a judgment is to be formed. It will be right to make great allowances for the difference of condition, of education, of conversation, of the sphere in which they move. Many millions of them have been brought to, and born in America. Most of them indeed have been confined to tillage, to their own homes, and their own society: yet many have been so situated, that they might have availed themselves of the conversation of their masters; many have been brought up to the handicraft arts, and from that circumstance have always been associated with the whites. Some have been liberally educated, and all have lived in countries where the arts and sciences are cultivated to a considerable degree, and have had before their eyes samples of the best works from abroad. The Indians, with no advantages of this kind, will often carve figures on their pipes not destitute of design and merit. They will crayon out an animal, a plant, or a country, so as to prove the existence of a germ in their minds which only wants cultivation. They astonish you with strokes of the most sublime oratory; such as prove their reason and sentiment strong, their imagination glowing and elevated. But never yet could I find that a black had uttered a thought above the level of plain narration; never see even an elementary trait of painting or sculpture. In music they are more generally gifted than the whites with accurate ears for tune and time, and they have been found capable of imagining a small catch. Whether they will be equal to the composition of a more extensive run of melody, or of complicated harmony, is yet to be proved. Misery is often the parent of the most affecting touches in poetry.—Among the blacks is misery enough, God knows, but no poetry. Love is the peculiar œstrum of the poet. Their love is ardent, but it kindles the senses only, not the imagination. Religion indeed has produced a Phyllis Whately; but it could not produce a poet. The compositions published under her name are below the dignity of criticism. The heroes of the Dunciad are to her, as Hercules to the author of that poem. Ignatius Sancho has approached nearer to merit in composition; yet his letters do more honour to the heart than the head. They breathe the purest effusions of friendship and general philanthropy, and shew how great a degree of the latter may be compounded with strong religious zeal. He is often happy in the turn of his compliments, and his stile is easy and familiar, except when he affects a Shandean fabrication of words. But his imagination is wild and extravagant, escapes incessantly from every restraint of reason and taste, and, in the course of its vagaries, leaves a tract of thought as incoherent and eccentric, as is the course of a meteor through the sky. His subjects should often have led him to a process of sober reasoning: yet we find him always substituting sentiment for demonstration. Upon the whole, though we admit him to the first place among those of his own colour who have presented themselves to the public judgment, yet when we compare him with the writers of the race among whom he lived, and particularly with the epistolary class, in which he has taken his own stand, we are compelled to enroll him at the bottom of the column. This criticism supposes the letters published under his name to be genuine, and to have received amendment from no other hand; points which would not be of easy investigation. The improvement of the blacks in body and mind, in the first instance of their mixture with the whites, has been observed by every one, and proves that their inferiority is not the effect merely of their condition of life. We know that among the Romans, about the Augustan age especially, the condition of their slaves was much more deplorable than that of the blacks on the continent of America. The two sexes were confined in separate apartments, because to raise a child cost the master more than to buy one. Cato, for a very restricted indulgence to his slaves in this particular, took from them a certain price. But in this country the slaves multiply as fast as the free inhabitants. Their situation and manners place the commerce between the two sexes almost without restraint.— The same Cato, on a principle of œconomy, always sold his sick and superannuated slaves. He gives it as a standing precept to a master visiting his farm, to sell his old oxen, old waggons, old tools, old and diseased servants, and every thing else become useless. "Vendat boves vetulos, plaustrum vetus, ferramenta, vetera, servum senem, servum morbosum, & si quid aliud supersit vendat." The American slaves cannot enumerate this among the injuries and insults they receive. It was the common practice to expose in the island of Æsculapius, in the Tyber, diseased slaves, whose cure was like to become tedious. The Emperor Claudius, by an edict, gave freedom to such of them as should recover, and first declared, that if any person chose to kill rather than to expose them, it should be deemed homicide. The exposing them is a crime of which no instance has existed with us; and were it to be followed by death, it would be punished capitally. We are told of a certain Vedius Pollio, who, in the presence of Augustus, would have given a slave as food to his fish, for having broken a glass. With the Romans, the regular method of taking the evidence of their slaves was under torture. Here it has been thought better never to resort to their evidence. When a master was murdered, all his slaves, in the same house, or within hearing, were condemned to death. Here punishment falls on the guilty only, and as precise proof is required against him as against a freeman. Yet notwithstanding these and other discouraging circumstances among the Romans, their slaves were often their rarest artists. They excelled too in science, insomuch as to be usually employed as tutors to their master's children. Epictetus, [Diogenes, Phaedon], Terence, and Phædrus, were slaves. But they were of the race of whites. It is not their condition then, but nature, which has produced the distinction.—Whether further observation will or will not verify the conjecture, that nature has been less bountiful to them in the endowments of the head, I believe that in those of the heart she will be found to have done them justice. That disposition to theft with which they have been branded, must be ascribed to their situation, and not to any depravity of the moral sense. The man, in whose favour no laws of property exist, probably feels himself less bound to respect those made in favour of others. When arguing for ourselves, we lay it down as a fundamental, that laws, to be just, must give a reciprocation of right: that, without this, they are mere arbitrary rules of conduct, founded in force, and not in conscience: and it is a problem which I give to the master to solve, whether the religious precepts against the violation of property were not framed for him as well as his slave? And whether the slave may not as justifiably take a little from one, who has taken all from him, as he may slay one who would slay him? That a change in the relations in which a man is placed should change his ideas of moral right and wrong, is neither new, nor peculiar to the colour of the blacks. Homer tells us it was so 2600 years ago.

ἥμισυ γάρ τ' ἀρετῆς ἀποαίνυται εὐρύοπα Ζεὺς
ἀνέρος, εὖτ' ἄν μιν κατὰ δούλιον ἦμαρ ἕλησιν. *Od.* 17. 323.
Jove fix'd it certain, that whatever day
Makes man a slave, takes half his worth away.

But the slaves of which Homer speaks were whites. Notwithstanding these considerations which must weaken their respect for the laws of property, we find among them numerous instances of the most rigid integrity, and as many as among their better instructed masters, of benevolence, gratitude, and unshaken fidelity.—The opinion, that they are inferior in the faculties of reason and imagination, must be hazarded with great diffidence. To justify a general conclusion, requires many observations, even where the subject may be submitted to the Anatomical knife, to Optical glasses, to analysis by fire, or by solvents. How much more then where it is a faculty, not a substance, we are examining; where it eludes the research of all the senses; where the conditions of its existence are various and variously combined; where the effects of those which are present or absent bid defiance to calculation; let me add too, as a circumstance of great tenderness, where our conclusion would degrade a whole race of men from the rank in the scale of beings which their Creator may perhaps have given them. To our reproach it must be said, that though for a century and a half we have had under our eyes the races of black and of red men, they have never yet been viewed by us as subjects of natural history. I advance it therefore as a suspicion only, that the blacks, whether originally a distinct race, or made distinct by time and circumstances, are inferior to the whites in the endowments both of body and mind. It is not against experience to suppose, that different species of the same genus, or varieties of the same species, may possess different qualifications. Will not a lover of natural history then, one who views the gradations in all the races of animals with the eye of philosophy, excuse an effort to keep those in the department of man as distinct as nature has formed them? This unfortunate difference of colour, and perhaps of faculty, is a powerful obstacle to the emancipation of these people. Many of their advocates, while they wish to vindicate the liberty of human nature, are anxious also to preserve its dignity and beauty. Some of these, embarrassed by the question "What further is to be done with them?" join themselves in opposition with those who are actuated by sordid avarice only. Among the Romans emancipation required but one effort. The slave, when made free, might mix with, without staining the blood of his master. But with us a second is necessary, unknown to history. When freed, he is to be removed beyond the reach of mixture.

. . . . . .

Another object of the revisal is, to diffuse knowledge more generally through the mass of the people. This bill proposes to lay off every county into small districts of five or six miles square, called hundreds, and in each of them to establish a school for teaching reading, writing, and arithmetic. The tutor to be supported by the hundred, and every person in it entitled to send their children three years gratis, and as much longer as they please, paying for it. These schools to be under a visitor, who is annually to chuse the boy, of best genius in the school, of those whose parents are too poor to give them further education, and to send him forward to one of the grammar schools, of which twenty are proposed to be erected in different parts of the country, for teaching Greek, Latin, geography, and the higher branches of numerical arithmetic. Of the boys thus sent in any one year, trial is to be made at the grammar schools one or two years, and the best genius of the whole selected, and continued six years, and the residue dismissed. By this means twenty of the best geniusses will be raked from the rubbish annually, and be instructed, at the pubic expence, so far as the grammar schools go. At the end of six years instruction, one half are to be discontinued (from among whom the grammar schools will probably be supplied with future masters); and the other half, who are to be chosen for the superiority of their parts and disposition, are to be sent and continued three years in the study of such sciences as they shall chuse, at William and Mary college, the plan of which is proposed to be enlarged, as will be hereafter explained, and extended to all the useful sciences. The ultimate result of the whole scheme of education would be the teaching all children of the state reading, writing, and common arithmetic: turning out ten annually of superior genius, well taught in Greek, Latin, geography, and the higher branches of arithmetic: turning out ten others annually, of still superior parts, who, to those branches of learning, shall have added such of the sciences as their genius shall have led them to: the furnishing to the wealthier part of the people convenient schools, at which their children may be educated, at their own expence.—The general objects of this law are to provide an education adapted to the years, to the capacity, and the condition of every one, and directed to their freedom and happiness. Specific details were not proper for the law. These must be the business of the visitors entrusted with its execution. The first stage of this education being the schools of the hundreds, wherein the great mass of the people will receive their instruction, the principal foundations of future order will be laid here. Instead therefore of putting the Bible and Testament into the hands of the children, at an age when their judgments are not sufficiently matured for religious enquiries, their memories may here be stored with the most useful facts from Grecian, Roman, European and American history. The first elements of morality too may be instilled into their minds; such as, when further developed as their judgments advance in strength, may teach them how to work out their own greatest happiness, by shewing them that it does not depend on the condition of life in which chance has placed them, but is always the result of a good conscience, good health, occupation, and freedom in all just pursuits.—Those whom either the wealth of their parents or the adoption of the state shall destine to higher degrees of learning, will go on to the grammar schools, which constitute the next stage, there to be instructed in the languages. The learning Greek and Latin, I am told, is going into disuse in Europe. I know not what their manners and occupations may call for: but it would be very ill-judged in us to follow their example in this instance. There is a certain period of life, say from eight to fifteen or sixteen years of age, when the mind, like the body, is not yet firm enough for laborious and close operations. If applied to such, it falls an early victim to premature exertion; exhibiting indeed at first, in these young and tender subjects, the flattering appearance of their being men while they are yet children, but ending in reducing them to be children when they should be men. The memory is then most susceptible and tenacious of impressions; and the learning of languages being chiefly a work of memory, it seems precisely fitted to the powers of this period, which is long enough too for acquiring the most useful languages antient and modern. I do not pretend that language is science. It is only an instrument for the attainment of science. But that time is not lost which is employed in providing tools for future operation: more especially as in this case the books put into the hands of the youth for this purpose may be such as will at the same time impress their minds with useful facts and good principles. If this period be suffered to pass in idleness, the mind becomes lethargic and impotent, as would the body it inhabits if unexercised during the same time. The sympathy between body and mind during their rise, progress and decline, is too strict and obvious to endanger our being misled while we reason from the one to the other.—As soon as they are of sufficient age, it is supposed they will be sent on from the grammar schools to the university, which constitutes our third and last stage, there to study those sciences which may be adapted to their views.—By that part of our plan which prescribes the selection of the youths of genius from among the classes of the poor, we hope to avail the state of those talents which nature has sown as liberally among the poor as the rich, but which perish without use, if not sought for and cultivated.—But of all the views of this law none is more important, none more legitimate, than that of rendering the people the safe, as they are the ultimate, guardians of their own liberty. For this purpose the reading in the first stage, where *they* will receive their whole education, is proposed, as has been said, to be chiefly historical. History by apprising them of the past will enable them to judge of the future; it will avail them of the experience of other times and other nations; it will qualify them as judges of the actions and designs of men; it will enable them to know ambition under every disguise it may assume; and knowing it, to defeat its views. In every government on earth is some trace of human weakness, some germ of corruption and degeneracy, which cunning will discover, and wickedness insensibly open, cultivate, and improve. Every government degenerates when trusted to the rulers of the people alone. The people themselves therefore are its only safe depositories. And to render even them safe their minds must be improved to a certain degree. This indeed is not all that is necessary, though it be essentially necessary. An amendment of our constitution must here come in aid of the public education. The influence over government must be shared among all the people. If every individual which composes their mass participates of the ultimate authority, the government will be safe; because the corrupting the whole mass will exceed any private resources of wealth: and public ones cannot be provided but by levies on the people. In this case every man would have to pay his own price. The government of Great-Britain has been corrupted, because but one man in ten has a right to vote for members of parliament. The sellers of the government therefore get nine-tenths of their price clear. It has been thought that corruption is restrained by confining the right of suffrage to a few of the wealthier of the people: but it would be more effectually restrained by an extension of that right to such numbers as would bid defiance to the means of corruption.

Lastly, it is proposed, by a bill in this revisal, to begin a public library and gallery, by laying out a certain sum annually in books, paintings, and statues.

QUERY XVII.

Religion

The different religions received into that state?

. . . . . .

The error seems not sufficiently eradicated, that the operations of the mind, as well as the acts of the body, are subject to the coercion of the laws. But our rulers can have authority over such natural rights only as we have submitted to them. The rights of conscience we never submitted, we could not submit. We are answerable for them to our God. The legitimate powers of government extend to such acts only as are injurious to others. But it does me no injury for my neighbour to say there are twenty gods, or no god. It neither picks my pocket nor breaks my leg. If it be said, his testimony in a court of justice cannot be relied on, reject it then, and be the stigma on him. Constraint may make him worse by making him a hypocrite, but it will never make him a truer man. It may fix him obstinately in his errors, but will not cure them. Reason and free enquiry are the only effectual agents against error. Give a loose to them, they will support the true religion, by bringing every false one to their tribunal, to the test of their investigation. They are the natural enemies of error, and of error only. Had not the Roman government permitted free enquiry, Christianity could never have been introduced. Had not free enquiry been indulged, at the æra of the reformation, the corruptions of Christianity could not have been purged away. If it be restrained now, the present corruptions will be protected, and new ones encouraged. Was the government to prescribe to us our medicine and diet, our bodies would be in such keeping as our souls are now. Thus in France the emetic was once forbidden as a medicine, and the potatoe as an article of food. Government is just as infallible too when it fixes systems in physics. Galileo was sent to the inquisition for affirming that the earth was a sphere: the government had declared it to be as flat as a trencher, and Galileo was obliged to adjure his error. This error however at length prevailed, the earth became a globe, and Descartes declared it was whirled round its axis by a vortex. The government in which he lived was wise enough to see that this was no question of civil jurisdiction, or we should all have been involved by authority in vortices. In fact, the vortices have been exploded, and the Newtonian principle of gravitation is now more firmly established, on the basis of reason, than it would be were the government to step in, and to make it an article of necessary faith. Reason and experiment have been indulged, and error has fled before them. It is error alone which needs the support of government. Truth can stand by itself. Subject opinion to coercion: whom will you make your inquisitors? Fallible men; men governed by bad passions, by private as well as public reasons. And why subject it to coercion? To produce uniformity. But is uniformity of opinion desireable? No more than of face and stature. Introduce the bed of Procrustes then, and as there is danger that the large men may beat the small, make us all of a size, by lopping the former and stretching the latter. Difference of opinion is advantageous in religion. The several sects perform the office of a Censor morum over each other. Is uniformity attainable? Millions of innocent men, women, and children, since the introduction of Christianity, have been burnt, tortured, fined, imprisoned; yet we have not advanced one inch towards uniformity. What has been the effect of coercion? To make one half the world fools, and the other half hypocrites. To support roguery and error all over the earth. Let us reflect that it is inhabited by a thousand millions of people. That these profess probably a thousand different systems of religion. That ours is but one of that thousand. That if there be but one right, and ours that one, we should wish to see the 999 wandering sects gathered into the fold of truth. But against such a majority we cannot effect this by force. Reason and persuasion are the only practicable instruments. To make way for these, free enquiry must be indulged; and how can we wish others to indulge it while we refuse it ourselves. But every state, says an inquisitor, has established some religion. No two, say I, have established the same. Is this a proof of the infallibility of establishments? Our sister states of Pennsylvania and New York, however, have long subsisted without any establishment at all. The experiment was new and doubtful when they made it. It has answered beyond conception. They flourish infinitely. Religion is well supported; of various kinds, indeed, but all good enough; all sufficient to preserve peace and order: or if a sect arises, whose tenets would subvert morals, good sense has fair play, and reasons and laughs it out of doors, without suffering the state to be troubled with it. They do not hang more malefactors than we do. They are not more disturbed with religious dissensions. On the contrary, their harmony is unparalleled, and can be ascribed to nothing but their unbounded tolerance, because there is no other circumstance in which they differ from every nation on earth. They have made the happy discovery, that the way to silence religious disputes, is to take no notice of them. Let us too give this experiment fair play, and get rid, while we may, of those tyrannical laws. It is true, we are as yet secured against them by the spirit of the times. I doubt whether the people of this country would suffer an execution for heresy, or a three years imprisonment for not comprehending the mysteries of the Trinity. But is the spirit of the people an infallible, a permanent reliance? Is it government? Is this the kind of protection we receive in return for the rights we give up? Besides, the spirit of the times may alter, will alter. Our rulers will become corrupt, our people careless. A single zealot may commence persecutor, and better men be his victims. It can never be too often repeated, that the time for fixing every essential right on a legal basis is while our rulers are honest, and ourselves united. From the conclusion of this war we shall be going down hill. It will not then be necessary to resort every moment to the people for support. They will be forgotten, therefore, and their rights disregarded. They will forget themselves, but in the sole faculty of making money, and will never think of uniting to effect a due respect for their rights. The shackles, therefore, which shall not be knocked off at the conclusion of this war, will remain on us long, will be made heavier and heavier, till our rights shall revive or expire in a convulsion.

QUERY XVIII.

Manners

The particular customs and manners that may happen to be received in that state?

It is difficult to determine on the standard by which the manners of a nation may be tried, whether *catholic,* or *particular*. It is more difficult for a native to bring to that standard the manners of his own nation, familiarized to him by habit. There must doubtless be an unhappy influence on the manners of our people produced by the existence of slavery among us. The whole commerce between master and slave is a perpetual exercise of the most boisterous passions, the most unremitting despotism on the one part, and degrading submissions on the other. Our children see this, and learn to imitate it; for man is an imitative animal. This quality is the germ of all education in him. From his cradle to his grave he is learning to do what he sees other do. If a parent could find no motive either in his philanthropy or his self-love, for restraining the intemperance of passion towards his slave, it should always be a sufficient one that his child is present. But generally it is not sufficient. The parent storms, the child looks on, catches the lineaments of wrath, puts on the same airs in the circle of smaller slaves, gives a loose to his worst of passions, and thus nursed, educated, and daily exercised in tyranny, cannot but be stamped by it with odious peculiarities. The man must be a prodigy who can retain his manners and morals undepraved by such circumstances. And with what execration should the statesman be loaded, who permitting one half the citizens thus to trample on the rights of the other, transforms those into despots, and these into enemies, destroys the morals of the one part, and the amor patriæ of the other. For if a slave can have a country in this world, it must be any other in preference to that in which he is born to live and labour for another: in which he must lock up the faculties of his nature, contribute as far as depends on his individual endeavours to the evanishment of the human race, or entail his own miserable condition on the endless generations proceeding from him. With the morals of the people, their industry also is destroyed. For in a warm climate, no man will labour for himself who can make another labour for him. This is so true, that of the proprietors of slaves a very small proportion indeed are ever seen to labour. And can the liberties of a nation be thought secure when we have removed their only firm basis, a conviction in the minds of the people that these liberties are of the gift of God? That they are not to be violated but with his wrath? Indeed I tremble for my country when I reflect that God is just: that his justice cannot sleep for ever: that considering numbers, nature and natural means only, a revolution of the wheel of fortune, an exchange of situation, is among possible events: that it may become probable by supernatural interference! The Almighty has no attribute which can take side with us in such a contest.— But it is impossible to be temperate and to pursue this subject through the various considerations of policy, of morals, of history natural and civil. We must be contented to hope they will force their way into every one's mind. I think a change already perceptible, since the origin of the present revolution. The spirit of the master is abating, that of the slave rising from the dust, his condition mollifying, the way I hope preparing, under the auspices of heaven, for a total emancipation, and that this is disposed, in the order of events, to be with the consent of the masters, rather than by their extirpation.

QUERY XIX.

Manufactures

The present state of manufactures, commerce, interior and exterior trade?

We never had an interior trade of any importance. Our exterior commerce has suffered very much from the beginning of the present contest. During this time we have manufactured within our families the most necessary articles of cloathing. Those of cotton will bear some comparison with the same kinds of manufacture in Europe; but those of wool, flax and hemp are very coarse, unsightly, and unpleasant: and such is our attachment to agriculture, and such our preference for foreign manufactures, that be it wise or unwise, our people will certainly return as soon as they can, to the raising raw materials, and exchanging them for finer manufactures than they are able to execute themselves.

The political œconomists of Europe have established it as a principle that every state should endeavour to manufacture for itself: and this principle, like many others, we transfer to America, without calculating the difference of circumstance which should often produce a difference of result. In Europe the lands are either cultivated, or locked up against the cultivator. Manufacture must therefore be resorted to of necessity not of choice, to support the surplus of their people. But we have an immensity of land courting the industry of the husbandman. Is it best then that all our citizens should be employed in its improvement, or that one half should be called off from that to exercise manufactures and handicraft arts for the other? Those who labour in the earth are the chosen people of God, if ever he had a chosen people, whose breasts he has made his peculiar deposit for substantial and genuine virtue. It is the focus in which he keeps alive that sacred fire, which otherwise might escape from the face of the earth. Corruption of morals in the mass of cultivators is a phænomenon of which no age nor nation has furnished an example. It is the mark set on those, who not looking up to heaven, to their own soil and industry, as does the husbandman, for their subsistance, depend for it on the casualties and caprice of customers. Dependance begets subservience and venality, suffocates the germ of virtue, and prepares fit tools for the designs of ambition. This, the natural progress and consequence of the arts, has sometimes perhaps been retarded by accidental circumstances: but, generally speaking, the proportion which the aggregate of the other classes of citizens bears in any state to that of its husbandmen, is the proportion of its unsound to its healthy parts, and is a good-enough barometer whereby to measure its degree of corruption. While we have land to labour then, let us never wish to see our citizens occupied at a work-bench, or twirling a distaff. Carpenters, masons, smiths, are wanting in husbandry: but, for the general operations of manufacture, let our work-shops remain in Europe. It is better to carry provisions and materials to workmen there, than bring them to the provisions and materials, and with them their manners and principles. The loss by the transportation of commodities across the Atlantic will be made up in happiness and permanence of government. The mobs of great cities add just so much to the support of pure government, as sores do to the strength of the human body. It is the manners and spirit of a people which preserve a republic in A degeneracy in these is a canker which soon eats to the heart of its laws and constitution.

Letters to John Adams, October 28, 1813;
to Benjamin Rush, with a Syllabus, April 21, 1803;
and to Thomas Law, June 13, 1814

To John Adams

Monticello Oct. 28. [18]13.

DEAR SIR

According to the reservation between us, of taking up one of the subjects of our correspondence at a time, I turn to your letters of Aug. 16. and Sep. 2.

The passage you quote from Theognis, I think has an Ethical, rather than a political object. The whole piece is a moral *exhortation, παραίνεσις*, and this passage particularly seems to be a reproof to man, who, while with his domestic animals he is curious to improve the race by employing always the finest male, pays no attention to the improvement of his own race, but intermarries with the vicious, the ugly, or the old, for considerations of wealth or ambition. It is in conformity with the principle adopted afterwards by the Pythagoreans, and expressed by Ocellus in another form. Περι δε τῆς ἐκ τῶν αλλήλων ανθρωπων γενεσεως, etc.—ουχ ἡδονης ἐνεκα ἡ μιξις. Which, as literally as intelligibility will admit, may be thus translated. 'Concerning the interprocreation of men, how, and of whom it shall be, in a perfect manner, and according to the laws of modesty and sanctity, conjointly, this is what I think right. First to lay it down that we do not commix for the sake of pleasure, but of the procreation of children. For the powers, the organs and desires for coition have not been given by god to man for the sake of pleasure, but for the procreation of the race. For as it were incongruous for a mortal born to partake of divine life, the immortality of the race being taken away, god fulfilled the purpose by making the generations uninterrupted and continuous. This therefore we are especially to lay down as a principle, that coition is not for the sake of pleasure.' But Nature, not trusting to this moral and abstract motive, seems to have provided more securely for the perpetuation of the species by making it the effect of the oestrum implanted in the constitution of both sexes. And not only has the commerce of love been indulged on this unhallowed impulse, but made subservient also to wealth and ambition by marriages without regard to the beauty, the healthiness, the understanding, or virtue of the subject from which we are to breed. The selecting the best male for a Haram of well chosen females also, which Theognis seems to recommend from the example of our sheep and asses, would doubtless improve the human, as it does the brute animal, and produce a race of veritable αριστοι ["aristocrats"]. For experience proves that the moral and physical

Source: The Adams-Jefferson Letters: The Complete Correspondence Between Thomas Jefferson and Abigail and John Adams, 2 vols., ed. Lester J. Cappon, vol. 2 (Chapel Hill: University of North Carolina Press, 1959), 387–92; *The Papers of Thomas Jefferson, Second Series,* ed. Charles T. Cullen, *Jefferson's Extracts from the Gospels: "The Philosophy of Jesus" and "The Life and Morals of Jesus,"* ed. Dickinson W. Adams (Princeton: Princeton University Press, 1983), 331–34, 355–58. Editor's notes in Cappon altered; editor's notes in Adams omitted. Reprinted by permission of The University of North Carolina Press, Copyright © 1955; Princeton University Press, Copyright © 1983.

qualities of man, whether good or evil, are transmissible in a certain degree from father to son. But I suspect that the equal rights of men will rise up against this privileged Solomon, and oblige us to continue acquiescence under the Ἀμαυρωσις γενεος ἀστων ["the degeneration of the race of men"] which Theognis complains of, and to content ourselves with the accidental aristoi produced by the fortuitous concourse of breeders. For I agree with you that there is a natural aristocracy among men. The grounds of this are virtue and talents. Formerly bodily powers gave place among the aristoi. But since the invention of gunpowder has armed the weak as well as the strong with missile death, bodily strength, like beauty, good humor, politeness and other accomplishments, has become but an auxiliary ground of distinction. There is also an artificial aristocracy founded on wealth and birth, without either virtue or talents; for with these it would belong to the first class. The natural aristocracy I consider as the most precious gift of nature for the instruction, the trusts, and government of society. And indeed it would have been inconsistent in creation to have formed man for the social state, and not to have provided virtue and wisdom enough to manage the concerns of the society. May we not even say that that form of government is the best which provides the most effectually for a pure selection of these natural aristoi into the offices of government? The artificial aristocracy is a mischievous ingredient in government, and provision should be made to prevent it's ascendancy. On the question, What is the best provision, you and I differ; but we differ as rational friends, using the free exercise of our own reason, and mutually indulging it's errors. *You* think it best to put the Pseudo-aristoi into a separate chamber of legislation where they may be hindered from doing mischief by their coordinate branches, and where also they may be a protection to wealth against the Agrarian and plundering enterprises of the Majority of the people. I think that to give them power in order to prevent them from doing mischief, is arming them for it, and increasing instead of remedying the evil. For if the coordinate branches can arrest their action, so may they that of the coordinates. Mischief may be done negatively as well as positively. Of this a cabal in the Senate of the U.S. has furnished many proofs. Nor do I believe them necessary to protect the wealthy; because enough of these will find their way into every branch of the legislation to protect themselves. From 15. to 20. legislatures of our own, in action for 30. years past, have proved that no fears of an equalisation of property are to be apprehended from them.

I think the best remedy is exactly that provided by all our constitutions, to leave to the citizens the free election and separation of the aristoi from the pseudo-aristoi, of the wheat from the chaff. In general they will elect the real good and wise. In some instances, wealth may corrupt, and birth blind them; but not in sufficient degree to endanger the society.

It is probable that our difference of opinion may in some measure be produced by a difference of character in those among whom we live. From what I have seen of Massachusets and Connecticut myself, and still more from what I have heard, and the character given of the former by yourself, [vol. I. p. 3.] who know them so much better, there seems to be in those two states a traditionary reverence for certain families, which has rendered the offices of the government nearly hereditary in those families. I presume that from an early period of your history, members of these families happening to posses virtue and talents, have honestly exercised them for the good of the people, and by their services have endeared their names to them.

In coupling Connecticut with you, I mean it politically only, not morally. For having made the Bible the Common law of their land they seem to have modelled their morality on the story of Jacob and Laban. But altho' this hereditary succession to office with you may in some degree be founded in real family merit, yet in a much higher degree it has proceeded from your strict alliance of church and state. These families are canonised in the eyes of the people on the common principle "you tickle me, and I will tickle you." In Virginia we have nothing of this. Our clergy, before the revolution, having been secured against rivalship by fixed salaries, did not give themselves the trouble of acquiring influence over the people. Of wealth, there were great accumulations in particular families, handed down from generation to generation under the English law of entails. But the only object of ambition for the wealthy was a set in the king's council. All their court then was paid to the crown and it's creatures; and they Philipised in all collisions between the king and people. Hence they were unpopular; and that unpopularity continues attached to their names. A Randolph, a Carter, or a Burwell must have great personal superiority over a common competitor to be elected by the people, even at this day.

At the first session of our legislature after the Declaration of Independance, we passed a law abolishing entails. And this was followed by one abolishing the privilege of Primogeniture, and dividing the lands of intestates equally among all their children, or other representatives. These laws, drawn by myself, laid the axe to the root of Pseudo-aristocracy. And had another which I prepared been adopted by the legislature, our work would have been compleat. It was a Bill for the more general diffusion of learning. This proposed to divide every county into wards of 5. or 6. miles square, like your townships; to establish in each ward a free school for reading, writing and common arithmetic; to provide for the annual selection of the best subjects from these schools who might recieve at the public expence a higher degree of education at a district school; and from these district schools to select a certain number of the most promising subjects to be compleated at an University, where all the useful sciences should be taught. Worth and genius would thus have been sought out from every condition of life, and compleatly prepared by education for defeating the competition of wealth and birth for public trusts.

My proposition had for a further object to impart to these wards those portions of self-government for which they are best qualified, by confiding to them the care of their poor, their roads, police, elections, the nomination of jurors, administration of justice in small cases, elementary exercises of militia, in short, to have made them little republics, with a Warden at the head of each, for all those concerns which, being under their eye, they would better manage than the larger republics of the county or state. A general call of ward-meetings by their Wardens on the same day thro' the state would at any time produce the genuine sense of the people on any required point, and would enable the state to act in mass, as your people have so often done, and with so much effect, by their town meetings. The law for religious freedom, which made a part of this system, having put down the aristocracy of the clergy, and restored to the citizen the freedom of the mind, and those of entails and descents nurturing an equality of condition among them, this on Education would have raised the mass of the people to the high ground of moral respectability necessary to their own safety, and to orderly government; and would have compleated the great object of qualifying them to select the veritable aristoi, for the trusts of government, to the exclusion of the Pseudalists: and the same Theognis who has furnished the epigraphs of your two letters assures us that 'ουδεμιαν πω, Κυρν' ἀγαθοι πολιν ὤλεσαν ἀνδρες ["Curnis, good men have never harmed any city"]'. Altho' this law has not yet been acted on but in a small and inefficient degree, it is still considered as before the legislature, with other bills of the revised code, not yet taken up, and I have great hope that some patriotic spirit will, at a favorable moment, call it up, and make it the key-stone of the arch of our government.

With respect to Aristocracy, we should further consider that, before the establishment of the American states, nothing was known to History but the Man of the old world, crouded within limits either small or overcharged, and steeped in the vices which that situation generates. A government adapted to such men would be one thing; but a very different one that for the Man of these states. Here every one may have land to labor for himself if he chuses; or, preferring the exercise of any other industry, may exact for it such compensation as not only to afford a comfortable subsistence, but wherewith to provide for a cessation from labor in old age. Every one, by his property, or by his satisfactory situation, is interested in the support of law and order. And such men may safely and advantageously reserve to themselves a wholsome controul over their public affairs, and a degree of freedom, which in the hands of the Canaille of the cities of Europe, would be instantly perverted to the demolition and destruction of every thing public and private. The history of the last 25. years of France, and of the last 40. years in America, nay of it's last 200. years, proves the truth of both parts of this observation.

But even in Europe a change has sensibly taken place in the mind of Man. Science had liberated the ideas of those who read and reflect, and the American example has kindled feelings of right in the people. An insurrection has consequently begun, of science, talents and courage against rank and birth, which have fallen into contempt. It has failed in it's first effort, because the mobs of the cities, the instrument used for it's accomplishment, debased by ignorance, poverty and vice, could not be restrained to rational action. But the world will recover from the panic of this first catastrophe. Science is progressive, and talents and enterprize on the alert. Resort may be had to the people of the country, a more governable power from their principles and subordination; and rank, and birth, and tinsel-aristocracy will finally shrink into insignificance, even there. This however we have no right to meddle with. It suffices for us, if the moral and physical condition of our own citizens qualifies them to select the able and good for the direction of their government, with a recurrence of elections at such short periods as will enable them to displace an unfaithful servant before the mischief he meditates may be irremediable.

I have thus stated my opinion on a point on which we differ, not with a view to controversy, for we are both too old to change opinions which are the result of a long life of inquiry and reflection; but on the suggestion of a former letter of yours, that we ought not to die before we have explained ourselves to each other. We acted in perfect harmony thro' a long and perilous contest for our liberty and independance. A constitution has been acquired which, tho neither of us think perfect, yet both consider as competent to render our fellow-citizens the happiest and the securest on whom the sun has ever shone. If we do not think exactly alike as to it's imperfections, it matters little to our country which, after devoting to it long lives of disinterested labor, we have delivered over to our successors in life, who will be able to take care of it, and of themselves.

Of the pamphlet on aristocracy which has been sent to you, or who may be it's author, I have heard nothing but thro' your letter. If the person you suspect[1] it may be known from the quaint, mystical and hyperbolical ideas, involved in affected, new-fangled and pedantic terms, which stamp his writings. Whatever it be, I hope your quiet is not to be affected at this day by the rudeness of intemperance of scribblers; but that you may continue in tranquility to live and to rejoice in the prosperity of our country until it shall be your own wish to take your seat among the Aristoi who have gone before you. Ever and affectionately yours.

TH: JEFFERSON . . .

To Benjamin Rush, with a Syllabus

Washington April 21, 1803.

DEAR SIR

In some of the delightful conversations with you, in the evenings of 1798.99., which served as an Anodyne to the afflictions of the crisis through which our country was then labouring, the Christian religion was sometimes our topic: and I then promised you that, one day or other, I would give you my views of it. They are the result of a life of enquiry and reflection, and very different from that Anti-Christian system, imputed to me by those who know nothing of my opinions. To the corruptions of Christianity, I am indeed opposed; but not to the genuine precepts of Jesus himself. I am a Christian, in the only sense in which he wished any one to be; sincerely attached to his doctrines, in preference to all others; ascribing to himself every human excellence, and believing he never claimed any other. At the short intervals, since these conversations, when I could justifiably abstract my mind from public affairs, this subject has been under my contemplation. But the more I considered it, the more it expanded beyond the measure of either my time or information. In the moment of my late departure from Monticello, I recieved from Doctr. Priestly his little treatise of "Socrates and Jesus compared." This being a section of the general view I had taken of the field, it became a subject of reflection, while on the road, and unoccupied otherwise. The result was, to arrange in my mind a Syllabus, or Outline, of such an Estimate of the comparative merits of Christianity, as I wished to see executed, by some one of more leisure and information for the task than myself. This I now send you, as the only discharge of my promise I can probably ever execute. And, in confiding it to you, I know it will not be exposed to the malignant perversions of those who make every word from me a text for new misrepresentations and calumnies. I am moreover averse to the communication of my religious tenets to the public; because it would countenance the presumption of those who have endeavored to draw them before that tribunal, and to seduce public opinion to erect itself into that Inquisition over the rights of conscience, which the laws have so justly proscribed. It behoves every man, who values liberty of conscience for himself, to resist invasions of it in the case of others; or their case may, by change of circumstances, become his own. It behoves him too, in his own case, to give no example of concession, betraying the common right of independant opinion, by answering questions of faith, which the laws have left between god and himself. Accept my affectionate salutations.

TH: JEFFERSON

1. John Taylor of Caroline.

ENCLOSURE

Syllabus of an Estimate of the merit of the doctrines of Jesus, compared with those of others.

In a comparative view of the Ethics of the enlightened nations of antiquity, of the Jews, and of Jesus, no notice should be taken of the corruptions of reason, among the antients, to wit, the idolatry and superstition of their vulgar, Nor of the corruptions of Christianity by the over learned among it's professors.

Let a just view be taken of the moral principles inculcated by the most esteemed of the sects of antt. philosophy, or of their individuals; particularly Pythagoras, Socrates, Epicurus, Cicero, Epictetus, Seneca, Antoninus.

I. Philosophers. 1. Their precepts related chiefly to ourselves, and the government of those passions which, unrestrained, would disturb our tranquility of mind.[2] In this branch of Philosophy they were really great.

2. In developing our duties to others, they were short and defective. They embraced indeed the circles of kindred and friends: and inculcated patriotism, or the love of our country in the aggregate, as a primary obligation: towards our neighbors and countrymen, they taught justice, but scarcely viewed them as within the circle of benevolence. Still less have they inculcated peace, charity, and love to our fellow men, or embraced with benevolence, the whole family of mankind.

II. Jews. 1. Their system was Deism, that is, the belief of one only god. But their ideas of him, and of his attributes, were degrading and injurious.

2. Their Ethics were not only imperfect, but often irreconcileable with the sound dictates of reason and morality, as they respect intercourse with those around us: and repulsive, and anti-social, as respecting other nations. They needed reformation therefore in an eminent degree.

III. Jesus. In this state of things among the Jews, Jesus appeared. His parentage was obscure, his condition poor, his education null, his natural endowments great, his life correct and innocent; he was meek, benevolent, patient, firm, disinterested, and of the sublimest eloquence.

The disadvantgages under which his doctrines appear are remarkeable.

1. Like Socrates and Epictetus he wrote nothing himself.

2. But he had not, like them, a Xenophon or an Arrian to write for him. On the contrary, all the learned of his country, entrenched in it's power and riches, were opposed to him lest his labours should undermine their advantages:

and the committing to writing his life and doctrines, fell on the most unlettered, and ignorant of men:

---

2. To explain, I will exhibit the heads of Seneca's and Cicero's philosophical works, the most extensive of any we have recieved from the antients. Of 10. heads in Seneca, 7. relate to ourselves, to wit, de irâ, Consolatio, de tranquilitate, de constantiâ sapientis, de otio sapientis, de vitâ beatâ, de brevitate vitae. 2. relate to others, de clementia, de beneficiis, and 1. relates to the government of the world, de providentiâ. Of 11. tracts of Cicero, 5 respect ourselves, viz. de finibus, Tusculana, Academica, Paradoxa, de Senectute. 1. de officiis, partly to ourselves, partly to others. 1. de amicitiâ, relates to others: and 4. are on different subjects, to wit, de naturâ deorum, de divinatione, de fato, Somnium Scipionis. [T.J. note]

who wrote too from memory, and not till long after the transactions had passed.

3. According to the ordinary fate of those who attempt to enlighten and reform mankind,

he fell an early victim to the jealousy and combination of the altar and the throne;

at about 33. years of age, his reason having not yet attained the maximum of it's energy,

nor the course of his preaching, which was but of about 3. years, presented occasions for developing a compleat system of morals.

4. Hence the doctrines which he really delivered were defective as a whole.

And fragments only of what he did deliver have come to us, mutilated, mistated, and often unintelligible.

5. They have been still more disfigured by the corruptions of schismatising followers,

who have found an interest in sophisticating and perverting the simple doctrines he taught,

by engrafting on them the mysticisms of a Graecian Sophist, frittering them into subtleties, and obscuring them with jargon,

until they have caused good men to reject the whole in disgust, and to view Jesus himself as an impostor.

Notwithstanding these disadvantages, a system of morals is presented to us, which,

if filled up in the true style and spirit of the rich fragments he left us,

would be the most perfect and sublime that has ever been taught by man.

The question of his being a member of the god-head, or in direct communication with it,

claimed for him by some of his followers, and denied by others,

is foreign to the present view, which is merely an estimate of the intrinsic merit of his doctrines.

1. He corrected the Deism of the Jews, confirming them in their belief of one only god,

and giving them juster notions of his attributes and government.

2. His moral doctrines relating to kindred and friends were more pure and perfect, than those of the most correct of the philosophers, and greatly more so than those of the Jews.

And they went far beyond both in inculcating universal philanthropy,

not only to kindred and friends, to neighbors and countrymen,

but to all mankind, gathering all into one family, under the bonds of love, charity, peace, common wants, and common aids. A development of this head will evince the peculiar superiority of the system of Jesus over all others.

3. The precepts of Philosophy, and of the Hebrew code, laid hold of actions only.

He pushed his scrutinies into the heart of man; erected his tribunal in the region of his thoughts, and purified the waters at the fountain head.

4. He taught, emphatically, the doctrine of a future state: which was either doubted or disbelieved by the Jews:

and wielded it with efficacy, as an important incentive, supplementory to the other motives to moral conduct.

To Thomas Law

Poplar Forest near Lynchburg. June 13. [18]14.

Dear Sir

The copy of your Second thoughts on Instinctive impulses with the letter accompanying it, was recieved just as I was setting out on a journey to this place, two or three days distant from Monticello. I brought it with me, and read it with great satisfaction; and with the more, as it contained exactly my own creed on the foundation of morality in man. It is really curious that, on a question so fundamental, such a variety of opinions should have prevailed among men; and those too of the most exemplary virtue and first order of understanding. It shews how necessary was the care of the Creator in making the moral principle so much a part of our constitution as that no errors of reasoning or of speculation might lead us astray from it's observance in practice. Of all the theories on this question, the most whimsical seems to have been that of Woollaston, who considers *truth* as the foundation of morality. The thief who steals your guinea does wrong only inasmuch as he acts a lie, in using your guinea as if it were his own. Truth is certainly a branch of morality, and a very important one to society. But, presented as it's foundation, it is as if a tree, taken up by the roots, had it's stem reversed in the air, and one of it's branches planted in the ground.—Some have made the *love of god* the foundation of morality. This too is but a branch of our moral duties, which are generally divided into duties to god, and duties to man. If we did a good act merely from the love of god, and a belief that it is pleasing to him, whence arises the morality of the Atheist? It is idle to say as some do, that no such being exists. We have the same evidence of the fact as of most of those we act on, to wit, their own affirmations, and their reasonings in support of them. I have observed indeed generally that, while in protestant countries the defections from the Platonic Christianity of the priests is to Deism, in Catholic countries they are to Atheism. Diderot, Dalembert, D'Holbach, Condorcet, are known to have been among the most virtuous of men. Their virtue then must have had some other foundation than the love of god.

The *το καλον* of others is founded in a different faculty, that of taste, which is not even a branch of morality. We have indeed an innate sense of what we call beautiful: but that is exercised chiefly on subjects addressed to the fancy, whether thro' the eye, in visible forms, as landscape, animal figure, dress, drapery, architecture, the composition of colours &c. or to the imagination directly, as imagery, style, or measure in prose or poetry, or whatever else constitutes the domain of criticism or taste, a faculty entirely distinct from the moral one. Self-interest, or rather Self love, or *Egoism,* has been more plausibly substituted as the basis of morality. But I consider our relations with others as constituting the boundaries of morality. With ourselves we stand on the ground of identity, not of relation; which last, requiring two subjects, excludes self-love confined to a single one. To ourselves, in strict language, we can owe no duties, obligation requiring also two parties. Self-love therefore is no part of morality. Indeed it is exactly it's counterpart. It is the sole antagonist of virtue, leading us constantly by our propensities to self-gratification in violation of our moral duties to others. Accordingly it is against this enemy that are erected the batteries of moralists and religionists, as the only obstacle to the practice of morality. Take from man his selfish propensities, and he can have nothing to seduce him from the practice of virtue. Or subdue those propensities by education, instruction, or restraint, and virtue remains without a competitor. Egoism, in a broader sense, has been thus presented as the source of moral action. It has been said that we feed the hungry, clothe the naked, bind up the wounds of the man beaten by thieves, pour oil and wine into them, set him on our own beast, and bring him to the inn, because we recieve ourselves pleasure from these acts. So Helvetius, one of the best men on earth, and the most ingenious advocate of this principle, after defining 'interest' to mean, not merely that which is pecuniary, but whatever may procure us pleasure or withdraw us from pain, [de l'Es-prit.2.1.] says [ib. 2.2.] 'the humane man is he to whom the sight of misfortune is insupportable and who, to rescue himself from this spectacle, is forced to succour the unfortunate object.' This indeed is true. But it is one step short of the ultimate question. These good acts give us pleasure: but how happens it that they give us pleasure? Because nature hath implanted in our breasts a love of others, a sense of duty to them, a moral instinct in short, which prompts us irresistibly to feel and to succour their distresses; and protests against the language of Helvetius [ib. 2.5.] 'what other motive than self interest could determine a man to generous actions? It is as impossible for him to love what is good for the sake of good, as to love evil for the sake of evil.' The creator would indeed have been a bungling artist, had he intended man for a social animal, without planting in him social dispositions. It is true they are not planted in every man; because there is no rule without exceptions; but it is false reasoning which converts exceptions into the general rule. Some men are born without the organs of sight, or of hearing, or without hands. Yet it would be wrong to say that man is born without these faculties; and sight, hearing and hands may with truth enter into the general definition of Man. The want or imperfection of the moral sense in some men, like the want or imperfection of the senses of sight and hearing in others, is no proof that it is a general characteristic of the species. When it is wanting we endeavor to supply the defect by education, by appeals to reason and calculation, by presenting to the being so unhappily conformed other motives to do good, and to eschew evil; such as the love, or the hatred or rejection of those among whom he lives and whose society is necessary to his happiness, and even existence; demonstrations by sound calculation that honesty promotes interest in the long run; the rewards and penalties established by the laws; and ultimately the prospects of a future state of retribution for the evil as well as the good done while here. These are the correctives which are supplied by education, and which exercise the functions of the moralist, the preacher and legisla-tor: and they lead into a course of correct action all those whose depravity is not too profound to be eradicated. Some have argued against the existence of a moral sense, by saying that if nature had given us such a sense, impelling us to virtuous actions, and warning us against those which are vicious, then nature must also have desig-nated, by some particular ear-marks, the two sets of actions which are, in themselves, the one virtuous, and the other vicious: whereas we find in fact, that the same actions are deemed virtuous in one country, and vicious in another. The answer is that nature has constituted *utility* to man the standard and test of virtue. Men living in different countries, under different circumstances, different habits, and regimens, may have dif-ferent utilities. The same act therefore may be useful, and consequently virtuous, in one country, which is injurious and vicious in another differently circumstanced. I sincerely then believe with you in the general existence of a moral instinct. I think it the brightest gem with which the human character is studded; and the want of it as more degrading than the most hideous of the bodily deformities. I am happy in reviewing the roll of associates in this principle which you present in your 2d. letter, some of which I had not before met with. To these might be added Ld. Kaims, one of the ablest of our advocates, who goes so far as to say, in his Principles of Natural religion, that a man owes no duty to which he is not urged by some impulsive feeling. This is correct if referred to the standard of general feeling in the given case, and not to the feeling of a single individual. Perhaps I may misquote him, it being fifty years since I read his book.

The leisure and solitude of my situation here has led me to the indiscretion of taxing you with a long letter on a subject whereon nothing new can be offered you. I will indulge myself no further than to repeat the assurances of my continued esteem & respect.

TH: JEFFERSON

GEORGE MASON

"Objections to the Constitution of Government Formed by the Convention"
1787

Like many losers in history, the Antifederalists, as the opponents of ratification of the Constitution were called, have been given rather short shrift by historians. Yet their ideas contributed vitally to the shaping of the document itself, the nature of the defense made of it, and its later evolution. Furthermore, in the case of at least one Antifederalist, George Mason (1725–92), intellectual historians have a figure fully worthy of historical restitution. An erudite Virginia planter and the author of several important state papers, including the Virginia Declaration of Rights, which influenced Jefferson's Delcaration of Independence and formed the basis of the Constitution's Bill of Rights, Mason was generally recognized by his contemporaries as being, after Jefferson, the most intellectually influential of all the Virginia revolutionaries. He was also admired for his prominent role in the movement to form a stronger national government out of the Articles of Confederation and his active participation in the Constitutional Convention. But unlike most of his Convention colleagues, he refused to sign the final document, and he actively campaigned against its ratification. His objections to the Constitution were many, but they focused principally on two issues: the absence of any explicit guarantees against federal encroachment on citizens' individual rights and the inclusion of forms of representation that, in his view, promoted an unrepresentative legislative aristocracy. Although sketchy, the "Objections" succinctly demonstrated how much of the Revolution's liberal Enlightenment and republican heritage could be exploited to provide powerful ammunition to the critics of the Constitution. Helen Hill Miller, *George Mason: Gentleman Revolutionary* (Chapel Hill, 1975) is an informative biography. John M. Murrin cogently places Mason's thought in the context of the dominant traditions of eighteenth-century politics in "Can Liberals Be Patriots? Natural Right, Virtue, and Moral Sense in the America of George Mason and Thomas Jefferson," in Robert P. Davidow, ed., *Natural Rights and Natural Law: The Legacy of George Mason* (Fairfax, Va., 1986), 35–65. For an incisive discussion of Antifederalist thought, see Herbert J. Storing, *What the Anti-Federalists Were For* (Chicago, 1981).

There is no Declaration of Rights; and the Laws of the general Government being paramount to the Laws and Constitutions of the several States, the Delcaration of Rights in the separate States are no Security. Nor are the people secured even in the Enjoyment of the Benefits of the common-Law: which stands here upon no other Foundation than it's having been adopted by the respective Acts forming the Constitutions of the several States.

In the House of Representatives there is not the Substance, but the Shadow only of Representation; which can never produce proper Information in the Legislature, or inspire Confidence in the People: the Laws will therefore be generally made by Men little concern'd in, and unacquainted with their Effects and Consequences.[1]

The Senate have the Power of altering all Money-Bills, and of originating Appropriations of Money and the Sallerys of the Officers of their own Appointment in Conjunction with the President of the United States; altho' they are not the Representatives of the People, or amenable to them.

These with their other great Powers (vizt. their Power in the Appointment of Ambassadors and all public Officers, in making Treaties, and in trying all Impeachments) their Influence upon and Connection with the supreme Executive from these Causes, their Duration of Office, and their being a constant existing Body almost continually sitting, joined with their being one compleat Branch of the Legislature, will destroy any Balance in the Government, and enable them to accomplish what Usurpations they please upon the Rights and Libertys of the People.

The Judiciary of the United States is so constructed and extended, as to absorb and destroy the Judiciarys of the several States; thereby rendering Law as tedious[,] intricate and expensive, and Justice as unattainable, by a great part of the Community, as in England, and enabling the Rich to oppress and ruin the Poor.

The President of the United States has no constitutional Council (a thing unknown in any safe and regular Government) he will therefore be unsupported by proper Information and Advice; and will generally be directed by Minions and Favourites—or He will become a Tool to the Senate—or a Council of State will grow out of the principal Officers of the great Departments; the worst and most dangerous of all Ingredients for such a Council, in a free Country; for they may be induced to join in any dangerous or oppressive Measures, to shelter themselves, and prevent an Inquiry into their own Misconduct in Office; whereas had a constitutional Council been formed (as was proposed) of six Members; vizt. two from the Eastern, two from the Middle, and two from the Southern States, to be appointed by Vote of the States in the House of Representatives, with the same Duration and Rotation of Office as the Senate, the Executive wou'd always have had safe and proper Information and Advice, the President of such a Council might have acted as Vice President of the United States, pro tempore, upon any Vacancy or Disability of the chief Magistrate; and long continued Sessions of the Senate wou'd in a great Measure have been prevented.

From this fatal Defect of a constitutional Council has arisen the improper Power

---

1. This Objection has been in some Degree lessened by an Amendment, often before refused, and at last made by an Erasure, after the Engrossment upon Parchment, of the word *forty,* and inserting *thirty,* in the 3d Clause of the 2d Section of the 1st Article. [G.M. note]

Source: The Complete Anti-Federalist, ed. Herbert J. Storing, vol. 2 (Chicago: University of Chicago Press, 1981), 11–13. Editor's notes omitted. Reprinted by permission of The University of Chicago Press, Copyright © 1981.

of the Senate, in the Appointment of public Officers, and the alarming Dependence and Connection between that Branch of the Legislature, and the supreme Executive.

Hence also sprung that unnecessary and dangerous Officer, the Vice President; who for want of other Employment, is made President of the Senate; thereby dangerously blending the executive and legislative Powers; besides always giving to some one of the States an unnecessary and unjust Pre-eminence over the others.

The President of the United States has the unrestrained Power of granting Pardon for Treason; which may be sometimes exercised to screen from Punishment those whom he had secretly instigated to commit the Crime, and thereby prevent a Discovery of his own Guilt.

By declaring all Treaties supreme Laws of the Land, the Executive and the Senate have in many Cases, an exclusive Power of Legislation; which might have been avoided by proper Distinctions with Respect to Treaties, and requiring the Assent of the House of Representatives, where it cou'd be done with Safety.

By requiring only a Majority to make all commercial and navigation Laws, the five Southern States (whose Produce and Circumstances are totally different from that of the eight Northern and Eastern States) will be ruined; for such rigid and premature Regulations may be made, as will enable the Merchants of the Northern and Eastern States not only to demand an exorbitant Freight, but to monopolize the Purchase of the Commodities at their own Price, for many years: to the great Injury of the landed Interest, and Impoverishment of the People: and the Danger is the greater, as the Gain on one Side will be in Proportion to the Loss on the other. Whereas requiring two thirds of the Members present in both Houses wou'd have produced mutual moderation, promoted the general Interest, and removed an insuperable Objection to the Adoption of the Government.

Under their own Construction of the general Clause at the End of the enumerated powers the Congress may grant Monopolies in Trade and Commerce, constitute new Crimes, inflict unusual and severe punishments, and extend their Power as far as they shall think proper; so that the State Legislatures have no Security for the Powers now presumed to remain to them; or the People for their Rights.

There is no Delaration of any kind for preserving the Liberty of the Press, the Tryal by Jury in civil Causes; nor against the Danger of standing Armys in time of Peace.

The State Legislatures are restrained from laying Export Duties on their own Produce.

The general Legislature is restrained from prohibiting the further Importation of Slaves for twenty odd Years; tho' such Importations render the United States weaker, more vulnerable, and less capable of Defence.

Both the general Legislature and the State Legislatures are expressly prohibited making ex post facto Laws; tho' there never was, or can be a Legislature but must and will make such Laws, when necessity and the public Safety require them; which will hereafter be a Breach of all the Constitutions in the Union, and afford precedents for other Innovations.

This Government will commence in a moderate Aristocracy; it is at present impossible to foresee whether it will, in it's Operation, produce a Monarchy, or a corrupt oppressive Aristocracy; it will most probably vibrate some Years between the two, and then terminate in the one or the other.

ALEXANDER HAMILTON

"Constitutional Convention Speech on a Plan of Government"
1787

As aide-de-camp to General Washington, brilliant secretary of treasury in the Washington administration, and ill-fated Federalist party leader, Alexander Hamilton (1755–1804) was American republicanism's sometimes consummate man of action. As treasury secretary, he was also the author of a series of influential financial reports that advocated the most far-reaching program of governmental support for capitalist economic development in the early republic. But at the bottom of these public actions and policies, no less than with those of the more scholarly Adams and Jefferson, was a strongly held conception of the ideal republican state. Ironically, the one text where he developed his conception most completely was his speech before the Constitutional Convention, arguing for a political system considerably different from the adopted one he wound up vigorously defending in the ensuing ratification debate. Nevertheless, Hamilton canvassed many of his later ideas in this pointed critique of the Convention's two plans for a new government—specifically his notion that a strong central government could be relied on to promote the public welfare better than state and local governments, his claim that an industrious society inevitably nurtured clashing passions and interests that government needed to convert into springs of support for itself, and his belief that both private property and public virtue could be best promoted by making representation in the upper house and the executive branch as little subject to popular accountability as was still consistent with a nonhereditary republican society. For a discerning study of Hamilton's political thought, see Gerald Stourzh, *Alexander Hamilton and the Idea of Republican Government* (Stanford, Ca. 1970). But for an older yet still valuable counterview, see Cecelia M. Kenyon, "Alexander Hamilton: Rousseau of the Right," *Political Science Quarterly,* 73 (June 1958), 161–78.

James Madison's Version

[Philadelphia, June 18, 1787]

MR. HAMILTON, had been hitherto silent on the business before the Convention, partly from respect to others whose superior abilities age & experience rendered him unwilling to bring forward ideas dissimilar to theirs, and partly from his delicate situation with respect to his own State, to whose sentiments as expressed by his Colleagues, he could by no means accede. The crisis however which now marked our affairs, was too serious to permit any scruples whatever to prevail over the duty imposed on every man to contribute his efforts for the public safety & happiness. He was obliged therefore to declare himself unfriendly to both plans. He was particularly opposed to that from N. Jersey, being fully convinced, that no amendment of the Confederation, leaving the States in possession of their Sovereignty could possibly answer the purpose. On the other hand he confessed he was much discouraged by the amazing extent of Country in expecting the desired blessings from any general sovereignty that could be substituted. As to the powers of the Convention, he thought the doubts started on that subject had arisen from distinctions & reasonings too subtle. A *federal* Govt. he conceived to mean an association of independent Communities into one. Different Confederacies have different powers, and exercise them in different ways. In some instances the powers are exercised over collective bodies; in others over individuals, as in the German Diet—& among ourselves in cases of piracy. Great latitude therefore must be given to the signification of the term. The plan last proposed[1] departs itself from the *federal* idea, as understood by some, since it is to operate eventually on individuals. He agreed moreover with the Honble gentleman from Va. (Mr. R.) that we owed it to our Country, to do on this emergency whatever we should deem essential to its happiness. The States sent us here to provide for the exigences of the Union. To rely on & propose any plan not adequate to these exigences, merely because it was not clearly within our powers, would be to sacrifice the means to the end. It may be said that the *States* can not *ratify* a plan not within the purview of the article of Confederation providing for alterations & amendments. But may not the States themselves in which no constitutional authority equal to this purpose exists in the Legislatures, have had in view a reference to the people at large. In the Senate of N. York, a proviso was moved, that no act of the Convention should be binding untill it should be referred to the people & ratified; and the motion was lost by a single voice only, the reason assigned agst. it being, that it might possibly be found an inconvenient shackle.

The great question is what provision shall we make for the happiness of our Country? He would first make a comparative examination of the two plans—prove that there were essential defects in both —and point out such changes as might render a *national one,* efficacious. The great & essential principles necessary for the support of Government are 1. an active & constant interest in supporting it. This principle does not exist in the States in favor of the federal Govt. They have evidently in a high degree, the esprit de corps. They constantly pursue internal interests adverse to those

1. The New Jersey Plan.

Source: The Papers of Alexander Hamilton, vol. 4, ed. Harold C. Syrett and Jacob E. Cooke (New York: Columbia University Press, 1962), 187–95. Editors' notes altered. Reprinted by permission of Columbia University Press, Copyright © 1962.

of the whole. They have their particular debts—their particular plans of finance &c. All these when opposed to, invariably prevail over the requisitions & plans of Congress. 2. The love of power. Men love power. The same remarks are applicable to this principle. The States have constantly shewn a disposition rather to regain the powers delegated by them than to part with more, or to give effect to what they had parted with. The ambition of their demagogues is known to hate the controul of the Genl. Government. It may be remarked too that the Citizens have not that anxiety to prevent a dissolution of the Genl. Govt. as of the particular Govts. A dissolution of the latter would be fatal; of the former would still leave the purposes of Govt. attainable to a considerable degree. Consider what such a State as Virga. will be in a few years, a few compared with the life of nations. How strongly will it feel its importance & self-sufficiency? 3. An habitual attachment of the people. The whole force of this tie is on the side of the State Govt. Its sovereignty is immediately before the eyes of the people: its protection is immediately enjoyed by them. From its hand distributive justice, and all those acts which familiarize & endear Govt. to a people, are dispensed to them. 4. *Force* by which may be understood a *coertion of laws* or *coertion of arms*. Congs. have not the former except in few cases. In particualr States, this coercion is nearly sufficient; tho' he held it in most cases, not entirely so. A certain portion of military force is absolutely necessary in large communities. Masss. is now feeling this necessity & making provision for it. But how can this force be exerted on the States collectively. It is impossible. It amounts to a war between the parties. Foreign powers also will not be idle spectators. They will interpose, the confusion will increase, and a dissolution of the Union will ensue. 5. *influence*. he did not mean corruption, but a dispensation of those regular honors & emoluments, which produce an attachment to the Govt. Almost all the weight of these is on the side of the States; and must continue so as long as the States continue to exist. All the passions then we see, of avarice, ambition, interest, which govern most individuals, and all public bodies, fall into the current of the States, and do not flow in the stream of the Genl. Govt. The former therefore will generally be an overmatch for the Genl. Govt. and render any confederacy, in its very nature precarious. Theory is in this case fully confirmed by experience. The Amphyctionic Council had it would seem ample powers for general purposes. It had in particular the power of fining and using force agst. delinquent members. What was the consequence. Their decrees were mere signals of war. The Phocian war is a striking example of it. Philip at length taking advantage of their disunion, and insinuating himself into their Councils, made himself master of their fortunes. The German Confederacy affords another lesson. The authority of Charlemagne seemed to be as great as could be necessary. The great feudal chiefs however, exercising their local sovereignties, soon felt the spirit & found the means of, encroachments, which reduced the imperial authority to a nominal sovereignty. The Diet has succeeded, which tho' aided by a Prince at its head, of great authority independently of his imperial attributes, is a striking illustration of the weakness of Confederated Governments. Other examples instruct us in the same truth. The Swiss cantons have scarce any Union at all, and have been more than once at war with one another. How then are all these evils to be avoided? only by such a compleat sovereignty in the general Governmt. as will turn all the strong principles & passions above mentioned on its side. Does the scheme of N. Jersey produce this effect? does it afford any substantial remedy whatever? On the contrary it labors under great defects, and the defect of some of its provisions will destroy the efficacy of others. It gives a direct revenue to Congs. but this will not be sufficient. The balance can only be supplied by requisitions: which experience proves can not be relied on. If States are to deliberate on the mode, they will also deliberate on the object of the supplies, and will grant or not grant as they approve or disapprove of it. The delinquency of one will invite and countenance it in others. Quotas too must in the nature of things be so unequal as to produce the same evil. To what standard will you resort? Land is a fallacious one. Compare Holland with Russia: France or Engd. with other countries of Europe. Pena. with N. Carola. will the relative pecuniary abilities in those instances, correspond with the relative value of land. Take numbers of inhabitants for the rule and make like comparison of different countries, and you will find it to be equally unjust. The different degrees of industry and improvement in different Countries render the first object a precarious measure of wealth. Much depends too on *situation*. Cont. N. Jersey & N. Carolina, not being commercial States & contributing to the wealth of the commercial ones, can never bear quotas assessed by the ordinary rules of proportion. They will & must fail in their duty, their example will be followed, and the Union itself be dissolved. Whence then is the national revenue to be drawn? from Commerce? even from exports which notwithstanding the common opinion are fit objects of moderate taxation, from excise, &c &c. These tho' not equal, are less unequal than quotas. Another destructive ingredient in the plan, is that equality of suffrage which is so much desired by the small States. It is not in human nature that Va. & the large States should consent to it, or if they did that they shd. long abide by it. It shocks too much the ideas of Justice, and every human feeling. Bad principles in a Govt. tho slow are sure in their operation, and will gradually destroy it. A doubt has been raised whether Congs. at present have a right to keep Ships or troops in time of peace. He leans to the negative. Mr. Ps. plan provides no remedy. If the powers proposed were adequate, the organization of Congs. is such that they could never be properly & effectually exercised. The members of Congs. being chosen by the States & subject to recall, represent all the local prejudices. Should the powers be found effectual, they will from time to time be heaped on them, till a tyrannic sway shall be established. The general power whatever be its form if it preserves itself, must swallow up the State powers. Otherwise it will be swallowed up by them. It is agst. all the principles of a good Government to vest the requisite powers in such a body as Congs. Two Sovereignties can not co-exist within the same limits. Giving powers to Congs. must eventuate in a bad Govt. or in no Govt. The plan of N. Jersey therefore will not do. What then is to be done? Here he was embarrassed. The extent of the Country to be governed, discouraged him. The expence of a general Govt. was also formidable; unless there were such a diminution of expence on the side of the State Govts. as the case would admit. If they were extinguished, he was persuaded that great œconomy might be obtained by substituting a general Govt. He did not mean however to shock the public opinion by proposing such a measure. On the other hand he saw no *other* necessity for declining it. They are not necessary for any of the great purposes of commerce, revenue, or agriculture. Subordinate authorities he was aware would be necessary. There must be district tribunals: corporations for local purposes. But cui bono, the vast & expensive apparatus now appertaining to the States. The only difficulty of a serious nature which occurred to him, was that of drawing representatives from the extremes to the center of the Community. What inducements can be offered that will suffice? The moderate wages for the 1st. branch would only be a bait to little demagogues. Three dollars or thereabouts he supposed would be the utmost. The Senate he feared from a similar cause, would be filled by certain undertakers who wish for particular offices under the Govt. This view of the subject almost led him to despair that a Republican Govt. could be established over so great an extent. He was sensible at the same time that it would be unwise to propose one of any other form. In his private opinion he had no scruple in declaring, supported as he was by the opinions of so many of the wise & good, that the British Govt. was the best in the world: and that he doubted much whether any thing short of it would do in America. He hoped Gentlemen of different opnions would bear with him in this, and begged them to recollect the change of opinion on this subject which had taken place and was still going on. It was once thought that the power of Congs. was amply sufficient to secure the end of their institution. The error was now seen by every one. The members most tenacious of republicanism, he observed, were as loud as any in declaiming agst. the vices of democracy. This progress of the public mind led him to anticipate the time, when others as well as himself would join in the praise bestowed by Mr. Neckar on the British Constitution, namely, that it is the only Govt. in the world "which unites public strength with individual security." In every community where industry is encouraged, there will be a division of it into the few & the many. Hence separate interests will arise. There will be debtors & creditors &c. Give all power to the many, they will oppress the few. Give all power to the few, they will oppress the many. Both therefore ought to have power, that each may defend itself agst. the other. To the want of this check we owe our paper money, instalment laws &c. To the proper adjustment of it the British owe the excellence of their Constitution. Their house of Lords is a most noble institution. Having nothing to hope for by a change, and a sufficient inter-est by means of their property, in being faithful to the national interest, they form a permanent barrier agst. every pernicious innovation, whether attempted on the part of the Crown or of the Commons. No temporary Senate will have the firmness eno' to answer the purpose. The Senate (of Maryland) which seems to be so much appealed to, has not yet been sufficiently tried. Had the people been unanimous & eager, in the late appeal to them on the subject of a paper emission they would have yielded to the torrent. Their acquiescing in such an appeal is a proof of it. Gentlemen differ in their opinions concerning the necessary checks, from the different estimates they form of the human passions. They suppose seven years a sufficient period to give the senate an adequate firmness, from not duly considering the amazing violence & turbulence of the democratic spirit. When a great object of Govt. is pursued, which seizes the popular passions, they spread like wild fire, and become irresistable. He appealed to the gentlemen from the N. England States whether experience had not there verified the remark. As to the Executive, it seemed to be admitted that no good one could be established on Republican principles. Was not this giving up the merits of the question: for can there be a good Govt. without a good Executive. The English model was the only good one on this subject. The Hereditary interest of the King was so interwoven with that of the Nation, and his personal emoluments so great, that he was placed above the danger of being corrupted from abroad—and at the same time was both sufficiently independent and sufficiently controuled, to answer the purpose of the insti-tution at home. one of the weak sides of Republics was their being liable to foreign influence & corruption. Men of little character, acquiring great power become easily the tools of intermedling Neibours. Sweeden was a striking instance. The French & English had each their parties during the late Revolution which was effected by the predominant influence of the former. What is the inference from all these observa-tions? That we ought to go as far in order to attain stability and permanency, as republican principles will admit. Let one branch of the Legislature hold their places for life or at least during good behaviour. Let the Executive also be for life. He appealed to the feelings of the members present whether a term of seven years, would induce the sacrifices of private affairs which an acceptance of public trust would require, so so as to ensure the services of the best Citizens. On this plan we should have in the Senate a permanent will, a weighty interest, which would answer essential purposes. But is this a Republican Govt., it will be asked? Yes if all the Magistrates are appointed, and vacancies are filled, by the people, or a process of election originating with the people. He was sensible that an Executive constituted as he proposed would have in fact but little of the power and independence that might be necessary. On the other plan of appointing him for 7 years, he thought the Executive ought to have but little power. He would be ambitious, with the means of making creatures; and as the object of his ambition wd. be to *prolong* his power, it is probable that in case of a war, he would avail himself of the emergence, to evade or refuse a degradation from his place. An Executive for life has not this motive for forgetting his fidelity, and will therefore be a safer depository of power. It will be objected probably, that such an Executive will be an *elective Monarch,* and will give birth to the tumults which characterize that form of Govt. He wd. reply that *Monarch* is an indefinite term. It marks not either the degree or duration of power. If this Executive Magistrate wd. be a monarch for life—the other propd. by the Report from the Comtte of the whole, wd. be a monarch for seven years. The circumstance of being elective was also applicable to both. It had been observed by judicious writers that elective monarchies wd. be the best if they could be guarded agst. the *tumults* excited by the ambition and intrigues of competitors. He was not sure that tumults were an inseparable evil. He rather thought this character of Elective Monarchies had been taken rather from particular cases than from general principles. The election of Roman Emperors was made by the *Army.* In *Poland* the election is made by great rival *princes* with independent power, and ample means, of raising commotions. In the German Empire, the appointment is made by the Electors & Princes, who have equal motives & means, for exciting cabals & parties. Might not such a mode of election be devised among ourselves as will defend the community agst. these effects in any dangerous degree? Having made these observations he would read to the Committee a sketch of a plan which he shd. prefer to either of those under consideration. He was aware that it went beyond the ideas of most members. But will such a plan be adopted out of doors? In return he would ask will the people adopt the other plan? At present they will adopt neither. But he sees the Union dissolving or already dissolved—he sees evils operating in the States which must soon cure the people of their fondness for democracies—he sees that a great progress has been already made & is still going on in the public mind. He thinks therefore that the people will in time be unshackled from their prejudices; and whenever that happens, they will themselves not be satisfied at stopping where the plan of Mr. R. wd. place them, but be ready to go as far at least as he proposes.

JAMES MADISON

The Federalist, "Number 10" and "Number 51"
1787–88

Republican party leader and fourth president of the United States James Madison (1751–1836) is the only American statesman whose political theories have nearly eclipsed in historical importance his not inconsiderable career as a politician. This is mainly because of his contributions to *The Federalist,* the series of New York newspaper articles that he and Hamilton and John Jay contributed to win ratification of the Constitution. His *Federalist* writings remain to this day the most influential work in American political thought ever published, and for good reasons. In these writings, but particularly in numbers 10 and 51, Madison achieved a modern breakthrough in American republican theory. In essence he placed republican concerns for virtue on a new sociological basis. In *The Federalist* "Number 10" he argued that the proposed national government's extensive territory—which opponents of the Constitution, in line with traditional republican theory, feared would produce self-seeking factionalism—would have the very opposite effect because it would multiply and thereby neutralize competing interests. He also argued that a large republic would produce popularly elected representatives who were more cosmopolitan in their vision and therefore likely wiser and more patriotic than those representing smaller states. Madison's revisionist argument in *The Federalist* "Number 51," although less sociological, was no less elite-minded *and* protodemocratic. Here he detached the entire structure of mixed government from its historical roots in differing social orders and converted it into a system of popularly originated powers that, by checking each other, could thereby fulfill the traditional concern of republican ideology—the protection of liberty against the encroachments of power. With passions and interests so controlled and manipulated rather than suppressed or denied, self-government, Madison concluded, could be safely, if indirectly, guided by reason, either through the enlightened self-interest of the masses or through the wise and the virtuous who devised systems like those of the *Federalist.* For a valuable introduction to Madison the political thinker, see Marvin Meyers, ed., *The Mind of the Founder: Sources of the Political Thought of James Madison* (Hanover, N.H., 1981), xi–xlvii. The outstanding interpretation of Madisonian and Federalist ideas of the Constitution is Gordon S. Wood, *The Creation of the American Republic, 1776–1787* (Chapel Hill, 1969), 469–564. For two excellent studies of the philosophical bases of Madison, Hamilton, and Jay's political theories, see Morton White, *Philosophy, "The Federalist," and the Constitution* (New York, 1987); and Daniel W. Howe, "The Political Psychology of *The Federalist,*" *William and Mary Quarterly,* 44 (July 1987), 485–509.

"Number 10"

[22 November 1787]

Among the numerous advantages promised by a well constructed union, none deserves to be more accurately developed than its tendency to break and control the violence of faction. The friend of popular governments, never finds himself so much alarmed for their character and fate, as when he contemplates their propensity to this danger-ous vice. He will not fail therefore to set a due value on any plan which, without violating the principles to which he is attached, provides a proper cure for it. The instability, injustice and confusion introduced into the public councils, have in truth been the mortal diseases under which popular governments have every where per-ished; as they continue to be the favorite and fruitful topics from which the adversaries to liberty derive their most specious declamations. The valuable improvements made by the American constitutions on the popular models, both antient and modern, cannot certainly be too much admired; but it would be an unwarrantable partiality, to contend that they have as effectually obviated the danger on this side as was wished and expected. Complaints are every where heard from our most considerate and virtuous citizens, equally the friends of public and private faith, and of public and personal liberty; that our governments are too unstable; that the public good is disregarded in the conflicts of rival parties; and that measures are too often decided, not according to the rules of justice, and the rights of the minor party; but by the superior force of an interested and over-bearing majority. However anxiously we may wish that these com-plaints had no foundation, the evidence of known facts will not permit us to deny that they are in some degree true. It will be found indeed, on a candid review of our situ-ation, that some of the distresses under which we labour, have been erroneously charged on the operation of our governments; but it will be found at the same time, that other causes will not alone account for many of our heaviest misfortunes; and particularly, for that prevailing and increasing distrust of public engagements, and alarm for private rights, which are echoed from one end of the continent to the other. These must be chiefly, if not wholly, effects of the unsteadiness and injustice, with which a factious spirit has tainted our public administration.

By a faction I understand a number of citizens, whether amounting to a majority or minority of the whole, who are united and actuated by some common impulse of passion, or of interest, adverse to the rights of other citizens, or to the permanent and aggregate interests of the community.

There are two methods of curing the mischiefs of faction: The one, by removing its causes; the other, by controlling its effects.

There are again two methods of removing the causes of faction: The one by destroying the liberty which is essential to its existence; the other, by giving to every citizen the same opinions, the same passions, and the same interests.

It could never be more truly said than of the first remedy, that it is worse than the disease. Liberty is to faction, what air is to fire, an aliment without which it instantly expires. But it could not be a less folly to abolish liberty, which is essential to political life, because it nourishes faction, than it would be to wish the annihilation of air, which is essential to animal life because it imparts to fire its destructive agency.

Source: The Papers of James Madison, vol. 10, ed. Robert A. Rutland et al. (Chicago: University of Chicago Press, 1977), 263–70, 476–80. Editors' notes omitted. Reprinted by permission of The University of Chicago Press, Copyright © 1977.

The second expedient is as impracticable, as the first would be unwise. As long as the reason of man continues fallible, and he is at liberty to exercise it, different opinions will be formed. As long as the connection subsists between his reason and his self-love, his opinions and his passions will have a reciprocal influence on each other; and the former will be objects to which the latter will attach themselves. The diversity in the faculties of men from which the rights of property originate, is not less an insuperable obstacle to an uniformity of interests. The protection of these faculties is the first object of government. From the protection of different and unequal faculties of acquiring property, the possession of different degrees and kinds of property immediately results: And from the influence of these on the sentiments and views of the respective proprietors, ensues a division of the society into different interests and parties.

The latent causes of faction are thus sown in the nature of man; and we see them every where brought into different degrees of activity, according to the different circumstances of civil society. A zeal for different opinions concerning religion, concerning government, and many other points, as well of speculation as of practice; an attachment to different leaders ambitiously contending for pre-eminence and power; or to persons of other descriptions whose fortunes have been interesting to the human passions, have in turn divided mankind into parties, inflamed them with mutual animosity, and rendered them much more disposed to vex and oppress each other, than to co-operate for their common good. So strong is this propensity of mankind to fall into mutual animosities, that where no substantial occasion presents itself, the most frivolous and fanciful distinctions have been sufficient to kindle their unfriendly passions, and excite their most violent conflicts. But the most common and durable source of factions, has been the various and unequal distribution of property. Those who hold, and those who are without property, have ever formed distinct interests in society. Those who are creditors, and those who are debtors, fall under a like discrimination. A landed interest, a manufacturing interest, a mercantile interest, a monied interest, with many lesser interests, grow up of necessity in civilized nations, and divide them into different classes, actuated by different sentiments and views. The regulation of these various and interfering interests forms the principal task of modern legislation, and involves the spirit of party and faction in the necessary and ordinary operations of government.

No man is allowed to be a judge in his own cause; because his interest would certainly bias his judgment, and, not improbably, corrupt his integrity. With equal, nay with greater reason, a body of men, are unfit to be both judges and parties, at the same time; yet, what are many of the most important acts of legislation, but so many judicial determinations, not indeed concerning the rights of single persons, but concerning the rights of large bodies of citizens; and what are the different classes of legislators, but advocates and parties to the causes which they determine? Is a law proposed concerning private debts? It is a question to which the creditors are parties on one side, and the debtors on the other. Justice ought to hold the balance between them. Yet the parties are and must be themselves the judges; and the most numerous party, or, in other words, the most powerful faction must be expected to prevail. Shall domestic manufactures be encouraged, and in what degree, by restrictions on foreign manufactures? are questions which would be differently decided by the landed and the manufacturing classes; and probably by neither, with a sole regard to justice and the public good. The apportionment of taxes on the various descriptions of property, is an act which seems to require the most exact impartiality, yet there is perhaps no legislative act in which greater opportunity and temptation are given to a predominant party, to trample on the rules of justice. Every shilling with which they over-burden the inferior number, is a shilling saved to their own pockets.

It is in vain to say, that enlightened statesmen will be able to adjust these clashing interests, and render them all subservient to the public good. Enlightened statesmen will not always be at the helm: Nor, in many cases, can such an adjustment be made at all, without taking into view indirect and remote considerations, which will rarely prevail over the immediate interest which one party may find in disregarding the rights of another, or the good of the whole.

The inference to which we are brought, is, that the *causes* of faction cannot be removed; and that relief is only to be sought in the means of controlling its *effects*.

If a faction consists of less than a majority, relief is supplied by the republican principle, which enables the majority to defeat its sinister views by regular vote: It may clog the administration, it may convulse the society; but it will be unable to execute and mask its violence under the forms of the constitution. When a majority is included in a faction, the form of popular government on the other hand enables it to sacrifice to its ruling passion or interest, both the public good and the rights of other citizens. To secure the public good, and private rights against the danger of such a faction, and at the same time to preserve the spirit and the form of popular government, is then the great object to which our enquiries are directed. Let me add that it is the great desideratum, by which alone this form of government can be rescued from the opprobrium under which it has so long labored, and be recommended to the esteem and adoption of mankind.

By what means is this object attainable? Evidently by one of two only. Either the existence of the same passion or interest in a majority at the same time, must be prevented; or the majority, having such co-existent passion or interest, must be rendered, by their number and local situation, unable to concert and carry into effect schemes of oppression. If the impulse and the opportunity be suffered to coincide, we well know that neither moral nor religious motives can be relied on as an adequate control. They are not found to be such on the injustice and violence of individuals, and lose their efficacy in proportion to the number combined together; that is, in proportion as their efficacy becomes needful.

From this view of the subject, it may be concluded that a pure democracy, by which I mean a society, consisting of a small number of citizens, who assemble and administer the government in person, can admit of no cure for the mischiefs of faction. A common passion or interest will, in almost every case, be felt by a majority of the whole; a communication and concert results from the form of government itself; and there is nothing to check the inducements to sacrifice the weaker party, or an obnoxious individual. Hence it is, that such democracies have ever been spectacles of turbulence and contention; have ever been found incompatible with personal security, or the rights of property; and have in general been as short in their lives, as they have been violent in their deaths. Theoretic politicians, who have patronized this species of government, have erroneously supposed, that by reducing mankind to a perfect equality in their political rights, they would, at the same time, be perfectly equalized, and assimilated in their possessions, their opinions, and their passions.

A republic, by which I mean a government in which the scheme of representation takes place, opens a different prospect, and promises the cure for which we are seeking. Let us examine the points in which it varies from pure democracy, and we shall comprehend both the nature of the cure, and the efficacy which it must derive from the union.

The two great points of difference between a democracy and a republic, are first, the delegation of the government, in the latter, to a small number of citizens elected by the rest; secondly, the greater number of citizens, and greater sphere of country, over which the latter may be extended.

The effect of the first difference is, on the one hand, to refine and enlarge the public views, by passing them through the medium of a chosen body of citizens, whose wisdom may best discern the true interest of their country, and whose patriotism and love of justice, will be least likely to sacrifice it to temporary or partial considerations. Under such a regulation, it may well happen that the public voice pronounced by the representatives of the people, will be more consonant to the public good, than if pronounced by the people themsleves convened for the purpose. On the other hand, the effect may be inverted. Men of factious tempers, of local prejudices, or of sinister designs, may by intrigue, by corruption, or by other means, first obtain the suffrages, and then betray the interests of the people. The question resulting is, whether small or extensive republics are most favourable to the election of proper guardians of the public weal; and it is clearly decided in favour of the latter by two obvious considerations.

In the first place it is to be remarked, that however small the republic may be, the representatives must be raised to a certain number, in order to guard against the cabals of a few; and that however large it may be, they must be limited to a certain number, in order to guard against the confusion of a multitude. Hence the number of representatives in the two cases not being in proportion to that of the constituents, and being proportionally greatest in the small republic, it follows, that if the proportion of fit characters be not less in the large than in the small republic, the former will present a greater option, and consequently a greater probability of a fit choice.

In the next place, as each representative will be chosen by a greater number of citizens in the large than in the small republic, it will be more difficult for unworthy candidates to practise with success the vicious arts, by which elections are too often carried; and the suffrages of the people being more free, will be more likely to centre on men who possess the most attractive merit, and the most diffusive and established characters.

It must be confessed, that in this, as in most other cases, there is a mean, on both sides of which inconveniencies will be found to lie. By enlarging too much the number of electors, you render the representative too little acquainted with all their local circumstances and lesser interests; as by reducing it too much, you render him unduly attached to these, and too little fit to comprehend and pursue great and national objects. The federal constitution forms a happy combination in this respect; the great and aggregate interests being referred to the national, the local and particular to the state legislatures.

The other point of difference is, the greater number of citizens and extent of territory which may be brought within the compass of republican, than of democratic government; and it is this circumstance principally which renders factious combinations less to be dreaded in the former, than in the latter. The smaller the society, the fewer probably will be the distinct parties and interests composing it; the fewer the distinct parties and interests, the more frequently will a majority be found of the same party; and the smaller the number of individuals composing a majority, and the smaller the compass within which they are placed, the more easily will they concert and execute their plans of oppression. Extend the sphere, and you take in a greater variety of parties and interests; you make it less probable that a majority of the whole will have a common motive to invade the rights of other citizens; or if such a common motive exists, it will be more difficult for all who feel it to discover their own strength, and to act in unison with each other. Besides other impediments, it may be remarked, that where there is a consciousness of unjust or dishonourable purposes, communication is always checked by distrust, in proportion to the number whose concurrence is necessary.

Hence it clearly appears, that the same advantage, which a republic has over a democracy, in controlling the effects of faction, is enjoyed by a large over a small republic—is enjoyed by the union over the states composing it. Does this advantage consist in the substitution of representatives, whose enlightened views and virtuous sentiments render them superior to local prejudices, and to schemes of injustice? It will not be denied, that the representation of the union will be most likely to possess these requisite endowments. Does it consist in the greater security afforded by a greater variety of parties, against the event of any one party being able to outnumber and oppress the rest? In an equal degree does the encreased variety of parties, comprised within the union, encrease this security. Does it, in fine, consist in the greater obstacles opposed to the concert and accomplishment of the secret wishes of an unjust and interested majority? Here, again, the extent of the union gives it the most palpable advantage.

The influence of factious leaders may kindle a flame within their particular states, but will be unable to spread a general conflagration through the other states: A religious sect, may degenerate into a political faction in a part of the confederacy; but the variety of sects dispersed over the entire face of it, must secure the national councils against any danger from that source: A rage for paper money, for an abolition of debts, for an equal division of property, or for any other improper or wicked project, will be less apt to pervade the whole body of the union, than a particular member of it; in the same proportion as such a malady is more likely to taint a particular county or district, than an entire state.

In the extent and proper structure of the union, therefore, we behold a republican remedy for the diseases most incident to republican government. And according to the degree of pleasure and pride, we feel in being republicans, ought to be our zeal in cherishing the spirit, and supporting the character of federalists.

PUBLIUS.

"Number 51"

[6 February 1788]

To what expedient then shall we finally resort for maintaining in practice the necessary partition of power among the several departments, as laid down in the constitution? The only answer that can be given is, that as all these exterior provisions are found to be inadequate, the defect must be supplied, by so contriving the interior structure of the government, as that its several constituent parts may, by their mutual relations, be the means of keeping each other in their proper places. Without presuming to undertake a full developement of this important idea, I will hazard a few general observations, which may perhaps place it in a clearer light, and enable us to form a more correct judgment of the principles and structure of the government planned by the convention.

In order to lay a due foundation for that separate and distinct exercise of the different powers of government, which to a certain extent, is admitted on all hands to be essential to the preservation of liberty, it is evident that each department should have a will of its own; and consequently should be so constituted that the members of each should have as little agency as possible in the appointment of the members of the others. Were this principle rigorously adhered to, it would require that all the appointments for the supreme executive, legislative and judiciary magistracies should be drawn from the same fountain of authority, the people, through channels, having no communication whatever with one another. Perhaps such a plan of constructing the several departments would be less difficult in practice than it may in contemplation appear. Some difficulties however, and some additional expence, would attend the execution of it. Some deviations therefore from the principle must be admitted. In the constitution of the judiciary department in particular, it might be inexpedient to insist rigorously on the princple; first, because peculiar qualifications being essential in the members, the primary consideration ought to be to select that mode of choice, which best secures these qualifications; secondly, because the permanent tenure by which the appointments are held in that department, must soon destroy all sense of dependence on the authority conferring them.

It is equally evident that the members of each department should be as little dependent as possible on those of the others, for the emoluments annexed to their offices. Were the executive magistrate, or the judges, not independent of the legislature in this particular, their independence in every other, would be merely nominal.

But the great security against a gradual concentration of the several powers in the same department, consists in giving to those who administer each department, the necessary constitutional means, and personal motives, to resist encroachments of the others. The provision for defence must in this, as in all other cases, be made commensurate to the danger of attack. Ambition must be made to counteract ambition. The interest of the man must be connected with the constitutional rights of the place. It may be a reflection on human nature, that such devices should be necessary to control the abuses of government. But what is government itself but the greatest of all reflections on human nature? If men were angels, no government would be necessary. If angels were to govern men, neither external nor internal controls on government would be necessary. In framing a government which is to be administered by men over men, the great difficulty lies in this: You must first enable the government to control the governed; and in the next place, oblige it to control itself. A dependence on the people is no doubt the primary control on the government; but experience has taught mankind the necessity of auxiliary precautions.

This policy of supplying by opposite and rival interests, the defect of better motives, might be traced through the whole system of human affairs, private as well as public. We see it particularly displayed in all the subordinate distributions of power; where the constant aim is to divide and arrange the several offices in such a manner as that each may be a check on the other; that the private interest of every individual, may be a centinel over the public rights. These inventions of prudence cannot be less requisite in the distribution of the supreme powers of the state.

But it is not possible to give to each department an equal power of self-defence. In republican government the legislative authority necessarily predominates. The remedy for this inconveniency is, to divide the legislature into different branches; and to render them by different modes of election, and different principles of action, as little connected with each other, as the nature of their common functions, and their common dependence on the society, will admit. It may even be necessary to guard against dangerous encroachments by still further precautions. As the weight of the legislative authority requires that it should be thus divided, the weakness of the executive may require, on the other hand, that it should be fortified. An absolute negative, on the legislature, appears at first view to be the natural defence with which the executive magistrate should be armed. But perhaps it would be neither altogether safe, nor alone sufficient. On ordinary occasions, it might not be exerted with the requisite firmness; and on extraordinary occasions, it might be perfidiously abused. May not this defect of an absolute negative be supplied by some qualified connection between this weaker department, and the weaker branch of the stronger department, by which the latter may be led to support the constitutional rights of the former, without being too much detached from the rights of its own department?

If the principles on which these observations are founded be just, as I persuade myself they are, and they be applied as a criterion to the several state constitutions, and to the federal constitution, it will be found, that if the latter does not perfectly correspond with them, the former are infinitely less able to bear such a test.

There are moreover two considerations particularly applicable to the federal system of America, which place that system in a very interesting point of view.

First. In a single republic, all the power surrendered by the people, is submitted to the administration of a single government; and the usurpations are guarded against by a division of the government into distinct and separate departments. In the compound republic of America, the power surrendered by the people, is first divided between two distinct governments, and then the portion allotted to each, subdivided among distinct and separate departments. Hence a double security arises to the rights of the people. The different governments will control each other; at the same time that each will be controled by itself.

Second. It is of great importance in a republic, not only to guard the society against the oppression of its rulers; but to guard one part of the society against the injustice of the other part. Different interests necessarily exist in different classes of citizens. If a majority be united by a common interest, the rights of the minority will be insecure. There are but two methods of providing against this evil: The one by creating a will in the community independent of the majority, that is, of the society itself; the other by comprehending in the society so many separate descriptions of citizens, as will render an unjust combination of a majority of the whole very improbable, if not impracticable. The first method prevails in all governments possessing an hereditary or self-appointed authority. This at best is but a precarious security; because a power independent of the society may as well espouse the unjust views of the major, as the rightful interests of the minor party, and may possibly be turned against both parties. The second method will be exemplified in the federal republic of the United States. Whilst all authority in it will be derived from, and dependent on the society, the society itself will be broken into so many parts, interests and classes of citizens, that the rights of individuals or of the minority, will be in little danger from interested combinations of the majority. In a free government, the security for civil rights must be the same as that for religious rights. It consists in the one case in the multiplicity of interests, and in the other, in the multiplicity of sects. The degree of security in both cases will depend on the number of interests and sects; and this may be presumed to depend on the extent of country and number of people comprehended under the same government. This view of the subject must particularly recommend a proper federal system to all the sincere and considerate friends of republican government: Since it shews that in exact proportion as the territory of the union may be formed into more circumscribed confederacies or states, oppressive combinations of a majority will be facilitated, the best security under the republican form, for the rights of every class of citizens, will be diminished; and consequently, the stability and independence of some member of the government, the only other security must be proportionally increased. Justice is the end of government. It is the end of civil society. It ever has been, and ever will be pursued, until it be obtained, or until liberty be lost in the pursuit. In a society under the forms of which the stronger faction can readily unite and oppress the weaker, anarchy may as truly be said to reign, as in a state of nature where the weaker individual is not secured against the violence of the stronger: And as in the latter state even the stronger individuals are prompted by the uncertainty of their condition, to submit to a government which may protect the weak as well as themselves: So in the former state, will the more powerful factions or parties be gradually induced by a like motive, to wish for a government which will protect all parties, the weaker as well as the more powerful. It can be little doubted, that if the state of Rhode-Island was separated from the confederacy, and left to itself, the insecurity of rights under the popular form of government within such narrow limits, would be displayed by such reiterated oppressions of factious majorities, that some power altogether independent of the people would soon be called for by the voice of the very factions whose misrule had proved the necessity of it. In the extended republic of the United States, and among the great variety of interests, parties and sects which it embraces, a coalition of a majority of the whole society could seldom take place upon any other principles than those of justice and the general good: Whilst there being thus less danger to a minor from the will of the major party, there must be less pretext also, to provide for the security of the former, by introducing into the government a will not dependent on the latter; or in other words, a will independent of the society itself. It is no less certain than it is important, notwithstanding the contrary opinions which have been entertained, that the larger the society, provided it lie within a practicable sphere, the more duly capable it will be of self government. And happily for the *republican cause,* the practicable sphere may be carried to a very great extent, by a judicious modification and mixture of the *federal principle*.

PUBLIUS.

Part Three

Evangelical Democracy

Introduction

Four years before he died, Jefferson confidently predicted to a Unitarian correspondent that a thoroughly rationalized Unitarian Christianity would become within a generation the religion of America. He could hardly have been more wrong. In fact, at the very moment Jefferson wrote, there were occurring throughout the country stirrings of religious excitements that would soon swell into the greatest nationwide revival of emotion-laden Christian evangelicalism in American history. Indeed, by the time of the Civil War, evangelical Christianity had virtually become the religion, if not of America, at least of most Americans. No greater proof would seem to be needed to show how little the American Enlightenment had accomplished in weakening the hold on American culture of generations of Puritan- and revival-nurtured piety.

Actually, however, the Second Great Awakening of the early nineteenth century was not exactly untouched by rationalistic elements of its own. First of all, compared with earlier, more strictly Calvinistic revivals of American piety, the revivals of the Second Awakening often embraced a good many appeals to human ability and responsibility for helping to win salvation. Furthermore, evangelical preachers and academics often put a particular stress on the "common sense" and sometimes even "scientific" basis of their faith. These didactically liberalizing characteristics were developed with particular force and authority in the writings of Charles Grandison Finney. In the lecture on revivals that follows, Finney fashioned, out of a stirring yet legalistic theology of sin and accountability, an entire technology of conversion and religious awakening. Finally, leading evangelical intellectuals were sometimes quite emphatic about their faith being the religion of the common man and thus the primary engine of American social progress. Mostly the sort of popular social movements evangelicals supported were those, like temperance, that authoritatively inculcated or evidenced on a wide scale an individualistic ethic of personal self-government and liberation from sin. Some, however, derived from the quasidemocratic strain in evangelicalism a radically perfectionist vision of society. John Humphrey Noyes was especially creative in this regard. In the selection from *The Berean,* Noyes asserted an evangelical, antinomian millennialism that substituted the rule of "perfect holiness" for all purely human theological and social systems of contract and authority.

However variously democratic, evangelical Protestantism was still fundamentally a religious movement. For an understanding of the substance of democratic political thought, one needs to turn to the antebellum period's political intellectuals, particularly the writers and journalists who, as partisans of Andrew Jackson's Democratic party, made the largest claims for their democratic credentials. Jacksonian democracy is often regarded as more or less continuous with Jeffersonian republicanism, which in several important respects it was. Both ideologies associated economic independence with moral virtue, favored limited governments, and were deeply hostile to government-engendered special privileges. But many Jacksonian intellectuals went further in parlaying these stances into a full-blown philosphy of "equal rights," which they rigorously applied in denouncing a large range of not only political programs, but also social tendencies—about which Jefferson was sometimes ambiguous—that they thought interfered with individual freedom and economic equality. William Leggett was particularly famous for arguing this philosophy. In his two editorials contained herein, he advanced somewhat contrasting versions of this democratic ethic. Another distinguishing quality of Jacksonian thought was its investment of the "common man" and the "common judgment" with unprecedented moral and intellectual value. No Jacksonian intellectual made this argument more thoroughly than George Bancroft. In his oration "The Office of the People," Bancroft defended, in both sweeping and circumspect ways, the philosophical validity and cultural utility of identifying majoritarian rule with divine authority.

Like the Democratic party, the Whig party also had its intellectual defenders. And like their Jacksonian opponents, most of these Whig intellectuals too embraced the era's talisman of equality, although usually in a very different form. In their hands it appeared not as equality of rights or condition but of opportunity—to rise socially and economically or to benefit from increasing prosperity—that they believed was facilitated precisely by the tariffs, banks, internal improvements, and other programs of national institution building that the Jacksonians furiously opposed. Consistent with their optimistic conservative nationalism, these Whigs also celebrated the given fact and public virtues of American democracy and therefore denounced as unnecessary and dangerous the class envy and hostility that they believed the Jacksonian assaults on privilege encouraged. There were other Whigs, however, who joined these views with more nervously liberal views of America's prospects. More in line with the evangelicals or the morally concerned Protestant liberals from whom they drew many of their followers, they worried about the moral selfishness and social atomization that an expanding capitalist democracy seemed to them to be engendering. Intellectuals sometimes with only very tenuous ties to the Whig party were particularly attracted to this sort of thinking, and the solutions they put forward were often Whiggish but with a distinct social and moral twist: they advocated promoting egalitarian opportunity and social cohesion by shoring up, through various political and voluntaristic means, America's ostensibly nonpolitical institutions, especially the family, the school, and the church. Catharine Beecher was a particularly fascinating representative of this current. Her *Treatise on Domestic Economy* linked Whiggish concern for upward mobility with the imperative of moral influence and social cohesion in the person of the American middle-class woman. Henry C. Carey accomplished something of the same synthesis in a more extreme form in the area of economics. In the selected chapter from his *Principles of Social Science,* Carey argued that wealth, technology, and division of labor could facilitate, if properly promoted, an infinite "tendency" toward cultural perfection and social benevolence unprecedented in the history of the world. Few evangelicals could have conjured up a more glorious picture of the coming age.

Recommendations for Further Reading

Perry Miller, *The Life of the Mind in America: From the Revolution to the Civil War* (New York, 1965); Rush Welter, *The Mind of America, 1820–1860* (New York, 1975); David Brion Davis, ed., *Antebellum American Culture: An Interpretive Anthology* (Lexington, Mass., 1979); Wilson Smith, *Professors & Public Ethics: Studies of Northern Moral Philosophers Before the Civil War* (Ithaca, N.Y., 1956); Timothy L. Smith, *Revivalism and Social Reform: American Protestantism on the Eve of the Civil War* (New York, 1957); D. H. Meyer, *The Instructed Conscience: The Shaping of the American National Ethic* (Philadelphia, 1972); Theodore Dwight Bozeman, *Protestants in an Age of Science: The Baconian Ideal and Antebellum American Religious Thought* (Chapel Hill, 1977); Donald G. Mathews, *Religion in the Old South* (Chicago, 1977); E. Brooks Holifield, *The Gentlemen Theologians: American Theology in Southern Culture, 1795–1860* (Durham, N.C., 1978); Herbert Hovenkamp, *Science and Religion in America, 1800–1860* (Philadelphia, 1978); William G. McLoughlin, *Revivals, Awakenings, and Reform* (Chicago, 1978); Anne C. Loveland, *Southern Evangelicals and the Social Order, 1800–1860* (Baton Rouge, La., 1980); Leonard I. Sweet, ed., *The Evangelical Tradition in America* (Macon, Ga., 1984); Bruce Kuklick, *Churchmen and Philosophers: From Jonathan Edwards to John Dewey* (New Haven, 1985); James Turner, *Without God, Without Creed: The Origins of Unbelief in America* (Baltimore, 1985); Louise L. Stevenson, *Scholarly Means to Evangelical Ends: The New Haven Scholars and the Transformation of Higher Learning in America, 1830–1890* (Baltimore, 1986); Louis Hartz, *The Liberal Tradition in America* (New York, 1955); John William Ward, *Andrew Jackson: Symbol for an Age* (New York, 1955); Marvin Meyers, *The Jacksonian Persuasion: Politics and Belief* (Stanford, Ca., 1957); John F. Kasson, *Civilizing the Machine: Technology and Republican Values in America, 1776–1900* (New York, 1976); Daniel Walker Howe, *The Political Culture of the American Whigs* (Chicago, 1979); Robert Kelley, *The Cultural Pattern in American Politics: The First Century* (New York, 1979); John Ashworth, *'Agrarians' and 'Aristocrats': Party Political Ideology in the United States, 1837–1846* (London, 1983); Sean Wilentz, *New York City & the Rise of the American Working Class, 1788–1850* (New York, 1984).

CHARLES GRANDISON FINNEY

"What a Revival of Religion Is"
1835

Charles Grandison Finney (1792–1875), evangelical preacher and later president of Ober-
lin College, was indisputably the most influential American revivalist of the nineteenth
century. This influence was partly due, of course, to his enormous talents as a theatrical,
lawyerlike persuader of souls and his ingenuity in introducing to urban audiences controversial "new measures" like protracted meetings and the "anxious seat." But much of it
was also due to the appeal of his systematic and thoroughly post-Calvinist revivalist theology. In place of the deterministic and partly mystical Calvinist drama of sin and salvation, Finney offered unconverted sinners in his famous *Lectures on Revivals of Religion* a
way that was libertarian and rational yet strongly coercive. "Sluggish" men, Finney
argued in this introductory lecture, had but one choice—to obey or not to obey God's
moral law. It is true he stressed that the decision itself was influenced by God and ultimately was determined by the sinners' wills. Nonetheless, here and elsewhere in his *Lectures* Finney dwelled on the elaborate and calculated manipulation of "excitements" that
were needed to be contrived to facilitate that decision. The process, Finney emphasized,
was much the same cause-and-effect one as any valid scientific technique. William G.
McLoughlin, Jr., *Modern Revivalism: Charles Grandison Finney to Billy Graham* (New
York, 1959), 3–121, provides an excellent survey of Finney's career and thought. Keith
J. Hardman, *Charles Grandison Finney, 1792–1875: Revivalist and Reformer* (Syracuse,
N.Y., 1987) is a good critical biography. For a judicious study of the legalistic dimension
of Finney's theology, see David L. Weddle, *The Law as Gospel: Revival and Reform in the
Theology of Charles G. Finney* (Metuchen, N.J., 1985).

TEXT.—*O Lord, revive thy work in the midst of the years, in the midst of the years make known; in wrath remember mercy.*—HAB. iii.2.

It is supposed that the prophet Habakkuk was contemporary with Jeremiah, and that this prophecy was uttered in anticipation of the Babylonish captivity. Looking at the judgments which were speedily to come upon his nation, the soul of the prophet was wrought up to an agony, and he cries out in his distress, "O Lord, revive thy work." As if he had said, "O Lord, grant that thy judgments may not make Israel desolate. In the midst of these awful years, let the judgments of God be made the means of reviving religion among us. In wrath remember mercy."

Religion is the work of man. It is something for man to do. It consists in obeying God. It is man's duty. It is true, God induces him to do it. He influences him by his Spirit, because of his great wickedness and reluctance to obey. If it were not necessary for God to influence men—if men were disposed to obey God, there would be no occasion to pray, "O Lord, revive thy work." The ground of necessity for such a prayer is, that men are wholly indisposed to obey; and unless God interpose the influence of his Spirit, not a man on earth will ever obey the commands of God.

A "Revival of Religion" presupposes a declension. Almost all the religion in the world has been produced by revivals. God has found it necessary to take advantage of the excitability there is in mankind, to produce powerful excitements among them, before he can lead them to obey. Men are so sluggish, there are so many things to lead their minds off from religion, and to oppose the influence of the gospel, that it is necessary to raise an exictement among them, till the tide rises so high as to sweep away the opposing obstacles. They must be so excited that they will break over these counteracting influences, before they will obey God.

Look back at the history of the Jews, and you will see that God used to maintain religion among *them* by special occasions, when there would be a great excitement, and people would turn to the Lord. And after they had been thus revived, it would be but a short time before there would be so many counteracting influences brought to bear upon them, that religion would decline, and keep on declining, till God could have time—so to speak—to shape the course of events so as to produce another excitement, and then pour out his Spirit again to convert sinners. Then the counteracting causes would again operate, and religion would decline, and the nation would be swept away in the vortex of luxury, idolatry, and pride.

There is so little *principle* in the church, so little firmness and stability of purpose, that unless they are greatly excited, they will not obey God. They have so little knowledge, and their principles are so weak, that unless they are excited, they will go back from the path of duty, and do nothing to promote the glory of God. The state of the world is still such, and probably will be till the millennium is fully come, that religion must be mainly promoted by these excitements. How long and how often has the experiment been tried, to bring the church to act steadily for God, without these periodical excitements! Many good men have supposed, and still suppose, that the best

Source: Charles Grandison Finney, *Lectures on Revivals of Religion,* ed. William G. McLoughlin (Cambridge, Mass.: Harvard University Press, Belknap Press, 1960), 9–23. Editor's notes omitted. Reprinted by permission of The Belknap Press of Harvard University Press, Copyright © 1960; © 1988 by The President and Fellows of Harvard College.

way to promote religion, is to go along *uniformly,* and gather in the ungodly gradually, and without excitement. But however such reasoning may appear in the abstract, *facts* demonstrate its futility. If the church were far enough advanced in knowledge, and had stability of principle enough to *keep awake,* such a course would do; but the church is so little enlightened, and there are so many counteracting causes, that the church will not go steadily to work without a special excitement. As the millennium advances, it is probable that these periodical excitements will be unknown. Then the church will be enlightened, and the counteracting causes removed, and the entire church will be in a state of habitual and steady obedience to God. The entire church will stand and take the infant mind, and cultivate it for God. Children will be trained up in the way they should go, and there will be no such torrents of worldliness, and fashion, and covetousness, to bear away the piety of the church, as soon as the excitement of a revival is withdrawn.

It is very desirable it should be so. It is very desirable that the church should go on steadily in a course of obedience without these excitements. Such excitements are liable to injure the health. Our nervous system is so strung that any powerful excitement, if long continued, injures our health and unfits us for duty. If religion is ever to have a pervading influence in the world, it can't be so; this spasmodic religion must be done away. Then it will be uncalled for. Christians will not sleep the greater part of the time, and once in a while wake up, and rub their eyes, and bluster about, and vociferate, a little while, and then go to sleep again. Then there will be no need that ministers should wear themselves out, and kill themselves, by their efforts to roll back the flood of worldly influence that sets in upon the church. But as yet the state of the Christian world is such, that to expect to promote religion without excitements is unphilosophical and absurd. The great political, and other worldly excitements that agitate Christendom, are all unfriendly to religion, and divert the mind from the interests of the soul. Now these excitements can only be counteracted by *religious* excitements. And until there is religious principle in the world to put down irreligious excitements, it is in vain to try to promote religion, except by counteracting excitements. This is true in philosophy, and it is a historical fact.

It is altogether improbable that religion will ever make progress among *heathen* nations except through the influence of revivals. The attempt is now making to do it by education, and other cautious and gradual improvements. But so long as the laws of mind remain what they are, it cannot be done in this way. There must be excitement sufficient to wake up the dormant moral powers, and roll back the tide of degradation and sin. And precisely so far as our own land approximates to heathenism, it is impossible for God or man to promote religion in such a state of things but by powerful excitements.—This is evident from the fact that this has always been the way in which God has done it. God does not create these excitements, and choose this method to promote religion for nothing, or without reason. Where mankind are so reluctant to obey God, they will not act until they are excited. For instance, how many there are who know that they ought to be religious, but they are afraid if they become pious they shall be laughed at by their companions. Many are wedded to idols, others are procrastinating repentance, until they are settled in life, or until they have secured some favorite worldly interest. Such persons never will give up their false shame, or relinquish their ambitious schemes, till they are so excited that they cannot contain themselves any longer.

These remarks are designed only as an introduction to the discourse. I shall now proceed with the main design, to show,

I. What a revival of religion is not;

II. What it is; and,

III. The agencies employed in promoting it.

I. A REVIVAL OF RELIGION NOT A MIRACLE.

1. A miracle has been generally defined to be, a Divine interference, setting aside or suspending the laws of nature. It is not a miracle, in this sense. All the laws of matter and mind remain in force. They are neither suspended nor set aside in a revival.

2. It is not a miracle according to another definition of the term miracle—*something above the powers of nature.* There is nothing in religion beyond the ordinary powers of nature. It consists entirely in the *right exercise* of the powers of nature. It is just that, and nothing else. When mankind become religious, they are not *enabled* to put forth exertions which they were unable before to put forth. They only exert the powers they had before in a different way, and use them for the glory of God.

3. It is not a miracle, or dependent on a miracle, in any sense. It is a purely philosophical result of the right use of the constituted means—as much so as any other effect produced by the application of means. There may be a miracle among its antecedent causes, or there may not. The apostles employed miracles, simply as a means by which they arrested attention to their message, and established its Divine authority. But the miracle was not the revival. The miracle was one thing; the revival that followed it was quite another thing. The revivals in the apostles' days were connected with miracles, but they were not miracles.

I said that a revival is the result of the *right* use of the appropriate means. The means which God has enjoyed for the production of a revival, doubtless have a natural tendency to produce a revival. Otherwise God would not have enjoined them. But means will not produce a revival, we all know, without the blessing of God. No more will grain, when it is sowed, produce a crop without the blessing of God. It is impossible for us to say that there is not as direct an influence or agency from God, to produce a crop of grain, as there is to produce a revival. What are the laws of nature, according to which, it is supposed, that grain yields a crop? They are nothing but the constituted manner of the operations of God. In the Bible, the word of God is compared to grain, and preaching is compared to sowing seed, and the results to the springing up and growth of the crop. And the result is just as philosophical in the one case, as in the other, and is as naturally connected with the cause.

I wish this idea to be impressed on all your minds, for there has long been an idea prevalent that promoting religion has something very peculiar in it, not to be judged of by the ordinary rules of cause and effect; in short, that there is no connection of the means with the result, and no tendency in the means to produce the effect. No doctrine is more dangerous than this to the prosperity of the church, and nothing more absurd.

Suppose a man were to go and preach this doctrine among farmers, about their sowing grain. Let him tell them that God is a sovereign, and will give them a crop only when it pleases him, and that for them to plow and plant and labor as if they expected to raise a crop is very wrong, and taking the work out of the hands of God, that it interferes with his sovereignty, and is going on in their own strength; and that there is no connection between the means and the result on which they can depend. And now, suppose the farmers should believe such doctrine. Why, they would starve the world to death.

Just such results will follow from the church's being persuaded that promoting religion is somehow so mysteriously a subject of Divine sovereignty, that there is no natural connection between the means and the end. What *are* the results? Why, generation after generation have gone down to hell. No doubt more than five thousand millions have gone down to hell, while the church has been dreaming, and waiting for God to save them without the use of means. It has been the devil's most successful means of destroying souls. The connection is as clear in religion as it is when the farmer sows his grain.

There is one fact under the government of God, worthy of universal notice, and of everlasting remembrance; which is, that the most useful and important things are most easily and certainly obtained by the use of the appropriate means. This is evidently a principle in the Divine administration. Hence, all the *necessaries* of life are obtained with great *certainty* by the use of the simplest means. The luxuries are more difficult to obtain; the means to procure them are more intricate and less certain in their results; while things absolutely hurtful and poisonous, such as alcohol and the like, are often obtained only by torturing nature, and making use of a kind of infernal sorcery to procure the death-dealing abomination. This principle holds true in moral government, and as spiritual blessings are of surpassing importance, we should expect their attainment to be connected with *great certainty* with the use of the appropriate means; and such we find to be the fact; and I fully believe that could facts be known, it would be found that when the appointed means have been *rightly* used, spiritual blessings have been obtained with greater uniformity than temporal ones.

II. I AM TO SHOW WHAT A REVIVAL IS.

It presupposes that the church is sunk down in a backslidden state, and a revival consists in the return of the church from her backslidings, and in the conversion of sinners.

1. A revival always includes conviction of sin on the part of the church. Backslidden professors cannot wake up and begin right away in the service of God, without deep searchings of heart. The fountains of sin need to be broken up. In a true revival, Christians are always brought under such convictions; they see their sins in such a light, that often they find it impossible to maintain a hope of their acceptance with God. It does not always go to that extent; but there are always, in a genuine revival, deep convictions of sin, and often cases of abandoning all hope.

2. Backslidden Christians will be brought to repentance. A revival is nothing else than a new beginning of obedience to God. Just as in the case of a converted sinner, the first step is a deep repentance, a breaking down of heart, a getting down into the dust before God, with deep humility, and forsaking of sin.

3. Christians will have their faith renewed. While they are in their backslidden state they are blind to the state of sinners. Their hearts are as hard as marble. The truths of the Bible only appear like a dream. They admit it to be all true; their con-

science and their judgment assent to it; but their faith does not see it standing out in bold relief, in all the burning realities of eternity. But when they enter into a revival, they no longer see men as trees walking, but they see things in that strong light which will renew the love of God in their hearts. This will lead them to labor zealously to bring others to him. They will feel grieved that others do not love God, when they love him so much. And they will set themselves feelingly to persuade their neighbors to give him their hearts. So their love to men will be renewed. They will be filled with a tender and burning love for souls. They will have a longing desire for the salvation of the whole world. They will be in agony for individuals whom they want to have saved; their friends, relations, enemies. They will not only be urging them to give their hearts to God, but they will carry them to God in the arms of faith, and with strong crying and tears beseech God to have mercy on them, and save their souls from endless burnings.

4. A revival breaks the power of the world and of sin over Christians. It brings them to such vantage ground that they get a fresh impulse towards heaven. They have a new foretaste of heaven, and new desires after union to God; and the charm of the world is broken, and the power of sin overcome.

5. When the churches are thus awakened and reformed, the reformation and salvation of sinners will follow, going through the same stages of conviction, repentance, and reformation. Their hearts will be broken down and changed. Very often the most abandoned profligates are among the subjects. Harlots, and drunkards, and infidels, and all sorts of abandoned characters, are awakened and converted. The worst part of human society are softened, and reclaimed, and made to appear as lovely specimens of the beauty of holiness.

III. I AM TO CONSIDER THE AGENCIES EMPLOYED IN CARRYING FORWARD A REVIVAL OF RELIGION.

Ordinarily, there are three agents employed in the work of conversion, and one instrument. The agents are God,—some person who brings the truth to bear on the mind,—and the sinner himself. The instrument is the truth. There are *always two* agents, God and the sinner, employed and active in every case of genuine conversion.

1. The agency of God is two-fold; by his Providence and by his Spirit.

(1.) By his providential government, he so arranges events as to bring the sinner's mind and the truth in contact. He brings the sinner where the truth reaches his ears or his eyes. It is often interesting to trace the manner in which God arranges events so as to bring this about, and how he sometimes makes every thing seem to favor a revival. The state of the weather, and of the public health, and other circumstances concur to make every thing just right to favor the application of truth with the greatest possible efficacy. How he sometimes sends a minister along, just at the time he is wanted! How he brings out a particular truth, just at the particular time when the individual it is fitted to reach is in the way to hear!

(2.) God's special agency by his Holy Spirit. Having direct access to the mind, and knowing infinitely well the whole history and state of each individual sinner, he employs that truth which is best adapted to his particular case, and then sets it home with Divine power. He gives it such vividness, strength, and power, that the sinner quails, and throws down his weapons of rebellion, and turns to the Lord. Under his influence, the truth burns and cuts its way like fire. He makes the truth stand out in such aspects, that it crushes the proudest man down with the weight of a mountain. If men were *disposed* to obey God, the truth is given with sufficient clearness in the Bible; and from preaching they could learn all that is necessary for them to know. But because they are wholly *disinclined* to obey it, God clears it up before their minds, and pours in a blaze of convincing light upon their souls, which they cannot withstand, and they yield to it, and obey God, and are saved.

2. The agency of men is commonly employed. Men are not mere *instruments* in the hands of God. Truth is the instrument. The preacher is a moral agent in the work; he acts; he is not a mere passive instrument; he is voluntary in promoting the conversion of sinners.

3. The agency of the sinner himself. The conversion of a sinner consists in his obeying the truth. It is therefore impossible it should take place without his agency, for it consists in *his* acting right. He is influenced to this by the agency of God, and by the agency of men. Men act on their fellow-men, not only by language, but by their looks, their tears, their daily deportment. See that impenitent man there, who has a pious wife. Her very looks, her tenderness, her solemn, compassionate dignity, softened and moulded into the image of Christ, are a sermon to him all the time. He has to turn his mind away, because it is such a reproach to him. He feels a sermon ringing in his ears all day long.

Mankind are accustomed to read the countenances of their neighbors. Sinners often read the state of a Christian's mind in his eyes. If his eyes are full of levity, or worldly anxiety and contrivance, sinners read it. If they are full of the Spirit of God, sinners read it; and they are often led to conviction by barely seeing the countenance of Christians.

An individual once went into a manufactory to see the machinery. His mind was solemn, as he had been where there was a revival. The people who labored there all knew him by sight, and knew who he was. A young lady who was at work saw him, and whispered some foolish remark to her companion, and laughed. The person stopped and looked at her with a feeling of grief. She stopped, her thread broke, and she was so much agitated she could not join it. She looked out at the window to compose herself, and then tried again; again and again she strove to recover her self-command. At length she sat down, overcome with her feelings. The person then approached and spoke with her; she soon manifested a deep sense of sin. The feeling spread through the establishment like fire, and in a few hours almost every person employed there was under conviction, so much so, that the owners, though worldly men, were astounded, and requested to have the works stop and have a prayer meeting; for they said it was a great deal more important to have these people converted than to have the works go on. And in a few days, the owners and nearly every person employed in the establishment were hopefully converted. The eye of this individual, his solemn countenance, his compassionate feeling, rebuked the levity of the young woman, and brought her under conviction of sin; and this whole revival followed, probably in a great measure, from so small an incident.

If Christians have deep feeling on the subject of religion themselves, they will produce deep feeling wherever they go. And if they are cold, or light and trifling, they inevitably destroy all deep feeling, even in awakened sinners.

I knew a case, once, of an individual who was very anxious, but one day I was grieved to find that her convictions seemed to be all gone. I asked her what she had been doing. She told me she had been spending the afternoon at such a place, among some professors of religion, not thinking that it would dissipate her convictions to spend an afternoon with professors of religion. But they were trifling and vain, and thus her convictions were lost. And no doubt those professors of religion, by their folly, destroyed a soul, for her convictions did not return.

The church is required to use the means for the conversion of sinners. Sinners cannot properly be said to use the means for their own conversion. The church uses the means. What sinners do is to submit to the truth, or to resist it. It is a mistake of sinners, to think they are using means for their own conversion. The whole drift of a revival, and every thing about it, is designed to present the truth *to* your mind, for your obedience or resistance.

REMARKS.

1. Revivals were formerly regarded as miracles. And it has been so by some even in our day. And others have ideas on the subject so loose and unsatisfactory, that if they would only *think,* they would see their absurdity. For a long time, it was supposed by the church, that a revival was a miracle, an interposition of Divine power which they had nothing to do with, and which they had no more agency in producing, than they had in producing thunder, or a storm of hail, or an earthquake. It is only within a few years that ministers generally have supposed revivals were to be *promoted,* by the use of means designed and adapted specially to that object. Even in New England, it has been supposed that revivals came just as showers do, sometimes in one town, and sometimes in another, and that ministers and churches could do nothing more to produce them, than they could to make showers of rain come on their own town, when they are falling on a neighboring town.

It used to be supposed that a revival would come about once in fifteen years, and all would be converted that God intended to save, and then they must wait until another crop came forward on the stage of life. Finally, the time got shortened down to five years, and they supposed there might be a revival about as often as that.

I have heard a fact in relation to one of these pastors, who supposed revivals might come about once in five years. There had been a revival in his congregation. The next year, there was a revival in a neighboring town, and he went there to preach, and staid several days, till he got his soul all engaged in the work. He returned home on Saturday, and went into his study to prepare for the Sabbath. And his soul was in an agony. He thought how many adult persons there were in his congregation at enmity with God—so many still unconverted—so many persons *die* yearly—such a portion of them unconverted—if a revival does not come under five years, so many adult heads of families will be in hell. He put down his calculations on paper, and embodied them in his sermon for the next day, with his heart bleeding at the dreadful picture. As I understood it, he did not do this with any expectation of a revival, but he felt deeply, and poured out his heart to his people. And that sermon awakened *forty heads of families,* and a powerful revival followed; and so his theory about a revival once in five years was all exploded.

Thus God has overthrown, generally, the theory that revivals are miracles.

2. Mistaken notions concerning the sovereignty of God, have greatly hindered revivals.

Many people have supposed God's sovereignty to be something very different from what it is. They have supposed it to be such an arbitrary disposal of events, and particularly of the gift of his Spirit, as precluded a rational employment of means for promoting a revival of religion. But there is no evidence from the Bible, that God exercises any such sovereignty as that. There are no facts to prove it. But every thing goes to show, that God has connected means with the end through all the departments of his government—in nature and in grace. There is no *natural* event in which his own agency is not concerned. He has not built the creation like a vast machine, that will go on alone without his further care. He has not retired from the universe, to let it work for itself. This is mere atheism. He exercises a universal superintendence and control. And yet every event in nature has been brought about by means. He neither administers providence nor grace with that sort of sovereignty, that dispenses with the use of means. There is no more sovereignty in one than in the other.

And yet some people are terribly alarmed at all direct efforts to promote a revival, and they cry out, "You are trying to get up a revival in your own strength. Take care, you are interfering with the sovereignty of God. Better keep along in the usual course, and let God give a revival when he thinks it is best. God is a sovereign, and it is very wrong for you to attempt to get up a revival, just because *you think* a revival is needed." This is just such preaching as the devil wants. And men cannot do the devil's work more effectually, than by preaching up the sovereignty of God, as a reason why we should not put forth efforts to produce a revival.

3. You see the error of those who are beginning to think that religion can be better promoted in the world without revivals, and who are disposed to give up all efforts to produce religious excitements. Because there are evils arising in some instances out of great excitements on the subject of religion, they are of opinion that it is best to dispense with them altogether. This cannot, and must not be. True, there is danger of abuses. In cases of great *religious* as well as all other excitements, more or less incidental evils may be expected of course. But this is no reason why they should be given up. The best things are always liable to abuses. Great and manifold evils have originated in the providential and moral governments of God. But these *foreseen* perversions and evils were not considered a sufficient reason for giving them up. For the establishment of these governments was on the whole the best that could be done for the production of the greatest amount of happiness. So in revivals of religion, it is found by experience, that in the present state of the world, religion cannot be promoted to any considerable extent without them. The evils which are sometimes complained of, when they are real, are incidental, and of small importance when compared with the amount of good produced by revivals. The sentiment should not be admitted by the church for a moment, that revivals may be given up. It is fraught with all that is dangerous to the interests of Zion, is death to the cause of missions, and brings in its train the damnation of the world.

FINALLY—I have a proposal to make to you who are here present. I have not commenced this course of Lectures on Revivals to get up a curious theory of my own on the subject. I would not spend my time and strength merely to give you instructions, to gratify your curiosity, and furnish you something to talk about. I have no idea of preaching *about* revivals. It is not my design to preach so as to have you able to say at the close, "We *understand* all about revivals now," while you do *nothing*. But I wish to ask you a question. What do you hear lectures on revivals for? Do you mean that whenever you are convinced what your duty is in promoting a revival, you will go to work and practise it?

Will you follow the instructions I shall give you from the word of God, and put them in practice in your own hearts? Will you bring them to bear upon your families, your acquaintances, neighbors, and through the city? Or will you spend the winter in learning *about* revivals, and do nothing *for* them? I want you, as fast as you learn any thing of the subject of revivals, to put it in practice, and go to work and see if you cannot promote a revival among sinners here. If you will not do this, I wish you to let me know at the beginning, so that I need not waste my strength. You ought to decide *now* whether you will do this or not. You know that we call sinners to decide on the spot whether *they* will obey the gospel. And we have no more authority to let you take time to deliberate whether *you* will obey God, than we have to let sinners do so. We call on you to unite now in a solemn pledge to God, that you will do your duty as fast as you learn what it is, and to pray that He will pour out his Spirit upon this church and upon all the city this winter.

JOHN HUMPHREY NOYES

Selection from *The Berean*
1847

"Be ye therefore perfect, even as your Father which is in Heaven is perfect." Upon this injunction of Matthew, Finney built his doctrine of perfect holiness, which posited that the converted were capable of receiving a "second blessing" that made them able to commit sinless acts of disinterested benevolence and, by this means, help bring about the coming millennium. Other evangelicals utilized similar ideas as a justification for antislavery activism and other kinds of radical reform. The most extreme version of this evangelical perfectionism was espoused by John Humphrey Noyes (1811–86). A graduate of Dartmouth and a student of theology at Yale, the center of the post-Calvinist "new divinity," Noyes went on to found the Oneida Community, which put into practice, in line with Noyes's theories, a Bible-based communist economy and a highly regulated system of multiple sexual partnerships. These activities earned him the nearly universal condemnation of his evangelical associates, but he always regarded them as logical deductions from the basic premise of evangelical perfectionism, which abjured selfishness and promised perfect holiness. Furthermore, the security of this perfect holiness, Noyes argued in the two articles printed herein, was no mere subjective fancy or external moral law, but faith in the marvelous character of the Bible itself and the reality of Christ's crucifixion and resurrection. Because men and women had already been redeemed through Christ and the millennium already begun with his second coming (which Noyes dated at A.D. 70), individuals had only to receive the grace that made possible complete salvation from sin in this world. Robert David Thomas, *The Man Who Would Be Perfect: John Humphrey Noyes and the Utopian Impulse* (Philadelphia, 1977) is a psychobiographical study. But the best approach to Noyes's thought is still through the fascinating, if discursive, collections of his writings and papers edited by George Wallingford Noyes, *Religious Experience of John Humphrey Noyes: Founder of the Oneida Community* (New York, 1923), and *John Humphrey Noyes: The Putney Community* (Oneida, N.Y., 1931).

The Faith Once Delivered to the Saints

It is apparent to the most superficial inspection of the scriptures, that the religion even of the Old Testament saints, and much more that of the primitive church, was one which placed man in direct communication with God. Not a saint can be found among all whose names are enrolled on the inspired record—from Abel to the last of the apostles—whose biography does not savor strongly of that marvelousness which necessarily waits upon the open manifestations of Divinity. Dreams, visions, oracles, angelic visitations, conversations with God, inspirations, infusions of superhuman power, &c., are profusely scattered through the history of Judaism. And yet the glory of New Testament Christianity as far exceeds that of the preceding dispensation, in respect to all these and many other manifestations of God's presence, as sun-light exceeds star-light.[1]

1. Phrenologists define marvelousness to be 'credulity—disposition to believe what is not proved, or what are considered supernatural manifestations.' (*Fowler & Kirkham, p.* 141.) Spurzheim says it is 'a tendency to believe in inspirations, presentiments, phantoms,' &c. Combe says the organ of marvelousness 'is uniformly large in fanatics. It predominates in the Rev. Edward Irving, and in all his followers whom I have seen.' (*Combe's Phrenology, p.* 79.) By the marvelousness of the Bible, we mean that characteristic of the Bible which requires 'marvelousness' in those who receive it. The following statistics give the result of a running examination of the whole Bible with reference to this point:

MARVELOUS EVENTS RECORDED IN THE BIBLE.

Supernatural omens,	14
Significant dreams,	23
Appearances of angels and other supernatural beings,	51
Supernatural visions,	66
Miracles specifically mentioned, (not including the vast number alluded to in Matt. 8: 16, and like passages,)	175
Inspired prophecies, revelations, and other direct communications from the Lord	449
Total,	778

The items here enumerated, by no means embrace all the matter in the Bible that might be classed under the head of marvelousness. Special providences, religious exercises like those described in many of the psalms, and in short every recognition of the presence and direct agency of God or any other invisible being, might be placed in the same category. But the statistics already given are sufficient for our purpose. It is manifest that marvelousness is a very prominent characteristic of the Bible; and any one who will take the trouble to examine, may see that it pervades every part, we might almost say, every page of the book. It is not confined to those portions which were written in the earlier and darker ages of Judaism. Modern philosophy teaches that supernatural wonders diminish, as light increases. But we find the contrary of this true of the Bible. The character and history of Jesus Christ is surrounded with more of the materials of marvelousness, than that of Moses and the prophets. The new dispensation which he introduced, with all its increase of light, was accompanied by dreams, visions, appearances of angels, miracles, revelations and wonders of every kind, in greater abundance than ever was known before. The New Testament begins with the record of the supernatural conception of Jesus Christ, and ends with a gorgeous vision of the spiritual world.

Thus it is manifest that the Bible is fitted to feed and perpetuate what the sages of these philosophical times call *fanaticism.* A book, filled with excellent stories of special providences, miraculous deliverances, angelic visions, spiritual ecstasies, &c. &c.,—and especially a book which is so implicitly credited as the Bible—cannot be generally read without begetting in many minds the image of its own spirit. Such

Source: John Humphrey Noyes, *The Berean: A Manual for the Help of Those Who Seek the Faith of the Primitive Church* (Putney, Vt.: Spiritual Magazine, 1847), 47–51, 178–81.

The main difference between the two dispensations, was this: In accordance with the general character of the introductory dispensation, God manifested himself to the Jewish saints in an *external* manner; i.e., by visions, vocal oracles, angels, or at the most by those external influences of the Spirit which affect, as it were, only the outer surface of the soul, as in the case of prophetic inspiration. Whereas he manifested himself to Christian believers in the deep sanctuary of their hearts, making them radically new creatures, taking away their sins, and giving them full and permanent fellowship with his own vitality. The *indwelling* of God was a mystery which was 'hid from the ages and generations' of Judaism, but was manifested to the primitive church. There was also this further difference. God manifested himself, even externally, only to a *few* under the Jewish dispensation. Whereas the promise of Christianity was, 'I will pour out my spirit upon *all flesh*: and your sons and your daughters shall prophesy, and your young men shall see visions, and your old men shall dream dreams.' This promise was fulfilled. The special manifestations which had before been confined to a few individuals in every age, were given, on the day of Pentecost and afterwards, to the whole church of God.

These differences, however, do not destroy the identity of faith under the two dispensations. The religion of both—i.e. the religion of the whole Bible—was based on immediate communication with God. The later manifestations were more complete, spiritual and universal, and of course produced greater changes of character, than the earlier; but the faith which invited and apprehended those manifestations, was the same in all ages. Hence Paul, in the 11th of Hebrews, traces the history of one and the same faith, by a continuous line, from the beginning of the world till the advent of perfection by Christianity. The generic element in all the instances of faith which he adduces—and in the faith of Christianity as well as Judaism,—is an apprehension of, and confidence in the living God, as actually present, manifesting himself by signs and wonders, communicating superhuman wisdom and power, overruling, for the believer's comfort and protection, the powers of the spiritual and natural worlds.

We must distinctly mark the difference between this faith, and several counterfeits which have been extensively substituted for it.

1. Many talk about 'contending earnestly for the faith once delivered to the saints,' as though this were to be referred to *theological controversy,* and as though the faith of the saints were belief in a mere scheme of doctrine. But was it by belief in an orthodox creed that the saints 'stopped the mouths of lions, quenched the violence of fire, escaped the edge of the sword, out of weakness were made strong?' Nothing can be plainer than that 'the faith once delivered to the saints,' as exemplified by Paul in the 11th of Hebrews, was directed, not toward doctrines, but *toward the living God*.

2. Philosophers and poets have an apprehension of God as manifested in '*the works of nature,*' which they call faith. But this implies no personal acquaintance with

---

men as Swedenborg and Irving, however false and pernicious may have been their views in other respects, were certainly more nearly in spiritual concord with the Bible, in respect to marvelousness, than the philosophers and theologians who deride them. And while marvelousness remains a part of human nature, and the Bible is allowed to feed it, we may assuredly look for the appearance of such 'fanatics' *ad infinitum*. Those conservators therefore, of the public morals, whose business it is to put down 'pestilent heresies,' must either return to the policy of Popery, and forbid the reading of the Bible by any but the clergy, (and even then some *clerical* enthusiast like Luther will break forth,) or they must give up their business, and seek the welfare of mankind by endeavoring to *enlighten* and *purify* the fanatical propensities, which they can neither smother nor control.

God. Believers of this kind sustain no nearer relation to God than one man would to another, in case the parties had never seen each other or had any communication—but only had seen each other's productions. Whereas the faith exhibited in the Bible, manifestly introduced the saints to personal fellowship with God, so that they walked with him, conversed with him, received messages and messengers from him, and lived under his immediate protection and superintendence.

3. The faith of many religious persons consists in receiving the Bible as the word of God. They apprehend God as revealed *through the scriptures.*—This kind of faith is like that last mentioned—only the believer in this case has not merely seen the works of the unknown being, but has received a letter from him, which he reveres and believes. The letter however is not addressed to him individually, but is a circular sent 'to all whom it may concern.' So that there is still no personal acquaintance.

4. Another class of religionists, a little in advance of the former, by systematizing the legal developments of the Bible, build up in their minds what they call a *moral government,* and place God at the head of it as king over moral beings. Their faith apprehends God in his *official* capacity. The relation between him and them is that of king and subject. Their king, like the kings of this world, is high and lifted up, far above his common subjects, distant and reserved. They see him only through his laws and state transactions. In all this there is no personal acquaintance, no vital union. God thus apprehended, is not *in* the believer, ruling by spiritual power, but [']over him' ruling by written laws. This is not 'the faith once delivered to the saints.'

5. Many of those already mentioned, and others, go so far as to admit certain measures of God's *personal* infuence. They conceive of him not only as manifested through his works, his word, and his moral government, but as operating by his spirit on the mind. But they are careful to disclaim any thing like revelation, inspiration, and supernatural power. They regard the operations of the Spirit as only imperceptible auxiliaries to the truth, influences which never manifest themselves directly to the consciousness, or in any other way; and which never would be recognized at all, if the Bible did not testify of their existence. This is the worst counterfeit of all; for while it appropriates to itself much of the language of the ancient saints, and so makes itself the most respectable substitute for Bible faith, it as effectually excludes the living God from his proper place in the heart, and in the church, as any of the grosser forms of unbelief. It is this kind of faith which, while pretending to honor the spiritual power of God as the chief agent of salvation, yet dares not trust it, but thrusts the law into its place as the great presiding influence; and makes the Spirit its secondary adjunct. It is this kind of faith which daubs over the apostasy of Christendom from the standard of the primitive saints, by teaching that 'the age of miracles is past'—an assumption, or rather a presumptuous falsehood, which is better fitted to destroy the legitimate influence of the Bible than all the enactments of Popery; since the Bible relates only to an age of miracles—its entire religion and morality is indissolubly interwoven with supernatural manifestations: it is therefore adapted only to an age of miracles, and if it were true that the age of miracles is past, men of the present day would have little more practical interest in it than they have in the Arabian Nights' Entertainment. It is this kind of faith, which, while it loudly praises the prophets and apostles, derides as visionary enthusiasm every approach toward that direct communication with God which was the glory of prophets and apostles; and thus covertly, but really casts infamy on the entire religion of the Bible, and on all the saints of God.

The true faith, of which the foregoing are counterfeits, while it recognizes the reflection of divine radiance in the works of nature, in the Bible, and in the moral government of the universe, still turns with chief interest to the direct manifestations of God by his Spirit; and it limits not the Holy One to imperceptible and dubious influences, but gives him room to reveal himself now, as in past ages, by all the appropriate operations of his infinite energy.

There is an intrinsic and palpable absurdity in the idea of admitting the Spirit of God into the world, and yet curtailing its appropriate and formerly actual manifestations, under the plea that the age of miracles is past. The age of miracles certainly is not past with God. He is as mighty as ever; and wherever his Spirit comes at all, there is superhuman, i.e., miraculous power; and if miraculous power is admitted into the world in the smallest degree, it cannot be said that the age of miracles is past with reference to man; and the way is therefore open for all the primitive manifestations of divine power. And then, how irrational it is to suppose that the same agent which once gave to man gifts of superhuman wisdom and power, is still present, *but only as a latent auxiliary of the clergy!* What a blasphemous descent is this, from the sublime to the ridiculous! As well might a purblind dotard say that the sun still shines, but the age of daylight is past, and only one of the seven colors which were the elements of ancient sunlight,—and that the dimmest—is now given to the world!

We repeat it—the great central idea of 'the faith once delivered to the saints,' was that of *the living God present in individual believers and in the church, and manifest by manifold tokens of superhuman wisdom and power.* And let it be observed that the relation between God and man which this idea involves, is not, as unbelief would suggest, unnatural, and foreign from the original design of man's constitution. God made man in his own image, with the very intent that this relation should exist between them— that man should be the temple, or, we may say, the *complement* of God. Adam at the beginning lived in open companionship with his Maker. As woman was married to man, so man was married to God. And it was to restore this union, which sin had severed, that the Son of God was made flesh, and suffered death. The renewal and everlasting confirmation of the *at-one-ment* which existed between God and the first Adam, was the great achievement of the second Adam. Moreover, it is plainly predicted in scripture that the human race in its final glory, shall return to open companionship with God—that 'his tabernacle shall be with men, and he shall dwell with them, and shall be their God.' A relation which existed at the beginning—which Christ came and died to establish—which will exist in the final state of man, cannot be unnatural. On the contrary, the present ordinary condition of mankind, living without God, is unnatural—at variance utterly with their original constitution. Man without his original spiritual Head, is as much out of the order of nature, as woman without a husband. The apostasy is the widowhood of the human race.

As the manifest indwelling of God is the essence of Bible religion, so it is the corner stone of Bible morality, education, social order, and physical well-being. All schemes of reform and improvement for soul and body, which have not this for their starting point and their end, however popular and promising they may be, are as certainly impostures as the Bible is a book of truth, and man was made to be the temple of his Maker. Who but a madman can expect to check the spiritual and physical disorders of social life, and restore mankind to harmony and happiness, while the first great wheel of the whole machinery by which the result is to be attained, is wanting? Trees without roots will as soon bud and blossom and bring forth fruit, as man will attain holiness of heart, vitue of action, wisdom of thought and health of body, without the indwelling of God.

The true reason why the great Reformation by Luther has failed, is that it turned the faith of the world to the Bible, rather than to God. Protestants are learning by sore experience that the Bible is *not* a 'sufficient rule of faith and practice.' The numberless and still multiplying schisms of the reformed churches, are making it more and more manifest that the balance-wheel of original Christianity is not yet recovered—that the Bible, without *inspiration* as the regulator of interpretation, is but an 'apple of discord.' In like manner all the subordinate reforms of more recent date which have any thing but the living God for their centre and propelling power, will sooner or later fail.

On the other hand, let the foundation of Bible faith be laid,—let God be invited by believing hearts to make his tabernacle with men, and reveal all the glory of his wisdom and power as he revealed it to the primitive church; let Him be installed and acknowledged as the ever-present and presiding Genius of Reform, and speedily sin and death will flee away, and the earth become as Eden.

Let all, then, who seek salvation for themselves, or long for the regeneration of the world—'*content earnestly for the* FAITH ONCE DELIVERED TO THE SAINTS.'

Perfectionism

Perceiving nothing in the sound or form of the word Perfectionist, essentially odious, and assuredly anticipating the time of its redemption from infamy, we will take the liberty to explain the meaning of it, as used by those who consent to bear it.

We will not attempt to state what a Perfectionist *is not;*—for this would require us to dissect and disclaim all the varying and incongruous images of perfection conjured up by the word in the various fancies of men, from a picture of a monk in sackcloth and ashes, to that of a seraph with six wings. If it is sufficient to say, that in the minds of those who consent to bear the name, so far as we know, perfection is predicated of only a single attribute, viz., holiness; and of that only in a limited sense. We find in the Bible, as well as in the nature of the case, three modifications of *perfect holiness:*—perfection of obedience; perfection of security of obedience; and perfection of holiness by experience or suffering. These distinctions may be easily understood by a simple illustration. The success of a general on a battlefield, may be perfect in a threefold manner. 1. He may be simply successful at the outset. 2. He may be successful at the outset, with an assurance of final victory. 3. He may be successful by the actual accomplishment of the victory.

1. The holiness of Adam, and of the angels that left their first estate, was perfect, considered simply as obedience to law, but destitute of prospective security, as was proved by their apostacy.

2. The holiness of Christ, the second Adam, was perfect, both as present obedience to law, and as prospectively secure. Yet in another sense it was imperfect, during his residence on earth. For 'though he were a *son,* yet *learned he obedience* by the things which he suffered; and *being made perfect,* he became the author of eternal salvation to all them that obey him.'—'For it became him, by whom are all things, and for whom are all things, in bringing many sons unto glory to make the captain of their salvation *perfect through sufferings.*' Previous to his crucifixion, this captain of

our salvation was perfectly successful in his conflict with sin, both presently and pro-spectively; yet the battle was before him. So Paul, while counting all things but loss, that he might overcome death by knowing the fellowship of the sufferings of Christ, denied that he had already attained the victory, or was already perfect; and yet in the next breath, falling back upon an inferior meaning of the word, he could say, 'Let us therefore, as many as be perfect be thus minded.'

3. The present holiness of Christ, on the throne of his glory, and of those who, having overcome by his blood, have attained that likeness of his resurrection toward which Paul was urging his way, is perfected in the highest sense. The battle is fought; the victory won; their holiness is perfect as obedience—perfect in security—and per-fect by victory over suffering. Perfectionists, then, if they may be allowed to designate the place which they suppose they hold on the scale of perfection, universally dis-claim the profession of attainments above those of the *suffering* Son of God. They covet not the premature glory of victory before battle. They stand with Paul on the middle ground, between the perfection of Adam and of Christ, saved from sin—eternally saved—yet 'saved by hope, waiting for the adoption, to wit, the redemption of their bodies.'

We acknowledge that the phrase *perfect holiness* is almost a solecism in the first of the three senses above mentioned; for any thing short of perfect *present* obedience, is perfect disobedience; and we might as well speak of the imperfect success of a gen-eral who never began to conquer, as to speak of the imperfect holiness of one who has not yet obeyed God. The truth is too simple to need expansion, that every individual action is either wholly sinful or wholly righteous; and that every being in the universe, at any given time, is either entirely wicked or entirely holy, i.e. either conformed to law or not conformed to law: yet the prevailing modes of thought and speech force us to recognize a quality of action and character, called *imperfect holiness,* which takes rank somewhere indefinitely below what may seem the lowest possible or conceivable modification of holiness. So that, with reference to this, we must name *mere* holiness, *perfect* holiness—consigning the censure due to the impropriety of our langauge, to those who maintain the possibility of serving God and mammon, i.e. of being holy and sinful, at the same time. A profession, then of *perfect* holiness, thus understood, is in truth merely a profession of holiness, without which, confessedly, none can claim the name of sons or servants of God; and instead of derserving the charge of arrogance, should rather be censured, if at all, for conveying, in the language of it, the implication that men may be less than perfectly holy, and yet not perfectly sinful. But we take higher ground. The first Adam was holy; the second Adam was, in a more proper sense, perfectly holy—his holiness was secure. The gospel platform is as much above the ground of mere holiness, as a deed in fee simple is above mere possession.

As obedience is the test of all holiness, so we believe, under the gospel, *perpetuity of obedience* is the test of all holiness. Here we may speak, without solecism, of perfect holiness; and here we are exposed to a more plausible charge of arrogance. Let us examine the ground of this charge. Without entering the wide field of scripture argu-ment, it is sufficient for our purpose to notice a single fact in relation to the views of those who most freely stigmatize the supposed self-righteousness of Perfectionists. These very persons universally and confessedly expect, at death, to become Perfec-tionists, and that not merely of the second, but of the third degree: in other words, while earthly Perfectionists claim only secure deliverance from sin, their accusers anticipate, within a brief space, secure deliverance from sin and all evil. What is the consideration which exempts their anticipation from the charge of self-righteous pre-sumption, and yet leaves the burden upon our claim? Their answer assuredly must be—'We anticipate, at death, secure redemption from sin and evil, as the *gift of the grace of God.*' But the self-same apology relieves our claim. We *receive* present redemp-tion from sin as the gift of the grace of God; we only enter, 'by a new and living way,' upon the possession of a portion of that gratuitous inheritance which they expect to receive at death. We must be permitted, then, to say boldly, that the same rule which allows men to *hope* for heaven without presumption, allows us to *receive* heaven here without self-righteousness: and the charge of arrogance is due to those who hope for the gift, while they daily displease the Giver. The same Christ who will be the believ-er's portion in heaven, is our righteousness and sanctification here. While, therefore, we shrink not from the odium connected with the name *Perfectionist,* we cannot despair of disabusing all honest men, ere long, of a portion of their prejudices against it, by convincing them that we join in the testimony of our living head, that 'there is none good but one, that is God,' and believe that by the energy of his goodness alone we are delivered from sin.

The standard by which every man judges of the nature of true humility, and of its opposite, spiritual pride, is determined by the answer which his heart gives to the question—[']Who is the author of righteousness?['] If the credit of holiness is due to him who professes it, then his profession exalts himself at the expense of God, and justly exposes him to the charge of spiritual arrogance, however high or low may be his claim. But if God alone is acknowledged as the author of righteousness, a profes-sion of holiness is only the acknowledgment of a gift—and not only consistent with, but necessary to, the exercise of true humility. The man who has no conception of any righteousness other than his own, may well count the confession of imperfection—genuine modesty. From such we expect no mercy. But if there are any who ascribe all righteousness to God, we hope to convince them that the arrogance which boasts of the 'Lord our righteousness' is the perfection of humility; and that the profession of humility which delights in the confession of sin and in the expectation of a continued commission of it, is only a modest way of robbing Christ of the crown of his glory.

Is it imagined that the man to whom God in truth has given perfect holiness, has done some great thing? He has done nothing. The great achievement of his will which, be it remembered, the grace of God has secured, is the cessation from his own works, and the commencement of an everlasting repose on the energy of the living God, as the basis and hope of his righteousness. He has simply died—and with his dying breath bequeathed his body, soul and spirit to his Maker, rolling the responsibility of his future and eternal obedience upon the everlasting arm.

We believe it is incomparably easier to receive deliverance from all sins, than to conquer one. Paul clearly presents the principle in Rom. 1:21–32, which accounts for the difficulty men find in obtaining freedom from sin.—Because they refuse to glorify God, he *gives them up* to vile affections. The affections of men are rightfully under the perfect control of God. When he is dethroned, he abandons his kingdom, and anarchy ensues; every effort to quell the rebellion of desires, which falls short of a reinstate-ment of God in his sovereignty over the heart, must result in disheartening failure. But why should it be difficult for Him who 'stands at the door,' if his petition for entrance is heard, and his claim for dominion admitted, to restore peace and security to the ruined kingdom? Why should it be thought an incredible thing, that God should raise the dead? Pride, envy, anger, sensuality, &c., are but limbs of the tree of sin, the stock of which is that *unbelief which rejects the righteousness of God*. The man who commences the work of exterminating sin at the top of the tree, or among any of the branches will soon be disheartened by the discovery that the branches he has once lopped off, soon grow again, or send their juice into other limbs. We say, therefore, it is easier to lay the ax at the root and fell the whole tree at once, than to exterminate effectually a single limb. In view of these considerations, though we object not to the name, Perfectionist—and though we verily believe and unblushingly maintain that we are free from sin—we beg to be relieved of the glory, and of the shame of the achievement; as we have been taught with the scourge, that the day has come when 'all the haughtiness of men shall be brought low, and the Lord alone exalted.'

WILLIAM LEGGETT

Selection from *Political Writings*
1834

As the editor of New York City's leading Democratic newspaper, the *Evening Post*, William Leggett (1801–39) wielded a supple and acerbic pen that earned him admiring recognition among the city's literati. He was also a fiercely independent ideologue whose implacably principled editorial defenses of free trade, free banking, and labor organizing won him a large following among the radical "Loco Foco" wing of the city's Democrats. His equally principled defense of abolitionists and denunciation of the Jackson administration's acquiescence in the destruction of their literature by Southern postmasters triggered venomous attacks and ostracism by regular Democratic party organizations. The doctrine at the center of all these positions was equal rights, which Leggett utilized in different ways. On the one hand, equal rights meant natural rights, anterior to society and goods in and of themselves regardless of their consequences in the marketplace. (Like heaven's Calvinistic rains, Leggett wrote, quoting President Jackson, they "shower its favours alike on the high and low.") On the other hand, in his editorial "Rich and Poor," he made it clear that his libertarian ethic was also good *because* it favored the laboring poor, who appeared in Leggett's analysis as a homogeneous class of productive, middle-class, equal individuals. At the same time the ethic curtailed the opportunities of the rich, who in his view were not real aristocrats at all, but especially grasping, greedy examples of the middle classes lured on by the speculative promises of "mincing and bowing" demagogues. Marvin Meyers has an excellent chapter on Leggett's political and economic ideas in his *The Jacksonian Persuasion: Politics and Belief* (Stanford, Ca., 1957), 185–205. But still worth consulting is an older portrait by Richard Hofstadter, "William Leggett, Spokesman of Jacksonian Democracy," *Political Science Quarterly*, 58 (December 1943), 581–94. For a fairly complete recent compilation of Leggett's writings, see William Leggett, *Democratick Editorials: Essays in Jacksonian Political Economy*, ed. Lawrence H. White (Indianapolis, Ind., 1984).

True Functions of Goverment

[*From the* Evening Post, *Nov. 21, 1834.*]

"There are no necessary evils in Government. Its evils exist only in its abuses. If it would confine itself to *equal protection,* and, as heaven does its rains, shower its favours alike on the high and the low, the rich and the poor, it would be an unqualified blessing."

This is the language of our venerated President, and the passage deserves to be written in letters of gold, for neither in truth of sentiment or beauty of expression can it be surpassed. We choose it as our text for a few remarks on the true functions of Government.

The fundamental principle of all governments is the protection of person and property from domestic and foreign enemies; in other words, to defend the weak against the strong. By establishing the social feeling in a community, it was intended to counteract that selfish feeling, which, in its proper exercise, is the parent of all worldly good, and, in its excesses, the root of all evil. The functions of Government, when confined to their proper sphere of action, are therefore restricted to the making of *general laws,* uniform and universal in their operation, for these purposes, and for no other.

Governments have no right to interfere with the pursuits of individuals, as guarantied by those general laws, by offering encouragements and granting privileges to any particular class of industry, or any select bodies of men, inasmuch as all classes of industry and all men are equally important to the general welfare, and equally entitled to protection.

Whenever a Government assumes the power of discriminating between the different classes of the community, it becomes, in effect, the arbiter of their prosperity, and exercises a power not contemplated by any intelligent people in delegating their sovereignty to their rulers. It then becomes the great regulator of the profits of every species of industry, and reduces men from a dependence on their own exertions, to a dependence on the caprices of their Government. Governments possess no delegated right to tamper with individual industry a single hair's-breadth beyond what is essential to protect the rights of person and property.

In the exercise of this power of intermeddling with the private pursuits and individual occupations of the citizen, a Government may at pleasure elevate one class and depress another; it may one day legislate exclusively for the farmer, the next for the mechanic, and the third for the manufacturer, who all thus become the mere puppets of legislative cobbling and tinkering, instead of independent citizens, relying on their own resources for their prosperity. It assumes the functions which belong alone to an overruling Providence, and affects to become the universal dispenser of good and evil.

This power of regulating—of increasing or diminishing the profits of labour and the value of property of all kinds and degrees, by direct legislation, in a great measure destroys the essential object of all civil compacts, which, as we said before, is to make the social a counterpoise to the selfish feeling. By thus operating directly on the latter, by offering one class a bounty and another a discouragement, they involve the selfish feeling in every struggle of party for the ascendancy, and give to the force of political

Source: *A Collection of the Political Writings of William Leggett,* 2 vols., ed. Theodore Sedgwick, Jr., vol. 1 (New York: Taylor & Dodd, 1840), 162–66, 106–10.

rivalry all the bitterest excitement of personal interests conflicting with each other. Why is it that parties now exhibit excitement aggravated to a degree dangerous to the existence of the Union and to the peace of society? Is it not that by frequent exercises of partial legislation, almost every man's personal interests have become deeply involved in the result of the contest? In common times, the strife of parties is the mere struggle of ambitious leaders for power; now they are deadly contests of the whole mass of the people, whose pecuniary interests are implicated in the event, because the Government has usurped and exercised the power of legislating on their private affairs. The selfish feeling has been so strongly called into action by this abuse of authority as almost to overpower the social feeling, which it should be the object of a good Government to foster by every means in its power.

No nation, knowingly and voluntarily, with its eyes open, ever delegated to its Government this enormous power, which places at its disposal the property, the industry, and the fruits of the industry, of the whole people. As a general rule, the prosperity of rational men depends on themselves. Their talents and their virtues shape their fortunes. They are therefore the best judges of their own affairs, and should be permitted to seek their own happiness in their own way, untrammelled by the capricious interference of legislative bungling, so long as they do not violate the equal rights of others, nor transgress the general laws for the security of person and property.

But modern refinements have introduced new principles in the science of Government. Our own Government, most especially, has assumed and exercised an authority over the people, not unlike that of weak and vacillating parents over their children, and with about the same degree of impartiality. One child becomes a favourite because he has made a fortune, and another because he has failed in the pursuit of that object; one because of its beauty, and another because of its deformity. Our Government has thus exercised the right of dispensing favours to one or another class of citizens at will; of directing its patronage first here and then there; of bestowing one day and taking back the next; of giving to the few and denying to the many; of investing wealth with new and exclusive privileges, and distributing, as it were at random, and with a capricous policy, in unequal portions, what it ought not to bestow, or what, if given away, should be equally the portion of all.

A government administered on such a system of policy may be called a Government of Equal Rights, but it is in its nature and essence a disguised despotism. It is the capricious dispenser of good and evil, without any restraint, except its own sovereign will. It holds in its hand the distribution of the goods of this world, and is consequently the uncontrolled master of the people.

Such was not the object of the Government of the United States, nor such the powers delegated to it by the people. The object was beyond doubt to protect the weak against the strong, by giving them an equal voice and equal rights in the state; not to make one portion stronger, the other weaker at pleasure, by crippling one or more classes of the community, or making them tributary to one alone. This is too great a power to entrust to Government. It was never given away by the people, and is not a right, but a usurpation.

Experience will show that this power has always been exercised under the influence and for the exclusive benefit of wealth. It was never wielded in behalf of the community. Whenever an exception is made to the general law of the land, founded on the principle of equal rights, it will always be found to be in favour of wealth. These immunities are never bestowed on the poor. They have no claim to a dispensation of exclusive benefits, and their only business is to *"take care of the rich that the rich may take care of the poor."*

Thus it will be seen that the sole reliance of the labouring classes, who constitute a vast majority of every people on the earth, is the great principle of Equal Rights; that their only safeguard against oppression is a system of legislation which leaves all to the free exercise of their talents and industry, within the limits of the GENERAL LAW, and which, on no pretence of public good, bestows on any particular class of industry, or any particular body of men, rights or privileges not equally enjoyed by the great aggregate of the body politic.

Time will remedy the departures which have already been made from this sound republican system, if the people but jealously watch and indignantly frown on any future attempts to invade their equal rights, or appropriate to the few what belongs to all alike. To quote, in conclusion, the langauge of the great man, with whose admirable sentiment we commenced these remarks, "it is time to pause in our career—if we cannot at once, in justice to the interests vested under improvident legislation, make our government what it ought to be, we can at least take a stand against all new grants of monopolies and exclusive privileges, and against any prostitution of our Government to the advancement of the few at the expense of the many."

Rich and Poor

[*From the* Evening Post, *December 6, 1834.*]

The rich perceive, acknowledge, and act upon a common interest, and why not the poor? Yet the moment the latter are called up to combine for the preservation of their rights, forsooth the community is in danger! Property is no longer secure, and life in jeopardy. This cant has descended to us from those times when the poor and labouring classes had no stake in the community, and no rights except such as they could acquire by force. But the times have changed, though the cant remains the same. The scrip nobility of this Republic have adopted towards the free people of this Republic the same language which the Feudal Barons and the despot who contested with them the power of oppressing the people, used towards their serfs and villains, as they were opprobiously called.

These would-be lordlings of the Paper Dynasty, cannot or will not perceive, that there is some difference in the situation and feelings of the people of the United States, and those of the despotic governments of Europe. They forget that at this moment our people, we mean emphatically the class which labours with its own hands, is in possession of a greater portion of the property and intelligence of this country, ay, ten times over, than all the creatures of the paper credit system put together. This property is indeed more widely and equally distributed among the people than among the phantoms of the paper system, and so much the better. And as to their intelligence, let any man talk with them, and if he does not learn something it is his own fault. They are as well acquainted with the rights of person and property, and have as just a regard for them, as the most illustrious lordling of the scrip nobility. And why should they not? Who and what are the great majority of the wealthy people of this city—we may say of this country? Are they not (we say it not in disparagement, but in high commendation) are they not men who began the world comparatively poor with ordinary education and ordinary means? And what should make them so much wiser than their neighbours? Is it because they live in better style, ride in carriages, and have more money—or at least more credit than their poorer neighbours? Does a man become wiser, stronger, or more virtuous and patriotic, because he has a fine house over his head? Does he love his country the better because he has a French cook, and a box at the opera? Or does he grow more learned, logical and profound by intense study of the daybook, ledger, bills of exchange, bank promises, and notes of hand?

Of all the countries on the face of the earth, or that ever existed on the face of the earth, this is the one where the claims of wealth and aristocracy are the most unfounded, absurd and ridiculous. With no claim to hereditary distinctions; with no exclusive rights except what they derive from monopolies, and no power of perpetuating their estates in their posterity, the assumption of aristocratic airs and claims is supremely ridiculous. To-morrow they themselves may be beggars for aught they know, or at all events their children may become so. Their posterity in the second generation will have to begin the world again, and work for a living as did their forefathers. And yet the moment a man becomes rich among us, he sets up for wisdom—he despises the poor and ignorant—he sets up for patriotism: he is your only man who has a stake in the community, and therefore the only one who ought to have a voice in the state. What folly is this? And how contemptible his presumption? He is not a whit wiser, better or more patriotic than when he commenced the world, a waggon driver. Nay not half so patriotic, for he would see his country disgraced a thousand times, rather than see one fall of the stocks, unless perhaps he had been speculating on such a contingency. To him a victory is only of consequence, as it raises, and a defeat only to be lamented, as it depresses a loan. His soul is wrapped up in a certificate of scrip, or a Bank note. Witness the conduct of these pure patriots, during the late war, when they, at least a large proportion of them, not only withheld all their support from the Government, but used all their influence to prevent others from giving their assistance. Yet these are the people who alone have a stake in the community, and of course exclusively monopolize patriotism.

But let us ask what and where is the danger of a combination of the labouring classes in vindication of their political principles, or in defence of their menaced rights? Have they not the right to act in concert, when their opponents act in concert? Nay, is it not their bounden duty to combine against the only enemy they have to fear as yet in this free country, monopoly and a great paper system that grinds them to the dust? Truly this is strange republican doctrine, and this is a strange republican country, where men cannot unite in one common effort, in one common cause, without rousing the cry of danger to the rights of person and property. Is not this a government of the people, founded on the rights of the people, and instituted for the express object of guarding them against the encroachments and usurpations of power? And if they are not permitted the possession of common interest; the exercise of a common feeling; if they cannot combine to resist by constitutional means, these encroachments; to what purpose were they declared free to exercise the right of suffrage in the choice of rulers, and the making of laws?

And what we ask is the power against which the people, not only of this country, but of almost all Europe, are called upon to array themselves, and the encroachment on their rights, they are summoned to resist? Is it not emphatically, the power of monopoly, and the encroachments of corporate privileges of every kind, which the cupidity of the rich engenders to the injury of the poor?

It was to guard against the encroachments of power, the insatiate ambition of wealth that this government was instituted, by the people themselves. But the objects which call for the peculiar jealousy and watchfulness of the people, are not now what they once were. The cautions of the early writers in favour of the liberties of mankind, have in some measure become obsolete and inapplicable. We are menaced by our old enemies, avarice and ambition, under a new name and form. The tyrant is changed from a steel-clad feudal baron, or a minor despot, at the head of thousands of ruffian followers, to a mighty civil gentleman who comes mincing and bowing to the people with a quill behind his ear, at the head of countless millions of magnificent *promises*. He promises to make every body rich; he promises to pave cities with gold; and he promises to pay. In short he is made up of promises. He will do wonders, such as never were seen or heard of, provided the people will only allow him to make his promises, equal to silver and gold, and human labour, and grant him the exclusive benefits of all the great blessings he intends to confer on them. He is the sly, selfish, grasping and insatiable tyrant, the people are now to guard against. A CONCENTRATED MONEY POWER; a usurper in the disguise of a benefactor; an agent exercising privileges which his principal never possessed; an impostor who, while he affects to wear chains, is placed above those who are free? a chartered libertine, that pretends to be manacled only that he may the more safely pick our pockets, and lord it over our rights. This is the enemy we are now to encounter and overcome, before we can expect to enjoy the substantial realities of freedom.

GEORGE BANCROFT

"The Office of the People in Art, Government, and Religion"
1835

The man of letters as politician was a recognizable type in antebellum America. What made George Bancroft (1800–91) unusual was the fact that, despite his Harvard education and Whig and banker connected family interests, he was a Democrat—indeed, for some years the Democratic boss of Massachusetts. Furthermore, although he was one of the first Americans to be awarded a Ph.D. degree at a European university, he was also a highly popular professional author. His best selling ten-volume *History of the United States* boasted the largest readership of any historical work published in America in the nineteenth century. One key to understanding both his unexpected embrace of the Democratic party and his success as an author lay in his knack for formulating an idea of democracy that was at once idealistic, populistic, and—despite the overlay of romantic philosophy—deeply conservative. In Bancroft's oration, which follows, "reason" or truth is the product, not of an active mind, but of a ready and passive assent to the universal or common opinions of men and women. Bancroft admitted the existence of conflicting sects, but only those aspects of their outlook that comported easily with other or past opinions were "received into the common inheritance." History moved, in Bancroft's view, but only very slowly and ineluctably toward the very present that middle-class Christian democracy had already achieved. The future, happily, could only bring more of the same. For a severe but very discerning study of Bancroft's intellectual and political career, see Lilian Handlin, *George Bancroft: The Intellectual as Democrat* (New York, 1984). Russell B. Nye, *George Bancroft: Brahmin Rebel* (New York, 1944) is still a useful work on Bancroft's literary career.

An Oration Delivered Before the Adelphi Society
of Williamstown College in August, 1835.

I.

The material world does not change in its masses or in its powers. The stars shine with no more lustre than when they first sang together in the glory of their birth. The flowers that gemmed the fields and the forests, before America was discovered, now bloom around us in their season. The sun that shone on Homer shines on us in unchanging lustre. The bow that beamed on the patriarch still glitters in the clouds. Nature is the same. For her no new forces are generated; no new capacities are discovered. The earth turns on its axis, and perfects its revolutions, and renews its seasons, without increase or advancement.

But a like passive destiny does not attach to the inhabitants of the earth. For them the expectations of social improvement are no delusion; the hopes of philanthropy are more than a dream. The five senses do not constitute the whole inventory of our sources of knowledge. They are the organs by which thought connects itself with the external universe; but the power of thought is not merged in the exercise of its instruments. We have functions which connect us with heaven, as well as organs which set us in relation with earth. We have not merely the senses opening to us the external world, but an internal sense, which places us in connexion with the world of intelligence and the decrees of God.

There is a *spirit in man*: not in the privileged few; not in those of us only who by the favor of Providence have been nursed in public schools: IT IS IN MAN: it is the attribute of the race. The spirit, which is the guide to truth, is the gracious gift to each member of the human family.

Reason exists within every breast. I mean not that faculty which deduces inferences from the experience of the senses, but that higher faculty, which from the infinite treasures of its own consciousness, originates truth, and assents to it by the force of intuitive evidence; that faculty which raises us beyond the control of time and space, and gives us faith in things eternal and invisible. There is not the difference between one mind and another, which the pride of philosophers might conceive. To them no faculty is conceded, which does not belong to the meanest of their countrymen. In them there can not spring up a truth which does not equally have its germ in every mind. They have not the power of creation; they can but reveal what God has implanted in every breast.

The intellectual functions, by which relations are perceived, are the common endowments of the race. The differences are apparent, not real. The eye in one person may be dull, in another quick, in one distorted, and in another tranquil and clear; yet the relation of the eye to light is in all men the same. Just so judgment may be liable in individual minds to the bias of passion, and yet its relation to truth is immutable, and is universal.

Source: George Bancroft, *Literary and Historical Miscellanies* (New York: Harper & Bros., 1855), 408–11, 413–16, 417–29, 430–32, 433–35.

In questions of practical duty, conscience is God's umpire, whose light illumines every heart. There is nothing in books, which had not first, and has not still its life within us. Religion itself is a dead letter, wherever its truths are not renewed in the soul. Individual conscience may be corrupted by interest, or debauched by pride, yet the rule of morality is distinctly marked; its harmonies are to the mind like music to the ear; and the moral judgment, when carefully analyzed and referred to its principles, is always founded in right. The eastern superstition, which bids its victims prostrate themselves before the advancing car of their idols, springs from a noble root, and is but a melancholy perversion of that self-devotion, which enables the Christian to bear the cross, and subject his personal passions to the will of God. Immorality of itself never won to its support the inward voice; conscience if questioned, never forgets to curse the guilty with the memory of sin, to cheer the upright with the meek tranquillity of approval. And this admirable power, which is the instinct of Deity, is the attribute of every man; it knocks at the palace gate, it dwells in the meanest hovel. Duty, like death, enters every abode, and delivers its message. Conscience, like reason and judgment, is universal.

. . . . . .

But I am asked if I despise learning? Shall one who has spent much of his life in schools and universities plead the equality of uneducated nature? Is there no difference between the man of refinement and the savage?

"I am a man," said Black Hawk nobly to the chief of the first republic in the world; "I am a man," said the barbarous chieftain, "and you are another."

I speak for the universal diffusion of human powers, not of human attainments; for the capacity for progress, not for the perfection of undisciplined instincts. The fellowship which we should cherish with the race, receives the Comanche warrior and the Caffre within the pale of equality. Their functions may not have been exercised, but they exist. Immure a person in a dungeon; as he comes to the light of day, his vision seems incapable of performing its office. Does that destroy your conviction in the relation between the eye and light? The rioter over his cups resolves to eat and drink and be merry; he forgets his spiritual nature in his obedience to the senses; but does that destroy the relation between conscience and eternity? "What ransom shall we give?" exclaimed the senators of Rome to the savage Attila. "Give," said the barbarian, "all your gold and jewels, your costly furniture and treasures, and set free every slave." "Ah," replied the degenerate Romans, "what then will be left to us?" "I leave you your souls," replied the unlettered invader from the steppes of Asia, who had learnt in the wilderness to value the immortal mind, and to despise the servile herd, that esteemed only their fortunes, and had no true respect for themselves. You cannot discover a tribe of men, but you also find the charities of life, and the proofs of spiritual existence. Behold the ignorant Algonquin deposit a bow and quiver by the side of the departed warrior; and recognise his faith in immortality. See the Comanche chieftain, in the heart of our continent, inflict on himself severest penance; and reverence his confession of the needed atonement for sin. The Barbarian who roams our western prairies has like passions and like endowments with ourselves. He bears within him the instinct of Deity; the consciousness of a spiritual nature; the love of beauty; the rule of morality.

And shall we reverence the dark-skinned Caffre? Shall we respect the brutal Hottentot? You may read the right answer written on every heart. It bids me not despise the sable hunter, that gathers a livelihood in the forests of Southern Africa. All are men. When we know the Hottentot better, we shall despise him less.

II.

If it be true, that the gifts of mind and heart are universally diffused, if the sentiment of truth, justice, love, and beauty exists in every one, then it follows, as a necessary consequence, that the common judgment in taste, politics, and religion, is the highest authority on earth, and the nearest possible approach to an infallible decision. From the consideration of individual powers I turn to the action of the human mind in masses.

If reason is a universal faculty, the universal decision is the nearest criterion of truth. The common mind winnows opinions; it is the sieve which separates error from certainty. The exercise by many of the same faculty on the same subject would naturally lead to the same conclusions. But if not, the very differences of opinion that arise prove the supreme judgment of the general mind. Truth is one. It never contradicts itself. One truth cannot contradict another truth. Hence truth is a bond of union. But error not only contradicts truth, but may contradict itself; so that there may be many errors, and each at variance with the rest. Truth is therefore of necessity an element of harmony; error as necessarily an element of discord. Thus there can be no continuing universal judgment but a right one. Men cannot agree in an absurdity; neither can they agree in a falsehood.

If wrong opinions have often been cherished by the masses, the cause always lies in the complexity of the ideas presented. Error finds its way into the soul of a nation, only thorugh the channel of truth. It is to a truth that men listen; and if they accept error also, it is only because the error is for the time so closely interwoven with the truth, that the one cannot readily be separated from the other.

Unmixed error can have no existence in the public mind. Wherever you see men clustering together to form a party, you may be sure that however much error may be there, truth is there also. Apply this principle boldly; for it contains a lesson of candor, and a voice of encouragement. There never was a school of philosophy, nor a clan in the realm of opinion, but carried along with it some important truth. And therefore every sect that has ever flourished has benefited Humanity; for the errors of a sect pass away and are forgotten; its truths are received into the common inheritance. To know the seminal thought of every prophet and leader of a sect, is to gather all the wisdom of mankind.

. . . . . .

The sentiment of beauty, as it exists in the human mind, is the criterion in works of art, inspires the conceptions of genius, and exercises a final judgment on its productions. For who are the best judges in matters of taste? Do you think the cultivated individual? Undoubtedly not; but the collective mind. The public is wiser than the wisest critic. In Athens, the arts were carried to perfection, when "the fierce democracie" was in the ascendant; the temple of Minerva and the works of Phidias were planned and perfected to please the common people. When Greece yielded to tyrants, her genius for excellence in art expired; or rather, the purity of taste disappeared; because the artist then endeavored to gratify a patron, and therefore, humored his caprice; while before he had endeavored to delight the race.

When, after a long eclipse, the arts again burst into a splendid existence, it was equally under a popular influence. During the rough contests and feudal tyrannies of the middle age, religion had opened in the church an asylum for the people. There the serf and the beggar could kneel; there the pilgrim and the laborer were shrived; and the children of misfortune not less than the prosperous were welcomed to the house of prayer. The church was, consequently, at once the guardian of equality, and the nurse of the arts; and the souls of Giotto, and Perugino, and Raphael, moved by an infinite sympathy with the crowd, kindled into divine conceptions of beautiful forms. Appealing to the sentiment of devotion in the common mind, they dipped their pencils in living colors, to decorate the altars where man adored. By degrees the wealthy nobility desired in like manner to adorn their palaces; but at the attempt, the quick familiarity of the artist with the beautiful declined. Instead of the brilliant works which spoke to the soul, a school arose, who appealed to the senses; and in the land which had proudced the most moving pictures, addressed to the religious feeling, and instinct with the purest beauty, the banquet halls were covered with grotesque forms, such as float before the imagination, when excited and bewildered by sensual indulgence. Instead of holy families, the ideal representations of the virgin mother and the godlike child, of the enduring faith of martyrs, of the blessed benevolence of evangelic love, there came the motley group of fawns and satyrs, of Diana stooping to Endymion, of voluptuous beauty, and the forms of licentiousness. Humanity frowned on the dese-cration of the arts; and painting, no longer vivified by a fellow-feeling with the mul-titude, lost its greatness in the attempt to adapt itself to personal humors.

If with us the arts are destined to a brilliant career, the inspiration must spring from the vigor of the people. Genius will not create, to flatter patrons or decorate saloons. It yearns for larger influences; it feeds on wider sympathies; and its perfect display can never exist, except in an appeal to the general sentiment for the beautiful.

Again. Italy is famed for its musical compositions, its inimitable operas. It is a well-known fact, that the best critics are often deceived in their judgment of them; while the pit, composed of the throng, does, without fail, render a true verdict.

But the taste for music, it may be said, is favored by natural organization. Pre-cisely a statement that sets in a clearer light the natural capacity of the race; for taste is then not an acquisition, but in part a gift. But let us pass to works of literature.

Who are by way of eminence the poets of all mankind? Surely Homer and Shak-speare. Now Homer formed his taste, as he wandered from door to door, a vagrant minstrel, paying for hospitality by a song; and Shakspeare wrote for an audience, com-posed in a great measure of the common people.

The little story of Paul and Virginia is a universal favorite. When it was first writ-ten, the author read it aloud to a circle in Paris, composed of the wife of the prime minister, and the choicest critics of France. They condemned it, as dull and insipid. The author appealed to the public; and the children of all Europe reversed the decree of the Parisians. The judgment of children, that is, the judgment of the common mind under its most innocent and least imposing form, was more trustworthy than the crit-icism of the select refinement of the most polished city in the world.

Demosthenes of old formed himself to the perfection of eloquence by means of addresses to the crowd. The great comic poet of Greece, emphatically the poet of the vulgar mob, is distinguished above all others for the incomparable graces of his diction; and it is related of one of the most skilful writers in the Italian, that when inquired of where he had learned the purity and nationality of his style, he replied, from listening to the country people, as they brought their produce to market.

At the revival of letters a distinguishing feature of the rising literature was the employment of the dialect of the vulgar. Dante used the language of the populace and won immortality; Wickliffe, Luther, and at a later day Descartes, each employed his mother tongue, and carried truth directly to all who were familiar with its accents. Every beneficent revolution in letters has the character of popularity; every great reform among authors has sprung from the power of the people in its influence on the development and activity of mind.

The same influence continues unimpaired. Scott, in spite of his reverence for the aristocracy, spurned a drawing-room reputation; the secret of Byron's superiority lay in part in the agreement which existed between his muse and the democratic tendency of the age. German literature is almost entirely a popular creation. It was fostered by no monarch; it was dandled by no aristocracy. It was plebeian in its origin, and therefore manly in its results.

III.

In like manner the best government rests on the people and not on the few, on persons and not on property, on the free development of public opinion and not on authority; because the munificent Author of our being has conferred the gifts of mind upon every member of the human race without distinction of outward circumstances. Whatever of other possessions may be engrossed, mind asserts its own independence. Lands, estates, the produce of mines, the prolific abundance of the seas, may be usurped by a privileged class. Avarice, assuming the form of ambitious power, may grasp realm after realm, subdue continents, compass the earth in its schemes of aggrandizement, and sigh after other worlds; but mind eludes the power of appropriation; it exists only in its own individuality; it is a property which cannot be confiscated and cannot be torn away; it laughs at chains; it bursts from imprisonment; it defies monopoly. A government of equal rights must, therefore, rest upon mind; not wealth, not brute force, the sum of the moral intelligence of the community should rule the State. Prescription can no more assume to be a valid plea for political injustice; society studies to eradicate established abuses, and to bring social institutions and laws into harmony with moral right; not dismayed by the natural and necessary imperfections of all human effort, and not giving way to despair, because every hope does not at once ripen into fruit.

The public happiness is the true object of legislation, and can be secured only by the masses of mankind themselves awakening to the knowledge and the care of their own interests. Our free institutions have reversed the false and ignoble distinctions between men; and refusing to gratify the pride of caste, have acknowledged the common mind to be the true material for a commonwealth. Every thing has hitherto been done for the happy few. It is not possible to endow an aristocracy with greater benefits than they have already enjoyed; there is no room to hope that individuals will be more highly gifted or more fully developed than the greatest sages of past times. The world can advance only through the culture of the moral and intellectual powers of the people. To accomplish this end by means of the people themselves, is the highest purpose of government. If it be the duty of the individual to strive after a perfection like the perfection of God, how much more ought a nation to be the image of Deity. The common mind is the true Parian marble, fit to be wrought into likeness to a God. The duty of America is to secure the culture and the happiness of the masses by their reliance on themselves.

The absence of the prejudices of the old world leaves us here the opportunity of consulting independent truth; and man is left to apply the instinct of freedom to every social relation and public interest. We have approached so near to nature, that we can hear her gentlest whispers; we have made Humanity our lawgiver and our oracle; and, therefore, the nation receives, vivifies and applies principles, which in Europe the wisest accept with distrust. Freedom of mind and of conscience, freedom of the seas, freedom of industry, equality of franchises, each great truth is firmly grasped, comprehended and enforced; for the multitude is neither rash nor fickle. In truth, it is less fickle than those who profess to be its guides. Its natural dialectics surpass the logic of the schools. Political action has never been so consistent and so unwavering, as when it results from a feeling or a principle, diffused through society. The people is firm and tranquil in its movements, and necessarily acts with moderation, because it becomes but slowly impregnated with new ideas; and effects no changes, except in harmony with the knowledge which it has acquired. Besides, where it is permanently possessed of power, there exists neither the occasion nor the desire for frequent change. It is not the parent of tumult; sedition is bred in the lap of luxury, and its chosen emissaries are the beggared spendthrift and the impoverished libertine. The government by the people is in very truth the strongest government in the world. Discarding the implements of terror, it dares to rule by moral force, and has its citadel in the heart.

Such is the political system which rests on reason, reflection, and the free expression of deliberate choice. There may be those who scoff at the suggestion, that the decision of the whole is to be preferred to the judgement of the enlightened few. They say in their hearts that the masses are ignorant; that farmers know nothing of legislation; that mechanics should not quit their workshops to join in forming public opinion. But true political science does indeed venerate the masses. It maintains, not as has been perversely asserted, that "the people can make right," but that the people can DISCERN right. Individuals are but shadows, too often engrossed by the pursuit of shadows; the race is immortal: individuals are of limited sagacity; the common mind is infinite in its experience: individuals are languid and blind; the many are ever wakeful: individuals are corrupt; the race has been redeemed: individuals are time-serving; the masses are fearless: individuals may be false, the masses are ingenuous and sincere: individuals claim the divine sanction of truth for the deceitful conceptions of their own fancies; the Spirit of God breathes through the combined intelligence of the people. Truth is not to be ascertained by the impulses of an individual; it emerges from the contradictions of personal opinion; it raises itself in majestic serenity above the strifes of parties and the conflict of sects; it acknowledges neither the solitary mind, nor the separate faction as its oracle; but owns as its only faithful interpreter the dictates of pure reason itself, proclaimed by the general voice of mankind. The decrees of the universal conscience are the nearest approach to the presence of God in the soul of man.

Thus the opinion which we respect is, indeed, not the opinion of one or of a few, but the sagacity of the many. It is hard for the pride of cultivated philosophy to put its ear to the ground, and listen reverently to the voice of lowly humanity; yet the people collectively are wiser than the most gifted individual, for all his widsom constitutes but a part of theirs. When the great sculptor of Greece was endeavoring to fashion the perfect model of beauty, he did not passively imitiate the form of the loveliest woman of his age; but he gleaned the several lineaments of his faultless work from the many. And so it is, that a perfect judgment is the result of comparison, when error eliminates error, and truth is established by concurring witnesses. The organ of truth is the invisible decision of the unbiased world; she pleads before no tribunal but public opinion; she owns no safe interpreter but the common mind; she knows no court of appeals but the soul of humanity. It is when the multitude give counsel, that right purposes find safety; theirs is the fixedness that cannot be shaken; theirs is the understanding which exceeds in wisdom; theirs is the heart, of which the largeness is as the sand on the sea-shore.

It is not by vast armies, by immense natural resources, by accumulations of treasure, that the greatest results in modern civilization have been accomplished. The traces of the career of conquest pass away, hardly leaving a scar on the national intelligence. The famous battle grounds of victory are, most of them, comparatively indifferent to the human race; barren fields of blood, the scourges of their times, but affecting the social condition as little as the raging of a pestilence. Not one benevolent institution, not one ameliorating principle in the Roman state, was a voluntary concession of the aristocracy; each useful element was borrowed from the Democracies of Greece, or was a reluctant concession to the demands of the people. The same is true in modern political life. It is the confession of an enemy to Democracy, that "ALL THE GREAT AND NOBLE INSTITUTIONS OF THE WORLD HAVE COME FROM POPULAR EFFORTS."

It is the uniform tendency of the popular element to elevate and bless Humanity. The exact measure of the progress of civilization is the degree in which the intelligence of the common mind has prevailed over wealth and brute force; in other words, the measure of the progress of civilization is the progress of the people. Every great object, connected with the benevolent exertions of the day, has reference to the culture of those powers which are alone the common inheritance. For this the envoys of religion cross seas, and visit remotest isles; for this the press in its freedom teems with the production of maturest thought; for this the philanthropist plans new schemes of education; for this halls in every city and village are open to the public instructor. Not that we view with indifference the glorious efforts of material industry; the increase in the facility of internal intercourse; the accumulations of thrifty labor; the varied results of concentrated action. But even there it is mind that achieves the triumph. It is the genius of the architect that gives beauty to the work of human hands, and makes the temple, the dwelling, or the public edifice, an outward representation of the spirit of propriety and order. It is science that guides the blind zeal of cupidity to the construction of the vast channels of communication, which are fast binding the world into one family. And it is as a method of moral improvement, that these swifter means of intercourse derive their greatest value. Mind becomes universal property; the poem that is published on the soil of England, finds its response on the shores of lake Erie and the banks of the Missouri, and is admired near the sources of the Ganges. The defence of public liberty in our own halls of legislation penetrates the plains of Poland, is echoed along the mountains of Greece, and pierces the darkest night of eastern despotism.

The universality of the intellectual and moral powers, and the necessity of their development for the progress of the race, proclaim the great doctrine of the natural right of every human being to moral and intellectual culture. It is the glory of our fathers to have established in their laws the equal claims of every child to the public care of its morals and its mind. From this principle we may deduce the universal right to leisure; that is, to time not appropriated to material purposes, but reserved for the culture of the moral affections and the mind. It does not tolerate the exclusive enjoyment of leisure by a privileged class; but defending the rights of labor, would suffer none to sacrifice the higher purposes of existence in unceasing toil for that which is not life. Such is the voice of nature; such the conscious claim of the human mind. The universe opens its pages to every eye; the music of creation resounds in every ear; the glorious lessons of immortal truth, that are written in the sky and on the earth, address themselves to every mind, and claim attention from every human being. God has made man upright, that he might look before and after; and he calls upon every one not merely to labor, but to reflect; not merely to practise the revelations of divine will, but to contemplate the displays of divine power. Nature claims for every man leisure, for she claims every man as a witness to the divine glory, manifested in the created world.

. . . . . .

The right to universal education being thus acknowledged by our conscience, not less than by our laws, it follows, that the people is the true recipient of truth. Do not seek to conciliate individuals; do not dread the frowns of a sect; do not yield to the proscriptions of a party; but pour out truth into the common mind. Let the waters of intelligence, like the rains of heaven, descend on the whole earth. And be not discouraged by the dread of encountering ignorance. *The prejudices of ignorance are more easily removed than the prejudices of interest; the first are blindly adopted; the second wilfully preferred.* Intelligence must be diffused among the whole people; truth must be scatted among those who have no interest to suppress its growth. The seeds that fall on the exchange, or in the hum of business, may be choked by the thorns that spring up in the hotbed of avarice; the seeds that are let fall in the saloon, may be like those dropped by the wayside, which take no root. Let the young aspirant after glory scatter the seeds of truth broadcast on the wide bosom of Humanity; in the deep, fertile soil of the public mind. There it will strike deep root and spring up, and bear an hundred-fold, and bloom for ages, and ripen fruit through remote generations.

It is alone by infusing great principles into the common mind, that revolutions in human society are brought about. They never have been, they never can be, effected by superior individual excellence. The age of the Antonines is the age of the greatest glory of the roman empire. Men distinguished by every accomplishment of culture and science, for a century in succession, possessed undisputed sway over more than a hundred millions of men; till at last, in the person of Mark Aurelian, philosophy herself seemed to mount the throne. And did she stay the downward tendencies of the Roman empire? Did she infuse new elements of life into the decaying constitution? Did she commence one great, beneficent reform? Not one permanent amelioration was effected; philosophy was clothed with absolute power; and yet absolute power accomplished nothing for Humanity. It could accomplish nothing. Had it been possible, Aurelian would have wrought a change. Society can be regenerated, the human race can be advanced, only by moral principles diffused through the multitude.

And now let us take an opposite instance; let us see, if amelioration follows, when in despite of tryanny truth finds access to the common people; and Christianity itself shall furnish my example.

When Christianity first made its way into Rome, the imperial city was the seat of wealth, philosophy, and luxury. Absolute government was already established; and had the will of Claudius been gained, or the conscience of Messalina been roused, or the heart of Narcissus, once a slave, then prime minister, been touched by the recollections of his misfortunes, the aid of the sovereign of the civilized world would have been engaged. And did the messenger of divine truth make his appeal to them? Was his mission to the emperor and his minions? to the empress and her flatterers? to servile senators? to wealthy favorites? Paul preserves for us the names of the first converts; the Roman Mary and Junia; Julia and Nerea; and the beloved brethren; all plebeian names, unknown to history.

. . . . . .

Yes, reforms in society are only effected through the masses of the people, and through them have continually taken place. New truths have been successively developed, and, becoming the common property of the human family, have improved its condition. This progress is advanced by every sect, precisely because each sect, to obtain vitality, does of necessity embody a truth; by every political party, for the conflicts of party are the war of ideas; by every nationality, for a nation cannot exist as such, till humanity makes it a special trustee of some part of its wealth for the ultimate benefit of all. The irresistible tendency of the human race is therefore to advancement, for absolute power has never succeeded, and can never succeed, in suppressing a single truth. An idea once revealed may find its admission into every living breast and live there. Like God it becomes immortal and omnipresent. The movement of the species is upward, irresistibly upward. The individual is often lost; Providence never disowns the race. No principle once promulgated, has ever been forgotten. No "timely tramp" of a despot's foot ever trod out one idea. The world cannot retrograde; the dark ages cannot return. Dynasties perish; cities are buried; nations have been victims to error, or martyrs for right; Humanity has always been on the advance; gaining maturity, universality, and power.

Yes, truth is immortal; it cannot be destroyed; it is invincible, it cannot long be resisted. Not every great principle has yet been generated; but when once proclaimed and diffused, it lives without end, in the safe custody of the race. States may pass away; every just principle of legislation which has been once established will endure. Philosophy has sometimes forgotten God; a great people never did. The skepticism of the last century could not uproot Christianity, because it lived in the hearts of the millions. Do you think that infidelity is spreading? Christianity never lived in the hearts of so many millions as at this moment. The forms under which it is professed may decay, for they, like all that is the work of man's hands, are subject to the changes and chances of mortal being; but the spirit of truth is incorruptible; it may be developed, illustrated, and applied; it never can die; it never can decline.

No truth can perish; not truth can pass away. The flame is undying, though generations disappear. Wherever moral truth has started into being, Humanity claims and guards the bequest. Each generation gathers together the imperishable children of the past, and increases them by new sons of light, alike radiant with immortality.

CATHARINE BEECHER

Selection from *A Treatise on Domestic Economy*
1841

As the sister of the novelist Harriet Beecher Stowe and the daughter and sister, respectively, of two of America's most illustrious preachers, Lyman and Henry Ward Beecher, Catharine Beecher (1800–78) was born to the evangelical purple. Nonetheless, by her own right and in her own sphere (to borrow one of her favored terms), she was fully as influential as they in theirs. That sphere was American middle-class female culture. An indefatigable organizer of women's schools and colleges and a resourceful battler for the advancement of women teachers in public education, Beecher was the antebellum era's leader in the takeoff of American female education. Equally important was her role in intellectually reconciling, for the many women who read her books, existing patterns of female subordination with the values of American democracy. In the opening chapters of her popular *Treatise on Domestic Economy*, she managed this feat in three main ways. She showed that a Christian and liberal idea of democracy was perfectly consistent with social hierarchies. She argued that women's domestic and teaching sphere, properly defined, was not only the basis of women's social advancement, but was central to the very functioning of American democracy and the evangelical regeneration of the world. Finally, she sought to show, by providing a new scheme of professionalized domestic work and female schooling, that women's activities as well as their mental health necessitated autonomous and utilitarian rationalistic thinking skills—or the very same skills that had often been considered by educational reformers since Locke the primary ingredients of *masculine* success in school and work. Kathryn Kish Sklar, *Catharine Beecher: A Study in American Domesticity* (New Haven, 1973) is a first-rate biographical study that gives full attention to Beecher's social thought. For two stimulating interpretations of Beecher's educational theories, see Joan N. Burstyn, "Catharine Beecher and the Education of Women," *New England Quarterly*, 47 (September 1974), 386–403; and Jane Roland Martin, *Reclaiming a Conversation: The Ideal of the Educated Woman* (New Haven, 1985), 103–38. Jeanne Boydston, Mary Kelley, and Anne Margolis, *The Limits of Sisterhood: The Beecher Sisters on Women's Rights and Woman's Sphere* (Chapel Hill, 1988) is an imaginative collection of writings and commentary. For an excellent study of republican antecedents of Beecher's ideology of intellectual domesticity, see Linda K. Kerber, *Women of the Republic: Intellect and Ideology in Revolutionary America* (Chapel Hill, 1980). For a similarly fine study of the domestic theme in antebellum women's literature, see Mary Kelley, *Private Woman, Public Stage: Literary Domesticity in Nineteenth-Century America* (New York, 1984).

Chapter I.

THE PECULIAR RESPONSIBILITIES OF AMERICAN WOMEN.

There are some reasons, why American women should feel an interest in the support of the democratic institutions of their Country, which it is important that they should consider. The great maxim, which is the basis of all our civil and political institutions, is, that "all men are created equal," and that they are equally entitled to "life, liberty, and the pursuit of happiness."

But it can readily be seen, that this is only another mode of expressing the fundamental principle which the Great Ruler of the Universe has established, as the law of His eternal government. "Thou shalt love they neighbor as theyself;" and "Whatsoever ye would that men should do to you, do ye even so to them," are the Scripture forms, by which the Supreme Lawgiver requires that each individual of our race shall regard the happiness of others, as of the same value as his own; and which forbid any institution, in private or civil life, which secures advantages to one class, by sacrificing the interests of another.

The principles of democracy, then, are identical with the principles of Christianity.

But, in order that each individual may pursue and secure the highest degree of happiness within his reach, unimpeded by the selfish interests of others, a system of laws must be established, which sustain certain relations and dependencies in social and civil life. What these relations and their attending obligations shall be, are to be determined, not with reference to the wishes and interests of a few, but solely with reference to the general good of all; so that each individual shall have his own interest, as well as the public benefit, secured by them.

For this purpose, it is needful that certain relations be sustained, which involve the duties of subordination. There must be the magistrate and the subject, one of whom is the superior, and the other the inferior. There must be the relations of husband and wife, parent and child, teacher and pupil, employer and employed, each involving the relative duties of subordination. The superior, in certain particulars, is to direct, and the inferior is to yield obedience. Society could never go forward, harmoniously, nor could any craft or profession be successfully pursued, unless these superior and subordinate relations be instituted and sustained.

But who shall take the higher, and who the subordinate, stations in social and civil life? This matter, in the case of parents and children, is decided by the Creator. He has given children to the control of parents, as their superiors, and to them they remain subordinate, to a certain age, or so long as they are members of their household. And parents can delegate such a portion of their authority to teachers and employers, as the interests of their children require.

In most other cases, in a truly democratic state, each individual is allowed to choose for himself, who shall take the position of his superior. No woman is forced to obey any husband but the one she chooses for herself; nor is she obliged to take a husband, if she prefers to remain single. So every domestic, and every artisan or

Source: Catharine E. Beecher, *A Treatise on Domestic Economy, for the Use of Young Ladies at Home, at School,* rev. ed. (New York: Harper & Bros., 1846), 25–28, 32–34, 35–41, 43–44, 45–46, 47–49, 50–53, 53–54, 54–62.

laborer, after passing from parental control, can choose the employer to whom he is to accord obedience, or, if he prefers to relinquish certain advantages, he can remain wihtout taking a subordinate place to any employer.

Each subject, also, has equal power with every other, to decide who shall be his superior as a ruler. The weakest, the poorest, the most illiterate, has the same opportunity to determine this question, as the richest, the most learned, and the most exalted.

And the various privileges that wealth secures, are equally open to all classes. Every man may aim at riches, unimpeded by any law or institution which secures peculiar privileges to a favored class, at the expense of another. Every law, and every institution, is tested by examining whether it secures equal advantages to all; and, if the people become convinced that any regulation sacrifices the good of the majority to the interests of the smaller number, they have power to abolish it.

The institutions of monarchical and aristocratic nations are based on precisely opposite principles. They secure, to certain small and favored classes, advantages, which can be maintained, only by sacrificing the interests of the great mass of the people. Thus, the throne and aristocracy of England are supported by laws and customs, which burden the lower classes with taxes, so enormous, as to deprive them of all the luxuries, and of most of the comforts, of life. Poor dwellings, scanty food, unhealthy employments, excessive labor, and entire destitution of the means and time for education, are appointed for the lower classes, that a few may live in palaces, and riot in every indulgence.

The tendencies of democratic institutions, in reference to the rights and interests of the female sex, have been fully developed in the United States; and it is in this aspect, that the subject is one of peculiar interest to American women. In this Country, it is established, both by opinion and by practice, that woman has an equal interest in all social and civil concerns; and that no domestic, civil, or political, institution, is right, which sacrifices her interest to promote that of the other sex. But in order to secure her the more firmly in all these privileges, it is decided, that, in the domestic relation, she take a subordinate station, and that, in civil and political concerns, her interests be intrusted to the other sex, without her taking any part in voting, or in making and administering laws. The result of this order of things has been fairly tested, and is thus portrayed by M. De Tocqueville, a writer, who, for intelligence, fidelity, and ability, ranks second to none.

"There are people in Europe, who, confounding together the different characteristics of the sexes, would make of man and woman, beings not only equal, but alike. They would give to both the same functions, impose on both the same duties, and grant to both the same rights. They would mix them in all things—their business, their occupations, their pleasures. It may readily be conceived that, by *thus* attempting to make one sex equal to the other, both are degraded; and, from so preposterous a medley of the works of Nature, nothing could ever result, but weak men and disorderly women.

"It is not thus that the Americans understand the species of democratic equality, which may be established between the sexes. They admit, that, as Nature has appointed such wide differences between the physical and moral constitutions of man and woman, her manifest design was, to give a distinct employment to their various faculties; and they hold, that improvement does not consist in making beings so dissimilar do pretty nearly the same things, but in getting each of them to fulfil their respective tasks, in the best possible manner. The Americans have applied to the sexes the great principle of political economy, which governs the manufactories of our age, by carefully dividing the duties of man from those of woman, in order that the great work of society may be the better carried on.

. . . . . .

"Thus the Americans do not think that man and woman have either the duty, or the right, to perform the same offices, but they show an equal regard for both their respective parts; and, though their lot is different, they consider both of them, as beings of equal value. They do not give to the courage of woman the same form, or the same direction, as to that of man; but they never doubt her courage: and if they hold that man and his partner ought not always to exercise their intellect and understanding in the same manner, they at least believe the understanding of the one to be as sound as that of the other, and her intellect to be as clear. Thus, then, while they have allowed the social inferiority of woman to subsist, they have done all they could to raise her, morally and intellectually, to the level of man; and, in this respect, they appear to me to have excellently understood the true principle of democratic improvement.

"As for myself, I do not hesitate to avow, that, although the women of the United States are confined within the narrow circle of domestic life, and their situation is, in some respects, one of extreme dependence, I have nowhere seen women occupying a loftier position; and if I were asked, now I am drawing to the close of this work, in which I have spoken of so many important things done by the Americans, to what the singular prosperity and growing strength of that people ought mainly to be attributed, I should reply,—to the superiority of their women."

This testimony of a foreigner, who has had abundant opportunities of making a comparison, is sanctioned by the assent of all candid and intelligent men, who have enjoyed similar opportunities.

It appears, then, that it is in America, alone, that women are raised to an equality with the other sex; and that, both in theory and practice, their interests are regarded as of equal value. They are made subordinate in station, only where a regard to their best interests demands it, while, as if in compensation for this, by custom and courtesy, they are always treated as superiors. Universally, in this Country, through every class of society, precedence is given to woman, in all the comforts, conveniences, and courtesies, of life.

In civil and political affairs, American women take no interest or concern, except so far as they sympathize with their family and personal friends; but in all cases, in which they do feel a concern, their opinions and feelings have a consideration, equal, or even superior, to that of the other sex.

In matters pertaining to the education of their children, in the selection and support of a clergyman, in all benevolent enterprises, and in all questions relating to morals or manners, they have a superior influence. In such concerns, it would be impossible to carry a point, contrary to their judgment and feelings; while an enterprise, sustained by them, will seldom fail of success.

If those who are bewailing themselves over the fancied wrongs and injuries of women in this Nation, could only see things as they are, they would know, that, whatever remnants of a barbarous or aristocratic age may remain in our civil institutions, in reference to the interests of women, it is only because they are ignorant of them, or do not use their influence to have them rectified; for it is very certain that there is nothing reasonable, which American women would unite in asking, that would not readily be bestowed.

The preceding remarks, then, illustrate the position, that the democratic institutions of this Country are in reality no other than the principles of Christianity carried into operation, and that they tend to place woman in her true position in society, as having equal rights with the other sex; and that, in fact, they have secured to American women a lofty and fortunate position, which, as yet, has been attained by the women of no other nation.

There is another topic, presented in the work of the above author, which demands the profound attention of American women.

The following is taken from that part of the Introduction to the work, illustrating the position, that, for ages, there has been a constant progress, in all civilized nations, towards the democratic equality attained in this Country.

"The various occurrences of national existence have every where turned to the advantage of democracy; all men have aided it by their exertions; those who have intentionally labored in its cause, and those who have served it unwittingly; those who have fought for it, and those who have declared themselves its opponents, have all been driven along in the same track, have all labored to one end;" "all have been blind instruments in the hands of God."

"The gradual developement of the equality of conditions, is, therefore, a Providential fact; and it possesses all the characteristics of a Divine decree: it is universal, it is durable, it constantly eludes all human interference, and all events, as well as all men, contribute to its progress."

· · · · · ·

It thus appears, that the sublime and elevating anticipations which have filled the mind and heart of the religious world, have become so far developed, that philosophers and statesmen are perceiving the signs, and are predicting the approach, of the same grand consummation. There is a day advancing, "by seers predicted, and by poets sung," when the curse of selfishness shall be removed; when "scenes surpassing fable, and yet true," shall be realized; when all nations shall rejoice and be made blessed, under those benevolent influences, which the Messiah came to establish on earth.

And this is the Country, which the Disposer of events designs shall go forth as the cynosure of nations, to guide them to the light and blessedness of that day. To us is committed the grand, the responsible privilege, of exhibiting to the world, the beneficent influences of Christianity, when carried into every social, civil, and political institution; and, though we have, as yet, made such imperfect advances, already the light is streaming into the dark prison-house of despotic lands, while startled kings and sages, philosophers and statesmen, are watching us with that interest, which a career so illustrious, and so involving their own destiny, is calculated to excite. They are studying our institutions, scrutinizing our experience, and watching for our mistakes, that they may learn whether "a social revolution, so irresistible, be advantageous or prejudicial to mankind."

There are persons, who regard these interesting truths merely as food for national vanity; but evey reflecting and Christian mind, must consider it as an occasion for solemn and anxious reflection. Are we, then, a spectacle to the world? Has the Eternal Lawgiver appointed us to work out a problem, involving the destiny of the whole earth? Are such momentous interests to be advanced or retarded, just in proportion as we are faithful to our high trust? "What manner of persons, then, ought we to be," in attempting to sustain so solemn, so glorious a responsibility?

But the part to be enacted by American women, in this great moral enterprise, is the point to which special attention should here be directed.

The success of democratic institutions, as is conceded by all, depends upon the intellectual and moral character of the mass of the people. If they are intelligent and virtuous, democracy is a blessing; but if they are ignorant and wicked, it is only a curse, and as much more dreadful than any other form of civil government, as a thousand tyrants are more to be dreaded than one. It is equally conceded, that the formation of the moral and intellectual character of the young is committed mainly to the female hand. The mother forms the character of the future man; the sister bends the fibres that are hereafter to be the forest tree; the wife sways the heart, whose energies may turn for good or for evil the destinies of a nation. Let the women of a country be made virtuous and intelligent, and the men will certainly be the same. The proper education of a man decides the welfare of an individual; but educate a woman, and the interests of a whole family are secured.

If this be so, as none will deny, then to American women, more than to any others on earth, is committed the exalted privilege of extending over the world those blessed influences, which are to renovate degraded man, and "clothe all climes with beauty."

No American woman, then, has any occasion for feeling that hers is an humble or insignificant lot. The value of what an individual accomplishes, is to be estimated by the importance of the enterprise achieved, and not by the particular position of the laborer. The drops of heaven which freshen the earth, are each of equal value, whether they fall in the lowland meadow, or the princely parterre. The builders of a temple are of equal importance, whether they labor on the foundations, or toil upon the dome.

Thus, also, with those labors which are to be made effectual in the regeneration of the Earth. And it is by forming a habit of regarding the apparently insignificant efforts of each isolated laborer, in a comprehensive manner, as indispensible portions of a grand result, that the minds of all, however humble their sphere of service, can be invigorated and cheered. The woman, who is rearing a family of children; the woman, who labors in the schoolroom; the woman, who, in her retired chamber, earns, with her needle, the mite, which contributes to the intellectual and moral elevation of her Country; even the humble domestic, whose example and influence may be moulding and forming young minds, while her faithful services sustain a prosperous domestic state;—each and all may be animated by the consciousness, that they are agents in accomplishing the greatest work that ever was committed to human responsibility. It is the building of a glorious temple, whose base shall be coextensive with the bounds of the earth, whose summit shall pierce the skies, whose splendor shall beam on all lands; and those who hew the lowliest stone, as much as those who carve the highest capital, will be equally honored, when its top-stone shall be laid, with new rejoicings of the morning stars, and shoutings of the sons of God.

Chapter II.

DIFFICULTIES PECULIAR TO AMERICAN WOMEN.

In the preceding chapter, were presented those views, which are calculated to inspire American women with a sense of their high responsibilities to their Country, and to the world; and of the excellence and grandeur of the object to which their energies may be consecrated.

But it will be found to be the law of moral action, that whatever involves great results and great benefits, is always attended with great hazards and difficulties. And as it has been shown, that American women have a loftier position, and a more elevated object of enterprise, than the females of any other nation, so it will appear, that they have greater trials and difficulties to overcome, than any other women are called to encounter.

Properly to appreciate the nature of these trials, it must be borne in mind, that the estimate of evils and privations depends, not so much on their positive nature, as on the character and habits of the person who meets them. A women, educated in the savage state, finds it no trial to be destitute of many conveniences, which a woman, even of the lowest condition, in this Country, would deem indispensable to existence. So a woman, educated with the tastes and habits of the best New England or Virginia housekeepers, would encounter many deprivations and trials, which would never occur to one reared in the log cabin of a new settlement. So, also, a woman, who has been accustomed to carry forward her arrangements with well-trained domestics, would meet a thousand trials to her feelings and temper, by the substitution of ignorant foreigners, or shiftless slaves, which would be of little account to one who had never enjoyed any better service.

Now, the larger portion of American women are the descendants of English progenitors, who, as a nation, are distinguished for systematic housekeeping, and for a great love of order, cleanliness, and comfort. And American women, to a greater or less extent, have inherited similar tastes and habits. But the posperity and democratic tendencies of this Country produce results, materially affecting the comfort of housekeepers, which the females of monarchical and aristocratic lands are not called to meet. In such countries, all ranks and classes are fixed in a given position, and each person is educated for a particular sphere and style of living. And the dwellings, conveniences, and customs of life, remain very nearly the same, from generation to generation. This secures the preparation of all classes for their particular station, and makes the lower orders more dependent, and more subservient to employers.

But how different is the state of things in this Country. Every thing is moving and changing. Persons in poverty, are rising to opulence, and persons of wealth, are sinking to poverty. The children of common laborers, by their talents and enterprise, are becoming nobles in intellect, or wealth, or office; while the children of the wealthy, enervated by indulgence, are sinking to humbler stations. The sons of the wealthy are leaving the rich mansions of their fathers, to dwell in the log cabins of the forest, where very soon they bear away the daughters of ease and refinement, to share the privations of a new settlement. Meantime, even in the more stationary portions of the community, there is a mingling of all grades of wealth, intellect, and education. There are no distinct classes, as in aristocratic lands, whose bounds are protected by distinct and impassable lines, but all are thrown into promiscuous masses. Thus, persons of humble means are brought into contact with those of vast wealth, while all intervening grades are placed side by side. Thus, too, there is a constant comparison of conditons, among equals, and a constant temptation presented to imitate the customs, and to strive for the enjoyments, of those who possess larger means.

In addition to this, the flow of wealth, among all classes, is constantly increasing the number of those who live in a style demanding much hired service, while the number of those, who are compelled to go to service, is constantly diminishing. Our manufactories, also, are making increased demands for female labor, and offering larger compensation. In consequence of these things, there is such a disproportion between those who wish to hire, and those who are willing to go to domestic service, that, in the non-slaveholding States, were it not for the supply of poverty-stricken foreigners, there would not be a domestic for each family who demands one. And this resort to foreigners, poor as it is, scarcely meets the demand; while the disproportion must every year increase, especially if our prosperity increases. For, just in proportion as wealth rolls in upon us, the number of those, who will give up their own independent homes to serve strangers, will be diminished.

The difficulties and sufferings, which have accrued to American women, from this cause, are almost incalculable. There is nothing, which so much demands system and regularity, as the affairs of a housekeeper, made up, as they are, of ten thousand desultory and minute items; and yet, this perpetually fluctuating state of society seems forever to bar any such system and regularity. The anxieties, vexations, perplexities, and even hard labor, which come upon American women, from this state of domestic service, are endless; and many a woman has, in consequence, been disheartened, discouraged, and ruined in health. The only wonder is, that, amid so many real difficulties, American women are still able to maintain such a character for energy, fortitude, and ambiableness, as is universally allowed to be their due.

But the second, and still greater difficulty, peculiar to American women, is, a delicacy of constitution, which renders them early victims to disease and decay.

. . . . . .

A perfectly healthy woman, especially a perfectly healthy mother, is so unfrequent, in some of the wealthier classes, that those, who are so, may be regarded as the exceptions, and not as the general rule. The writer has heard some of her friends declare, that they would ride fifty miles, to see a perfectly healthy and vigorous woman, out of the laboring classes. This, although somewhat jocose, was not an entirely unfair picture of the true state of female health in the wealthier classes.

There are many causes operating, which serve to perpetuate and increase this evil. It is a well-known fact, that mental excitement tends to weaken the physical system, unless it is counterbalanced by a corresponding increase of exercise and fresh air. Now, the people of this Country are under the influence of high commercial, political, and religious stimulus, altogether greater than was ever known by any other nation; and in all this, women are made the sympathizing companions of the other sex. At the same time, young girls, in pursuing an education, have ten times greater an amount of intellectual taxation demanded, than was ever before exacted. Let any daughter, educated in our best schools at this day, compare the course of her study with that pursued in her mother's early life, and it will be seen that this estimate of the increase of mental taxation probably falls below the truth. Though, in some countries, there are small classes of females, in the higher circles, who pursue literature and science to a far greater extent than in any corresponding circles in this Country, yet, in no nation in the world are the advantages of a good intellectual education enjoyed, by so large a proportion of the females. And this education has consisted far less of accomplishments, and far more of those solid studies which demand the exercise of the various powers of mind, than the education of the women of other lands.

And when American women are called to the responsibilities of domestic life, the degree in which their minds and feelings are taxed, is altogether greater than it is in any other nation.

No women on earth have a higher sense of their moral and religious responsibilities, or better understand, not only what is demanded of them, as housekeepers, but all the claims that rest upon them as wives, mothers, and members of a social community. An American woman, who is the mistress of a family, feels her obligations, in reference to her influence over her husband, and a still greater responsibility in rearing and educating her children. She feels, too, the claims which the moral interests of her domestics have on her watchful care. In social life, she recognises the claims of hospitality, and the demands of friendly visiting. Her responsibility, in reference to the institutions of benevolence and religion, is deeply realized. The regular worship of the Lord's day, and all the various religious meetings and benevolent societies which place so much dependence on female influence and example, she feels obligated to sustain. Add to these multiplied responsibilities, the perplexities and evils which have been pointed out, resulting from the fluctuating state of society, and the deficiency of domestic service, and no one can deny that American women are exposed to a far greater amount of intellectual and moral excitement, than those of any other land. Of course, in order to escape the danger resulting from this, a greater amount of exercise in the fresh air, and all those methods which strengthen the constitution, are imperiously required.

But, instead of this, it will be found, that, owing to the climate and customs of this Nation, there are no women who secure so little of this healthful and protecting regimen, as ours. Walking and riding and gardening, in the open air, are practised by the women of other lands, to a far greater extent, than by American females.

. . . . . .

But there is one peculiarity of situation, in regard to American women, which makes this delicacy of constitution still more disastrous. It is the liability to the exposures and hardships of a newly-settled country.

. . . . . .

. . . If the American women of the East merit the palm, for their skill and success as accomplished housekeepers, still more is due to the heroines of the West, who, with such unyielding fortitude and cheeerful endurance, attempt similar duties, amid so many disadvantages and deprivations.

But, though American women have those elevated principles and feelings, which enable them to meet such trials in so exemplary a manner, their physical energies are not equal to the exertions demanded. Though the mind may be bright and firm, the casket is shivered; though the spirit may be willing, the flesh is weak. A woman of firm health, with the hope and elasticity of youth, may be envied rather than pitied, as she shares with her young husband the hopes and enterprises of pioneer life. But, when the body fails, then the eye of hope grows dim, the heart sickens, the courage dies; and, in solitude, weariness, and suffering, the wanderer pines for the dear voices and the tender sympathies of a far distant home. Then it is, that the darkest shade is presented, which marks the peculiar trials and liabilities of American women, and which exhibits still more forcibly the disastrous results of that delicacy of constitution which has been pointed out. For, though all American women, or even the greater part of them, are not called to encounter such trials, yet no mother, who rears a family of daughters, can say, that such a lot will not fall to one of her flock; nor can she know which will escape. The reverses of fortune, and the chances of matrimony, expose every woman in the Nation to such liabilities, for which she needs to be prepared.

Chapter III.

REMEDIES FOR THE PRECEDING DIFFICULTIES.

Having pointed out the peculiar responsibilities of American women, and the peculiar embarrassments which they are called to encounter, the folliwng suggestions are offered, as remedies for such difficulties.

In the first place, the physical and domestic education of daughters should occupy the principal attention of mothers, in childhood; and the stimulation of the intellect should be very much reduced. As a general rule, daughters should not be sent to school before they are six years old; and, when they are sent, far more attention should be paid to their physical developement, than is usually done. They should never be confined, at any employment, more than an hour at a time; and this confinement should be followed by sports in the open air. Such accommodations should be secured, that, at all seasons, and in all weathers, the teacher can every half hour send out a portion of her school, for sports. And still more care should be given to preserve pure air in the schoolroom. The close stoves, crowded condition, and poisonous air, of most schoolrooms, act as constant drains on the health and strength of young children.

In addition to this, much less time should be given to school, and much more to domestic employments, especially in the wealthier classes. A little girl may begin, at five or six years of age, to assist her mother; and, if properly trained, by the time she is ten, she can render essential aid. From this time, until she is fourteen or fifteen, it should be the principal object of her education to secure a strong and healthy constitution, and a thorough practical knowledge of all kinds of domestic employments.

. . . . . .

It is in this point of view, that the dearth of good domestics in this Country may, in its results, prove a substantial blessing. If all housekeepers, who have the means, could secure good servants, there would be little hope that so important a revolution, in the domestic customs of the wealthy classes, could be effected. And so great is the natural indolence of mankind, that the amount of exercise, needful for health, will never be secured by those who are led to it through no necessity, but merely from rational considerations. Yet the pressure of domestic troubles, from the want of good domestics, has already determined many a mother, in the wealthy classes, to train her daughters to aid her in domestic service; and thus necessity is compelling mothers to do what abstract principles of expediency could never secure.

A second method of promoting the same object, is, to raise the science and practice of Domestic Economy to its appropriate place, as a regular study in female seminaries. . . . But it is to the mothers of our Country, that the community must look for this change. It cannot be expected, that teachers, who have their attention chiefly absorbed by the intellectual and moral interests of their pupils, should properly realize the importance of this department of education. But if mothers generally become convinced of this, their judgement and wishes will meet the respectful consideration they deserve, and the object will be accomplished.

The third method of securing a remedy for the evils pointed out, is, the endowment of female institutions, under the care of suitable trustees, who shall secure a proper course of education. The importance of this measure cannot be realized by those, who have not turned their attention to this subject; and for such, the following considerations are presented.

The endowment of colleges, and of law, medical, and divinity, schools, for the other sex, is designed to secure a thorough and proper education, for those who have the most important duties of society to perform. The men who are to expound the laws, the men who have the care of the public health, and the men who are to communicate religious instruction, should have well-disciplined and well-informed minds; and it is mainly for this object that collegiate and professional institutions are established. Liberal and wealthy individuals contribute funds, and the legislatures of the States also lend assistance, so that every State in this Nation has from one to twenty such endowed institutions, supplied with buildings, apparatus, a library, and a faculty of learned men to carry forward a superior course of instruction. And the use of all these advantages is secured, in many cases, at an expense, no greater than is required to send a boy to a common school and pay his board there. No private school could offer these advantages, without charging such a sum, as would forbid all but the rich from securing its benefits. By furnishing such superior advantages, on low terms, multitudes are properly educated, who would otherwise remain in ignorance; and thus the professions are supplied, by men properly qualified for them.

Were there no such institutions, and no regular and appropriate course of study demanded for admission to the bar, the pulpit, and to medical practice, the education of most professional men would be desultory, imperfect, and deficient. Parents and children would regulate the course of study according to their own crude notions; and, instead of having institutions which agree in carrying on a similar course of study, each school would have its own peculiar system, and compete and conflict with every other. Meantime, the public would have no means of deciding which was best, nor any opportunity for learning when a professional man was properly qualified for his duties. But as it is, the diploma of a college, and the license of an appointed body of judges, must both be secured, before a young man feels that he has entered the most promising path to success in his profession.

Our Country, then, is most abundantly supplied with endowed institutions, which secure a liberal education, on such low terms as make them accessible to all classes, and in which the interests of edcuation are watched over, sustained, and made permanent, by an appropriate board of trustees.

But are not the most responsible of all duties committed to the charge of woman? Is it not her profession to take care of mind, body, and soul? and that, too, at the most critical of all periods of existence? And is it not as much a matter of public concern, that she should be properly qualified for her duties, as that ministers, lawyers, and physicians, should be prepared for theirs? And is it not as important to endow institutions which shall make a superior education accessible to all classes,—for females, as for the other sex? And is it not equally important, that institutions for females be under the supervision of intelligent and responsible trustees, whose duty it shall be to secure a uniform and appropriate education for one sex as much as for the other? It would seem as if every mind must accord an affirmative reply, as soon as the matter is fairly considered.

. . . . . .

In attempting a sketch of the kind of institutions which are demanded, it is very fortunate that there is no necessity for presenting a theory, which may, or may not, be approved by experience. It is the greatest honor of one of our newest Western States, that it can boast of such an Institution, endowed, too, wholly by the munificence of a single individual. A slight sketch of this Institution, which the writer has examined in all its details, will give an idea of what can be done, by showing what has actually been accomplished.

. . . . . .

To secure adequate exercise for the pupils, two methods are adopted. By the first, each young lady is required to spend a certain portion of time in domestic employments, either in sweeping, dusting, setting and clearing tables, washing and ironing, or other household concerns.

Let not the aristocratic mother and daughter express their dislike of such an arrangement, till they can learn how well it succeeds. Let them walk, as the writer has done, through the large airy halls, kept clean and in order by their fair occupants, to the washing and ironing-rooms. There they will see a long hall, conveniently fitted up with some thirty neatly-painted tubs, with a clean floor, and water conducted so as to save both labor and slopping. Let them see some thirty or forty merry girls, superintended by a motherly lady, chatting and singing, washing and starching, while every convenience is at hand, and every thing around is clean and comfortable. Two hours, thus employed, enable each young lady to wash the articles she used during the previous week, which is all that is demanded, while thus they are all practically initaited into the arts and mysteries of the wash-tub. The Superintendent remarked to the writer, that, after a few weeks of probation, most of her young washers succeeded quite as well as those whom she could hire, and who made it their business. Adjacent to the washing-room, is the ironing establishment; where another class are arranged, on the ironing-day, around long, extended tables, with heating-furnaces, clothes-frames, and all needful applicances.

By as sytematic arrangement of school and domestic duties, a moderate portion of time, usually not exceeding two hours a day, from each of the pupils, accomplished all the domestic labor of a family of ninety, except the cooking, which was done by two hired domestics. This part of domestic labor it was deemed inexpedient to incorporate as a portion of the business of the pupils, inasmuch as it could not be accommodated to the arrangements of the school, and was in other respects objectionable.

Is it asked, how can young ladies paint, play the piano, and study, when their hands and dresses must be unfitted by such drudgery? The woman who asks this question, has yet to learn that a pure and delicate skin is better secured by healthful exercise, than by any other method; and that a young lady, who will spend two hours a day at the wash-tub, or with a broom, is far more likely to have rosy cheeks, a finely-moulded form, and a delicate skin, than one who lolls all day in her parlor or chamber, or only leaves it, girt in tight dresses, to make fashionable calls. It is true, that long-protracted daily labor hardens the hand, and unfits it for delicate employments; but the amount of labor needful for health produces no such effect. As to dress, and appearance, if neat and convenient accommodations are furnished, there is no occasion for the exposures which demand shabby dresses. A dark calico, genteelly made, with an oiled-silk apron, and wide cuffs of the same material, secures both good looks and good service. This plan of domestic employments for the pupils in this Institution, not only secures regular healthful exercise, but also aids to reduce the expenses of education, so that, with the help of the endowments, it is brought within the reach of many, who otherwise could never gain such advantages.

In addition to this, a system of Calisthenic exercises is introduced, which secures all the advantages which dancing is supposed to effect, and which is free from the dangerous tendencies of that fascinating and fashionable amusement. This system is so combined with music, and constantly varying evolutions, as to serve as an amusement, and also as a mode of curing distortions, particularly all tendencies to curvature of the spine; while, at the same time, it tends to promote grace of movement, and easy manners.

Another advantage of this Institution, is, an elevated and invigorating course of mental discipline. Many persons seem to suppose, that the chief object of an intellectual education is the acquisition of knowledge. But it will be found, that this is only a secondary object. The formation of habits of investigation, of correct reasoning, of persevering attention, of regular system, of accurate analysis, and of vigorous mental action, is the primary object to be sought in preparing American women for their arduous duties; duties which will demand not only quickness of perception, but steadiness of purpose, regularity of system, and perseverance in action.

It is for such purposes, that the discipline of the Mathematics is so important an element in female education; and it is in this aspect, that the mere acquisition of facts, and the attainment of accomplishments, should be made of altogether secondary account.

In the Insitution here described, a systematic course of study is adopted, as in our colleges; designed to occupy three years. The following slight outline of the course, will exhibit the liberal plan adopted in this respect.

In Mathematics, the whole of Arithmetic contained in the larger works used in schools, the whole of Euclid, and such portions from Day's Mathematics as are requisite to enable the pupils to demonstrate the various problems in Olmsted's larger work on Natural Philosophy. In Language, besides English Grammar, a short course in Latin is required, sufficient to secure an understanding of the philosophy of the language, and that kind of mental discipline which the exercise of translating affords. In Philosophy, Chemistry, Astronomy, Botany, Geology and Mineralogy, Intellectual and Moral Philosophy, Political Economy, and the Evidences of Christianity, the same textbooks are used as are required at our best colleges. In Geography, the most thorough course is adopted; and in History, a more complete knowledge is secured, by means of charts and textbooks, than most of our colleges offer. To these branches, are added Griscom's Physiology, Bigelow's Technology, and Jahn's Archaeology, together with a course of instruction in polite literature, for which Chambers's English Literature is employed as the textbook, each recitation being attended with selections and criticisms, from teacher or pupils, on the various authors brought into notice. Vocal Music, on the plan of the Boston Academy, is a part of the daily instructions. Linear drawing, and pencilling, are designed also to be a part of the course. Instrumental Music is taught, but not as a part of the regular course of study.

To secure the proper instruction in all these branches, the division of labor, adopted in colleges, is pursued. Each teacher has distinct branches as her department, for which she is responsible, and in which she is independent. One teacher performs the duties of a *governess,* in maintaining rules, and attending to the habits and manners of the pupils. By this method, the teachers have sufficient time, both to prepare themselves, and to impart instruction and illustration in the classroom. In this Institiution it is made a direct object of effort *to cure defects of character and habits.* At the frequent meetings of the Principal and teachers, the peculiarities of each pupil are made the subjects of inquiry; and methods are devised for remedying defects through the personal influence of the several teachers. This, when thus made a direct object of combined effort, often secures results most gratifying and encouraging.

One peculiarity of this Insitution demands consideration. By the method adopted here, the exclusive business of educating their own sex is, as it ever ought to be, confined to females. The Principal of the Institution, indeed, is a gentleman; but, while he takes the position of a father of the family, and responsible head of the whole concern, the entire charge of instruction, and most of the responsibilities in regard to health, morals, and manners, rest upon the female teachers, in their several departments. The Principal is the chaplain and religious teacher; and is a member of the board of instructers, so far as to have a right to advise, and an equal vote, in every question pertaining to the concerns of the School; and thus he acts as a sort of regulator and mainspring in all the various departments. But no one person in the Institution is loaded with the excessive responsibilities, which rest upon one, where a large institution of this kind has a Principal, who employs and directs all the subordinate assistants. The writer has never before seen the principle of the division of labor and responsibility so perfectly carried out in any female institution; and she believes that experience will prove that this is the true model for combining, in appropriate proportions, the agency of both sexes in carrying forward such an institution. There are cases where females are well qualified, and feel williing to take the place occupied by the Principal but such cases are rare.

One thing more should be noticed, to the credit of the rising State where this Institution is located. A female association has been formed, embracing a large portion of the ladies of standing and wealth, the design of which, is, to educate, gratuitously, at this, and other similar, institutions, such females as are anxious to obtain a good education, and are destitute of the means. If this enterprise is continued, with the same energy and perseverance as has been manifested during the last few years, that State will take the lead of her sister States in well-educated women; and if the views in the preceding pages are correct, this will give her precedence in every intellectual and moral advantage.

Many, who are not aware of the great economy secured by a proper division of labor, will not understand how so extensive a course can be properly completed in three years. But in this Institution, none are received under fourteen; and a certain amount of previous acquisition is required, in order to admission, as is done in our colleges. This secures a diminution of classes, so that but few studies are pursued at one time; while the number of well-qualified teachers is so adequate, that full time is afforded for all needful instruction and illustration. Where teachers have so many classes, that they merely have time to find out what the pupils learn from books, without any aid from their teachers, the acquisitions of the pupils are vague and imperfect, and soon pass away; so that an immense amount of expense, time, and labor, is spent in acquiring or recalling what is lost about as fast as it is gained.

Parents are little aware of the immense waste incurred by the present mode of conducting female education. In the wealthy classes, young girls are sent to school, as a matter of course, year after year, confined, for six hours a day, to the schoolhouse, and required to add some time out of school to learning their lessons. Thus, during the most critical period of life, they are for a long time immured in a room, filled with an atmosphere vitiated by many breaths, and are constantly kept under some sort of responsibility in regard to mental effort. Their studies are pursued at random, often changed with changing schools, while book after book (heavily taxing the parent's purse) is conned awhile, and then supplanted by others. Teachers have usually so many pupils, and such a variety of branches to teach, that little time can be afforded to each pupil; while scholars, at this thoughtless period of life, feeling sure of going to school as long as they please, manifest little interest in their pursuits.

The writer believes that the actual amount of education, permanently secured by most young ladies from the age of ten to fourteen, could all be acquired in one year, at the Institution described, by a young lady at the age of fifteen or sixteen.

Instead of such a course as the common one, if mothers would keep their daughters as their domestic assistants, until they are fourteen, requiring them to study one lesson, and go out, once a day, to recite it to a teacher, it would abundantly prepare them, after their constitutions are firmly established, to enter such an institution, where, in three years, they could secure more, than almost any young lady in the Country now gains by giving the whole of her youth to school pursuits.

In the early years of female life, reading, writing, needlework, drawing, and music, should alternate with domestic duties; and one hour a day, devoted to some study, in addition to the above pursuits, would be all that is needful to prepare them for a thorough education after growth is attained, and the constitution established. This is the time when young women would feel the value of an education, and pursue their studies with that maturity of mind, and vividness of interest, which would double the perpetuity and value of all their acquisitions.

The great difficulty, which opposes such a plan, is, the want of institutions that would enable a young lady to complete, in three years, the liberal course of study, here described. But if American mothers become convinced of the importance of such advantages for their daughters, and will use their influence appropriately and efficiently, they will certainly be furnished. There are other men of liberality and wealth, besides the individual referred to, who can be made to feel that a fortune, expended in securing an appropriate education to American women, is as wisely bestowed, as in founding colleges for the other sex, who are already so abundantly supplied. We ought to have institutions, similar to the one described in every part of this Nation; and funds should be provided, for educating young women destitute of means: and if American women think and feel, that, by such a method, their own trials will be lightened, and their daughters will secure a healthful constitution and a thorough domestic and intellectual education, the appropriate expression of their wishes will secure the necessary funds. The tide of charity, which has been so long flowing from the female hand to provide a liberal education for young men, will flow back with abundant remuneration.

The last method suggested for lessening the evils peculiar to American women, is, a decided effort to oppose the aristocratic feeling, that labor is degrading; and to bring about the impression, that it is refined and lady-like to engage in domestic pursuits. In past ages, and in aristocratic countries, leisure and indolence and frivolous pursuits have been deemed lady-like and refined, because those classes, which were most refined, countenanced such an opinion. But whenever ladies of refinement, as a general custom, patronise domestic pursuits, then these employments will be deemed lady-like. It may be urged, however, that is is impossible for a woman who cooks, washes, and sweeps, to appear in the dress, or acquire the habits and manners, of a lady; that the drudgery of the kitchen is dirty work, and that no one can appear delicate and refined, while engaged in it. Now all this depends on circumstances. If a woman has a house, destitute of neat and convenient facilities; if she has no habits of order and system; is she is remiss and careless in person and dress;—then all this may be true. But, if a woman will make some sacrifices of costly ornaments in her parlor, in order to make her kitchen neat and tasteful; if she will sacrifice expensive dishes, in order to secure such conveniences for labor as protect from exposures; if she will take pains to have the dresses, in which she works, made of suitable materials, and in good taste; if she will rise early, and systematize and oversee the work of her family, so as to have it done thoroughly, neatly, and in the early part of the day; she will find no necessity for any such apprehensions. It is because such work has generally been done by vulgar people, and in a vulgar way, that we have such associations; and when ladies manage such things, as ladies should, then such associations will be removed. There are pursuits, deemed very refined and genteel, which involve quite as much exposure as kitchen employments. For example, to draw a large landscape, in colored crayons, would be deemed very lady-like; but the writer can testify, from sad experience, that no cooking, washing, sweeping, or any other domestic duty, ever left such deplorable traces on hands, face, and dress, as this same lady-like pursuit. Such things depend entirely on custom and associations; and every American woman, who values the institutions of her Country, and wishes to lend her influence in extending and perpetuating such blessings, may feel that she is doing this, whenever, by her example and influence, she destroys the aristocratic association, which would render domestic labor degrading.

HENRY C. CAREY

"Of Wealth"
1858

The "harmony of interests" was a cliché among Whig intellectuals and politicians, but none of them strove harder to put that idea on firm theoretical ground than Henry C. Carey (1793–1879). The son of the Irish immigrant Philadephia publisher Matthew Carey and himself a publisher and successful investor and the doyen of a large and admiring circle of journalists, entrepreneurs, and politicians, Carey was the incarnation of the era's ideal of the civically active, enterprising, and upwardly mobile citizen. But his greatest fame in America and Europe came from his series of multivolume treatises on political economy. In each of them he made—often with an array of statistical evidence—the same central argument he presented in this chapter from his most ambitious work: the pessimistic conclusions of classical economists about the inevitability of poverty caused by increasing population pressing on limited land and resources were wrong because labor's value and, therefore, share of wealth could be increased by the application of capital, invention, and local "associations" of production and exchange. Elsewhere he spelled out the political implications of this analysis: unlike the pseudo free-trade policies that supported independent agricultural laborers exchanging their products with distant monopolistic urban capitalists, government-supported tariffs along with banking and general incorporation laws were good because they facilitated the accumulation of domestic capital needed to promote these equality-engendering centers of associated wealth. But in "Of Wealth" he underlined his equally favorite moral argument that these "laws" of human wealth ultimately depended on men and women's rational self-mastery and power over nature's infinitely exploitable "machine." Because such powers were so self-flattering *and* altruistic, Carey concluded, they deserved our complete "reverence." For an excellent discussion of Carey's social thought in the context of American Whiggery, see Daniel Walker Howe, *The Political Culture of the American Whigs* (Chicago, 1979), 108–22. Paul K. Conkin cogently analyzes Carey's economic ideas in *Prophets of Prosperity: America's First Political Economists* (Bloomington, Ind., 1980), 261–307.

§ 1. Robinson Crusoe had made a bow, and had thus acquired wealth. In what, however, did that wealth consist? In the possession of the instrument? Assuredly not; but in the *power* that it gave him over the natural properties of the wood and the cord—enabling him to substitute the elasticity of the one, and the tenacity of the other, for the muscular contraction by help of which, alone, he had thus far been enabled to obtain supplies of food. Having made a canoe, he found his wealth increased, because by help of his new machine he could command the services of water—and, as nature always works gratuitously, all the addition he was now enabled to make to his supplies, was obtained wholly free of cost. Having erected a pole in his canoe, and placed upon it a skin by way of sail, he was enabled to command the services of the wind, and thus still further to increase his power to move from place to place; and so did his wealth steadily increase.

Let us suppose, however, that instead of having been led by observation of the properties of wood to make a bow, he had found one, and had been so deficient in knowledge as to be unable to use it; would his wealth in this case have been increased? Certainly not. The bow would have been as useless as the trees with which the land was covered. Or, suppose he had found a canoe, and had been as ignorant of the properties of water, or of wood, as we may well suppose to have been the case with the wild men of Germany and of India; would he not have remained as poor as he before had been? That such would have been the case, cannot be doubted. If so, then wealth cannot consist in the mere possession of an instrument, unconnected with the knowledge how to use it. Were a thousand bows given to a man who had been blind from birth, he would be no richer than before—and were we to transfer to the savages of the Rocky Mountains, all property in the mills and furnaces of the Union, they would find therein no addition to their wealth—for their liability to perish of hunger, or of cold, would remain unchanged; although they had thus become the owners of machinery capable of producing all the implements required for enabling them to obtain food and clothing in abundance, were they but possessed of knowledge. Books and newspapers would not be wealth to the man who could not read, but food would be—and he might gladly give a whole library for as much grain as would support him for a single year.

For thousands of years, the people of England were in possession of almost boundless supplies of that fuel, a bushel of which is capable of raising one hundred thousand pounds a foot in a minute, and thus doing as much work as could be done by hundreds of men; and yet that fuel was not wealth, because of the want of knowledge how to utilize its powers. The force was there, latent; but it was not until the days of Watt, that man was enabled to compel it to labor in his service. So it has been with the anthracite coal-mines of Pennsylvania. That fuel was purer and better than any other—and capable, therefore, of doing a greater amount of work; but, *for that reason,* it required a higher degree of knowledge for the development of its latent powers. The greater the power to be useful—the greater the amount of utility latent in a commodity, or thing—the greater is always the amount of resistance to be overcome, in subjecting it to the control of man. That once done, the power thus acquired, centres in THE MAN, whose value steadily rises, as the utility of the raw material by which he is surrounded, becomes more and more developed.

Source: Henry C. Carey, *Principles of Social Science,* 3 vols., vol. 1 (Philadelphia: J. B. Lippincott & Co., 1871), 181–92, 193, 194–97.

The first poor cultivator commences . . . his operations on the hill-side. Below him are lands that have, for ages, received the washings of those above, as well as the leaves of trees, and the fallen trees themselves, all of which have, from time immemorial, decayed and become incorporated with the earth—thus forming soils fitted to yield the largest returns to labor; yet for that reason are they inaccessible. Their character exhibits itself in the large trees with which they are covered, and in their capacity for retaining the water required for aiding the process of decomposition; but the poor settler has no power either to clear them of their timber, or to drain them of the superfluous moisture. He begins on the hill-side; but with the increase of his family, and the improvement of his machinery of cultivation, we find him descending the hill, and obtaining not only more food for himself, but also the means of feeding the horse, or the ox, required to assist him in his labors. Aided by the manure yielded to him by the better lands, we see his successors next retracing his steps, improving the hill-side, and compelling it to yield a return twice greater than had been at first obtained. With each step down the hill, they obtain still larger reward for labor; and from each they return, with increased power, to the cultivation of the original poor soil. They have now horses and oxen; and while, by their aid, they extract from the new soils the manure that had for ages accumulated, they have also carts and wagons to carry it up the hill; and with every additional step, their rewards become increased, while their labors are lessened. They go back to the sand and raise the marl, with which they cover the surface; or return to the clay and sink into the limestone, by aid of which they double their products. They are all the time making a machine which feeds them while making it, and which increases in its powers the more there is taken from it. At first, it was worthless; but now—having fed and clothed them for years—it has become so greatly useful, that those who might desire to use it would pay largely for the permission so to do.

The earth is a great machine given to man to be fashioned to his purpose. The more he fashions it, the better it feeds him, because each step is but preparatory to a new one more productive than the last—requiring less labor and yielding larger return. The labor of clearing is great; yet the return is small, the earth being covered with stumps, and filled with roots. With each year the latter decay, and the ground becomes enriched; while the labor of ploughing is diminished. At length, the stumps having disappeared, the return is doubled, while the labor is less by one half than at first. To forward this process the owner has done nothing but crop the ground—nature having done the rest. The aid she thus grants him, yields far more food than had been at first obtained in return to the labor of clearing the land. This, however, is not all. The surplus thus yielded has given him the means of improving the poorer lands—furnishing manure with which to enrich them—and thus has he trebled, or quadrupled, his original return without further effort; that which he saves in working the new soils, sufficing to carry the manure to the older ones. He is thus obtaining a daily increased power over the various treasures of the earth.

With every operation connected with the subjection of the earth to the control of man, the result is the same—the first step being, invariably, the most costly one, and the least productive.[1] The drain commences necessarily near the stream, where the

---

1. The French proverb—*Ce n'est que le premier pas qui coute* [Beginning is the difficulty]—is true in regard to all the relations of life; but in none is it more emphatically so than in reference to the occupation

labor is heaviest; yet it frees from water but little land. Further distant, the same quantity of labor, profiting by what has been already done, frees thrice the extent; and now the most perfect system of thorough drainage may be established with less effort than had been at first required for one of the most imperfect kind. To bring the lime into connection with the clay, upon fifty acres, is lighter labor than had been the clearing of a single one; yet the process doubles the return for every acre of the fifty. The man who requires a little fuel for his own use, expends much labor in opening the neighboring vein of coal. To enlarge this, so as to double the product, is a work of comparatively small effort; as is the next enlargement, by which he is enabled to use a wagon, giving him a return fifty times greater than had been obtained while still dependent upon his own unassisted powers. To sink a shaft to the first vein below the surface, and erect a steam engine, are expensive operations—but then to sink to a second, and tunnel to a third, are trifles in comparison with the first; yet each is equally productive. The first line of railroad runs by houses and towns occupied by a few hundred thousand persons. Little branches are next made, costing altogether far less labor than the first, but bringing into connection with it probably thrice the amount of population. The trade increasing, a second track, a third, or a fourth, may be required. The original one facilitating the passage of the materials and the removal of the obstructions, three new ones may now be made for less than had been expended upon the first.

All labor thus given to fashioning the great machine is but the prelude to its further application, with increased returns and rise of wages; and hence it is that portions of the machine, as it exists, invariably exchange, when brought to market, for far less labor than they have cost. The man who cultivated the thin soils was happy to obtain a hundred bushels for his year's work—but with the progress of himself and his neighbors down the hill, into the more fertile soils, wages have risen, and two hundred bushels may be now required. His farm will yield a thousand bushels—but it requires the labor of four men, who must have two hundred bushels each; and the surplus is but two hundred bushels. At twenty years' purchase, this gives a capital of four thousand bushels, or the equivalent of twenty years' wages; whereas it may have cost—in the labor of himself, his sons, and his assistants—the equivalent of a hundred years of labor, or perhaps far more. During all this time, however, it has fed and clothed them all; and the farm has been produced by insensible contributions made from year to year, unthought of and unfelt.

It is now worth twenty years' wages, because its owner has for years taken from it a thousand bushels annually; but when it had lain for centuries, accumulating power to serve the purposes of man, it was worth nothing. Such is the case with the earth everywhere. The more there is taken from it the more there is found to exist. When the coal-mines of England were untouched, they were valueless. Now their value is almost countless; yet the land contains abundant supplies for thousands of years. Iron ore, a century since, being held in low esteem, leases were granted for almost nominal rents. Now, notwithstanding the great quantities that have been removed, such leases are deemed equivalent to the possession of large fortunes; although the amount of ore elsewhere known to exist, is probably a hundred times increased.

---

of land. Such being the case, it will readily be seen how destructive of the best interests of man must be a system which, looking to the constant exhaustion of the soil, produces a perpetually increasing necessity for commencing the work of cultivation on new lands, to be in their turn exhausted. [H.C.C. note]

The rich lands above described—the coal, the lime, and the ore—were, a century since as much as they are now, possessed of the power to contribute to the comfort and enjoyment of man; yet they were not wealth, because he himself was deficient in the knowledge required for enabling him to compel them to labor in his service. Their utility was latent, waiting the action of the human mind for its development.

In the man of that day we find, however, a state of things precisely similar. His powers were then as great as are those of the men of the present day; but they, too, were latent. His brain was ready to serve him, had he made the demand for its services; but that he could not do. It, too, would have labored gratuitously; not only so, but by lessening the demand upon his muscular powers, it would largely have diminished the quantity of food required for repairing the waste consequent upon exertion. The time required for the supply of his necessities would thus have been reduced, with corresponding increase in the quantity at his command for further study of the powers of nature—and for preparation of the machinery needed for subjecting them to his service.

Wealth consists *in the power to command the always gratuitous services of nature*— whether rendered by the brain of man, or by the matter by which he is surrounded, and upon which it is required to operate. The greater the *power* of association—the greater the diversity of the demands upon the human intellect—the greater, as we have seen, must be the development of the peculiar faculties—or individuality—of each member of the society; and the greater the *capacity* for association. With the latter comes increase of power over nature and over himself; and the more perfect his capacity for self-government, the more rapid must be the motion of society—the greater the tendency towards further progress—and the more rapid the growth of wealth.

The supply of power waiting the demands of man is, as has been said, unlimited. To the world at large, it is what the accumulations in the robbers' cave were to Ali Baba, who needed but the magic word to make the doors fly open, and thus to become master of their wealth. To enable man to do the same, and thus to do, in his case, all that the genii, in the other, had power to do, he has only to qualify himself for crying "open sesame," by combining his efforts with those of his fellow-men.

§ 2. The greater the tendency towards combination of action among men, the greater is the rapidity with which knowledge is diffused, power is gained, and wealth accumulated. That there may be combination, there must be difference—and that the latter may exist, there must be diversity of employment. Where that is found, man is seen to be obtaining constantly increasing power over nature and over himself—thus acquiring freedom in the direct ratio of the development of his latent powers.

In the early periods of society, when men cultivate the poor soils, there can be little association, and, consequently, little combination of action. Having neither horse nor cart, the solitary settler is dependent, mainly, upon his hands and arms for power to harvest his little crop. Carrying a hide to his place of exchange, distant many miles, he seeks to obtain for it leather, shoes, or cloth.—Population increasing, roads are made, and richer soils are cultivated. The store and the mill coming nearer to him, he obtains shoes and flour with the use of less machinery of exchange; and having now more leisure for the preparation of his machine, the returns to labor are increased. More people now obtaining food from the same surface, new places of exchange appear. The wool being, on the spot, converted into cloth, he exchanges directly with the clothier. The saw-mill being at hand, he exchanges with the miller. The tanner gives him leather for his hides, and the paper-maker exchanges paper for his rags. His *power to command* the use of the machinery of exchange is thus a constantly augmenting one; whereas his *necessity* for its use is a constantly decreasing one—there being, with each successive year, a greater tendency towards having the consumer and the producer take their places by each other's side. With each, he finds increase of power to devote his time and mind to the process of fashioning the great instrument to which he is indebted for food and wool; and thus it is that increase of the consuming population is essential to the progress of production.

The loss from the use of machinery of exchange, is in the ratio of the bulk of the article to be exchanged. Food stands first; fuel next, stone for building, third; iron, fourth; cotton, fifth; and so on—diminishing until we come to laces and nutmegs. The raw material being that in the formation of which the earth has most co-operated and by the production of which the land is most improved—the nearer the place of exchange or conversion can be brought to the place of production, the less must be the loss in the process, and the greater the power of accumulating capital to aid in the production of further wealth. That this must necessarily be so, will be obvious to all who reflect that, in physical science, it is a law, that whatever tends to diminish the quantity of machinery required, tends to the diminution of friction, and to the increase of power.

The man who raises food on his own land, is building up the machine for doing so to more advantage in the following year. His neighbor, to whom it is *given*, on condition of sitting still, loses a year's work on his machine, and all he has gained has been the pleasure of idling away his time. If he has employed himself and his horses and wagon in bringing it home, the same number of days that would have been required for raising it, he has misemployed his time, for the farm is unimproved. He has wasted labor and manure. As nobody, however, gives, it is obvious that the man who has a farm, and obtains his food elsewhere, must pay for raising it, and also for transporting it; that although he may have obtained as good wages in some other pursuit, his farm, instead of being improved by a year's cultivation, is deteriorated by a year's neglect; and that he is a poorer man than he would have been had he raised his own food.

The article of next greatest bulk is fuel. While warming his house, he is clearing his land. He would lose by sitting idle, if his neighbor brought his fuel to him, and still more if he had to spend the same time in hauling it; because he would be wearing out his wagon, and losing the manure. Were he to hire himself and his wagon to another, and for the same quantity of fuel he could have cut on his own property, he would be a loser, for his farm would be uncleared.

In taking the stone from his own fields to build his house, he gains doubly, for as his house is built, his land is being cleared. If he remains idle, and lets his neighbor bring him stone, he loses—for his fields remain unfit for cultivation. If he performs as much work for a neighbor, receiving the same apparent wages, he is a loser, by the fact that he has yet to remove the stones—and, until they shall be removed, he cannot cultivate his land.

With every improvement in the machinery of exchange, there is a diminution in the proportion which that machinery bears to the mass of commodities susceptible of being exchanged—because of the extraordinary increase of product consequent upon the increased labor that may be given to building up the great machine. It is a matter of daily observation, that the demand for horses and men increases as railroads drive them from the turnpikes—and the reason is, that the farmer's means of improving his land increase more rapidly than men and horses for the work. The man who has, thus far, sent to market his half-fed cattle, accompanied by horses and men to drive them—and wagons and horses loaded with hay, or turnips, with which to feed them on the road, and to fatten them when at market—now fattens them on the ground and sends them by railroad ready for the slaughter-house; and thus is his demand for machinery of exchange greatly diminished. He keeps his men, his horses and wagons, and the refuse of his hay and oats, at home; the former employed in ditching and draining, while the latter fertilizes the soil he has thus far cultivated. His production doubling, he accumulates rapidly, while the people around him have more to eat, more to spend in clothing, and can accumulate more themselves. He wants laborers in the field, and these require clothes and dwellings. The shoemaker and the carpenter, finding that there is a demand for their labor, now join the community—eating the food on the ground on which it is produced; and thus is the machinery of exchange improved. The quantity of flour consumed on the spot inducing the miller to come and eat his share, while preparing that of others, the labor of exchanging is again diminished, leaving more to be given to the land. The lime being now turned up, *tons* of turnips are obtained from the same surface that before gave *bushels* of rye. The quantity to be consumed increasing faster than the population, more mouths are needed on the spot; and next the woollen-mill comes. The wool no longer requiring wagons and horses, they are now turned to transporting coal; enabling the farmer to clear his woodland, and to reduce to cultivation the fine soil that has, for centuries, produced nothing but timber. Production again increasing, the new wealth now takes the form of a cotton-mill; and with every step in that direction the farmer finds new demands on the great machine he has constructed, attended with constant increase of power to build it up higher and stronger, and to sink its foundations deeper. He now supplies beef and mutton, wheat, butter, eggs, poultry, cheese, and every other of the comforts and luxuries of life, for which the climate is suited; and all of these from the same land which, when his predecessors commenced the work of cultivation on the light soil of the hills, had given scarcely the rye required for the support of life.

We have here the establishment of a local attraction tending to neutralize the attraction of the capital, or great commercial city; and where such local centres most exist, there, invariably, is found the greatest tendency to the development of individuality, and the combination of action—and the most rapid progress in knowledge, wealth, and power. The more nearly the social system approximates, in its arrangements, to that we see to have been established for the maintenance of order throughout the great system of which our planet forms a part, the greater will be the motion, and the more perfect the harmony—and the more will man be enabled to control and direct the various forces provided for his use; and the more rapidly will he pass from being a creature of necessity towards attaining his true position, that of a being of power.

With every step in this direction, there is, as has been shown, a decline in the value of all existing accumulations; because, on the one side, of the steady diminution in the resistance offered by nature to the gratification of man's desires; and, on the other, of the steady increase in the power of man to overcome the resistance which yet remains. That this must necessarily be the case, will be obvious to all who reflect that if coal, iron, cloth, or any other commodity, could be supplied as freely as is now the atmospheric air, the former could have no more value in our eyes than we are now accustomed to attach to the latter. Existing accumulations are the result of past labors. Whatever tends to increase the power of the present man, tends to give him increased control over the accumulations of the past, and to diminish the *proportion* of the product of labor that can be demanded by the owner of the latter for their use. All, therefore, who desire to diminish the control of capital over labor, and thus increase the freedom of man, should desire to promote the growth of wealth.

Wealth grows with the growth of the power of association and the development of individuality. Individuality is developed as employments become diversified; and hence it is that man has always become more free as the farmer and the artisan have tended more to take their places by each other's side.

§3. We are accustomed to measure the wealth of individuals, or of communities, by the *value* of the property they hold; whereas wealth grows, as we see, with the decline of values, which are only a measure of the resistance to be overcome before similar property, or commodities, can be reproduced. This view might, therefore, seem to be in opposition to the general idea of wealth, but, when examined, the difference will be seen to be only apparent. The *positive* wealth of an individual is to be measured by the power he exercises; but his *relative* wealth, by the amount of effort that would be required to be given by others before they could acquire similar power. A man, owning a house that affords him shelter, and a farm giving him food and clothing, has positive wealth, although neither of them has any value in the estimation of other parties. If asked to fix a price at which he would part with them, he would estimate the amount of effort that would be required of others before they could acquire similar power—and that would be the measure of his wealth as compared with another who had neither house nor farm. His positive wealth consists in the extent of his power over nature. His relative wealth is the measure of his power, as compared with that exercised by his fellow-men.

At this moment, however, an improvement takes place in the mode of making bricks and clearing lands, and forthwith there is a diminution of his *comparative,* but without alteration in his *positive* wealth—the house still continuing to shelter him, and the farm to feed him, as before. The decline in the former is a consequence of increase in the wealth and power of the whole community of which he is a member—and that decline becomes more rapid as improvements multiply; because with each successive one, there is a diminution in the obstacles offered by nature to the production of houses and farms, and an increase in the number produced, with steady improvement in the condition of the community. The positive wealth of the individual remains unchanged, and yet his relative wealth is steadily diminishing; and this is equally true, whether considered with reference to intellectual or material accumulations. The man who can read, has wealth; and the more ignorant those around him, the greater is its value. Place him among others who can both read and write, and he becomes poorer than before, by comparison, although his positive wealth remains undiminished.

The wealth of a community is in the ratio of its power to command the services of nature; and the greater that power, the less will be the value of commodities, and the greater the quantity that may be obtained in return for any given amount of labor. With every step in this direction, there will be a diminution in the *proportion* borne by the time required for producing the necessaries of life, to that which may be given to the preparation of machinery required for obtaining further control over nature; or to the purposes of education, recreation, or enjoyment. The progress of man is, therefore, in the ratio of the decline in the value of commodities, and of the increase in his own.

§4. The tendency of modern political economy having been towards excluding from consideration all phenomena not directly connected with the production and consumption of *material* wealth, there had arisen a necessity for giving to the new science a title that should be more in harmony with this limitation in its field of action; and hence it is, that we have had various propositions looking to the adoption of Chrematistics, Catallactics, or other words which should expressly exclude the idea that the mind and morals of man were within the range of the economist. These names have never, it is true, been adopted; but the mere suggestion of them by distinguished economists, is evidence of the thoroughly material character of the system.

. . . . . .

Modern political economy, having made for itself a being which it denominated man, and from the composition of which it excluded all those parts of the ordinary man that were common to him and the angel—retaining carefully all those common to him and the beast of the forest—found itself forced, necessarily, to the exclusion from its definition of wealth, of every thing pertaining to the feelings, affections, or intellect. In its view, man is an animal that *will* procreate, and *can be made* to work, but, in order that it may do so, it *must* be fed; and it is as a necessary consequence of this, that not only those named above, but numerous other distinguished economists, have found themselves driven to the necessity of treating as unproductive, all employments of time or mind that do not take a material form. Magistrates and men of letters, teachers, men of science, artists, and others—the Humboldts and the Thierrys, the Savignys and the Kents, the Aragos and the Davys, the Canovas and the Davids—are regarded by this school as unproductive, except so far as they produce *things.*

. . . . . .

§5. By the definition of wealth above given, such inconsistencies are avoided, and the word is brought back to its original signification of general happiness, prosperity, and power—not the power of man over his fellow-man, but over himself, his faculties, and the numerous and wonderful forces provided for his use. Such, to no inconsiderable extent, was the idea of Adam Smith. . . . He shows how greatly happiness, wealth, and progress, would be promoted by the adoption of a policy in accordance with those "natural inclinations of man" which lead him to combine with his fellow-men for the development of the various faculties of all the members of society—facilitating the extension of commerce, and emancipating him from the exactions of the trader and the soldier.

Dr. Smith was no advocate of centralization. On the contrary, he fully believed in a policy tending to the creation of local centres of action; and he did not believe in that one which looked to prevent association, by compelling all the farmers of the world to resort to a single and distant market when they desired to convert their food and wool into cloth. Such, however, was the policy of his country; and therefore did it become necessary for Mr. Malthus to prove that the pauperism which was the necessary consequence of centralization, had its origin in a great natural law, which forbade that the quantity of food should keep pace with the demands of an increasing population. Next came Mr. Ricardo, to whom the world is indebted for the idea that cultivation had always commenced on the rich soils of the earth—and that the men who were then flying from England to the colonies, were going from the cultivation of poor soils to that of rich ones; when directly the reverse had ever been the case. His doctrine, and that of his followers, is therefore that of dispersion, centralization, and large cities; whereas that of Dr. Smith looked to association, to local self-government, and to countries abounding in villages and towns, in which should be performed the exchanges of the surrounding country.

The whole tendency of modern political economists has been in a direction opposite to that indicated as the true one, by the author of the Wealth of Nations; and therefore it has been, that their science has become limited to the single consideration, how it is that material wealth may be increased—leaving altogether out of view the consideration of the morality, or the happiness, of the communities they desired to teach. Hence it is that it has gradually taken so repulsive a form, and that one among its most eminent teachers has found himself called upon to say to his readers, that the political economist is required to look to the growth of wealth alone, and to limit himself to the discussion of the measures by help of which he thinks it may be promoted—allowing "neither sympathy with indigence, nor disgust at profusion or at avarice—neither reverence for existing institutions, nor detestation of existing abuses—neither love of popularity, nor of paradox, nor of system, to deter him from stating what he believes to be the facts, or from drawing from those facts what appear to him to be the legitimate conclusions."[2]

Happily, true science is required to make no such calls upon its teachers. The more it is studied, the more must the "indigence" they see around them excite their "sympathy," and the more free must they become in its expression—because the more fully must they become satisfied that the existence of such a state of things is a consequence of human, and not of divine, laws; the greater must be the "disgust" excited by both "profusion and avarice," as tending to the production of "indigence"; the greater must be their "reverence" for all institutions tending to promote the growth of that habit of association by help of which, alone, man acquires the power over nature in which consists his wealth; the greater the "detestation of existing abuses" tending to perpetuate the existing poverty and wretchedness; and the stronger their determination honestly to labor for their extirpation.

Wealth grows with the growth of the power of man to satisfy that first and greatest want of his nature—the desire for association with his fellow-men. The more rapid

2. Senior: *Outlines of Political Economy*, p. 130. [H.C.C. note]

its growth, the greater is the tendency towards the disappearance of "indigence," on the one hand, and "profusion and avarice," on the other—towards the termination of existing "abuses," tending to limit the exercise of the power of association, to restrain the development of individuality, and to impair the feeling of strict responsibility towards God and man—and towards having society assume that form which is most calculated for facilitating the progress of the latter towards the high position for which he was originally intended; and therefore the form most calculated to inspire respect and "reverence."

Part Four

Romanticism and Reform

Introduction

"The key to the period appeared to be that the mind had become aware of itself." So Ralph Waldo Emerson characterized, fifty years afterward, the spirit of that intensely enthusiastic circle of young ministers, teachers, writers and their followers, who from Boston, Cambridge, Concord, and other New England outposts disseminated America's most important philosophy of romanticism. At the heart of their romanticism—or Transcendentalism, as their outlook came to be known—lay a gigantic paradox. On the one hand, the young Transcendentalists, "born [as Emerson wrote] with knives in their brain," turned to the mind itself as an object of inquiry quite independent of the external world of common sense perceptions their rationalist elders had taught them were the proper objects of thought. On the other hand, they often went beyond these transcendental dialectics to conclude, as did the post-Kantian writers they generally followed, that the mind could not only *transcend* sense perceptions but *substitute for them* and so constitute the world. Reinforcing this last tendency was their religious commitment; like their European romantic counterparts, they sought not just to understand the world but to bring it in line with qualities they believed authentic religion promoted—principally the capacity for wonder and a sense of wholeness. Vibrating among these three poles, but rarely reconciling them, the Transcendentalists managed to produce a body of cultural criticism as trenchant, buoyant, and innocent as any in American intellectual history.

No Transcendentalist text captures so fully both the critical and the visionary sides of the movement as Emerson's "Divinity School Address." It is therefore fitting that this section opens with Emerson's startling attack on all Christian sects, whether orthodox or liberal, that base their claims to authority on evidence external to human consciousness. In place of these dead faiths, Emerson preached "the God within" and a nature vibrant with symbolic meaning. Emerson also wrote a good deal of social criticism along similar lines, criticizing modern society's deadening mechanism and fragmentation and advocating as antidotes ways of seeing that facilitated organic wholeness and spiritual vitality. But for Emerson the greatest threat to the divine self came from the tendency of America's business civilization to breed a stifling cultural conformity. In his essay on "Self-Reliance," Emerson argued that the ultimate solution to this self-alienation was the creation of an "aboriginal Self" whose very rootlessness guaranteed its sense of power and security.

Emerson's essay is included also because it demonstrates so well the theoretical ambiguities of Transcendentalism's relation to the practice of reform. Although Emerson in his essay frequently pitted the "active soul" *against* social reformers, other Transcendentalists were (as Emerson himself was at times) more sympathetic toward at least certain kinds of organized reform. These included, of course, those Transcendentalists who sought to achieve individual self-sufficiency through the collective association of work in the socialistic community Brook Farm. But they also included Transcendentalist intellectuals who preferred more individualistic vehicles of social change. Schools that stressed intuitive learning through the medium of "conversations" was one reform effort many favored. Another was the long, lusty, personal-critico-prophetic essays designed (as Henry David Thoreau said of his *Walden*) "to wake my neighbors up." Of these discursive odes Margaret Fuller's "Great Lawsuit" startled many because of both its subject matter and its point of view. In her essay Fuller presented a scheme of feminine self-culture that aimed at achieving transcendental wholeness, though in a rather un-Emersonian social and evolutionary form. Even more than women, American slaves were obviously denied opportunites for self-development and as a consequence won the sympathy of Transcendentalist adherents. Still, the most elaborate Transcendentalist statement on the slavery question, Thoreau's famous essay on civil resistance, was primarily concerned not with slaves, but with the moral and political slavishness that he saw as endemic in the free democratic North. As a corrective Thoreau offered one of the most complete theories of principled social activism ever written.

Of all the Transcendentalists' reform writings, none had greater long-range cultural impact than their literary criticism. The Transcendentalist call for "new demands on literature" to be realized by the symbol-making powers of independent American writers has been heeded repeatedly in literary and academic circles down to our own time. Yet the romantic era's greatest imaginative prose writers wrote in a vein that was certainly inward-turned but by no means wholly Transcendentalist. For writers like Hawthorne and Melville, the mind disclosed demonic impulses rarely turned up by Emerson's young psychic probers. Curiously, though, their fascination with dissonances in the romantic mind made them more not less concerned with America's *collective* destiny. In his essay on Hawthorne that concludes Part Four, Melville argued not only for the recognition of these "powers of darkness," but also daringly insisted that writers like Hawthorne who exposed them ought to be embraced as the true exponents of American democratic culture. Only Melville's fellow New Yorker Walt Whitman was more sanguine about the prospects for America's comradely hug of the delinquent romantic self.

Recommendations for Further Reading

F. O. Matthiessen, *American Renaissance: Art and Expression in the Age of Emerson and Whitman* (New York, 1941); Perry Miller, ed., *The Transcendentalists: An Anthology* (Cambridge, Mass., 1950); Charles Feidelson, Jr., *Symbolism and American Literature* (Chicago, 1953); William R. Hutchison, *The Transcendentalist Ministers: Church Reform in the New England Renaissance* (New Haven, 1959); Leo Marx, *The Machine in the Garden: Technology and the Pastoral Ideal in America* (New York, 1964); Tony Tanner, *The Reign of Wonder: Naivety and Reality in American Literature* (Cambridge, 1965); Daniel Walker Howe, *The Unitarian Conscience: Harvard Moral Philosophy, 1805–1861* (Cambridge, Mass., 1970); M. H. Abrams, *Natural Supernaturalism: Tradition and Revolution in Romantic Literature* (New York, 1971); Lawrence Buell, *Literary Transcendentalism: Style and Vision in the American Renaissance* (Ithaca, N.Y., 1973); Ann Douglas, *The Feminization of American Culture* (New York, 1977); Taylor Stoehr, *Nay-Saying in Concord: Emerson, Alcott, and Thoreau* (Hamden, Conn., 1979); Michael Davitt Bell, *The Development of American Romance: The Sacrifice of Relation* (Chicago, 1980); Anne C. Rose, *Transcendentalism as a Social Movement, 1830–1850* (New Haven, 1981); Larzer Ziff,

Literary Democracy: The Declaration of Cultural Independence in America (New York, 1981); Philip F. Gura and Joel Myerson, eds., *Critical Essays on American Transcendentalism* (Boston, 1982); Michael T. Gilmore, *American Romanticism and the Marketplace* (Chicago, 1985); Lawrence Buell, *New England Literary Culture: From Revolution Through Renaissance* (Cambridge, 1986); Irving Howe, *The American Newness: Culture and Politics in the Age of Emerson* (Cambridge, Mass., 1986); Donald Meyer, *Sex and Power: The Rise of Women in America, Russia, Sweden, and Italy* (Middletown, Conn., 1987); David S. Reynolds, *Beneath the American Renaissance: The Subversive Imagination in America in the Age of Emerson and Melville* (New York, 1988).

RALPH WALDO EMERSON

"The Divinity School Address"
1838

"Self-Reliance"
1841

"A believer in Unity, a seer of Unity, I yet behold two." This self-described ruling characteristic of Ralph Waldo Emerson (1803–82)—which both epitomized his position as a Transcendentalist and defined his power as a writer and thinker—is well displayed in the two works presented herein. The first was his harsh critique of the Unitarian church delivered in 1838 before a mixed audience of sympathetic graduating Harvard Divinity School students and their mostly perplexed and exasperated teachers. Historians have long recognized that Emerson's portrayal of his inherited faith as "corpse-cold" was something of a caricature. Yet in reading this address it is easy to see why for Emerson this was no hyperbole. *Any* religion that put God "outside of me" vitiated itself, Emerson thought, and to Emerson Unitarianism did just that in a doubly deadening way—first, by asserting that the intellectual authority of its faith rested on a certain class of supernatural events (Christ's miracles); second, by claiming that such events could be demonstrated on entirely empirical grounds. Emerson, on the contrary, sought to demonstrate—both poetically and discursively—that a religious faith became living only when submerged in nature, which, in turn, was brought to life by men and women perceiving, through their godlike "Reason," both its physical and symbolic character. Such divine double vision obviously required not only expunging an external god, but external society as well, a subject Emerson explored in his essay "Self-Reliance" published three years later. Now he struck a new note of defiance: he no longer offered himself as a "new Teacher" in a renewed church but as a seer-sayer imparting to his readers "truth and health in rough electric shocks." The truth they needed to know was that in order to be self-reliant they had to be nonconforming. Yet his social vision was neither anarchic nor hermetic. What he desired—and what obviously tied him to the bustling democratic society for which he would soon become a national spokesman—was a society so fluid that all of its parts would be capable of constantly moving and changing and therefore feeling their "power." Meanwhile, the "Self-reliance" that such a society facilitated was for Emerson ultimately God-reliance: in a culture so freed of external fixity and so stripped of psychic relations with family and property, individuals had only one source of secure and unchanging "Principles"—the God within. No one in nineteenth-century Western thought, not even Nietzsche (who admired Emerson greatly), offered a more exhilaratingly—or chillingly—transvalued vision of emerging modern culture. Stephen E. Whicher, *Freedom and Fate: An Inner Life of Ralph Waldo Emerson* (Philadelphia, 1953) is a profound study of the evolution of Emerson's thought. For two excellent renderings of Emerson's thought in the context of his life and times, see Joel Porte, *Representative Man: Ralph Waldo Emerson in His Time* (New York, 1979); and Maurice Gonnaud, *An Uneasy Solitude: Individual and Society in the Work of Ralph Waldo Emerson* (Princeton, 1987). A good sampling of criticism may be found in Harold Bloom, ed., *Ralph Waldo Emerson* (New York, 1985).

"The Divinity School Address"
1838

*An Address Delivered Before the Senior Class
in Divinity College, Cambridge, Sunday Evening, 15 July, 1838*

In this refulgent summer it has been a luxury to draw the breath of life. The grass grows, the buds burst, the meadow is spotted with fire and gold in the tint of flowers. The air is full of birds, and sweet with the breath of the pine, the balm-of-Gilead, and the new hay. Night brings no gloom to the heart with its welcome shade. Through the transparent darkness the stars pour their almost spiritual rays. Man under them seems a young child, and his huge globe a toy. The cool night bathes the world as with a river, and prepares his eyes again for the crimson dawn. The mystery of nature was never displayed more happily. The corn and the wine have been freely dealt to all creatures, and the never-broken silence with which the old bounty goes forward, has not yielded yet one word of explanation. One is constrained to respect the perfection of this world, in which our senses converse. How wide; how rich; what invitation from every property it gives to every faculty of man! In its fruitful soils; in its navigable sea; in its mountains of metal and stone; in its forests of all woods; in its animals; in its chemical ingredients; in the powers and path of light, heat, attraction, and life, it is well worth the pith and heart of great men to subdue and enjoy it. The planters, the mechanics, the inventors, the astronomers, the builders of cities, and the captains, history delights to honor.

But the moment the mind opens, and reveals the laws which traverse the universe, and make things what they are, then shrinks the great world at once into a mere illustration and fable of this mind. What am I? and What is? asks the human spirit with a curiosity new-kindled, but never to be quenched. Behold these outrunning laws, which our imperfect apprehension can see tend this way and that, but not come full circle. Behold these infinite relations, so like, so unlike; many, yet one. I would study, I would know, I would admire forever. These works of thought have been the entertainments of the human spirit in all ages.

A more secret, sweet, and overpowering beauty appears to man when his heart and mind open to the sentiment of virtue. Then instantly he is instructed in what is above him. He learns that his being is without bound; that, to the good, to the perfect, he is born, low as he now lies in evil and weakness. That which he venerates is still his own, though he has not realized it yet. *He ought.* He knows the sense of that grand word, though his analysis fails entirely to render account of it. When in innocency, or when by intellectual perception, he attains to say,—'I love the Right; Truth is beautiful within and without, forevermore. Virtue, I am thine: save me: use me: thee will I serve,

Source: *The Collected Works of Ralph Waldo Emerson,* ed. Alfred R. Ferguson, vol. 1, *Nature, Addresses, and Lectures,* ed. Robert E. Spiller and Alfred R. Ferguson (Cambridge, Mass.: Harvard University Press, Belknap Press, 1971), 76–93. Reprinted by permission of The Belknap Press of Harvard University Press, Copyright © 1971 by The President and Fellows of Harvard College.

day and night, in great, in small, that I may be not virtuous, but virtue;'—then is the end of the creation answered, and God is well pleased.

The sentiment of virtue is a reverence and delight in the presence of certain divine laws. It perceives that this homely game of life we play, covers, under what seem foolish details, principles that astonish. The child amidst his baubles, is learning the action of light, motion, gravity, muscular force; and in the game of human life, love, fear, justice, appetite, man, and God, interact. These laws refuse to be adequately stated. They will not by us or for us be written out on paper, or spoken by the tongue. They elude, evade our persevering thought, and yet we read them hourly in each other's faces, in each other's actions, in our own remorse. The moral traits which are all globed into every virtuous act and thought,—in speech, we must sever, and describe or suggest by painful enumeration of many particulars. Yet, as this sentiment is the essence of all religion, let me guide your eye to the precise objects of the sentiment, by an enumeration of some of those classes of facts in which this element is conspicuous.

The intuition of the moral sentiment is an insight of the perfection of the laws of the soul. These laws execute themselves. They are out of time, out of space, and not subject to circumstance. Thus; in the soul of man there is a justice whose retributions are instant and entire. He who does a good deed, is instantly ennobled himself. He who does a mean deed, is by the action itself contracted. He who puts off impurity, thereby puts on purity. If a man is at heart just, then in so far is he God; the safety of God, the immortality of God, the majesty of God do enter into that man with justice. If a man dissemble, deceive, he deceives himself, and goes out of acquaintance with his own being. A man in the view of absolute goodness, adores, with total humility. Every step so downward, is a step upward. The man who renounces himself, comes to himself by so doing.

See how this rapid intrinsic energy worketh everywhere, righting wrongs, correcting appearances, and bringing up facts to a harmony with thoughts. Its operation in life, though slow to the senses, is, at last, as sure as in the soul. By it, a man is made the Providence to himself, dispensing good to his goodness, and evil to his sin. Character is always known. Thefts never enrich; alms never impoverish; murder will speak out of stone walls. The least admixture of a lie,—for example, the smallest mixture of vanity, the least attempt to make a good impression, a favorable appearance,—will instantly vitiate the effect. But speak the truth, and all nature and all spirits help you with unexpected furtherance. Speak the truth, and all things alive or brute are vouchers, and the very roots of the grass underground there, do seem to stir and move to bear you witness. See again the perfection of the Law as it applies itself to the affections, and becomes the law of society. As we are, so we associate. The good, by affinity, seek the good; the vile, by affinity, the vile. Thus of their own volition, souls proceed into heaven, into hell.

These facts have always suggested to man the sublime creed, that the world is not the product of manifold power, but of one will, of one mind; and that one mind is everywhere active, in each ray of the star, in each wavelet of the pool; and whatever opposes that will, is everywhere baulked and baffled, because things are made so, and not otherwise. Good is positive. Evil is merely privative, not absolute. It is like cold, which is the privation of heat. All evil is so much death or nonentity. Benevolence is absolute and real. So much benevolence as a man hath, so much life hath he. For all things proceed out of this same spirit, which is differently named love, justice, temperance, in its different applications, just as the ocean receives different names on the several shores which it washes. All things proceed out of the same spirit, and all things conspire with it. Whilst a man seeks good ends, he is strong by the whole strength of nature. In so far as he roves from these ends, he bereaves himself of power, of auxiliaries; his being shrinks out of all remote channels, he becomes less and less, a mote, a point, until absolute badness is absolute death.

The perception of this law of laws always awakens in the mind a sentiment which we call the religious sentiment, and which makes our highest happiness. Wonderful is its power to charm and to command. It is a mountain air. It is the embalmer of the world. It is myrrh and storax, and chlorine and rosemary. It makes the sky and the hills sublime, and the silent song of the stars is it. By it, is the universe made safe and habitable, not by science or power. Thought may work cold and intransitive in things, and find no end or unity. But the dawn of the sentiment of virtue on the heart, gives and is the assurance that Law is sovereign over all natures; and the worlds, time, space, eternity, do seem to break out into joy.

This sentiment is divine and deifying. It is the beatitude of man. It makes him illimitable. Through it, the soul first knows itself. It corrects the capital mistake of the infant man, who seeks to be great by following the great, and hopes to derive advantages *from another,*—by showing the fountain of all good to be in himself, and that he, equally with every man, is an inlet into the deeps of Reason. When he says, "I ought;" when love warms him; when he chooses, warned from on high, the good and great deed; then, deep melodies wander through his soul from Supreme Wisdom. Then he can worship, and be enlarged by his worship; for he can never go behind this sentiment. In the sublimest flights of the soul, rectitude is never surmounted, love is never outgrown.

This sentiment lies at the foundation of society, and successively creates all forms of worship. The principle of veneration never dies out. Man fallen into superstition, into sensuality, is never wholly without the visions of the moral sentiment. In like manner, all the expressions of this sentiment are sacred and permanent in proportion to their purity. The expressions of this sentiment affect us deeper, greatlier, than all other compositions. The sentences of the oldest time, which ejaculate this piety, are still fresh and fragrant. This thought dwelled always deepest in the minds of men in the devout and contemplative East; not alone in Palestine, where it reached its purest expression, but in Egypt, in Persia, in India, in China. Europe has always owed to oriental genius, its divine impulses. What these holy bards said, all sane men found agreeable and true. And the unique impression of Jesus upon mankind, whose name is not so much written as ploughed into the history of this world, is proof of the subtle virtue of this infusion.

Meanwhile, whilst the doors of the temple stand open, night and day, before every man, and the oracles of this truth cease never, it is guarded by one stern condition; this, namely; It is an intuition. It cannot be received at second hand. Truly speaking, it is not instruction, but provocation, that I can receive from another soul. What he announces, I must find true in me, or wholly reject; and on his word, or as his second, be he who he may, I can accept nothing. On the contrary, the absence of this primary faith is the presence of degradation. As is the flood so is the ebb. Let this faith depart, and the very words it spake, and the things it made, become false and hurtful. Then falls the church, the state, art, letters, life. The doctrine of the divine nature being forgotten, a sickness infects and dwarfs the constitution. Once man was all; now he is an appendage, a nuisance. And because the indwelling Supreme Spirit cannot wholly be got rid of, the doctrine of it suffers this perversion, that the divine nature is attributed to one or two persons, and denied to all the rest, and denied with fury. The doctrine of inspiration is lost; the base doctrine of the majority of voices, usurps the place of the doctrine of the soul. Miracles, prophecy, poetry, the ideal life, the holy life, exist as ancient history merely; they are not in the belief, nor in the aspiration of society; but, when suggested, seem ridiculous. Life is comic or pitiful, as soon as the high ends of being fade out of sight, and man becomes near-sighted, and can only attend to what addresses the senses.

These general views, which, whilst they are general, none will contest, find abundant illustration in the history of religion, and especially in the history of the Christian church. In that, all of us have had our birth and nurture. The truth contained in that, you, my young friends, are now setting forth to teach. As the Cultus, or established worship of the civilized world, it has great historical interest for us. Of its blessed words, which have been the consolation of humanity, you need not that I should speak. I shall endeavor to discharge my duty to you, on this occasion, by pointing out two errors in its administration, which daily appear more gross from the point of view we have just now taken.

Jesus Christ belonged to the true race of prophets. He saw with open eye the mystery of the soul. Drawn by its severe harmony, ravished with its beauty, he lived in it, and had his being there. Alone in all history, he estimated the greatness of man. One man was true to what is in you and me. He saw that God incarnates himself in man, and evermore goes forth anew to take possession of his world. He said, in this jubilee of sublime emotion, 'I am divine. Through me, God acts; through me, speaks. Would you see God, see me; or, see thee, when thou also thinkest as I now think.' But what a distortion did his doctrine and memory suffer in the same, in the next, and the following ages! There is no doctrine of the Reason which will bear to be taught by the Understanding. The understanding caught this high chant from the poet's lips, and said, in the next age, 'This was Jehovah come down out of heaven. I will kill you, if you say he was a man.' The idioms of his language, and the figures of his rhetoric, have usurped the place of his truth; and churches are not built on his principles, but on his tropes. Christianity became a Mythus, as the poetic teaching of Greece and of Egypt, before. He spoke of miracles; for he felt that man's life was a miracle, and all that man doth, and he knew that this daily miracle shines, as the man is diviner. But the very word Miracle, as pronounced by Christian churches, gives a false impression; it is Monster. It is not one with the blowing clover and the falling rain.

He felt respect for Moses and the prophets; but no unfit tenderness at postponing their initial revelations, to the hour and the man that now is; to the eternal revelation in the heart. Thus was he a true man. Having seen that the law in us is commanding, he would not suffer it to be commanded. Boldly, with hand, and heart, and life, he declared it was God. Thus was he a true man. Thus is he, as I think, the only soul in history who has appreciated the worth of a man.

1. In thus contemplating Jesus, we become very sensible of the first defect of historical Christianity. Historical Christianity has fallen into the error that corrupts all attempts to communicate religion. As it appears to us, and as it has appeared for ages, it is not the doctrine of the soul, but an exaggeration of the personal, the positive, the ritual. It has dwelt, it dwells, with noxious exaggeration about the *person* of Jesus. The soul knows no persons. It invites every man to expand to the full circle of the universe,

and will have no preferences but those of spontaneous love. But by this eastern monarchy of a Christianity, which indolence and fear have built, the friend of man is made the injurer of man. The manner in which his name is surrounded with expressions, which were once sallies of admiration and love, but are now petrified into official titles, kills all generous sympathy and liking. All who hear me, feel, that the language that describes Christ to Europe and America, is not the style of friendship and enthusiasm to a good and noble heart, but is appropriated and formal,—paints a demigod, as the Orientals or the Greeks would describe Osiris or Apollo. Accept the injurious impositions of our early catechetical instruction, and even honesty and self-denial were but splendid sins, if they did not wear the Christian name. One would rather by

'A pagan suckled in a creed outworn,'

than to be defrauded of his manly right in coming into nature, and finding not names and places, not land and professions, but even virtue and truth foreclosed and monopolized. You shall not be a man even. You shall not own the world; you shall not dare, and live after the infinite Law that is in you, and in company with the infinite Beauty which heaven and earth reflect to you in all lovely forms; but you must subordinate your nature to Christ's nature; you must accept our interpretations; and take his portrait as the vulgar draw it.

That is always best which gives me to myself. The sublime is excited in me by the great stoical doctrine, Obey thyself. That which shows God in me, fortifies me. That which shows God out of me, makes me a wart and a wen. There is no longer a necessary reason for my being. Already the long shadows of untimely oblivion creep over me, and I shall decease forever.

The divine bards are the friends of my virtue, of my intellect, of my strength. They admonish me, that the gleams which flash across my mind, are not mine, but God's; that they had the like, and were not disobedient to the heavenly vision. So I love them. Noble provocations go out from them, inviting me also to emancipate myself; to resist evil; to subdue the world; and to Be. And thus by his holy thoughts, Jesus serves us, and thus only. To aim to convert a man by miracles, is a profanation of the soul. A true conversion, a true Christ, is now, as always, to be made, by the reception of beautiful sentiments. It is true that a great and rich soul, like his, falling among the simple, does so preponderate, that, as his did, it names the world. The world seems to them to exist for him, and they have not yet drunk so deeply of his sense, as to see that only by coming again to themselves, or to God in themselves, can they grow forevermore. It is a low benefit to give me something; it is a high benefit to enable me to do somewhat of myself. The time is coming when all men will see, that the gift of God to the soul is not a vaunting, overpowering, excluding sanctity, but a sweet, natural goodness, a goodness like thine and mine, and that so invites thine and mine to be and to grow.

The injustice of the vulgar tone of preaching is not less flagrant to Jesus, than it is to the souls which it profanes. The preachers do not see that they make his gospel not glad, and shear him of the locks of beauty and the attributes of heaven. When I see a majestic Epaminondas, or Washington; when I see among my contemporaries, a true orator, an upright judge, a dear friend; when I vibrate to the melody and fancy of a poem; I see beauty that is to be desired. And so lovely, and with yet more entire consent of my human being, sounds in my ear the severe music of the bards that have sung of the true God in all ages. Now do not degrade the life and dialogues of Christ out of the circle of this charm, by insulation and peculiarity. Let them lie as they befel, alive and warm, part of human life, and of the landscape, and of the cheerful day.

2. The second defect of the traditionary and limited way of using the mind of Christ is a consequence of the first; this, namely; that the Moral Nature, that Law of laws, whose revelations introduce greatness,—yea, God himself, into the open soul, is not explored as the fountain of the established teaching in society. Men have come to speak of the revelation as somewhat long ago given and done, as if God were dead. The injury to faith throttles the preacher; and the goodliest of institutions becomes an uncertain and inarticulate voice.

It is very certain that it is the effect of conversation with the beauty of the soul, to beget a desire and need to impart to others the same knowledge and love. If utterance is denied, the thought lies like a burden on the man. Always the seer is a sayer. Somehow his dream is told. Somehow he publishes it with solemn joy. Sometimes with pencil on canvas; sometimes with chisel on stone; sometimes in towers and aisles of granite, his soul's worship is builded; sometimes in anthems of indefinite music; but clearest and most permanent, in words.

The man enamored of this excellency, becomes its priest or poet. The office is coeval with the world. But observe the condition, the spiritual limitation of the office. The spirit only can teach. Not any profane man, not any sensual, not any liar, not any slave can teach, but only he can give, who has; he only can create, who is. The man on whom the soul descends, through whom the soul speaks, alone can teach. Courage, piety, love, wisdom, can teach; and every man can open his door to these angels, and they shall bring him the gift of tongues. But the man who aims to speak as books enable, as synods use, as the fashion guides, and as interest commands, babbles. Let him hush.

To this holy office, you propose to devote yourselves. I wish you may feel your call in throbs of desire and hope. The office is the first in the world. It is of that reality, that it cannot suffer the deduction of any falsehood. And it is my duty to say to you, that the need was never greater of new revelation than now. From the views I have already expressed, you will infer the sad conviction, which I share, I believe, with numbers, of the universal decay and now almost death of faith in society. The soul is not preached. The Church seems to totter to its fall, almost all life extinct. On this occasion, any complaisance, would be criminal, which told you, whose hope and commission it is to preach the faith of Christ, that the faith of Christ is preached.

It is time that this ill-suppressed murmur of all thoughtful men against the famine of our churches; this moaning of the heart because it is bereaved of the consolation, the hope, the grandeur, that come alone out of the culture of the moral nature; should be heard through the sleep of indolence, and over the din of routine. This great and perpetual office of the preacher is not discharged. Preaching is the expression of the moral sentiment in application to the duties of life. In how many churches, by how many prophets, tell me, is man made sensible that he is an infinite Soul; that the earth and heavens are passing into his mind; that he is drinking forever the soul of God? Where now sounds the persuasion, that by its very melody imparadises my heart, and so affirms its own origin in heaven? Where shall I hear words such as in elder ages drew men to leave all and follow,—father and mother, house and land, wife and child? Where shall I hear these august laws of moral being so pronounced, as to fill my ear, and I feel ennobled by the offer of my uttermost action and passion? The test of the true faith, certainly, should be its power to charm and command the soul, as the laws of nature control the activity of the hands,—so commanding that we find pleasure and honor in obeying. The faith should blend with the light of rising and of setting suns, with the flying cloud, the singing bird, and the breath of flowers. But now the priest's Sabbath has lost the splendor of nature; it is unlovely; we are glad when it is done; we can make, we do make, even sitting in our pews, a far better, holier, sweeter, for ourselves.

Whenever the pulpit is usurped by a formalist, then is the worshipper defrauded and disconsolate. We shrink as soon as the prayers begin, which do not uplift, but smite and offend us. We are fain to wrap our cloaks about us, and secure, as best we can, a solitude that hears not. I once heard a preacher who sorely tempted me to say, I would go to church no more. Men go, thought I, where they are wont to go, else had no soul entered the temple in the afternoon. A snowstorm was falling around us. The snowstorm was real; the preacher merely spectral; and the eye felt the sad contrast in looking at him, and then out of the window behind him, into the beautiful meteor of the snow. He had lived in vain. He had no one word intimating that he had laughed or wept, was married or in love, had been commended, or cheated, or chagrined. If he had ever lived and acted, we were none the wiser for it. The capital secret of his profession, namely, to convert life into truth, he had not learned. Not one fact in all his experience, had he yet imported into his doctrine. This man had ploughed, and planted, and talked, and bought, and sold; he had read books; he had eaten and drunken; his head aches; his heart throbs; he smiles and suffers; yet was there not a surmise, a hint, in all the discourse, that he had ever lived at all. Not a line did he draw out of real history. The true preacher can always be known by this, that he deals out to the people his life,—life passed through the fire of thought. But of the bad preacher, it could not be told from his sermon, what age of the world he fell in; whether he had a father or a child; whether he was a freeholder or a pauper; whether he was a citizen or a countryman; or any other fact of his biography.

It seemed strange that the people should come to church. It seemed as if their houses were very unentertaining, that they should prefer this thoughtless clamor. It shows that there is a commanding attraction in the moral sentiment, that can lend a faint tint of light to dulness and ignorance, coming in its name and place. The good hearer is sure he has been touched sometimes; is sure there is somewhat to be reached, and some word that can reach it. When he listens to these vain words, he comforts himself by their relation to his remembrance of better hours, and so they clatter and echo unchallenged.

I am not ignorant that when we preach unworthily, it is not always quite in vain. There is a good ear, in some men, that draws supplies to virtue out of very indifferent nutriment. There is poetic truth concealed in all the common-places of prayer and of sermons, and though foolishly spoken, they may be wisely heard; for, each is some select expression that broke out in a moment of piety from some stricken or jubilant soul, and its excellency made it remembered. The prayers and even the dogmas of our church, are like the zodiac of Denderah, and the astronomical monuments of the Hindoos, wholly insulated from anything now extant in the life and business of the people. They mark the height to which the waters once rose. But this docility is a check upon the mischief from the good and devout. In a large portion of the community, the religious service gives rise to quite other thoughts and emotions. We need not chide the negligent servant. We are struck with pity, rather, at the swift retribution of his sloth. Alas for the unhappy man that is called to stand in the pulpit, and *not* give bread of life. Everything that befals, accuses him. Would he ask contributions for the missions, foreign or domestic? Instantly his face is suffused with shame, to propose to his parish, that they should send money a hundred or a thousand miles, to furnish such poor fare as they have at home, and would do well to go the hundred or the thousand miles, to escape. Would he urge people to a godly way of living;—and can he ask a fellow creature to come to Sabbath meetings, when he and they all know what is the poor uttermost they can hope for therein? Will he invite them privately to the Lord's Supper? He dares not. If no heart warm this rite, the hollow, dry, creaking formality is too plain, than that he can face a man of wit and energy, and put the invitation without terror. In the street, what has he to say to the bold village blasphemer? The village blasphemer sees fear in the face, form, and gait of the minister.

Let me not taint the sincerity of this plea by any oversight of the claims of good men. I know and honor the purity and strict conscience of numbers of the clergy. What life the public worship retains, it owes to the scattered company of pious men, who minister here and there in the churches, and who, sometimes accepting with too great tenderness the tenet of the elders, have not accepted from others, but from their own heart, the genuine impulses of virtue, and so still command our love and awe, to the sanctity of character. Moreover, the exceptions are not so much to be found in a few eminent preachers, as in the better hours, the truer inspirations of all,—nay, in the sincere moments of every man. But with whatever exception, it is still true, that tradition characterizes the preaching of this country; that it comes out of the memory, and not out of the soul; that it aims at what is usual, and not at what is necessary and eternal; that thus, historical Christianity destroys the power of preaching, by withdrawing it from the exploration of the moral nature of man, where the sublime is, where are the resources of astonishment and power. What a cruel injustice it is to that Law, the joy of the whole earth, which alone can make thought dear and rich; that Law whose fatal sureness the astronomical orbits poorly emulate, that it is travestied and depreciated, that it is behooted and behowled, and not a trait, not a word of it articulated. The pulpit in losing sight of this Law, loses all its inspiration, and gropes after it knows not what. And for want of this culture, the soul of the community is sick and faithless. It wants nothing so much as a stern, high, stoical, Christian discipline, to make it know itself and the divinity that speaks through it. Now man is ashamed of himself; he skulks and sneaks through the world, to be tolerated, to be pitied, and scarcely in a thousand years does any man dare to be wise and good, and so draw after him the tears and blessings of his kind.

Certainly there have been periods when, from the inactivity of the intellect on certain truths, a greater faith was possible in names and persons. The Puritans in England and America, found in the Christ of the Catholic Church, and in the dogmas inherited from Rome, scope for their austere piety, and their longings for civil freedom. But their creed is passing away, and none arises in its room. I think no man can go with his thoughts about him, into one of our churches, without feeling that what hold the public worship had on men, is gone or going. It has lost its grasp on the affection of the good, and the fear of the bad. In the country,—neighborhoods, half parishes are *signing off*,—to use the local term. It is already beginning to indicate character and religion to withdraw from the religious meetings. I have heard a devout person, who prized the Sabbath, say in bitterness of heart, "On Sundays, it seems wicked to go to church." And the motive, that holds the best there, is now only a hope and a waiting. What was once a mere circumstance, that the best and the worst men in the parish, the poor and the rich, the learned and the ignorant, young and old, should meet one day as fellows in one house, in sign of an equal right in the soul,—has come to be a paramount motive for going thither.

My friends, in these two errors, I think, I find the causes of that calamity of a decaying church and a wasting unbelief, which are casting malignant influences around us, and making the hearts of good men sad. And what greater calamity can fall upon a nation, than the loss of worship? Then all things go to decay. Genius leaves the temple, to haunt the senate, or the market. Literature becomes frivolous. Science is cold. The eye of youth is not lighted by the hope of other worlds, and age is without honor. Society lives to trifles, and when men die, we do not mention them.

And now, my brothers, you will ask, What in these desponding days can be done by us? The remedy is already declared in the ground of our complaint of the Church. We have contrasted the Church with the Soul. In the soul, then, let the redemption be sought. In one soul, in your soul, there are resources for the world. Wherever a man comes, there comes revolution. The old is for slaves. When a man comes, all books are legible, all things transparent, all religions are forms. He is religious. Man is the wonderworker. He is seen amid miracles. All men bless and curse. He saith yea and nay, only. The stationariness of religion; the assumption that the age of inspiration is past, that the Bible is closed; the fear of degrading the character of Jesus by representing him as a man; indicate with sufficient clearness the falsehood of our theology. It is the office of a true teacher to show us that God is, not was; that He speaketh, not spake. The true Christianity,—a faith like Christ's in the infinitude of man,—is lost. None believeth in the soul of man, but only in some man or person old and departed. Ah me! no man goeth alone. All men go in flocks to this saint or that poet, avoiding the God who seeth in secret. They cannot see in secret; they love to be blind in public. They think society wiser than their soul, and know not that one soul, and their soul, is wiser than the whole world. See how nations and races flit by on the sea of time, and leave no ripple to tell where they floated or sunk, and one good soul shall make the name of Moses, or of Zeno, or of Zoroaster, reverend forever. None assayeth the stern ambition to be the Self of the nation, and of nature, but each would be an easy secondary to some Christian scheme, or sectarian connexion, or some eminent man. Once leave your own knowledge of God, your own sentiment, and take secondary knowledge, as St. Paul's, or George Fox's, or Swedenborg's, and you get wide from God with every year this secondary form lasts, and if, as now, for centuries,—the chasm yawns to that breadth, that men can scarcely be convinced there is in them anything divine.

Let me admonish you, first of all, to go alone; to refuse the good models, even those most sacred in the imagination of men, and dare to love God without mediator or veil. Friends enough you shall find who will hold up to your emulation Wesleys and Oberlins, Saints and Prophets. Thank God for these good men, but say, 'I also am a man.' Imitation cannot go above its model. The imitator dooms himself to hopeless mediocrity. The inventor did it, because it was natural to him, and so in him it has a charm. In the imitator, something else is natural, and he bereaves himself of his own beauty, to come short of another man's.

Yourself a newborn bard of the Holy Ghost,—cast behind you all conformity, and acquaint men at first hand with Deity. Be to them a man. Look to it first and only, that you are such; that fashion, custom, authority, pleasure, and money are nothing to you,—are not bandages over your eyes, that you cannot see,—but live with the privilege of the immeasurable mind. Not too anxious to visit periodically all families and each family in your parish connexion,—when you meet one of these men or women, be to them a divine man; be to them thought and virtue; let their timid aspirations find in you a friend; let their trampled instincts be genially tempted out in your atmosphere; let their doubts know that you have doubted, and their wonder feel that you have wondered. By trusting your own soul, you shall gain a greater confidence in other men. For all our penny-wisdom, for all our soul-destroying slavery to habit, it is not to be doubted, that all men have sublime thoughts; that all men do value the few real hours of life; they love to be heard; they love to be caught up into the vision of principles. We mark with light in the memory the few interviews, we have had in the dreary years of routine and of sin, with souls that made our souls wiser; that spoke what we thought; that told us what we knew; that gave us leave to be what we inly were. Discharge to men the priestly office, and, present or absent, you shall be followed with their love as by an angel.

And, to this end, let us not aim at common degrees of merit. Can we not leave, to such as love it, the virtue that glitters for the commendation of society, and ourselves pierce the deep solitudes of absolute ability and worth? We easily come up to the standard of goodness in society. Society's praise can be cheaply secured, and almost all men are content with those easy merits; but the instant effect of conversing with God, will be, to put them away. There are sublime merits; persons who are not actors, not speakers, but influences; persons too great for fame, for display; who disdain eloquence; to whom all we call art and artist, seems too nearly allied to show and by-ends, to the exaggeration of the finite and selfish, and loss of the universal. The orators, the poets, the commanders encroach on us only as fair women do, by our allowance and homage. Slight them by preoccupation of mind, slight them, as you can well afford to do, by high and universal aims, and they instantly feel that you have right, and that it is in lower places that they must shine. They also feel your right; for they with you are open to the influx of the all-knowing Spirit, which annihilates before its broad noon the little shades and gradations of intelligence in the compositions we call wiser and wisest.

In such high communion, let us study the grand strokes of rectitude: a bold benevolence, an independence of friends, so that not the unjust wishes of those who love us, shall impair our freedom, but we shall resist for truth's sake the freest flow of kindness, and appeal to sympathies far in advance; and,—what is the highest form in which we know this beautiful element,—a certain solidity of merit, that has nothing to do with opinion, and which is so essentially and manifestly virtue, that it is taken for granted, that the right, the brave, the generous step will be taken by it, and nobody thinks of commending it. You would compliment a coxcomb doing a good act, but you would not praise an angel. The silence that accepts merit as the most natural thing in the world, is the highest applause. Such souls, when they appear, are the Imperial Guard of Virtue, the perpetual reserve, the dictators of fortune. One needs not praise their courage,—they are the heart and soul of nature. O my friends, there are resources in us on which we have not drawn. There are men who rise refreshed on hearing a threat; men to whom a crisis which intimidates and paralyzes the majority—demanding not the faculties of prudence and thrift, but comprehension, immovableness, the readiness of sacrifice,—comes graceful and beloved as a bride. Napoleon said of Massena, that he was not himself until the battle began to go against him; then, when the dead began to fall in ranks around him, awoke his powers of combination, and he put on terror and victory as a robe. So it is in rugged crises, in unweariable endurance, and in aims which put sympathy out of question, that the angel is shown. But these are heights that we can scarce remember and look up to, without contrition and shame. Let us thank God that such things exist.

And now let us do what we can to rekindle the smouldering, nigh quenched fire on the altar. The evils of the church that now is, are manifest. The question returns, What shall we do? I confess, all attempts to project and establish a Cultus with new rites and forms, seem to me vain. Faith makes us, and not we it, and faith makes its own forms. All attempts to contrive a system, are as cold as the new worship introduced by the French to the goddess of Reason,—to-day, pasteboard and fillagree, and ending to-morrow in madness and murder. Rather let the breath of new life be breathed by you through the forms already existing. For, if once you are alive, you shall find they shall become plastic and new. The remedy to their deformity is, first, soul, and second, soul, and evermore, soul. A whole popedom of forms, one pulsation of virtue can uplift and vivify. Two inestimable advantages Christianity has given us; first; the Sabbath, the jubilee of the whole world; whose light dawns welcome alike into the closet of the philosopher, into the garret of toil, and into prison cells, and everywhere suggests, even to the vile, a thought of the dignity of spiritual being. Let it stand forevermore, a temple, which new love, new faith, new sight shall restore to more than its first splendor to mankind. And secondly, the institution of preaching,— the speech of man to men,—essentially the most flexible of all organs, of all forms. What hinders that now, everywhere, in pulpits, in lecture-rooms, in houses, in fields, wherever the invitation of men or your own occasions lead you, you speak the very truth, as your life and conscience teach it, and cheer the waiting, fainting hearts of men with new hope and new revelation?

I look for the hour when that supreme Beauty, which ravished the souls of those Eastern men, and chiefly of those Hebrews, and through their lips spoke oracles to all time, shall speak in the West also. The Hebrew and Greek Scriptures contain immortal sentences, that have been bread of life to millions. But they have no epical integrity; are fragmentary; are not shown in their order to the intellect. I look for the new Teacher, that shall follow so far those shining laws, that he shall see them come full circle; shall see their rounding complete grace; shall see the world to be the mirror of the soul; shall see the identity of the law of gravitation with purity of heart; and shall show that the Ought, that Duty, is one thing with Science, with Beauty, and with Joy.

"Self-Reliance"
1841

"Ne te quæsiveris extra."[1]

"Man is his own star; and the soul that can
Render an honest and a perfect man,
Commands all light, all influence, all fate;
Nothing to him falls early or too late
Our acts our angels are, or good or ill,
Our fatal shadows that walk by us still."

Epilogue to Beaumont and Fletcher's
Honest Man's Fortune.

Cast the bantling on the rocks,
Suckle him with the she-wolf's teat;
Wintered with the hawk and fox,
Power and speed be hands and feet.

I read the other day some verses written by an eminent painter which were original and not conventional. The soul always hears an admonition in such lines, let the subject be what it may. The sentiment they instil is of more value than any thought they may contain. To believe your own thought, to believe that what is true for you in your private heart, is true for all men,—that is genius. Speak your latent conviction and it shall be the universal sense; for the inmost in due time becomes the outmost,—and our first thought is rendered back to us by the trumpets of the Last Judgment. Familiar as the voice of the mind is to each, the highest merit we ascribe to Moses, Plato, and Milton, is that they set at naught books and traditions, and spoke not what men but what they thought. A man should learn to detect and watch that gleam of light which flashes across his mind from within, more than the lustre of the firmament of bards and sages. Yet he dismisses without notice his thought, because it is his. In every work of genius we recognize our own rejected thoughts: they come back to us with a certain alienated majesty. Great works of art have no more affecting lesson for us than this. They teach us to abide by our spontaneous impression with good-humored inflexibility then most when the whole cry of voices is on the other side. Else, to-morrow a stranger will say with masterly good sense precisely what we have thought and felt all the time, and we shall be forced to take with shame our own opinion from another.

1. "Look to no one outside yourself." Persius, *Satires*, 1.7.

Source: The Collected Works of Ralph Waldo Emerson, ed. Joseph Slater and Douglas Emory Wilson, vol. 2, *Essays: First Series*, ed. Joseph Slater, Alfred R. Ferguson, and Jean Ferguson Carr (Cambridge: Harvard University Press, Belknap Press, 1979), 25–51. Reprinted by permission of The Belknap Press of Harvard University Press, Copyright © 1979 by The President and Fellows of Harvard College.

There is a time in every man's education when he arrives at the conviction that envy is ignorance; that imitation is suicide; that he must take himself for better, for worse, as his portion; that though the wide universe is full of good, no kernel of nourishing corn can come to him but through his toil bestowed on that plot of ground which is given to him to till. The power which resides in him is new in nature, and none but he knows what that is which he can do, nor does he know until he has tried. Not for nothing one face, one character, one fact makes much impression on him, and another none. This sculpture in the memory is not without preestablished harmony. The eye was placed where one ray should fall, that it might testify of that particular ray. We but half express ourselves, and are ashamed of that divine idea which each of us represents. It may be safely trusted as proportionate and of good issues, so it be faithfully imparted, but God will not have his work made manifest by cowards. A man is relieved and gay when he has put his heart into his work and done his best; but what he has said or done otherwise, shall give him no peace. It is a deliverance which does not deliver. In the attempt his genius deserts him; no muse befriends; no invention, no hope.

Trust thyself: every heart vibrates to that iron string. Accept the place the divine Providence has found for you; the society of your contemporaries, the connexion of events. Great men have always done so and confided themselves childlike to the genius of their age, betraying their perception that the absolutely trustworthy was seated at their heart, working through their hands, predominating in all their being. And we are now men, and must accept in the highest mind the same transcendent destiny; and not minors and invalids in a protected corner, not cowards fleeing before a revolution, but guides, redeemers, and benefactors, obeying the Almighty effort, and advancing on Chaos and the Dark.

What pretty oracles nature yields us on this text in the face and behavior of children, babes and even brutes. That divided and rebel mind, that distrust of a sentiment because our arithmetic has computed the strength and means opposed to our purpose, these have not. Their mind being whole, their eye is as yet unconquered, and when we look in their faces, we are disconcerted. Infancy conforms to nobody: all conform to it, so that one babe commonly makes four or five out of the adults who prattle and play to it. So God has armed youth and puberty and manhood no less with its own piquancy and charm, and made it enviable and gracious and its claims not to be put by, if it will stand by itself. Do not think the youth has no force because he cannot speak to you and me. Hark! in the next room his voice is sufficiently clear and emphatic. It seems he knows how to speak to his contemporaries. Bashful or bold, then, he will know how to make us seniors very unnecessary.

The nonchalance of boys who are sure of a dinner, and would disdain as much as a lord to do or say aught to conciliate one, is the healthy attitude of human nature. A boy is in the parlour what the pit is in the playhouse; independent, irresponsible, looking out from his corner on such people and facts as pass by, he tries and sentences them on their merits, in the swift summary way of boys, as good, bad, interesting, silly, eloquent, troublesome. He cumbers himself never about consequences, about interests: he gives an independent, genuine verdict. You must court him: he does not court you. But the man is, as it were, clapped into jail by his consciousness. As soon as he has once acted or spoken with eclat, he is a committed person, watched by the sympathy or the hatred of hundreds whose affections must now enter into his account. There is no Lethe for this. Ah, that he could pass again into his neutrality! Who can thus avoid all pledges, and having observed, observe again from the same unaffected, unbiassed, unbribable, unaffrighted innocence, must always be formidable. He would utter opinions on all passing affairs, which being seen to be not private but necessary, would sink like darts into the ear of men, and put them in fear.

These are the voices which we hear in solitude, but they grow faint and inaudible as we enter into the world. Society everywhere is in conspiracy against the manhood of every one of its members. Society is a joint-stock company in which the members agree for the better securing of his bread to each shareholder, to surrender the liberty and culture of the eater. The virtue in most request is conformity. Self-reliance is its aversion. It loves not realities and creators, but names and customs.

Whoso would be a man must be a nonconformist. He who would gather immortal palms must not be hindered by the name of goodness, but must explore if it be goodness. Nothing is at last sacred but the integrity of your own mind. Absolve you to yourself, and you shall have the suffrage of the world. I remember an answer which when quite young I was prompted to make to a valued adviser who was wont to importune me with the dear old doctrines of the church. On my saying, What have I to do with the sacredness of traditions, if I live wholly from within? my friend suggested— "But these impulses may be from below, not from above." I replied, "They do not seem to me to be such; but if I am the Devil's child, I will live then from the Devil." No law can be sacred to me but that of my nature. Good and bad are but names very readily transferable to that or this; the only right is what is after my constitution, the only wrong what is against it. A man is to carry himself in the presence of all opposition as if every thing were titular and ephemeral but he. I am ashamed to think how easily we capitulate to badges and names, to large societies and dead institutions. Every decent and well-spoken individual affects and sways me more than is right. I ought to go upright and vital, and speak the rude truth in all ways. If malice and vanity wear the coat of philanthropy, shall that pass? If an angry bigot assumes this bountiful cause of Abolition, and comes to me with his last news from Barbadoes, why should I not say to him, 'Go love thy infant; love thy wood-chopper: be good-natured and modest: have that grace; and never varnish your hard, uncharitable ambition with this incredible tenderness for black folk a thousand miles off. Thy love afar is spite at home.' Rough and graceless would be such greeting, but truth is handsomer than the affectation of love. Your goodness must have some edge to it—else it is none. The doctrine of hatred must be preached as the counteraction of the doctrine of love when that pules and whines. I shun father and mother and wife and brother, when my genius calls me. I would write on the lintels of the door-post, Whim. I hope it is somewhat better than whim at last, but we cannot spend the day in explanation. Expect me not to show cause why I seek or why I exclude company. Then, again, do not tell me, as a good man did to-day, of my obligation to put all poor men in good situations. Are they my poor? I tell thee, though foolish philanthropist, that I grudge the dollar, the dime, the cent I give to such men as do not belong to me and to whom I do not belong. There is a class of persons to whom by all spiritual affinity I am bought and sold; for them I will go to prison, if need be; but your miscellaneous popular charities; the education at college of fools; the building of meeting-houses to the vain end to which many now stand; alms to sots; and the thousandfold Relief Societies;—though I confess with shame I sometimes succumb and give the dollar, it is a wicked dollar which by and by I shall have the manhood to withhold.

Virtues are in the popular estimate rather the exception than the rule. There is the man *and* his virtues. Men do what is called a good action, as some piece of courage or charity, much as they would pay a fine in expiation of daily non-appearance on parade. Their works are done as an apology or extenuation of their living in the world,—as invalids and the insane pay a high board. Their virtues are penances. I do not wish to expiate, but to live. My life is for itself and not for a spectacle. I much prefer that it should be of a lower strain, so it be genuine and equal, than that it should be glittering and unsteady. I wish it to be sound and sweet, and not to need diet and bleeding. I ask primary evidence that you are a man, and refuse this appeal from the man to his actions. I know that for myself it makes no difference whether I do or forbear those actions which are reckoned excellent. I cannot consent to pay for a privilege where I have intrinsic right. Few and mean as my gifts may be, I actually am, and do not need for my own assurance or the assurance of my fellows any secondary testimony.

What I must do, is all that concerns me, not what the people think. This rule, equally arduous in actual and in intellectual life, may serve for the whole distinction between greatness and meanness. It is the harder, because you will always find those who think they know what is your duty better than you know it. It is easy in the world to live after the world's opinion; it is easy in solitude to live after our own; but the great man is he who in the midst of the crowd keeps with perfect sweetness the independence of solitude.

The objection to conforming to usages that have become dead to you, is, that it scatters your force. It loses your time and blurs the impression of your character. If you maintain a dead church, contribute to a dead Bible-Society, vote with a great party either for the Government or against it, spread your table like base housekeepers,—under all these screens, I have difficulty to detect the precise man you are. And, of course, so much force is withdrawn from your proper life. But do your work, and I shall know you. Do your work, and you shall reinforce yourself. A man must consider what a blindman's buff is this game of conformity. If I know your sect, I anticipate your argument. I hear a preacher announce for his text and topic the expediency of one of the institutions of his church. Do I not know beforehand that not possibly can he say a new and spontaneous word? Do I not know that with all this ostentation of examining the grounds of the institution, he will do no such thing? Do I not know that he is pledged to himself not to look but at one side,—the permitted side, not as a man, but as a parish minister? He is a retained attorney, and these airs of the bench are the emptiest affectation. Well, most men have bound their eyes with one or another handkerchief, and attached themselves to some one of these communities of opinion. This conformity makes them not false in a few particulars, authors of a few lies, but false in all particulars. Their every truth is not quite true. Their two is not the real two, their four not the real four: so that every word they say chagrins us, and we know not where to begin to set them right. Meantime nature is not slow to equip us in the prison-uniform of the party to which we adhere. We come to wear one cut of face and figure, and acquire by degrees the gentlest asinine expression. There is a mortifying experience in particular which does not fail to wreak itself also in the general history; I mean "the foolish face of praise," the forced smile which we put on in company where we do not feel at ease in answer to conversation which does not interest us. The muscles, not spontaneously moved, but moved by a low usurping wilfulness, grow tight about the outline of the face with the most disagreeable sensation.

For nonconformity the world whips you with its displeasure. And therefore a man must know how to estimate a sour face. The bystanders look askance on him in the public street or in the friend's parlor. If this aversation had its origin in contempt and resistance like his own, he might well go home with a sad countenance; but the sour faces of the multitude, like their sweet faces, have no deep cause, but are put on and off as the wind blows, and a newspaper directs. Yet is the discontent of the multitude more formidable than that of the senate and the college. It is easy enough for a firm man who knows the world to brook the rage of the cultivated classes. Their rage is decorous and prudent, for they are timid as being very vulnerable themselves. But when to their feminine rage the indignation of the people is added, when the ignorant and the poor are aroused, when the unintelligent brute force that lies at the bottom of society is made to growl and mow, it needs the habit of magnanimity and religion to treat it godlike as a trifle of no concernment.

The other terror that scares us from self-trust is our consistency; a reverence for our past act or word, because the eyes of others have no other data for computing our orbit than our past acts, and we are loath to disappoint them.

But why should you keep your head over your shoulder? Why drag about this corpse of your memory, lest you contradict somewhat you have stated in this or that public place? Suppose you should contradict yourself; what then? It seems to be a rule of wisdom never to rely on your memory alone, scarcely even in acts of pure memory, but to bring the past for judgment into the thousand-eyed present, and live ever in a new day. In your metaphysics you have denied personality to the Deity: yet when the devout motions of the soul come, yield to them heart and life, though they should clothe God with shape and color. Leave your theory as Joseph his coat in the hand of the harlot, and flee.

A foolish consistency is the hobgoblin of little minds, adored by little statesmen and philosophers and divines. With consistency a great soul has simply nothing to do. He may as well concern himself with his shadow on the wall. Speak what you think now in hard words, and to-morrow speak what to-morrow thinks in hard words again, though it contradict every thing you said to-day.—'Ah, so you shall be sure to be misunderstood.'—Is it so bad then to be misunderstood? Pythagoras was misunderstood, and Socrates, and Jesus, and Luther, and Copernicus, and Galileo, and Newton, and every pure and wise spirit that ever took flesh. To be great is to be misunderstood.

I suppose no man can violate his nature. All the sallies of his will are rounded in by the law of his being as the inequalities of Andes and Himmaleh are insignificant in the curve of the sphere. Nor does it matter how you gauge and try him. A character is like an acrostic or Alexandrian stanza;—read it forward, backward, or across, it still spells the same thing. In this pleasing contrite wood-life which God allows me, let me record day by day my honest thought without prospect or retrospect, and, I cannot doubt, it will be found symmetrical, though I mean it not, and see it not. My book should smell of pines and resound with the hum of insects. The swallow over my window should interweave that thread or straw he carries in his bill into my web also. We pass for what we are. Character teaches above our wills. Men imagine that they communicate their virtue or vice only by overt actions and do not see that virtue or vice emit a breath every moment.

There will be an agreement in whatever variety of actions, so they be each honest and natural in their hour. For of one will, the actions will be harmonious, however unlike they seem. These varieties are lost sight of at a little distance, at a little height of thought. One tendency unites them all. The voyage of the best ship is a zigzag line of a hundred tacks. See the line from a sufficient distance, and it straightens itself to the average tendency. Your genuine action will explain itself and will explain your other genuine actions. Your conformity explains nothing. Act singly, and what you have already done singly, will justify you now. Greatness appeals to the future. If I can be firm enough to-day to do right and scorn eyes, I must have done so much right before, as to defend me now. Be it how it will, do right now. Always scorn appearances, and you always may. The force of character is cumulative. All the foregone days of virtue work their health into this. What makes the majesty of the heroes of the senate and the field, which so fills the imagination? The consciousness of a train of great days and victories behind. They shed an united light on the advancing actor. He is attended as by a visible escort of angels. That is it which throws thunder into Chatham's voice, and dignity into Washington's port, and America into Adams's eye. Honor is venerable to us because it is no ephemeris. It is always ancient virtue. We worship it to-day, because it is not of to-day. We love it and pay it homage, because it is not a trap for our love and homage, but is self-dependent, self-derived, and therefore of an old immaculate pedigree, even if shown in a young person.

I hope in these days we have heard the last of conformity and consistency. Let the words be gazetted and ridiculous henceforward. Instead of the gong for dinner, let us hear a whistle from the Spartan fife. Let us never bow and apologize more. A great man is coming to eat at my house. I do not wish to please him: I wish that he should wish to please me. I will stand here for humanity, and though I would make it kind, I would make it true. Let us affront and reprimand the smooth mediocrity and squalid contentment of the times, and hurl in the face of custom, and trade, and office, the fact which is the upshot of all history, that there is a great responsible Thinker and Actor working wherever a man works; that a true man belongs to no other time or place, but is the centre of things. Where he is, there is nature. He measures you, and all men, and all events. Ordinarily every body in society reminds us of somewhat else or of some other person. Character, reality, reminds you of nothing else; it takes place of the whole creation. The man must be so much that he must make all circumstances indifferent. Every true man is a cause, a country, and an age; requires infinite spaces and numbers and time fully to accomplish his design;—and posterity seem to follow his steps as a train of clients. A man Cæsar is born, and for ages after, we have a Roman Empire. Christ is born, and millions of minds so grow and cleave to his genius, that he is confounded with virtue and the possible of man. An institution is the lengthened shadow of one man; as, Monachism, of the Hermit Antony; the Reformation, of Luther; Quakerism, of Fox; Methodism, of Wesley; Abolition, of Clarkson. Scipio, Milton called "the height of Rome;" and all history resolves itself very easily into the biography of a few stout and earnest persons.

Let a man then know his worth, and keep things under his feet. Let him not peep or steal, or skulk up and down with the air of a charity-boy, a bastard, or an interloper, in the world which exists for him. But the man in the street finding no worth in himself which corresponds to the force which built a tower or sculptured a marble god, feels poor when he looks on these. To him a palace, a statue, or a costly book have an alien and forbidding air, much like a gay equipage, and seem to say like that, "Who are you, sir?" Yet they all are his, suitors for his notice, petitioners to his faculties that they will come out and take possession. The picture waits for my verdict: it is not to command me, but I am to settle its claims to praise. That popular fable of the sot who was picked up dead drunk in the street, carried to the duke's house, washed and dressed and laid in the duke's bed, and, on his waking, treated with all obsequious ceremony like the duke, and assured that he had been insane, owes its popularity to the fact, that it symbolizes so well the state of man, who is in the world a sort of sot, but now and then wakes up, exercises his reason, and finds himself a true prince.

Our reading is mendicant and sycophantic. In history, our imagination plays us false. Kingdom and lordship, power and estate are a gaudier vocabulary than private John and Edward in a small house and common day's work: but the things of life are the same to both: the sum total of both is the same. Why all this deference to Alfred, and Scanderbeg, and Gustavus? Suppose they were virtuous: did they wear out virtue? As great a stake depends on your private act to-day, as followed their public and renowned steps. When private men shall act with original views, the lustre will be transferred from the actions of kings to those of gentlemen.

The world has been instructed by its kings, who have so magnetized the eyes of nations. It has been taught by this colossal symbol the mutual reverence that is due from man to man. The joyful loyalty with which men have everywhere suffered the king, the noble, or the great proprietor to walk among them by a law of his own, make his own scale of men and things, and reverse theirs, pay for benefits not with money but with honor, and represent the Law in his person, was the hieroglyphic by which they obscurely signified their consciousness of their own right and comeliness, the right of every man.

The magnetism which all original action exerts is explained when we inquire the reason of self-trust. Who is the Trustee? What is the aboriginal Self on which a universal reliance may be grounded? What is the nature and power of that science-baffling star, without parallax, without calculable elements, which shoots a ray of beauty even into trivial and impure actions, if the least mark of independence appear? The inquiry leads us to that source, at once the essence of genius, of virtue, and of life, which we call Spontaneity or Instinct. We denote this primary wisdom as Intuition, whilst all later teachings are tuitions. In that deep force, the last fact behind which analysis cannot go, all things find their common origin. For the sense of being which in calm hours rises, we know not how, in the soul, is not diverse from things, from space, from light, from time, from man, but one with them, and proceeds obviously from the same source whence their life and being also proceed. We first share the life by which things exist, and afterwards see them as appearances in nature, and forget that we have shared their cause. Here is the fountain of action and of thought. Here are the lungs of that inspiration which giveth man wisdom, and which cannot be denied without impiety and atheism. We lie in the lap of immense intelligence, which makes us receivers of its truth and organs of its activity. When we discern justice, when we discern truth, we do nothing of ourselves, but allow a passage to its beams. If we ask whence this comes, if we seek to pry into the soul that causes, all philosophy is at fault. Its presence or its absence is all we can affirm. Every man discriminates between the voluntary acts of his mind, and his involuntary perceptions, and knows that to his involuntary perceptions a perfect faith is due. He may err in the expression of them, but he knows that these things are so, like day and night, not to be disputed. My wilful actions and acquisitions are but roving;—the idlest reverie, the faintest native emotion, command my curiosity and respect. Thoughtless people contradict as readily the statement of perceptions as of opinions, or rather much more readily; for, they do not distinguish between perception and notion. They fancy that I choose to see this or that thing. But perception is not whimsical, but fatal. If I see a trait, my children will see it after me, and in course of time, all mankind,—although it may chance that no one has seen it before me. For my perception of it is as much a fact as the sun.

The relations of the soul to the divine spirit are so pure that it is profane to seek to interpose helps. It must be that when God speaketh, he should communicate not one thing, but all things; should fill the world with his voice; should scatter forth light, nature, time, souls, from the centre of the present thought; and new date and new create the whole. Whenever a mind is simple, and receives a divine wisdom, old things pass away,—means, teachers, texts, temples fall; it lives now and absorbs past and future into the present hour. All things are made sacred by relation to it,—one as much as another. All things are dissolved to their centre by their cause, and in the universal miracle petty and particular miracles disappear. If, therefore, a man claims to know and speak of God, and carries you backward to the phraseology of some old mouldered nation in another country, in another world, believe him not. Is the acorn better than the oak which is its fulness and completion? Is the parent better than the child into whom he has cast his ripened being? Whence then this worship of the past? The centuries are conspirators against the sanity and authority of the soul. Time and space are but physiological colors which the eye makes, but the soul is light; where it is, is day; where it was, is night; and history is an impertinence and an injury, if it be anything more than a cheerful apologue or parable of my being and becoming.

Man is timid and apologetic; he is no longer upright; he dares not say 'I think,' 'I am,' but quotes some saint or sage. He is ashamed before the blade of grass or the blowing rose. These roses under my window make no reference to former roses or to better ones; they are for what they are; they exist with God to-day. There is no time to them. There is simply the rose; it is perfect in every moment of its existence. Before a leaf-bud has burst, its whole life acts; in the full-blown flower, there is no more; in the leafless root, there is no less. Its nature is satisfied, and it satisfies nature, in all moments alike. But man postpones or remembers; he does not live in the present, but with reverted eye laments the past, or, heedless of the riches that surround him, stands on tiptoe to foresee the future. He cannot be happy and strong until he too lives with nature in the present, above time.

This should be plain enough. Yet see what strong intellects dare not yet hear God himself, unless he speak the phraseology of I know not what David, or Jeremiah, or Paul. We shall not always set so great a price on a few texts, on a few lives. We are like children who repeat by rote the sentences of grandames and tutors, and, as they grow older, of the men of talents and character they chance to see,—painfully recollecting the exact words they spoke; afterwards, when they come into the point of view which those had who uttered these sayings, they understand them, and are willing to let the words go; for, at any time, they can use words as good, when occasion comes. If we live truly, we shall see truly. It is as easy for the strong man to be strong, as it is for the weak to be weak. When we have new perception, we shall gladly disburden the memory of its hoarded treasures as old rubbish. When a man lives with God, his voice shall be as sweet as the murmur of the brook and the rustle of the corn.

And now at last the highest truth on this subject remains unsaid; probably, cannot be said; for all that we say is the far off remembering of the intuition. That thought, by what I can now nearest approach to say it, is this. When good is near you, when you have life in yourself, it is not by any known or accustomed way; you shall not discern the foot-prints of any other; you shall not see the face of man; you shall not hear any name;—the way, the thought, the good shall be wholly strange and new. It shall exclude example and experience. You take the way from man, not to man. All persons that ever existed are its forgotten ministers. Fear and hope are alike beneath it. There is somewhat low even in hope. In the hour of vision, there is nothing that can be called gratitude, nor properly joy. The soul raised over passion beholds identity and eternal causation, perceives the self-existence of Truth and Right, and calms itself with knowing that all things go well. Vast spaces of nature, the Atlantic Ocean, the South Sea,—long intervals of time, years, centuries,—are of no account. This which I think and feel underlay every former state of life and circumstances, as it does underlie my present, and what is called life, and what is called death.

Life only avails, not the having lived. Power ceases in the instant of repose; it resides in the moment of transition from a past to a new state, in the shooting of the gulf, in the darting to an aim. This one fact the world hates, that the soul *becomes;* for, that forever degrades the past, turns all riches to poverty, all reputation to a shame, confounds the saint with the rogue, shoves Jesus and Judas equally aside. Why then do we prate of self-reliance? Inasmuch as the soul is present, there will be power not confident but agent. To talk of reliance, is a poor external way of speaking. Speak rather of that which relies, because it works and is. Who has more obedience than I, masters me, though he should not raise his finger. Round him I must revolve by the gravitation of spirits. We fancy it rhetoric when we speak of eminent virtue. We do not yet see that virtue is Height, and that a man or a company of men plastic and permeable to principles, by the law of nature must overpower and ride all cities, nations, kings, rich men, poets, who are not.

This is the ultimate fact which we so quickly reach on this as on every topic, the resolution of all into the ever blessed ONE. Self-existence is the attribute of the Supreme Cause, and it constitutes the measure of good by the degree in which it enters into all lower forms. All things real are so by so much virtue as they contain. Commerce, husbandry, hunting, whaling, war, eloquence, personal weight, are somewhat, and engage my respect as examples of its presence and impure action. I see the same law working in nature for conservation and growth. Power is in nature the essential measure of right. Nature suffers nothing to remain in her kingdom which cannot help itself. The genesis and maturation of a planet, its poise and orbit, the bended tree recovering itself from the strong wind, the vital resources of every animal and vegetable, are demonstrations of the self-sufficing, and therefore self-relying soul.

Thus all concentrates; let us not rove; let us sit at home with the cause. Let us stun and astonish the intruding rabble of men and books and institutions by a simple declaration of the divine fact. Bid the invaders take the shoes from off their feet, for God is here within. Let our simplicity judge them, and our docility to our own law demonstrate the poverty of nature and fortune beside our native riches.

But now we are a mob. Man does not stand in awe of man, nor is his genius admonished to stay at home, to put itself in communication with the internal ocean, but it goes abroad to beg a cup of water of the urns of other men. We must go alone. I like the silent church before the service begins, better than any preaching. How far off, how cool, how chaste the persons look, begirt each one with a precinct or sanctuary. So let us always sit. Why should we assume the faults of our friend, or wife, or father, or child, because they sit around our hearth, or are said to have the same blood? All men have my blood, and I have all men's. Not for that will I adopt their petulance or folly, even to the extent of being ashamed of it. But your isolation must not be mechanical, but spiritual, that is, must be elevation. At times the whole world seems to be in conspiracy to importune you with emphatic trifles. Friend, client, child, sickness, fear, want, charity, all knock at once at thy closet door and say,—'Come out unto us.' But keep thy state; come not into their confusion. The power men possess to annoy me, I give them by a weak curiosity. No man can come near me but through my act. "What we love that we have, but by desire we bereave ourselves of the love."

If we cannot at once rise to the sanctities of obedience and faith, let us at least resist our temptations; let us enter into the state of war, and wake Thor and Woden, courage and contancy, in our Saxon breasts. This is to be done in our smooth times by speaking the truth. Check this lying hospitality and lying affection. Live no longer to the expectation of these deceived and deceiving people with whom we converse. Say to them, O father, O mother, O wife, O brother, O friend, I have lived with you after appearances hitherto. Henceforward I am the truth's. Be it known unto you that henceforward I obey no law less than the eternal law. I will have no covenants but proximities. I shall endeavor to nourish my parents, to support my family, to be the chaste husband of one wife,—but these relations I must fill after a new and unprecedented way. I appeal from your customs. I must be myself. I cannot break myself any longer for you, or you. If you can love me for what I am, we shall be the happier. If you cannot, I will still seek to deserve that you should. I will not hide my tastes or aversions. I will so trust that what is deep is holy, that I will do strongly before the sun and moon whatever inly rejoices me, and the heart appoints. If you are noble, I will love you; if you are not, I will not hurt you and myself by hypocritical attentions. If you are true, but not in the same truth with me, cleave to your companions; I will seek my own. I do this not selfishly, but humbly and truly. It is alike your interest and mine and all men's, however long we have dwelt in lies, to live in truth. Does this sound harsh to-day? You will soon love what is dictated by your nature as well as mine, and if we follow the truth, it will bring us out safe at last.—But so you may give these friends pain. Yes, but I cannot sell my liberty and my power, to save their sensibility. Besides, all persons have their moments of reason when they look out into the region of absolute truth; then will they justify me and do the same thing.

The populace think that your rejection of popular standards is a rejection of all standard, and mere antinomianism; and the bold sensualist will use the name of philosophy to gild his crimes. But the law of consciousness abides. There are two confessionals, in one or the other of which we must be shriven. You may fulfil your round of duties by clearing yourself in the *direct,* or, in the *reflex* way. Consider whether you have satisfied your relations to father, mother, cousin, neighbor, town, cat, and dog; whether any of these can upbraid you. But I may also neglect this reflex standard, and absolve me to myself. I have my own stern claims and perfect circle. It denies the name of duty to many offices that are called duties. But if I can discharge its debts, it enables me to dispense with the popular code. If any one imagines that this law is lax, let him keep its commandment one day.

And truly it demands something godlike in him who has cast off the common motives of humanity, and has ventured to trust himself for a taskmaster. High be his heart, faithful his will, clear his sight, that he may in good earnest be doctrine, society, law to himself, that a simple purpose may be to him as strong as iron necessity is to others.

If any man consider the present aspects of what is called by distinction *society,* he will see the need of these ethics. The sinew and heart of man seem to be drawn out, and we are become timorous desponding whimperers. We are afraid of truth, afraid of fortune, afraid of death, and afraid of each other. Our age yields no great and perfect persons. We want men and women who shall renovate life and our social state, but we see that most natures are insolvent, cannot satisfy their own wants, have an ambition out of all proportion to their practical force, and do lean and beg day and night continually. Our housekeeping is mendicant, our arts, our occupations, our marriages, our religion we have not chosen, but society has chosen for us. We are parlor soldiers. We shun the rugged battle of fate, where strength is born.

If our young men miscarry in their first enterprizes, they lose all heart. If the young merchant fails, men say he is *ruined.* If the finest genius studies at one of our colleges, and is not installed in an office within one year afterwards in the cities or suburbs of Boston or New York, it seems to his friends and to himself that he is right in being disheartened and in complaining the rest of his life. A sturdy lad from New Hampshire or Vermont, who in turn tries all the professions, who *teams it, farms it, peddles,* keeps a school, preaches, edits a newspaper, goes to Congress, buys a township, and so forth, in successive years, and always, like a cat, falls on his feet, is worth a hundred of these city dolls. He walks abreast with his days, and feels no shame in not 'studying a profession,' for he does not postpone his life, but lives already. He has not one chance, but a hundred chances. Let a Stoic open the resources of man, and tell men they are not leaning willows, but can and must detach themselves; that with the exercise of self-trust, new powers shall appear; that a man is the word made flesh, born to shed healing to the nations, that he should be ashamed of our compassion, and that the moment he acts from himself, tossing the laws, the books, idolatries, and customs out of the window, we pity him no more but thank and revere him,—and that teacher shall restore the life of man to splendor, and make his name dear to all History.

It is easy to see that a greater self-reliance must work a revolution in all the offices and relations of men; in their religion; in their education; in their pursuits; their modes of living; their association; in their property; in their speculative views.

1. In what prayers do men allow themselves! That which they call a holy office, is not so much as brave and manly. Prayer looks abroad and asks for some foreign addition to come through some foreign virtue, and loses itself in endless mazes of natural and supernatural, and mediatorial and miraculous. Prayer that craves a particular commodity,—any thing less than all good,—is vicious. Prayer is the contemplation of the facts of life from the highest point of view. It is the soliloquy of a beholding and jubilant soul. It is the spirit of God pronouncing his works good. But prayer as a means to effect a private end, is meanness and theft. It supposes dualism and not unity in nature and consciousness. As soon as the man is at one with God, he will not beg. He will then see prayer in all action. The prayer of the farmer kneeling in his field to weed it, the prayer of the rower kneeling with the stroke of his oar, are true prayers

heard throughout nature, though for cheap ends. Caratach, in Fletcher's Bonduca, when admonished to inquire the mind of the god Audate, replies,—

> "His hidden meaning lies in our endeavors,
> Our valors are our best gods."

Another sort of false prayers are our regrets. Discontent is the want of self-reliance: it is infirmity of will. Regret calamities, if you can thereby help the sufferer; if not, attend your own work, and already the evil begins to be repaired. Our sympathy is just as base. We come to them who weep foolishly, and sit down and cry for company, instead of imparting to them truth and health in rough electric shocks, putting them once more in communication with their own reason. The secret of fortune is joy in our hands. Welcome evermore to gods and men is the self-helping man. For him all doors are flung wide: him all tongues greet, all honors crown, all eyes follow with desire. Our love goes out to him and embraces him, because he did not need it. We solicitously and apologetically caress and celebrate him, because he held on his way and scorned our disapprobation. The gods love him because men hated him. "To the persevering mortal," said Zoroaster, "the blessed Immortals are swift."

As men's prayers are a disease of the will, so are their creeds a disease of the intellect. They say with those foolish Israelites, 'Let not God speak to us, lest we die. Speak thou, speak any man with us, and we will obey.' Everywhere I am hindered of meeting God in my brother, because he has shut his own temple doors, and recites fables merely of his brother's, or his brother's brother's God. Every new mind is a new classification. If it prove a mind of uncommon activity and power, a Locke, a Lavoisier, a Hutton, a Bentham, a Fourier, it imposes its classification on other men, and lo! a new system. In proportion to the depth of the thought, and so to the number of the objects it touches and brings within reach of the pupil, is his complacency. But chiefly is this apparent in creeds and churches, which are also classifications of some powerful mind acting on the elemental thought of Duty, and man's relation to the Highest. Such is Calvinism, Quakerism, Swedenborgianism. The pupil takes the same delight in subordinating every thing to the new terminology, as a girl who has just learned botany in seeing a new earth and new seasons thereby. It will happen for a time, that the pupil will find his intellectual power has grown by the study of his master's mind. But in all unbalanced minds, the classification is idolized, passes for the end, and not for a speedily exhaustible means, so that the walls of the system blend to their eye in the remote horizon with the walls of the universe; the luminaries of heaven seem to them hung on the arch their master built. They cannot imagine how you aliens have any right to see,—how you can see; 'It must be somehow that you stole the light from us.' They do not yet perceive, that light, unsystematic, indomitable, will break into any cabin, even into theirs. Let them chirp awhile and call it their own. If they are honest and do well, presently their neat new pinfold will be too strait and low, will crack, will lean, will rot and vanish, and the immortal light, all young and joyful, million-orbed, million-colored, will beam over the universe as on the first morning.

2. It is for want of self-culture that the superstition of Travelling, whose idols are Italy, England, Egypt, retains its fascination for all educated Americans. They who made England, Italy, or Greece venerable in the imagination, did so by sticking fast where they were, like an axis of the earth. In manly hours, we feel that duty is our place. The soul is no traveller: the wise man stays at home, and when his necessities,

his duties, on any occasion call him from his house, or into foreign lands, he is at home still, and shall make men sensible by the expression of his countenance, that he goes the missionary of wisdom and virtue, and visits cities and men like a sovereign, and not like an interloper or a valet.

I have no churlish objection to the circumnavigation of the globe, for the purposes of art, of study, and benevolence, so that the man is first domesticated, or does not go abroad with the hope of finding somewhat greater than he knows. He who travels to be amused, or to get somewhat which he does not carry, travels away from himself, and grows old even in youth among old things. In Thebes, in Palmyra, his will and mind have become old and dilapidated as they. He carries ruins to ruins.

Travelling is a fool's paradise. Our first journeys discover to us the indifference of places. At home I dream that at Naples, at Rome, I can be intoxicated with beauty, and lose my sadness. I pack my trunk, embrace my friends, embark on the sea, and at last wake up in Naples, and there beside me is the stern Fact, the sad self, unrelenting, identical, that I fled from. I seek the Vatican, and the palaces. I affect to be intoxicated with sights and suggestions, but I am not intoxicated. My giant goes with me wherever I go.

3. But the rage of travelling is a symptom of a deeper unsoundness affecting the whole intellectual action. The intellect is vagabond, and our system of education fosters restlessness. Our minds travel when our bodies are forced to stay at home. We imitate; and what is imitation but the travelling of the mind? Our houses are built with foreign taste; our shelves are garnished with foreign ornaments; our opinions, our tastes, our faculties, lean, and follow the Past and the Distant. The soul created the arts wherever they have flourished. It was in his own mind that the artist sought his model. It was an application of his own thought to the thing to be done and the conditions to be observed. And why need we copy the Doric or the Gothic model? Beauty, convenience, grandeur of thought, and quaint expression are as near to us as to any, and if the American artist will study with hope and love the precise thing to be done by him, considering the climate, the soil, the length of the day, the wants of the people, the habit and form of the government, he will create a house in which all these will find themselves fitted, and taste and sentiment will be satisfied also.

Insist on yourself; never imitate. Your own gift you can present every moment with the cumulative force of a whole life's cultivation; but of the adopted talent of another, you have only an extemporaneous, half possession. That which each can do best, none but his Maker can teach him. No man yet knows what it is, nor can, till that person has exhibited it. Where is the master who could have taught Shakspeare? Where is the master who could have instructed Franklin, or Washington, or Bacon, or Newton? Every great man is a unique. The Scipionism of Scipio is precisely that part he could not borrow. Shakspeare will never be made by the study of Shakspeare. Do that which is assigned you, and you cannot hope too much or dare too much. There is at this moment for you an utterance brave and grand as that of the colossal chisel of Phidias, or trowel of the Egyptians, or the pen of Moses, or Dante, but different from all these. Not possibly will the soul all rich, all eloquent, with thousand-cloven tongue, deign to repeat itself; but if you can hear what these patriarchs say, surely you can reply to them in the same pitch of voice: for the ear and the tongue are two organs of one nature. Abide in the simple and noble regions of thy life, obey thy heart, and thou shalt reproduce the Foreworld again.

4. As our Religion, our Education, our Art look abroad, so does our spirit of society. All men plume themselves on the improvement of society, and no man improves.

Society never advances. It recedes as fast on one side as it gains on the other. It undergoes continual changes: it is barbarous, it is civilized, it is christianized, it is rich, it is scientific; but this change is not amelioration. For every thing that is given, something is taken. Society acquires new arts and loses old instincts. What a contrast between the well-clad, reading, writing, thinking American, with a watch, a pencil, and a bill of exchange in his pocket, and the naked New Zealander, whose property is a club, a spear, a mat, and an undivided twentieth of a shed to sleep under. But compare the health of the two men, and you shall see that the white man has lost his aboriginal strength. If the traveller tell us truly, strike the savage with a broad axe, and in a day or two the flesh shall unite and heal as if you struck the blow into soft pitch, and the same blow shall send the white to his grave.

The civilized man has built a coach, but has lost the use of his feet. He is supported on crutches, but lacks so much support of muscle. He has a fine Geneva watch, but he fails of the skill to tell the hour by the sun. A Greenwich nautical almanac he has, and so being sure of the information when he wants it, the man in the street does not know a star in the sky. The solstice he does not observe; the equinox he knows as little; and the whole bright calendar of the year is without a dial in his mind. His note-books impair his memory; his libraries overload his wit; the insurance office increases the number of accidents; and it may be a question whether machinery does not encumber; whether we have not lost by refinement some energy, by a christianity entrenched in establishments and forms, some vigor of wild virtue. For every stoic was a stoic; but in Christendom where is the Christian?

There is no more deviation in the moral standard than in the standard of height or bulk. No greater men are now than ever were. A singular equality may be observed between the great men of the first and of the last ages; nor can all the science, art, religion and philosophy of the nineteenth century avail to educate greater men than Plutarch's heroes, three or four and twenty centuries ago. Not in time is the race progressive. Phocion, Socrates, Anaxagoras, Diogenes, are great men, but they leave no class. He who is really of their class will not be called by their name, but will be his own man, and, in his turn the founder of a sect. The arts and inventions of each period are only its costume, and do not invigorate men. The harm of the improved machinery may compensate its good. Hudson and Behring accomplished so much in their fishing-boats, as to astonish Parry and Franklin, whose equipment exhausted the resources of science and art. Galileo, with an opera-glass, discovered a more splendid series of celestial phenomena than any one since. Columbus found the New World in an undecked boat. It is curious to see the periodical disuse and perishing of means and machinery which were introduced with loud laudation, a few years or centuries before. The great genius returns to essential man. We reckoned the improvements of the art of war among the triumphs of science, and yet Napoleon conquered Europe by the Bivouac, which consisted of falling back on naked valor, and disencumbering it of all aids. The Emperor held it impossible to make a perfect army, says Las Cases, "without abolishing our arms, magazines, commissaries, and carriages, until in imitation of the Roman custom, the soldier should receive his supply of corn, grind it in his hand-mill, and bake his bread himself."

Society is a wave. The wave moves onward, but the water of which it is composed, does not. The same particle does not rise from the valley to the ridge. Its unity is only phenomenal. The persons who make up a nation to-day, next year die, and their experience with them.

And so the reliance on Property, including the reliance on governments which protect it, is the want of self-reliance. Men have looked away from themselves and at things so long, that they have come to esteem the religious, learned, and civil institutions, as guards of property, and they deprecate assaults on these, because they feel them to be assaults on property. They measure their esteem of each other, by what each has, and not by what each is. But a cultivated man becomes ashamed of his property, out of new respect for his nature. Especially he hates what he has, if he see that it is accidental,—came to him by inheritance, or gift, or crime; then he feels that it is not having; it does not belong to him, has no root in him, and merely lies there, because no revolution or no robber takes it away. But that which a man is, does always by necessity acquire, and what the man acquires is living property, which does not wait the beck of rulers, or mobs, or revolutions, or fire, or storm, or bankruptcies, but perpetually renews itself wherever the man breathes. "Thy lot or portion of life," said the Caliph Ali, "is seeking after thee; therefore be at rest from seeking after it." Our dependence on these foreign goods leads us to our slavish respect for numbers. The political parties meet in numerous conventions; the greater the concourse, and with each new uproar of announcement, The delegation from Essex! The Democrats from New Hampshire! The Whigs of Maine! the young patriot feels himself stronger than before by a new thousand of eyes and arms. In like manner the reformers summon conventions, and vote and resolve in multitude. Not so, O friends! will the God deign to enter and inhabit you, but by a method precisely the reverse. It is only as a man puts off all foreign support, and stands alone, that I see him to be strong and to prevail. He is weaker by every recruit to his banner. Is not a man better than a town? Ask nothing of men, and in the endless mutation, thou only firm column must presently appear the upholder of all that surrounds thee. He who knows that power is inborn, that he is weak because he has looked for good out of him and elsewhere, and so perceiving, throws himself unhesitatingly on his thought, instantly rights himself, stands in the erect position, commands his limbs, works miracles; just as a man who stands on his feet is stronger than a man who stands on his head.

So use all that is called Fortune. Most men gamble with her, and gain all, and lose all, as her wheel rolls. But do thou leave as unlawful these winnings, and deal with Cause and Effect, the chancellors of God. In the Will work and acquire, and thou hast chained the wheel of Chance, and shalt sit hereafter out of fear from her rotations. A political victory, a rise of rents, the recovery of your sick, or the return of your absent friend, or some other favorable event, raises your spirits, and you think good days are preparing for you. Do not believe it. Nothing can bring you peace but yourself. Nothing can bring you peace but the triumph of principles.

MARGARET FULLER

"The Great Lawsuit: Man Versus Men, Woman Versus Women"
1843

As the editor of the Transcendentalists' journal the *Dial,* the assistant editor of Horace Greeley's *New York Tribune,* and a leading foreign correspondent and revolutionary activitist in Italy, Margaret Fuller (1810–50) was well known for crossing boundaries. But the boundaries she was most famous for crossing were those of gender in her book *Woman in the Nineteenth Century* (1845). As the first major philosophical American work on the woman question, Fuller's book was of decisive importance in shaping the thought of many of nineteenth-century America's leading feminists. The bulk of her book, though, including its main theoretical arguments, Fuller first presented in her earlier article in the *Dial.* In her article, as in the book, Fuller applied to the problem of gender roles the romantic concept of self-culture, or the cultivated unfolding of the soul to a state of perfect wholeness of being. Although somewhat ambiguous about the ultimate nature of male and female identities, she nonetheless made clear that women's growth in wholeness required a radical alteration of the conventional two-spheres structure of American gender relations. In particular she argued that "masculine" and "feminine" elements in women's character had to be given complete freedom for realization and women's mental cultivation, if it was to be active, had to give rise to new opportunities for employment. Although the ends she proposed for female emancipation were thus individualistic, the *means* she suggested were at least partly social. They were also conflict-ridden. In order to break women's psychic dependency on men and achieve soul-dependency, she proposed that women for the time being look to themselves as teachers. Her hope, however, was thoroughly Emersonian: if women lived truly "self-centered," and therefore God-centered, lives, they would stimulate a new race of men to do likewise and so usher in a new harmony between the sexes. The best entry to Margaret Fuller's life and thought is the current ongoing edition of her letters edited by Robert N. Hudspeth, *The Letters of Margaret Fuller* (Ithaca, N.Y., 1983–87). For two stimulating, recent articles on her social thought, see David M. Robinson, "Margaret Fuller and the Transcendental Ethos: *Woman in the Nineteenth Century,*" *PMLA,* 97 (January 1982), 83–98; and Bell Gale Chevigny, "To the Edges of Ideology: Margaret Fuller's Centrifugal Evolution," *American Quarterly,* 38 (Summer 1986), 173–201. For a discussion of Fuller as a women's intellectual leader, see Charles Capper, "Margaret Fuller as Cultural Reformer: The Conversations in Boston," *American Quarterly,* 39 (Winter 1987), 509–28.

This great suit has now been carried on through many ages, with various results. The decisions have been numerous, but always followed by appeals to still higher courts. How can it be otherwise, when the law itself is the subject of frequent elucidation, constant revision? Man has, now and then, enjoyed a clear, triumphant hour, when some irresistible conviction warmed and purified the atmosphere of his planet. But, presently, he sought repose after his labors, when the crowd of pigmy adversaries bound him in his sleep. Long years of inglorious imprisonment followed, while his enemies revelled in his spoils, and no counsel could be found to plead his cause, in the absence of that all-promising glance, which had, at times, kindled the poetic soul to revelation of his claims, of his rights.

Yet a foundation for the largest claim is now established. It is known that his inheritance consists in no partial sway, no exclusive possession, such as his adversaries desire. For they, not content that the universe is rich, would, each one for himself, appropriate treasure; but in vain! The many-colored garment, which clothed with honor an elected son, when rent asunder for the many, is a worthless spoil. A band of robbers cannot live princely in the prince's castle; nor would he, like them, be content with less than all, though he would not, like them, seek it as fuel for riotous enjoyment, but as his principality, to administer and guard for the use of all living things therein. He cannot be satisfied with any one gift of the earth, any one department of knowledge, or telescopic peep at the heavens. He feels himself called to understand and aid nature, that she may, through his intelligence, be raised and interpreted; to be a student of, and servant to, the universe-spirit; and only king of his planet, that, as an angelic minister, he may bring it into conscious harmony with the law of that spirit.

Such is the inheritance of the orphan prince, and the illegitimate children of his family will not always be able to keep it from him, for, from the fields which they sow with dragon's teeth, and water with blood, rise monsters, which he alone has power to drive away.

But it is not the purpose now to sing the prophecy of his jubilee. We have said that, in clear triumphant moments, this has many, many times been made manifest, and those moments, though past in time, have been translated into eternity by thought. The bright signs they left hang in the heavens, as single stars or constellations, and, already, a thickly-sown radiance consoles the wanderer in the darkest night. Heroes have filled the zodiac of beneficent labors, and then given up their mortal part to the fire without a murmur. Sages and lawgivers have bent their whole nature to the search for truth, and thought themselves happy if they could buy, with the sacrifice of all temporal ease and pleasure, one seed for the future Eden. Poets and priests have strung the lyre with heart-strings, poured out their best blood upon the alter which, reared anew from age to age, shall at last sustain the flame which rises to highest heaven. What shall we say of those who, if not so directly, or so consciously, in connection with the central truth, yet, led and fashioned by a divine instinct, serve no less to develop and interpret the open secret of love passing into life, the divine energy creating for the purpose of happiness;—of the artist, whose hand, drawn by a preëxistent harmony to a certain medium, moulds it to expressions of life more highly and completely organized than are seen elsewhere, and, by carrying out the intention of nature, reveals her meaning to those who are not yet sufficiently matured to divine it; of the philosopher, who listens steadily for causes, and, from those obvious, infers

Source: Dial, 4 (July 1843), 1, 3–5, 7–8, 9–17, 17–18, 18–20, 22–24, 28, 32–33, 35–37, 38, 43–47.

those yet unknown; of the historian, who, in faith that all events must have their reason and their aim, records them, and lays up archives from which the youth of prophets may be fed. The man of science dissects the statement, verifies the facts, and demonstrates connection even where he cannot its purpose.

Lives, too, which bear none of these names, have yielded tones of no less significance. The candlestick, set in a low place, has given light as faithfully, where it was needed, as that upon the hill. In close alleys, in dismal nooks, the Word has been read as distinctly, as when shown by angels to holy men in the dark prison. Those who till a spot of earth, scarcely larger than is wanted for a grave, have deserved that the sun should shine upon its sod till violets answer.

So great has been, from time to time, the promise, that, in all ages, men have said the Gods themselves came down to dwell with them; that the All-Creating wandered on the earth to taste in a limited nature the sweetness of virtue, that the All-Sustaining incarnated himself, to guard, in space and time, the destinies of his world; that heavenly genius dwelt among the shepherds, to sing to them and teach them how to sing. Indeed,

"Der stets den Hirten gnädig sich bewies."
"He has constantly shown himself favorable to shepherds."

And these dwellers in green pastures and natural students of the stars, were selected to hail, first of all, the holy child, whose life and death presented the type of excellence, which has sustained the heart of so large a portion of mankind in these later generations.

Such marks have been left by the footsteps of man, whenever he has made his way through the wilderness of men. And whenever the pigmies stepped in one of these, they felt dilate within the breast somewhat that promised larger stature and purer blood. They were tempted to forsake their evil ways, to forsake the side of selfish personal existence, of decrepit skepticism,. and covetousness of corruptible possessions. Conviction flowed in upon them. They, too, raised the cry; God is living, all is his, and all created beings are brothers, for they are his children. These were the triumphant moments; but, as we have said, man slept and selfishness awoke.

Thus he is still kept out of his inheritance, still a pleader, still a pilgrim. But his reinstatement is sure. And now, no mere glimmering consciousness, but a certainty, is felt and spoken, that the highest ideal man can form of his own capabilities is that which he is destined to attain. Whatever the soul knows how to seek, it must attain. Knock, and it shall be opened; seek, and ye shall find. It is demonstrated, it is a maxim. He no longer paints his proper nature in some peculiar form and says, "Prometheus had it," but "Man must have it." However disputed by many, however ignorantly used, or falsified, by those who do receive it, the fact of an universal, unceasing revelation, has been too clearly stated in words, to be lost sight of in thought, and sermons preached from the text, "Be ye perfect," are the only sermons of a pervasive and deep-searching influence.

But among those who meditate upon this text, there is great difference of view, as to the way in which perfection shall be sought.

Through the intellect, say some; Gather from every growth of life its seed of thought; look behind every symbol for its law. If thou canst *see* clearly, the rest will follow.

Through the life, say others; Do the best thou knowest to-day. Shrink not from incessant error, in this gradual, fragmentary state. Follow thy light for as much as it will show thee, be faithful as far as thou canst, in hope that faith presently will lead to sight. Help others, without blame that they need thy help. Love much, and be forgiven.

It needs not intellect, needs not experience, says a third. If you took the true way, these would be evolved in purity. You would not learn through them, but express through them a higher knowledge. In quietness, yield thy soul to the causal soul. Do not disturb its teachings by methods of thine own. Be still, seek not, but wait in obedience. Thy commission will be given.

Could we, indeed, say what we want, could we give a description of the child that is lost, he would be found. As soon as the soul can say clearly, that a certain demonstration is wanted, it is at hand. When the Jewish prophet described the Lamb, as the expression of what was required by the coming era, the time drew nigh. But we say not, see not, as yet, clearly, what we would. Those who call for a more triumphant expression of love, a love that cannot be crucified, show not a perfect sense of what has already been expressed. Love has already been expressed, that made all things new, that gave the worm its ministry as well as the eagle; a love, to which it was alike to descend into the depths of hell, or to sit at the right hand of the Father.

Yet, no doubt, a new manifestation is at hand, a new hour in the day of man. We cannot expect to see him a completed being, when the mass of men lie so entangled in the sod, or use the freedom of their limbs only with wolfish energy. The tree cannot come to flower till its root be freed from the cankering worm, and its whole growth open to air and light. Yet something new shall presently be shown of the life of man, for hearts crave it now, if minds do not know how to ask it.

. . . . . .

Meanwhile, not a few believe, and men themselves have expressed the opinion, that the time is come when Euridice is to call for an Orpheus, rather than Orpheus for Euridice; that the idea of man, however imperfectly brought out, has been far more so than that of woman, and that an improvement in the daughters will best aid the reformation of the sons of this age.

It is worthy of remark, that, as the principle of liberty is better understood and more nobly interpreted, a broader protest is made in behalf of woman. As men become aware that all men have not had their fair chance, they are inclined to say that no women have had a fair chance. The French revolution, that strangely disguised angel, bore witness in favor of woman, but intrepreted her claims no less ignorantly than those of man. Its idea of happiness did not rise beyond outward enjoyment, unobstructed by the tyranny of others. The title it gave was Citoyen, Citoyenne, and it is not unimportant to woman that even this species of equality was awarded her. Before, she could be condemned to perish on the scaffold for treason, but not as a citizen, but a subject. This right with which this title then invested a human being, was that of bloodshed and license. The Goddess of Liberty was impure. Yet truth was prophesied in the ravings of that hideous fever induced by long ignorance and abuse. Europe is conning a valued lesson from the blood-stained page. The same tendencies, farther unfolded, will bear good fruit in this country.

Yet, in this country, as by the Jews, when Moses was leading them to the promised land, everything has been done that inherited depravity could, to hinder the promise of heaven from its fulfilment. The cross, here as elsewhere, has been planted only to be blasphemed by cruelty and fraud. The name of the Prince of Peace has been profaned by all kinds of injustice towards the Gentile whom he said he came to save. But I need not speak of what has been done towards the red man, the black man. These deeds are the scoff of the world; and they have been accompanied by such pious words, that the gentlest would not dare to intercede with, "Father forgive them, for they know not what they do."

Here, as elsewhere, the gain of creation consists always in the growth of individual minds, which live and aspire, as flowers bloom and birds sing, in the midst of morasses; and in the continual development of that thought, the thought of human destiny, which is given to eternity to fulfil, and which ages of failure only seemingly impede. Only seemingly, and whatever seems to the contrary, this country is as surely destined to elucidate a great moral law, as Europe was to promote the mental culture of man.

Though the national independence be blurred by the servility of individuals; though freedom and equality have been proclaimed only to leave room for a monstrous display of slave dealing, and slave keeping; though the free American so often feels himself free, like the Roman, only to pamper his appetites and his indolence through the misery of his fellow beings, still it is not in vain, that the verbal statement has been made, "All men are born free and equal." There it stands, a golden certainty, wherewith to encourage the good, to shame the bad. The new world may be called clearly to perceive that it incurs the utmost penalty, if it reject the sorrowful brother. And if men are deaf, the angels hear. But men cannot be deaf. It is inevitable that an external freedom, such as has been achieved for the nation, should be so also for every member of it. That, which has once been clearly conceived in the intelligence, must be acted out.

. . . . . .

We sicken no less at the pomp than the strife of words. We feel that never were lungs so puffed with the wind of declamation, on moral and religious subjects, as now. We are tempted to implore these "word-heroes," these word-Catos, word-Christs, to beware of cant above all things; to remember that hypocrisy is the most hopeless as well as the meanest of crimes, and that those must surely be polluted by it, who do not keep a little of all this morality and religion for private use. We feel that the mind may "grow black and rancid in the smoke" even of altars. We start up from the harangue to go into our closet and shut the door. But, when it has been shut long enough, we remember that where there is so much smoke, there must be some fire; with so much talk about virture and freedom must be mingled some desire for them; that it cannot be in vain that such have become the common topics of conversation among men; that the very newspapers should proclaim themselves Pilgrims, Puritans, Heralds of Holiness. The king that maintains so costly a retinue cannot be a mere Count of Carabbas fiction. We have waited here long in the dust; we are tired and hungry, but the triumphal procession must appear at last.

Of all its banners, none has been more steadily upheld, and under none has more valor and willingness for real sacrifices been shown, than that of the champions of the enslaved African. And this band it is, which, partly in consequence of a natural following out of principles, partly because many women have been prominent in that cause, makes, just now, the warmest appeal in behalf of woman.

Though there has been a growing liberality on this point, yet society at large is not so prepared for the demands of this party, but that they are, and will be for some time, coldly regarded as the Jacobins of their day.

"Is it not enough," cries the sorrowful trader, "that you have done all you could to break up the national Union, and thus destroy the prosperity of our country, but now you must be trying to break up family union, to take my wife away from the cradle, and the kitchen hearth, to vote at polls, and preach from a pulpit? Of course, if she does such things, she cannot attend to those of her own sphere. She is happy enough as she is. She has more leisure than I have, every means of improvement, every indulgence."

"Have you asked her whether she was satisfied with these indulgences?"

"No, but I know she is. She is too amiable to wish what would make me unhappy, and too judicious to wish to step beyond the sphere of her sex. I will never consent to have our peace disturbed by any such discussions."

"'Consent'—you? it is not consent from you that is in question, it is assent from your wife."

"Am not I the head of my house?"

"You are not the head of your wife. God has given her a mind of her own."

"I am the head and she the heart."

"God grant you play true to one another then. If the head represses no natural pulse of the heart, there can be no question as to your giving your consent. Both will be of one accord, and there needs but to present any question to get a full and true answer. There is no need of precaution, of indulgence, or consent. But our doubt is whether the heart consents with the head, or only acquiesces in its decree; and it is to ascertain the truth on this point, that we propose some liberating measures."

Thus vaguely are these questions proposed and discussed at present. But their being proposed at all implies much thought, and suggests more. Many women are considering within themselves what they need that they have not, and what they can have, if they find they need it. Many men are considering whether women are capable of being and having more than they are and have, and whether, if they are, it will be best to consent to improvement in their condition.

The numerous party, whose opinions are already labelled and adjusted too much to their mind to admit of any new light, strive, by lectures on some model-woman of bridal-like beauty and gentleness, by writing or lending little treatises, to mark out with due precision the limits of woman's sphere, and woman's mission, and to prevent other than the rightful shepherd from climbing the wall, or the flock from using any chance gap to run astray.

Without enrolling ourselves at once on either side, let us look upon the subject from that point of view which to-day offers. No better, it is to be feared, than a high house-top. A high hill-top, or at least a cathedral spire, would be desirable.

It is not surprising that it should be the Anti-Slavery party that pleads for woman, when we consider merely that she does not hold property on equal terms with men; so that, if a husband dies without a will, the wife, instead of stepping at once into his place as head of the family, inherits only a part of his fortune, as if she were a child, or ward only, not an equal partner.

We will not speak of the innumerable instances, in which profligate or idle men live upon the earnings of industrious wives; or if the wives leave them and take with them the children, to perform the double duty of mother and father, follow from place to place, and threaten to rob them of the children, if deprived of the rights of a husband, as they call them, planting themselves in their poor lodgings, frightening them into paying tribute by taking from them the children, running into debt at the expense of these otherwise so overtasked helots. Though such instances abound, the public opinion of his own sex is against the man, and when cases of extreme tyranny are made known, there is private action in the wife's favor. But if woman be, indeed, the weaker party, she ought to have legal protection, which would make such oppression impossible.

And knowing that there exists, in the world of men, a tone of feeling towards women as towards slaves, such as is expressed in the common phrase, "Tell that to women and children;" that the infinite soul can only work through them in already ascertained limits; that the prerogative of reason, man's highest portion, is allotted to them in a much lower degree; that it is better for them to be engaged in active labor, which is to be furnished and directed by those better able to think, &c. &c.; we need not go further, for who can review the experience of last week, without recalling words which imply, whether in jest or earnest, these views, and views like these? Knowing this, can we wonder that many reformers think that measures are not likely to be taken in behalf of women, unless their wishes could be publicly represented by women?

That can never be necessary, cry the other side. All men are privately influenced by women; each has his wife, sister, or female friends, and is too much biassed by these relations to fail of representing their interests. And if this is not enough, let them propose and enforce their wishes with the pen. The beauty of home would be destroyed, the delicacy of the sex be violated, the dignity of halls of legislation destroyed, by an attempt to introduce them there. Such duties are inconsistent with those of a mother; and then we have ludicrous pictures of ladies in hysterics at the polls, and senate chambers filled with cradles.

But if, in reply, we admit as truth that woman seems destined by nature rather to the inner circle, we much add that the arrangements of civilized life have not been as yet such as to secure it to her. Her circle, if the duller, is not the quieter. If kept from excitement, she is not from drudgery. Not only the Indian carries the burdens of the camp, but the favorites of Louis the Fourteenth accompany him in his journeys, and the washerwoman stands at her tub and carries home her work at all seasons, and in all states of health.

As to the use of the pen, there was quite as much opposition to woman's possessing herself of that help to free-agency as there is now to her seizing on the rostrum or the desk; and she is likely to draw, from a permission to plead her cause that way, opposite inferences to what might be wished by those who now grant it.

As to the possibility of her filling, with grace and dignity, any such position, we should think those who had seen the great actresses, and heard the Quarker preachers of modern times, would not doubt, that woman can express publicly the fulness of thought and emotion, without losing any of the peculiar beauty of her sex.

As to her home, she is not likely to leave it more than she now does for balls, theatres, meetings for promoting missions, revival meetings, and others to which she flies, in hope of an animation for her existence, commensurate with what she sees enjoyed by men. Governors of Ladies' Fairs are no less engrossed by such a charge, than the Governor of the State by his; presidents of Washingtonian societies, no less away from home than presidents of conventions. If men look straitly to it, they will find that, unless their own lives are domestic, those of the women will not be. The female Greek, of our day, is as much in the street as the male, to cry, What news? We doubt not it was the same in Athens of old. The women, shut out from the market-place, made up for it at the religious festivals. For human beings are not so constituted, that they can live without expansion; and if they do not get it one way, must another, or perish.

And, as to men's representing women fairly, at present, while we hear from men who owe to their wives not only all that is comfortable and graceful, but all that is wise in the arrangement of their lives, the frequent remark, "You cannot reason with a woman," when from those of delicacy, nobleness, and poetic culture, the contemp-tuous phrase, "Women and children," and that in no light sally of the hour, but in works intended to give a permanent statement of the best experiences, when not one man in the million, shall I say, no, not in the hundred million, can rise above the view that woman was made *for man,* when such traits as these are daily forced upon the attention, can we feel that man will always do justice to the interests of woman? Can we think that he takes a sufficiently discerning and religious view of her office and destiny, ever to do her justice, except when prompted by sentiment; accidentally or transiently, that is, for his sentiment will vary according to the relations in which he is placed. The lover, the poet, the artist, are likely to view her nobly. The father and the philosopher have some chance of liberality; the man of the world, the legislator for expediency, none.

Under these circumstances, without attaching importance in themselves to the changes demanded by the champions of woman, we hail them as signs of the times. We would have every arbitrary barrier thrown down. We would have every path laid open to woman as freely as to man. Were this done, and a slight temporary fermen-tation allowed to subside, we believe that the Divine would ascend into nature to a height unknown in the history of past ages, and nature, thus instructed, would regulate the spheres not only so as to avoid collision, but to bring forth ravishing harmony.

Yet then, and only then, will human beings be ripe for this, when inward and outward freedom for woman, as much as for man, shall be acknowledged as a right, not yielded as a concession. As the friend of the negro assumes that one man cannot, by right, hold another in bondage, so should the friend of woman assume that man cannot, by right, lay even well-meant restrictions on woman. If the negro be a soul, if the woman be a soul, apparelled in flesh, to one master only are they accountable. There is but one law for all souls, and, if there is to be an interpreter of it, he comes not as man, or son of man, but as Son of God.

Were thought and feeling once so far elevated that man should esteem himself the brother and friend, but nowise the lord and tutor of woman, were he really bound with her in equal worship, arrangements as to function and employment would be of no consequence. What woman needs is not as a woman to act or rule, but as a nature to grow, as an intellect to discern, as a soul to live freely, and unimpeded to unfold such powers as were given her when we left our common home. If fewer talents were given her, yet, if allowed the free and full employment of these, so that she may render back to the giver his own with usury, she will not complain, nay, I dare to say she will bless and rejoice in her earthly birth-place, her earthly lot.

Let us consider what obstructions impede this good era, and what signs give rea-son to hope that it draws near.

I was talking on this subject with Miranda, a woman, who, if any in the world, might speak without heat or bitterness of the position of her sex. Her father was a man who cherished no sentimental reverence for woman, but a firm belief in the equality of the sexes. She was his eldest child, and came to him at an age when he needed a companion. From the time she could speak and go alone, he addressed her not as a plaything, but as a living mind. Among the few verses he ever wrote were a copy addressed to this child, when the first locks were cut from her head, and the reverence expressed on this occasion for that cherished head he never belied. It was to him the temple of immortal intellect. He respected his child, however, too much to be an indulgent parent. He called on her for clear judgment, for courage, for honor and fidelity, in short for such virtues as he knew. In so far as he possessed the keys to the wonders of this universe, he allowed free use of them to her, and by the incentive of a high expectation he forbade, as far as possible, that she should let the privilege lie idle.

Thus this child was early led to feel herself a child of the spirit. She took her place easily, not only in the world of organized being, but in the world of mind. A dignified sense of self dependence was given as all her portion, and she found it a sure anchor. Herself securely anchored, her relations with others were established with equal security. She was fortunate, in a total absence of those charms which might have drawn to her bewildering flatteries, and of a strong electric nature, which repelled those who did not belong to her, and attracted those who did. With men and women her relations were noble; affectionate without passion, intellectual without coldness. The world was free to her, and she lived freely in it. Outward adversity came, and inward conflict, but that faith and self-respect had early been awakened, which must always lead at last to an outward serenity, and an inward peace.

Of Miranda I had always thought as an example, that the restraints upon the sex were insuperable only to those who think them so, or who noisily strive to break them. She had taken a course of her own, and no man stood in her way. Many of her acts had been unusual, but excited no uproar. Few helped, but none checked her; and the many men, who knew her mind and her life, showed to her confidence as to a brother, gentleness as to a sister. And not only refined, but very coarse men approved one in whom they saw resolution and clearness of design. Her mind was often the leading one, always effective.

When I talked with her upon these matters, and had said very much what I have written, she smilingly replied, And yet we must admit that I have been fortunate, and this should not be. My good father's early trust gave the first bias, and the rest followed of course. It is true that I have had less outward aid, in after years, than most women, but that is of little consequence. Religion was early awakened in my soul, a sense that what the soul is capable to ask it must attain, and that, though I might be aided by others, I must depend on myself as the only constant friend. This self-dependence, which was honored in me, is deprecated as a fault in most women. They are taught to learn their rule from without, not to unfold it from within.

This is the fault of man, who is still vain, and wishes to be more important to woman than by right he should be.

Men have not shown this disposition towards you, I said.

No, because the position I early was enabled to take, was one of self-reliance. And were all women as sure of their wants as I was, the result would be the same. The difficulty is to get them to the point where they shall naturally develop self-respect, the question how it is to be done.

Once I thought that men would help on this stage of things more than I do now. I saw so many of them wretched in the connections they had formed in weakness and vanity. They seemed so glad to esteem women whenever they could!

But early I perceived that men never, in any extreme of despair, wished to be women. Where they admired any woman they were inclined to speak of her as above her sex. Silently I observed this, and feared it argued a rooted skepticism, which for ages had been fastening on the heart, and which only an age of miracles could eradicate.

Ever I have been treated with great sincerity; and I look upon it as a most signal instance of this, that an intimate friend of the other sex said in a fervent moment, that I deserved in some star to be a man. Another used as highest praise, in speaking of a character in literature, the words "a manly woman."

It is well known that of every strong woman they say she has a masculine mind.

This by no means argues a willing want of generosity towards woman. Man is as generous towards her, as he knows how to be.

Whenever she has herself arisen in national or private history, and nobly shone forth in any ideal of excellence, men have received her, not only willingly, but with triumph. Their encomiums indeed are always in some sense mortifying, they show too much surprise.

In every-day life the feelings of the many are stained with vanity. Each wishes to be lord in a little world, to be superior at least over one; and he does not feel strong enough to retain a life-long ascendant over a strong nature. Only a Brutus would rejoice in a Portia. Only Theseus could conquer before he wed the Amazonian Queen. Hercules wished rather to rest from his labors with Dejanira, and received the poisoned robe, as a fit guerdon. The tale should be interpreted to all those who seek repose with the weak.

But not only is man vain and fond of power, but the same want of development, which thus affects him morally in the intellect, prevents his discerning the destiny of woman. The boy wants no woman, but only a girl to play ball with him, and mark his pocket handkerchief.

. . . . . .

The sexes should not only correspond to and appreciate one another, but prophesy to one another. In individual instances this happens. Two persons love in one another the future good which they aid one another to unfold. This is very imperfectly done as yet in the general life. Man has gone but little way, now he is waiting to see whether woman can keep step with him, but instead of calling out like a good brother; You can do it if you only think so, or impersonally; Any one can do what he tries to do, he often discourages with school-boy brag; Girls cant do that, girls cant play ball. But let any one defy their taunts, break through, and be brave and secure, they rend the air with shouts.

No! man is not willingly ungenerous. He wants faith and love, because he is not yet himself an elevated being. He cries with sneering skepticism; Give us a sign. But if the sign appears, his eyes glisten, and he offers not merely approval, but homage.

. . . . . .

We will not speak of the enthusiasm excited by actresses, improvisatrici, female singers, for here mingles the charm of beauty and grace, but female authors, even learned women, if not insufferably ugly and slovenly, from the Italian professor's daughter, who taught behind the curtain, down to Mrs. Carter and Madame Dacier, are sure of an admiring audience, if they can once get a platform on which to stand.

But how to get this platform, or how to make it of reasonably easy access is the difficulty. Plants of great vigor will almost always struggle into blossom, despite impediments. But there should be encouragement, and a free, genial atmosphere for those of more timid sort, fair play for each in its own kind. Some are like the little, delicate flowers, which love to hide in the dripping mosses by the sides of mountain torrents, or in the shade of tall trees. But others require an open field, a rich and loosened soil, or they never show their proper hues.

It may be said man does not have his fair play either; his energies are repressed and distorted by the interposition of artifical obstacles. Aye, but he himself has put them there; they have grown out of his own imperfections. If there *is* a misfortune in woman's lot, it is in obstacles being interposed by men, which do *not* mark her state, and if they express her past ignorance, do not her present needs. As every man is of woman born, she has slow but sure means of redress, yet the sooner a general justness of thought makes smooth the path, the better.

Man is of woman born, and her face bends over him in infancy with an expression he can never quite forget. Eminent men have delighted to pay tribute to this image, and it is a hacknied observation, that most men of genius boast some remarkable development in the mother. The rudest tar brushes off a tear with his coat-sleeve at the hallowed name. The other day I met a decrepit old man of seventy, on a journey, who challenged the stage-company to guess where he was going. They guessed aright, "To see your mother." "Yes," said he, "she is ninety-two, but has good eye-sight still, they say. I've not seen her these forty years, and I thought I could not die in peace without." I should have liked his picture painted as a companion piece to that of a boisterous little boy, whom I saw attempt to declaim at a school exhibition.

> "O that those lips had language! Life has passed
> With me but roughly since I heard thee last."

He got but very little way before sudden tears shamed him from the stage.

. . . . . .

. . . [T]he idea of woman has not failed to be often and forcibly represented. So many instances throng on the mind. . . .

Neither can she complain that she has not had her share of power. This, in all ranks of society, except the lowest, has been hers to the extent that vanity could crave, far beyond what wisdom would accept. In the very lowest, where man, pressed by poverty, sees in woman only the partner of toils and cares, and cannot hope, scarcely has an idea of a comfortable home, he maltreats her, often, and is less influenced by her. In all ranks, those who are amiable and uncomplaining, suffer much. They suffer long, and are kind; verily, they have their reward. But wherever man is sufficiently raised above extreme poverty, or brutal stupidity, to care for the comforts of the fireside, or the bloom and ornament of life, woman has always power enough, if she choose to exert it, and is usually disposed to do so in proportion to her ignorance and childish vanity. Unacquainted with the importance of life and its purposes, trained to a selfish coquetry and love of petty power, she does not look beyond the pleasure of making herself felt at the moment, and governments are shaken and commerce broken up to gratify the pique of a female favorite. The English shopkeeper's wife does not vote, but it is for her interest that the politician canvasses by the coarsest flattery. France suffers no woman on her throne, but her proud nobles kiss the dust at the feet of Pompadour and Dubarry, for such flare in the lighted foreground where a Roland would modestly aid in the closet. Spain shuts up her women in the care of duennas, and allows them no book but the Breviary; but the ruin follows only the more surely from the worthless favorite of a worthless queen.

It is not the transient breath of poetic incense, that women want; each can receive that from a lover. It is not life-long sway; it needs but to become a coquette, a shrew, or a good cook, to be sure of that. It is not money, nor notoriety, nor the badges of authority, that men have appropriated to themselves. If demands made in their behalf lay stress on any of these particulars, those who make them have not searched deeply into the need. It is for that which at once includes all these and precludes them; which would not be forbidden power, lest there be temptation to steal and misuse it; which would not have the mind perverted by flattery from a worthiness of esteem. It is for that which is the birthright of every being capable to receive it,—the freedom, the religious, the intelligent freedom of the universe, to use its means, to learn its secret as far as nature has enabled them, with God alone for their guide and their judge.

Ye cannot believe it, men; but the only reason why women ever assume what is more appropriate to you, is because you prevent them from finding out what is fit for themselves. Were they free, were they wise fully to develop the strength and beauty of woman, they would never wish to be men, or manlike. The well-instructed moon flies not from her orbit to seize on the glories of her partner. No; for she knows that the one law rules, one heaven contains, one universe replies to them alike. It is with women as with the slave.

> "Vor dem Sklaven, wenn er die Kette bricht,
> Vor dem freien Menschen erzittert nicht."

Tremble not before the free man, but before the slave who has chains
to break.

In slavery, acknowledged slavery, women are on a par with men. Each is a work-tool, an article of property,—no more! In perfect freedom, such as is painted in Olympus, in Swedenborg's angelic state, in the heaven where there is no marrying nor giving in marriage, each is a purified intelligence, an enfranchised soul,—no less!

. . . . . .

Where the thought of equality has become pervasive, it shows itself in four kinds.
The household partnership. In our country the woman looks for a "smart but kind" husband, the man for a "capable, sweet-tempered" wife.
The man furnishes the house, the woman regulates it. Their relation is one of mutual esteem, mutual dependence. Their talk is of business, their affection shows itself by practical kindness. They know that life goes more smoothly and cheerfully to

each for the other's aid; they are grateful and content. The wife praises her husband as a "good provider," the husband in return compliments her as a "capital house-keeper." This relation is good as far as it goes.

Next comes a closer tie which takes the two forms, either of intellectual compan-ionship, or mutual idolatry. The last, we suppose, is to no one a pleasing subject of contemplation. The parties weaken and narrow one another; they lock the gate against all the glories of the universe that they may live in a cell together. To themselves they seem the only wise, to all others steeped in infatuation, the gods smile as they look forward to the crisis of cure, to men the woman seems an unlovely syren, to women the man an effeminate boy.

The other form, of intellectual companionship, has become more and more fre-quent. Men engaged in public life, literary men, and artists have often found in their wives companions and confidants in thought no less than in feeling. And, as in the course of things the intellectual development of woman has spread wider and risen higher, they have, not unfrequently, shared the same employment. As in the case of Roland and his wife, who were friends in the household and the nation's councils, read together, regulated home affairs, or prepared public documents together indifferently.

. . . . . .

I have not spoken of the higher grade of marriage union, the religious, which may be expressed as pilgrimage towards a common shrine. This includes the others; home sympathies, and household wisdom, for these pilgrims must know how to assist one another to carry their burdens along the dusty way; intellectual communion, for how sad it would be on such a journey to have a companion to whom you could not com-municate thoughts and aspirations, as they sprang to life, who would have no feeling for the more and more glorious prospects that open as we advance, who would never see the flowers that may be gathered by the most industrious traveller. It must include all these.

. . . . . .

We cannot wonder at the aversion with which old bachelors and old maids have been regarded. Marriage is the natural means of forming a sphere, of taking root on the earth: it requires more strength to do this without such an opening, very many have failed of this, and their imperfections have been in every one's way. They have been more partial, more harsh, more officious and impertinent than others. Those, who have a complete experience of the human instincts, have a distrust as to whether they can be thoroughly human and humane, such as is hinted at in the saying, "Old maids' and bachelors' children are well cared for," which derides at once their igno-rance and their presumption.

Yet the business of society has become so complex, that it could now scarcely be carried on without the presence of these despised auxiliaries, and detachments from the army of aunts and uncles are wanted to stop gaps in every hedge. They rove about, mental and moral Ishmaelites, pitching their tents amid the fixed and ornamented hab-itations of men.

They thus gain a wider, if not so deep, experience. They are not so intimate with others, but thrown more upon themselves, and if they do not there find peace and incessant life, there is none to flatter them that they are not very poor and very mean.

A position, which so constantly admonishes, may be of inestimable benefit. The person may gain, undistracted by other relationships, a closer communion with the One. Such a use is made of it by saints and sibyls. Or she may be one of the lay sisters of charity, or more humbly only the useful drudge of all men, or the intellectual interpreter of the varied life she sees.

Or she may combine all these. Not "needing to care that she may please a husband," a frail and limited being, all her thoughts may turn to the centre, and by steadfast contemplation enter into the secret of truth and love, use it for the use of all men, instead of a chosen few, and interpret through it all the forms of life.

Saints and geniuses have often chosen a lonely position, in the faith that, if undisturbed by the pressure of near ties they could give themselves up to the inspiring spirit, it would enable them to understand and reproduce life better than actual experience could.

How many old maids take this high stand, we cannot say; it is an unhappy fact that too many of those who come before the eye are gossips rather, and not always good-natured gossips. But, if these abuse, and none make the best of their vocation, yet, it has not failed to produce some good fruit. It has been seen by others, if not by themselves, that beings likely to be left alone need to be fortified and furnished within themselves, and education and thought have tended more and more to regard beings as related to absolute Being, as well as to other men. It has been seen that as the loss of no bond ought to destroy a human being, so ought the missing of none to hinder him from growing. And thus a circumstance of the time has helped to put woman on the true platform. Perhaps the next generation will look deeper into this matter, and find that contempt is put on old maids, or old women at all, merely because they do not use the elixir which will keep the soul always young. No one thinks of Michael Angelo's Persian Sibyl, or St. Theresa, or Tasso's Leonora, or the Greek Electra as an old maid, though all had reached the period in life's course appointed to take that degree.

· · · · · ·

Women are indeed the easy victims of priestcraft, or self-delusion, but this might not be, if the intellect was developed in proportion to the other powers. They would then have a regulator and be in better equipoise, yet must retain the same nervous susceptibility, while their physical structure is such as it is.

It is with just that hope, that we welcome everything that tends to strengthen the fibre and develop the nature on more sides. When the intellect and affections are in harmony, when intellectual consciousness is calm and deep, inspiration will not be confounded with fancy.

The electrical, the magnetic element in woman has not been fairly developed at any period. Everything might be expected from it; she has far more of it than man. This is commonly expressed by saying, that her intuitions are more rapid and more correct.

· · · · · ·

The especial genius of woman I believe to be electrical in movement, intuitive in function, spiritual in tendency. She is great not so easily in classification, or recreation, as in an instinctive seizure of causes, and a simple breathing out of what she receives that has the singleness of life, rather than the selecting or energizing of art.

More native to her is it to be the living model of the artist, than to set apart from herself any one form in objective reality; more native to inspire and receive the poem than to create it. In so far as soul is in her completely developed, all soul is the same; but as far as it is modified in her as woman, it flows, it breathes, it sings, rather than deposits soil, or finishes work, and that which is especially feminine flushes in blossom the face of earth, and pervades like air and water all this seeming solid globe, daily renewing and purifying its life. Such may be the especially feminine element, spoken as of Femality. But it is no more the order of nature that it should be incarnated pure in any form, than that the masculine energy should exist unmingled with it in any form.

Male and female represent the two sides of the great radical dualism. But, in fact, they are perpetually passing into one another. Fluid hardens to solid, solid rushes to fluid. There is no wholly masculine man, no purely feminine woman.

History jeers at the attempts of physiologists to bind great original laws by the forms which flow from them. They make a rule; they say from observation, what can and cannot be. In vain! Nature provides exceptions to every rule. She sends women to battle, and sets Hercules spinning; she enables women to bear immense burdens, cold, and frost; she enables the man, who feels maternal love, to nourish his infant like a mother. Of late she plays still gayer pranks. Not only she deprives organizations, but organs, of a necessary end. She enables people to read with the top of the head, and see with the pit of the stomach. Presently she will make a female Newton, and a male Syren.

Man partakes of the feminine in the Apollo, woman of the masculine as Minerva.

Let us be wise and not impede the soul. Let her work as she will. Let us have one creative energy, one incessant revelation. Let it take what form it will, and let us not bind it by the past to man or woman, black or white. Jove sprang from Rhea, Pallas from Jove. So let it be.

If it has been the tendency of the past remarks to call woman rather to the Minerva side,—if I, unlike the more generous writer, have spoken from society no less than the soul,—let it be pardoned. It is love that has caused this, love for many incarcerated souls, that might be freed could the idea of religious self-dependence be established in them, could the weakening habit of dependence on others be broken up.

Every relation, every gradation of nature, is incalculably precious, but only to the soul which is poised upon itself, and to whom no loss, no change, can bring dull discord, for it is in harmony with the central soul.

If any individual live too much in relations, so that he becomes a stranger to the resources of his own nature, he falls after a while into a distraction, or imbecility, from which he can only be cured by a time of isolation, which gives the renovating fountains time to rise up. With a society it is the same. Many minds, deprived of the traditionary or instinctive means of passing a cheerful existence, must find help in self-impulse or perish. It is therefore that while any elevation, in the view of union, is to be hailed with joy, we shall not decline celibacy as the great fact of the time. It is one from which no vow, no arrangement, can at present save a thinking mind. For now the rowers are pausing on their oars, they wait a change before they can pull together. All tends to illustrate the thought of a wise contemporary. Union is only possible to those who are units. To be fit for relations in time, souls, whether of man or woman, must be able to do without them in the spirit.

It is therefore that I would have woman lay aside all thought, such as she habitually cherishes, of being taught and led by men. I would have her, like the Indian girl, dedicate herself to the Sun, the Sun of Truth, and go no where if his beams did not make clear the path. I would have her free from compromise, from complaisance, from helplessness, because I would have her good enough and strong enough to love one and all beings, from the fulness, not the poverty of being.

Men, as at present instructed, will not help this work, because they also are under the slavery of habit. I have seen with delight their poetic impulses. A sister is the fairest ideal, and how nobly Wordsworth, and even Byron, have written of a sister.

There is no sweeter sight than to see a father with his little daughter. Very vulgar men become refined to the eye when leading a little girl by the hand. At that moment the right relation between the sexes seems established, and you feel as if the man would aid in the noblest purpose, if you ask him in behalf of his little daughter. Once two fine figures stood before me, thus. The father of very intellectual aspect, his falcon eye softened by affection as he looked down on his fair child, she the image of himself, only more graceful and brilliant in expression. I was reminded of Southey's Kehama, when lo, the dream was rudely broken. They were talking of education, and he said,

"I shall not have Maria brought too forward. If she knows too much, she will never find a husband; superior women hardly ever can."

"Surely," said his wife, with a blush, "you wish Maria to be as good and wise as she can, whether it will help her to marriage or not."

"No," he persisted, "I want her to have a sphere and a home, and some one to protect her when I am gone."

It was a trifling incident, but made a deep impression. I felt that the holiest relations fail to instruct the unprepared and perverted mind. If this man, indeed, would have looked at it on the other side, he was the last that would have been willing to have been taken himself for the home and protection he could give, but would have been much more likely to repeat the tale of Alcibiades with his phials.

But men do *not* look at both sides, and women must leave off asking them and being influenced by them, but retire within themselves, and explore the groundwork of being till they find their peculiar secret. Then when they come forth again, renovated and baptized, they will know how to turn all dross to gold, and will be rich and free though they live in a hut, tranquil, if in a crowd. Then their sweet singing shall not be from passionate impulse, but the lyrical overflow of a divine rapture, and a new music shall be elucidated from this many-chorded world.

Grant her then for a while the armor and the javelin. Let her put from her the press of other minds and meditate in virgin loneliness. The same idea shall reappear in due time as Muse, or Ceres, the all-kindly, patient Earth-Spirit.

I tire every one with my Goethean illustrations. But it cannot be helped.

Goethe, the great mind which gave itself absolutely to the leadings of truth, and let rise through him the waves which are still advancing through the century, was its intellectual prophet. Those who know him, see, daily, his thought fulfilled more and more, and they must speak of it, till his name weary and even nauseate, as all great names have in their time. And I cannot spare the reader, if such there be, his wonderful sight as to the prospects and wants of women.

As his Wilhelm grows in life and advances in wisdom, he becomes acquainted with women of more and more character, rising from Mariana to Macária.

Macaria, bound with the heavenly bodies in fixed revolutions, the centre of all relations, herself unrelated, expresses the Minerva side.

Mignon, the electrical, inspired lyrical nature.

All these women, though we see them in relations, we can think of as unrelated. They all are very individual, yet seem nowhere restrained. They satisfy for the present, yet arouse an infinite expectation.

The economist Theresa, the benevolent Natalia, the fair Saint, have chosen a path, but their thoughts are not narrowed to it. The functions of life to them are not ends, but suggestions.

Thus to them all things are important, because none is necessary. Their different characters have fair play, and each is beautiful in its minute indications, for nothing is enforced or conventional, but everything, however slight, grows from the essential life of the being.

Mignon and Theresa wear male attire when they like, and it is graceful for them to do so, while Macaria is confined to her arm chair behind the green curtain, and the Fair Saint could not bear a speck of dust on her robe.

All things are in their places in this little world because all is natural and free, just as "there is room for everything out of doors." Yet all is rounded in by natural harmony which will always arise where Truth and Love are sought in the light of freedom.

Goethe's book bodes an era of freedom like its own, of "extraordinary generous seeking," and new revelations. New individualities shall be developed in the actual world, which shall advance upon it as gently as the figures come out upon his canvass.

A profound thinker has said "no married woman can represent the female world, for she belongs to her husband. The idea of woman must be represented by a virgin."

But that is the very fault of marriage, and of the present relation between the sexes, that the woman does belong to the man, instead of forming a whole with him. Were it otherwise there would be no such limitation to the thought.

Woman, self-centred, would never be absorbed by any relation; it would be only an experience to her as to man. It is a vulgar error that love, *a* love to woman is her whole existence; she also is born for Truth and Love in their universal energy. Would she but assume her inheritance, Mary would not be the only Virgin Mother. Not Manzoni alone would celebrate in his wife the virgin mind with the maternal wisdom and conjugal affections. The soul is ever young, ever virgin.

And will not she soon appear? The woman who shall vindicate their birthright for all women; who shall teach them what to claim, and how to use what they obtain? Shall not her name be for her era Victoria, for her country and her life Virginia? Yet predictions are rash; she herself must teach us to give her the fitting name.

HENRY DAVID THOREAU

"Resistance to Civil Government"
1849

No American writer is so thoroughly identified with his own acts as Henry David Thoreau (1817–62). A little over a year after the Independence Day of 1845, when Thoreau moved into his hut off Concord's Walden Pond so that he could live simply in order to "live deep and suck out all the marrow of life," he was arrested by the town's sheriff for refusing to pay the poll tax. His reason for refusing was his belief that the money raised by the tax went to a government that supported slavery and was just then prosecuting, in Thoreau's view and that of many Northerners, an imperialistic and slavery-expansionist war with Mexico. But his subsequently published essay justifying his stance was more than an agitational antislavery tract; it was also an imaginative work of political thought that was to inspire reformers as disparate in their causes as Tolstoy, Gandhi, and Martin Luther King. As a theoretical work it can be read on four levels: first, as a rationale for the priority of individual "conscience" over political "expediency"; second, as a cluster of differing governmental models for realizing that priority; third, as an argument for the practical power of symbolic actions of passive resistance in a morally confused democratic society; and finally, as a dramatization of the psychic rewards granted the Transcendentalist thinker willing to convert his revulsion from "a cheap and superficial life" into a struggle against his "underbred" townsmen and that "half-witted . . . timid" entity known to Thoreau as the democratic state. Sherman Paul, *The Shores of America: Thoreau's Inward Exploration* (Urbana, Ill., 1958), and Robert D. Richardson, Jr., *Henry Thoreau: A Life of the Mind* (Berkeley, 1986) are two fine intellectual biographies. For a provocative study that emphasizes the "deeply pessimistic" and "hostile" elements in Thoreau's intellectual makeup, see Richard Bridgman, *Dark Thoreau* (Lincoln, Neb., 1982). Of the many studies of Thoreau's politics, two stand out: William A. Herr, "A More Perfect State: Thoreau's Concept of Civil Government," *Massachusetts Review*, 16 (Summer 1975), 470–87; and Myron Simon, "Thoreau and Anarchism," *Michigan Quarterly Review*, 23 (Summer 1984), 360–84. For an excellent comparison of Thoreau's concept of "exemplary acts" compared with other Transcendentalist ideas of social change, see Taylor Stoehr, *Nay-Saying in Concord: Emerson, Alcott, and Thoreau* (Hamden, Conn., 1979), 13–66.

I heartily accept the motto,—"That government is best which governs least;" and I should like to see it acted up to more rapidly and systematically. Carried out, it finally amounts to this, which also I believe,—"That government is best which governs not at all;" and when men are prepared for it, that will be the kind of government which they will have. Government is at best but an expedient; but most governments are usually, and all governments are sometimes, inexpedient. The objections which have been brought against a standing army, and they are many and weighty, and deserve to prevail, may also at last be brought against a standing government. The standing army is only an arm of the standing government. The government itself, which is only the mode which the people have chosen to execute their will, is equally liable to be abused and perverted before the people can act through it. Witness the present Mexican war, the work of comparatively a few individuals using the standing government as their tool; for, in the outset, the people would not have consented to this measure.

This American government,—what is it but a tradition, though a recent one, endeavoring to transmit itself unimpaired to posterity, but each instant losing some of its integrity? It has not the vitality and force of a single living man; for a single man can bend it to his will. It is a sort of wooden gun to the people themselves; and, if ever they should use it in earnest as a real one against each other, it will surely split. But it is not the less necessary for this; for the people must have some complicated machinery or other, and hear its din, to satisfy that idea of government which they have. Governments show thus how successfully men can be imposed on, even impose on themselves, for their own advantage. It is excellent, we must all allow; yet this government never of itself furthered any enterprise, but by the alacrity with which it got out of its way. *It* does not keep the country free. *It* does not settle the West. *It* does not educate. The character inherent in the Ameican people has done all that has been accomplished; and it would have done somewhat more, if the government had not sometimes got in its way. For government is an expedient by which men would fain succeed in letting one another alone; and, as has been said, when it is most expedient, the governed are most let alone by it. Trade and commerce, if they were not made of India rubber, would never manage to bounce over the obstacles which legislators are continually putting in their way; and, if one were to judge these men wholly by the effects of their actions, and not partly by their intentions, they would deserve to be classed and punished with those mischievous persons who put obstructions on the railroads.

But, to speak practically and as a citizen, unlike those who call themselves no-government men, I ask for, not at once no government, but *at once* a better government. Let every man make known what kind of government would command his respect, and that will be one step toward obtaining it.

After all, the practical reason why, when the power is once in the hands of the people, a majority are permitted, and for a long period continue, to rule, is not because they are most likely to be in the right, nor because this seems fairest to the minority, but because they are physically the strongest. But a government in which the majority rule in all cases cannot be based on justice, even as far as men understand it. Can there not be a government in which majorities do not virtually decide right and wrong, but conscience?—in which majorities decide only those questions to which the rule of

Source: The Writings of Henry D. Thoreau, ed. William L. Howarth et al., *Reform Papers*, ed. Wendell Glick (Princeton: Princeton University Press, 1973), 63–90. Reprinted by permission of Princeton University Press, Copyright © 1973.

expediency is applicable? Must the citizen ever for a moment, or in the least degree, resign his conscience to the legislator? Why has every man a conscience, then? I think that we should be men first, and subjects afterward. It is not desirable to cultivate a respect for the law, so much as for the right. The only obligation which I have a right to assume, is to do at any time what I think right. It is truly enough said, that a corporation has no conscience; but a corporation of conscientious men is a corporation *with* a conscience. Law never made men a whit more just; and, by means of their respect for it, even the well-disposed are daily made the agents of injustice. A common and natural result of an undue respect for law is, that you may see a file of soldiers, colonel, captain, corporal, privates, powder-monkeys and all, marching in admirable order over hill and dale to the wars, against their wills, aye, against their common sense and consciences, which makes it very steep marching indeed, and produces a palpitation of the heart. They have no doubt that it is a damnable business in which they are concerned; they are all peaceably inclined. Now, what are they? Men at all? or small moveable forts and magazines, at the service of some unscrupulous man in power? Visit the Navy Yard, and behold a marine, such a man as an American government can make, or such as it can make a man with its black arts, a mere shadow and reminiscence of humanity, a man laid out alive and standing, and already, as one may say, buried under arms with funeral accompaniments, though it may be

> "Not a drum was heard, not a funeral note,
>   As his corse to the rampart we hurried;
> Not a soldier discharged his farewell shot
>   O'er the grave where our hero we buried."

The mass of men serve the State thus, not as men mainly, but as machines, with their bodies. They are the standing army, and the militia, jailers, constables, *posse comitatus*, &. In most cases there is no free exercise whatever of the judgment or of the moral sense; but they put themselves on a level with wood and earth and stones, and wooden men can perhaps be manufactured that will serve the purpose as well. Such command no more respect than men of straw, or a lump of dirt. They have the same sort of worth only as horses and dogs. Yet such as these even are commonly esteemed good citizens. Others, as most legislators, politicians, lawyers, ministers, and office-holders, serve the State chiefly with their heads; and, as they rarely make any moral distinctions, they are as likely to serve the devil, without intending it, as God. A very few, as heroes, patriots, martyrs, reformers in the great sense, and *men*, serve the State with their consciences also, and so necessarily resist it for the most part; and they are commonly treated by it as enemies. A wise man will only be useful as a man, and will not submit to be "clay," and "stop a hole to keep the wind away," but leave that office to his dust at least:—

> "I am too high-born to be propertied,
>   To be a secondary at control,
> Or useful serving-man and instrument
> To any sovereign state throughout the world."

He who gives himself entirely to his fellow-men appears to them useless and selfish; but he who gives himself partially to them is pronounced a benefactor and philanthropist.

How does it become a man to behave toward this American government to-day?

I answer that he cannot without disgrace be associated with it. I cannot for an instant recognize that political organization as *my* government which is the *slave's* government also.

All men recognize the right of revolution; that is, the right to refuse allegiance to and to resist the government, when its tyranny or its inefficiency are great and unendurable. But almost all say that such is not the case now. But such was the case, they think, in the Revolution of '75. If one were to tell me that this was a bad government because it taxed certain foreign commodities brought to its ports, it is most probable that I should not make an ado about it, for I can do without them: all machines have their friction; and possibly this does enough good to counterbalance the evil. At any rate, it is a great evil to make a stir about it. But when the friction comes to have its machine, and oppression and robbery are organized, I say, let us not have such a machine any longer. In other words, when a sixth of the population of a nation which has undertaken to be the refuge of liberty are slaves, and a whole country is unjustly overrun and conquered by a foreign army, and subjected to military law, I think that it is not too soon for honest men to rebel and revolutionize. What makes this duty the more urgent is the fact, that the country so overrun is not our own, but ours is the invading army.

Paley, a common authority with many on moral questions, in his chapter on the "Duty of Submission to Civil Government," resolves all civil obligation into expediency; and he proceeds to say, "that so long as the interest of the whole society requires it, that is, so long as the established government cannot be resisted or changed without public inconveniency, it is the will of God that the established government be obeyed, and no longer." . . . "This principle being admitted, the justice of every particular case of resistance is reduced to a computation of the quantity of the danger and grievance on the one side, and of the probability and expense of redressing it on the other." Of this, he says, every man shall judge for himself. But Paley appears never to have contemplated those cases to which the rule of expediency does not apply, in which a people, as well as an individual, must do justice, cost what it may. If I have unjustly wrested a plank from a drowning man, I must restore it to him though I drown myself. This, according to Paley, would be inconvenient. But he that would save his life, in such a case, shall lose it. This people must cease to hold slaves, and to make war on Mexico, though it cost them their existence as a people.

In their practice, nations agree with Paley; but does any one think that Massachusetts does exactly what is right at the present crisis?

> "A drab of state, a cloth-o'-silver slut,
> To have her train borne up, and her soul trail in the dirt."

Practically speaking, the opponents to a reform in Massachusetts are not a hundred thousand politicians at the South, but a hundred thousand merchants and farmers here, who are more interested in commerce and agriculture than they are in humanity, and are not prepared to do justice to the slave and to Mexico, *cost what it may.* I quarrel not with far-off foes, but with those who, near at home, co-operate with, and do the bidding of those far away, and without whom the latter would be harmless. We are accustomed to say, that the mass of men are unprepared; but improvement is slow, because the few are not materially wiser or better than the many. It is not so important that many should be as good as you, as that there be some absolute goodness somewhere; for that will leaven the whole lump. There are thousands who are *in opinion* opposed to slavery and to the war, who yet in effect do nothing to put an end to them; who, esteeming themselves children of Washington and Franklin, sit down with their hands in their pockets, and say that they know not what to do, and do nothing; who even postpone the question of freedom to the question of free-trade, and quietly read the prices-current along with the latest advices from Mexico, after dinner, and, it may be, fall asleep over them both. What is the price-current of an honest man and patriot to-day? They hesitate, and they regret, and sometimes they petition; but they do nothing in earnest and with effect. They will wait, well-disposed, for others to remedy the evil, that they may no longer have it to regret. At most, they give only a cheap vote, and a feeble countenance and God-speed, to the right, as it goes by them. There are nine hundred and ninety-nine patrons of virtue to one virtuous man; but it is easier to deal with the real possessor of a thing than with the temporary guardian of it.

All voting is a sort of gaming, like chequers or backgammon, with a slight moral tinge to it, a playing with right and wrong, with moral questions; and betting naturally accompanies it. The character of the voters is not staked. I cast my vote, perchance, as I think right; but I am not vitally concerned that that right should prevail. I am willing to leave it to the majority. Its obligation, therefore, never exceeds that of expediency. Even voting *for the right* is *doing* nothing for it. It is only expressing to men feebly your desire that it should prevail. A wise man will not leave the right to the mercy of chance, nor wish it to prevail through the power of the majority. There is but little virtue in the action of masses of men. When the majority shall at length vote for the abolition of slavery, it will be because they are indifferent to slavery, or because there is but little slavery left to be abolished by their vote. *They* will then be the only slaves. Only *his* vote can hasten the abolition of slavery who asserts his own freedom by his vote.

I hear of a convention to be held at Baltimore, or elsewhere, for the selection of a candidate for the Presidency, made up chiefly of editors, and men who are politicians by profession; but I think, what is it to any independent, intelligent, and respectable man what decision they may come to, shall we not have the advantage of his wisdom and honesty, nevertheless? Can we not count upon some independent votes? Are there not many individuals in the country who do not attend conventions? But no: I find that the respectable man, so called, has immediately drifted from his position, and despairs of his country, when his country has more reason to despair of him. He forthwith adopts one of the candidates thus selected as the only *available* one, thus proving that he is himself *available* for any purposes of the demagogue. His vote is of no more worth than that of any unprincipled foreigner or hireling native, who may have been bought. Oh for a man who is a *man*, and, as my neighbor says, has a bone in his back which you cannot pass your hand through! Our statistics are at fault: the population has been returned too large. How many *men* are there to a square thousand miles in this country? Hardly one. Does not America offer any inducement for men to settle here? The American has dwindled into an Odd Fellow,—one who may be known by the development of his organ of gregariousness, and a manifest lack of intellect and cheerful self-reliance; whose first and chief concern, on coming into the world, is to see that the alms-houses are in good repair; and, before yet he has lawfully donned the virile garb, to collect a fund for the support of the widows and orphans that may be; who, in short, ventures to live only by the aid of the mutual insurance company, which has promised to bury him decently.

It is not a man's duty, as a matter of course, to devote himself to the eradication of any, even the most enormous wrong; he may still properly have other concerns to engage him; but it is his duty, at least, to wash his hands of it, and, if he gives it no thought longer, not to give it practically his support. If I devote myself to other pursuits and contemplations, I must first see, at least, that I do not pursue them sitting upon another man's shoulders. I must get off him first, that he may pursue his contemplations too. See what gross inconsistency is tolerated. I have heard some of my townsmen say, "I should like to have them order me out to help put down an insurrection of the slaves, or to march to Mexico,—see if I would go;" and yet these very men have each, directly by their allegiance, and so indirectly, at least, by their money, furnished a substitute. The soldier is applauded who refuses to serve in an unjust war by those who do not refuse to sustain the unjust government which makes the war; is applauded by those whose own act and authority he disregards and sets at nought; as if the State were penitent to that degree that it hired one to scourge it while it sinned, but not to that degree that it left off sinning for a moment. Thus, under the name of order and civil government, we are all made at last to pay homage to and support our own meanness. After the first blush of sin, comes its indifference; and from immoral it becomes, as it were, *unmoral*, and not quite unnecessary to that life which we have made.

The broadest and most prevalent error requires the most disinterested virtue to sustain it. The slight reproach to which the virtue of patriotism is commonly liable, the noble are most likely to incur. Those who, while they disapprove of the character and measures of a government, yield to it their allegiance and support, are undoubtedly its most conscientious supporters, and so frequently the most serious obstacles to reform. Some are petitioning the State to dissolve the Union, to disregard the requisitions of the President. Why do they not dissolve it themselves,—the union between themselves and the State,—and refuse to pay their quota into its treasury? Do not they stand in the same relation to the State, that the State does to the Union? And have not the same reasons prevented the State from resisting the Union, which have prevented them from resisting the State?

How can a man be satisfied to entertain an opinion merely, and enjoy *it*? Is there any enjoyment in it, if his opinion is that he is aggrieved? If you are cheated out of a single dollar by your neighbor, you do not rest satisfied with knowing that you are cheated, or with saying that you are cheated, or even with petitioning him to pay you your due; but you take effectual steps at once to obtain the full amount, and see that you are never cheated again. Action from principle,—the perception and the performance of right,—changes things and relations; it is essentially revolutionary, and does not consist wholly with any thing which was. It not only divides states and churches, it divides families; aye, it divides the *individual,* separating the diabolical in him from the divine.

Unjust laws exist: shall we be content to obey them, or shall we endeavor to amend them, and obey them until we have succeeded, or shall we transgress them at once? Men generally, under such a government as this, think that they ought to wait until they have persuaded the majority to alter them. They think that, if they should resist, the remedy would be worse than the evil. But it is the fault of the government itself that the remedy *is* worse than the evil. *It* makes it worse. Why is it not more apt to anticipate and provide for reform? Why does it not cherish its wise minority? Why does it cry and resist before it is hurt? Why does it not encourage its citizens to be on the alert to point out its faults, and *do* better than it would have them? Why does it always crucify Christ, and excommunicate Copernicus and Luther, and pronounce Washington and Franklin rebels?

One would think, that a deliberate and practical denial of its authority was the only offence never contemplated by government; else, why has it not assigned its definite, its suitable and proportionate penalty? If a man who has no property refuses but once to earn nine shillings for the State, he is put in prison for a period unlimited by any law that I know, and determined only by the discretion of those who placed him there; but if he should steal ninety times nine shillings from the State, he is soon permitted to go at large again.

If the injustice is part of the necessary friction of the machine of government, let it go, let it go: perchance it will wear smooth,—certainly the machine will wear out. If the injustice has a spring, or a pulley, or a rope, or a crank, exclusively for itself, then perhaps you may consider whether the remedy will not be worse than the evil; but if it is of such a nature that it requires you to be the agent of injustice to another, then, I say, break the law. Let your life be a counter friction to stop the machine. What I have to do is to see, at any rate, that I do not lend myself to the wrong which I condemn.

As for adopting the ways which the State has provided for remedying the evil, I know not of such ways. They take too much time, and a man's life will be gone. I have other affairs to attend to. I came into this world, not chiefly to make this a good place to live in, but to live in it, be it good or bad. A man has not every thing to do, but something; and because he cannot do *every thing,* it is not necessary that he should do *something* wrong. It is not my business to be petitioning the governor or the legislature any more than it is theirs to petition me; and, if they should not hear my petition, what should I do then? But in this case the State has provided no way: its very Constitution is the evil. This may seem to be harsh and stubborn and unconciliatory; but it is to treat with the utmost kindness and consideration the only spirit that can appreciate or deserves it. So is all change for the better, like birth and death which convulse the body.

I do not hestiate to say, that those who call themselves abolitionists should at once effectually withdraw their support, both in person and property, from the government of Massachusetts, and not wait till they constitute a majority of one, before they suffer the right to prevail through them. I think that it is enough if they have God on their side, without waiting for that other one. Moreover, any man more right than his neighbors, constitutes a majority of one already.

I meet this American government, or its representative the State government, directly, and face to face, once a year, no more, in the person of its tax-gatherer; this is the only mode in which a man situated as I am necessarily meets it; and it then says distinctly, Recognize me; and the simplest, the most effectual, and, in the present posture of affairs, the indispensablest mode of treating with it on this head, of expressing your little satisfaction with and love for it, is to deny it then. My civil neighbor, the tax-gatherer, is the very man I have to deal with,—for it is, after all, with men and not with parchment that I quarrel,—and he has voluntarily chosen to be an agent of the government. How shall he ever know well what he is and does as an officer of the government, or as a man, until he is obliged to consider whether he shall treat me, his neighbor, for whom he has respect, as a neighbor and well-disposed man, or as a maniac and disturber of the peace, and see if he can get over this obstruction to his neighborliness without a ruder and more impetuous thought or speech corresponding with his action? I know this well, that if one thousand, if one hundred, if ten men whom I could name,—if ten *honest* men only,—aye, if *one* HONEST man, in this State of Massachusetts, *ceasing to hold slaves,* were actually to withdraw from this copartnership, and be locked up in the county jail therefor, it would be the abolition of slavery in America. For it matters not how small the beginning may seem to be: what is once well done is done for ever. But we love better to talk about it: that we say is our mission. Reform keeps many scores of newspapers in its service, but not one man. If my esteemed neighbor, the State's ambassador, who will devote his days to the settlement of the question of human rights in the Council Chamber, instead of being threatened with the prisons of Carolina, were to sit down the prisoner of Massachusetts, that State which is so anxious to foist the sin of slavery upon her sister,—though at present she can discover only an act of inhospitality to be the ground of a quarrel with her,— the Legislature would not wholly waive the subject the following winter.

Under a government which imprisons any unjustly, the true place for a just man is also a prison. The proper place to-day, the only place which Massachusetts has provided for her freer and less desponding spirits, is in her prisons, to be put out and locked out of the State by her own act, as they have already put themselves out by their principles. It is there that the fugitive slave, and the Mexican prisoner on parole, and the Indian come to plead the wrongs of his race, should find them; on that separate, but more free and honorable ground, where the State places those who are not *with* her but *against* her,—the only house in a slave-state in which a free man can abide with honor. If any think that their influence would be lost there, and their voices no longer afflict the ear of the State, that they would not be as an enemy within its walls, they do not know by how much truth is stronger than error, nor how much more eloquently and effectively he can combat injustice who has experienced a little in his own person. Cast your whole vote, not a strip of paper merely, but your whole influence. A minority is powerless while it conforms to the majority; it is not even a minority then; but it is irresistible when it clogs by its whole weight. If the alternative is to keep all just men in prison, or give up war and slavery, the State will not hesitate which to choose. If a thousand men were not to pay their tax-bills this year, that would not be a violent and bloody measure, as it would be to pay them, and enable the State to commit violence and shed innocent blood. This is, in fact, the definition of a peaceable revolution, if any such is possible. If the tax-gatherer, or any other public officer, asks me, as one has done, "But what shall I do?" my answer is, "If you really wish to do any thing, resign your office." When the subject has refused allegiance, and the officer has resigned his office, then the revolution is accomplished. But even suppose blood should flow. Is there not a sort of blood shed when the conscience is wounded? Through this wound a man's real manhood and immortality flow out, and he bleeds to an everlasting death. I see this blood flowing now.

I have contemplated the imprisonment of the offender, rather than the seizure of his goods,—though both will serve the same purpose,—because they who assert the purest right, and consequently are most dangerous to a corrupt State, commonly have not spent much time in accumulating property. To such the State renders comparatively small service, and a slight tax is wont to appear exorbitant, particularly if they are obliged to earn it by special labor with their hands. If there were one who lived wholly without the use of money, the State itself would hesitate to demand it of him. But the rich man—not to make any invidious comparison—is always sold to the institution which makes him rich. Absolutely speaking, the more money, the less virtue;

for money comes between a man and his objects, and obtains them for him; and it was certainly no great virtue to obtain it. It puts to rest many questions which he would otherwise be taxed to answer; while the only new question which it puts is the hard but superfluous one, how to spend it. Thus his moral ground is taken from under his feet. The opportunities of living are diminished in proportion as what are called the "means" are increased. The best thing a man can do for his culture when he is rich is to endeavour to carry out those schemes which he entertained when he was poor. Christ answered the Herodians according to their condition. "Show me the tribute-money," said he;—and one took a penny out his pocket;—If you use money which has the image of Cæsar on it, and which he has made current and valuable, that is, *if you are men of the State,* and gladly enjoy the advantages of Cæsar's government, then pay him back some of his own when he demands it; "Render therefore to Cæsar that which is Cæsar's, and to God those things which are God's,"—leaving them no wiser than before as to which was which; for they did not wish to know.

When I converse with the freest of my neighbors, I perceive that, whatever they may say about the magnitude and seriousness of the question, and their regard for the public tranquility, the long and the short of the matter is, that they cannot spare the protection of the existing government, and they dread the consequences of disobedience to it to their property and families. For my own part, I should not like to think that I ever rely on the protection of the State. But, if I deny the authority of the State when it presents its tax-bill, it will soon take and waste all my property, and so harass me and my children without end. This is hard. This makes it impossible for a man to live honestly and at the same time comfortably in outward respects. It will not be worth the while to accumulate property; that would be sure to go again. You must hire or squat somewhere, and raise but a small crop, and eat that soon. You must live within yourself, and depend upon yourself, always tucked up and ready for a start, and not have many affairs. A man may grow rich in Turkey even, if he will be in all respects a good subject of the Turkish government. Confucius said,—"If a State is governed by the principles of reason, poverty and misery are subjects of shame; if a State is not governed by the principles of reason, riches and honors are the subjects of shame." No: until I want the protection of Massachusetts to be extended to me in some distant southern port, where my liberty is endangered, or until I am bent solely on building up an estate at home by peaceful enterprise, I can afford to refuse allegiance to Massachusetts, and her right to my property and life. It costs me less in every sense to incur the penalty of disobedience to the State, than it would to obey. I should feel as if I were worth less in that case.

Some years ago, the State met me in behalf of the church, and commanded me to pay a certain sum toward the support of a clergyman whose preaching my father attended, but never I myself. "Pay it," it said, "or be locked up in the jail." I declined to pay. But, unfortunately, another man saw fit to pay it. I did not see why the school-master should be taxed to support the priest, and not the priest the schoolmaster; for I was not the State's schoolmaster, but I supported myself by voluntary subscription. I did not see why the lyceum should not present its tax-bill, and have the State to back its demand, as well as the church. However, at the request of the selectmen, I condescended to make some such statement as this in writing:—"Know all men by these presents, that I, Henry Thoreau, do not wish to be regarded as a member of any incorporated society which I have not joined." This I gave to the town-clerk; and he has it. The State, having thus learned that I did not wish to be regarded as a member of that church, has never made a like demand on me since; though it said that it must adhere to its original presumption that time. If I had known how to name them, I should then have signed off in detail from all the societies which I never signed on to; but I did not know where to find a complete list.

I have paid no poll-tax for six years. I was put into a jail once on this account, for one night; and, as I stood considering the walls of solid stone, two or three feet thick, the door of wood and iron, a foot thick, and the iron grating which strained the light, I could not help being struck with the foolishness of that institution which treated me as if I were mere flesh and blood and bones, to be locked up. I wondered that it should have concluded at length that this was the best use it could put me to, and had never thought to avail itself of my services in some way. I saw that, if there was a wall of stone between me and my townsmen, there was a still more difficult one to climb or break through, before they could get to be as free as I was. I did not for a moment feel confined, and the walls seemed a great waste of stone and mortar. I felt as if I alone of all my townsmen had paid my tax. They plainly did not know how to treat me, but behaved like persons who are underbred. In every threat and in every compliment there was a blunder; for they thought that my chief desire was to stand the other side of that stone wall. I could not but smile to see how industriously they locked the door on my meditations, which followed them out again without let or hinderance, and *they* were really all that was dangerous. As they could not reach me, they had resolved to punish my body; just as boys, if they cannot come at some person against whom they have a spite, will abuse his dog. I saw that the State was half-witted, that it was timid as a lone woman with her silver spoons, and that it did not know its friends from its foes, and I lost all my remaining respect for it, and pitied it.

Thus the State never intentionally confronts a man's sense, intellectual or moral, but only his body, his senses. It is not armed with superior wit or honesty, but with superior physical strength. I was not born to be forced. I will breathe after my own fashion. Let us see who is the strongest. What force has a multitude? They only can force me who obey a higher law than I. They force me to become like themselves. I do not hear of *men* being *forced* to live this way or that by masses of men. What sort of life were that to live? When I meet a government which says to me, "Your money or your life," why should I be in haste to give it my money? It may be in a great strait, and not know what to do: I cannot help that. It must help itself; do as I do. It is not worth the while to snivel about it. I am not responsible for the successful working of the machinery of society. I am not the son of the engineer. I perceive that, when an acorn and a chestnut fall side by side, the one does not remain inert to make way for the other, but both obey their own laws, and spring and grow and flourish as best they can, till one, perchance, overshadows and destroys the other. If a plant cannot live according to its nature, it dies; and so a man.

The night in prison was novel and interesting enough. The prisoners in their shirt-sleeves were enjoying a chat and the evening air in the door-way, when I entered. But the jailer said, "Come, boys, it is time to lock up;" and so they dispersed, and I heard the sound of their steps returning into the hollow apartments. My roommate was introduced to me by the jailer, as "a first-rate fellow and a clever man." When the door was locked, he showed me where to hang my hat, and how he managed matters there. The rooms were whitewashed once a month; and this one, at least, was the whitest, most simply furnished, and probably the neatest apartment in the town. He naturally wanted to know where I came from, and what brought me there; and, when I had told him, I asked him in my turn how he came there, presuming him to be an honest man, of course; and, as the world goes, I believe he was. "Why," said he, "they accuse me of burning a barn; but I never did it." As near as I could discover, he had probably gone to bed in a barn when drunk, and smoked his pipe there; and so a barn was burnt. He had the reputation of being a clever man, had been there some three months waiting for his trial to come on, and would have to wait as much longer; but he was quite domesticated and contented, since he got his board for nothing, and thought that he was well treated.

He occupied one window, and I the other; and I saw, that, if one stayed there long, his principal business would be to look out the window. I had soon read all the tracts that were left there, and examined where former prisoners had broken out, and where a grate had been sawed off, and heard the history of the various occupants of that room; for I found that even here there was a history and a gossip which never circulated beyond the walls of the jail. Probably this is the only house in the town where verses are composed, which are afterward printed in a circular form, but not published. I was shown quite a long list of verses which were composed by some young men who had been detected in an attempt to escape, who avenged themselves by singing them.

I pumped my fellow-prisoner as dry as I could, for fear I should never see him again; but at length he showed me which was my bed, and left me to blow out the lamp.

It was like travelling into a far country, such as I had never expected to behold, to lie there for one night. It seemed to me that I never had heard the town-clock strike before, nor the evening sounds of the village; for we slept with the windows open, which were inside the grating. It was to see my native village in the light of the middle ages, and our Concord was turned into a Rhine stream, and visions of knights and castles passed before me. They were the voices of old burghers that I heard in the streets. I was an involuntary spectator and auditor of whatever was done and said in the kitchen of the adjacent village-inn,—a wholly new and rare experience to me. It was a closer view of my native town. I was fairly inside of it. I never had seen its institutions before. This is one of its peculiar institutions; for it is a shire town. I began to comprehend what its inhabitants were about.

In the morning, our breakfasts were put through the hole in the door, in small oblong-square tin pans, made to fit, and holding a pint of chocolate, with brown bread, and an iron spoon. When they called for the vessels again, I was green enough to return what bread I had left; but my comrade seized it, and said that I should lay that up for lunch or dinner. Soon after, he was let out to work at haying in a neighboring field, whither he went every day, and would not be back till noon; so he bade me good-day, saying that he doubted if he should see me again.

When I came out of prison,—for some one interfered, and paid the tax,—I did not perceive that great changes had taken place on the common, such as he observed who went in a youth, and emerged a tottering and gray-headed man; and yet a change had to my eyes come over the scene,—the town, and State, and country,—greater than any that mere time could effect. I saw yet more distinctly the State in which I lived. I saw to what extent the people among whom I lived could be trusted as good neighbors and friends; that their friendship was for summer weather only; that they did not greatly purpose to do right; that they were a distinct race from me by their prejudices and superstitions, as the Chinamen and Malays are; that, in their sacrifices to humanity, they ran no risks, not even to their property; that, after all, they were not so noble but they treated the thief as he had treated them, and hoped, by a certain outward observance and a few prayers, and by walking in a particular straight though useless path from time to time, to save their souls. This may be to judge my neighbors harshly; for I believe that most of them are not aware that they have such an institution as the jail in their village.

It was formerly the custom in our village, when a poor debtor came out of jail, for his acquaintances to salute him, looking through their fingers, which were crossed to represent the grating of a jail window, "How do ye do?" My neighbors did not thus salute me, but first looked at me, and then at one another, as if I had returned from a long journey. I was put into jail as I was going to the shoemaker's to get a shoe which was mended. When I was let out the next morning, I proceeded to finish my errand, and, having put on my mended shoe, joined a huckleberry party, who were impatient to put themselves under my conduct; and in half an hour,—for the horse was soon tackled,—was in the midst of a huckleberry field, on one of our highest hills, two miles off; and then the State was nowhere to be seen.

This is the whole history of "My Prisons."

I have never declined paying the highway tax, because I am as desirous of being a good neighbor as I am of being a bad subject; and, as for supporting schools, I am doing my part to educate my fellow-countrymen now. It is for no particular item in the tax-bill that I refuse to pay it. I simply wish to refuse allegiance to the State, to withdraw and stand aloof from it effectually. I do not care to trace the course of my dollar, if I could, till it buys a man, or a musket to shoot one with,—the dollar is innocent,—but I am concerned to trace the effects of my allegiance. In fact, I quietly declare war with the State, after my fashion, though I will still make what use and get what advantage of her I can, as is usual in such cases.

If others pay the tax which is demanded of me, from a sympathy with the State, they do but what they have already done in their own case, or rather they abet injustice to a greater extent than the State requires. If they pay the tax from a mistaken interest in the individual taxed, to save his property or prevent his going to jail, it is because they have not considered wisely how far they let their private feelings interfere with the public good.

This, then, is my position at present. But one cannot be too much on his guard in such a case, lest his action be biassed by obstinacy, or an undue regard for the opinions of men. Let him see that he does only what belongs to himself and to the hour.

I think sometimes, Why, this people mean well; they are only ignorant; they would do better if they knew how: why give your neighbors this pain to treat you as they are not inclined to? But I think, again, this is no reason why I should do as they do, or permit others to suffer much greater pain of a different kind. Again, I sometimes say to myself, When many millions of men, without heat, without ill-will, without personal feeling of any kind, demand of you a few shillings only, without the possibility, such is their constitution, of retracting or altering their present demand, and without the possibility, on your side, of appeal to any other millions, why expose yourself to this overwhelming brute force? You do not resist cold and hunger, the winds and the waves, thus obstinately; you quietly submit to a thousand similar necessities. You do not put your head into the fire. But just in proportion as I regard this as not wholly a brute force, but partly a human force, and consider that I have relations to those millions as to so many millions of men, and not of mere brute or inanimate things, I see that appeal is possible, first and instantaneously, from them to the Maker of them, and, secondly, from them to themselves. But, if I put my head deliberately into the fire, there is no appeal to fire or to the Maker of fire, and I have only myself to blame. If I could convince myself that I have any right to be satisfied with men as they are, and to treat them accordingly, and not according, in some respects, to my requisitions and expectations of what they and I ought to be, then, like a good Mussulman and fatalist, I should endeavor to be satisfied with things as they are, and say it is the will of God. And, above all, there is this difference between resisting this and a purely brute or natural force, that I can resist this with some effect; but I cannot expect, like Orpheus, to change the nature of the rocks and trees and beasts.

I do not wish to quarrel with any man or nation. I do not wish to split hairs, to make fine distinctions, or set myself up as better than my neighbors. I seek rather, I may say, even an excuse for conforming to the laws of the land. I am but too ready to conform to them. Indeed I have reason to suspect myself on this head; and each year, as the tax-gatherer comes round, I find myself disposed to review the acts and position of the general and state governments, and the spirit of the people, to discover a pretext for conformity. I believe that the State will soon be able to take all my work of this sort out of my hands, and then I shall be no better a patriot than my fellow-countrymen. Seen from a lower point of view, the Constitution, with all its faults, is very good; the law and the courts are very respectable; even this State and this American government are, in many respects, very admirable and rare things, to be thankful for, such as a great many have described them; but seen from a point of view a little higher, they are what I have described them; seen from a higher still, and the highest, who shall say what they are, or that they are worth looking at or thinking of at all?

However, the government does not concern me much, and I shall bestow the fewest possible thoughts on it. It is not many moments that I live under a government, even in this world. If a man is thought-free, fancy-free, imagination-free, that which *is not* never for a long time appearing *to be* to him, unwise rulers or reformers cannot fatally interrupt him.

I know that most men think differently from myself; but those whose lives are by profession devoted to the study of these or kindred subjects, content me as little as any. Statesmen and legislators, standing so completely within the institution, never distinctly and nakedly behold it. They speak of moving society, but have no resting-place without it. They may be men of a certain experience and discrimination, and have no doubt invented ingenious and even useful systems, for which we sincerely thank them; but all their wit and usefulness lie within certain not very wide limits. They are wont to forget that the world is not governed by policy and expediency. Webster never goes behind government, and so cannot speak with authority about it. His words are wisdom to those legislators who contemplate no essential reform in the existing government; but for thinkers, and those who legislate for all time, he never once glances at the subject. I know of those whose serene and wise speculations on this theme would soon reveal the limits of his mind's range and hospitality. Yet, compared with the cheap professions of most reformers, and the still cheaper wisdom and eloquence of politicians in general, his are almost the only sensible and valuable words, and we thank Heaven for him. Comparatively, he is always strong, original, and, above all, practical. Still his quality is not wisdom, but prudence. The lawyer's truth is not Truth, but consistency, or a consistent expediency. Truth is always in harmony with herself, and is not concerned chiefly to reveal the justice that may consist with wrong-doing. He well deserves to be called, as he has been called, the Defender of the Constitution. There are really no blows to be given by him but defensive ones. He is not a leader, but a follower. His leaders are the men of '87. "I have never made an effort," he says, "and never propose to make an effort; I have never countenanced an effort, and never mean to countenance an effort, to disturb the arrangement as originally made, by which the various States came into the Union." Still thinking of the sanction which the Constitution gives to slavery, he says, "Because it was a part of the original compact,—let it stand." Notwithstanding his special acuteness and ability, he is unable to take a fact out of its merely political relations, and behold it as it lies absolutely to be disposed of by the intellect,—what, for instance, it behoves a man to do here in America to-day with regard to slavery,—but ventures, or is driven, to make some such desperate answer as the following, while professing to speak absolutely, and as a private man,—from which what new and singular code of social duties might be inferred?—"The manner," says he, "in which the governments of those States where slavery exists are to regulate it, is for their own consideration, under their responsibility to their constituents, to the general laws of propriety, humanity, and justice, and to God. Associations formed elsewhere, springing from a feeling of humanity, or any other cause, have nothing whatever to do with it. They have never received any encouragement from me, and they never will."[1]

They who know of no purer sources of truth, who have traced up its stream no higher, stand, and wisely stand, by the Bible and the Constitution, and drink at it there with reverence and humility; but they who behold where it comes trickling into this lake or that pool, gird up their loins once more, and continue their pilgrimage toward its fountain-head.

No man with a genius for legislation has appeared in America. They are rare in the history of the world. There are orators, politicians, and eloquent men, by the thousand; but the speaker has not yet opened his mouth to speak, who is capable of settling the much-vexed questions of the day. We love eloquence for its own sake, and not for any truth which it may utter, or any heroism it may inspire. Our legislators have not yet learned the comparative value of free-trade and of freedom, of union, and of rectitude, to a nation. They have no genius or talent for comparatively humble questions of taxation and finance, commerce and manufactures and agriculture. If we were left solely to the wordy wit of legislators in Congress for our guidance, uncorrected by the seasonable experience and the effectual complaints of the people, America would not long retain her rank among the nations. For eighteen hundred years, though perchance I have no right to say it, the New Testament has been written; yet where is the legislator who has wisdom and practical talent enough to avail himself of the light which it sheds on the science of legislation?

The authority of government, even such as I am willing to submit to,—for I will cheerfully obey those who know and can do better than I, and in many things even those who neither know nor can do so well,—is still an impure one: to be strictly just, it must have the sanction and consent of the governed. It can have no pure right over my person and property but what I concede to it. The progress from an absolute to a limited monarchy, from a limited monarchy to a democracy, is a progress toward a true respect for the individual. Is a democracy, such as we know it, the last improvement possible in government? Is it not possible to take a step further towards recog-

1. These extracts have been inserted since the Lecture was read. [H.D.T. note].

nizing and organizing the rights of man? There will never be a really free and enlightened State, until the State comes to recognize the individual as a higher and independent power, from which all its own power and authority are derived, and treats him accordingly. I please myself with imagining a State at last which can afford to be just to all men, and to treat the individual with respect as a neighbor; which even would not think it inconsistent with its own repose, if a few were to live aloof from it, not meddling with it, nor embraced by it, who fulfilled all the duties of neighbors and fellow-men. A State which bore this kind of fruit, and suffered it to drop off as fast as it ripened, would prepare the way for a still more perfect and glorious State, which also I have imagined, but not yet anywhere seen.

HERMAN MELVILLE

"Hawthorne and His Mosses"
1850

"I love all men who dive." In announcing this preference Herman Melville (1819–91) could have been holding a mirror up to himself. Certainly no writer in America—indeed in modern literature—has sought to plunge more deeply into the philosophical and psychological depths of human consciousness in his fiction than Melville. The tour de force of this sort of plunging was, of course, *Moby-Dick.* But it was also much in evidence in his extraordinary review of a collection of short stories by Nathaniel Hawthorne (1804–64), whom he had just opportunely met. Hawthorne was then most admired, despite his recently published *Scarlet Letter,* as a writer of brightly idealized tales and genteel sketches. In his review Melville exploded this view, emphasizing instead the "blackness" that he found displayed in Hawthorne's best stories. But the most interesting aspect of this essay was Melville's assimilation of Hawthorne to his powerful, if tension-filled, call for the integration of the romantic intellect with American democratic culture. Thus, through his hot-souled Virginian persona, Melville thundered for the end to "literary flunkeyism towards England" and for a new collective, democratic literature to match America's new and future political greatness. Yet in other places Melville also argued that such a democratic literature, if it was to be truly great, could only be constituted, as Hawthorne's was, by *both* a sensibility of all-embracing "love and humor" and a deep intellectual vision too disturbing and profound to be easily accessible to the multitude. Herein, according to Melville, lay the genius of writers like Shakespeare and now Hawthorne: they contrived genial masks to soothe the complacent and cowardly while flashing forth in "cunning glimpses" the fearful but vital truths that would be "all but madness for any good man, in his own proper character, to utter, or even hint of." With his prescription for genius *and* popularity announced, Melville turned to completing the novel that would prove him right by half. Two recent, contrasting interpretations of Melville's "highbrow" romanticism are Henry Nash Smith, *Democracy and the Novel: Popular Resistance to Classic American Writers* (New York, 1978), 3–15, 35–55; and Michael T. Gilmore, *American Romanticism and the Marketplace* (Chicago, 1985), 52–62, 132–53. The cultural background of Melville's critical outlook are helpfully illuminated in Perry Miller, *The Raven and the Whale: The War of Words and Wits in the Era of Poe and Melville* (New York, 1956); and Thomas Bender, *New York Intellect: A History of Intellectual Life in New York City, from 1750 to the Beginnings of Our Own Time* (New York, 1987), 119–68. Michael Paul Rogin, *Subversive Genealogy: The Politics and Art of Herman Melville* (New York, 1983) is a suggestive psychohistorical study of Melville's cultural and political ideology.

By a Virginian Spending July in Vermont

A papered chamber in a fine old farm-house—a mile from any other dwelling, and dipped to the eaves in foliage—surrounded by mountains, old woods, and Indian ponds,—this, surely, is the place to write of Hawthorne. Some charm is in this northern air, for love and duty seem both impelling to the task. A man of a deep and noble nature has seized me in this seclusion. His wild, witch voice rings through me; or, in softer cadences, I seem to hear it in the songs of the hill-side birds, that sing in the larch trees at my window.

Would that all excellent books were foundlings, without father or mother, that so it might be, we could glorify them, without including their ostensible authors. Nor would any true man take exception to this;—least of all, he who writes,—"When the Artist rises high enough to achieve the Beautiful, the symbol by which he makes it perceptible to mortal senses becomes of little value in his eyes, while his spirit possesses itself in the enjoyment of the reality."

But more than this. I know not what would be the right name to put on the title-page of an excellent book, but this I feel, that the names of all fine authors are fictitious ones, far more so than that of Junius,—simply standing, as they do, for the mystical, ever-eluding Spirit of all Beauty, which ubiquitously possesses men of genius. Purely imaginative as this fancy may appear, it nevertheless seems to receive some warranty from the fact, that on a personal interview no great author has ever come up to the idea of his reader. But that dust of which our bodies are composed, how can it fitly express the nobler intelligences among us? With reverence be it spoken, that not even in the case of one deemed more than man, not even in our Saviour, did his visible frame betoken anything of the augustness of the nature within. Else, how could those Jewish eyewitnesses fail to see heaven in his glance.

It is curious, how a man may travel along a country road, and yet miss the grandest, or sweetest of prospects, by reason of an intervening hedge, so like all other hedges, as in no way to hint of the wide landscape beyond. So has it been with me concerning the enchanting landscape in the soul of this Hawthorne, this most excellent Man of Mosses. His "Old Manse" has been written now four years, but I never read it till a day or two since. I had seen it in the book-stores—heard of it often—even had it recommended to me by a tasteful friend, as a rare, quiet book, perhaps too deserving of popularity to be popular. But there are so many books called "excellent", and so much unpopular merit, that amid the thick stir of other things, the hint of my tasteful friend was disregarded; and for four years the Mosses on the old Manse never refreshed me with their perennial green. It may be, however, that all this while, the book, like wine, was only improving in flavor and body. At any rate, it so chanced that this long procrastination eventuated in a happy result. At breakfast the other day, a mountain girl, a cousin of mine, who for the last two weeks has every morning helped me to strawberries and raspberries,—which, like the roses and pearls in the fairy-tale, seemed to fall into the saucer from those strawberry-beds her cheeks,—this delightful creature, this charming Cherry says to me—"I see you spend your mornings in the hay-mow; and yesterday I found there 'Dwight's Travels in New England'. Now I have

Source: *The Writings of Herman Melville: The Northwestern-Newberry Edition*, ed. Harrison Hayford, Hershel Parker, and G. Thomas Tanselle, vol. 9, *The Piazza Tales and Other Prose Pieces, 1839–1860*, ed. Harrison Hayford et al. (Evanston, Ill.: Northwestern University Press; Chicago: Newberry Library, 1987), 239–53. Reprinted by permission of Northwestern University Press, Copyright © 1987.

something far better than that,—something more congenial to our summer on these hills. Take these raspberries, and then I will give you some moss."—"Moss!" said I.— "Yes, and you must take it to the barn with you, and good-bye to 'Dwight'".

With that she left me, and soon returned with a volume, verdantly bound, and garnished with a curious frontispiece in green,—nothing less, than a fragment of real moss cunningly pressed to a fly-leaf.—"Why this," said I spilling my raspberries, "this is the 'Mosses from an Old Manse'". "Yes" said cousin Cherry "yes, it is that flowery Hawthorne."—"Hawthorne and Mosses" said I "no more: it is morning: it is July in the country: and I am off for the barn".

Stretched on that new mown clover, the hill-side breeze blowing over me through the wide barn door, and soothed by the hum of the bees in the meadows around, how magically stole over me this Mossy Man! and how amply, how bountifully, did he redeem that delicious promise to his guests in the Old Manse, of whom it is written— "Others could give them pleasure, or amusement, or instruction—these could be picked up anywhere—but it was for me to give them rest. Rest, in a life of trouble! What better could be done for weary and world-worn spirits? what better could be done for anybody, who came within our magic circle, than to throw the spell of a magic spirit over him?"—So all that day, half-buried in the new clover, I watched this Hawthorne's "Assyrian dawn, and Paphian sunset and moonrise, from the summit of our Eastern Hill."

The soft ravishments of the man spun me round about in a web of dreams, and when the book was closed, when the spell was over, this wizard "dismissed me with but misty reminiscences, as if I had been dreaming of him".

What a mild moonlight of contemplative humor bathes that Old Manse!—the rich and rare distilment of a spicy and slowly-oozing heart. No rollicking rudeness, no gross fun fed on fat dinners, and bred in the lees of wine,—but a humor so spiritually gentle, so high, so deep, and yet so richly relishable, that it were hardly inappropriate in an angel. It is the very religion of mirth; for nothing so human but it may be advanced to that. The orchard of the Old Manse seems the visible type of the fine mind that has described it. Those twisted, and contorted old trees, "that stretch out their crooked branches, and take such hold of the imagination, that we remember them as humorists, and odd-fellows." And then, as surrounded by these grotesque forms, and hushed in the noon-day repose of this Hawthorne's spell, how aptly might the still fall of his ruddy thoughts into your soul be symbolized by "the thump of a great apple, in the stillest afternoon, falling without a breath of wind, from the mere necessity of perfect ripeness"! For no less ripe than ruddy are the apples of the thoughts and fancies in this sweet Man of Mosses.

"Buds and Bird-voices"—What a delicious thing is that!—"Will the world ever be so decayed, that Spring may not renew its greenness?"—And the "Fire-Worship". Was ever the hearth so glorified into an altar before? The mere title of that piece is better than any common work in fifty folio volumes. How exquisite is this:—"Nor did it lessen the charm of his soft, familiar courtesy and helpfulness, that the mighty spirit, were opportunity offered him, would run riot through the peaceful house, wrap its inmates in his terrible embrace, and leave nothing of them save their whitened bones. This possibility of mad destruction only made his domestic kindness the more beautiful and touching. It was so sweet of him, being endowed with such power, to dwell, day after day, and one long, lonesome night after another, on the dusky hearth, only now and then betraying his wild nature, by thrusting his red tongue out of the chimney-top! True, he had done much mischief in the world, and was pretty certain to do more, but his warm heart atoned for all. He was kindly to the race of man."

But he has still other apples, not quite so ruddy, though full as ripe;—apples, that have been left to wither on the tree, after the pleasant autumn gathering is past. The sketch of "The Old Apple Dealer" is conceived in the subtlest spirit of sadness; he whose "subdued and nerveless boyhood prefigured his abortive prime, which, likewise, contained within itself the prophecy and image of his lean and torpid age". Such touches as are in this piece can not proceed from any common heart. They argue such a depth of tenderness, such a boundless sympathy with all forms of being, such an omnipresent love, that we must needs say, that this Hawthorne is here almost alone in his generation,—at least, in the artistic manifestation of these things. Still more. Such touches as these,—and many, very many similar ones, all through his chapters— furnish clews, whereby we enter a little way into the intricate, profound heart where they originated. And we see, that suffering, some time or other and in some shape or other,—this only can enable any man to depict it in others. All over him, Hawthorne's melancholy rests like an Indian Summer, which though bathing a whole country in one softness, still reveals the distinctive hue of every towering hill, and each far-winding vale.

But it is the least part of genius that attracts admiration. Where Hawthorne is known, he seems to be deemed a pleasant writer, with a pleasant style,—a sequestered, harmless man, from whom any deep and weighty thing would hardly be anticipated:—a man who means no meanings. But there is no man, in whom humor and love, like mountain peaks, soar to such a rapt height, as to receive the irradiations of the upper skies;—there is no man in whom humor and love are developed in that high form called genius; no such man can exist without also possessing, as the indispensable complement of these, a great, deep intellect, which drops down into the universe like a plummet. Or, love and humor are only the eyes, through which such an intellect views this world. The great beauty in such a mind is but the product of its strength. What, to all readers, can be more charming than the piece entitled "Monsieur du Miroir"; and to a reader at all capable of fully fathoming it, what, at the same time, can possess more mystical depth of meaning?—Yes, there he sits, and looks at me,— this "shape of mystery", this "identical Monsieur du Miroir".—Methinks I should tremble now, were his wizard power of gliding through all impediments in search of me, to place him suddenly before my eyes".

How profound, nay appalling, is the moral evolved by the "Earth's Holocaust"; where—beginning with the hollow follies and affectations of the world,—all vanities and empty theories and forms, are, one after another, and by an admirably graduated, growing comprehensiveness, thrown into the allegorical fire, till, at length, nothing is left but the all-engendering heart of man; which remaining still unconsumed, the great conflagration is nought.

Of a piece with this, is the "Intelligence Office", a wondrous symbolizing of the secret workings in men's souls. There are other sketches, still more charged with ponderous import.

"The Christmas Banquet", and "The Bosom Serpent" would be fine subjects for a curious and elaborate analysis, touching the conjectural parts of the mind that produced them. For spite of all the Indian-summer sunlight on the hither side of Hawthorne's soul, the other side—like the dark half of the physical sphere—is shrouded in a blackness, ten times black. But this darkness but gives more effect to the ever-moving dawn, that forever advances through it, and circumnavigates his world. Whether Hawthorne has simply availed himself of this mystical blackness as a means to the wondrous effects he makes it to produce in his lights and shades; or whether there really lurks in him, perhaps unknown to himself, a touch of Puritanic gloom,—this, I cannot altogether tell. Certain it is, however, that this great power of blackness in him derives its force from its appeals to that Calvinistic sense of Innate Depravity and Original Sin, from whose visitations, in some shape or other, no deeply thinking mind is always and wholly free. For, in certain moods, no man can weigh this world, without throwing in something, somehow like Original Sin, to strike the uneven balance. At all events, perhaps no writer has ever wielded this terrific thought with greater terror than this same harmless Hawthorne. Still more: this black conceit pervades him, through and through. You may be witched by his sunlight,—transported by the bright gildings in the skies he builds over you;—but there is the blackness of darkness beyond; and even his bright gildings but fringe, and play upon the edges of thunder-clouds.—In one word, the world is mistaken in this Nathaniel Hawthorne. He himself must often have smiled at its absurd misconception of him. He is immeasurably deeper than the plummet of the mere critic. For it is not the brain that can test such a man; it is only the heart. You cannot come to know greatness by inspecting it; there is no glimpse to be caught of it, except by intuition; you need not ring it, you but touch it, and you find it is gold.

Now it is that blackness in Hawthorne, of which I have spoken, that so fixes and fascinates me. It may be, nevertheless, that it is too largely developed in him. Perhaps he does not give us a ray of his light for every shade of his dark. But however this may be, this blackness it is that furnishes the infinite obscure of his back-ground,—that back-ground, against which Shakespeare plays his grandest conceits, the things that have made for Shakespeare his loftiest, but most circumscribed renown, as the profoundest of thinkers. For by philosophers Shakespeare is not adored as the great man of tragedy and comedy.—"Off with his head! so much for Buckingham!" this sort of rant, interlined by another hand, brings down the house,—those mistaken souls, who dream of Shakespeare as a mere man of Richard-the-Third humps, and Macbeth daggers. But it is those deep far-away things in him; those occasional flashings-forth of the intuitive Truth in him; those short, quick probings at the very axis of reality;—these are the things that make Shakespeare, Shakespeare. Through the mouths of the dark characters of Hamlet, Timon, Lear, and Iago, he craftily says, or sometimes insinuates the things, which we feel to be so terrifically true, that it were all but madness for any good man, in his own proper character, to utter, or even hint of them. Tormented into desperation, Lear the frantic King tears off the mask, and speaks the sane madness of vital truth. But, as I before said, it is the least part of genius that attracts admiration. And so, much of the blind, unbridled admiration that has been heaped upon Shakespeare, has been lavished upon the least part of him. And few of his endless commentators and critics seem to have remembered, or even perceived, that the immediate products of a great mind are not so great, as that undeveloped, (and sometimes undevelopable) yet dimly-discernable greatness, to which these immediate products are but the infallible indices. In Shakespeare's tomb lies infinitely more than Shakespeare ever wrote. And if I magnify Shakespeare, it is not so much for what he did do, as for what he did not do, or refrained from doing. For in this world of lies,

Truth is forced to fly like a scared white doe in the woodlands; and only by cunning glimpses will she reveal herself, as in Shakespeare and other masters of the great Art of Telling the Truth,—even though it be covertly, and by snatches.

But if this view of the all-popular Shakespeare be seldom taken by his readers, and if very few who extol him, have ever read him deeply, or, perhaps, only have seen him on the tricky stage, (which alone made, and is still making him his mere mob renown)—if few men have time, or patience, or palate, for the spiritual truth as it is in that great genius;—it is, then, no matter of surprise that in a contemporaneous age, Nathaniel Hawthorne is a man, as yet, almost utterly mistaken among men. Here and there, in some quiet arm-chair in the noisy town, or some deep nook among the noiseless mountains, he may be appreciated for something of what he is. But unlike Shakespeare, who was forced to the contrary course by circumstances, Hawthorne (either from simple disinclination, or else from inaptitude) refrains from all the popularizing noise and show of broad farce, and blood-besmeared tragedy; content with the still, rich utterances of a great intellect in repose, and which sends few thoughts into circulation, except they be arterialized at his large warm lungs, and expanded in his honest heart.

Nor need you fix upon that blackness in him, if it suit you not. Nor, indeed, will all readers discern it, for it is, mostly, insinuated to those who may best understand it, and account for it; it is not obtruded upon every one alike.

Some may start to read of Shakespeare and Hawthorne on the same page. They may say, that if an illustration were needed, a lesser light might have sufficed to elucidate this Hawthorne, this small man of yesterday. But I am not, willingly, one of those, who, as touching Shakespeare at least, exemplify the maxim of Rochefoucault, that "we exalt the reputation of some, in order to depress that of others";—who, to teach all noble-souled aspirants that there is no hope for them, pronounce Shakespeare absolutely unapproachable. But Shakespeare has been approached. There are minds that have gone as far as Shakespeare into the universe. And hardly a mortal man, who, at some time or other, has not felt as great thoughts in him as any you will find in Hamlet. We must not inferentially malign mankind for the sake of any one man, whoever he may be. This is too cheap a purchase of contentment for conscious mediocrity to make. Besides, this absolute and unconditional adoration of Shakespeare has grown to be a part of our Anglo Saxon superstitions. The Thirty Nine articles are now Forty. Intolerance has come to exist in this matter. You must believe in Shakespeare's unapproachability, or quit the country. But what sort of a belief is this for an American, a man who is bound to carry republican progressiveness into Literature, as well as into Life? Believe me, my friends, that Shakespeares are this day being born on the banks of the Ohio. And the day will come, when you shall say who reads a book by an Englishman that is a modern? The great mistake seems to be, that even with those Americans who look forward to the coming of a great literary genius among us, they somehow fancy he will come in the costume of Queen Elizabeth's day,—be a writer of dramas founded upon old English history, or the tales of Boccaccio. Whereas, great geniuses are parts of the times; they themselves are the times; and possess a correspondent coloring. It is of a piece with the Jews, who while their Shiloh was meekly walking in their streets, were still praying for his magnificent coming; looking for him in a chariot, who was already among them on an ass. Nor must we forget, that, in his own life-time, Shakespeare was not Shakespeare, but only Master William Shakespeare of the shrewd, thriving, business firm of Condell, Shakespeare & Co., proprietors of the Globe Theatre in London; and by a courtly author, of the name of Greene, was hooted at, as an "upstart crow" beautified "with other birds' feathers". For, mark it well, imitation is often the first charge brought against real originality. Why this is so, there is not space to set forth here. You must have plenty of sea-room to tell the Truth in; especially, when it seems to have an aspect of newness, as America did in 1492, though it was then just as old, and perhaps older than Asia, only those sagacious philosophers, the common sailors, had never seen it before; swearing it was all water and moonshine there.

Now, I do not say that Nathaniel of Salem is a greater than William of Avon, or as great. But the difference between the two men is by no means immeasurable. Not a very great deal more, and Nathaniel were verily William.

This, too, I mean, that if Shakespeare has not been equalled, he is sure to be surpassed, and surpassed by an American born now or yet to be born. For it will never do for us who in most other things out-do as well as out-brag the world, it will not do for us to fold our hands and say, In the highest department advance there is none. Nor will it at all do to say, that the world is getting grey and grizzled now, and has lost that fresh charm which she wore of old, and by virtue of which the great poets of past times made themselves what we esteem them to be. Not so. The world is as young today, as when it was created; and this Vermont morning dew is as wet to my feet, as Eden's dew to Adam's. Nor has Nature been all over ransacked by our progenitors, so that no new charms and mysteries remain for this latter generation to find. Far from it. The trillionth part has not yet been said; and all that has been said, but multiplies the avenues to what remains to be said. It is not so much paucity, as superabundance of material that seems to incapacitate modern authors.

Let America then prize and cherish her writers; yea, let her glorify them. They are not so many in number, as to exhaust her good-will. And while she has good kith and kin of her own, to take to her bosom, let her not lavish her embraces upon the household of an alien. For believe it or not England, after all, is, in many things, an alien to us. China has more bowels of real love for us than she. But even were there no Hawthorne, no Emerson, no Whittier, no Irving, no Bryant, no Dana, no Cooper, no Willis (not the author of the "Dashes", but the author of the "Belfry Pigeon")— were there none of these, and others of like calibre among us, nevertheless, let America first praise mediocrity even, in her own children, before she praises (for everywhere, merit demands acknowledgment from every one) the best excellence in the children of any other land. Let her own authors, I say, have the priority of appreciation. I was much pleased with a hot-headed Carolina cousin of mine, who once said,—"If there were no other American to stand by, in Literature,—why, then I would stand by Pop Emmons and his 'Fredoniad,' and till a better epic came along, swear it was not very far behind the Iliad." Take away the words, and in spirit he was sound.

Not that American genius needs patronage in order to expand. For that explosive sort of stuff will expand though screwed up in a vice, and burst it, though it were triple steel. It is for the nation's sake, and not for her authors' sake, that I would have America be heedful of the increasing greatness among her writers. For how great the shame, if other nations should be before her, in crowning her heroes of the pen. But this is almost the case now. American authors have received more just and discriminating praise (however loftily and ridiculously given, in certain cases) even from some Englishmen, then from their own countrymen. There are hardly five critics in America; and several of them are asleep. As for patronage, it is the American author who now patronizes his country, and not his country him. And if at times some among them appeal to the people for more recognition, it is not always with selfish motives, but patriotic ones.

It is true, that but few of them as yet have evinced that decided originality which merits great praise. But that graceful writer, who perhaps of all Americans has received the most plaudits from his own country for his production,—that very popular and amiable writer, however good, and self-reliant in many things, perhaps owes his chief reputation to the self-acknowledged imitation of a foreign model, and to the studied avoidance of all topics but smooth ones. But it is better to fail in originality, than to succeed in imitation. He who has never failed somewhere, that man can not be great. Failure is the true test of greatness. And if it be said, that continual success is a proof that a man wisely knows his powers,—it is only to be added, that, in that case, he knows them to be small. Let us believe it, then, once for all, that there is no hope for us in these smooth pleasing writers that know their powers. Without malice, but to speak the plain fact, they but furnish an appendix to Goldsmith, and other English authors. And we want no American Goldsmiths; nay, we want no American Miltons. It were the vilest thing you could say of a true American author, that he were an American Tompkins. Call him an American, and have done; for you can not say a nobler thing of him.—But it is not meant that all American writers should studiously cleave to nationality in their writings; only this, no American writer should write like an Englishman, or a Frenchman; let him write like a man, for then he will be sure to write like an American. Let us away with this Bostonian leaven of literary flunkeyism towards England. If either must play the flunkey in this thing, let England do it, not us. And the time is not far off when circumstances may force her to it. While we are rapidly preparing for that political supremacy among the nations, which prophetically awaits us at the close of the present century; in a literary point of view, we are deplorably unprepared for it; and we seem studious to remain so. Hitherto, reasons might have existed why this should be; but no good reason exists now. And all that is requisite to amendment in this matter, is simply this: that, while freely acknowledging all excellence, everywhere, we should refrain from unduly lauding foreign writers and, at the same time, duly recognize the meritorious writers that are our own;—those writers, who breathe that unshackled, democratic spirit of Christianity in all things, which now takes the practical lead in this world, though at the same time led by ourselves— us Americans. Let us boldly contemn all imitation, though it comes to us graceful and fragrant as the morning; and foster all originality, though, at first, it be crabbed and ugly as our own pine knots. And if any of our authors fail, or seem to fail, then, in the words of my enthusiastic Carolina cousin, let us clap him on the shoulder, and back him against all Europe for his second round. The truth is, that in our point of view, this matter of a national literature has come to such a pass with us, that in some sense we must turn bullies, else the day is lost, or superiority so far beyond us, that we can hardly say it will ever be ours.

And now, my countrymen, as an excellent author, of your own flesh and blood,— an unimitating, and, perhaps, in his way, an inimitable man—whom better can I commend to you, in the first place, than Nathaniel Hawthorne. He is one of the new, and far better generation of your writers. The smell of your beeches and hemlocks is upon him; your own broad praries are in his soul; and if you travel away inland into his deep and noble nature, you will hear the far roar of his Niagara. Give not over to future generations the glad duty of acknowledging him for what he is. Take that joy to your self, in your own generation; and so shall he feel those grateful impulses in him, that may possibly prompt him to the full flower of some still greater achievement in your eyes. And by confessing him, you thereby confess others; you brace the whole brotherhood. For genius, all over the world, stands hand in hand, and one shock of recognition runs the whole circle round.

In treating of Hawthorne, or rather of Hawthorne in his writings (for I never saw the man; and in the chances of a quiet plantation life, remote from his haunts, perhaps never shall) in treating of his works, I say, I have thus far omitted all mention of his "Twice Told Tales", and "Scarlet Letter". Both are excellent; but full of such manifold, strange and diffusive beauties, that time would all but fail me, to point the half of them out. But there are things in those two books, which, had they been written in England a century ago, Nathaniel Hawthorne had utterly displaced many of the bright names we now revere on authority. But I am content to leave Hawthorne to himself, and to the infallible finding of posterity; and however great may be the praise I have bestowed upon him, I feel, that in so doing, I have more served and honored myself, than him. For, at bottom, great excellence is praise enough to itself; but the feeling of a sincere and appreciative love and admiration towards it, this is relieved by utterance; and warm, honest praise ever leaves a pleasant flavor in the mouth; and it is an honorable thing to confess to what is honorable in others.

But I cannot leave my subject yet. No man can read a fine author, and relish him to his very bones, while he reads, without subsequently fancying to himself some ideal image of the man and his mind. And if you rightly look for it, you will almost always find that the author himself has somewhere furnished you with his own picture.—For poets (whether in prose or verse), being painters of Nature, are like their brethren of the pencil, the true portrait-painters, who, in the multitude of likenesses to be sketched, do not invariably omit their own; and in all high instances, they paint them without any vanity, though, at times, with a lurking something, that would take several pages to properly define.

I submit it, then, to those best acquainted with the man personally, whether the following is not Nathaniel Hawthorne;—and to himself, whether something involved in it does not express the temper of his mind,—that lasting temper of all true, candid men—a seeker, not a finder yet:—

> "A man now entered, in neglected attire, with the aspect of a thinker, but somewhat too rough-hewn and brawny for a scholar. His face was full of sturdy vigor, with some finer and keener attribute beneath; though harsh at first, it was tempered with the glow of a large, warm heart, which had force enough to heat his powerful intellect through and through. He advanced to the Intelligencer, and looked at him with a glance of such stern sincerity, that perhaps few secrets were beyond its scope.
> "'I seek for Truth', said he."

* * * * *

Twenty four hours have elapsed since writing the foregoing. I have just returned from the hay mow, charged more and more with love and admiration of Hawthorne. For I have just been gleaning through the Mosses, picking up many things here and there that had previously escaped me. And I found that but to glean after this man, is better than to be in at the harvest of others. To be frank (though, perhaps, rather foolish) notwithstanding what I wrote yesterday of these Mosses, I had not then culled them all; but had, nevertheless, been sufficiently sensible of the subtle essence, in them, as to write as I did. To what infinite height of loving wonder and admiration I may yet be borne, when by repeatedly banquetting on these Mosses, I shall have thoroughly incorporated their whole stuff into my being,—that, I can not tell. But already I feel that this Hawthorne has dropped germinous seeds into my soul. He expands and deepens down, the more I contemplate him; and further, and further, shoots his strong New-England roots into the hot soil of my Southern soul.

By careful reference to the "Table of Contents", I now find, that I have gone through all the sketches; but that when I yesterday wrote, I had not at all read two particular pieces, to which I now desire to call special attention,—"A Select Party", and "Young Goodman Brown". Here, be it said to all those whom this poor fugitive scrawl of mine may tempt to the perusal of the "Mosses," that they must on no account suffer themselves to be trifled with, disappointed, or deceived by the triviality of many of the titles to these Sketches. For in more than one instance, the title utterly belies the piece. It is as if rustic demijohns containing the very best and costliest of Falernian and Tokay, were labelled "Cider", "Perry," and "Elderberry wine". The truth seems to be, that like many other geniuses, this Man of Mosses takes great delight in hoodwinking the world,—at least, with respect to himself. Personally, I doubt not, that he rather prefers to be generally esteemed but a so-so sort of author; being willing to reserve the thorough and acute appreciation of what he is, to that party most qualified to judge—that is, to himself. Besides, at the bottom of their natures, men like Hawthorne, in many things, deem the plaudits of the public such strong presumptive evidence of mediocrity in the object of them, that it would in some degree render them doubtful of their own powers, did they hear much and vociferous braying concerning them in the public pastures. True, I have been braying myself (if you please to be witty enough, to have it so) but then I claim to be the first that has so brayed in this particular matter; and therefore, while pleading guilty to the charge still claim all the merit due to originality.

But with whatever motive, playful or profound, Nathaniel Hawthorne has chosen to entitle his pieces in the manner he has, it is certain, that some of them are directly calculated to deceive—egregiously deceive, the superficial skimmer of pages. To be downright and candid once more, let me cheerfully say, that two of these titles did dolefully dupe no less an eagle-eyed reader than myself; and that, too, after I had been impressed with a sense of the great depth and breadth of this American man. "Who in the name of thunder" (as the country-people say in this neighborhood) "who in the name of thunder", would anticipate any marvel in a piece entitled "Young Goodman Brown"? You would of course suppose that it was a simple little tale, intended as a supplement to "Goody Two Shoes". Whereas, it is deep as Dante; nor can you finish it, without addressing the author in his own words—"It is yours to penetrate, in every bosom, the deep mystery of sin". And with Young Goodman, too, in allegorical pursuit of his Puritan wife, you cry out in your anguish,—

> "'Faith!' shouted Goodman Brown, in a voice of agony and desperation; and
> the echoes of the forest mocked him, crying—'Faith! Faith!' as if bewildered
> wretches were seeking her all through the wilderness."

Now this same piece, entitled "Young Goodman Brown", is one of the two that I had not all read yesterday; and I allude to it now, because it is, in itself, such a strong positive illustration of that blackness in Hawthorne, which I had assumed from the mere occasional shadows of it, as revealed in several of the other sketches. But had I previously perused "Young Goodman Brown", I should have been at no pains to draw the conclusion, which I came to, at a time, when I was ignorant that the book contained one such direct and unqualified manifestation of it.

The other piece of the two referred to, is entitled "A Select Party", which, in my first simplicity upon originally taking hold of the book, I fancied must treat of some pumpkin-pie party in Old Salem, or some chowder party on Cape Cod. Whereas, by all the gods of Peedee! it is the sweetest and sublimest thing that has been written since Spencer wrote. Nay, there is nothing in Spencer that surpasses it, perhaps, nothing that equals it. And the test is this: read any canto in "The Faery Queen", and then read "A Select Party", and decide which pleases you the most,—that is, if you are qualified to judge. Do not be frightened at this; for when Spencer was alive, he was thought of very much as Hawthorne is now,— was generally accounted just such a "gentle" harmless man. It may be, that to common eyes, the sublimity of Hawthorne seems lost in his sweetness,—as perhaps in this same "Select Party" of his; for whom, he has builded so august a dome of sunset clouds, and served them on richer plate, than Belshazzar's when he banquetted his lords in Babylon.

But my chief business now, is to point out a particular page in this piece, having reference to an honored guest, who under the name of "The Master Genius" but in the guise of "a young man of poor attire, with no insignia of rank or acknowledged eminence", is introduced to the Man of Fancy, who is the giver of the feast. Now the page having reference to this "Master Genius", so happily expresses much of what I yesterday wrote, touching the coming of the literary Shiloh of America, that I cannot but be charmed by the coincidence; especially, when it shows such a parity of ideas, at least in this one point, between a man like Hawthorne and a man like me.

And here, let me throw out another conceit of mine touching this American Shiloh, or "Master Genius", as Hawthorne calls him. May it not be, that this commanding mind has not been, is not, and never will be, individually developed in any one man? And would it, indeed, appear so unreasonable to suppose, that this great fullness and overflowing may be, or may be destined to be, shared by a plurality of men of genius? Surely, to take the very greatest example on record, Shakespeare cannot be regarded as in himself the concretion of all the genius of his time; nor as so immeasurably beyond Marlow, Webster, Ford, Beaumont, Jonson, that those great men can be said to share none of his power? For one, I conceive that there were dramatists in Elizabeth's day, between whom and Shakespeare the distance was by no means great. Let anyone, hitherto little acquainted with those neglected old authors, for the first time read them thoroughly, or even read Charles Lamb's Specimens of them, and he will be amazed at the wondrous ability of those Anaks of men, and shocked at this renewed example of the fact, that Fortune has more to do with fame than merit,—though, without merit, lasting fame there can be none.

Nevertheless, it would argue too illy of my country were this maxim to hold good concerning Nathaniel Hawthorne, a man, who already, in some few minds, has shed "such a light, as never illuminates the earth, save when a great heart burns as the household fire of a grand intellect."

The words are his,—in the "Select Party"; and they are a magnificent setting to a coincident sentiment of my own, but ramblingly expressed yesterday, in reference to himself. Gainsay it who will, as I now write, I am Posterity speaking by proxy— and after times will make it more than good, when I declare—that the American, who up to the present day, has evinced, in Literature, the largest brain with the largest

heart, that man is Nathaniel Hawthorne. Moreover, that whatever Nathaniel Hawthorne may hereafter write, "The Mosses from an Old Manse" will be ultimately
accounted his masterpiece. For there is a sure, though a secret sign in some works
which prove the culmination of the powers (only the developable ones, however) that
produced them. But I am by no means desirous of the glory of a prophet. I pray Heaven
that Hawthorne may *yet* prove me an impostor in this prediction. Especially, as I somehow cling to the strange fancy, that, in all men, hiddenly reside certain wondrous,
occult properties—as in some plants and minerals—which by some happy but very
rare accident (as bronze was discovered by the melting of the iron and brass in the
burning of Corinth) may chance to be called forth here on earth; not entirely waiting
for their better discovery in the more congenial, blessed atmosphere of heaven.

Once more—for it is hard to be finite upon an infinite subject, and all subjects
are infinite. By some people, this entire scrawl of mine may be esteemed altogether
unnecessary, inasmuch, "as years ago" (they may say) "we found out the rich and rare
stuff in this Hawthorne, whom you now parade forth, as if only *yourself* were the
discoverer of this Portuguese diamond in our Literature".—But even granting all this;
and adding to it, the assumption that the books of Hawthorne have sold by the five-
thousand,—what does that signify?—They should be sold by the hundred-thousand;
and read by the million; and admired by every one who is capable of admiration.

Part Five

The Quest for Union

Introduction

The fervent calls by literary intellectuals for a new national literature mingled in the antebellum period with a swelling national chorus for strengthening and expanding the American union. In fact, so strong was this sentiment that Democrats and Whigs each put forward their own favored ideology of either majoritarian democracy or state-supported economic growth as the key to sustaining it. Of course, for political intellectuals the idea of an American union was hardly absolute. Inherited and to some extent competing republican ideas of liberty, federalism, and fundamental moral law dictated modifications. The most difficult modifications were those required by the question of slavery. It was not just that the issue was divisive, nor ever that, with the emergence of the controversy over the extension of slavery in the territories, it had become so all-engrossing. The fundamental intellectual problem was much more basic: in contesting the issue of slavery, ideologists and intellectuals advanced such radically counterposed notions of society and government as to call into question, even while supporting union in the abstract, the substance of American nationhood.

Southern writers were particularly insistent in claiming that Northern paeans to a strong union masked schemes subversive of a national polity. For many Southerners the greatest of these schemes was the common Northern assertion of the supremacy of the federal government in matters that affected fundamental Southern minority interests, of which slavery was the most important. The Southern thinker who was among the earliest to sound this alarm and who subsequently constructed the most elaborate countertheory of federal–state relations was John C. Calhoun. In his *Disquisition on Government* he argued that only a national government based on a concurrence of "interests" as represented by the various states could protect minorities from oppression by majorities and foster political leaders dedicated to the good of the whole.

In his *Disquisition* Calhoun made it clear that the good he sought depended on restricting the sphere of liberty to the "intelligent" and "deserving." This fact should remind us that Southern intellectual apologists for slavery were hardly mere ideologists of the popular sentiments of their section. Many Southern political leaders, it is true, defended slavery on the grounds that it guaranteed a *white* democratic society by providing opportunities for small slaveholders and obviating the need for a white proletariat. But most leading antebellum Southern intellectuals preferred to portray slavery as a cultivated, patriarchal system beneficial to slaves and slaveholders alike. No Southern intellectual was more adept at this kind of argumentation than George Fitzhugh. In his *Sociology for the South,* Fitzhugh not only delineated the organic social solidarity he claimed Southern slavery fostered, but he also went one step further: he proposed that the entire anarchical Northern "free trade" social system be supplanted by some version of "slavery."

Like Southern proslavery writers, Northern antislavery intellectuals and ideologues also articulated visions of an ideal American polity. But because Northern writers had the benefit of a freer and more sophisticated popular culture, their visions were correspondingly wider. At one extreme were evangelical antislavery writers like Harriet Beecher Stowe, who indicted the slave system because it was, contra Fitzhugh, predatory and mammon-embracing and thus just the opposite of the familial, altruistic culture they hoped somehow their *own* capitalistic society could become. At another extreme were those radical abolitionists whose libertarian antislavery views led them to make the individual sacrosanct and forswear all use of physical coercion as a violation of "the government of God." Most abolitionists, however, were more moderate in their social philosophy. One of the most influential of these was Frederick Douglass. In his July Fourth oration Douglass mixed Enlightenment, republican, and humanized Christian ideals to produce an extraordinarily damning yet hopeful view of the democratic possibilities of American middle-class civilization. The Northern thinker who went the furthest, though, in trying to integrate an antislavery perspective with a moral vision of the American union was Abraham Lincoln. Eschewing both abolitionism and complete racial equality, Lincoln nonetheless in both his speeches on slavery and on labor, imbued his Whiggishly nationalist solutions of self-government and upward mobility with an intense moral—egalitarian fervor. But it was in his two greatest Civil War addresses that he disclosed his view of the ultimate forces behind the union's moral redemption—namely, righteousness actualized through divine vengeance, human suffering, and human forgiveness. No public statement, discursive or poetic, has synthesized so many strands in the American intellectual tradition while seeming to express something beyond it.

Recommendations for Further Reading:

William R. Taylor, *Cavalier and Yankee: The Old South and American National Character* (New York, 1961); Edmund Wilson, *Patriotic Gore: Studies in the Literature of the American Civil War* (New York, 1962); Paul C. Nagel, *One Nation Indivisible: The Union in American Thought, 1776–1861* (New York, 1964); John Higham, *From Boundlessness to Consolidation: The Transformation of American Culture, 1848–1860* (Ann Arbor, Mich., 1969); Paul C. Nagel, *This Sacred Trust: American Nationality, 1798–1898* (New York, 1971); George M. Fredrickson, *The Black Image in the White Mind: The Debate on Afro-American Character and Destiny, 1817–1914* (New York, 1971); David Brion Davis, *The Problem of Slavery in the Age of Revolution, 1770–1823* (Ithaca, N.Y., 1975); Stanley M. Elkins, *Slavery: A Problem in American Institutional and Intellectual Life,* rev. ed. (Chicago, 1976); David Brion Davis, *Slavery and Human Progress* (New York, 1984); Anne Norton, *Alternative Americas: A Reading of Antebellum Political Culture* (Chicago, 1986); Larry E. Tise, *Proslavery: A History of the Defense of Slavery in America, 1701–1840* (Athens, Ga., 1988); Clement Eaton, *The Mind of the Old South* (Baton Rouge, La., 1967); Drew Gilpin Faust, *A Sacred Circle: The Dilemma of the Intellectual in the Old South, 1840–1860* (Baltimore, 1977); Bertram Wyatt-Brown, *Southern Honor: Ethics and Behavior in the Old South* (New York, 1982); David T. Bailey, *Shadow on the Church: Southwestern Evangelical Religion and the Issue of Slavery, 1783–1860* (Ithaca, N.Y., 1985); Michael O'Brien, *Rethinking the South: Essays in Intellectual History* (Baltimore, 1988); George M. Fredrickson, *The Inner Civil War: Northern Intellectuals and the Crisis of the Union* (New York, 1965); Eric Foner, *Free Soil, Free Labor, Free Men: The Ideology of the Republican Party Before the Civil War* (New York, 1970); Lewis Perry, *Radical Abolitionism: Anarchy and the Government of God in Antislavery Thought* (Ithaca, N.Y., 1973); Ronald G. Walters, *The Antislavery Appeal: American Abolitionism After 1830* (Baltimore, 1976); Leonard I. Sweet, *Black Images of America, 1784–1870* (New York, 1976); George B. Forgie, *Patricide in the House Divided: A Psychological Interpretation of Lincoln and His Age* (New York, 1979); Lawrence J. Friedman, *Gregarious Saints: Self and Community in American Abolitionism, 1830–1870* (Cambridge, 1982).

JOHN C. CALHOUN

Selection from *A Disquisition on Government* (c. late 1840s)

Throughout most of his long career as, among other roles, vice president, senator, secretary of state, and persistent presidential aspirant, John C. Calhoun (1782–1850) devoted himself overwhelmingly to two efforts—an unflagging defense of slavery and slaveholder political interests and the contrivance of a governmental structure that would protect those interests while, if possible, preserving the American union. His favored solution, which he formulated as a universally applicable proposition in his posthumously published *Disquisition on Government,* was the "concurrent majority," or government by the majority of each of the interests in a community considered separately and concurring unanimously. By thus providing an absolute veto to each interest, Calhoun argued, oppressive majorities—the hobgoblin of classical republican theory—would be prevented. But Calhoun's scheme was not just negative. Interests that under the democratic system of numerical majorities warred against each other, egged on by demagogic spoilsmen, would be converted into cooperative communities, although of a very special sort. Monolithic and elite-dominated, they would guarantee rule and even relative "liberty" only to those virtuous and intelligent enough to contribute to "the march of progress" and the improvement of the race. For democrats North and South the price of Calhoun's utopian union was high indeed. For two contrasting studies of Calhoun's political thought, see August O. Spain, *The Political Theory of John C. Calhoun* (New York, 1951); and Richard N. Current, *John C. Calhoun* (New York, 1963). For a good collection of interpretive writings on Calhoun, see John L. Thomas, ed., *John C. Calhoun: A Profile* (New York, 1968). Gillis J. Harp, "Taylor, Calhoun, and the Decline of a Theory of Political Disharmony," *Journal of the History of Ideas,* 46 (January–March 1985), 107–20, helpfully places Calhoun's theories in the context of eighteenth- and early nineteenth-century postliberal intellectual developments.

[G]overnment, although intended to protect and preserve society, has itself a strong tendency to disorder and abuse of its powers, as all experience and almost every page of history testify. The cause is to be found in the same constitution of our nature which makes government indispensable. The powers which it is necessary for government to possess, in order to repress violence and preserve order, cannot execute themselves. They must be administered by men in whom, like others, the individual are stronger than the social feelings. And hence, the powers vested in them to prevent injustice and oppression on the part of others, will, if left unguarded, be by them converted into instruments to oppress the rest of the community. That, by which this is prevented, by whatever name called, is what is meant by CONSTITUTION, in its most comprehensive sense, when applied to GOVERNMENT.

Having its origin in the same principle of our nature, *constitution* stands to *government,* as *government* stands to *society;* and, as the end for which society is ordained, would be defeated without government, so that for which government is ordained would, in a great measure, be defeated without constitution. But they differ in this striking particular. There is no difficulty in forming government. It is not even a matter of choice, whether there shall be one or not. Like breathing, it is not permitted to depend on our volition. Necessity will force it on all communities in some one form or another. Very different is the case as to constitution. Instead of a matter of necessity, it is one of the most difficult tasks imposed on man to form a constitution worthy of the name; while, to form a perfect one,—one that would completely counteract the tendency of government to oppression and abuse, and hold it strictly to the great ends for which it is ordained,—has thus far exceeded human wisdom, and possibly ever will. From this, another striking difference results. Constitution is the contrivance of man, while government is of Divine ordination. Man is left to perfect what the wisdom of the Infinite ordained, as necessary to preserve the race.

. . . . . .

How government, then, must be constructed, in order to counteract, through its organism, this tendency on the part of those who make and execute the laws to oppress those subject to their operation, . . . next . . . claims attention.

There is but one way in which this can possibly be done; and that is, by such an organism as will furnish the ruled with the means of resisting successfully this tendency on the part of the rulers to oppression and abuse. Power can only be resisted by power,—and tendency by tendency. Those who exercise power and those subject to its exercise,—the rulers and the ruled,—stand in antagonistic relations to each other. The same constitution of our nature which leads rulers to oppress the ruled,— regardless of the object for which government is ordained,—will, with equal strength, lead the ruled to resist, when possessed of the means of making peaceable and effective resistance. Such an organism, then, as will furnish the means by which resistance may be systematically and peaceably made on the part of the ruled, to oppression and abuse of power on the part of the rulers, is the first and indispensable step towards *forming* a constitutional government. And as this can only be effected by or through

Source: *The Works of John C. Calhoun,* vol. 1, *A Disquisition on Government and a Discourse on the Constitution and Government of the United States,* ed. Richard K. Crallé (Charleston, S.C.: Steam Power-Press of Walker and James, 1851), 7–8, 12–17, 24–31, 35–36, 45–49, 55–59.

the right of suffrage,—(the right on the part of the ruled to choose their rulers at proper intervals, and to hold them thereby responsible for their conduct,)—the responsibility of the rulers to the ruled, through the right of suffrage, is the indispensable and primary principle in the *foundation* of a constitutional government. When this right is properly guarded, and the people sufficiently enlightened to understand their own rights and the interests of the community, and duly to appreciate the motives and conduct of those appointed to make and execute the laws, it is all-sufficient to give to those who elect, effective control over those they have elected.

I call the right of suffrage the indispensable and primary principle; for it would be a great and dangerous mistake to suppose, as many do, that it is, of itself, sufficient to form constitutional governments. To this erroneous opinion may be traced one of the causes, why so few attempts to form constitutional governments have succeeded; and why, of the few which have, so small a number have had durable existence. It has led, not only to mistakes in the attempts to form such governments, but to their overthrow, when they have, by some good fortune, been correctly formed. So far from being, of itself, sufficient,—however well guarded it might be, and however enlightened the people,—it would, unaided by other provisions, leave the government as absolute, as it would be in the hands of irresponsible rulers; and with a tendency, at least as strong, towards oppression and abuse of its powers; as I shall next proceed to explain.

The right of suffrage, of itself, can do no more than give complete control to those who elect, over the conduct of those they have elected. In doing this, it accomplishes all it possibly can accomplish. This is its aim,—and when this is attained, its end is fulfilled. It can do no more, however enlightened the people, or however widely extended or well guarded the right may be. The sum total, then, of its effects, when most successful, is, to make those elected, the true and faithful representatives of those who elected them,—instead of irresponsible rulers,—as they would be without it; and thus, by converting it into an agency, and the rulers into agents, to divest government of all claims to sovereignty, and to retain it unimpaired to the community. But it is manifest that the right of suffrage, in making these changes, transfers, in reality, the actual control over the government, from those who make and execute the laws, to the body of the community; and, thereby, places the powers of the government as fully in the mass of the community, as they would be if they, in fact, had assembled, made, and executed the laws themselves, without the intervention of representatives or agents. The more perfectly it does this, the more perfectly it accomplishes its ends; but in doing so, it only changes the seat of authority, without counteracting, in the least, the tendency of the government to oppression and abuse of its powers.

If the whole community had the same interests, so that the interests of each and every portion would be so affected by the action of the government, that the laws which oppressed or impoverished one portion, would necessarily oppress and impoverish all others,—or the reverse,—then the right of suffrage, of itself, would be all-sufficient to counteract the tendency of the government to oppression and abuse of its powers; and, of course, would form, of itself, a perfect constitutional government. The interest of all being the same, by supposition, as far as the action of the government was concerned, all would have like interests as to what laws should be made, and how they should be executed. All strife and struggle would cease as to who should be elected to make and execute them. The only question would be, who was most fit; who the wisest and most capable of understanding the common interest of the whole.

This decided, the election would pass off quietly, and without party discord; as no one portion could advance its own peculiar interest without regard to the rest, by electing a favorite candidate.

But such is not the case. On the contrary, nothing is more difficult than to equalize the action of the government, in reference to the various and diversified interests of the community; and nothing more easy than to pervert its powers into instruments to aggrandize and enrich one or more interests by oppressing and impoverishing the others; and this too, under the operation of laws, couched in general terms;—and which, on their face, appear fair and equal. Nor is this the case in some particular communities only. It is so in all; the small and the great,—the poor and the rich,—irrespective of pursuits, productions, or degrees of civilization;—with, however, this difference, that the more extensive and populous the country, the more diversified the condition and pursuits of its population, and the richer, more luxurious, and dissimilar the people, the more difficult is it to equalize the action of the government,—and the more easy for one portion of the community to pervert its powers to oppress, and plunder the other.

Such being the case, it necessarily results, that the right of suffrage, by placing the control of the government in the community must, from the same constitution of our nature which makes government necessary to preserve society, lead to conflict among its different interests,—each striving to obtain possession of its powers, as the means of protecting itself against the others;—or of advancing its respective interests, regardless of the interests of others. For this purpose, a struggle will take place between the various interests to obtain a majority, in order to control the government. If no one interest be strong enough, of itself, to obtain it, a combination will be formed between those whose interests are most alike;—each conceding something to the others, until a sufficient number is obtained to make a majority. The process may be slow, and much time may be required before a compact, organized majority can be thus formed; but formed it will be in time, even without preconcert or design, by the sure workings of that principle or constitution of our nature in which government itself originates. When once formed, the community will be divided into two great parties,—a major and minor,—between which there will be incessant struggles on the one side to retain, and on the other to obtain the majority,—and, thereby, the control of the government and the advantages it confers.

So deeply seated, indeed, is this tendency to conflict between the different interests or portions of the community, that it would result from the action of the government itself, even though it were possible to find a community, where the people were all of the same pursuits, placed in the same condition of life, and in every respect, so situated, as to be without inequality of condition or diversity of interests. The advantages of possessing the control of the powers of the government, and, thereby, of its honors and emoluments, are, of themselves, exclusive of all other considerations, ample to divide even such a community into two great hostile parties.

. . . . . .

As, then, the right of suffrage, without some other provision, cannot counteract this tendency of government, the next question for consideration is—What is that other provision? This demands the most serious consideration; for of all the questions embraced in the science of government, it involves a principle, the most important, and the least understood; and when understood, the most difficult of application in practice. It is, indeed, emphatically, that principle which *makes* the constitution, in its strict and limited sense.

From what has been said, it is manifest, that this provision must be of a character calculated to prevent any one interest, or combination of interests, from using the powers of government to aggrandize itself at the expense of the others. Here lies the evil: and just in proportion as it shall prevent, or fail to prevent it, in the same degree it will effect, or fail to effect the end intended to be accomplished. There is but one certain mode in which this result can be secured; and that is, by the adoption of some restriction or limitation, which shall so effectually prevent any one interest, or combination of interests, from obtaining the exclusive control of the government, as to render hopeless all attempts directed to that end. There is, again, but one mode in which this can be effected; and that is, by taking the sense of each interest or portion of the community, which may be unequally and injuriously affected by the action of the government, separately, through its own majority, or in some other way by which its voice may be fairly expressed; and to require the consent of each interest, either to put or to keep the government in action. This, too, can be accomplished only in one way,—and that is, by such an organism of the government,—and, if necessary for the purpose, of the community also,—as will, by dividing and distributing the powers of government, give to each division or interest, through its appropriate organ, either a concurrent voice in making and executing the laws, or a veto on their execution. It is only by such an organism, that the assent of each can be made necessary to put the government in motion; or the power made effectual to arrest its action, when put in motion;—and it is only by the one or the other that the different interests, orders, classes, or portions, into which the community may be divided, can be protected, and all conflict and struggle between them prevented,—by rendering it impossible to put or to keep it in action, without the concurrent consent of all.

Such an organism as this, combined with the right of suffrage, constitutes, in fact, the elements of constitutional government. The one, by rendering those who make and execute the laws responsible to those on whom they operate, prevents the rulers from oppressing the ruled; and the other, by making it impossible for any one interest or combination of interests or class, or order, or portion of the community, to obtain exclusive control, prevents any one of them from oppressing the other. It is clear, that oppression and abuse of power must come, if at all, from the one or the other quarter. From no other can they come. It follows, that the two, suffrage and proper organism combined, are sufficient to counteract the tendency of government to oppression and abuse of power; and to restrict it to the fulfilment of the great ends for which it is ordained.

In coming to this conclusion, I have assumed the organism to be perfect, and the different interests, portions, or classes of the community, to be sufficiently enlightened to understand its character and object, and to exercise, with due intelligence, the right of suffrage. To the extent that either may be defective, to the same extent the government would fall short of fulfilling its end. But this does not impeach the truth of the principles on which it rests. In reducing them to proper form, in applying them to practical uses, all elementary principles are liable to difficulties; but they are not, on this account, the less true, or valuable. Where the organism is perfect, every interest will be truly and fully represented, and of course the whole community must be so. It may be difficult, or even impossible, to make a perfect organism,—but, although this be true, yet even when, instead of the sense of each and of all, it takes that of a few great and prominent interests only, it would still, in a great measure, if not altogether, fulfil the end intended by a constitution. For, in such case, it would require so large a portion of the community, compared with the whole, to concur, or acquiesce in the action of the government, that the number to be plundered would be too few, and the number to be aggrandized too many, to afford adequate motives to oppression and the abuse of its powers. Indeed, however imperfect the organism, it must have more or less effect in diminishing such tendency.

It may be readily inferred, from what has been stated, that the effect of organism is neither to supersede nor diminish the importance of the right of suffrage; but to aid and perfect it. The object of the latter is, to collect the sense of the community. The more fully and perfectly it accomplishes this, the more fully and perfectly it fulfils its end. But the most it can do, of itself, is to collect the sense of the greater number; that is, of the stronger interests, or combination of interests; and to assume this to be the sense of the community. It is only when aided by a proper organism, that it can collect the sense of the entire community,—of each and all its interests; of each, through its appropriate organ, and of the whole, through all of them united. This would truly be the sense of the entire community; for whatever diversity each interest might have within itself,—as all would have the same interest in reference to the action of the government, the individuals composing each would be fully and truly represented by its own majority or appropriate organ, regarded in reference to the other interests. In brief, every individual of every interest might trust, with confidence, its majority or appropriate organ, against that of every other interest.

It results, from what has been said, that there are two different modes in which the sense of the community may be taken; one, simply by the right of suffrage, unaided; the other, by the right through a proper organism. Each collects the sense of the majority. But one regards numbers only, and considers the whole community as a unit, having but one common interest throughout; and collects the sense of the greater number of the whole, as that of the community. The other, on the contrary, regards interests as well as numbers;—considering the community as made up of different and conflicting interests, as far as the action of the government is concerned; and takes the sense of each, through its majority or appropriate organ, and the united sense of all, as the sense of the entire community. The former of these I shall call the numerical, or absolute majority; and the latter, the concurrent, or constitutional majority. I call it the constitutional majority, because it is an essential element in every constitutional government,—be its form what it may. So great is the difference, politically speaking, between the two majorities, that they cannot be confounded, without leading to great and fatal errors; and yet the distinction between them has been so entirely overlooked, that when the term *majority* is used in political discussions, it is applied exclusively to designate the numerical,—as if there were no other. Until this distinction is recognized, and better understood, there will continue to be great liability to error in properly constructing constitutional governments, especially of the popular form, and of preserving them when properly constructed. Until then, the latter will have a strong tendency to slide, first, into the government of the numerical majority, and, finally, into absolute government of some other form. To show that such must be the case, and at the same time to mark more strongly the difference between the two, in order to guard against the danger of overlooking it, I propose to consider the subject more at length.

The first and leading error which naturally arises from overlooking the distinction referred to, is, to confound the numerical majority with the people; and this so completely as to regard them as identical. This is a consequence that necessarily results from considering the numerical as the only majority. All admit, that a popular government, or democracy, is the government of the people; for the terms imply this. A perfect government of the kind would be one which would embrace the consent of every citizen or member of the community; but as this is impracticable, in the opinion of those who regard the numerical as the only majority, and who can perceive no other way by which the sense of the people can be taken,—they are compelled to adopt this as the only true basis of popular government, in contradistinction to governments of the aristocratical or monarchical form. Being thus constrained, they are, in the next place, forced to regard the numerical majority, as, in effect, the entire people; that is, the greater part as the whole; and the government of the greater part as the government of the whole. It is thus the two come to be confounded, and a part made identical with the whole. And it is thus, also, that all the rights, powers, and immunities of the whole people come to be attributed to the numerical majority; and, among others, the supreme, sovereign authority of establishing and abolishing governments at pleasure.

This radical error, the consequence of confounding the two, and of regarding the numerical as the only majority, has contributed more than any other cause, to prevent the formation of popular constitutional governments,—and to destroy them even when they have been formed. It leads to the conclusion that, in their formation and establishment nothing more is necessary than the right of suffrage,—and the allotment to each division of the community a representation in the government, in proportion to numbers. If the numerical majority were really the people; and if, to take its sense truly, were to take the sense of the people truly, a government so constituted would be a true and perfect model of a popular constitutional government; and every departure from it would detract from its excellence. But, as such is not the case,—as the numerical majority, instead of being the people, is only a portion of them,—such a government, instead of being a true and perfect model of the people's government, that is, a people self-governed, is but the government of a part, over a part,—the major over the minor portion.

But this misconception of the true elements of constitutional government does not stop here. It leads to others equally false and fatal, in reference to the best means of preserving and perpetuating them, when, from some fortunate combination of circumstances, they are correctly formed. For they who fall into these errors regard the restrictions which organism imposes on the will of the numerical majority as restrictions on the will of the people, and, therefore, as not only useless, but wrongful and mischievous. And hence they endeavor to destroy organism, under the delusive hope of making government more democratic.

Such are some of the consequences of confounding the two, and of regarding the numerical as the only majority. And in this may be found the reason why so few popular governments have been properly constructed, and why, of these few, so small a number have proved durable. Such must continue to be the result, so long as these errors continue to be prevalent.

. . . . . .

The necessary consequence of taking the sense of the community by the concurrent majority is, as has been explained, to give to each interest or portion of the community a negative on the others. It is this mutual negative among its various conflicting interests, which invests each with the power of protecting itself;—and places the rights and safety of each, where only they can be securely placed, under its own guardianship. Without this there can be no systematic, peaceful, or effective resistance to the natural tendency of each to come into conflict with the others: and without this there can be no constitution. It is this negative power,—the power of preventing or arresting the action of the government,—be it called by what term it may,—veto, interposition, nullification, check, or balance of power,—which, in fact, forms the constitution. They are all but different names for the negative power. In all its forms, and under all its names, it results from the concurrent majority. Without this there can be no negative; and, without a negative, no constitution. The assertion is true in reference to all constitutional governments, be their forms what they may. It is, indeed, the negative power which makes the constitution,—and the positive which makes the government. The one is the power of acting;—and the other the power of preventing or arresting action. The two, combined, make constitutional governments.

But, as there can be no constitution without the negative power, and no negative power without the concurrent majority;—it follows, necessarily, that where the numerical majority has the sole control of the government, there can be no constitution; as constitution implies limitation or restriction,—and, of course, is inconsistent with the idea of sole or exclusive power. And hence, the numerical, unmixed with the concurrent majority, necessarily forms, in all cases, absolute government.

. . . . . .

Among the other advantages which governments of the concurrent have over those of the numerical majority,—and which strongly illustrates their more popular character, is,—that they admit, with safety, a much greater extension of the right of suffrage. It may be safely extended in such governments to universal suffrage: that is,—to every male citizen of mature age, with few ordinary exceptions; but it cannot be so far extended in those of the numerical majority, without placing them ultimately under the control of the more ignorant and dependent portions of the community. For, as the community becomes populous, wealthy, refined, and highly civilized, the difference between the rich and the poor will become more strongly marked; and the number of the ignorant and dependent greater in proportion to the rest of the community. With the increase of this difference, the tendency to conflict between them will become stronger; and, as the poor and dependent become more numerous in proportion, there will be, in governments of the numerical majority, no want of leaders among the wealthy and ambitious, to excite and direct them in their efforts to obtain the control.

The case is different in governments of the concurrent majority. There, mere numbers have not the absolute control; and the wealthy and intelligent being identified in interest with the poor and ignorant of their respective portions or interests of the community, become their leaders and protectors. And hence, as the latter would have neither hope nor inducement to rally the former in order to obtain the control, the right of suffrage, under such a government, may be safely enlarged to the extent stated, without incurring the hazard to which such enlargement would expose governments of the numerical majority.

In another particular, governments of the concurrent majority have greatly the advantage. I allude to the difference in their respective tendency, in reference to dividing or uniting the community. That of the concurrent . . . is to unite the community, let its interests be ever so diversified or opposed; while that of the numerical is to divide it into two conflicting portions, let its interests be, naturally, ever so united and identified.

That the numerical majority will divide the community, let it be ever so homogeneous, into two great parties, which will be engaged in perpetual struggles to obtain the control of the government, has already been established. The great importance of the object at stake, must necessarily form strong party attachments and party antipathies;—attachments on the part of the members of each to their respective parties, through whose efforts they hope to accomplish an object dear to all; and antipathies to the opposite party, as presenting the only obstacle to success.

In order to have a just conception of their force, it must be taken into consideration, that the object to be won or lost appeals to the strongest passions of the human heart,—avarice, ambition, and rivalry. It is not then wonderful, that a form of government, which periodically stakes all its honors and emoluments, as prizes to be contended for, should divide the community into two great hostile parties; or that party attachments, in the progress of the strife, should become so strong among the members of each respectively, as to absorb almost every feeling of our nature, both social and individual; or that their mutual antipathies should be carried to such an excess as to destroy, almost entirely, all sympathy between them, and to substitute in its place the strongest aversion. Nor is it surprising, that under their joint influence, the community should cease to be the common centre of attachment, or that each party should find that centre only in itself. It is thus, that, in such governments, devotion to party becomes stronger than devotion to country,—the promotion of the interests of party more important than the promotion of the common good of the whole, and its triumph and ascendency, objects of far greater solicitude, than the safety and prosperity of the community. It is thus, also, that the numerical majority, by regarding the community as a unit, and having, as such, the same interests throughout all its parts, must, by its necessary operation, divide it into two hostile parts, waging, under the forms of law, incessant hostilities against each other.

The concurrent majority, on the other hand, tends to unite the most opposite and conflicting interests, and to blend the whole in one common attachment to the country. By giving to each interest, or portion, the power of self-protection, all strife and struggle between them for ascendency, is prevented; and, thereby, not only every feeling calculated to weaken the attachment to the whole is suppressed, but the individual and the social feelings are made to unite in one common devotion to country. Each sees and feels that it can best promote its own prosperity by conciliating the goodwill, and promoting the prosperity of the others. And hence, there will be diffused throughout the whole community kind feelings between its different portions; and, instead of antipathy, a rivalry amongst them to promote the interests of each other, as far as this can be done consistently with the interest of all. Under the combined influence of these causes, the interests of each would be merged in the common interests of the whole; and thus, the community would become a unit, by becoming the common centre of attachment of all its parts. And hence, instead of faction, strife, and struggle for party ascendency, there would be patriotism, nationality, harmony, and a struggle only for supremacy in promoting the common good of the whole.

. . . . . .

. . . [I]t is a great and dangerous error to suppose that all people are equally entitled to liberty. It is a reward to be earned, not a blessing to be gratuitously lavished on all alike;—a reward reserved for the intelligent, the patriotic, the virtuous and deserving;—and not a boon to be bestowed on a people too ignorant, degraded and vicious, to be capable either of appreciating or of enjoying it. Nor is it any disparagement to liberty, that such is, and ought to be the case. On the contrary, its greatest praise,—its proudest distinction is, that an all-wise Providence has reserved it, as the noblest and highest reward for the development of our faculties, moral and intellectual. A reward more appropriate than liberty could not be conferred on the deserving;—nor a punishment inflicted on the undeserving more just, than to be subject to lawless and despotic rule. This dispensation seems to be the result of some fixed law;—and every effort to disturb or defeat it, by attempting to elevate a people in the scale of liberty, above the point to which they are entitled to rise, must ever prove abortive, and end in disappointment. The progress of a people rising from a lower to a higher point in the scale of liberty, is necessarily slow;—and by attempting to precipitate, we either retard, or permanently defeat it.

There is another error, not less great and dangerous, usually associated with the one which has just been considered. I refer to the opinion, that liberty and equality are so intimately united, that liberty cannot be perfect without perfect equality.

That they are united to a certain extent,—and that equality of citizens, in the eyes of the law, is essential to liberty in a popular government, is conceded. But to go further, and make equality of *condition* essential to liberty, would be to destroy both liberty and progress. The reason is, that inequality of condition, while it is a necessary consequence of liberty, is, at the same time, indispensable to progress. In order to understand why this is so, it is necessary to bear in mind, that the main spring to progress is, the desire of individuals to better their condition; and that the strongest impulse which can be given to it is, to leave individuals free to exert themselves in the manner they may deem best for that purpose, as far at least as it can be done consistently with the ends for which government is ordained,—and to secure to all the fruits of their exertions. Now, as individuals differ greatly from each other, in intelligence, sagacity, energy, perseverance, skill, habits of industry and economy, physical power, position and opportunity,—the necessary effect of leaving all free to exert themselves to better their condition, must be a corresponding inequality between those who may possess these qualities and advantages in a high degree, and those who may be deficient in them. The only means by which this result can be prevented are, either to impose such restrictions on the exertions of those who may possess them in a high degree, as will place them on a level with those who do not; or to deprive them of the fruits of their exertions. But to impose such restrictions on them would be destructive of liberty,—while, to deprive them of the fruits of their exertions, would be to destroy the desire of bettering their condition. It is, indeed, this inequality of condition between the front and rear ranks, in the march of progress, which gives so strong an impulse to the former to maintain their position, and to the latter to press forward into their files. This gives to progress its greatest impulse. To force the front rank back to the rear, or attempt to push forward the rear into line with the front, by the interposition of the government, would put an end to the impulse, and effectually arrest the march of progress.

These great and dangerous errors have their origin in the prevalent opinion that all men are born free and equal;—than which nothing can be more unfounded and false. It rests upon the assumption of a fact, which is contrary to universal observation, in whatever light it may be regarded. It is, indeed, difficult to explain how an opinion so destitute of all sound reason, ever could have been so extensively entertained, unless we regard it as being confounded with another, which has some semblance of truth;—but which, when properly understood, is not less false and dangerous. I refer to the assertion, that all men are equal in the state of nature; meaning, by a state of nature, a state of individuality, supposed to have existed prior to the social and political state; and in which men lived apart and independent of each other. If such a state ever did exist, all men would have been, indeed, free and equal in it; that is, free to do as they pleased, and exempt from the authority or control of others—as, by supposition, it existed anterior to society and government. But such a state is purely hypothetical. It never did, nor can exist; as it is inconsistent with the preservation and perpetuation of the race. It is, therefore, a great misnomer to call it *the state of nature*. Instead of being the natural state of man, it is, of all conceivable states, the most opposed to his nature—most repugnant to his feelings, and most incompatible with his wants. His natural state is, the social and political—the one for which his Creator made him, and the only one in which he can preserve and perfect his race. As, then, there never was such a state as the, so called, state of nature, and never can be, it follows, that men, instead of being born in it, are born in the social and political state; and of course, instead of being born free and equal, are born subject, not only to parental authority, but to the laws and institutions of the country where born, and under whose protection they draw their first breath.

GEORGE FITZHUGH

Selection from *Sociology for the South*
1854

The self-educated Port Royal, Virginia lawyer–journalist George Fitzhugh (1806–81) was a paradoxical figure among Southern intellectuals. He was often by turns parochial, naive, and hopelessly addicted to special pleading. Yet he was also the one Southern writer who more than any other tried to cast a defense of slavery that would be almost universal in its scope. In *Sociology for the South,* Fitzhugh's first major work, he argued essentially four things: that slavery was an organic system that, therefore, could not be criticized *or* defended on any mechanistic or purely rationalistic basis; that slavery's essential feature was the master–slave relationship, which was both interdependent (as in feudalism) and protective (as in an ideal patriarchal family); that the absence of such a feature in the North and in Europe made their capitalist systems and cultures inherently predatory and anarchic and, therefore, vastly inferior both economically and morally to the slave system and culture in the South. But what made Fitzhugh's argument so unique and radical was the soft bombshell he dropped in the closing section of his chapter "Negro Slavery": that because the essence of slavery was "protection" through "government," the system so defined ought in various ways to be applied to the North and *extended* in various ways in what Fitzhugh implicitly conceded was a less than perfectly patriarchal South. The supreme irony of Fitzhugh's position was that in advancing such protective schemes he was merely echoing, as he pointed out, many of the liberal and radical sentiments of reformers and critics in capitalist Europe and the North. As a picture of Southern slavery, Fitzhugh's critique was obviously perverse, but as a window on the contradictions of nineteenth-century capitalist culture, it was extraordinarily illuminating. Harvey Wish, *George Fitzhugh: Propagandist of the Old South* (Baton Rouge, La., 1943) is a useful biography. For two provocative, but divergent, interpretations of the ideological significance of Fitzhugh's proslavery thought, see C. Vann Woodward's introduction, "George Fitzhugh, *Sui Generis,*" to his edition of Fitzhugh's *Cannibals All! or Slaves Without Masters* (Cambridge, Mass., 1960), vii–xxxix; and Eugene D. Genovese, *The World the Slaveholders Made: Two Essays in Interpretation* (New York, 1969), 115–244, 258–65.

Chapter I.

FREE TRADE.

Political economy is the science of free society. Its theory and its history alike establish this position. Its fundamental maxims, *Laissez-faire* and *"Pas trop gouverner,"* are at war with all kinds of slavery, for they in fact assert that individuals and peoples prosper most when governed least. It is not, therefore, wonderful that such a science should not have been believed or inculcated whilst slavery was universal. Roman and Greek masters, feudal lords and Catholic priests, if conscientious, must have deemed such maxims false and heritical, or if unconscientious, would find in their self-interest sufficient reasons to prevent their propagation.

. . . . . .

Until now, industry had been controlled and directed by a few minds. Monopoly in its every form had been rife. Men were suddenly called on to walk alone, to act and work for themselves without guide, advice or control from superior authority. In the past, nothing like it had occurred; hence no assistance could be derived from books. The prophets themselves had overlooked or omitted to tell of the advent of this golden era, and were no better guides than the historians and philosophers. A philosophy that should guide and direct industry was equally needed with a philosophy of morals. The occasion found and made the man. For writing a one-sided philosophy, no man was better fitted than Adam Smith.

. . . . . .

Adam Smith's philosophy is simple and comprehensive, *(teres et rotundus.)* Its leading and almost its only doctrine is, that individual well-being and social and national wealth and prosperity will be best promoted by each man's eagerly pursuing his own selfish welfare unfettered and unrestricted by legal regulations, or governmental prohibitions, farther than such regulations may be necessary to prevent positive crime. That some qualifications of this doctrine will not be found in his book, we shall not deny; but this is his system. It is obvious enough that such a governmental policy as this doctrine would result in, would stimulate energy, excite invention and industry, and bring into livelier action, genius, skill and talent. It had done so before Smith wrote, and it was no doubt the observation of those effects that suggested the theory. His friends and acquaintances were of that class, who, in the war of the wits to which free competition invited, were sure to come off victors. His country, too, England and Scotland, in the arts of trade and in manufacturing skill, was an overmatch for the rest of the world. International free trade would benefit his country as much as social free trade would benefit his friends. This was his world, and had it been the only world his philosophy would have been true. But there was another and much larger world, whose misfortunes, under his system, were to make the fortunes of his friends and his country. A part of that world, far more numerous than his friends and acquaintance was at his door, they were the unemployed poor, the weak in mind or

Source: George Fitzhugh, *Sociology for the South, or the Failure of Free Society* (Richmond, Va.: A. Morris, 1854), 7, 9–10, 11–14, 20–21, 22–28, 29–33, 80–84, 85–86, 88–89, 89–95.

body, the simple and unsuspicious, the prodigal, the dissipated, the improvident and the vicious. *Laissez-faire* and *pas trop gouverner* suited not them; one portion of them needed support and protection; the other, much and rigorous government. Still they were fine subjects out of which the astute and designing, the provident and avaricious, the cunning, the prudent and the industrious might make fortunes in the field of free competition. Another portion of the world which Smith overlooked, were the countries with which England traded, covering a space many hundred times larger than England herself. She was daily growing richer, more powerful and intellectual, by her trade, and the countries with which she traded poorer, weaker, and more ignorant. Since the vast extension of trade, consequent on the discoveries of Columbus and Vasco de Gama, the civilized countries of Europe which carried on this trade had greatly prospered, but the savages and barbarians with whom they traded had become more savage and barbarous or been exterminated. Trade is a war of the wits, in which the stronger witted are as sure to succeed as the stronger armed in a war with swords. Strength of wit has this great advantage over strength of arm, that it never tires, for it gathers new strength by appropriating to itself the spoils of the vanquished. And thus, whether between nations or individuals, the war of free trade is constantly widening the relative abilities of the weak and the strong. It has been justly observed that under this system the rich are continually growing richer and the poor poorer. The remark is true as well between nations as between individuals. Free trade, when the American gives a bottle of whiskey to the Indian for valuable furs, or the Englishman exchanges with the African blue-beads for diamonds, gold and slaves, is a fair specimen of all free trade when unequals meet. Free trade between England and Ireland furnishes the latter an excellent market for her beef and potatoes, in exchange for English manufactures. The labor employed in manufacturing pays much better than that engaged in rearing beeves and potatoes. On the average, one hour of English labor pays for two of Irish. Again, manufacturing requires and encourages skill and intelligence; grazing and farming require none. But far the worst evils of this free trade remain to be told. Irish pursuits depressing education and refinement, England becomes a market for the wealth, the intellect, the talent, energy and enterprise of Ireland. All men possessing any of these advantages or qualities retreat to England to spend their incomes, to enter the church, the navy, or the army, to distinguish themselves as authors, to engage in mechanic or manufacturing pursuits. Thus is Ireland robbed of her very life's blood, and thus do our Northern States rob the Southern.

. . . . . .

Political economy is quite as objectionable, viewed as a rule of morals, as when viewed as a system of economy. Its authors never seem to be aware that they are writing an ethical as well as an economical code; yet it is probable that no writings, since the promulgation of the Christian dispensation, have exercised so controlling an influence on human conduct as the writings of these authors. The morality which they teach is one of simple and unadulterated selfishness. The public good, the welfare of society, the prosperity of one's neighbors, is, according to them, best promoted by each man's looking solely to the advancement of his own pecuniary interests. They maintain that national wealth, happiness and prosperity being but the aggregate of individual wealth, happiness and prosperity, if each man pursues exclusively his own selfish good, he is doing the most he can to promote the general good. They seem to forget that men eager in the pursuit of wealth are never satisfied with the fair earnings of their own bodily labor, but find their wits and cunning employed in over-reaching others much more profitable than their hands. *Laissez-faire*, free competition begets a war of the wits, which these economists encourage, quite as destructive to the weak, simple, and guileless, as the war of the sword.

. . . . . .

It begets another war in the bosom of society still more terrible than this. It arrays captial against labor. Every man is taught by political economy that it is meritorious to make the best bargains one can. In all old countries, labor is superabundant, employers less numerous than laborers; yet all the laborers must live by the wages they receive from the capitalists. The capitalist cheapens their wages; they compete with and underbid each other, for employed they must be on any terms. This war of the rich with the poor and the poor with one another, is the morality which political economy inculcates. It is the only morality, save the Bible, recognized or acknowledged in free society, and is far more efficacious in directing worldly men's conduct than the Bible, for that teaches self-denial, not self-indulgence and aggrandizement. This process of underbidding each other by the poor, which universal liberty necessarily brings about, has well been compared by the author of Alton Locke to the prisoners in the Black Hole of Calcutta strangling one another. A beautiful system of ethics this, that places all mankind in antagonistic positions, and puts all society at war. What can such a war result in but the oppression and ultimate extermination of the weak? In such society the astute capitalist, who is very skilful and cunning, gets the advantage of every one with whom he competes or deals; the sensible man with moderate means gets the advantage of most with whom he has business, but the mass of the simple and poor are outwitted and cheated by everybody.

Woman fares worst when thrown into this warfare of competition. The delicacy of her sex and her nature prevents her exercising those coarse arts which men do in the vulgar and promiscuous jostle of life, and she is reduced to the necessity of getting less than half price for her work. To the eternal disgrace of human nature, the men who employ her value themselves on the Adam Smith principle for their virtuous and sensible conduct. "Labor is worth what it will bring; they have given the poor woman more than any one else would, or she would not have taken the work." Yet she and her children are starving, and the employer is growing rich by giving her half what her work is worth. Thus does free competition, the creature of free society, throw the whole burden of the social fabric on the poor, the weak and ignorant. They produce every thing and enjoy nothing. They are "the muzzled ox that treadeth out the straw."

In free society none but the selfish virtues are in repute, because none other help a man in the race of competition. In such society virtue loses all her loveliness, because of her selfish aims. Good men and bad men have the same end in view: self-promotion, self-elevation. The good man is prudent, cautious, and cunning of fence; he knows well, the arts (the virtues, if you please) which enable him to advance his fortunes at the expense of those with whom he deals; he does not "cut too deep"; he does not cheat and swindle, he only makes good bargains and excellent profits. He gets more subjects by this course; everybody comes to him to be bled. He bides his time; takes advantage of the follies, the improvidence and vices of others, and makes his fortune out of the follies and weaknesses of his fellow-men. The bad man is rash, hasty, unskilful and impolitic. He is equally selfish, but not half so prudent and cunning. Selfishness is almost the only motive of human conduct in free society, where every man is taught that it is his first duty to change and better his pecuniary situation.

The first principles of the science of political economy inculcate separate, individual action, and are calculated to prevent that association of labor without which nothing great can be achieved; for man isolated and individualized is the most helpless of animals. We think this error of the economists proceeded from their adoping Locke's theory of the social contract. We believe no heresy in moral science has been more pregnant of mischief than this theory of Locke. It lies at the bottom of all moral speculations, and if false, must infect with falsehood all theories built on it. Some animals are by nature gregarious and associative. Of this class are men, ants and bees. An isolated man is almost as helpless and ridiculous as a bee setting up for himself. Man is born a member of society, and does not form society. Nature, as in the cases of bees and ants, has it ready formed for him. He and society are congenital. Society is the being—he one of the members of that being. He has no rights whatever, as opposed to the interests of society; and that society may very properly make any use of him that will redound to the public good. Whatever rights he has are subordinate to the good of the whole; and he has never ceded rights to it, for he was born its slave, and had no rights to cede.

Government is the creature of society, and may be said to derive its powers from the consent of the governed; but society does not owe its sovereign power to the separate consent, volition or agreement of its members. Like the hive, it is as much the work of nature as the individuals who compose it. Consequences, the very opposite of the doctrine of free trade, result from this doctrine of ours. It makes each society a band of brothers, working for the common good, instead of a bag of cats biting and worrying each other. The competitive system is a system of antagonism and war; ours of peace and fraternity. The first is the system of free society; the other that of slave society. The Greek, the Roman, Judaistic, Egyptian, and all ancient polities, were founded on our theory. The loftiest patrician in those days, valued himself not on selfish, cold individuality, but on being the most devoted servant of society and his country. In ancient times, the individual was considered nothing, the State every thing. And yet, under this system, the noblest individuality was evolved that the world has ever seen. The prevalence of the doctrines of political economy has injured Southern character, for in the South those doctrines most prevail. Wealthy men, who are patterns of virtue in the discharge of their domestic duties, value themselves on never intermeddling in public matters. They forget that property is a mere creature of law and society, and are willing to make no return for that property to the public, which by its laws gave it to them, and which guard and protect them in its possession.

All great enterprises owe their success to association of capital and labor. The North is indebted for its great wealth and prosperity to the readiness with which it forms associations for all industrial and commercial purposes. The success of Southern farming is a striking instance of the value of the association of capital and laborers, and ought to suggest to the South the necessity of it for other purposes.

The dissociation of labor and disintegration of society, which liberty and free competition occasion, is especially injurious to the poorer class; for besides the labor necessary to support the family, the poor man is burdened with the care of finding a home, and procuring employment, and attending to all domestic wants and concerns. Slavery relieves our slaves of these cares altogether, and slavery is a form, and the very best form, of socialism. In fact, the ordinary wages of common labor are insufficient to keep up separate domestic establishments for each of the poor, and association or starvation is in many cases inevitable. In free society, as well in Europe as in America, this is the accepted theory, and various schemes have been resorted to, all without success, to cure the evil. The association of labor properly carried out under a common head or ruler, would render labor more efficient, relieve the laborer of many of the cares of household affairs, and protect and support him in sickness and old age, besides preventing the too great reduction of wages by redundancy of labor and free competition. Slavery attains all these results. What else will?

. . . . . .

A maxim well calculated not only to retard the progress of civilization, but to occasion its retrogression, has grown out of the science of political economy. "The world is too much governed," has become quite an axiom with many politicians. Now the need of law and government is just in proportion to man's wealth and enlightenment. Barbarians and savages need and will submit to but few and simple laws, and little of government. The love of personal liberty and freedom from all restraint, are distinguishing traits of wild men and wild beasts. Our Anglo-Saxon ancestors loved personal liberty because they were barbarians, but they did not love it half so much as North American Indians or Bengal tigers, because they were not half so savage. As civilization advances, liberty recedes; and it is fortunate for man that he loses his love of liberty just as fast as he becomes more moral and intellectual. The wealthy, virtuous and religious citizens of large towns enjoy less of liberty than any other persons whatever, and yet they are the most useful and rationally happy of all mankind. The best governed countries, and those which have prospered most, have always been distinguished for the number and stringency of their laws. Good men obey superior authority, the laws of God, of morality, and of their country; bad men love liberty and violate them. It would be difficult very often for the most ingenious casuist to distinguish between sin and liberty; for virtue consists in the performance of duty, and the obedience to that law or power that imposes duty, whilst sin is but the violation of duty and disobedience to such law and power. It is remarkable, in this connection, that sin began by the desire for liberty and the attempt to attain it in the person of Satan and his fallen angels. The world wants good government and a plenty of it—not liberty. It is deceptive in us to boast of our Democracy, to assert the capacity of the people for self-government, and then refuse to them its exercise. In New England, and in all our large cities, where the people govern most, they are governed best. If government be not too much centralized, there is little danger of too much government. The danger and evil with us is of too little. Carlyle says of our institutions, that they are "anarchy plus a street constable." We ought not to be bandaged up too closely in our infancy, it might prevent growth and development; but the time is coming when we shall need more of government, if we would secure the permanency of our institutions.

All men concur in the opinion that some government is necessary. Even the political economist would punish murder, theft, robbery, gross swindling, &c.; but they encourage men to compete with and slowly undermine and destroy one another by means quite as effective as those they forbid. We have heard a distinguished member of this school object to negro slavery, because the protection it afforded to an inferior race would perpetuate that race, which, if left free to compete with the whites, must be starved out in a few generations. Members of Congress, of the Young American party, boast that the Anglo-Saxon race is manifestly destined to eat out all other races, as the wire-grass destroys and takes the place of other grasses. Nay, they allege this competitive process is going on throughout all nature; the weak are everywhere devouring the strong; the hardier plants and animals destroying the weaker, and the superior races of man exterminating the inferior. They would challenge our admiration for this war of nature, by which they say Providence is perfecting its own work— getting rid of what is weak and indifferent, and preserving only what is strong and hardy. We see the war, but not the improvement. This competitive, destructive system has been going on from the earliest records of history; and yet the plants, the animals, and the men of to-day are not superior to those of four thousand years ago. To restrict this destructive, competitive propensity, man was endowed with reason, and enabled to pass laws to protect the weak against the strong. To encourage it, is to encourage the strong to oppress the weak, and to violate the primary object of all government. It is strange it should have entered the head of any philosopher to set the weak, who are the majority of mankind, to competing, contending and fighting with the strong, in order to improve their condition.

Hobbes maintains that "a state of nature is a state of war." This is untrue of a state of nature, because men are naturally associative; but it is true of a civilized state of universal liberty, and free competition, such as Hobbes saw around him, and which no doubt suggested his theory. The wants of man and his history alike prove that slavery has always been part of his social organization. A less degree of subjection is inadequate for the government and protection of great numbers of human beings.

An intelligent English writer, describing society as he saw it, uses this language:

"There is no disguising from the cool eye of philosophy, that all living creatures exist in a state of natural warfare; and that man (in hostility with all) is at enmity also with his own species; man is the natural enemy of man; and society, unable to change his nature, succeeds but in establishing a hollow truce by which fraud is substituted for violence."

Such is free society, fairly portrayed; such are the infidel doctrines of political economy, when candidly avowed. Slavery and Christianity bring about a lasting peace, not "a hollow truce." But we mount a step higher. We deny that there is a society in free countries. They who act each for himself, who are hostile, antagonistic and competitive, are not social and do not constitute a society. We use the term free society, for want of a better; but, like the term free government, it is an absurdity: those who are governed are not free—those who are free are not social.

. . . . . .

Chapter IV.

THE TWO PHILOSOPHIES.

In the three preceding chapters we have shewn that the world is divided between two philosophies. The one the philosophy of free trade and universal liberty—the philosophy adapted to promote the interests of the strong, the wealthy and the wise. The other, that of socialism, intended to protect the weak, the poor and the ignorant. The latter is almost universal in free society; the former prevails in the slaveholding States

of the South. Thus we see each section cherishing theories at war with existing institutions. The people of the North and of Europe are pro-slavery men in the abstract;
those of the South are theoretical abolitionists. This state of opinions is readily
accounted for. The people in free society feel the evils of universal liberty and free
competition, and desire to get rid of those evils. They propose a remedy, which is in
fact slavery; but they are wholly unconscious of what they are doing, because never
having lived in the midst of slavery, they know not what slavery is. The citizens of
the South, who have seen none of the evils of liberty and competition, but just enough
of those agencies to operate as healthful stimulants to energy, enterprise and industry,
believe free competition to be an unmixed good.

The South, quiet, contented, satisfied, looks upon all socialists and radical reformers as madmen or knaves. It is as ignorant of free society as that society is of slavery.
Each section sees one side of the subject alone; each, therefore, takes partial and erroneous views of it. Social science will never take a step in advance till some Southern
slaveholder, competent for the task, devotes a life-time to its study and elucidation;
for slavery can only be understood by living in its midst, whilst thousands of books
daily exhibit the minutest workings of free society. The knowledge of the numerous
theories of radical reform proposed in Europe, and the causes that have led to their
promulgation, is of vital importance to us. Yet we turn away from them with disgust,
as from something unclean and vicious. We occupy high vantage ground for observing,
studying and classifying the various phenomena of society; yet we do not profit by the
advantages of our position. We should do so, and indignantly hurl back upon our
assailants the charge, that there is something wrong and rotten in our system. From
their own mouths we can show free society to be a monstrous abortion, and slavery
to be the healthy, beautiful and natural being which they are trying, unconsciously, to
adopt.

Chapter V.

NEGRO SLAVERY.

We have already stated that we should not attempt to introduce any new theories of
government and of society, but merely try to justify old ones, so far as we could deduce
such theories from ancient and almost universal practices. Now it has been the practice in all countries and in all ages, in some degree, to accommodate the amount and
character of government control to the wants, intelligence, and moral capacities of the
nations or individuals to be governed. A highly moral and intellectual people, like the
free citizens of ancient Athens, are best governed by a democracy. For a less moral
and intellectual one, a limited and constitutional monarchy will answer. For a people
either very ignorant or very wicked, nothing short of military despotism will suffice.
So among individuals, the most moral and well-informed members of society require
no other government than law. They are capable of reading and understanding the
law, and have sufficient self-control and virtuous disposition to obey it. Children cannot be governed by mere law; first, because they do not understand it, and secondly,
because they are so much under the influence of impulse, passion and appetite, that
they want sufficient self-control to be deterred or governed by the distant and doubtful
penalties of the law. They must be constantly controlled by parents or guardians,
whose will and orders shall stand in the place of law for them. Very wicked men must

be put into penitentiaries; lunatics into asylums, and the most wild of them into straight jackets, just as the most wicked of the sane are manacled with irons; and idiots must have committees to govern and take care of them. Now, it is clear the Athenian democracy would not suit a negro nation, nor will the government of mere law suffice for the individual negro. He is but a grown up child, and must be governed as a child, not as a lunatic or criminal. The master occupies towards him the place of parent or guardian. We shall not dwell on this view, for no one will differ with us who thinks as we do of the negro's capacity, and we might argue till dooms-day, in vain, with those who have a high opinion of the negro's moral and intellectual capacity.

Secondly. The negro is improvident; will not lay up in summer for the wants of winter; will not accumulate in youth for the exigencies of age. He would become an insufferable burden to society. Society has the right to prevent this, and can only do so by subjecting him to domestic slavery.

In the last place, the negro race is inferior to the white race, and living in their midst, they would be far outstripped or outwitted in the chase of free competition. Gradual but certain extermination would be their fate. We presume the maddest abolitionist does not think the negro's providence of habits and money-making capacity at all to compare to those of the whites. This defect of character would alone justify enslaving him, if he is to remain here. In Africa or the West Indies, he would become idolatrous, savage and cannibal, or be devoured by savages and cannibals. At the North he would freeze or starve.

. . . . . .

. . . [A]bolish negro slavery, and how much of slavery still remains. Soldiers and sailors in Europe enlist for life; here, for five years. Are they not slaves who have not only sold their liberties, but their lives also? And they are worse treated than domestic slaves. No domestic affection and self-interest extend their ægis over them. No kind mistress, like a guardian angel, provides for them in health, tends them in sickness, and soothes their dying pillow. Wellington at Waterloo was a slave. He was bound to obey, or would, like admiral Bying, have been shot for gross misconduct, and might not, like a common laborer, quit his work at any moment. He had sold his liberty, and might not resign without the consent of his master, the king. The common laborer may quit his work at any moment, whatever his contract; declare that liberty is an inalienable right, and leave his employer to redress by a useless suit for damages. The highest and most honorable position on earth was that of the slave Wellington; the lowest, that of the free man who cleaned his boots and fed his hounds. The African cannibal, caught, christianized and enslaved, is as much elevated by slavery as was Wellington. The kind of slavery is adapted to the men enslaved. Wives and apprentices are slaves; not in theory only, but often in fact. Children are slaves to their parents, guardians and teachers. Imprisoned culprits are slaves. Lunatics and idiots are slaves also. Three-fourths of free society are slaves, no better treated, when their wants and capacities are estimated, than negro slaves. The masters in free society, or slave society, if they perform properly their duties, have more cares and less liberty than the slaves themselves. "In the sweat of thy face shalt thou earn thy bread!" made all men slaves, and such all *good men* continue to be.

. . . . . .

We have a further question to ask. If it be right and incumbent to subject children to the authority of parents and guardians, and idiots and lunatics to committees, would it not be equally right and incumbent to give the free negroes masters, until at least they arrive at years of discretion, which very few ever did or will attain? What is the difference between the authority of a parent and of a master? Neither pay wages, and each is entitled to the services of those subject to him. The father may not sell his child forever, but may hire him out till he is twenty-one. The free negro's master may also be restrained from selling. Let him stand in *loco parentis,* and call him papa instead of master. Look closely into slavery, and you will see nothing so hideous in it; or if you do, you will find plenty of it at home in its most hideous form.

. . . . . .

It is a common remark, that the grand and lasting architectural structures of antiquity were the results of slavery. The mighty and continued association of labor requisite to their construction, when mechanic art was so little advanced, and labor-saving processes unknown, could only have been brought about by a despotic authority, like that of the master over his slaves. It is, however, very remarkable, that whilst in taste and artistic skill the world seems to have been retrograding ever since the decay and abolition of feudalism, in mechanical invention and in great utilitarian operations requiring the wielding of immense capital and much labor, its progress has been unexampled. Is it because capital is more despotic in its authority over free laborers than Roman masters and feudal lords were over their slaves and vassals?

Free society has continued long enough to justify the attempt to generalize its phenomena, and calculate its moral and intellectual influences. It is obvious that, in whatever is purely utilitarian and material, it incites invention and stimulates industry. Benjamin Franklin, as a man and a philosopher, is the best exponent of the working of the system. His sentiments and his philosophy are low, selfish, atheistic and material. They tend directly to make man a mere "featherless biped," well-fed, well-clothed and comfortable, but regardless of his soul as "the beasts that perish.[']

Since the Reformation the world has as regularly been retrograding in whatever belongs to the departments of genius, taste and art, as it has been progressing in physical science and its application to mechanical construction. Mediæval Italy rivalled if it did not surpass ancient Rome, in poetry, in sculpture, in painting, and many of the fine arts. Gothic architecture reared its monuments of skill and genius throughout Europe, till the 15th century; but Gothic architecture died with the Reformation. The age of Elizabeth was the Augustan age of England. The men who lived then acquired their sentiments in a world not yet deadened and vulgarized by puritanical cant and levelling demagoguism. Since then men have arisen who have been the fashion and the go for a season, but none have appeared whose names will descend to posterity. Liberty and equality made slower advances in France. The age of Louis XIV. was the culminating point of French genius and art. It then shed but a flickering and lurid light. Frenchmen are servile copyists of Roman art, and Rome had no art of her own. She borrowed from Greece; distorted and deteriorated what she borrowed; and France imitates and falls below Roman distortions. The genius of Spain disappeared with Cervantes; and now the world seems to regard nothing as desirable except what will make money and what costs money. There is not a poet, an orator, a sculptor, or painter in the world. The tedious elaboration necessary to all the productions of high art would be ridiculed in this money-making, utilitarian charlatan age. Nothing now but what is gaudy and costly excites admiration. The public taste is debased.

But far the worst feature of modern civilization, which is the civilization of free society, remains to be exposed. Whilst labor-saving processes have probably lessened by one half, in the last century, the amount of work needed for comfortable support, the free laborer is compelled by capital and competition to work more than he ever did before, and is less comfortable. The organization of society cheats him of his earnings, and those earnings go to swell the vulgar pomp and pageantry of the ignorant millionaires, who are the only great of the present day. These reflections might seem, at first view, to have little connexion with negro slavery; but it is well for us of the South not to be deceived by the tinsel glare and glitter of free society, and to employ ourselves in doing our duty at home, and studying the past, rather than in insidious rivalry of the expensive pleasures and pursuits of men whose sentiments and whose aims are low, sensual and grovelling.

Human progress, consisting in moral and intellectual improvement, and there being no agreed and conventional standard weights or measures of moral and intellectual qualities and quantities, the question of progress can never be accurately decided. We maintain that man has not improved, because in all save the mechanic arts he reverts to the distant past for models to imitate, and he never imitates what he can excel.

We need never have white slaves in the South, because we have black ones. Our citizens, like those of Rome and Athens, are a privileged class. We should train and educate them to deserve the privileges and to perform the duties which society confers on them. Instead, by a low demagoguism depressing their self-respect by discourses on the equality of man, we had better excite their pride by reminding them that they do not fulfil the menial offices which white men do in other countries. Society does not feel the burden of providing for the few helpless paupers in the South. And we should recollect that here we have but half the people to educate, for half are negroes; whilst at the North they profess to educate all. It is in our power to spike this last gun of the abolitionists. We should educate all the poor. The abolitionists say that it is one of the necessary consequences of slavery that the poor are neglected. It was not so in Athens, and in Rome, and should not be so in the South. If we had less trade with and less dependence on the North, all our poor might be profitable and honorably employed in trades, professions and manufactures. Then we should have a rich and denser population. Yet we but marshal her in the way that she was going. The South is already aware of the necessity of a new policy, and has begun to act on it. Every day more and more is done for education, the mechanic arts, manufactures and internal improvements. We will soon be independent of the North.

We deem this peculiar question of negro slavery of very little importance. The issue is made throughout the world on the general subject of slavery in the abstract. The argument has commenced. One set of ideas will govern and control after awhile the civilized world. Slavery will every where be abolished, or every where be re-instituted. We think the opponents of practical, existing slavery, are estopped by their own admission; nay, that unconsciously, as socialists, they are the defenders and propagandists of slavery, and have furnished the only sound arguments on which its defence and justification can be rested. We have introduced the subject of negro slavery to afford us a better opportunity to disclaim the purpose of reducing the white man any where to the condition of negro slaves here. It would be very unwise and unscientific to govern white men as you would negroes. Every shade and variety of slavery has existed in the world. In some cases there has been much of legal regulation, much restraint of the master's authority; in others, none at all. The character of slavery necessary to protect the whites in Europe should be much milder than negro slavery, for slavery is only needed to protect the white man, whilst it is more necessary for the government of the negro even than for his protection. But even negro slavery should not be outlawed. We might and should have laws in Virginia, as in Louisiana, to make the master subject to presentment by the grand jury and to punishment, for any inhuman or improper treatment or neglect of his slave.

We abhor the doctrine of the "Types of Mankind;" first, because it is at war with scripture, which teaches us that the whole human race is descended from a common parentage; and, secondly, because it encourages and incites brutal masters to treat negroes, not as weak, ignorant and dependent brethren, but as wicked beasts, without the pale of humanity. The Southerner is the negro's friend, his only friend. Let no intermeddling abolitionist, no refined philosophy, dissolve this friendship.

FREDERICK DOUGLASS

"What to the Slave Is the Fourth of July?"
1852

Frederick Douglass (1818–95) was the foremost Afro-American leader of the early nineteenth century. He was also the author of three autobiographies that collectively, in their record of his relentless climb from slave to Republican party statesman, rivaled Franklin's as a great American exemplary saga. Hardly less important, though, was his role in defining, through his writings on antislavery, a powerful philosophy of American reform. Douglass's primary strength as a reform thinker was his ability to extract from the major traditions of post-Revolutionary American political thought both a sharply defined argument for black emancipation and a culturally resonant vision of a just American society. Nowhere was this dual exploitation better exemplified than in Douglass's oration on the Fourth of July. On the one hand, Douglass used the egalitarian ideals of the Declaration of Independence and a humanistic Christianity to puncture the moral pretensions of a system that converted men and women into property and to excoriate Americans who in the overwhelming majority hypocritically celebrated the Fourth of July while tolerating a system that mocked it. On the other hand, in identifying antislavery with two of the most basic beliefs in American culture, along with the Constitution, which he interpreted as "a GLORIOUS LIBERTY DOCUMENT," Douglass presented antislavery as almost the essence of American nationhood. Finally, linking antislavery's progress with the very forces most Americans associated with their nation's progress—knowledge, technology, and commerce—Douglass all but foretold the movement's ultimate triumph. All, then, that was needed was "a fiery stream of biting ridicule, blasting reproach, withering sarcasm, and stern rebuke" to awaken Americans to an urgent sense of their duty to do the right. And this the ex-slave Douglass gave them in heaping portions. For a comprehensive study of Douglass's social and political thought, see Waldo E. Martin, Jr., *The Mind of Frederick Douglass* (Chapel Hill, 1984). August Meier, "Frederick Douglass' Vision for America: A Case Study in Nineteenth-Century Negro Protest," in Harold M. Hyman and Leonard W. Levy, eds., *Freedom and Reform: Essays in Honor of Henry Steele Commager* (New York, 1967), 127–48, cogently places Douglass's reform ideas in their Afro-American intellectual context. For a sensitive discussion of the psychological roots of Douglass's social ideology, see Peter F. Walker, *Moral Choices: Memory, Desire, and Imagination in Nineteenth-Century American Abolition* (Baton Rouge, La., 1978), 207–61.

An Address Delivered in Rochester, New York, on 5 July 1852

Mr. President, Friends and Fellow Citizens: He who could address this audience without a quailing sensation, has stronger nerves than I have.

. . . . . .

The papers and placards say, that I am to deliver a 4th [of] July oration. This certainly sounds large, and out of the common way, for me. It is true that I have often had the privilege to speak in this beautiful Hall, and to address many who now honor me with their presence. But neither their familiar faces, nor the perfect gage I think I have of Corinthian Hall, seems to free me from embarrassment.

The fact is, ladies and gentlemen, the distance between this platform and the slave plantation, from which I escaped, is considerable—and the difficulties to be overcome in getting from the latter to the former, are by no means slight. That I am here to-day is, to me, a matter of astonishment as well as of gratitude. You will not, therefore, be surprised, if in what I have to say, I evince no elaborate preparation, nor grace my speech with any high sounding exordium. With little experience and with less learning, I have been able to throw my thoughts hastily and imperfectly together, and trusting to your patient and generous indulgence, I will proceed to lay them before you.

This, for the purpose of this celebration, is the 4th of July. It is the birthday of your National Independence, and of your political freedom. This, to you, is what the Passover was to the emancipated people of God. It carries your minds back to the day, and to the act of your great deliverance; and to the signs, and to the wonders, associated with that act, and that day. This celebration also marks the beginning of another year of your national life; and reminds you that the Republic of America is now 76 years old. I am glad, fellow-citizens, that your nation is so young. Seventy-six years, though a good old age for a man, is but a mere speck in the life of a nation. Three score years and ten is the allotted time for individual men, but nations number their years by thousands. According to this fact, you are, even now, only in the beginning of your national career, still lingering in the period of childhood. I repeat, I am glad this is so. There is hope in the thought, and hope is much needed, under the dark clouds which lower above the horizon. The eye of the reformer is met with angry flashes, portending disastrous times; but his heart may well beat lighter at the thought that America is young, and that she is still in the impressible stage of her existence.

. . . . . .

Citizens, your fathers . . . succeeded; and to-day you reap the fruits of their success. The freedom gained is yours; and you, therefore, may properly celebrate this anniversary. The 4th of July is the first great fact in your nation's history—the very ring-bolt in the chain of your yet undeveloped destiny.

Pride and patriotism, not less than gratitude, prompt you to celebrate and to hold it in perpetual remembrance. I have said that the Declaration of Independence is the RING-BOLT to the chain of your nation's destiny; so, indeed, I regard it. The principles contained in that instrument are saving principles. Stand by those principles, be true to them on all occasions, in all places, against all foes, and at whatever cost.

Source: The Frederick Douglass Papers, Series One: Speeches, Debates, and Interviews, vol. 2, ed. John W. Blassingame et al. (New Haven: Yale University Press, 1982), 359, 360, 363–88. Editors' notes omitted. Reprinted by permission of Yale University Press, Copyright © 1982.

From the round top of your ship of state, dark and threatening clouds may be seen. Heavy billows, like mountains in the distance, disclose to the leeward huge forms of flinty rocks! That *bolt* drawn, that *chain* broken, and all is lost. *Cling to this day— cling to it,* and to its principles, with the grasp of a storm-tossed mariner to a spar at midnight.

. . . . . .

Fellow Citizens, I am not wanting in respect for the fathers of this republic. The signers of the Declaration of Independence were brave men. They were great men too—great enough to give fame to a great age. It does not often happen to a nation to raise, at one time, such a number of truly great men. The point from which I am compelled to view them is not, certainly, the most favorable; and yet I cannot contemplate their great deeds with less than admiration. They were statesmen, patriots and heroes, and for the good they did, and the principles they contended for, I will unite with you to honor their memory.

They loved their country better than their own private interests; and, though this is not the highest form of human excellence, all will concede that it is a rare virtue, and that when it is exhibited, it ought to command respect. He who will, intelligently, lay down his life for his country, is a man whom it is not in human nature to despise. Your fathers staked their lives, their fortunes, and their sacred honor, on the cause of their country. In their admiration of liberty, they lost sight of all other interests.

They were peace men; but they preferred revolution to peaceful submission to bondage. They were quiet men; but they did not shrink from agitating against oppression. They showed forbearance; but that they knew its limits. They believed in order; but not in the order of tyranny. With them, nothing was *"settled"* that was not right. With them, justice, liberty and humanity were *"final;"* not slavery and oppression. You may well cherish the memory of such men. They were great in their day and generation. Their solid manhood stands out the more as we contrast it with these degenerate times.

How circumspect, exact and proportionate were all their movements! How unlike the politicians of an hour! Their statesmanship looked beyond the passing moment, and stretched away in strength into the distant future. They seized upon eternal principles, and set a glorious example in their defence. Mark them!

Fully appreciating the hardship to be encountered, firmly believing in the right of their cause, honorably inviting the scrutiny of an on-looking world, reverently appealing to heaven to attest their sincerity, soundly comprehending the solemn responsibility they were about to assume, wisely measuring the terrible odds against them, your fathers, the fathers of this republic, did, most deliberately, under the inspiration of a glorious patriotism, and with a sublime faith in the great principles of justice and freedom, lay deep the corner-stone of the national superstructure, which has risen and still rises in grandeur around you.

Of this fundamental work, this day is the anniversary. Our eyes are met with demonstrations of joyous enthusiasm. Banners and pennants wave exultingly on the breeze. The din of business, too, is hushed. Even Mammon seems to have quitted his grasp on this day. The ear-piercing fife and the stirring drum unite their accents with the ascending peal of a thousand church bells. Prayers are made, hymns are sung, and sermons are preached in honor of this day; while the quick martial tramp of a great and multitudinous nation, echoed back by all the hills, valleys and mountains of a vast continent, bespeak the occasion one of thrilling and universal interest—a nation's jubilee.

Friends and citizens, I need not enter further into the causes which led to this anniversary. Many of you understand them better than I do. You could instruct me in regard to them. That is a branch of knowledge in which you feel, perhaps, a much deeper interest than your speaker. The causes which led to the separation of the colonies from the British crown have never lacked for a tongue. They have all been taught in your common schools, narrated at your firesides, unfolded from your pulpits, and thundered from your legislative halls, and are as familiar to you as household words. They form the staple of your national poetry and eloquence.

I remember, also, that, as a people, Americans are remarkably familiar with all facts which make in their own favor. This is esteemed by some as a national trait— perhaps a national weakness. It is a fact, that whatever makes for the wealth or for the reputation of Americans, and can be had *cheap!* will be found by Americans. I shall not be charged with slandering Americans, if I say I think the American side of any question may be safely left in American hands.

I leave, therefore, the great deeds of your fathers to other gentlemen whose claim to have been regularly descended will be less likely to be disputed than mine!

The Present.

My business, if I have any here to-day, is with the present. The accepted time with God and his cause is the ever-living now.

> "Trust no future, however pleasant,
>   Let the dead past bury its dead;
> Act, act in the living present,
>   Heart within, and God overhead."

We have to do with the past only as we can make it useful to the present and to the future. To all inspiring motives, to noble deeds which can be gained from the past, we are welcome. But now is the time, the important time. Your fathers have lived, died, and have done their work, and have done much of it well. You live and must die, and you must do your work. You have no right to enjoy a child's share in the labor of your fathers, unless your children are to be blest by your labors. You have no right to wear out and waste the hard-earned fame of your fathers to cover your indolence. Sydney Smith tells us that men seldom eulogize the wisdom and virtues of their fathers, but to excuse some folly or wickedness of their own. This truth is not a doubtful one. There are illustrations of it near and remote, ancient and modern. It was fashionable, hundreds of years ago, for the children of Jacob to boast, we have "Abraham to our father," when they had long lost Abraham's faith and spirit. That people contented themselves under the shadow of Abraham's great name, while they repudiated the deeds which made his name great. Need I remind you that a similar thing is being done all over this country to-day? Need I tell you that the Jews are not the only people who built the tombs of the prophets, and garnished the sepulchres of the righteous? Washington could not die till he had broken the chains of his slaves. Yet his monument is built up by the price of human blood, and the traders in the bodies and souls of men, shout—"We have Washington to *our father*." Alas! that it should be so; yet so it is.

> "The evil that men do, lives after them,
> The good is oft' interred with their bones."

Fellow-citizens, pardon me, allow me to ask, why am I called upon to speak here to-day? What have I, or those I represent, to do with your national independence? Are the great principles of political freedom and of natural justice, embodied in that Declaration of Independence, extended to us? and am I, therefore, called upon to bring our humble offering to the national altar, and to confess the benefits and express devout gratitude for the blessings resulting from your independence to us?

Would to God, both for your sakes and ours, than an affirmative answer could be truthfully returned to these questions! Then would my task be light, and my burden easy and delightful. For *who* is there so cold, that a nation's sympathy could not warm him? Who so obdurate and dead to the claims of gratitude, that would not thankfully acknowledge such priceless benefits? Who so stolid and selfish, that would not give his voice to swell the hallelujahs of a nation's jubilee, when the chains of servitude had been torn from his limbs? I am not that man. In a case like that, the dumb might eloquently speak, and the "lame man leap as an hart."

But, such is not the state of the case. I say it with a sad sense of the disparity between us. I am not included within the pale of this glorious anniversary! Your high independence only reveals the immeasurable distance between us. The blessings in which you, this day, rejoice, are not enjoyed in common. The rich inheritance of justice, liberty, prosperity and independence, bequeathed by your fathers, is shared by you, not by me. The sunlight that brought life and healing to you, has brought stripes and death to me. This Fourth [of] July is *yours,* not *mine. You* may rejoice, *I* must mourn. To drag a man in fetters into the grand illuminated temple of liberty, and call upon him to join you in joyous anthems, were inhuman mockery and sacrilegious irony. Do you mean, citizens, to mock me, by asking me to speak to-day? If so, there is a parallel to your conduct. And let me warn you that it is dangerous to copy the example of a nation whose crimes, towering up to heaven, were thrown down by the breath of the Almighty, burying that nation in irrecoverable ruin! I can to-day take up the plaintive lament of a peeled and woe-smitten people!

"By the rivers of Babylon, there we sat down. Yea! we wept when we remembered Zion. We hanged our harps upon the willows in the midst thereof. For there, they that carried us away captive, required of us a song; and they who wasted us required of us mirth, saying, Sing us one of the songs of Zion. How can we sing the Lord's song in a strange land? If I forget thee, O Jerusalem, let my right hand forget her cunning. If I do not remember thee, let my tongue cleave to the roof of my mouth."

Fellow-citizens; above your national, tumultous joy, I hear the mournful wail of millions! whose chains, heavy and grievous yesterday, are, to-day, rendered more intolerable by the jubilee shouts that reach them. If I do forget, if I do not faithfully remember those bleeding children of sorrow this day, "may my right hand forget her cunning, and may my tongue cleave to the roof of my mouth!" To forget them, to pass lightly over their wrongs, and to chime in with the popular theme, would be treason most scandalous and shocking, and would make me a reproach before God and the world. My subject, then fellow-citizens, is ᴀᴍᴇʀɪᴄᴀɴ Sʟᴀᴠᴇʀʏ. I shall see, this day, and its popular characteristics, from the slave's point of view. Standing, there, identified with the American bondman, making his wrongs mine, I do not hesitate to declare, with all my soul, that the character and conduct of this nation never looked blacker to me than on this 4th of July! Whether we turn to the declarations of the past, or to the professions of the present, the conduct of the nation seems equally hideous and revolting. America is false to the past, false to the present, and solemnly binds herself to be false to the future. Standing with God and the crushed and bleeding slave on this occasion, I will, in the name of humanity which is outraged, in the name of liberty which is fettered, in the name of the constitution and the Bible, which are disregarded and trampled upon, dare to call in question and to denounce, with all the emphasis I can command, everything that serves to perpetuate slavery—the great sin and shame of America! "I will not equivocate; I will not excuse;" I will use the severest language I can command; and yet not one word shall escape me that any man, whose judgement is not blinded by prejudice, or who is not at heart a slaveholder, shall not confess to be right and just.

But I fancy I hear some one of my audience say, it is just in this circumstance that you and your brother abolitionists fail to make a favorable impression on the public mind. Would you argue more, and denounce less, would you persuade more, and rebuke less, your cause would be much more likely to succeed. But, I submit, where all is plain there is nothing to be argued. What point in the anti-slavery creed would you have me argue? On what branch of the subject do the people of this country need light? Must I undertake to prove that the slave is a man? That point is conceded already. Nobody doubts it. The slaveholders themselves acknowledge it in the enactment of laws for their government. They acknowledge it when they punish disobedience on the part of the slave. There are seventy-two crimes in the State of Virginia, which, if committed by a black man, (no matter how ignorant he be), subject him to the punishment of death; while only two of the same crimes will subject a white man to the like punishment. What is this but the acknowledgement that the slave is a moral, intellectual and responsible being? The manhood of the slave is conceded. It is admitted in the fact that Southern statute books are covered with enactments forbidding, under severe fines and penalties, the teaching of the slave to read or to write. When you can point to any such laws, in reference to the beasts of the field, then I may consent to argue the manhood of the slave. When the dogs in your streets, when the fowls of the air, when the cattle on your hills, when the fish of the sea, and the reptiles that crawl, shall be unable to distinguish the slave from a brute, *then* will I argue with you that the slave is a man!

For the present, it is enough to affirm the equal manhood of the negro race. Is it not astonishing that, while we are ploughing, planting and reaping, using all kinds of mechanical tools, erecting houses, constructing bridges, building ships, working in metals of brass, iron, copper, silver and gold; that, while we are reading, writing and cyphering, acting as clerks, merchants and secretaries, having among us lawyers, doctors, ministers, poets, authors, editors, orators, and teachers; that, while we are engaged in all manner of enterprises common to other men, digging gold in California, capturing the whale in the Pacific, feeding sheep and cattle on the hill-side, living, moving, acting, thinking, planning, living in families as husbands, wives and children, and, above all, confessing and worshipping the Christian's God, and looking hopefully for life and immortality beyond the grave, we are called upon to prove that we are men!

Would you have me argue that man is entitled to liberty? that he is the rightful owner of his own body? You have already declared it. Must I argue the wrongfulness of slavery? Is that a question for Republicans? Is it to be settled by the rules of logic and argumentation, as a matter beset with great difficulty, involving a doubtful application of the principle of justice, hard to be understood? How should I look to-day, in the presence of Americans, dividing, and subdividing a discourse, to show that men have a natural right to freedom? speaking of it relatively, and positively, negatively, and affirmatively. To do so, would be to make myself ridiculous, and to offer an insult to your understanding. There is not a man beneath the canopy of heaven, that does not know that slavery is wrong *for him*.

What, am I to argue that it is wrong to make men brutes, to rob them of their liberty, to work them without wages, to keep them ignorant of their relations to their fellow men, to beat them with sticks, to flay their flesh with the lash, to load their limbs with irons, to hunt them with dogs, to sell them at auction, to sunder their families, to knock out their teeth, to burn their flesh, to starve them into obedience and submission to their masters? Must I argue that a system thus marked with blood, and stained with pollution, is *wrong*? No! I will not. I have better employments for my time and strength, than such arguments would imply.

What, then, remains to be argued? Is it that slavery is not divine; that God did not establish it; that our doctors of divinity are mistaken? There is blasphemy in the · thought. That which is inhuman, cannot be divine! *Who* can reason on such a proposition? They that can, may; I cannot. The time for such argument is past.

At a time like this, scorching irony, not convincing argument, is needed. O! had I the ability, and could I reach the nation's ear, I would, to-day, pour out a fiery stream of biting ridicule, blasting reproach, withering sarcasm, and stern rebuke. For it is not light that is needed, but fire; it is not the gentle shower, but thunder. We need the storm, the whirlwind, and the earthquake. The feeling of the nation must be quickened; the conscience of the nation must be roused; the propriety of the nation must be startled; the hypocrisy of the nation must be exposed; and its crimes against God and man must be proclaimed and denounced.

What, to the American slave, is your 4th of July? I answer; a day that reveals to him, more than all other days in the year, the gross injustice and cruelty to which he is the constant victim. To him, your celebration is a sham; your boasted liberty, an unholy license; your national greatness, swelling vanity; your sounds of rejoicing are empty and heartless; your denunciations of tyrants, brass fronted impudence; your shouts of liberty and equality, hollow mockery; your prayers and hymns, your sermons and thanksgivings, with all your religious parade, and solemnity, are, to him, mere bombast, fraud, deception, impiety, and hyprocrisy—a thin veil to cover up crimes which would disgrace a nation of savages. There is not a nation on the earth guilty of practices, more shocking and bloody, than are the people of these United States, at this very hour.

Go where you may, search where you will, roam through all the monarchies and despotisms of the old world, travel through South America, search out every abuse, and when you have found the last, lay your facts by the side of the everyday practices of this nation, and you will say with me, that, for revolting barbarity and shameless hypocrisy, America reigns without a rival.

The Internal Slave Trade.

Take the American slave-trade, which, we are told by the papers, is especially prosperous just now. Ex-Senator Benton tells us that the price of men was never higher
than now. He mentions the fact to show that slavery is in no danger. This trade is one
of the peculiarities of American institutions. It is carried on in all the large towns and
cities in one-half of this confederacy; and millions are pocketed every year, by dealers
in this horrid traffic. In several states, this trade is a chief source of wealth. It is called
(in contradistinction to the foreign slave-trade) *"the internal slave-trade."* It is, probably, called so, too, in order to divert from it the horror with which the foreign slave-
trade is contemplated. That trade has long since been denounced by this government,
as piracy. It has been denounced with burning words, from the high places of the
nation, as an execrable traffic. To arrest it, to put an end to it, this nation keeps a
squadron, at immense cost, on the coast of Africa. Everywhere, in this country, it is
safe to speak of this foreign slave-trade, as a most inhuman traffic, opposed alike to
the laws of God and of man. The duty to extirpate and destory it, is admitted even by
our DOCTORS OF DIVINITY. In order to put an end to it, some of these last have consented
that their colored brethren (nominally free) should leave this country, and establish
themselves on the western coast of Africa! It is, however, a notable fact that, while so
much execration is poured out by Americans upon those engaged in the foreign slave-
trade, the men engaged in the slave-trade between the states pass without condemnation, and their business is deemed honorable.

Behold the practical operation of this internal slave-trade, the American slave-
trade, sustained by American politics and American religion. Here you will see men
and women reared like swine for the market. You know what is a swine-drover? I will
show you a man-drover. They inhabit all our Southern States. They perambulate the
country, and crowd the highways of the nation, with droves of human stock. You will
see one of these human flesh-jobbers, armed with pistol, whip and bowie-knife, driving
a company of a hundred men, women, and children, from the Potomac to the slave
market at New Orleans. These wretched people are to be sold singly, or in lots, to suit
purchasers. They are food for the cotton-field, and the deadly sugar-mill. Mark the sad
procession, as it moves wearily along, and the inhuman wretch who drives them. Hear
his savage yells and his blood-chilling oaths, as he hurries on his affrighted captives!
There, see the old man, with locks thinned and gray. Cast one glance, if you please,
upon that young mother, whose shoulders are bare to the scorching sun, her briny
tears falling on the brow of the babe in her arms. See, too, that girl of thirteen, weeping, *yes!* weeping, as she thinks of the mother from whom she has been torn! The drove
moves tardily. Heat and sorrow have nearly consumed their strength; suddenly you
hear a quick snap, like the discharge of a rifle; the fetters clank, and the chain rattles
simultaneously; your ears are saluted with a scream, that seems to have torn its way
to the centre of your soul! The crack you heard, was the sound of the slave-whip; the
scream you heard, was from the woman you saw with the babe. Her speed had faltered
under the weight of her child and her chains! that gash on her shoulder tells her to
move on. Follow this drove to New Orleans. Attend the auction, see men examined
like horses; see the forms of women rudely and brutally exposed to the shocking gaze
of American slave-buyers. See this drove sold and separated forever; and never forget
the deep, sad sobs that arose from that scattered multitude. Tell me citizen, WHERE,
under the sun, you can witness a spectacle more fiendish and shocking. Yet this is but

a glance at the American slave-trade, as it exists, at this moment, in the ruling part of the United States.

I was born amid such sights and scenes. To me the American slave-trade is a terrible reality. When a child, my soul was often pierced with a sense of its horrors. I lived on Philpot Street, Fell's Point, Baltimore, and have watched from the wharves, the slave ships in the Basin, anchored from the shore, with their cargoes of human flesh, waiting for favorable winds to waft them down the Chesapeake. There was, at that time, a grand slave market kept at the head of Pratt Street, by Austin Woldfolk. His agents were sent into every town and county in Maryland, announcing their arrival, through the papers, and on flaming *"hand-bills,"* headed CASH FOR NEGROES. These men were generally well dressed men, and very captivating in their manners. Ever ready to drink, to treat, and to gamble. The fate of many a slave has depended upon the turn of a single card; and many a child has been snatched from the arms of its mother by bargains arranged in a state of brutal drunkenness.

The flesh-mongers gather up their victims by dozens, and drive them, chained, to the general depot at Baltimore. When a sufficient number have been collected here, a ship is chartered, for the purpose of conveying the forlorn crew to Mobile, or to New Orleans. From the slave prison to the ship, they are usually driven in the darkness of night; for since the anti-slavery agitation, a certain caution is observed.

In the deep still darkness of midnight, I have been often aroused by the dead heavy footsteps, and the piteous cries of the chained gangs that passed our door. The anguish of my boyish heart was intense; and I was often consoled, when speaking to my mistress in the morning, to hear her say that the custom was very wicked; that she hated to hear the rattle of the chains, and the heart-rending cries. I was glad to find one who sympathised with me in my horror.

Fellow-citizens, this murderous traffic is, to-day, in active operation in this boasted republic. In the solitude of my spirit, I see clouds of dust raised on the high-ways of the South; I see the bleeding footsteps; I hear the doleful wail of fettered humanity, on the way to the slave-markets, where the victims are to be sold like *horses, sheep,* and *swine,* knocked off to the highest bidder. There I see the tenderest ties ruthlessly broken, to gratify the lust, caprice and rapacity of the buyers and sellers of men. My soul sickens at the sight.

> "Is this the land your Fathers loved,
>   The freedom which they toiled to win?
> Is this the earth whereon they moved?
>   Are these the graves they slumber in?"

But a still more inhuman, disgraceful, and scandalous state of things remains to be presented.

By an act of the American Congress, not yet two years old, slavery has been nationalized in its most horrible and revolting form. By that act, Mason & Dixon's line has been obliterated; New York has become as Virginia; and the power to hold, hunt, and sell men, women, and children as slaves remains no longer a mere state institution, but is now an institution of the whole United States. The power is co-extensive with the star-spangled banner and American Christianity. Where these go, may also go the merciless slave-hunter. Where these are, man is not sacred. He is a bird for the sportsman's gun. By that most foul and fiendish of all human decrees, the liberty and person of every man are put in peril. Your broad republican domain is hunting ground for men. *Not* for thieves and robbers, enemies of society, merely, but for men guilty of no crime. Your law-makers have commanded all good citizens to engage in this hellish sport. Your President, your Secretary of State, your *lords, nobles,* and ecclesiastics, enforce, as a duty you owe to your free and glorious country, and to your God, that you do this accursed thing. Not fewer than forty Americans have, within the past two years, been hunted down and, without a moment's warning, hurried away in chains, and consigned to slavery and excruciating torture. Some of these have had wives and children, dependent on them for bread; but of this, no account was made. The right of the hunter to his prey stands superior to the right of marriage, and to *all* rights in this republic, the rights of God included! For black men there are neither law, justice, humanity, nor religion. The Fugitive Slave *Law* makes MERCY TO THEM, A CRIME; and bribes the judge who tries them. An American JUDGE GETS TEN DOLLARS FOR EVERY VICTIM HE CONSIGNS to slavery, and five, when he fails to do so. The oath of any two villains is sufficient, under this hell-black enactment, to send the most pious and exemplary black man into the remorseless jaws of slavery! His own testimony is nothing. He can bring no witnesses for himself. The minister of American justice is bound by the law to hear but *one* side; and *that* side, is the side of the oppressor. Let this damning fact be perpetually told. Let it be thundered around the world, that, in tyrant-killing, king-hating, people-loving, democratic, Christian America, the seats of justice are filled with judges, who hold their offices under an open and palpable *bribe,* and are bound, in deciding in the case of a man's liberty, *to hear only his accusers!*

In glaring violation of justice, in shameless disregard of the forms of administering law, in cunning arrangment to entrap the defenceless, and in diabolical intent, this Fugitive Slave Law stands alone in the annals of tyrannical legislation. I doubt if there be another nation on the glove, having the brass and the baseness to put such a law on the statute-book. If any man in this assembly thinks differently from me in this matter, and feels able to disprove my statements, I will gladly confront him at any suitable time and place he may select.

Religious Liberty.

I take this law to be one of the grossest infringements of Christian Liberty, and, if the churches and ministers of our country were not stupidly blind, or most wickedly indifferent, they, too, would so regard it.

At the very moment that they are thanking God for the enjoyment of civil and religious liberty, and for the right to worship God according to the dictates of their own consciences, they are utterly silent in respect to a law which robs religion of its chief significance, and makes it utterly worthless to a world lying in wickedness. Did this law concern the "*mint, anise* and *cummin*"—abridge the right to sing psalms, to partake of the sacrament, or to engage in any of the ceremonies of religion, it would be smitten by the thunder of a thousand pulpits. A general shout would go up from the church, demanding *repeal, repeal, instant repeal!* And it would go hard with that politician who presumed to solicit the votes of the people without inscribing this motto on his banner. Further, if this demand were not complied with, another Scotland would be added to the history of religious liberty, and the stern old Covenanters would be thrown into the shade. A John Knox would be seen at every church door, and heard from every pulpit, and Fillmore would have no more quarter than was shown by Knox, to the beautiful, but treacherous Queen Mary of Scotland. The fact that the church of our country, (with fractional exceptions), does not esteem "the Fugitive Slave Law" as a declaration of war against religious liberty, implies that that church regards religion simply as a form of worship, an empty ceremony, and *not* a vital principle, requiring active benevolence, justice, love and good will towards man. It esteems sacrifice above mercy; psalm-singing above right doing; solemn meetings above practical righteousness. A worship that can be conducted by persons who refuse to give shelter to the houseless, to give bread to the hungry, clothing to the naked, and who enjoin obedience to a law forbidding these acts of mercy, is a curse, not a blessing to mankind. The Bible addresses all such persons as "scribes, pharisees, hypocrites, who pay tithe of *mint, anise,* and *cummin,* and have omitted the weighter matters of the law, judgement, mercy and faith."

The Church Responsible.

But the church of this country is not only indifferent to the wrongs of the slave, it actually takes sides with the oppressors. It has made itself the bulwark of American slavery, and the shield of American slave-hunters. Many of its most eloquent Divines, who stand as the very lights of the church, have shamelessly given the sanction of religion and the Bible to the whole slave system. They have taught that man may, properly, be a slave; that the relation of master and slave is ordained of God; that to send back an escaped bondman to his master is clearly the duty of all the followers of the Lord Jesus Christ; and this horrible blasphemy is palmed off upon the world for Christianity.

For my part, I would say, welcome infidelity! welcome atheism! welcome anything! in preference to the gospel, *as preached by those Divines!* They convert the very name of religion into an engine of tyranny, and barbarous cruelty, and serve to confirm more infidels, in this age, than all the infidel writings of Thomas Paine, Voltaire, and Bolingbroke, put together, have done! These ministers make religion a cold and flinty-hearted thing, having neither principles of right action, nor bowels of compassion. They strip the love of God of its beauty, and leave the throne of religion a huge, horrible, repulsive form. It is a religion for oppressors, tyrants, man-stealers, and *thugs.* It is not that *"pure and undefiled religion"* which is from above, and which is *"first pure, then peaceable, easy to be entreated,* full of mercy and good fruits, *without partiality, and without hypocrisy."* But a religion which favors the rich against the poor; which exalts the proud above the humble; which divides mankind into two classes, tyrants and slaves; which says to the man in chains, *stay there;* and to the oppressor, *oppress on;* it is a religion which may be professed and enjoyed by all the robbers and enslavers of mankind; it makes God a respecter of persons, denies his fatherhood of the race, and tramples in the dust the great truth of the brotherhood of man. All this we affirm to be true of the popular church, and the popular worship of our land and nation—a religion, a church, and a worship which, on the authority of inspired wisdom, we pronounce to be an abomination in the sight of God. In the language of Isaiah, the American church might be well addressed. "Bring no more vain oblations; incense is an abomination unto me: the new moons and Sabbaths, the calling of assemblies, I cannot away with; it is iniquity, even the solemn meeting. Your new moons and your appointed feasts my soul hateth. They are a trouble to me; I am weary to bear them;

and when ye spread forth your hands I will hide mine eyes from you. Yea! when ye make many prayers, I will not hear. YOUR HANDS ARE FULL OF BLOOD; cease to do evil, learn to do well; seek judgement; relieve the oppressed; judge for the fatherless; plead for the widow."

The American church is guilty, when viewed in connection with what it is doing to uphold slavery; but it is superlatively guilty when viewed in connection with its ability to abolish slavery.

The sin of which it is guilty is one of omission as well as of commission. Albert Barnes but uttered what the common sense of every man at all observant of the actual state of the case will receive as truth, when he declared that "There is no power out of the church that could sustain slavery an hour, if it were not sustained in it."

Let the religious press, the pulpit, the Sunday school, the conference meeting, the great ecclesiastical, missionary, Bible and tract associations of the land array their immense powers against slavery and slave-holding; and the whole system of crime and blood would be scattered to the winds; and that they do not do this involves them in the most awful responsibility of which the mind can conceive.

In prosecuting the anti-slavery enterprise, we have been asked to spare the church, to spare the ministry; but *how*, we ask, could such a thing be done? We are met on the threshold of our efforts for the redemption of the slave, by the church and ministry of the country, in battle arrayed against us; and we are compelled to fight or flee. From what *quarter*, I beg to know, has proceeded a fire so deadly upon our ranks, during the last two years, as from the Northern pulpit? As the champions of oppressors, the chosen men of American theology have appeared—men, honored for their so-called piety, and their real learning. The LORDS of Buffalo, the SPRINGS of New York, the LATHROPS of Auburn, the COXES and SPENCERS of Brooklyn, the GANNETS and SHARPS of Boston, the DEWEYS of Washington, and other great religious lights of the land, have, in utter denial of the authority of *Him*, by whom they professed to be called to the ministry, deliberately taught us, against the example of the Hebrews and against the remonstrance of the Apostles, they teach *"that we ought to obey man's law before the law of God."*

My spirit wearies of such blasphemy; and how such men can be supported, as the "standing types and representatives of Jesus Christ," is a mystery which I leave others to penetrate. In speaking of the American church, however, let it be distinctly understood that I mean the *great mass* of the religious organizations of our land. There are exceptions, and I thank God that there are. Noble men may be found scattered all over these Northern States, of whom Henry Ward Beecher of Brooklyn, Samuel J. May of Syracuse, and my esteemed friend[1] on the platform, are shining examples; and let me say further, that upon these men lies the duty to inspire our ranks with high religious faith and zeal, and to cheer us on in the great mission of the slave's redemption from his chains.

Religion in England and Religion in America.

One is struck with the difference between the attitude of the American church towards the anti-slavery movement, and that occupied by the churches in England towards a

---

1. Rev. R. R. Raymond. [F.D. note]

similar movement in that country. There, the church, true to its mission of ameliorating, elevating, and improving the condition of mankind, came forward promptly, bound up the wounds of the West Indian slave, and restored him to his liberty. There, the question of emancipation was a high[ly] religious question. It was demanded, in the name of humanity, and according to the law of the living God. The Sharps, the Clarksons, the Wilberforces, the Buxtons, and Burchells and the Knibbs, were alike famous for their piety, and for their philanthropy. The anti-slavery movement *there* was not an anti-church movement, for the reason that the church took its full share in prosecuting that movement: and the anti-slavery movement in this country will cease to be an anti-church movement, when the church of this country shall assume a favorable, instead of a hostile position towards that movement.

Americans! your republican politics, not less than your republican religion, are flagrantly inconsistent. You boast of your love of liberty, your superior civilization, and your pure Christianity, while the whole political power of the nation (as embodied in the two great political parties), is solemnly pledged to support and perpetuate the enslavement of three millions of your countrymen. You hurl your anathemas at the crowned headed tyrants of Russia and Austria, and pride yourselves on your Democratic institutions, while you yourselves consent to be the mere *tools* and *body-guards* of the tyrants of Virginia and Carolina. You invite to your shores fugitives of oppression from abroad, honor them with banquets, greet them with ovations, cheer them, toast them, salute them, protect them, and pour out your money to them like water; but the fugitives from your own land you advertise, hunt, arrest, shoot and kill. You glory in your refinement and your universal education; yet you maintain a system as barbarous and dreadful as ever stained the character of a nation—a system begun in avarice, supported in pride, and perpetuated in cruelty. You shed tears over fallen Hungary, and make the sad story of her wrongs the theme of your poets, statesmen and orators, till your gallant sons are ready to fly to arms to vindicate her cause against her oppressors; but, in regard to the ten thousand wrongs of the American slave, you would enforce the strictest silence, and would hail him as an enemy of the nation who dares to make those wrongs the subject of public discourse! You are all on fire at the mention of liberty for France or for Ireland; but are as cold as an iceberg at the thought of liberty for the enslaved of America. You discourse eloquently on the dignity of labor; yet, you sustain a system which, in its very essence, casts a stigma upon labor. You can bare your bosom to the storm of British artillery to throw off a threepenny tax on tea; and yet wring the last hard-earned farthing from the grasp of the black laborers of your country. You profess to believe "that, of one blood, God made all nations of men to dwell on the face of all the earth," and hath commanded all men, everywhere to love one another; yet you notoriously hate, (and glory in your hatred), all men whose skins are not colored like your own. You declare, before the world, and are understood by the world to declare, that you *hold these truths to be self evident, that all men are created equal; and are endowed by their Creator with certain inalienable rights; and that, among these are, life, liberty, and the pursuit of happiness;"* and yet, you hold securely, in a bondage which, according to your own Thomas Jefferson, "is *worse than ages of that which your fathers rose in rebellion to oppose,"* a seventh part of the inhabitants of your country.

Fellow-citizens! I will not enlarge further on your national inconsistencies. The existence of slavery in this country brands your republicanism as a sham, your humanity as a base pretence, and your Christianity as a lie. It destroys your moral power abroad; it corrupts your politicians at home. It saps the foundation of religion; it makes your name a hissing, and a byword to a mocking earth. It is the antagonistic force in your government, the only thing that seriously disturbs and endangers your *Union*. It fetters your progress; it is the enemy of improvement, the deadly foe of education; it fosters pride; it breeds insolence; it promotes vice; it shelters crime; it is a curse to the earth that supports it; and yet, you cling to it, as if it were the sheet anchor of all your hopes. Oh! be warned! be warned! a horrible reptile is coiled up in your nation's bosom; the venomous creature is nursing at the tender breast of your youthful republic; *for the love of God, tear away,* and fling from you the hideous monster, and *let the weight of twenty millions crush and destroy it forever!*

The Constitution.

But it is answered in reply to all this, that precisely what I have now denounced is, in fact, guaranteed and sanctioned by the Constitution of the United States; that the right to hold and to hunt slaves is a part of that Constitution framed by the illustrious Fathers of this Republic.

Then, I dare to affirm, notwithstanding all I have said before, your fathers stooped, basely stooped

> "To palter with us in a double sense:
> And keep the word of promise to the ear,
> But break it to the heart."

And instead of being the honest men I have before declared them to be, they were the veriest imposters that ever practised on mankind. *This* is the inevitable conclusion, and from it there is no escape. But I differ from those who charge this baseness on the framers of the Constitution of the United States. *It is a slander upon their memory,* at least, so I believe. There is not time now to argue the constitutional question at length; nor have I the ability to discuss it as it ought to be discussed. The subject has been handled with masterly power by Lysander Spooner, Esq., by William Goodell, by Samuel E. Sewall, Esq., and last, though not least, by Gerritt Smith, Esq. These gentlemen have, as I think, fully and clearly vindicated the Constitution from any design to support slavery for an hour.

Fellow-citizens! there is no matter in respect to which, the people of the North have allowed themselves to be so ruinously imposed upon, as that of the pro-slaverly character of the Constitution. In *that* instrument I hold there is neither warrant, license, nor sanction of the hateful thing; but, interpreted as it *ought* to be interpreted, the Constitution is a GLORIOUS LIBERTY DOCUMENT. Read its preamble, consider its purposes. Is slavery among them? Is it at the gateway? or is it in the temple? It is neither. While I do not intend to argue this question on the present occasion, let me ask, if it be not somewhat singular that, if the Constitution were intended to be, by its framers and adopters, a slave-holding instrument, why neither *slavery, slaveholding,* nor *slave* can anywhere be found in it. What would be thought of an instrument, drawn up, *legally* drawn up, for the purpose of entitling the city of Rochester to a track of land, in which no mention of land was made? Now, there are certain rules of interpretation, for the proper understanding of all legal instruments. These rules are well established. They are plain, common-sense rules, such as you and I, and all of us, can understand and apply, without having passed years in the study of law. I scout the idea that the question of the constitutionality or unconstitutionality of slavery is not a question for the people. I hold that every American citizen has a right to form an opinion of the constitution, and to propagate that opinion, and to use all honorable means to make his opinion the prevailing one. Without this right, the liberty of an American citizen would be as insecure as that of a Frenchman. Ex-Vice-President Dallas tells us that the constitution is an object to which no American mind can be too attentive, and no American heart too devoted. He further says, the constitution, in its words, is plain and intelligible, and is meant for the home-bred, unsophisticated understandings of our fellow-citizens. Senator Berrien tells us that the Constitution is the fundamental law, that which controls all others. The charter of our liberties, which every citizen has a personal interest in understanding thoroughly. The testimony of Senator Breese, Lewis Cass, and many others that might be named, who are everywhere esteemed as sound lawyers, so regard the constitution. I take it, therefore, that it is not presumption in a private citizen to form an opinion of that instrument.

Now, take the constitution according to its plain reading, and I defy the presentation of a single pro-slavery clause in it. On the other hand it will be found to contain principles and purposes, entirely hostile to the existence of slavery.

I have detained my audience entirely too long already. At some future period I will gladly avail myself of an opportunity to give this subject a full and fair discussion.

Allow me to say, in conclusion, notwithstanding the dark picture I have this day presented of the state of the nation, I do not despair of this country. There are forces in operation, which must inevitably work the downfall of slavery. *"The arm of the Lord is not shortened,"* and the doom of slavery is certain. I, therefore, leave off where I began, with *hope*. While drawing encouragement from the Declaration of Independence, the great principles it contains, and the genius of American Institutions, my spirit is also cheered by the obvious tendencies of the age. Nations do not now stand in the same relation to each other that they did ages ago. No nation can now shut itself up from the surrounding world, and trot round in the same old path of its fathers without interference. The time *was* when such could be done. Long established customs of hurtful character could formerly fence themselves in, and do their evil work with social impunity. Knowledge was then confined and enjoyed by the privileged few, and the multitude walked on in mental darkness. But a change has now come over the affairs of mankind. Walled cities and empires have become unfashionable. The arm of commerce has borne away the gates of the strong city. Intelligence is penetrating the darkest corners of the globe. It makes its pathway over and under the sea, as well as on the earth. Wind, steam, and lightning are its chartered agents. Oceans no longer divide, but link nations together. From Boston to London is now a holiday excursion. Space is comparatively annihilated. Thoughts expressed on one side of the Atlantic are distinctly heard on the other.

The far off and almost fabulous Pacific rolls in grandeur at our feet. The Celestial Empire, the mystery of ages, is being solved. The fiat of the Almightly, *"Let there be Light,"* has not yet spent its force. No abuse, no outrage whether in taste, sport or avarice, can now hide itself from the all-pervading light. The iron shoe, and crippled foot of China must be seen, in contrast with nature. *Africa must rise and put on her yet* unwoven garment, *"Ethiopia shall stretch out her hand unto God."* In the fervent aspirations of William Lloyd Garrison, I say, and let every heart join in saying it:

God speed the year of jubilee
The wide world o'er!
When from their galling chains set free,
Th' oppress'd shall vilely bend the knee,
And wear the yoke of tyranny
Like brutes no more
That year will come, and freedom's reign,
To man his plundered rights again
Restore.

God speed the day when human blood
Shall cease to flow!
In every clime be understood,
The claims of human brotherhood,
And each return for evil, good,
Not blow for blow;
That day will come all feuds to end,
And change into a faithful friend
Each foe.

God speed the hour, the glorious hour,
When none on earth
Shall exercise a lordly power,
Nor in a tyrant's presence cower;
But all to manhood's stature tower,
By equal birth!
THAT HOUR WILL COME, to each, to all,
And from his prison-house, the thrall
Go forth.

Until that year, day, hour, arrive,
With head, and heart, and hand I'll strive,
To break the rod, and rend the gyve,
The spoiler of his prey deprive—
So witness Heaven!
And never from my chosen post,
Whate'er the peril or the cost,
Be driven.

ABRAHAM LINCOLN

"Speech at Peoria, Illinois"
1854

"Address Before the Wisconsin State Agricultural Society"
1859

"Address Delivered at the Dedication of the Cemetery at Gettysburg"
1863

"Second Inaugural Address"
1865

Like Frederick Douglass, Abraham Lincoln (1809–65) was a political moralist. But unlike that of Douglass, Lincoln's egalitarian philosophy was complicated by his commitment to a semihistoricist and sometimes mystical conception of democratic union. In his Peoria speech against the Kansas-Nebraska Act, Lincoln demonstrated the ways in which such competing commitments both strengthened and weakened his antislavery outlook. Slavery, he argued, was intrinsically immoral and discontinuous with the founders' vision, and therefore Americans were both morally and historically obligated to take action to continue to keep the "cancer" isolated preparatory to some indefinitely defined later cutting. Meanwhile, social and historical circumstances justified not taking any further steps in the direction of either slave emancipation or black civil rights. A critical element in Lincoln's social thought was his concept of labor. Lincoln thought slavery particularly wrong because it allowed slaveholders to wring "their bread from the sweat of other men's faces." But it was not only a laborer's economic autonomy that defined Lincoln's idea of labor. In his Wisconsin address he presented an entire array of virtues democratic labor fostered—self-culture, small-scale capitalism, social mobility, even a hope of immortality. Lincoln's most profound considerations of democracy's transcendent meaning were provoked, though, not by the labor question but by Civil War. For Lincoln, in his two Civil War addresses, death was a tragic facilitator of democracy's consecration and rebirth. And not just death. In the Second Inaugural, Lincoln broke this process down further to a tension-filled synthesis of the war's multiple meanings—divine wrath, righteous human actions, atonement and redemption through human suffering, and finally, brooding over all, a hidden God's inscrutable purposes. The classic study of Lincoln's political ethics is Harry V. Jaffa, *Crisis of the House Divided: An Interpretation of the Issues in the Lincoln-Douglas Debates* (Garden City, N.Y., 1959), 181–409, 415–29. Two recent biographical studies argue for the close connection between Lincoln's psychology and his political ideology: Dwight G. Anderson, *Abraham Lincoln: The Quest for Immortality* (New York, 1982); and Charles B. Strozier, *Lincoln's Quest for Union: Public and Private Mean-*

ings (New York, 1982). For recent provocative discussions of Lincoln's "political reli-gion," see William S. Corlett, Jr., "The Availability of Lincoln's Political Religion" and Glen E. Thurow, "Reply to Corlett," *Political Theory*, 10 (November 1982), 520–46; and John P. Diggins, *The Lost Soul of American Politics: Virtue, Self-Interest, and the Founda-tions of Liberalism* (New York, 1984), 296–333, 389–91.

"Speech at Peoria, Illinois"
1854

[October 16, 1854]

This [Kansas-Nebraska Act] is the *repeal* of the Missouri Compromise. The foregoing history may not be precisely accurate in every particular; but I am sure it is sufficiently so, for all the uses I shall attempt to make of it, and in it, we have before us, the chief material enabling us to correctly judge whether the repeal of the Missouri Compromise is right or wrong.

I think, and shall try to show, that it is wrong; wrong in its direct effect, letting slavery into Kansas and Nebraska—and wrong in its prospective principle, allowing it to spread to every other part of the wide world, where men can be found inclined to take it.

This *declared* indifference, but as I must think, covert *real* zeal for the spread of slavery, I can not but hate. I hate it because of the monstrous injustice of slavery itself. I hate it because it deprives our republican example of its just influence in the world— enables the enemies of free institutions, with plausibility, to taunt us as hypocrites— causes the real friends of freedom to doubt our sincerity, and especially because it forces so many really good men amongst ourselves into an open war with the very fundamental principles of civil liberty—criticising the Declaration of Independence, and insisting that there is no right principle of action but *self-interest*.

Before proceeding, let me say I think I have no prejudice against the Southern people. They are just what we would be in their situation. If slavery did not now exist amongst them, they would not introduce it. If it did now exist amongst us, we should not instantly give it up. This I believe of the masses north and south. Doubtless there are individuals, on both sides, who would not hold slaves under any circumstances; and others who would gladly introduce slavery anew, if it were out of existence. We know that some southern men do free their slaves, go north, and become tip-top abolitionists; while some northern ones go south, and become most cruel slave-masters.

When southern people tell us they are no more responsible for the origin of slavery, than we; I acknowledge the fact. When it is said that the institution exists; and that it is very difficult to get rid of it, in any satisfactory way, I can understand and appreciate the saying. I surely will not blame them for not doing what I should not know how to do myself. If all earthly power were given me, I should not know what to do, as to the existing institution. My first impulse would be to free all the slaves, and send them to Liberia,—to their own native land. But a moment's reflection would convince me, that whatever of high hope, (as I think there is) there may be in this, in the long run, its sudden execution is impossible. If they were all landed there in a day, they would all perish in the next ten days; and there are not surplus shipping and

Source: *The Collected Works of Abraham Lincoln*, vol. 2, ed. Roy P. Basler, Marion Dolores Pratt, and Lloyd A. Dunlap (New Brunswick, N.J.: Rutgers University Press, 1953), 247, 254–56, 261–62, 264–66, 268, 270–71, 272–74, 275–76. Editors' notes omitted. Reprinted by permission of Rutgers University Press, Copyright © 1953 by the Abraham Lincoln Association.

surplus money enough in the world to carry them there in many times ten days. What then? Free them all, and keep them among us as underlings? Is it quite certain that this betters their condition? I think I would not hold one in slavery, at any rate; yet the point is not clear enough for me to denounce people upon. What next? Free them, and make them politically and socially, our equals? My own feelings will not admit of this; and if mine would, we well know that those of the great mass of white people will not. Whether this feeling accords with justice and sound judgment, is not the sole question, if indeed, it is any part of it. A universal feeling, whether well or ill-founded, can not be safely disregarded. We can not, then, make them equals. It does seem to me that systems of gradual emancipation might be adopted; but for their tardiness in this, I will not undertake to judge our brethren of the south.

When they remind us of their constitutional rights, I acknowledge them, not grudgingly, but fully, and fairly; and I would give them any legislation for the reclaiming of their fugitives, which should not, in its stringency, be more likely to carry a free man into slavery, than our ordinary criminal laws are to hang an innocent one.

But all this, to my judgment, furnishes no more excuse for permitting slavery to go into our own free territory, than it would for reviving the African slave trade by law. The law which forbids the bringing of slaves *from* Africa; and that which has so long forbid the taking them *to* Nebraska, can hardly be distinguished on any moral principle; and the repeal of the former could find quite as plausible excuses as that of the latter.

. . . . . .

I now come to consider whether the repeal, with its avowed principle, is intrinsically right. I insist that it is not. Take the particular case. A controversy had arisen between the advocates and opponents of slavery, in relation to its establishment within the country we had purchased of France. The southern, and then best part of the purchase, was already in as a slave State. The controversy was settled by also letting Missouri in as a slave State; but with the agreement that within all the remaining part of the purchase, North of a certain line, there should never be slavery. As to what was to be done with the remaining part south of the line, nothing was said; but perhaps the fair implication was, that it should come in with slavery if it should so choose. The southern part, except a portion heretofore mentioned, afterwards did come in with slavery, as the State of Arkansas. All these many years since 1820, the Northern part had remained a wilderness. At length settlements began in it also. In due course, Iowa, came in as a free State, and Minnesota was given a territorial government, without removing the slavery restriction. Finally the sole remaining part, North of the line, Kansas and Nebraska, was to be organized; and it is proposed, and carried, to blot out the old dividing line of thirty-four years standing, and to open the whole of that country to the introduction of slavery. Now, this, to my mind, is manifestly unjust. After an angry and dangerous controversy, the parties made friends by dividing the bone of contention. The one party first appropriates her own share, beyond all power to be disturbed in the possession of it; and then seizes the share of the other party. It is as if two starving men had divided their only loaf; the one had hastily swallowed his half, and then grabbed the other half just as he was putting it to his mouth!

. . . . . .

Equal justice to the south, it is said, requires us to consent to the extending of slavery to new countries. That is to say, inasmuch as you do not object to my taking my hog to Nebraska, therefore I must not object to you taking your slave. Now, I admit this is perfectly logical, if there is no difference between hogs and negroes. But while you thus require me to deny the humanity of the negro, I wish to ask whether you of the south yourselves, have even been willing to do as much? It is kindly provided that of all those who come into the world, only a small percentage are natural tyrants. That percentage is no larger in the slave States than in the free. The great majority, south as well as north, have human sympathies, of which they can no more divest themselves than they can of their sensibility to physical pain. These sympathies in the bosoms of the southern people, manifest in many ways, their sense of the wrong of slavery, and their consciousness that, after all, there is humanity in the negro. If they deny this, let me address them a few plain questions. In 1820 you joined the north, almost unanimously, in declaring the African slave trade piracy, and in annexing to it the punishment of death. Why did you do this? If you did not feel that it was wrong, why did you join in providing that men should be hung for it? The practice was no more than bringing wild negroes from Africa, to sell to such as would buy them. But you never thought of hanging men for catching and selling wild horses, wild buffaloes or wild bears.

Again, you have amongst you, a sneaking individual, of the class of native tyrants, known as the "SLAVE-DEALER." He watches your necessities, and crawls up to buy your slave, at a speculating price. If you cannot help it, you sell to him; but if you can help it, you drive him from your door. You despise him utterly. You do not recognize him as a friend, or even as an honest man. Your children must not play with his; they may rollick freely with the little negroes, but not with "slave-dealers" children. If you are obliged to deal with him, you try to get through the job without so much as touching him. It is common with you to join hands with the men you meet; but with the slave dealer you avoid the ceremony—instinctively shrinking from the snaky contact. If he grows rich and retires from business, you still remember him, and still keep up the ban of non-intercourse upon him and his family. Now why is this? You do not so treat the man who deals in corn, cattle or tobacco.

And yet again; there are in the United States and territories, including the District of Columbia, 433,643 free blacks. At $500 per head they are worth over two hundred millions of dollars. How comes this vast amount of property to be running about without owners? We do not see free horses or free cattle running at large. How is this? All these free blacks are the descendants of slaves, or have been slaves themselves, and they would be slaves now, but for SOMETHING which has operated on their white owners, inducing them, at vast pecuniary sacrifices, to liberate them. What is that SOMETHING? Is there any mistaking it? In all these cases it is your sense of justice, and human sympathy, continually telling you, that the poor negro has some natural right to himself—that those who deny it, and make mere merchandise of him, deserve kickings, contempt and death.

And now, why will you ask us to deny the humanity of the slave? and estimate him only as the equal of the hog? Why ask us to do what you will not do yourselves? Why ask us to do for *nothing,* what two hundred million of dollars could not induce you to do?

But one great argument in the support of the repeal of the Missouri Compromise, is still to come. That argument is "the sacred right of self government." It seems our distinguished Senator has found great difficulty in getting his antagonists, even in the Senate to meet him fairly on this argument—some poet has said

"Fools rush in where angels fear to tread."

At the hazzard of being thought one of the fools of this quotation, I meet that argument—I rush in, I take that bull by the horns.

I trust I understand, and truly estimate the right of self-government. My faith in the proposition that each man should do precisely as he pleases with all which is exclusively his own, lies at the foundation of the sense of justice there is in me. I extend the principles to communities of men, as well as to individuals. I so extend it, because it is politically wise, as well as naturally just: politically wise, in saving us from broils about matters which do not concern us. Here, or at Washington, I would not trouble myself with the oyster laws of Virginia, or the cranberry laws of Indiana.

The doctrine of self government is right—absolutely and eternally right—but it has no just application, as here attempted. Or perhaps I should rather say that whether it has such just application depends upon whether a negro is *not* or *is* a man. If he is *not* a man, why in that case, he who *is* a man may, as a matter of self-government, do just as he pleases with him. But if the negro *is* a man, is it not to that extent, a total destruction of self-government, to say that he too shall not govern *himself?* When the white man governs himself that is self-government; but when he governs himself, and also governs *another* man, that is *more* than self-government—that is despotism. If the negro is a *man,* why then my ancient faith teaches me that "all men are created equal;" and that there can be no moral right in connection with one man's making a slave of another.

Judge Douglas frequently, with bitter irony and sarcasm, paraphrases our argument by saying "The white people of Nebraska are good enough to govern themselves, *but they are not good enough to govern a few miserable negroes!!"*

Well I doubt not that the people of Nebraska are, and will continue to be as good as the average of people elsewhere. I do not say the contrary. What I do say is, that no man is good enough to govern another man, *without that other's consent.* I say this is the leading principle—the sheet anchor of American republicanism. Our Declaration of Independence says:

"We hold these truths to be self evident: that all men are created equal; that they are endowed by their Creator with certain inalienable rights; that among these are life, liberty and the pursuit of happiness. That to secure these rights, governments are instituted among men, DERIVING THEIR JUST POWERS FROM THE CONSENT OF THE GOVERNED."

I have quoted so much at this time merely to show that according to our ancient faith, the just powers of governments are derived from the consent of the governed. Now the relation of masters and slaves is, PRO TANTO, a total violation of this principle. The master not only governs the slave without his consent; but he governs him by a set of rules altogether different from those which he prescribes for himself. Allow ALL the governed an equal voice in the government, and that, and that only is self government.

Let it not be said I am contending for the establishment of political and social equality between the whites and blacks. I have already said the contrary. I am not now combating the argument of NECESSITY, arising from the fact that the blacks are already amongst us; but I am combating what is set up as MORAL argument for allowing them to be taken where they have never yet been—arguing against the EXTENSION of a bad thing, which where it already exists, we must of necessity, manage as we best can.

. . . . . .

Whether slavery shall go into Nebraska, or other new territories, is not a matter of exclusive concern to the people who may go there. The whole nation is interested that the best use shall be made of these territories. We want them for the homes of free white people. This they cannot be, to any considerable extent, if slavery shall be planted within them. Slave States are places for poor white people to remove FROM; not to remove TO. New free States are the places for poor people to go to and better their condition. For this use, the nation needs these territories.

. . . . . .

Finally, I insist, that if there is ANY THING which it is the duty of the WHOLE PEOPLE to never entrust to any hands but their own, that thing is the preservation and perpetuity, of their own liberties, and institutions. And if they shall think, as I do, that the extension of slavery endangers them, more than any, or all other causes, how recreant to themselves, if they submit the question, and with it, the fate of their country, to a mere hand-full of men, bent only on temporary self-interest. If this question of slavery extension were an insignificant one—one having no power to do harm—it might be shuffled aside in this way. But being, as it is, the great Behemoth of danger, shall the strong gripe of the nation be loosened upon him, to entrust him to the hands of such feeble keepers?

I have done with this mighty argument, of self-government. Go, sacred thing! Go in peace.

But Nebraska is urged as a great Union-saving measure. Well I too, go for saving the Union. Much as I hate slavery, I would consent to the extension of it rather than to see the Union dissolved, just as I would consent to any GREAT evil, to avoid a GREATER one. But when I go to Union saving, I must believe, at least, that the means I employ has some adaptation to the end. To my mind, Nebraska has no such adaptation.

"It hath no relish of salvation in it."

It is an aggravation, rather, of the only one thing which ever endangers the Union. When it came upon us, all was peace and quiet. The nation was looking to the forming of new bonds of Union; and a long course of peace and prosperity seemed to lie before us. In the whole range of possibility, there scarcely appears to me to have been any thing, out of which the slavery agitation could have been revived, except the very project of repealing the Missouri compromise. Every inch of territory we owned, already had a definite settlement of the slavery question, and by which, all parties were pledged to abide. Indeed, there was no uninhabited country on the continent, which we could acquire; if we except some extreme northern regions, which are wholly out of the question. In this state of case, the genius of Discord himself, could scarcely have invented a way of again getting [setting?] us by the ears, but by turning back and destroying the peace measures of the past. The councils of that genius seem to have prevailed, the Missouri compromise was repealed; and here we are, in the midst of a new slavery agitation, such, I think, as we have never seen before. Who is responsible for this? Is it those who resist the measure; or those who, causelessly, brought it forward, and pressed it through, having reason to know, and, in fact, knowing it must and would be so resisted? It could not but be expected by its author, that it would be looked upon as a measure for the extension of slavery, aggravated by a gross breach of faith. Argue as you will, and long as you will, this is the naked FRONT and ASPECT, of the measure. And in this aspect, it could not but produce agitation. Slavery is founded in the selfishness of man's nature—opposition to it, is [in?] his love of justice. These principles are an eternal antagonism; and when brought into collision so fiercely, as slavery extension brings them, shocks, and throes, and convulsions must ceaselessy follow. Repeal the Missouri compromise—repeal all compromises—repeal the declaration of independence—repeal all past history, you still can not repeal human nature. It still will be the abundance of man's heart, that slavery extension is wrong; and out of the abundance of his heart, his mouth will continue to speak.

. . . . . .

The Missouri Compromise ought to be restored. For the sake of the Union, it ought to be restored. We ought to elect a House of Representatives which will vote its restoration. If by any means, we omit to do this, what follows? Slavery may or may not be established in Nebraska. But whether it be or not, we shall have repudiated—discarded from the councils of the Nation—the SPIRIT of COMPROMISE; for who after this will ever trust in a national compromise? The spirit of mutual concession—that spirit which first gave us the constitution, and which has thrice saved the Union—we shall have strangled and cast from us forever. And what shall we have in lieu of it? The South flushed with triumph and tempted to excesses; the North, betrayed, as they believe, brooding on wrong and burning for revenge. One side will provoke; the other resent. The one will taunt, the other defy; one agrees [aggresses?], the other retaliates. Already a few in the North, defy all constitutional restraints, resist the execution of the fugitive slave law, and even menace the institution of slavery in the states where it exists.

Already a few in the South, claim the constitutional right to take to and hold slaves in the free states—demand the revival of the slave trade; and demand a treaty with Great Britain by which fugitive slaves may be reclaimed from Canada. As yet they are but few on either side. It is a grave question for the lovers of the Union, whether the final destruction of the Missouri Compromise, and with it the spirit of all compromise will or will not embolden and embitter each of these, and fatally increase the numbers of both.

But restore the compromise, and what then? We thereby restore the national faith, the national confidence, the national feeling of brotherhood. We thereby reinstate the spirit of concession and compromise—that spirit which has never failed us in past perils, and which may be safety trusted for all the future. The south ought to join in doing this. The peace of the nation is as dear to them as to us. In memories of the past and hopes of the future, they share as largely as we. It would be on their part, a great act—great in its spirit, and great in its effect. It would be worth to the nation a hundred years' purchase of peace and prosperity. And what of sacrifice would they make? They only surrender to us, what they gave us for a consideration long, long ago; what they have not now, asked for, struggled or cared for; what has been thrust upon them, not less to their own astonishment than to ours.

But it is said we cannot restore it; that though we elect every member of the lower house, the Senate is still against us. It is quite true, that of the Senators who passed the Nebraska bill, a majority of the whole Senate will retain their seats in spite of the elections of this and the next year. But if at these elections, their several constituencies shall clearly express their will against Nebraska, will these senators disregard their will? Will they neither obey, nor make room for those who will?

But even if we fail to technically restore the compromise, it is still a great point to carry a popular vote in favor of the restoration. The moral weight of such a vote can not be estimated too highly. The authors of Nebraska are not at all satisfied with the destruction of the compromise—an endorsement of this PRINCIPLE, they proclaim to be the great object. With them, Nebraska alone is a small matter—to establish a principle, for FUTURE USE, is what they particularly desire.

That future use is to be the planting of slavery wherever in the wide world, local and unorganized opposition can not prevent it. Now if you wish to give them this endorsement—if you wish to establish this principle—do so. I shall regret it; but it is your right. On the contrary if you are opposed to the principle—intend to give it no such endorsement—let no wheedling, no sophistry, divert you from throwing a direct vote against it.

Some men, mostly whigs, who condemn the repeal of the Missouri Compromise, nevertheless hesitate to go for its restoration, lest they be thrown in company with the abolitionist. Will they allow me as an old whig to tell them good humoredly, that I think this is very silly? Stand with anybody that stands RIGHT. Stand with him while he is right and PART with him when he goes wrong. Stand WITH the abolitionist in restoring the Missouri Compromise; and stand AGAINST him when he attempts to repeal the fugitive slave law. In the latter case you stand with the southern disunionist. What of that? you are still right. In both cases you are right. In both cases you oppose [expose?] the dangerous extremes. In both you stand on middle ground and hold the ship level and steady. In both you are national and nothing less than national. This is good old whig ground. To desert such ground, because of any company, is to be less than a whig—less than a man—less than an American.

I particularly object to the NEW position which the avowed principle of this Nebraska law gives to slavery in the body politic. I object to it because it assumes that there CAN be MORAL RIGHT in the enslaving of one man by another. I object to it as a dangerous dalliance for a few [free?] people—a sad evidence that, feeling prosperity we forget right—that liberty, as a principle, we have ceased to revere. I object to it because the fathers of the republic eschewed, and rejected it. The argument of "Necessity" was the only argument they ever admitted in favor of slavery; and so far, and so far only as it carried them, did they ever go. They found the institution existing among us, which they could not help; and they cast blame upon the British King for having permitted its introduction. BEFORE the constitution, they prohibited its introduction into the north-western Territory—the only country we owned, then free from it. AT the framing and adoption of the constitution, they forbore to so much as mention the word "slave" or "slavery" in the whole instrument. In the provision for the recovery

of fugitives, the slave is spoken of as a "PERSON HELD TO SERVICE OR LABOR." In that prohibiting the abolition of the African slave trade for twenty years, that trade is spoken
of as "The migration or importation of such persons as any of the States NOW EXISTING,
shall think proper to admit," &c. These are the only provisions alluding to slavery.
Thus, the thing is hid away, in the constitution, just as an afflicted man hides away a
wen or a cancer, which he dares not cut out once, lest he bleed to death; with the
promise, nevertheless, that the cutting may begin at the end of a given time. Less than
this our fathers COULD not do; and NOW [MORE?] they WOULD not do. Necessity drove
them so far, and farther, they would not go. But this is not all. The earliest Congress,
under the constitution, took the same view of slavery. They hedged and hemmed it in
to the narrowest limits of necessity.

. . . . . .

But NOW it is to be transformed into a "sacred right." Nebraska brings it forth,
places it on the high road to extension and perpetuity; and, with a pat on its back,
says to it, "Go, and God speed you." Henceforth it is to be the chief jewel of the
nation—the very figure-head of the ship of State. Little by little, but steadily as man's
march to the grave, we have been giving up the OLD for the NEW faith. Near eighty
years ago we began by declaring that all men are created equal; but now from that
beginning we have run down to the other declaration, that for SOME men to enslave
OTHERS is a "sacred right of self-government." These principles can not stand together.
They are as opposite as God and mammon; and whoever holds to the one, must
despise the other. When Pettit, in connection with his support of the Nebraska bill,
called the Declaration of Independence "a self-evident lie" he only did what consistency and candor require all other Nebraska men to do. Of the forty odd Nebraska
Senators who sat present and heard him, no one rebuked him. Nor am I apprized that
any Nebraska newspaper, or any Nebraska orator, in the whole nation, has ever yet
rebuked him. If this had been said among Marion's men, Southerners though they
were, what would have become of the man who said it? If this had been said to the
men who captured André, the man who said it, would probably have been hung sooner
than André was. If it had been said in old Independence Hall, seventy-eight years ago,
the very door-keeper would have throttled the man, and thrust him into the street.

Let no one be deceived. The spirit of seventy-six and the spirit of Nebraska, are
utter antagonisms; and the former is being rapidly displaced by the latter.

Fellow countrymen—Americans south, as well as north, shall we make no effort
to arrest this? Already the liberal party throughout the world, express the apprehension "that the one retrograde institution in America, is undermining the principles of
progress, and fatally violating the noblest political system the world ever saw." This
is not the taunt of enemies, but the warning of friends. Is it quite safe to disregard it—
to despise it? Is there no danger to liberty itself, in discarding the earliest practice, and
first precept of our ancient faith? In our greedy chase to make profit of the negro, let
us beware, lest we "cancel and tear to pieces" even the white man's charter of
freedom.

Our republican robe is soiled, and trailed in the dust. Let us repurify it. Let us
turn and wash it white, in the spirit, if not the blood, of the Revolution. Let us turn
slavery from its claims of "moral right," back upon its existing legal rights, and its

arguments of "necessity." Let us return it to the position our fathers gave it; and there let it rest in peace. Let us re-adopt the Declaration of Independence, and with it, the practices, and policy, which harmonize with it. Let north and south—let all Americans—let all lovers of liberty everywhere—join in the great and good work. If we do this, we shall not only have saved the Union; but we shall have so saved it, as to make, and to keep it, forever worthy of the saving. We shall have so saved it, that the succeeding millions of free happy people, the world over, shall rise up, and call us blessed, to the latest generations.

"Address Before the Wisconsin State Agricultural Society"
1859

[Milwaukee, Wisconsin, September 30, 1859]

The world is agreed that *labor* is the source from which human wants are mainly supplied. There is no dispute upon this point. From this point, however, men immediately diverge. Much disputation is maintained as to the best way of applying and controlling the labor element. By some it is assumed that labor is availabe only in connection with capital—that nobody labors, unless somebody else, owning capital, somehow, by the use of that capital, induces him to do it. Having assumed this, they proceed to consider whether it is best that capital shall *hire* laborers, and thus induce them to work by their own consent; or *buy* them, and drive them to it without their consent. Having proceeded so far they naturally conclude that all laborers are necessarily either *hired* laborers, or *slaves*. They further assume that whoever is once a *hired* laborer, is fatally fixed in that condition for life; and thence again that his condition is as bad as, or worse than that of a slave. This is the *"mud-sill"* theory.

But another class of reasoners hold the opinion that there is no *such* relation between capital and labor, as assumed; and that there is no such thing as a freeman being fatally fixed for life, in the condition of a hired laborer, that both these assumptions are false, and all inferences from them groundless. They hold that labor is prior to, and independent of, capital; that, in fact, capital is the fruit of labor, and could never have existed if labor had not *first* existed—that labor can exist without capital, but that capital could never have existed without labor. Hence they hold that labor is the superior—greatly the superior—of capital.

They do not deny that there is, and probably always will be, *a* relation between labor and capital. The error, as they hold, is in assuming that the *whole* labor of the world exists within that relation. A few men own capital; and that few avoid labor themselves, and with their capital, hire, or buy, another few to labor for them. A large majority belong to neither class—neither work for others, nor have others working for them. Even in all our slave States, except South Carolina, a majority of the whole people of all colors, are neither slaves nor masters. In these Free States, a large majority are neither *hirers* nor *hired*. Men, with their families—wives, sons and daughters—work for themselves, on their farms, in their houses and in their shops, taking the whole product to themselves, and asking no favors of capital on the one hand, nor of hirelings or slaves on the other. It is not forgotten that a considerable number of per-

Source: The Collected Works of Abraham Lincoln, vol. 3, ed. Roy P. Basler, Marion Dolores Pratt, and Lloyd A. Dunlap (New Brunswick, N.J.: Rutgers University Press, 1953), 477–82. Editors' notes omitted. Reprinted by permission of Rutgers University Press, Copyright © 1953 by the Abraham Lincoln Association.

sons mingle their own labor with capital; that is, labor with their own hands, and also buy slaves or hire freemen to labor for them; but this is only a *mixed,* and not a *distinct* class. No principle stated is disturbed by the existence of this mixed class. Again, as has already been said, the opponents of the *"mud-sill"* theory insist that there is not, of necessity, any such thing as the free hired laborer being fixed to that condition for life. There is demonstration for saying this. Many independent men, in this assembly, doubtless a few years ago were hired laborers. And their case is almost if not quite the general rule.

The prudent, penniless beginner in the world, labors for wages awhile, saves a surplus with which to buy tools or land, for himself; then labors on his own account another while, and at length hires another new beginner to help him. This, say its advocates, is *free* labor—the just and generous, and prosperous system, which opens the way for all—gives hope to all, and energy, and progress, and improvement of condition to all. If any continue through life in the condition of the hired laborer, it is not the fault of the system, but because of either a dependent nature which prefers it, or improvidence, folly, or singular misfortune. I have said this much about the elements of labor generally, as introductory to the consideration of a new phase which that element is in process of assuming. The old general rule was that *educated* people did not perform manual labor. They managed to eat their bread, leaving the toil of producing it to the uneducated. This was not an insupportable evil to the working bees, so long as the class of drones remained very small. But *now,* especially in these free States, nearly all are educated—quite too nearly all, to leave the labor of the uneducated, in any wise adequate to the support of the whole. It follows from this that henceforth educated people must labor. Otherwise, education itself would become a positive and intolerable evil. No country can sustain, in idleness, more than a small percentage of its numbers. The great majority must labor at something productive. From these premises the problem springs, "How can *labor* and *education* be the most satisfactorily combined?"

By the *"mud-sill"* theory it is assumed that labor and education are incompatible; and any practical combination of them impossible. According to that theory, a blind horse upon a tread-mill, is a perfect illustration of what a laborer should be—all the better for being blind, that he could not tread out of place, or kick understandingly. According to that theory, the education of laborers, is not only useless, but pernicious, and dangerous. In fact, it is, in some sort, deemed a misfortune that laborers should have heads at all. Those same heads are regarded as explosive materials, only to be safely kept in damp places, as far as possible from that peculiar sort of fire which ignites them. A Yankee who could invent a strong *handed* man without a head would receive the everlasting gratitude of the "mud-sill" advocates.

But Free Labor says "no!" Free Labor argues that, as the Author of man makes every individual with one head and one pair of hands, it was probably intended that heads and hands should cooperate as friends; and that that particular head, should direct and control that particular pair of hands. As each man has one mouth to be fed, and one pair of hands to furnish food, it was probably intended that that particular pair of hands should feed that particular mouth—that each head is the natural guardian, director, and protector of the hands and mouth inseparably connected with it; and that being so, every head should be cultivated, and improved, by whatever will add to its capacity for performing its charge. In one word Free Labor insists on universal education.

I have so far stated the opposite theories of *"Mud-Sill"* and "Free Labor" without declaring any preference of my own between them. On an occasion like this I ought not to declare any. I suppose, however, I shall not be mistaken, in assuming as a fact, that the people of Wisconsin prefer free labor, with its natural companion, education.

This leads to the further reflection, that no other human occupation opens so wide a field for the profitable and agreeable combination of labor with cultivated thought, as agriculture. I know of nothing so pleasant to the mind, as the discovery of anything which is at once *new* and *valuable*—nothing which so lightens and sweetens toil, as the hopeful pursuit of such discovery. And how vast, and how varied a field is agriculture, for such discovery. The mind, already trained to thought, in the country school, or higher school, cannot fail to find there an exhaustless source of profitable enjoyment. Every blade of grass is a study; and to produce two, where there was but one, is both a profit and a pleasure. And not grass alone; but soils, seeds, and seasons— hedges, ditches, and fences, draining, droughts, and irrigation—plowing, hoeing, and harrowing—reaping, mowing, and threshing—saving crops, pests of crops, diseases of crops, and what will prevent or cure them—implements, utensils, and machines, their relative merits, and [how] to improve them—hogs, horses, and cattle—sheep, goats, and poultry—trees, shrubs, fruits, plants, and flowers—the thousand things of which these are specimens—each a world of study within itself.

In all this, book-learning is available. A capacty, and taste, for reading, gives access to whatever has already been discovered by others. It is the key, or one of the keys, to the already solved problems. And not only so. It gives a relish, and facility, for successfully pursuing the [yet] unsolved ones. The rudiments of science, are available, and highly valuable. Some knowledge of Botany assists in dealing with the vegetable world—with all growing crops. Chemistry assists in the analysis of soils, selection, and application of manures, and in numerous other ways. The mechanical branches of Natural Philosophy, are ready help in almost everything; but especially in reference to implements and machinery.

The thought recurs that education—cultivated thought—can best be combined with agricultural labor, or any labor, on the principle of *thorough* work—that careless, half performed, slovenly work, makes no place for such combination. And thorough work, again, renders sufficient, the smallest quantity of ground to each man. And this again, conforms to what must occur in a world less inclined to wars, and more devoted to the arts of peace, than heretofore. Population must increase rapidly—more rapidly than in former times—and ere long the most valuable of all arts, will be the art of deriving a comfortable subsistence from the smallest area of soil. No community whose every member possesses this art, can ever be the victim of oppression in any of its forms. Such community will be alike independent of crowned-kings, money-kings, and land-kings.

But, according to your programme, the awarding of premiums awaits the closing of this address. Considering the deep interest necessarily pertaining to that performance, it would be no wonder if I am already heard with some impatience. I will detain you but a moment longer. Some of you will be successful, and such will need but little philosophy to take them home in cheerful spirits; others will be disappointed, and will be in a less happy mood. To such, let it be said, "Lay it not too much to heart." Let them adopt the maxim, "Better luck next time;" and then, by renewed exertion, make that better luck for themselves.

And by the successful, and the unsuccessful, let it be remembered, that while occasions like the present, bring their sober and durable benefits, the exultations and mortifications of them, are but temporary; that the victor shall soon be the vanquished, if he relax in his exertion; and that the vanquished this year, may be victor the next, in spite of all competition.

It is said an Eastern monarch once charged his wise men to invent him a sentence, to be ever in view, and which should be true and appropriate in all times and situations. They presented him the words: *"And this, too, shall pass away."* How much it expresses! How chastening in the hour of pride!—how consoling in the depths of affliction! "And this, too, shall pass away." And yet let us hope it is not *quite* true. Let us hope, rather, that by the best cultivation of the physical world, beneath and around us; and the intellectual and moral world within us, we shall secure an individual, social, and political prosperity and happiness, whose course shall be onward and upward, and which, while the earth endures, shall not pass away.

"Address Delivered at the Dedication of the Cemetery at Gettysburg" 1863

[November 19, 1863]

Four score and seven years ago our fathers brought forth on this continent, a new nation, conceived in Liberty, and dedicated to the proposition that all men are created equal.

Now we are engaged in a great civil war, testing whether that nation, or any nation so conceived and so dedicated, can long endure. We are met on a great battlefield of that war. We have come to dedicate a portion of that field, as a final resting place for those who here gave their lives that that nation might live. It is altogether fitting and proper that we should do this.

But, in a larger sense, we can not dedicate—we can not consecrate—we can not hallow—this ground. The brave men, living and dead, who struggled here, have consecrated it, far above our poor power to add or detract. The world will little note, nor long remember what we say here, but it can never forget what they did here. It is for us the living, rather, to be dedicated here to the unfinished work which they who fought here have thus far so nobly advanced. It is rather for us to be here dedicated to the great task remaining before us—that from these honored dead we take increased devotion to that cause for which they gave the last full measure of devotion—that we here highly resolve that these dead shall not have died in vain—that this nation, under God, shall have a new birth of freedom—and that government of the people, by the people, for the people, shall not perish from the earth.

Source: The Collected Works of Abraham Lincoln, vol. 7, ed. Roy P. Basler, Marion Dolores Pratt, and Lloyd A. Dunlap (New Brunswick, N.J.: Rutgers University Press, 1953), 23. Editors' notes omitted. Reprinted by permission of Rutgers University Press, Copyright © 1953 by the Abraham Lincoln Association.

"Second Inaugural Address"
1865

March 4, 1865

[Fellow Countrymen:]

At this second appearing to take the oath of the presidential office, there is less occasion for an extended address than there was at the first. Then a statement, somewhat in detail, of a course to be pursued, seemed fitting and proper. Now, at the expiration of four years, during which public declarations have been constantly called forth on every point and phase of the great contest which still absorbs the attention, and engrosses the energies of the nation, little that is new could be presented. The progress of our arms, upon which all else chiefly depends, is as well known to the public as to myself; and it is, I trust, reasonably satisfactory and encouraging to all. With high hope for the future, no prediction in regard to it is ventured.

On the occasion corresponding to this four years ago, all thoughts were anxiously directed to an impending civil-war. All dreaded it—all sought to avert it. While the inaugeral address was being delivered from this place, devoted altogether to *saving* the Union without war, insurgent agents were in the city seeking to *destroy* it without war—seeking to dissol[v]e the Union, and divide effects, by negotiation. Both parties deprecated war; but one of them would *make* war rather than let the nation survive; and the other would *accept* war rather than let it perish. And the war came.

One eighth of the whole population were colored slaves, not distributed generally over the Union, but localized in the Southern part of it. These slaves constituted a peculiar and powerful interest. All knew that this interest was, somehow, the cause of the war. To strengthen, perpetuate, and extend this interest was the object for which the insurgents would rend the Union, even by war; while the government claimed no right to do more than to restrict the territorial enlargement of it. Neither party expected for the war, the magnitude, or the duration, which it has already attained. Neither anticipated that the *cause* of the conflict might cease with, or even before, the conflict itself should cease. Each looked for an easier triumph, and a result less fundamental and astounding. Both read the same Bible, and pray to the same God; and each invokes His aid against the other. It may seem strange that any men should dare to ask a just God's assistance in wringing their bread from the sweat of other men's faces; but let us judge not that we be not judged. The prayers of both could not be answered; that of neither has been answered fully. The Almighty has His own purposes. "Woe unto the world because of offences! for it must needs be that offences come; but woe to that man by whom the offence cometh!" If we shall suppose that American Slavery is one of those offences which, in the providence of God, must needs

Source: The Collected Works of Abraham Lincoln, vol. 8, ed. Roy P. Basler, Marion Dolores Pratt, and Lloyd A. Dunlap (New Brunswick, N.J.: Rutgers University Press, 1953), 332–33. Editors' notes omitted. Reprinted by permission of Rutgers University Press, Copyright © 1953 by the Abraham Lincoln Association.

come, but which, having continued through His appointed time, He now wills to remove, and that He gives to both North and South, this terrible war, as the woe due to those by whom the offence came, shall we discern therein any departure from those divine attributes which the believers in a Living God always ascribe to Him? Fondly do we hope—fervently do we pray—that this mighty scourge of war may speedily pass away. Yet, if God wills that it continue, until all the wealth piled by the bond-man's two hundred and fifty years of unrequited toil shall be sunk, and until every drop of blood drawn with the lash, shall be paid by another drawn with the sword, as was said three thousand years ago, so still it must be said "the judgments of the Lord, are true and righteous altogether"

With malice toward none; with charity for all; with firmness in the right, as God gives us to see the right, let us strive on to finish the work we are in; to bind up the nation's wounds; to care for him who shall have borne the battle, and for his widow, and his orphan—to do all which may achieve and cherish a just, and a lasting peace, among ourselves, and with all nations.